# Lecture Notes in Computer Science 12127

More information about this series at http://www.springer.com/series/7409

Schahram Dustdar · Eric Yu ·
Camille Salinesi · Dominique Rieu ·
Vik Pant (Eds.)

# Advanced Information Systems Engineering

32nd International Conference, CAiSE 2020
Grenoble, France, June 8–12, 2020
Proceedings

 Springer

*Editors*
Schahram Dustdar
TU Wien
Vienna, Austria

Eric Yu
University of Toronto
Toronto, ON, Canada

Camille Salinesi
Université Paris 1 Panthéon-Sorbonne
Paris, France

Dominique Rieu
Université Grenoble Alpes
Saint-Martin-d'Hères, France

Vik Pant
University of Toronto
Toronto, ON, Canada

ISSN 0302-9743          ISSN 1611-3349   (electronic)
Lecture Notes in Computer Science
ISBN 978-3-030-49434-6          ISBN 978-3-030-49435-3   (eBook)
https://doi.org/10.1007/978-3-030-49435-3

LNCS Sublibrary: SL3 – Information Systems and Applications, incl. Internet/Web, and HCI

This Springer imprint is published by the registered company Springer Nature Switzerland AG
The registered company address is: Gewerbestrasse 11, 6330 Cham, Switzerland

# Preface

The 32nd International Conference on Advanced Information Systems Engineering (CAiSE 2020) was organized to be held in Grenoble, France, during June 8–12, 2020. Due to the outbreak of the COVID-19 pandemic, the conference was eventually moved online and held virtually over the same time period.

The CAiSE conference continues its tradition as the premiere venue for innovative and rigorous research across the whole spectrum of information systems (IS) engineering, with "Resilient Information Systems" as the special theme this year. When we decided on this special theme, we could not have anticipated how timely and real it would become. The circumstances brought about by the pandemic have highlighted the need for resilience in IS, as well as the contributions that IS are making towards the resilience of modern societies.

The CAiSE program included three invited keynotes, by Professor Edward Lee (UC Berkeley, USA), Dr. Thomas Baudel (IBM, France), and Professor Matthias Jarke (RWTH Aachen, Germany). The call for papers solicited research papers in the categories of formal and/or technical, empirical, experience, and exploratory papers, in all areas of IS engineering, including novel approaches to IS engineering; models, methods, and techniques in IS engineering; architectures and platforms for IS engineering; and domain-specific and multi-aspect IS engineering. 185 full paper submissions were received. We followed the selection process consolidated in the previous years: each paper was initially reviewed by at least two Program Committee (PC) members; papers with consistent negative evaluations were rejected; all papers with at least one positive evaluation were reviewed by a member of the Program Board (PB); all reviewers then engaged in an online discussion led by another PB member; finally, during the physical meeting of the PB in Paris (February 20–21, 2020), the final decision was made about the acceptance or rejection of each paper. The overall evaluation process of the papers resulted in the selection of 33 high-quality papers, which amounted to an acceptance rate of 15%. The final program of CAiSE 2020 was complemented by the CAiSE Forum, workshops, co-located working conferences, tutorials and panels, and a PhD consortium. For each of these events, separate proceedings were published.

We would like to thank the general chairs, Camille Salinesi and Dominique Rieu, organization chair, Agnes Front, and the whole organization team for their support and incredible work. We thank also the forum chairs, Nicolas Herbaut and Marcello La Rosa, workshop chairs, Sophie Dupuy-Chessa and Henderik A. Proper, tutorial and panel chairs, Xavier Franch and Samira Si Saïd, doctoral consortium chairs, Oscar Pastor and Mario Cortes-Cornax, publicity chairs, Sergio Espana, Naoufel Kraiem, Lin Liu, Gloria Lucia Giraldo Gómez, Birgit Penzenstadler, Motoshi Saeki, and Claudia Roncancio (coordinator), and web and social media chairs, Akram Idani and Sylvain Bouveret, for their extraordinary and professional work. We thank all PC and PB members, who played a fundamental role in the selection process. Finally, we would like to express our deepest gratitude to all those who served as organizers, session chairs, and hosts, who made great efforts to meet the online challenge to make the virtual conference a real success.

CAiSE 2020 was organized with the support of Université Grenoble Alpes and Université Paris 1 - Panthéon-Sorbonne.

April 2020                                                        Schahram Dustdar
                                                                          Eric Yu

# Organization

## General Chairs

Camille Salinesi      Université Paris 1 Panthéon-Sorbonne, France
Dominique Rieu      Université Grenoble Alpes, France

## Program Chairs

Eric Yu      University of Toronto, Canada
Schahram Dustdar      TU Wien, Austria

## Workshop Chairs

Sophie Dupuy-Chessa      Université Grenoble Alpes, France
Erik Proper      Institute of Science and Technology, Luxembourg

## Forum Chairs

Nicolas Herbaut      Université Paris 1 Panthéon-Sorbonne, France
Marcello La Rosa      The University of Melbourne, Australia

## Tutorial/Panel Chairs

Xavier Franch      Universitat Politècnica de Catalunya, Spain
Samira Si Saïd      Conservatoire National des Arts et Métiers Paris, France

## Doctoral Consortium Chairs

Oscar Pastor      Universidad Politécnica de Valencia, Spain
Mario Cortes-Cornax      Université Grenoble Alpes, France

## Industry Chairs (Innovation in and for Information Systems)

Fabrice Forest      Université Grenoble Alpes, France
Jean-Pierre Verjus      French Tech in the Alps – Grenoble, France
Adrian Mos      Naver Labs Europe

## Publicity Chairs

Sergio Espana      Utrecht University, The Netherlands
Naoufel Kraiem      University of Manouba, Tunisia

| Lin Liu | Tsinghua University, China |
| Gloria Lucia Giraldo Gómez | Universidad Nacional de Colombia, Colombia |
| Birgit Penzenstadler | California State University, Long Beach, USA |
| Claudia Roncancio (Publicity Coordinator) | Université Grenoble Alpes, France |
| Motoshi Saeki | Tokyo Institute of Technology School of Computing, Japan |

## Web and Social Media Chairs

| Akram Idani | Université Grenoble Alpes, France |
| Sylvain Bouveret | Université Grenoble Alpes, France |

## Proceedings Chair

| Vik Pant | University of Toronto, Canada |

## Organization Chair

| Agnes Front | Université Grenoble Alpes, France |

## Conference Steering Committee Chairs

| Johann Eder | Alpen Adria Universität Klagenfurt, Austria |
| John Krogstie | Norwegian University of Science and Technology, Norway |
| Eric Dubois | LIST, Luxembourg |

## Conference Advisory Board

| Janis Bubenko | KTH Stockholm, Sweden |
| Oscar Pastorv | Universidad Politécnica de Valencia, Spain |
| Barbara Pernici | Politecnico di Milano, Italy |
| Colette Rolland | Université Paris 1 Panthéon-Sorbonne, France |
| Arne Solvberg | Norwegian University of Science and Technology, Norway |

## Program Board Members

| Ernesto Damiani | University of Milan, Italy |
| Eric Dubois | Luxembourg Institute of Science and Technology, Luxembourg |
| Johann Eder | Alpen Adria Universität Klagenfurt, Austria |
| Xavier Franch | Universitat Politècnica de Catalunya, Spain |
| Matthias Jarke | RWTH Aachen University, Germany |

| John Krogstie | Norwegian University of Science and Technology, Norway |
| Heinrich C. Mayr | Alpen-Adria-Universität Klagenfurt, Austria |
| Selmin Nurcan | Université Paris 1 Panthéon-Sorbonne, France |
| Oscar Pastor Lopez | Universitat Politècnica de València, Spain |
| Barbara Pernici | Politecnico di Milano, Italy |
| Henderik Proper | Luxembourg Institute of Science and Technology, Luxembourg |
| Jolita Ralyté | University of Geneva, Switzerland |
| Manfred Reichert | Ulm University, Germany |
| Hajo A. Reijers | Utrecht University, The Netherlands |
| Stefanie Rinderle-Ma | University of Vienna, Austria |
| Antonio Ruiz-Cortés | University of Seville, Spain |
| Shazia Sadiq | The University of Queensland, Australia |
| Camille Salinesi | CRI, Université Paris 1 Panthéon-Sorbonne, France |
| Pnina Soffer | University of Haifa, Israel |
| Janis Stirna | Stockholm University, Sweden |
| Ernest Teniente | Universitat Politècnica de Catalunya, Spain |
| Yannis Vassiliou | National Technical University of Athens, Greece |
| Barbara Weber | University of St. Gallen, Switzerland |

## Program Committee Members

| Schahram Dustdar (Program Chair) | Vienna University of Technology, Austria |
| Eric Yu (Program Chair) | University of Toronto, Canada |
| Raian Ali | Hamad Bin Khalifa University, Qatar |
| Daniel Amyot | University of Ottawa, Canada |
| Joao Araujo | Universidade NOVA de Lisboa, Portugal |
| Marko Bajec | University of Ljubljana, Slovenia |
| Boualem Benatallah | The University of New South Wales, Australia |
| Alex Borgida | Rutgers University, USA |
| Sjaak Brinkkemper | Utrecht University, The Netherlands |
| Andrea Burattin | Technical University of Denmark, Denmark |
| Cristina Cabanillas | Vienna University of Economics and Business, Austria |
| Albertas Caplinskas | Vilnius University, Lithuania |
| Cinzia Cappiello | Politecnico di Milano, Italy |
| Carlo Combi | Università degli Studi di Verona, Italy |
| Fabiano Dalpiaz | Utrecht University, The Netherlands |
| Maya Daneva | University of Twente, The Netherlands |
| Valeria De Antonellis | University of Brescia, Italy |
| Adela Del Río Ortega | University of Seville, Spain |
| Claudio Di Ciccio | Vienna University of Economics and Business, Austria |
| Oscar Diaz | University of the Basque Country, Spain |
| João Falcão E. Cunha | University of Porto, Portugal |
| Pablo Fernandez | University of Seville, Spain |
| Ulrich Frank | Universität of Duisburg-Essen, Germany |

| Panos Vassiliadis | University of Ioannina, Greece |
| Matthias Weidlich | Humboldt-Universität zu Berlin, Germany |
| Hans Weigand | Tilburg University, The Netherlands |
| Mathias Weske | HPI, University of Potsdam, Germany |
| Jian Yang | Macquarie University, Australia |
| Yijun Yu | The Open University, UK |
| Jelena Zdravkovic | Stockholm University, Sweden |

## Additional Reviewers

Agostinelli, Simone
Andrews, Kevin
Azanza, Maider
Bagozi, Ada
Bondel, Gloria
Braun, Daniel
Böhm, Fabian
Chowdhury, Mohammad Jabed Morshed
de Kinderen, Sybren
El-Khawaga, Ghada
Englbrecht, Ludwig
Estrada Torres, Irene Bedilia
Fernandez, Pablo
Gall, Manuel
Gallersdörfer, Ulrich
García, José María
Garda, Massimiliano
Groefsema, Heerko
Guizzardi, Renata
Haarmann, Stephan
Holl, Patrick
Hoppenstedt, Burkhard
Hyrynsalmi, Sonja
Ihde, Sven
Iqbal, Mubashar
Jansen, Slinger
Jovanovic, Petar
Kaczmarek-Heß, Monika
Kalenkova, Anna
Kern, Sascha
Kostova, Blagovesta

Kraft, Robin
Kumara, Indika
Köpke, Julius
Lee, Jaejoon
Leno, Volodymyr
Lopez, Lidia
Marquez Chamorro, Alfonso
Molenaar, Sabine
Nalchigar, Soroosh
Nelissen, Klaas
Nikaj, Adriatik
Oliboni, Barbara
Palomares, Cristina
Parejo Maestre, José Antonio
Pereira, Juanan
Puchta, Alexander
Quintarelli, Elisa
Ramautar, Vijanti
Ras, Eric
Remy, Simon
Schlette, Daniel
Sottet, Jean-Sébastien
Spijkman, Tjerk
Stertz, Florian
Tantar, Alexandru
van der Werf, Jan Martijn
Velegrakis, Yannis
Verdecchia, Roberto
Wen, Lijie
Winter, Karolin
Zhao, Weiliang

# Extended Abstracts of Invited Keynote Talks

# The Coevolution of Humans and Machines (Extended Abstract)

Edward A. Lee ⓘ

UC Berkeley, Berkeley, CS, USA
eal@berkeley.edu
https://ptolemy.berkeley.edu/ eal/

**Abstract.** We humans are less in control of the trajectory of technology than we think. Technology shapes us as much as we shape it, and it may be more defensible to think of technology as the result of a Darwinian coevolution than the result of top-down intelligent design. To understand this question requires a deep dive into how evolution works, how humans are different from computers, and how technology development today resembles the emergence of a new life form on our planet.

**Keywords:** Technology and society · Evolutionary theory · Philosophy of technology

## 1  Coevolution

Richard Dawkins famously said that a chicken is an egg's way of making another egg. Is a human a computer's way of making another computer? We tend to think of technology as being created by humans in a top-down, intelligent-design manner, but we may actually have less control than we realize. The trajectory that technology takes is driven by many complex forces, including accidental mutations and feedback loops, where technology shapes the thinking of the engineers developing the technology.

In my new book, *The Coevolution* [1], I coin the term "digital creationism" for the idea that technology is the result of top-down intelligent design. This principle assumes that every technology is the outcome of a deliberate process, where every aspect of a design is the result of an intentional, human decision. I now know, after 40 years of experience, that this is not how it happens. Software engineers are more the agents of mutation in Darwinian evolutionary process. The outcome of their efforts is shaped more by the computers, networks, software tools, libraries, and programming languages than by their deliberate decisions. And the success and further development of their product is determined as much or more by the cultural milieu into which they launch their "creation" than their design decisions.

The French philosopher known as Alain (whose real name was Émile-Auguste Chartier), wrote about fishing boats in Brittany:

> Every boat is copied from another boat. ... Let's reason as follows in the manner of Darwin. It is clear that a very badly made boat will end up at the bottom after one or two voyages and thus

never be copied. ... One could then say, with complete rigor, that it is the sea herself who fashions the boats, choosing those which function and destroying the others [2].

Boat designers are agents of mutation, and sometimes their mutations result in a "badly made boat." From this perspective, perhaps Facebook has been fashioned more by teenagers than software engineers.

More deeply, digital technology coevolves with humans. Facebook changes its users, who then change Facebook. For software engineers, the tools we use, themselves earlier outcomes of software engineering, shape our thinking. Think about how integrated development environments (IDEs such as Eclipse), message boards (such as Stack Overflow), libraries (such the Standard Template Library), programming languages (Scala, Xtend, and JavaScript, for example), and Internet search (such as Google) affect the outcome of our software. These tools have more effect on the outcome than all of our deliberate decisions.

## 2    Public Policy

Today, the fear and hype around AI taking over the world and social media taking down democracy has fueled a clamor for more regulation. But if I am right about coevolution, we may be going about the project of regulating technology all wrong. Why have privacy laws, with all their good intentions, done little to protect our privacy and only overwhelmed us with small-print legalese?

Under the principle of digital creationism, bad outcomes are the result of unethical actions by individuals, for example by blindly following the profit motive with no concern for societal effects. Under the principle of coevolution, bad outcomes are the result of the procreative prowess of the technology itself. Technologies that succeed are those that more effectively propagate. The individuals we credit with (or blame for) creating those technologies certainly play a role, but so do the users of the technologies and their whole cultural context. Under this perspective, Facebook users bear some of the blame, along with Mark Zuckerberg, for distorted elections. They even bear some of the blame for the design of Facebook software that enables distorted elections. If they were willing to pay for social networking, for example, an entirely different software design would have emerged.

Under digital creationism, the purpose of regulation is to constrain the individuals who develop and market technology. In contrast, under coevolution, constraints can be about the use of technology, not just its design. The purpose of regulation becomes to nudge the process of both technology and cultural evolution through incentives and penalties. Nudging is probably the best we can hope for. Evolutionary processes do not yield easily to control.

## 3  Living Digital Beings

If we wish to nudge the process through regulation, we have to better understand the process. It may be more productive to think of the process as a coevolution, where software systems coevolve with our culture as if they were living symbiotic beings. To frame this line of thinking, I call these hypothetical beings "eldebees," short for LDBs, or living digital beings. They are creatures defined by bits, not DNA, and made of silicon and metal, not organic molecules. They are born and they die. Some are simple, with a genetic code of a few thousand bits, and some are extremely complex. Most live short lives, sometimes less than a second, while others live for months or years. Some even have prospects for immortality, prospects better than any organic being.

In this process, software engineers are doing more husbandry than design, combining bits of code from here with bits of code from there to create a new "codome," a mutation that, with high probability, will prove unfit and will either die out or further mutate. Users are midwives, bringing the eldebees to life, and culture is the ecosystem, itself evolving along with the technology.

Viewed this way, technology becomes analogous to an emerging new life form on our planet. This point of view sheds new light on many pressing questions, like whether artificial intelligences will annihilate us, turn us into cyborgs, or even become sentient. Technology already extends our minds and shapes our culture. Are we designing it, or are it designing us?

Understanding this perspective requires a deep dive into how evolution works, how humans are different from computers, and how the way technology develops resembles and does not resemble the emergence of a new life form on our planet. That is the subject of my book [1].

## References

1. Lee, E.A.: The Coevolution: The Entwined Futures of Humans and Machines. MIT Press, Cambridge (2020)
2. Rogers, D.S., Ehrlich, P.R.: Natural selection and cultural rates of change. Proc. Natl. Acad. Sci. USA **105**(9), 3416–3420 (2008)

# Data Sovereignty and the Internet of Production

Matthias Jarke ⓘ

Informatik 5, RWTH Aachen & Fraunhofer FIT, Ahornstr. 55, 52074 Aachen,
Germany
jarke@dbis.rwth-aachen.de

**Abstract.** While the privacy of personal data has captured great attention in the public debate, resulting, e.g., in the European GDPR guideline, the sovereignty of knowledge-intensive small and medium enterprises concerning the usage of their own data in the presence of dominant data-hungry players in the Internet needs more investigation. In Europe, even the legal concept of data ownership is unclear. We reflect on requirements analyses, reference architectures and solution concepts pursued by the International Data Spaces Initiative to address these issues. In this setting, massive amounts of heterogeneous data must be exchanged and analyzed across organizational and disciplinary boundaries, throughout the lifecycle from (re-)engineering, to production, usage and recycling, under hard resource and time constraints. A shared metaphor, borrowed from Plato's famous Cave Allegory, serves as the core modeling and data management approach from conceptual, logical, physical, and business perspectives.

**Keywords:** Data sovereignty · Data spaces · Digital shadows · Internet of production

## Introduction

The term "data sovereignty" is hotly debated in political, industrial, and privacy communities. Politicians understand sovereignty as national sovereignty over data in their territory, when it comes to the jurisdiction over the use of big data by the big international players.

One might think that data industries dislike the idea because – in whatever definition – it limits their opportunities to exploit "data as the new oil". However, some of them employ the vision of data sovereignty of citizens as a weapon to abolish mandatory data privacy rules as limiting customer sovereignty by viewing them as people in need of protection in an uneven struggle for data ownership. For exactly this reason, privacy proponents criticize data sovereignty as a tricky buzzword by the data industry, aiming to undermine the principles of real self-determination and data thriftiness (capturing only the minimal data necessary for a specified need) found in many privacy laws. The European GDPR regulation follows this argumentation to some degree by clearly specifying that you are the owner of all personal data about yourself.

Surprising to most participants, the well-known Göttingen-based law professor Gerald Spindler, one of the GDPR authors, pointed out at a recent Dagstuhl Seminar on Data Sovereignty (Cappiello et al. 2019) that this personal data ownership is the only formal concept of data ownership that legally exists in Europe. In particular, the huge group of knowledge-intensive small and medium enterprises (SMEs) or even larger user industries in Europe are lacking coherent legal, technical, and organizational concepts how to protect their data- and model-based knowledge in the globalized industrial ecosystems.

In late 2014, we introduced the idea to extend the concept of personal data spaces (Halevy et al. 2006) to the inter-organizational setting by introducing the idea of Industrial Data Spaces as the kernel of platforms in which specific industrial ecosystems could organize their cooperation in a data-sovereign manner (Jarke 2017, Jarke and Quix 2017). The idea was quickly taken up by European industry and political leaders. Since 2015, a number of large-scale German and EU projects have defined requirements (Otto and Jarke 2019). Via numerous use case experiments, the International Data Space (IDS) Association with currently roughly 100 corporate members worldwide has evolved, and agreed on a reference architecture now already in version 3 (Otto et al. 2019).

As recently pointed out by Loucopoulos et al. (2019), the production sector offers particularly complex challenges to such a setting due to the heterogeneity of its data and mathematical models, the structural and material complexity of many products, the globalized supply chains, and the international competition. Funded by the German "Excellence Competition 2019", an interdisciplinary group of researchers at RWTH Aachen University therefore started a 7-year Excellence Cluster "Internet of Production" aiming to address these challenges in a coherent manner.

# References

Cappiello, C., Gal, A., Jarke, M., Rehof, J.: Data ecosystems – sovereign data exchange among organizations. Dagstuhl Rep. **9**(9), 66–134 (2019)

Halevy, A., Franklin, M., Maier, D.: Principles of data space systems. In: Proceedings 25th ACM SIGMOD-PODS, pp. 1–9 (2006)

Jarke, M.: Data spaces – combining goal-driven and data-driven approaches in community decision and negotiation support. In: Schoop, M., Kilgour, D. (eds.) GDN 2017. LNBIP, vol. 293, pp. 3–14. Springer, Cham (2017). https://doi.org/10.1007/978-3-319-63546-0_1

Jarke, M., Quix, C.: On Warehouses, lakes, and spaces: the changing role of conceptual modeling for data integration. In: Cabot, J., Gómez, C., Pastor, O., Sancho, M., Teniente, E. (eds.) Conceptual Modeling Perspectives, pp. 231–245. Springer, Cham (2017). https://doi.org/10.1007/978-3-319-67271-7_16

Loucopoulos, P., Kavakli, E., Chechina, N.: Requirements engineering for cyber physical production systems. In: Giorgini, P., Weber, B. (eds.) CAiSE 2019. LNCS, vol. 11483, pp. 276–291. Springer, Cham (2019). https://doi.org/10.1007/978-3-030-21290-2_18

Otto, B., Jarke, M.: Designing a multi-sided data platform: findings from the international data spaces case. Electr. Markets **29**(4), 561–580 (2019). https://doi.org/10.1007/s12525-019-00362-x

Otto, B., Steinbuß, S., Teuscher, A., Lohmann, S. et al.: Reference Architecture Model Version 3.0. Dortmund: International Data Spaces Association (2019)

# Contents

**Distributed Applications**

Remodularization Analysis for Microservice Discovery Using Syntactic
and Semantic Clustering. . . . . . . . . . . . . . . . . . . . . . . . . . . . . . . . . . 3
    *Adambarage Anuruddha Chathuranga De Alwis, Alistair Barros,*
    *Colin Fidge, and Artem Polyvyanyy*

Decentralized Cross-organizational Application Deployment Automation:
An Approach for Generating Deployment Choreographies Based
on Declarative Deployment Models. . . . . . . . . . . . . . . . . . . . . . . . . . . 20
    *Karoline Wild, Uwe Breitenbücher, Kálmán Képes, Frank Leymann,*
    *and Benjamin Weder*

Modeling and Analyzing Architectural Diversity of Open Platforms . . . . . . . 36
    *Bahar Jazayeri, Simon Schwichtenberg, Jochen Küster,*
    *Olaf Zimmermann, and Gregor Engels*

Co-destruction Patterns in Crowdsourcing: Formal/Technical Paper . . . . . . . 54
    *Reihaneh Bidar, Arthur H. M. ter Hofstede, and Renuka Sindhgatta*

Information Systems Engineering with Digital Shadows: Concept
and Case Studies: An Exploratory Paper . . . . . . . . . . . . . . . . . . . . . . . . 70
    *Martin Liebenberg and Matthias Jarke*

Model-Driven Development of a Digital Twin for Injection Molding. . . . . . . 85
    *Pascal Bibow, Manuela Dalibor, Christian Hopmann, Ben Mainz,*
    *Bernhard Rumpe, David Schmalzing, Mauritius Schmitz,*
    *and Andreas Wortmann*

SIoTPredict: A Framework for Predicting Relationships in the Social
Internet of Things . . . . . . . . . . . . . . . . . . . . . . . . . . . . . . . . . . . . . . . 101
    *Abdulwahab Aljubairy, Wei Emma Zhang, Quan Z. Sheng,*
    *and Ahoud Alhazmi*

B-MERODE: A Model-Driven Engineering and Artifact-Centric Approach
to Generate Blockchain-Based Information Systems. . . . . . . . . . . . . . . . . . 117
    *Victor Amaral de Sousa, Corentin Burnay, and Monique Snoeck*

Smart Contract Invocation Protocol (SCIP): A Protocol for the Uniform
Integration of Heterogeneous Blockchain Smart Contracts . . . . . . . . . . . . . 134
    *Ghareeb Falazi, Uwe Breitenbücher, Florian Daniel,*
    *Andrea Lamparelli, Frank Leymann, and Vladimir Yussupov*

## AI and Big Data in IS

A System Framework for Personalized and Transparent
Data-Driven Decisions. . . . . . . . . . . . . . . . . . . . . . . . . . . . . . . . . . .    153
    *Sarah Oppold and Melanie Herschel*

Online Reinforcement Learning for Self-adaptive Information Systems . . . . .    169
    *Alexander Palm, Andreas Metzger, and Klaus Pohl*

Aspect Term Extraction Using Deep Learning Model with Minimal
Feature Engineering. . . . . . . . . . . . . . . . . . . . . . . . . . . . . . . . . . . . .    185
    *Felipe Zschornack Rodrigues Saraiva,
    Ticiana Linhares Coelho da Silva,
    and José Antônio Fernandes de Macêdo*

State Machine Based Human-Bot Conversation Model and Services . . . . . . .    199
    *Shayan Zamanirad, Boualem Benatallah, Carlos Rodriguez,
    Mohammadali Yaghoubzadehfard, Sara Bouguelia, and Hayet Brabra*

## Process Mining and Analysis

Stochastic-Aware Conformance Checking: An Entropy-Based Approach . . . .    217
    *Sander J. J. Leemans and Artem Polyvyanyy*

Conformance Checking Approximation Using Subset Selection
and Edit Distance . . . . . . . . . . . . . . . . . . . . . . . . . . . . . . . . . . . . . .    234
    *Mohammadreza Fani Sani, Sebastiaan J. van Zelst,
    and Wil M. P. van der Aalst*

Quantifying the Re-identification Risk of Event Logs for Process Mining:
Empiricial Evaluation Paper . . . . . . . . . . . . . . . . . . . . . . . . . . . . . . . .    252
    *Saskia Nuñez von Voigt, Stephan A. Fahrenkrog-Petersen,
    Dominik Janssen, Agnes Koschmider, Florian Tschorsch,
    Felix Mannhardt, Olaf Landsiedel, and Matthias Weidlich*

An Approach for Process Model Extraction by Multi-grained
Text Classification. . . . . . . . . . . . . . . . . . . . . . . . . . . . . . . . . . . . . .    268
    *Chen Qian, Lijie Wen, Akhil Kumar, Leilei Lin, Li Lin, Zan Zong,
    Shu'ang Li, and Jianmin Wang*

LoGo: Combining Local and Global Techniques for Predictive Business
Process Monitoring . . . . . . . . . . . . . . . . . . . . . . . . . . . . . . . . . . . . . .    283
    *Kristof Böhmer and Stefanie Rinderle-Ma*

Business Process Variant Analysis Based on Mutual Fingerprints
of Event Logs. . . . . . . . . . . . . . . . . . . . . . . . . . . . . . . . . . . . . . . . . .    299
    *Farbod Taymouri, Marcello La Rosa, and Josep Carmona*

DeepAlign: Alignment-Based Process Anomaly Correction Using
Recurrent Neural Networks . . . . . . . . . . . . . . . . . . . . . . . . . . . . . . . . . 319
    *Timo Nolle, Alexander Seeliger, Nils Thoma, and Max Mühlhäuser*

Workforce Upskilling: A History-Based Approach for Recommending
Unfamiliar Process Activities . . . . . . . . . . . . . . . . . . . . . . . . . . . . . . . . 334
    *Anastasiia Pika and Moe T. Wynn*

## Requirements and Modeling

Evaluating the Benefits of Model-Driven Development: Empirical
Evaluation Paper. . . . . . . . . . . . . . . . . . . . . . . . . . . . . . . . . . . . . . . . . 353
    *África Domingo, Jorge Echeverría, Óscar Pastor, and Carlos Cetina*

Workarounds in Business Processes: A Goal-Based Analysis . . . . . . . . . . . 368
    *Nesi Outmazgin, Pnina Soffer, and Irit Hadar*

Digging into Business Process Meta-models: A First Ontological Analysis. . . 384
    *Greta Adamo, Chiara Di Francescomarino, and Chiara Ghidini*

Mining User Opinions to Support Requirement Engineering:
An Empirical Study. . . . . . . . . . . . . . . . . . . . . . . . . . . . . . . . . . . . . . . 401
    *Jacek Dąbrowski, Emmanuel Letier, Anna Perini, and Angelo Susi*

Patterns for Certification Standards . . . . . . . . . . . . . . . . . . . . . . . . . . . . 417
    *Kevin Delmas, Claire Pagetti, and Thomas Polacsek*

Information Extraction and Graph Representation for the Design
of Formulated Products . . . . . . . . . . . . . . . . . . . . . . . . . . . . . . . . . . . . 433
    *Sagar Sunkle, Krati Saxena, Ashwini Patil, Vinay Kulkarni,*
    *Deepak Jain, Rinu Chacko, and Beena Rai*

## Information Systems Engineering

Resource-Based Adaptive Robotic Process Automation:
Formal/Technical Paper . . . . . . . . . . . . . . . . . . . . . . . . . . . . . . . . . . . . 451
    *Renuka Sindhgatta, Arthur H. M. ter Hofstede, and Aditya Ghose*

A Variability-Driven Analysis Method for Automatic Extraction
of Domain Behaviors. . . . . . . . . . . . . . . . . . . . . . . . . . . . . . . . . . . . . . 467
    *Iris Reinhartz-Berger and Sameh Abbas*

Mutation Operators for Large Scale Data Processing Programs
in Spark. . . . . . . . . . . . . . . . . . . . . . . . . . . . . . . . . . . . . . . . . . . . . . . 482
    *João Batista de Souza Neto, Anamaria Martins Moreira,*
    *Genoveva Vargas-Solar, and Martin Alejandro Musicante*

Recommendations for Evolving Relational Databases . . . . . . . . . . . . . . . .    498
   *Julien Delplanque, Anne Etien, Nicolas Anquetil, and Stéphane Ducasse*

A Combined Method for Usage of NLP Libraries Towards Analyzing
Software Documents . . . . . . . . . . . . . . . . . . . . . . . . . . . . . . . . . .    515
   *Xinyun Cheng, Xianglong Kong, Li Liao, and Bixin Li*

Query-Based Metrics for Evaluating and Comparing Document Schemas . . . .    530
   *Evandro Miguel Kuszera, Letícia M. Peres,*
   *and Marcos Didonet Del Fabro*

**Invited Keynote Talk**

Data Sovereignty and the Internet of Production . . . . . . . . . . . . . . . . . . . .    549
   *Matthias Jarke*

**Tutorials**

Volunteer Design of Data Warehouse . . . . . . . . . . . . . . . . . . . . . . . . . .    561
   *Sandro Bimonte*

Design of Service-Dominant Business Models for a Digital World . . . . . . . .    563
   *Paul Grefen and Oktay Turetken*

Using the Four-Component Instructional Design Model (4C/ID)
for Teaching Complex Learning Subjects in IS . . . . . . . . . . . . . . . . . . . . .    566
   *Monique Snoeck and Daria Bogdanova*

Open Source Software and Modern Information Systems: A Tutorial . . . . . . .    569
   *Anthony I. Wasserman*

Tutorial on Process Performance Management . . . . . . . . . . . . . . . . . . . . .    571
   *Adela del-Río-Ortega and Manuel Resinas*

**Author Index** . . . . . . . . . . . . . . . . . . . . . . . . . . . . . . . . . . . . . . . .    573

# Distributed Applications

# Remodularization Analysis for Microservice Discovery Using Syntactic and Semantic Clustering

Adambarage Anuruddha Chathuranga De Alwis[1](✉) ⓘ, Alistair Barros[1] ⓘ,
Colin Fidge[1] ⓘ, and Artem Polyvyanyy[2] ⓘ

[1] Queensland University of Technology, Brisbane, Australia
{adambarage.dealwis,alistair.barros,c.fidge}@qut.edu.au
[2] The University of Melbourne, Parkville, VIC 3010, Australia
artem.polyvyanyy@unimelb.edu.au

**Abstract.** This paper addresses the challenge of automated remodularization of large systems as microservices. It focuses on the analysis of enterprise systems, which are widely used in corporate sectors and are notoriously large, monolithic and challenging to manually decouple because they manage asynchronous, user-driven business processes and business objects (BOs) having complex structural relationships. The technique presented leverages semantic knowledge of enterprise systems, i.e., BO structure, together with syntactic knowledge of the code, i.e., classes and interactions as part of static profiling and clustering. On a semantic level, BOs derived from databases form the basis for prospective clustering of classes as modules, while on a syntactic level, structural and interaction details of classes provide further insights for module dependencies and clustering, based on K-Means clustering and optimization. Our integrated techniques are validated using two open source enterprise customer relationship management systems, SugarCRM and ChurchCRM. The results demonstrate improved feasibility of remodularizing enterprise systems (inclusive of coded BOs and classes) as microservices. Furthermore, the recommended microservices, integrated with 'backend' enterprise systems, demonstrate improvements in key non-functional characteristics, namely high execution efficiency, scalability and availability.

**Keywords:** Microservice discovery · System remodularization · Cloud migration

## 1 Introduction

Microservice architecture (MSA) has emerged as an evolution of service-oriented architecture (SOA) to enable effective execution of software applications in Cloud, Internet-of-Things and other distributed platforms [1]. Microservices (MSs) are fine-grained, in comparison to classical SOA components. They

© Springer Nature Switzerland AG 2020
S. Dustdar et al. (Eds.): CAiSE 2020, LNCS 12127, pp. 3–19, 2020.
https://doi.org/10.1007/978-3-030-49435-3_1

entail low coupling (inter-module dependency) and highly cohesive (intra-module dependency) functionality, down to individualised operations, e.g., single operation video-download as a MS component, versus a multi-operation video management SOA component [2]. This promotes systems performance properties, such as high processing efficiency, scalability and availability.

Reported experiences on MS development concern "greenfield" developments [1], where MSs are developed from "scratch". However, major uncertainty exists as to how MSs can be created by decoupling and reusing parts of a larger system, through refactoring. This is of critical importance for the corporate sectors which rely on large-scale enterprise systems (ESs), (e.g., Enterprise Resource Planning (ERP) and Customer-Relationship Management (CRM)), to manage their operations. Analysing ESs and identifying suitable parts for decoupling is technically cumbersome, given the millions of lines of code, thousands of database tables and extensive functional dependencies of their implementations. In particular, ESs manage business objects (BOs) [3], which have complex relationships and support highly asynchronous and typically user-driven processes [4–6]. For example, an order-to-cash process in SAP ERP has multiple sales orders, having deliveries shared across different customers, with shared containers in transportation carriers, and with multiple invoices and payments, which could be processed before or after delivery [7]. This poses challenges to identify suitable and efficient MSs from ES codes using classical software refactoring and optimal splitting/merging of code across software modules.

Software remodularization techniques [8–10] have been proposed based on static analysis, to identify key characteristics and dependencies of modules, and abstract these using graph formalisms. New modules are recommended using clustering algorithms and coupling and cohesion metrics. The focus of static analysis techniques includes inter-module structure (class inheritance hierarchies), i.e., *structural inheritance relationships*, and inter-module interactions (class object references), i.e., *structural interaction relationships*. Given that a degradation of logical design reflected in software implementations can result in classes with low cohesion, other techniques have been proposed to compare structural properties of classes using information retrieval techniques [10], i.e., *structural class similarity*. Despite these proposals, studies show that the success rate of software remodularisation remains low [11].

This paper presents a novel development of software remodularization applied to the contemporary challenge of discovering fine-grained MSs from an ES's code. It extends the syntactic focus of software remodularization, by exploiting the semantic structure of ESs, i.e., BOs and their relationships, which are, in principle, influential in class cohesion and coupling. Specifically, the paper presents the following:

- A novel MS discovery method for ESs combining syntactic properties, derived from extracted *structural inheritance relationships*, *structural interaction relationships*, *structural class similarity*, and *semantic properties*, derived in turn from databases and the relationships of BOs managed by classes.

– An evaluation of the MS discovery methods that addresses three research questions (refer Sect. 4.1) by implementing a prototype and experimenting on two open-source CRMs: SugarCRMonote[1] and ChurchCRM[2]. The results show that there is a 26.46% and 2.29% improvement in cohesion and a 18.75% and 16.74% reduction in coupling between modules of SugarCRM and ChurchCRM, respectively. Furthermore, SugarCRM and ChurchCRM manage to achieve 3.7% and 31.6% improved system execution efficiency and 36.2% and 47.8% scalability improvement, respectively, when MSs are introduced to the system as suggested by our approach while preserving overall system availability (refer to Tables 1, 2, 3, 4, 5 and 6).

The remainder of the paper is structured as follows. Section 2 describes the related works and background on system remodularization techniques. Section 3 provides a detailed description of our MS discovery approach while Sect. 4 describes the implementation and evaluation. The paper concludes with Sect. 5.

## 2 Background and Motivation

This section first provides an overview of existing software remodularization and MS discovery techniques with their relative strengths and weaknesses. It then provides an overview of the architectural context of ESs and their alignments with MSs. This context is assumed in the presentation of our software remodularization techniques (Sect. 3).

### 2.1 Related Work and Techniques Used for Software Remodularization

Software remodularization techniques involve automated analysis of different facets of systems, including software structure, behaviour, functional requirements, and non-functional requirements. Techniques have focussed on static analysis to analyse code structure and database schemas of the software systems while dynamic analysis studies interactions of systems. Both approaches provide complementary information for assessing properties of system modules based on high cohesion and low coupling, and make recommendations for improved modularity. However, static analysis is preferable for broader units of analysis (i.e., systems or subsystems level) as all cases of systems' execution are covered compared to dynamic analysis [9].

Traditionally, research into software remodularization based on static analysis has focused on a system's implementation through two areas of coupling and cohesion evaluation. The first is structural coupling and cohesion, which focuses on structural relationships between classes in the same module or in different modules. These include *structural inheritance relationships* between classes and *structural interaction relationships* resulting when one class creates another class

---

[1] https://www.sugarcrm.com/.
[2] http://churchcrm.io/.

and uses an object reference to invoke its methods [8]. Structural relationships such as these are automatically profiled through Module Dependency Graphs (MDG), capturing classes as nodes and structural relationships as edges [8,9], and are used to cluster classes using K-means, Hill-climbing, NSGA II and other clustering algorithms. The second is *structural class similarity* (otherwise known as *conceptual similarity* of the classes) [10]. This draws from information retrieval (IR) techniques, for source code comparison of classes, under the assumption that similarly named variables, methods, object references, tables and attributes in database query statements, etc., infer conceptual similarity of classes. Relevant terms are extracted from the classes and used for latent semantic indexing and cosine comparison to calculate the similarity value between them. Class similarity, thus, provides intra-module measurements for evaluating coupling and cohesion, in contrast to the inter-module measurements applied through structural coupling and cohesion described above.

Despite many proposals for automated analysis of systems, studies show that the success rate of software remodularization remains low [11]. A prevailing problem is the limited insights available from purely syntactic structures of software code to derive structural and interactional relationships of modules. More recently, semantic insights available through BO relationships were exploited to improve the feasibility of architectural analysis of applications. ESs manage domain-specific information using BOs, through their databases and business processes [5]. Evaluating the BO relationships and deriving valuable insights from them to remodularize software systems falls under the category of *semantic structural relationships* analysis. Such semantic relationships are highlighted by the experiments conducted by Pẽrez-Castillo *et al.* [12], in which the transitive closure of strong BO dependencies derived from databases was used to recommend software function hierarchies, and by the experiments conducted by Lu *et al.* [13], in which SAP ERP logs were used to demonstrate process discovery based on BOs. Research conducted by De Alwis *et al.* [14,15] on MS discovery based on BO relationship evaluation shows the impact of considering semantic structural relationships in software remodularization. However, to date, techniques related to semantic structural relationships have not been integrated with syntactic structural relationships and structural class similarity techniques. As a result, currently proposed design recommendation tools provide insufficient insights for software remodularization.

### 2.2   Architecture for Enterprise System to Microservice Remodularization

As detailed in Sect. 2.1, there are multiple factors which should be considered in the MS derivation process. In this section, we define the importance of considering such factors with respect to the architectural configuration of the ES and MSs.

As depicted in Fig. 1, an ES consists of a set of self-contained modules drawn from different subsystems and is deployed on a "backend" platform. Modules consist of a set of software classes which contain internal system

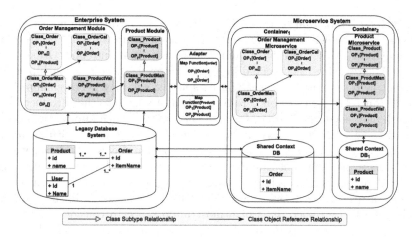

**Fig. 1.** Overview of an enterprise system extended with extracted microservices.

operations and operations which manage one or more BOs through create, read, update, and delete (CRUD) operations. For example 'Order Management Module' consists of several classes such as 'Class_Order', 'Class_OrderCal' and 'Class_OrderMan', which contain operations manipulating data related to 'Order' BO and 'Class_ProductVal', which contain operations manipulating data related to 'Product' BO. Furthermore, the modules are interrelated through method calls between classes in different modules (see the relationship of 'Class_ProductVal' and 'Class_ProductMan' in Fig. 1). In addition, classes inside each individual module can have generalization/specialization relationships (i.e., subtype-supertype relationships) between different classes as depicted by the relationships between 'Class_Order' and 'Class_OrderMan', and 'Class_Product' and 'Class_ProductMan' in Fig. 1.

The MSs, on the other hand, support a subset of operations through classes which are related to individual BOs. Such implementations lead to high cohesion within MSs and low coupling between the MSs (see the 'Order Management Microservice' and 'Product Microservice' in Fig. 1). The MSs communicate with each other through API calls in case they require information related to different BOs which reside in other MSs. For example, 'Order Management Microservice' can acquire Product values through an API call to 'Product Microservice' (refer arrow between the MSs in Fig. 1). The execution of operations across the ES and MS system is coordinated through business processes, which means that invocations of BO operations on the MSs will trigger operations on ES functions involving the same BOs. As required for consistency in an MS system, BO data will be synchronised across databases managed by ES and MSs periodically.

Based on this understanding of the structure of the ES and MSs, it is clear why we should consider semantic and syntactic information for the MS discovery process. In order to capture the *subtype relationships* and *object reference relationships* that exist in the ES system, we need *structural inheritance relationship* and *structural interaction relationship* analysis methods. Such methods can help to group classes which are highly coupled into one group, such as the grouping of 'Class_Order', 'Class_OrderCal' and 'Class_OrderMan' into one 'Order Management Microservice', as depicted in Fig. 1. However, those relationships alone would not help to capture class similarities at the code level. For example, the 'Class_ProductVal' operates on 'Product' BO and relates to the 'Product Module' much more than the 'Order Management Module'. Such information can be captured using *structural class similarity* measuring methods. With *structural inheritance and interaction relationships* and *structural class similarity* we can cluster classes into different modules. However, such modules might not align with the domain they are related to until we consider the BO relationships of different classes. In Fig. 1, one can notice that different classes in the ES relate to different BOs. As such, it is of utmost importance to consider the *semantic structural relationships* in the MS derivation process, since each MS should aim to contain classes that are related to each other and perform operations on the same BO (refer to the 'Order Management Microservice' and 'Product Microservice' in Fig. 1).

Previous research has extensively used *structural relationships* in system remodularization [8–10]. However, when it comes to MS derivation, combining the *semantic structural relationships* with the *syntactic structural relationships* should allow deriving better class clusters suitable for MS implementation. Given this system architecture context and our understanding of the features that should be evaluated for MS systems, we developed algorithms, as described in Sect. 3, for MS discovery. We use the following formalisation here onwards to describe the algorithms.

Let $\mathbb{I}$, $\mathbb{O}$, $\mathbb{OP}$, $\mathbb{B}$, $\mathbb{T}$ and $\mathbb{A}$ be a universe of *input* types, *output* types, *operations*, *BOs*, *database tables* and *attributes* respectively. We characterize a *database table* $t \in \mathbb{T}$ by a collection of attributes, i.e., $t \subseteq \mathbb{A}$, while a *business object* $b \in \mathbb{B}$ is defined as a collection of database tables, i.e., $b \subseteq \mathbb{T}$. An *operation* $op$, either of an ES or MS system, is given as a triple $(I, O, T)$, where $I \in \mathbb{I}^*$ is a sequence of *input types* the operation expects for input, $O \in \mathbb{O}^*$ is a sequence of *output types* the operation produces as output, and $T \subseteq \mathbb{T}$ is a set of *database tables* the operation accesses, i.e., either reads or augments.[3] Each *class* $cls \in CLS$ is defined as a collection of operations, i.e., $cls \subseteq \mathbb{OP}$.

## 3   Clustering Recommendation for Microservice Discovery

In order to derive the MSs while considering the factors defined in Sect. 2, we developed a six-step approach, which is illustrated in Fig. 2. In the first step, we derive the BOs by evaluating the SQL queries in the source code structure and also the database schemas and data as described by Nooijen *et al.* [16]. Next, we analyse the semantic structural relationships by deriving the class and BO

---

[3] $A^*$ denotes the application of the Kleene star operation to set $A$.

relationships. Steps 3–5 are used to discover the syntactic details related to the ES. In the third step, we measure the structural class similarities between the classes and in steps 4 and 5 we capture the structural details of the classes, step 4 discovers the structural inheritance relationships and step 5 discovers the structural interaction relationships. The details obtained through steps 2–5 are provided to the final step in which a K-means clustering algorithm is used to cluster and evaluate the best possible combination of classes for MS development and finally suggest them to the developers. Detailed descriptions of these steps and corresponding algorithms are provided in Sect. 3.1.

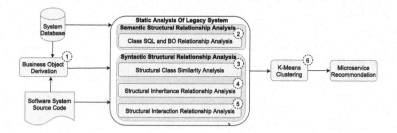

**Fig. 2.** Overview of our microservice discovery approach.

## 3.1   Clustering Discovery Algorithms

As depicted in Fig. 2, in order to derive a satisfactory clustering of system classes and operations and suggest MSs recommendations, we supply the K-means algorithm with four main feature sets. To derive these feature sets, we use Algorithm 1, which is composed of eight steps.

We define a BO $b \in B$ in an ES as a collection of database tables, i.e., $b \subseteq T$, since information related to a BO is often stored in several database tables. The $BOS$ function in Algorithm 1 used to derive BOs $B$ from ESs as detailed by Nooijen *et al.* [16] (see line 1). In the second step of the algorithm, the function $CLSEXT$ is used to extract code related to each class $cls \in CLS$ from the system code by searching through its folder and package structure (see line 2).

In the third step, we extract information required for the structural class similarity analysis using information retrieval (IR) techniques. As such, in the third step, the algorithm identifies unique words $UW$ related to all the classes using function $UWORDEXT$ (see line 3) which requires all the source codes of the classes $CLS$, and stop words $STW$, which should be filtered out from the classes. In general, IR techniques analyse documents and filter out the content which does not provide any valuable information for document analysis, which are referred to as 'stop words'. In our case, the stop words ($STW$) contain syntax related to the classes, common technical terms used in coding in that particular language (in this case PHP) and also common English words which would not provide any valuable insight about class purpose. These are specified by the user based on the language of the system they evaluate. The function $UWORDEXT$

first filters out the stop words $STW$ from the classes $CLS$ and then identifies the collection of unique words $UW$ in classes $CLS$, which is generally referred to as a 'bag of words' [17].

---

**Algorithm 1:** Discovery of BO and class relationships

---

**Input**: System code $SC$ of an ES $s$, stop words related to classes $STW$ and system database $DB$

**Output**: Feature set data *borel, cosine, subtyperel, referencerel* and BOs $B$

1  $B = \{b_1, \ldots, b_n\} := BOS(SC, DB)$
2  $CLS = \{cls_1, \ldots, cls_m\} := CLSEXT(SC)$
3  $UW = \langle uw_1, \ldots, uw_z \rangle := UWORDEXT(CLS, STW)$
4  **for** *each* $cls_i \in CLS$ **do**
5     **for** *each* $b_k \in B$ **do**
6       |  $borel[i][k] := BCOUNT(cls_i, b_k)$;
7     **end**
8     **for** *each* $uw_s \in UW$ **do**
9       |  $uwcount[i][s] := WCOUNT(uw_s, cls_i)$;
10    **end**
11 **end**
12 **for** *each* $cls_i, cls_k \in CLS$ **do**
13    |  $cosine[i][k] := COSINECAL(uwcount[i], uwcount[k])$;
14 **end**
15 $subtyperel := SUBTYPECAL(CLS)$;
16 $referencerel := REFERENCECAL(CLS)$;
17 **return** *borel, cosine, subtyperel, referencerel,* $B$

---

In the fourth step, the algorithm evaluates each class ($cls \in CLS$) extracted in step two and identifies the BOs which are related to each class. For this purpose, the algorithm uses the function $BCOUNT$ that processes the SQL statements, comments and method names related to the classes and counts the number of times tables relate to BOs. This information is stored in matrix *borel* (see lines 5–7). In this matrix, each row represents a class, and each column represents the number of relationships that class has with the corresponding BO, as depicted in Fig. 3(a). This helps to capture the semantic structural relationships (i.e., BO relationships) data, which provides an idea about the "boundness" of classes to BOs. For example Class 1 'Cls 1' is related to 'BO1' and 'BO2' in Fig. 3(a).

In the fifth step, the algorithm derives another matrix *uwcount*, which keeps the count of unique words related to each class using the function $WCOUNT$ (see lines 8–10). In this matrix, again, rows correspond to classes, and columns correspond to unique words identified in step three of the algorithm that appear in the corresponding classes. The values in *uwcount* are then used in the sixth step to calculate the cosine similarity between the documents using $COSINECAL$ function (see lines 12–14). First, this function normalizes the term frequencies with the respective magnitude L2 norms. Then it calculates the cosine similarity between different documents, by calculating the cosine value between two vectors of the *uwcount* (i.e., the rows related to two classes in *uwcount* matrix) and stores the values in the *cosine* matrix, as exemplified in Fig. 3(b). Note that the cosine similarity of a class to itself is always '1'. This provides the structural class similarity data for clustering.

Next, we extract the structural inheritance relationships (i.e., the class sub-type relationships) and structural interaction relationships (i.e., the class object reference relationships). This is achieved through steps seven and eight in the algorithm which use function *SUBTYPECAL* (see line 15) to identify the sub-type relationships and function *REFERENCECAL* (see line 16) to identify the class object reference relationships. In both of these functions, as the first step, the code is evaluated using Mondrian[4], which generates graphs based on class relationships. Then, the graphs are analyzed to create two matrices, namely *subtyperel* and *referencerel* which, respectively summarize the class subtype and reference relationships for further processing (see *subtyperel* depicted in Fig. 3(c) and *referencerel* depicted in Fig. 3(d)).

**(a) borel**

|       | BO1 | BO2 | BO3 |
|-------|-----|-----|-----|
| Cls 1 | 1   | 3   | 0   |
| Cls 2 | 0   | 3   | 0   |
| Cls 3 | 0   | 2   | 0   |
| Cls 4 | 1   | 0   | 3   |
| Cls 5 | 4   | 0   | 0   |

**(b) cosine**

|       | Cls 1 | Cls 2 | Cls 3 | Cls 4 | Cls 5 |
|-------|-------|-------|-------|-------|-------|
| Cls 1 | 1     | 0.75  | 0.83  | 0.44  | 0.05  |
| Cls 2 | 0.75  | 1     | 0.65  | 0.51  | 0.02  |
| Cls 3 | 0.83  | 0.65  | 1     | 0.53  | 0.03  |
| Cls 4 | 0.44  | 0.51  | 0.53  | 1     | 0.12  |
| Cls 5 | 0.05  | 0.02  | 0.03  | 0.12  | 1     |

**(c) subtyperel**

|       | Cls 1 | Cls 2 | Cls 3 | Cls 4 | Cls 5 |
|-------|-------|-------|-------|-------|-------|
| Cls 1 | 1     | 1     | 1     | 0     | 0     |
| Cls 2 | 1     | 1     | 0     | 1     | 0     |
| Cls 3 | 1     | 0     | 1     | 1     | 0     |
| Cls 4 | 0     | 1     | 1     | 1     | 0     |
| Cls 5 | 0     | 0     | 0     | 0     | 1     |

**(d) referencerel**

|       | Cls 1 | Cls 2 | Cls 3 | Cls 4 | Cls 5 |
|-------|-------|-------|-------|-------|-------|
| Cls 1 | 1     | 0     | 0     | 0     | 0     |
| Cls 2 | 0     | 1     | 1     | 1     | 0     |
| Cls 3 | 0     | 1     | 1     | 1     | 1     |
| Cls 4 | 0     | 1     | 1     | 1     | 0     |
| Cls 5 | 0     | 0     | 1     | 0     | 1     |

**Fig. 3.** Matrices derived from Algorithm 1.

The feature set data *borel*, *cosine*, *subtyperel*, *referencerel* and BOs $B$ obtained from Algorithm 1 are provided as input to the K-Means algorithm (i.e., Algorithm 2) to cluster the classes related to BOs based on their syntactic and semantic relationships. Note that each dataset captures different aspects of relationships between classes in the given system (see Fig. 3). Each initial centroid *intcent* $\in$ *IntCent* is a row number in the dataset that we provide. For example, one can select the first row of the dataset (as we have done in Fig. 3, see highlighted in red), as an initial centroid. In that situation, the *IntCent* will contain the data related to that specific row of the data set. Given these datasets as the first step in Algorithm 2, we initialize the distance difference value *distDif* to some constant, e.g., 10. The *distDif* is responsible for capturing the distance differences between the initial centroids *IntCent* and the newly calculated centroids *NewCent*. If this distance difference is zero, then it means that there is no difference between the initial centroid values and the newly calculated centroid values (in which case the algorithm terminates). After initializing the *distDif* value, the

---

[4] https://github.com/Trismegiste/Mondrian.

next steps of the algorithm are performed iteratively until the aforementioned condition of $distDif$ is met (see lines 2–21).

---

**Algorithm 2:** K-Means clustering for microservice discovery

---

**Input**: *borel, cosine, subtyperel, referencerel*, $k$ which is the number of BOs $B$ and an array of initial Centroid values $IntCent$

**Output**: $CLUS$ which captures the clustered MS recommendations.

1  $distDif := 10$ ;                                    // initialize $distDif$ value
2  **while** $distDif \neq 0$ **do**
3  | $CLUS = \{clus_1, \ldots, clus_k\} := INITCLUSTERS(k)$;
4  | **for** $0 \leq i < borel.size()$ **do**
5  | | $minEuclideanDis := MAX\_INTEGER$;   // initialize $minEuclideanDis$
6  | | **for each** $intcent_j \in IntCent$ **do**
7  | | | $newEuclideanDis := EUCAL(intcent_j, borel[i], cosine[i],$ $subtyperel[i], referencerel[i])$;
8  | | | **if** $newEuclideanDis < minEuclideanDis$ **then**
9  | | | | $minEuclideanDis := newEuclideanDis$;
10 | | | | $clusterNumber := j$;
11 | | | **end**
12 | | **end**
13 | | $clus_{clusterNumber} := clus_{clusterNumber} + i$;
14 | **end**
15 | **for each** $clus_i \in CLUS$ **do**
16 | | $NewCent = \{newcent_1, \ldots, newcent_n\} := NEWCENTCAL(clus_i)$;
17 | **end**
18 | $distDif := DISTANCECAL(IntCent, NewCent)$;   // Calculate distances
19 | $IntCent := NewCent$;
20 **end**
21 **return** $CLUS$

---

The first step of the iterative execution is to initialize the set of clusters $CLUS$, which we use to store the node groups identified by Algorithm 2. Next, we need to identify the cluster that each row (or the node) of our data should belong to by comparing the distance between each node in the dataset and each node in the initial centroids $intcent \in IntCent$. Hence we iterate through each row of the dataset we obtained from Algorithm 1 (see line 4 in Algorithm 2), while calculating the Euclidean distance between each row and each initial centroid $intcent \in IntCent$ (see lines 4–12 in Algorithm 2). For this calculation, as the initial step, we define the minimum Euclidean distance value $minEquclidianDis$ and initialize it to $MAX\_INTEGER$ (e.g., 100000). We assign this value to the $minEquclidianDis$ to ensure that it would be larger than the value we obtain for the $newEuclideanDis$ (line 7) at the end of the first iteration. Then, we calculate the Euclidean distance between one data set, for example, row 1 in Fig. 3 and each initial centroid point given. Next, we identify the centroid which has the minimum Euclidian distance to the node we obtained and allocate that node number to that particular cluster $clus \in CLUS$ (line 13). This process is carried out until all the nodes are clustered based on the Euclidean distance calculation. In the end, each node in the data set is clustered towards the centroid which has the minimal distance to it based on the four feature sets which emphasize that the classes related to that particular cluster are bound to the same BO and to each other syntactically and semantically.

The next step of Algorithm 2 is to calculate the new centroids based on the clusters obtained. For this, we take the mean value of the node data sets belonging to each cluster and assign it as the new centroid (see function $NEWCENTCAL$ at lines 15–17 in Algorithm 2). Then, we calculate the distance difference between the initial centroids and the new centroids. If this difference is zero, it means that there is no change of the centroid points and the algorithm has come to the optimum clustering point. If not, the newly calculated centroids becomes the initial centroids for the next iteration of the algorithm. At the end of the algorithm, the final set of clusters which contain the classes of the analysed ES are provided to the developers as recommendations for constructing MSs based on them.

## 4    Implementation and Validation

To demonstrate the applicability of the method described in Sect. 3, we developed a prototypical MS recommendation system[5] capable of discovering the class clusters related to different BOs, which lead to different MS configurations. The system was tested against two open-source customer relationship management systems: SugarCRM and ChurchCRM. SugarCRM consists of more than 8,000 files and 600 attributes in 101 tables, while ChurchCRM consists of more than 4,000 files and 350 attributes in 55 tables. However, most of the files are HTML files which are related to third-party components used by the systems. For the clustering, we only used the 1,400 classes of SugarCRM and 280 classes of ChurchCRM which capture the core functionality of the systems. Using our implementation, we performed static analysis of the source code to identify the BOs managed by the systems. As a result, 18 BOs were identified in Sugar-CRM, e.g., account, campaign, and user, and 11 BOs in ChurchCRM, e.g., user, family, and email. Then, we performed static analysis of both systems to derive matrices, similar to those depicted in Fig. 3, summarizing the BO relationships, class similarity relationships, class subtype relationships and class object reference relationships. All the obtained results were processed by the prototype to identify the class clusters to recommend MSs. Based on the input, the prototype identified 18 class clusters related to the BOs in SugarCRM and 11 class clusters related to the BOs in ChurchCRM. Consequently, each cluster suggests classes for developing an MS that relates to a single BO.

---

[5] https://github.com/AnuruddhaDeAlwis/KMeans.git.

### 4.1  Research Questions

Our evaluation aims to answer three research questions:

- **RQ1:** Do syntactic and semantic relationships between source code artifacts of an ES convey useful information for its remodularization into MSs?
- **RQ2:** Can our MS recommendation system discover MSs that have better cohesion and coupling than the original ES modules and lead to high scalability, availability, and execution efficiency in the cloud environment?
- **RQ3:** Can our MS recommendation system discover MSs that lead to better scalability, availability, and execution efficiency in the cloud environment than some MSs that do not follow the recommendations?

### 4.2  Experimental Setup

To answer the above research questions, we set up the following experiment consisting of three steps. In the first step, we evaluated the effectiveness of considering four different features (i.e., feature 1: *borel*, feature 2: *cosine*, feature 3: *referencerel* and feature 4: *subtyperel* extracted in Algorithm 1) in the clustering process. We evaluated this by measuring the Lack of Cohesion (LOC) and Structural Coupling (StrC) of the clusters, as detailed by Candela *et al.* [11], while incrementally adding different features in the clustering process. The values for the ES was calculated by clustering the classes into folders while conserving the original package structure, see first rows in Tables 1, 2, 3 and 4. Then, we clustered the classes several times, each time adding more features and calculating the LOC and StrC values. The obtained values are reported in Tables 1, 2, 3 and 4.

After evaluating the effectiveness of various features for clustering, we assessed the efficacy of introducing MSs to the ES. To this end, first, we hosted each ES in an AWS cloud by creating two EC2 instances having two virtual CPUs and a total memory of 2 GB, as depicted on the left side of Fig. 4. Systems' data were stored in a MySQL relational database instance which has one virtual CPU and total storage of 20 GB. Afterward, these systems were tested against 100 and 200 executions generated by four machines simultaneously, simulating the customer requests. We recorded the total execution time, average CPU consumption, and average network bandwidth consumption for these executions (refer to our technical report [18]). For SugarCRM, we test the functionality related to *campaign creation*, while for ChurchCRM we test the functionality related to *adding new people* to the system. The simulations were conducted using Selenuim[6] scripts which ran the system in a way similar to a real user.

Next, we introduced the 'campaign' and 'user' MSs to the SugarCRM system and 'person' and 'family' MSs to the ChurchCRM system. As depicted on the right side of Fig. 4, we hosted each MS on an AWS elastic container service (ECS), containing two virtual CPUs and a total memory of 1 GB. The BO data of each MS (i.e., campaign BO and user BO data of SugarCRM and person BO

---

[6] https://www.seleniumhq.org/.

and family BO data of ChurchCRM) was stored in separate MySQL relational database instances with one virtual CPU and total storage of 20 GB. Afterward, the test were performed on both ESs, again simulating *campaign creation* for SugarCRM and *adding new people* for ChurchCRM. Since MSs are refactored parts of the ESs in these tests, the ESs used API calls to pass the data to the MSs and the MSs processed and sent back the data to the ESs. MS databases and the ES databases were synchronized using the Amazon database migration service. Again, we recorded the total execution time, average CPU consumption, and average network bandwidth consumption for the entire system (i.e., ES and MS as a whole) (refer to our technical report [18]). The scalability, availability and execution efficiency of the systems were calculated based on the attained values. The results obtained are summarized in Tables 5 and 6 as *ES with MSs(1)* (refer to the second rows in Tables 5 and 6). Scalability was calculated according to the resource usage over time, as described by Tsai *et al.* [19]. To determine availability, first we calculated the packet loss for one minute when the system is down and then obtained the difference between the total up time and total time (i.e., up time + down time), as described by Bauer *et al.* [20]. Dividing the total time taken by the legacy system to process all requests by the total time taken by the corresponding ES system which has MSs led to the calculation of efficiency gain.

**Fig. 4.** System implementation in AWS.

In the third experiment, we disrupted the suggestions provided by our recommendation system and developed 'campaign' and 'user' MSs for SugarCRM, while introducing operations related to 'campaign' to 'user' MS and operations related to 'user' to 'campaign' MS. Similarly, for ChurchCRM, we developed 'person' and 'family' MSs such that 'person' MS contains operations related to 'family' MS and 'family' MS contains operations related to 'person' MS. With this change, again, we set up the experiment as described earlier and obtained the experimental results (refer to our technical report [18]). Then we calculated the scalability, availability and execution efficiencies of the systems which are summarized in Tables 5 and 6 as *ES with MSs(2)* (refer to the third rows in Tables 5 and 6). Based on these obtained experimental results we evaluate the effectiveness of the algorithms by answering the posed research questions.

*RQ1: Impact of Syntactic and Semantic Relationships.* The lower the lack of cohesion and structural coupling numbers, the better the cohesion and coupling of the system [11]. Consequently, it is evident from the average numbers reported in Tables 1, 2, 3 and 4 (refer to the orange color cells) that clustering improved the cohesion of software modules of SugarCRM and ChurchCRM by 26.46% and 2.29%, respectively, while reducing the coupling between modules by 18.75% and 16.74% respectively. Furthermore, it is evident that introducing additional features (i.e., syntactic and semantic information) in the clustering process increased the number of modules which obtain better coupling and cohesion values (refer to the blue cells in Tables 1, 2, 3 and 4). Thus, we conclude that there is a positive effect of introducing multiple syntactic and semantic relationships to the clustering process to improve the overall performance of the system.

*RQ2: Recommended MSs vs Original ES.* According to Tsai *et al.* [19], the lower the measured number, the better the scalability. Thus, it is evident that the MS systems derived based on our clustering algorithm managed to achieve 3.7% and 31.6% improved system execution efficiency and 36.2% and 47.8% scalability improvement (considering CPU scalability) (refer Tables 5 and 6), for SugarCRM and ChurchCRM, respectively, while also achieving better cohesion

**Table 1.** ChurchCRM ES vs MS system lack of cohesion value comparison.

| Features | 1 | 2 | 3 | 4 | 5 | 6 | 7 | 8 | 9 | 10 | 11 | Avg |
|---|---|---|---|---|---|---|---|---|---|---|---|---|
| Original ES | 61 | 188 | 853 | 7 | 4 | 1065 | 31 | 378 | 3064 | 13 | 17 | 516.45 |
| 1 and 2 | 61 | 77 | 666 | 33 | 8 | 1453 | 73 | 351 | 3802 | 3 | 10 | 594.27 |
| 1, 2 and 3 | 61 | 77 | 853 | 3 | 4 | 1564 | 23 | 351 | 3064 | 13 | 17 | 548.18 |
| 1, 2, 3 and 4 | 58 | 188 | 820 | 7 | 3 | 1059 | 31 | 351 | 3012 | 10 | 15 | 504.90 |

**Table 2.** ChurchCRM ES vs MS system structural coupling value comparison.

| Features | 1 | 2 | 3 | 4 | 5 | 6 | 7 | 8 | 9 | 10 | 11 | Avg |
|---|---|---|---|---|---|---|---|---|---|---|---|---|
| Original ES | 41 | 26 | 61 | 17 | 16 | 70 | 29 | 31 | 123 | 27 | 19 | 41.81 |
| 1 and 2 | 41 | 25 | 8 | 37 | 20 | 64 | 33 | 31 | 121 | 3 | 7 | 35.45 |
| 1, 2 and 3 | 41 | 25 | 61 | 16 | 16 | 68 | 29 | 27 | 123 | 7 | 19 | 41.09 |
| 1, 2, 3 and 4 | 42 | 25 | 34 | 17 | 15 | 63 | 29 | 3 | 112 | 26 | 17 | 34.81 |

**Table 3.** SugarCRM ES vs MS system lack of cohesion value comparison.

| Features | 1 | 2 | 3 | 4 | 5 | 6 | 7 | 8 | 9 | 10 | 11 | 12 | 13 | 14 | 15 | 16 | 17 | 18 | Avg |
|---|---|---|---|---|---|---|---|---|---|---|---|---|---|---|---|---|---|---|---|
| Original ES | 32 | 19 | 1255 | 698 | 1482 | 0 | 163 | 693 | 349 | 45 | 171 | 1803 | 1058 | 0 | 66 | 47 | 317 | 522 | 484.44 |
| 1 and 2 | 19 | 0 | 1067 | 1122 | 1173 | 0 | 86 | 459 | 170 | 21 | 120 | 953 | 587 | 0 | 36 | 6 | 453 | 187 | 358.83 |
| 1, 2 and 3 | 19 | 0 | 1201 | 626 | 1173 | 0 | 86 | 459 | 170 | 45 | 120 | 1027 | 587 | 0 | 36 | 7 | 590 | 268 | 356.33 |
| 1, 2, 3 and 4 | 19 | 0 | 1201 | 626 | 1173 | 0 | 86 | 459 | 170 | 45 | 120 | 1027 | 587 | 0 | 36 | 5 | 590 | 268 | 356.22 |

**Table 4.** SugarCRM ES vs MS system structural coupling value comparison.

| Features considered | 1 | 2 | 3 | 4 | 5 | 6 | 7 | 8 | 9 | 10 | 11 | 12 | 13 | 14 | 15 | 16 | 17 | 18 | Avg |
|---|---|---|---|---|---|---|---|---|---|---|---|---|---|---|---|---|---|---|---|
| Original ES | 24 | 12 | 121 | 63 | 48 | 4 | 99 | 24 | 29 | 29 | 28 | 101 | 67 | 0 | 16 | 10 | 82 | 85 | 46.77 |
| 1 and 2 | 12 | 2 | 117 | 76 | 48 | 4 | 87 | 18 | 25 | 20 | 27 | 85 | 45 | 0 | 15 | 5 | 52 | 64 | 39.00 |
| 1, 2 and 3 | 12 | 2 | 116 | 53 | 48 | 4 | 87 | 18 | 22 | 29 | 27 | 79 | 45 | 0 | 15 | 5 | 41 | 83 | 38.11 |
| 1, 2, 3 and 4 | 12 | 2 | 116 | 53 | 48 | 4 | 87 | 18 | 22 | 29 | 27 | 79 | 45 | 0 | 15 | 3 | 41 | 83 | 38.00 |

**Table 5.** Legacy vs MS system EC2 characteristics comparison for SugarCRM.

| System type | Scalability [CPU] | Scalability [DB CPU] | Scalability network | Availability [200] | Availability [400] | Efficiency [200] | Efficiency [400] |
|---|---|---|---|---|---|---|---|
| ES only | 3.521 | 2.972 | 2.759 | 99.115 | 99.087 | 1.000 | 1.000 |
| ES with MSs(1) | 2.246 | 2.532 | 2.352 | 99.082 | 99.086 | 1.037 | 1.000 |
| ES with MSs(2) | 2.667 | 2.546 | 2.684 | 99.099 | 99.099 | 1.018 | 0.986 |

**Table 6.** Legacy vs MS system EC2 characteristics comparison for ChurchCRM.

| System type | Scalability [CPU] | Scalability [DB CPU] | Scalability network | Availability [200] | Availability [400] | Efficiency [200] | Efficiency [400] |
|---|---|---|---|---|---|---|---|
| ES only | 3.565 | 3.109 | 3.405 | 99.385 | 99.418 | 1.000 | 1.000 |
| ES with MSs(1) | 1.859 | 2.751 | 3.663 | 95.000 | 94.871 | 1.316 | 1.189 |
| ES with MSs(2) | 2.876 | 2.667 | 2.779 | 95.238 | 95.000 | 1.250 | 1.158 |

and coupling values (refer Tables 1, 2, 3 and 4). As such, our recommendation system discovers MSs that have better cohesion and coupling values than the original enterprise system modules and can achieve improved cloud capabilities such as high scalability, high availability and high execution efficiency.

***RQ3: Recommended MSs vs Some MSs.*** MSs developed based on the suggestions provided by our recommendation system for SugarCRM and ChurchCRM managed to achieve: (i) 36.2% and 47.8% scalability improvement in EC2 instance CPU utilization, respectively; (ii) 14.8% and 11.5% scalability improvement in database instance CPU utilization, respectively; (iii) while achieving 3.7% and 31.6% improvement in execution efficiency, respectively. However, MSs that violate the recommendations reduced (i) EC2 instance CPU utilization to 24.24% and 19.32%; (ii) execution efficiency to 1.8% and 2.5%, for SugarCRM and ChurchCRM respectively and reduced database instance CPU utilization to 14.3% for SugarCRM. As such, it is evident that the MSs developed by following the recommendations of our system provided better cloud characteristics than the MSs developed against these recommendations.

### 4.3 Limitations

Next, we discuss an important limitation of our approach.

***Limitation of Structural Class Similarity Analysis:*** The cosine values might not provide an accurate idea about the structural class similarity since the structural similarity may also depend on the terms used in the definitions of the class names, method names and descriptions given in comments. This was mitigated to a certain extent by evaluating the code structure of the software systems before evaluating and verifying that the class names, method names and comments provide valuable insights into the logic behind the classes that implement the system.

## 5  Conclusion

This paper presented a novel technique for automated analysis and remodularization of ESs as MSs by combining techniques which consider semantic knowledge, together with syntactic knowledge about the code of the systems. A prototype recommendation system was developed and validation was conducted by implementing the MSs recommended by the prototype for two open source ESs: SugarCRM and ChurchCRM. The experiment showed that the proposed technique managed to derive class clusters which would lead to MSs with desired Cloud characteristics, such as high cohesion, low coupling, high scalability, high availability, and processing efficiency. In future work, we will enhance the technique by considering method level relationships in the analysis of MS candidates.

**Acknowledgment.** *This work was supported in part, through the Australian Research Council Discovery Project: DP190100314, "Re-Engineering Enterprise Systems for Microservices in the Cloud".*

## References

1. Newman, S.: Building Microservices. O'Reilly Media Inc., Sebastopol (2015)
2. https://www.nginx.com/blog/microservices-at-netflix-architectural-best-practices/
3. Barros, A., Duddy, K., Lawley, M., Milosevic, Z., Raymond, K., Wood, A.: Processes, roles, and events: UML concepts for enterprise architecture. In: Evans, A., Kent, S., Selic, B. (eds.) UML 2000. LNCS, vol. 1939, pp. 62–77. Springer, Heidelberg (2000). https://doi.org/10.1007/3-540-40011-7_5
4. Schneider, T.: SAP Business ByDesign Studio: Application Development, pp. 24–28. Galileo Press, Boston (2012)
5. Decker, G., Barros, A., Kraft, F.M., Lohmann, N.: Non-desynchronizable service choreographies. In: Bouguettaya, A., Krueger, I., Margaria, T. (eds.) ICSOC 2008. LNCS, vol. 5364, pp. 331–346. Springer, Heidelberg (2008). https://doi.org/10.1007/978-3-540-89652-4_26
6. Barros, A., Decker, G., Dumas, M.: Multi-staged and multi-viewpoint service choreography modelling. In: Proceedings of the Workshop on Software Engineering Methods for Service Oriented Architecture (SEMSOA), Hannover, Germany. CEUR Workshop Proceedings, vol. 244, May 2007
7. Barros, A., Decker, G., Dumas, M., Weber, F.: Correlation patterns in service-oriented architectures. In: Dwyer, M.B., Lopes, A. (eds.) FASE 2007. LNCS, vol. 4422, pp. 245–259. Springer, Heidelberg (2007). https://doi.org/10.1007/978-3-540-71289-3_20

8. Praditwong, K., Harman, M., Yao, X.: Software module clustering as a multi-objective search problem. IEEE Trans. Softw. Eng. **37**(2), 264–282 (2010)
9. Mitchell, B.S., Mancoridis, S.: On the automatic modularization of software systems using the bunch tool. IEEE Trans. Softw. Eng. **32**(3), 193–208 (2006)
10. Poshyvanyk, D., Marcus, A.: The conceptual coupling metrics for object-oriented systems. In: 22nd IEEE International Conference on Software Maintenance, pp. 469–478. IEEE, September 2006
11. Candela, I., Bavota, G., Russo, B., Oliveto, R.: Using cohesion and coupling for software remodularization: is it enough? ACM Trans. Softw. Eng. Methodol. (TOSEM) **25**(3), 24 (2016)
12. Pérez-Castillo, R., García-Rodríguez de Guzmán, I., Caballero, I., Piattini, M.: Software modernization by recovering web services from legacy databases. J. Softw.: Evol. Process **25**(5), 507–533 (2013)
13. Lu, X., Nagelkerke, M., van de Wiel, D., Fahland, D.: Discovering interacting artifacts from ERP systems. IEEE Trans. Serv. Comput. **8**(6), 861–873 (2015)
14. De Alwis, A.A.C., Barros, A., Fidge, C., Polyvyanyy, A.: Business object centric microservices patterns. In: Panetto, H., Debruyne, C., Hepp, M., Lewis, D., Ardagna, C.A., Meersman, R. (eds.) OTM 2019. LNCS, vol. 11877, pp. 476–495. Springer, Cham (2019). https://doi.org/10.1007/978-3-030-33246-4_30
15. De Alwis, A.A.C., Barros, A., Polyvyanyy, A., Fidge, C.: Function-splitting heuristics for discovery of microservices in enterprise systems. In: Pahl, C., Vukovic, M., Yin, J., Yu, Q. (eds.) ICSOC 2018. LNCS, vol. 11236, pp. 37–53. Springer, Cham (2018). https://doi.org/10.1007/978-3-030-03596-9_3
16. Nooijen, E.H.J., van Dongen, B.F., Fahland, D.: Automatic discovery of data-centric and artifact-centric processes. In: La Rosa, M., Soffer, P. (eds.) BPM 2012. LNBIP, vol. 132, pp. 316–327. Springer, Heidelberg (2013). https://doi.org/10.1007/978-3-642-36285-9_36
17. Lebanon, G., Mao, Y., Dillon, J.: The locally weighted bag of words framework for document representation. J. Mach. Learn. Res. **8**(Oct), 2405–2441 (2007)
18. https://drive.google.com/file/d/19niZYleVsuboNETCScYRB9LFVi3_5F2z/view?usp=sharing
19. Tsai, W.T., Huang, Y., Shao, Q.: Testing the scalability of SaaS applications. In: 2011 IEEE International Conference on Service-Oriented Computing and Applications (SOCA), pp. 1–4. IEEE, December 2011
20. Bauer, E., Adams, R.: Reliability and Availability of Cloud Computing. Wiley, Hoboken (2012)

# Decentralized Cross-organizational Application Deployment Automation: An Approach for Generating Deployment Choreographies Based on Declarative Deployment Models

Karoline Wild[(✉)] [iD], Uwe Breitenbücher [iD], Kálmán Képes [iD],
Frank Leymann [iD], and Benjamin Weder [iD]

Institute of Architecture of Application Systems, University of Stuttgart,
Stuttgart, Germany
{wild,breitenbuecher,kepes,leymann,weder}@iaas.uni-stuttgart.de

**Abstract.** Various technologies have been developed to automate the deployment of applications. Although most of them are not limited to a specific infrastructure and able to manage multi-cloud applications, they all require a central orchestrator that processes the deployment model and executes all necessary tasks to deploy and orchestrate the application components on the respective infrastructure. However, there are applications in which several organizations, such as different departments or even different companies, participate. Due to security concerns, organizations typically do not expose their internal APIs to the outside or leave control over application deployments to others. As a result, centralized deployment technologies are not suitable to deploy cross-organizational applications. In this paper, we present a concept for the decentralized cross-organizational application deployment automation. We introduce a global declarative deployment model that describes a composite cross-organizational application, which is split to local parts for each participant. Based on the split declarative deployment models, workflows are generated which form the deployment choreography and coordinate the local deployment and cross-organizational data exchange. To validate the practical feasibility, we prototypical implemented a standard-based end-to-end toolchain for the proposed method using TOSCA and BPEL.

**Keywords:** Distributed application · Deployment · Choreography · TOSCA · BPEL

## 1 Introduction

In recent years various technologies for the automated deployment, configuration, and management of complex applications have been developed. These *deployment automation technologies* include technologies such as Chef, Terraform,

© Springer Nature Switzerland AG 2020
S. Dustdar et al. (Eds.): CAiSE 2020, LNCS 12127, pp. 20–35, 2020.
https://doi.org/10.1007/978-3-030-49435-3_2

or Ansible to name some of the most popular [27]. Additionally, standards such as the Topology and Orchestration Specification for Cloud Applications (TOSCA) [20] have been developed to ensure portability and interoperability between different environments, e.g., different cloud providers or hypervisors. These deployment automation technologies and standards support a declarative deployment modeling approach [9]. The deployment is described as *declarative deployment model* that specifies the desired state of the application by its components and their relations. Based on this structural description a respective deployment engine derives the necessary actions to be performed for the deployment. Although most of these technologies and standards are not limited to a specific infrastructure and able to manage multi-cloud applications, they all use a central orchestrator for the deployment execution. This central orchestrator processes the declarative deployment model and either forwards the required actions in order to deploy and orchestrate the components to agents, e.g., in the case of Chef to the Chef clients running on the managed nodes, or executes them directly, e.g., via ssh on a virtual machine (VM), as done by Terraform [25].

However, today's applications often involve multiple participants, which can be different departments in a company or even different companies. Especially in Industry 4.0 the collaboration in the value chain network is of great importance, e.g., for remote maintenance or supply chain support [7]. All these applications have one thing in common: They are *cross-organizational applications* that composite distributed components, whereby different participants are responsible for different parts of the application. The deployment and management of such applications cannot be automated by common multi-cloud deployment automation technologies [22], since their central orchestrators require access to the internal infrastructure APIs of the different participants, e.g., the OpenStack API of the private cloud, or their credentials, e.g., to login to AWS. There are several reasons for the involved participants to disclose where and how exactly the application components are hosted internally: new security issues and potential attacks arose, legal and compliance rules must be followed, and the participant wants to keep the control over the deployment process [17]. This means that common centralized application deployment automation technologies are not suitable to meet the requirements of new emerging application scenarios that increasingly rely on cross-organizational collaborations.

In this paper, we address the following research question: *"How can the deployment of composite applications be executed across organizational boundaries involving multiple participants that do not open their infrastructure APIs to the outside in a fully automated decentralized manner?"* We present a concept for the decentralized cross-organizational application deployment automation that (i) is capable of globally coordinating the entire composite application deployment in a decentralized way while (ii) enabling the involved participants to control their individual parts locally. Therefore, we introduce a *global multi-participant deployment model* describing the composite cross-organizational application, which is split into local parts for each participant. Based on the local deployment models a deployment choreography is generated, which is executed in a decentralized manner. Based on the TOSCA and BPEL [19] standards the existing OpenTOSCA ecosystem [6] is extended for the proposed method and validated prototypically.

## 2   Declarative and Imperative Deployment Approaches

For application deployment automation two general approaches can be distinguished: declarative and imperative deployment modeling approaches [9]. For our decentralized cross-organizational application deployment automation concept both approaches are combined. Most of the deployment automation technologies use *deployment models* that can be processed by the respective deployment engine. Deployment models that specify the actions and their order to be executed, e.g., as it is done by workflows, are called *imperative deployment models*, deployment models that specify the desired state of an application are called *declarative deployment models* [9]. We explain the declarative deployment models in a technology-independent way based on the *Essential Deployment Meta Model (EDMM)* that has been derived from 13 investigated deployment technologies in previous work [27]. The meta model for declarative deployment models presented in Sect. 3 is based on the EDMM and is the basis for the declarative part of the presented concept.

In EDMM an application is defined by its *components* and their *relations*. For the semantic of these components and relations reusable *component* and *relation types* are specified. For example, it can be defined that a web application shall be hosted on an application server and shall be connected to a queue to publish data that are processed by other components. For specifying the configuration of the components *properties* are defined, e.g., to provide the credentials for the public cloud or to set the name of the database. For instantiating, managing, and terminating components and relations executable artifacts such as shell scripts or services are encapsulated as *operations* that can be executed to reach the desired state defined by the deployment model. The execution order of the operations is derived from the deployment model by the respective deployment engine [5].

In contrast, imperative deployment models explicitly specify the actions and their order to be executed to instantiate and manage an application [9]. Actions can be, e.g., to login to a public cloud or to install the WAR of a web application on an application server. Especially for complex applications or custom management behavior imperative deployment models are required, since even if declarative models are intuitive and easy to understand, they do not enable to customize the deployment and management. Imperative deployment technologies are, e.g., BPMN4TOSCA [16], and general-purpose technologies such as BPEL, BPMN [21], or scripting languages. In general, declarative deployment models are more intuitive but the execution is less customizable, while imperative deployment models are more complex to define but enable full control of the deployment steps. Therefore, there are hybrid approaches for using declarative models that are transformed into imperative models to get use of the benefits of both approaches [5]. In this paper, we follow this hybrid approach by transforming declarative models to imperative choreography models. This means, the user only has to specify the declarative model and, thus, we explain the declarative modeling approach in Sect. 4 using a motivating scenario. First, in the next section the meta model for declarative deployment models is introduced.

## 3   Meta Model for Declarative Deployment Models

Our approach presented in Sect. 5 is based on declarative deployment models that are transformed into imperative choreographies. Based on EDMM and inspired by the Declarative Application Management Modeling and Notation (DMMN) [3], the GENTL meta model [1], and TOSCA, a definition of declarative deployment models $d \in D$ is introduced:

**Definition 1 (Declarative Deployment Model).** *A declarative deployment model $d \in D$ is a directed, weighted, and possibly disconnected graph and describes the structure of an application with the required deployment operations:*

$$d = (C_d, R_d, CT_d, RT_d, O_d, V_d, type_d, operations_d, properties_d)$$

The elements of the tuple $d$ are defined as follows:

- $C_d$: Set of components in $d$, whereby each $c_i \in C_d$ represents one component.
- $R_d \subseteq C_d \times C_d$: Set of relations in $d$, whereby each $r_i = (c_s, c_t) \in R_d$ represents the relationship and $c_s$ is the source and $c_t$ the target component.
- $CT_d$ and $RT_d$: The set of component and relation types in $d$, whereby each $ct_i \in CT_d$ and $rt_i \in RT_d$ describes the semantics for components and relations having this type.
- $O_d \subseteq \wp(V_d) \times \wp(V_d)$: The set of operations in $d$, whereby each operation $o_i = (Input, Output) \in O_d$ specifies an operation that can be applied to components or relations with its input and output parameters.
- $V_d \subseteq \wp(\Sigma^+) \times \wp(\Sigma^+)$: Set of data elements, whereby $\Sigma^+$ is the set of characters in the ASCII table and $v_i = (datatype, value) \in V_d$.

Let the set of deployment model elements $DE_d := C_d \cup R_d$ be the union of components and relations of $d$. Let the set of deployment model element types $DET_d := CT_d \cup RT_d$ be the union of component types and relation types of $d$.

- $type_d$: The mapping assigning each $de_i \in DE_d$ to a component or relation type $det_i \in DET_d$: $type_d : DE_d \rightarrow DET_d$.
- $operations_d$: The mapping assigning each $de_i \in DE_d$ to a set of operations that can be applied to it: $operations_d : DE_d \rightarrow \wp(O_d)$.
- $properties_d$: The mapping assigning each $de_i \in DE_d$ to a set of data elements which are the properties of the element: $properties_d : DE_d \rightarrow \wp(V_d)$.  ∎

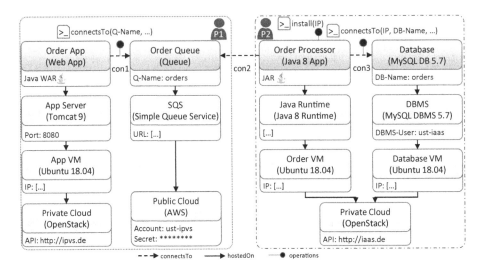

**Fig. 1.** Declarative deployment model specifying all details of the desired application. The notation is based on Vino4TOSCA with components as nodes, relations as edges, and the types in brackets [4]. In addition, sample operations are shown as dots.

## 4   Research Method and Motivating Scenario

Following the design cycle by Wieringa [26], we first examined the current situation in various research projects with industrial partners, namely in the projects IC4F[1], SePiA.Pro[2], and SmartOrchestra[3]. With regard to horizontal integration through the value chain network in the context of Industry 4.0, we focused on the requirements and challenges of collaboration between different companies [7]. Based on our previous research focus, the deployment and management of applications, the following research problems have emerged:

(a) How can the deployment of composite applications across organizational boundaries be automated in a decentralized manner?
(b) What is the minimal set of data to be shared between the involved participants to enable the automated decentralized deployment?

In Fig. 1 a declarative deployment model according to the meta model introduced in Sect. 3 is depicted for an order application to motivate the research problem. The application consists of four components: a web application *Order App* sending orders to the *Order Queue* and an *Order Processor* that processes the orders and stores them in the *Database*. These four components, depicted in dark gray with their component types in brackets, are the so-called *application-specific components*, since they represent the use case to be realized. For the Order Queue and Database, e.g., properties are specified to set the name of the

---

[1] https://www.ic4f.de/.
[2] http://projekt-sepiapro.de/en/.
[3] https://smartorchestra.de/en/.

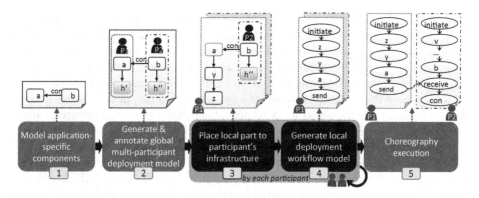

**Fig. 2.** Decentralized cross-organizational application deployment automation.

queue and database, respectively. In addition, three operations are exemplary shown: a *connectsTo* to establish a connection to the queue, a *connectsTo* to connect to the database, and an *install* operation to install the JAR artifact on the *Order VM*. The other properties and operations are abstracted.

Assuming that a single organization is responsible for deploying the entire application and has full control over the OpenStacks and AWS, the common deployment automation technologies examined by Wurster et al. [27] fit perfectly. However, in the depicted scenario two participants, *P1* and *P2*, who may be different departments or companies, intend to realize a cross-organizational application so that common deployment automation technologies are no longer applicable. While all participants must agree on the application-specific components, the underlying infrastructure is the responsibility of each participant. For security reasons, participants typically do not provide access to internal APIs, share the credentials for AWS, or leave the control over deployment to others.

To address the research problems, we propose a decentralized concept to enable the cross-organizational application deployment automation ensuring that (i) only as little data as necessary is exchanged between participants and (ii) each participant controls only his or her local deployment while the overall deployment is coordinated. The proposed solution is described in detail in the following section and in Sect. 6 the implementation and validation is presented. The motivating scenario in Fig. 1 serves as use case for the validation.

## 5   A Concept for Decentralized Cross-organizational Deployment Automation

For the decentralized cross-organizational application deployment automation with multiple participants, it has to be considered that (i) the participants want to exchange as little data as necessary and (ii) each participant controls only his or her local deployment while the global coordination of the deployment of the entire application is ensured. Taking these requirements into account, we have developed the deployment concept depicted in Fig. 2. In the first step, the application-specific components are modeled representing the use case to be realized. They typically include the business components such as the Order App, storage components such as the Database component, and communication components such as the Order Queue in Fig. 1. In the second step, the *global multi-participant deployment model (GDM)* is generated, a declarative deployment model containing all publicly visible information that is shared between the participants. This publicly visible information contains also data that must be provided by the respective infrastructure. For example, to execute the operation to establish a connection between Order Processor and Database in Fig. 1, the IP of the Database VM is required as input. Subgraphs, so called *local parts* of the GDM, are then assigned to participants responsible for the deployment of the respective components. The GDM is then processed by each participant. First, in step three, for each application-specific component a hosting environment is selected and the adapted model stored as *local multi-participant deployment model (LDM)*. In the motivating scenario in Fig. 1 participant P1 selected AWS for the Order Queue and the OpenStack for the Order App. However, this individual placement decision is not shared. For the deployment execution we use an hybrid approach: Based on the LDM a local deployment workflow model is generated in step four that orchestrates the local deployment and cross-organizational information exchange activities. All local workflows form implicitly the deployment choreography which enables the global coordination of the deployment across organizational boundaries. Each step is described in detail in the following.

### 5.1   Step 1: Application-Specific Component Modeling

In the initial step, the application-specific components representing the use case to be realized have to be modeled. They typically include business components, storage components, and communication components. In the motivating scenario in Fig. 1 the set of application-specific components contains the Order App, the Order Queue, the Order Processor, and the Database. In addition, the lifecycle operations, e.g., to install, start, stop, or terminate the components and relations, have to be defined for each of these components and their relations, since all input parameters of these operations must be provided as globally visible information in the GDM. Application-specific components are defined as follows:

**Definition 2 (Application-Specific Components).** *The set of application-specific components $C_s \subseteq C_d$ in d, where all $r_s = (c_s, c_t) \in R_d$ with $\{c_s, c_t\} \in C_s$ are of $type_d(r_s) = connectsTo$ and for each $c_i \in C_s : cap(type_d(c_i)) = \emptyset$, since they cannot offer hosting capabilities (see Definition 3).*   ∎

In addition, it has to be expressed that a component can have a certain requirement and that a component that provides a matching capability can serve as host, i.e., the component is the target of a relation of type *hostedOn*:

**Definition 3 (Hosting Requirements and Capability).** *Let RC the set of hosting requirement-capability pairs. The mapping $req : C_d \to \mathcal{P}(RC)$ and $cap : C_d \to \mathcal{P}(RC)$ assign to each component the set of capabilities and requirements,* respectively. The hosting capability of a component $c_y \in C_d$ matches the hosting requirement of a component $c_z \in C_d$, if it exists $rc \in RC$ with $rc \in req(c_z) \cap cap(c_y)$, then $c_y$ can host $c_z$. ∎

## 5.2   Step 2: Global Multi-Participant Deployment Model Generation

To ensure that the application-specific components can be deployed across organizational boundaries, the GDM is generated in the second step which contains the minimal set of necessary information that have to be globally visible, i.e., that have to be shared. Thus, the GDM is defined as follows:

**Definition 4 (Global Multi-Participant Deployment Model).** *A global multi-participant deployment model (GDM) is an annotated declarative deployment model that contains all globally visible information including the (i) application-specific components, (ii) necessary information about the hosting environment, and (iii) the participants assigned to parts of the GDM:*

$$g = (d, P_g, participant_g)$$

The elements of the tuple $g$ are defined as follows:

- $d \in D$: Declarative deployment model that is annotated with participants.
- $P_g \subseteq \wp(\Sigma^+) \times \wp(\Sigma^+)$: Set of participants with $p_i = (id, endpoint) \in P$, whereby $\Sigma^+$ is the set of characters in the ASCII table.
- $participant_g$: The mapping assigning a component $c_i \in C_d$ to a participant $p_i \in P_g participant_g : C_d \rightarrow P_g$. ∎

The example in Fig. 3 depicts a simplified GDM. The application-specific components, depicted in dark gray, specify requirements, e.g., the Order Queue requires a message queue middleware. These requirements have to be satisfied by the respective hosting environment. Furthermore, for these components as well as their connectsTo-relations operations with input parameters are defined. To establish a connection to the Order Queue the *URL* and *Q-Name* of the Queue are required. Either the target application-specific component provides respective matching properties such as the *Q-Name* property exposed by the Order Queue component or the environment has to provide it such as the input parameter *URL*. For this, in this step *placeholder host* components are generated that contain all capabilities and properties that have to be exposed by the hosting environment. Each placeholder host component $c_h$ is generated based on the following rules:

- For all $c_j \in C_s : req(c_j) \neq \emptyset$ a placeholder host component $c_h \in C_h$ and a hosting relation $r_h = (c_j, c_h) \in R_d$ with $type_d(r_h) = hostedOn$ are generated. Thus, $|C_h| \leq |C_s|$ since external services do not require a host.
- For each operation $op_j \in operations_s(c_j)$ all input data elements $v_j \in \pi_1(op_j) \backslash properties_d(c_j)$ are added to $properties_d(c_h)$.

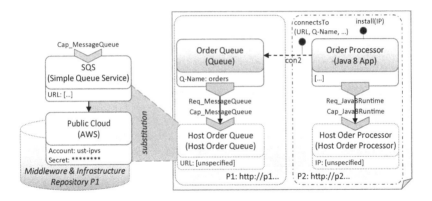

**Fig. 3.** Substitution of the database host from the motivating scenario.

– For each $r_j \in R_d : \pi_2(r_j) = c_j$ with $type_d(r_j) = connectsTo$ and for each operation $op_r \in operations_s(r_j)$ all data elements $v_r \in \pi_1(op_r) \setminus properties_s(c_j)$ are added to $properties_d(c_h)$.

In the example in Fig. 3 the *Host Order Queue* component provides the capability *MessageQueue* and exposes the property *URL*, which is required as input parameter for the *connectsTo* operations. Before the deployment model is processed by each participant, subgraphs of the GDM are assigned to the participants. This subgraph is called *local part* and indicates who is responsible for this part of the application. This is done by annotating the GDM as shown in Fig. 3 on the right.

### 5.3   Step 3: Local Part Placement

Since participants typically do not want to share detailed information about their hosting environment, the GDM is given to each participant for further processing. Each participant $p_i$ has to select a hosting environment for all $c_s \in C_s$ with $participant_g(c_s) = p_i$. In Fig. 3 the placement of the Order Queue component by substituting the placeholder host component *Order Queue Host* is shown. A placeholder host can be substituted by a stack that exposes the same capabilities and at least all properties of the placeholder host. These stacks are stored as declarative deployment models that contain middleware and infrastructure components available in the environment of the respective participant. In Fig. 3 a *SQS* hosted on AWS is shown. The substitution is based on the substitution mechanisms of TOSCA [20,24]: A placeholder host component $c_h \in C_h$ can be substituted by a deployment model $m$ if for each $prop_h \in properties_d(c_h)$ a component $c_f \in C_m : prop_h \in properties_m(c_f)$ and for each $cap_h \in cap(c_h)$ a component $c_k \in C_m : cap_h \in cap(c_k)$ exists.

The substitution in Fig. 3 is valid because the property *URL* is covered and the *SQS* exposes the required capability *MessageQueue*. The substitution is automated by our prototype described in Sect. 6. For the distribution of

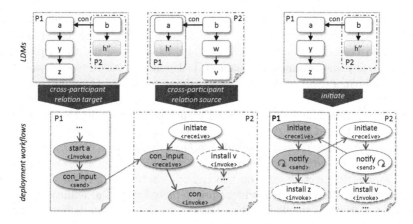

**Fig. 4.** Generated activities to (a) send information to relation source, (b) receive information from relation target, and (c) initiate the overall deployment.

components and matching to existing infrastructure and middleware several approaches exist [12,23,24]. Soldani et al. [24] introduced the ToscaMart method to reuse deployment models to derive models for new applications, Hirmer et al. [12] introduced a component wise completion, and we presented in previous work [23] how to redistribute a deployment model to different cloud offerings. These approaches use a requirement-capability matching mechanism to select appropriate components. We extended this mechanism to match the properties as well. The resulting *local multi-participant deployment model (LDM)* is a partially substituted GDM with detailed middleware and infrastructure components for the application-specific components managed by the respective participant. Up to this point we follow a purely declarative deployment modeling approach.

### 5.4   Step 4: Local Deployment Workflow Generation

The core step of our approach is the generation of local deployment workflow models that form the deployment choreography. They are derived from the LDMs by each participant and (i) orchestrate all local deployment activities and (ii) coordinate the entire deployment and data exchange to establish *cross-participant relations*. While centralized deployment workflows can already be generated [5], the global coordination and data exchange are not covered yet.

Cross-participant relations are of type *connectsTo* and between components managed by different participants. To establish cross-participant relations, the participants have to exchange the input parameters for the respective connectsTo-operations. In the example in Fig. 3 the relation *con2* establishes a connection from the Order Processor managed by P2 to the Order Queue managed by P1. The connectsTo-operation requires the *URL* and the *Q-Name* as input. Both parameters have to be provided by P1. Since this information is first available during deployment time, this data exchange has to be managed during deployment: For each cross-participant relation a sending and receiving activity is required to exchange the information after the target component is deployed and before the connection is established. In addition, the deployment of the entire application must be ensured. Independent which participant initiates the deployment, all other participants have to deploy their parts as well. This is covered by three cases that have to be distinguished for the local deployment workflow generation as conceptually shown in Fig. 4. In the upper part abstracted LDMs and in the lower part generated activities from the different participants perspectives are depicted. On the left (a) activities from a *cross-participant relation target* perspective, in the middle (b) from a *cross-participant relation source* perspective, and on the right (c) activities generated to ensure the *initiation* of the entire deployment are depicted. First, a definition of local deployment workflow models based on the production process definition [14,18] is provided:

**Definition 5 (Local Deployment Workflow Model).** *For each participant $p_i \in P$ a local deployment workflow model $w_i$ based on the LDM is defined as:*

$$w_i = (A_{w_i}, E_{w_i}, V_{w_i}, i_{w_i}, o_{w_i}, type_{w_i})$$

The elements of the tuple $w_i$ are defined as follows:

- $A_{w_i}$: Set of activities in $w_i$ with $a_y \in A_{w_i}$.
- $E_{w_i} \subseteq A_{w_i} \times A_{w_i}$: Set of control connectors between activities, whereby each $e_y = (a_s, a_t) \in E_{w_i}$ represents that $a_s$ has to be finished before $a_t$ can start.
- $V_{w_i} \subseteq \wp(\Sigma^+) \times \wp(\Sigma^+)$: Set of data elements, whereby $\Sigma^+$ is the set of characters in the ASCII table and $v_y = (datatype, value) \in V_{w_i}$.
- $i_{w_i}$: The mapping assigns to each activity $a_y \in A_{w_i}$ its input parameters and it is called the input container $i_{w_i} : A_{w_i} \rightarrow \wp(V_{w_i})$.
- $o_{w_i}$: The mapping assigns to each activity $a_y \in A_{w_i}$ its output parameters and it is called the output container $o_{w_i} : A_{w_i} \rightarrow \wp(V_{w_i})$.
- $type_{w_i}$: The mapping assigns each $a_y \in A_{w_i}$ to an activity type, $type_{w_i} : A_{w_i} \rightarrow \{\texttt{receive}, \texttt{send}, \texttt{invoke}\}$. ∎

Based on this definition, local deployment workflow models can be generated based on specific rules. In Fig. 4 the resulting activities are depicted:

(a) For each component $c_t \in C_d$ that is target of a cross-participant relation $r_c = (c_s, c_t)$ with $participant_g(c_t) = p_i$ and $participant_g(c_s) = p_j$, an activity $a_t \in A_{w_i} : type_{w_i}(a_t) = \texttt{invoke}$ is added that invokes the *start* operation of $c_t$. After a component is started, a connection to it can be established [5]. Thus, $a_c : type_{w_i}(a_c) = \texttt{send}$ is added to $w_i$ that contains all input parameters of the connectsTo-operation of $r_c$ provided by $p_i$ in $o_{w_i}(a_c)$.

(b) For the component $c_s \in C_d$, the source of the cross-participant relation $r_c$, an activity $a_{c'} : type_{w_j}(a_{c'}) = \texttt{receive}$ is add to $w_j$ of $p_j$. With the control connector $e(a_{init}, a_{c'})$ added to $w_j$ it is ensured that the activity is activated after the *initiate* activity of $p_j$. After the input values are received and the *start* operation of $c_s$ is successfully executed, the actual connectsTo-operation can be executed.

(c) Each workflow $w_i$ starts with the *initiate* activity $a_{init} \in A_{w_i} : type_{w_i}$ $(a_{init}) = \texttt{receive}$. To ensure that after $a_{init}$ is called the entire application deployment is initiated, a notification is sent to all other participants. For each $p_j \in P \setminus \{p_i\}$ an activity $a_n : type_{w_i}(a_n) = \texttt{send}$ with a control connector $e(a_{init}, a_n)$ is added to $w_i$. Since each participant notifies all others, for n participants, each participant has to discard n-1 messages. Since the payloads are at most a set of key-value pairs this is not critical.

Each participant generates a local deployment workflow model, which together implicitly form the deployment choreography. As correlation identifier the GDM id and application instance id are sufficient. While the GDM id is known in advance, the application instance id is generated by the initiating participant. The approach enables a decentralized deployment while each participant controls only his or her deployment and shares only necessary information.

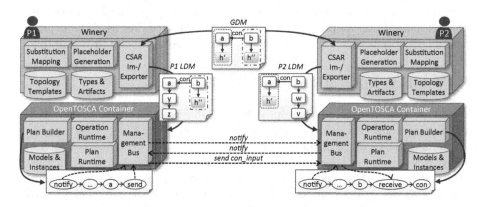

**Fig. 5.** System architecture and deployment choreography execution.

## 6 Implementation and Validation

To demonstrate the practical feasibility of the approach we extended the TOSCA-based open-source end-to-end toolchain *OpenTOSCA*[4] [6]. It consists of a modeling tool *Winery*, a deployment engine *OpenTOSCA Container*, and a self-service portal. In TOSCA, deployment models are modeled as *topology templates*, the components as *node*, and the relations as *relationship templates* with their *types*. The types define *properties, operations, capabilities*, and *requirements*. *Plans* are the imperative part of TOSCA, for which standard workflow languages such as BPMN or BPEL can be used. All TOSCA elements and executables, implementing operations and components, are packaged as *Cloud Service Archive (CSAR)*.

---

[4] https://github.com/OpenTOSCA.

In Fig. 5 the system architecture for two participants is depicted. Winery is extended by the *placeholder generation* and the *placeholder substitution*. Either P1 or P2 models the application-specific components and generates the GDM using the *Placeholder Generation* that generates node types with the respective properties and capabilities. The resulting GDM is then packaged with the *CSAR Im-/Exporter* and sent to each participant. The *Substitution Mapping* detects the local part of managed by the respective participant in the GDM and selects topology templates from the repository to substitute the placeholder host components. The substituted topology template is then uploaded to the OpenTOSCA Container. The *Plan Builder* generates a deployment plan based on the declarative model. We use BPEL for the implementation. Either P1 or P2 can then initiate the deployment. The *Plan Runtime* instantiates the plan and invokes the operations. The actual operation, e.g., to create a VM, is executed by the *Operation Runtime*. The communication between the OpenTOSCA Containers is managed by the *Management Bus*. The Management Bus is the participant's endpoint in our setup. However, also arbitrary messaging middleware or any other endpoint that can process the messages can be used. We used the deployment model presented in Fig. 1 with two and three participants for the validation.

## 7    Validity, Limitations, and Implications

In contrast to general workflow approaches [14,15], we do not have to deal with splitting workflows according to the participants, since we can completely rely on the declarative deployment model and only implicitly generates a choreography. However, a prerequisite is that each participant only uses the predefined interfaces so that the choreography can be executed. At present, we also limit ourselves to the deployment aspect and do not consider the subsequent management. While management functionalities such as scaling are often covered by the cloud providers themselves, other functionalities such as testing, backups, or updates are not offered. Management increases the complexity of automation, especially when local management affects components managed by other participants. We currently only support TOSCA as a modeling language and OpenTOSCA as a deployment engine. So far, we lack the flexibility to support technologies like Kubernetes, Terraform, or Chef, which are often already in use in practice. However, this is part of the planned future work.

## 8    Related Work

The research in the field of *multi-cloud*, *federated cloud*, and *inter-cloud* [10,22] focuses on providing unified access to different cloud providers, making placement decisions, migration, and management. All these approaches consider multiple cloud providers satisfying the requirements of a single user. The cloud forms differ in whether the user is aware of using several clouds or not. However, the collaboration between different users each using and controlling his or her environment, whether it is a private, public, or multi-cloud, is not considered, but this is highly important, especially in cross-company scenarios which arose with new emerging use cases in the fourth industrial revolution. Arcangeli et al. [2] examined the characteristics of deployment technologies for distributed applications and also considered the deployment control, whether it is centralized or decentralized. However, also the decentralized approaches with a peer-to-peer approach does not consider the sovereignty of the involved peers and the communication restrictions. In previous work [13], we introduced an approach to enable the deployment of parts of an application in environments that restrict incoming communication. However, the control is still held by a central orchestrator.

Kopp and Breitenbücher [17] motivated that choreographies are essential for distributed deployments. Approaches for modeling choreographies, e.g., with BPEL [8] or to split orchestration workflows into multiple workflows [14,15] have been published. However, most of the deployment technologies are based on a declarative deployment models [27], since defining the individual tasks to be performed in the correct order to reach a desired state are error-prone. Thus, instead of focusing on workflow choreographies we implicitly generated a choreography based on declarative deployment models. Breitenbücher et al. [5] demonstrated how to derive workflows from declarative deployment models. However, their approach only enables to generate orchestration workflows which cannot be used for decentralized cross-organizational deployments. Herry et al. [11] introduced a planning based approach to generate a choreography. However, they especially focus on generating an overall choreography that can be executed by several agents. For us the choreography is only an implicit artifact, since we mainly focus on enabling the cross-organizational deployment by minimizing the globally visible information and obtaining the sovereignty of the participants.

## 9    Conclusion and Future Work

In this paper, we presented an approach for the decentralized deployment automation of cross-organizational applications involving multiple participants. A cross-organizational deployment without a central trusted third-party is enabled based on a declarative deployment modeling approach. The approach facilitates that (i) each participant controls the local deployment, while the global deployment is coordinated and (ii) only the minimal set of information is shared. A declarative global multi-participant deployment model that contains all globally visible information is generated and split to local deployment models that are processed by each participant. Each participant adapts the local model with internal information and generates an imperative deployment workflow. These workflows form the deployment choreography that coordinates the entire application deployment. We implemented the concept by extending the OpenTOSCA ecosystem using TOSCA and BPEL. In future work the data exchange will be optimized since each participant sends notification messages to all other participant and thus for n participants n-1 messages have to be discarded. We further plan not only to enable multi-participant deployments but also multi-technology deployments by enabling to orchestrate multiple deployment technologies.

**Acknowledgments.** This work is partially funded by the BMWi project *IC4F* (01MA17008G), the DFG project *DiStOPT* (252975529), and the DFG's Excellence Initiative project SimTech (EXC 2075 - 390740016).

# References

1. Andrikopoulos, V., Reuter, A., Gómez Sáez, S., Leymann, F.: A GENTL approach for cloud application topologies. In: Villari, M., Zimmermann, W., Lau, K.-K. (eds.) ESOCC 2014. LNCS, vol. 8745, pp. 148–159. Springer, Heidelberg (2014). https://doi.org/10.1007/978-3-662-44879-3_11

2. Arcangeli, J.P., Boujbel, R., Leriche, S.: Automatic deployment of distributed software systems: definitions and state of the art. J. Syst. Softw. **103**, 198–218 (2015)

3. Breitenbücher, U.: Eine musterbasierte Methode zur Automatisierung des Anwendungsmanagements. Dissertation, Universität Stuttgart, Fakultaet Informatik, Elektrotechnik und Informationstechnik (2016)

4. Breitenbücher, U., Binz, T., Kopp, O., Leymann, F., Schumm, D.: Vino4TOSCA: a visual notation for application topologies based on TOSCA. In: Meersman, R., et al. (eds.) OTM 2012. LNCS, vol. 7565, pp. 416–424. Springer, Heidelberg (2012). https://doi.org/10.1007/978-3-642-33606-5_25

5. Breitenbücher, U., et al.: Combining declarative and imperative cloud application provisioning based on TOSCA. In: IC2E 2014. IEEE (2014)

6. Breitenbücher, U., et al.: The openTOSCA ecosystem - concepts & tools. In: European Space project on Smart Systems, Big Data, Future Internet - Towards Serving the Grand Societal Challenges. EPS Rome 2016, vol. 1. SciTePress (2016)

7. Camarinha-Matos, L.M., Fornasiero, R., Afsarmanesh, H.: Collaborative networks as a core enabler of industry 4.0. In: Camarinha-Matos, L.M., Afsarmanesh, H., Fornasiero, R. (eds.) PRO-VE 2017. IAICT, vol. 506, pp. 3–17. Springer, Cham (2017). https://doi.org/10.1007/978-3-319-65151-4_1

8. Decker, G., Kopp, O., Leymann, F., Weske, M.: BPEL4Chor: extending BPEL for modeling choreographies. In: ICWS 2007 (2007)

9. Endres, C., et al.: Declarative vs. imperative: two modeling patterns for the automated deployment of applications. In: PATTERNS (2017)

10. Grozev, N., Buyya, R.: Inter-cloud architectures and application brokering: taxonomy and survey. Softw.: Pract. Exper. **44**(3), 369–390 (2012)

11. Herry, H., Anderson, P., Rovatsos, M.: Choreographing configuration changes. In: CNSM 2013. IEEE (2013)

12. Hirmer, P., et al.: Automatic topology completion of TOSCA-based cloud applications. In: GI-Jahrestagung, GI, vol. P–251. GI (2014)

13. Képes, K., Breitenbücher, U., Leymann, F., Saatkamp, K., Weder, B.: Deployment of distributed applications across public and private networks. In: EDOC. IEEE (2019)

14. Khalaf, R.: Supporting business process fragmentation while maintaining operational semantics: a BPEL perspective. Dissertation, Universität Stuttgart, Fakultaet Informatik, Elektrotechnik und Informationstechnik (2006)

15. Khalaf, R., Leymann, F.: E role-based decomposition of business processes using BPEL. In: ICWS 2006 (2006)

16. Kopp, O., Binz, T., Breitenbücher, U., Leymann, F.: BPMN4TOSCA: a domain-specific language to model management plans for composite applications. In: Mendling, J., Weidlich, M. (eds.) BPMN 2012. LNBIP, vol. 125, pp. 38–52. Springer, Heidelberg (2012). https://doi.org/10.1007/978-3-642-33155-8_4

17. Kopp, O., Breitenbücher, U.: Choreographies are key for distributed cloud application provisioning. In: Proceedings of the 9th Central-European Workshop on Services and their Composition. CEUR-WS.org (2017)

18. Leymann, F., Roller, D.: Production Workflow: Concepts and Techniques. Prentice Hall PTR, Upper Saddle River (2000)

19. OASIS: Web Services Business Process Execution Language Version 2.0 (2007)

20. OASIS: TOSCA Simple Profile in YAML Version 1.2 (2019)

21. OMG: BPMN Version 2.0. Object Management Group (OMG) (2011)

22. Petcu, D.: Multi-Cloud: expectations and current approaches. In: 2013 International Workshop on Multi-Cloud Applications and Federated Clouds. ACM (2013)

23. Saatkamp, K., Breitenbücher, U., Kopp, O., Leymann, F.: Topology splitting and matching for multi-cloud deployments. In: CLOSER 2017. SciTePress (2017)

24. Soldani, J., Binz, T., Breitenbücher, U., Leymann, F., Brogi, A.: ToscaMart: a method for adapting and reusing cloud applications. J. Syst. Softw. **113**, 395–406 (2016)

25. Weerasiri, D., Barukh, M.C., Benatallah, B., Sheng, Q.Z., Ranjan, R.: A taxonomy and survey of cloud resource orchestration techniques. ACM Comput. Surv. **50**(2), 1–41 (2017)

26. Wieringa, R.J.: Design Science Methodology for Information Systems and Software Engineering. Springer, Heidelberg (2014). https://doi.org/10.1007/978-3-662-43839-8

27. Wurster, M., et al.: The essential deployment metamodel: a systematic review of deployment automation technologies. SICS (2019). https://doi.org/10.1007/s00450-019-00412-x

# Modeling and Analyzing Architectural Diversity of Open Platforms

Bahar Jazayeri[1]([✉]), Simon Schwichtenberg[1], Jochen Küster[2],
Olaf Zimmermann[3], and Gregor Engels[1]

[1] Paderborn University, Paderborn, Germany
{bahar.jazayeri,simon.schwichtenberg,gregor.engels}@upb.de
[2] Bielefeld University of Applied Sciences, Bielefeld, Germany
jochen.kuester@fh-bielefeld.de
[3] University of Applied Sciences of Eastern Switzerland, St. Gallen, Switzerland
ozimmerm@hsr.ch

**Abstract.** Nowadays, successful software companies attain enhanced business objectives by opening their platforms to thousands of third-party providers. When developing an open platform many architectural design decisions have to be made, which are driven from the companies' business objectives. The set of decisions results in an overwhelming design space of architectural variabilities. Until now, there are no architectural guidelines and tools that explicitly capture design variabilities of open platforms and their relation to business objectives. As a result, systematic knowledge is missing; platform providers have to fall back to ad-hoc decision-making; this bears consequences such as risks of failure and extra costs. In this paper, we present a pattern-driven approach called *SecoArc* to model diverse design decisions of open platforms and to analyze and compare alternative architectures with respect to business objectives. SecoArc consists of a *design process*, a *modeling language*, and an automated *architectural analysis technique*. It is implemented and ready-to-use in a tool. We evaluate the approach by means of a real-world case study. Results show that the approach improves the decision-making. Future platform providers can reduce risks by making informed decisions at design time.

## 1 Introduction

In recent years, prominent software companies succeed in growing by transforming their software products to platforms with open Application Programming Interfaces (APIs), so that third-party providers can develop software on top of them. Usually, online marketplaces are used to distribute the third-party developments of such *open platforms*. Success of open platforms highly depends on suitable design and governance of the ecosystem surrounding them, i.e., the arrangement of human actors and their interaction with the platforms [1]. Such an ecosystem is called *software ecosystem* and is the result of a variable and complex range of architectural design decisions whereas the decisions span across

© Springer Nature Switzerland AG 2020
S. Dustdar et al. (Eds.): CAiSE 2020, LNCS 12127, pp. 36–53, 2020.
https://doi.org/10.1007/978-3-030-49435-3_3

business, application, and infrastructure architectures [2]. Inevitably, different business decisions may result in completely different application and infrastructure architectures [3]. For instance, in ecosystems around mobile platforms (e.g., Apple iOS), the platform providers decide about technical standards like programming languages, which give them control over thousands of third-party providers. In contrary, open source software platforms (e.g., Mozilla Firefox) support innovation whereas developers are free to choose the development environment as well as to publish on the marketplaces. Another group is highly commercialized industrial platforms (e.g., belonging to Citrix and SAP) that are rigorously tested and verified and have networks of strategic partners around them.

Although a diverse range of open platforms has already been created in practice, there is still a lack of systematic architectural guidance to design the ecosystems surrounding them [4]. There is a multitude of Architecture Description Languages (ADLs) that focus on specific operational domains [5], while only supporting needs of those domains, e.g., for mobile applications [6]. In addition, general-purpose languages like UML and Enterprise Architecture Modeling (EAM) like ArchiMate do not allow architects to directly capture diverse design decisions of open platforms and more importantly to analyze suitability of ecosystem architecture with respect to business objectives and quality attributes [7]. The generality and abundance of notations in these languages lead in practice to laborious and time-consuming work [8]. More importantly, some crucial characteristics like *platform openness* are not addressed by these languages [9]. Therefore, the companies that also wish to open their own platforms have to only rely on ad-hoc decision-making and face the consequences such as extra costs of developing useless features, irreversible business risks of unwillingly exposing platform's intellectual property, or technical debt due to sub-optimal decisions [10]. A language that provides the suitable abstraction and captures the architectural diversity of open platforms can facilitate systematic creation of these systems in the future.

In this paper, we present a pattern-driven approach based on a study of 111 open platforms, called *SecoArc*, to model ecosystem architectures and analyze their suitability with respect to business objectives. The contribution of this paper is threefold. SecoArc provides: A) a systematic *design process* for stepwise development of ecosystem architecture. B) a *modeling language* to explicitly express design decisions of open platforms. The language is grounded on a rich *domain model* that embeds the architectural diversity of 111 platforms and a systematic literature review as our preliminary work [11–13]. C) a fully automated *architectural analysis technique* based on three patterns for suitability assessment and in-depth comparison of alternative architectures. SecoArc [14] has been implemented as a ready-to-use tool.

We evaluate the approach by means of a real-world case study called *On-The-Fly Computing Proof-of-Concept (PoC)*. The PoC platform is going to be open. However, there are several architectural variabilities and the possibility of achieving different architectures. The team would like to ensure the suitability of future ecosystem architecture with respect to crucial business objectives. Two alternative architectures are designed, analyzed, and compared. Using a semi-structured interview [15] aligned with ISO/IEC 25010 [16], functional suitability of SecoArc is evaluated. Results show that *i*) SecoArc contributes to familiarizing the architect with the domain knowledge of open platforms. *ii*) the automatic architectural analysis technique improves decision-making by disclosing enhanced and degraded business objectives and quality attributes. *iii*) availability of the tool and guide material directly impacts the uptake. In the future, platform providers can reduce risks by making informed decision-making and accordingly take actions at design time. In the following, Sect. 2 introduces three architectural patterns and the case study, PoC. In Sect. 3, we extract architectural variabilities of the PoC. Section 4 describes SecoArc and its elements. There, the applicability of SecoArc is demonstrated by means of the case study. Section 5 elaborates on the evaluation. After discussing related work in Sect. 6, Sect. 7 concludes and discusses future research directions.

## 2   Background

In this section, first, we present three architectural patterns that are the basis of architectural analysis in SecoArc. Afterwards, we introduce the case study.

### 2.1   Architectural Patterns of Software Ecosystems

In practice, patterns are used as powerful design instruments to communicate well-established knowledge [17]. In our previous work [11], we identify three architectural patterns that are derived from an examination of 111 open platforms from diverse application domains. Each pattern is characterized by an *organizational context* and a set of *design decisions*, and it helps to achieve certain *quality attributes* and *business objectives* as depicted in Fig. 1. The quality attributes are the attributes of business ecosystems from the quality model introduced by BEN HADJ SALEM MHAMDIA [18]. In the following, we present the architectural patterns.

**Open Source Software (OSS)-Based Ecosystem: Innovation.** This pattern aids to attract providers of open source software services. The providers are non-commercially motivated, and the platform is not safety-critical. The high degree of openness, e.g., open and free platforms, enhances creativity by opening the ecosystem for innovative services. Here, a platform is considered open when the third-party providers can directly contribute to the platform's code whereas a platform being free concerns the dimension of cost. Examples of ecosystems are Mozilla, Eclipse, and Apache Cordova.

**Partner-Based Ecosystem: Strategic Growth.** The pattern helps to grow complex and industrial software ecosystem while enhancing profitability. Platform provider strategically opens the platform by establishing partnerships with professional providers. The intellectual property is protected by applying monetization and openness policies, e.g., by defining entrance requirements and closing the source code. Exemplary ecosystems are Citrix, Symantec, and SAP.

**Resale Software Ecosystem: Business Scalability.** The pattern helps to gain business scalability and get control over a large market of third-party services. Platform provider is a large company. Providing testing frameworks and discovery features, e.g., rating and ranking, establish a sustainable development and marketing environment. Additionally, providing execution resources for services and Integrated Development Environment (IDE) enhance interoperability. Apple, Adobe, and Salesforce are the exemplary ecosystems.

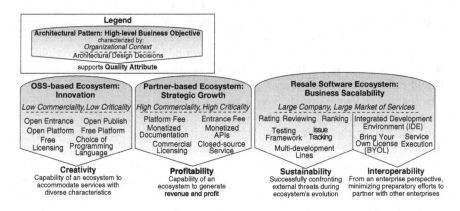

**Fig. 1.** Three architectural patterns for software ecosystems [11]

## 2.2   Case Study

*On-the-fly Computing (OTF)*[1] is a paradigm for the provision of tailor-made IT services that stems from a research project. Service providers publish basic services on a marketplace. Upon user's request, customized IT services are configured on-the-fly from a set of basic services. *The Proof-of-Concept (PoC)*[2] is a realization of the OTF paradigm with *60k+* lines of code. The basic services come from the Machine Learning (ML) libraries Weka[3], in Java, and Scikit-learn[4], in Python. With the help of PoC, users automatically create tailor-made ML services for typical classification problems without having any prior knowledge of ML. E.g., from labeled pictures of cats and dogs, the PoC learns a classification model that predicts if an unlabeled picture shows a dog or cat.

In dialogue with a *chatbot*, the user submits her (non-)functional requirements and the training data. The chatbot broadcasts the requirements to *configurators*.

---

[1]  sfb901.uni-paderborn.de, Last Access: March 20, 2020.
[2]  sfb901.uni-paderborn.de/poc, Last Access: March 20, 2020.
[3]  cs.waikato.ac.nz/ml/weka, Last Access: March 20, 2020.
[4]  scikit-learn.org, Last Access: March 20, 2020.

Configurators are computer programs to find and compose basic services. They try out different combinations of basic services. Once suitable combinations are found, the services with different non-functional properties are offered to the user. Upon the user's acceptance, her personal service is deployed for execution in a *compute center*.

## 3   Architectural Variabilities of the PoC

Goal of the PoC team is to open the platform to external service providers, so that their third-party ML services will be composed on the basis of the PoC platform. The team consists of managers responsible to take strategic decisions, e.g., defining business visions, ten domain experts for conceptualizing single components like the chatbot, a chief architect responsible for designing and integrating the system components, and ten programmers developing the components. The domain experts have an interdisciplinary background in business and economics, software engineering, and networking and infrastructure areas. Correspondingly, they hold different requirements.

The team is confronted with several variation points that can result in different architectures. In general, the variation points are the design decisions that can be changed at the design time, without violating core functional requirements. To extract the variation points, we conduct a workshop with the PoC team and two external service providers. During the workshop, the participants express important quality attributes in form of elaborated and prioritized scenarios. From these scenarios, the variation points and their variants are identified in three categories of business, application, and infrastructure. Table 1 shows the variabilities. The variants are not mutually exclusive, i.e., several variants of the same variation point can be applied at the same time. More details on the workshop can be found in [14].

While different ecosystem architectures can be built upon the variabilities, different architectures support different business objectives. The PoC team wants to decide on the most suitable architecture among two alternative choices:

> ***Architecture #1: Open Ecosystem** The platform remains an independent open-source project, so that the ecosystem grows by the direct contributions of service providers. All source codes should be free-to-use.*
>
> ***Architecture #2: Semi-Open Controlled Ecosystem** If the number of service providers drastically increases, the ecosystem openness might cause degradation in the quality of services. In this case, the PoC team wants to prevent unleashed growth of the ecosystem by establishing a controlled software development and marketing environment.*

Moreover, the following business vision should always be fulfilled:

> ***Business Vision:** The ecosystem should support innovation, while being sustainable in terms of confronting external threats that could have a long-term impact on the platform's success. Furthermore, the platform ownership should be managed by using the GNU General Public License (GPL).*

**Table 1.** Architectural variabilities of the PoC ecosystem

| | | |
|---|---|---|
| **Business** | **Entrance Quality Check (VP1)** | **(v1.1)** Entrance to the ecosystem is subject to no quality check. **(v1.2)** If necessary, using static code analysis, quality of third-party services should be checked. **(v1.3)** Third-party providers' qualification may need to be evaluated. |
| | **Entrance Fee (VP2)** | **(v2.1)** Entering the ecosystem is free. **(v2.2)** However, in some cases, the third-party providers need to pay an entrance fee. |
| | **Service Fee (VP3)** | The ecosystem supports **(v3.1)** free and **(v3.2)** paid third-party services. |
| | **Access to Platform (VP4)** | **(v4.1)** The platform's source code is open so far the platform quality is not threatened. **(v4.2)** The team might want to limit the access if necessary. |
| | **Access to Third-party Services (VP5)** | **(v5.1)** Basic services need to be open source. **(v5.2)** Protecting intellectual property of services becomes service providers' right. |
| **Application** | **Marketplace (VP6)** | **(v6.1)** While the default is to use available service repositories, **(v6.2)** the team is ready to establish own marketplace. |
| | **Programming Language (VP7)** | The ecosystem leverages two programming languages for third-party services, i.e., **(v7.1)** Java and **(v7.2)** Python. |
| **Infrastructure** | **Hardware Allocation (VP8)** | **(v8.1)** Compute centers dedicate fixed hardware resources to basic services. **(v8.2)** Compute centers dynamically allocate the resources at run-time based on resource availability and performance metrics. |
| | **Distribution of Execution (VP9)** | **(v9.1)** Execution of basic services is distributed on several compute centers. **(v9.2)** Each basic service is executed centralized by a compute center. |

Variation Point (VP$_i$) / Variant (v$_{i,j}$)

# 4   Modeling and Analyzing Architectural Diversity by Using SecoArc

SecoArc (Architecting Software Ecosystems) facilitates designing ecosystems around software platforms by means of three main elements, i.e., a **design process**, a **modeling language including a domain model and modeling workbench**, and an **architectural analysis technique**. These elements are already implemented by using Eclipse Modeling Framework[5] and Eclipse Sirius Framework[6] in a tool [14]. Figure 2 shows the SecoArc design process using Business Process Model and Notation (BPMN). The goal of the design process is to assist architects in a step-wise realization of suitable ecosystem architecture. It comprises the following activities: *specify organizational context of platform provider, model business, application, and infrastructure design decisions of ecosystem architecture using the SecoArc modeling language,* and *assess fulfillment of business objectives and quality attributes using the SecoArc architectural analysis technique.* If the architecture does not fulfill the objectives and attributes, further ecosystems can be modeled and then compared. After extracting the variabilities of PoC (cf. Table 1), the chief architect models, analyzes, and compares *Architectures #1* and *#2* using SecoArc. The architect familiarizes himself with the SecoArc using the user guide provided by the SecoArc specification [14].

---

[5] eclipse.org/emf, Last Access: March 20, 2020.
[6] eclipse.org/sirius, Last Access: March 20, 2020.

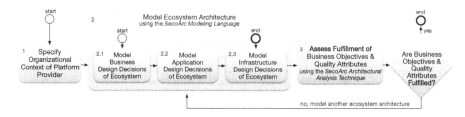

**Fig. 2.** SecoArc design process (Notation: BPMN)

### 4.1 Specify Organizational Context of Platform Provider

Designing an ecosystem begins with specifying the context of an organization. This is because a great part of architectural design decisions is derived from the organizational context. In addition, these contextual factors are considered during the SecoArc architectural analysis. Significance of four contextual factors are frequently supported by the literature on software ecosystems, e.g., [3]: *company size*, *market size*, *domain criticality*, and *commerciality*. Company size refers to the number of employees in an organization. Market size is the number of services on a marketplace. Domain criticality determines whether software failure is dangerous to human lives. Commerciality is the degree of protecting intellectual property.

#### 4.1.1 Organizational Context of the PoC

Since the contextual factors refer to the organizational context of PoC, they remain the same for both *Architectures #1* and *#2*. The platform is open, free-to-use, and not safety-critical. With *<100* employees and *<100* third-party services, the PoC is considered a small size organization with a medium size market. The relations between the range of values and the company and market size are specified in [11].

### 4.2 Model Ecosystem Architecture

Architects can use the modeling language to design an ecosystem architecture starting with the business decisions, and then the application and infrastructure decisions. The language aims at 1) facilitating explicit expression of design decisions of software ecosystems, 2) capturing architectural diversity, and 3) providing a modular integration of business, application, and infrastructure.

The modeling language is grounded on a rich *domain model* for software ecosystems. The domain model is a metamodel (a.k.a abstract syntax and its semantics) that covers key design decisions of software ecosystems. It is based on the examination of literature [13] and existing ecosystems [11,12]. In addition, a *modeling workbench* provides the visual notations (a.k.a. concrete syntax and its semantics) to design architecture. Both the domain model and modeling workbench span across business, application, and infrastructure architectures. Due to space limitations, the paper does not intend to describe complete lists of the language constructs. Complete lists are provided by the SecoArc specification [14].

### 4.2.1   Model Business Design Decisions of Ecosystem

Figure 3 presents the domain model of SecoArc. At the top, the BusinessArchitecture is shown. SoftwareEcosystem consists of HumanActor, BasicSoftwareElement, and BusinessAction. A HumanActor can be a User, EcosystemProvider, ServiceProvider, and Partner. A BasicSoftwareElement can be a SoftwarePlatform, Marketplace, and Service. The choice of BasicSoftwareElement is a fundamental decision that is taken early in the design phase with other business decisions. Using BusinessActions, business decisions can be defined, modified, or reused across the actors.

The domain model captures three significant groups of business decisions in software ecosystems, i.e., Fee, OpennessPolicy, and QualityCheck. Fee can be PlatformFee to use the platform, EntranceFee to enter the ecosystem, or ServiceFee to use a Service. A ServiceFee is defined by a ServiceProvider or Partner. Furthermore, using OpennessPolicy, the architect specifies which actors, and to which extend, can access or own a SoftwarePlatform or Service. Here, PlatformOpenness determines whether one can only contribute to the platform development or he/she has equity ownership of the platform. One way to regulate PlatformOpenness is where the third-party developers of the Mozilla Firefox web browser develop new functionality for the browser without having its ownership. Another OpennessPolicy is ServiceOpenness to grant a license to publish or to share intellectual property of services. For instance, in the Apple ecosystem, the developers receive license to publish on the Apple App Store whereas, in the Cloud Foundry ecosystem, third-party services belong to their providers and can be traded outside of the ecosystem [11]. Finally, using QualityCheck, it is defined whether a Service needs to pass StaticCodeAnalysis before being published or whether any of HumanActors should fulfill certain entrance requirements that are specified as an EntranceCertificate.

#### *4.2.1.1 Business Design Decisions of Architecture #1*

To keep the ecosystem fully open, entering the ecosystem is free for the users and service providers (Table 1: **v2.1**). The third-party services are free (**v3.1**) and released under the GPL license (**v5.1**). To enable third-party providers' contribution to a full extent, the team will provide open code repositories (**v4.1**). The only entrance barrier for the service providers is to pass a static code analysis (**v1.2**).

#### 4.2.1.2 Business Design Decisions of Architecture #2

To tackle an uncontrolled growth, several business decisions are to be taken into account. Figure 4 shows the business decisions designed using the SecoArc notations. Human actors, like `Providers of ML Services`, interact with the `BasicSoftwareElements` on the basis of `BusinessActions`. The symbols on the actions, e.g., $E_{\in}$ and $S_{\in}$, represent the business decisions that impact those actors.

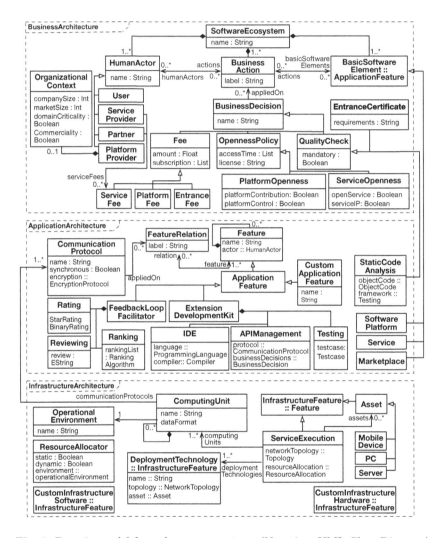

**Fig. 3.** Domain model for software ecosystems (Notation: UML Class Diagram)

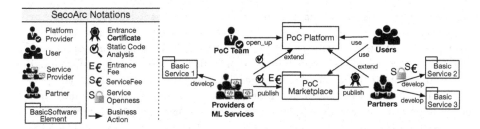

**Fig. 4.** *Architecture #2*: Business decisions modeled using SecoArc (For readability purposes, adopted from the original screenshot [14])

Firstly, to create a controlled marketing environment, the team considers providing an own marketplace (**v6.2**). This way, the providers are forced to continuously improve their services in order to beat the increased market competition. In addition, membership controls in terms of *1€* annual `EntranceFee` for the providers are to be set (**v2.2**) (shown by E€ in Fig. 4). Note that the notations in Fig. 4 do not show attributes of the business decisions. However, the SecoArc modeling workbench has a *properties view* that allows to define them. According to the business vision in Sect. 3, the PoC platform remains free and under the GPL license. Thus, `PlatformContribution` is true (**v4.1**).

Secondly, to ensure providing high quality services, the team considers partnering with other companies. In this case, `Partners` need to *"possess certain amount of annual revenue"*, which is specified using an `EntranceCertificate` in Fig. 4. Moreover, the partners are allowed to monetize their services and the belonging documentation by defining price models (**v3.2**), closing the source code, or use their own licenses (BYOL) (**v5.2**). Thereby, two types of services are created for `Partners`, i.e., `Basic Service` 2 and 3, whereas `Basic Service` 2 has `ServiceFee` and `ServiceOpenness` policies defined. The rest of business decisions remain the same as *Architecture #1*.

### 4.2.2  Model Application and Infrastructure Design Decisions of Ecosystem

The application architecture supports business decisions by its application merits whereas the infrastructure architecture provides the application architecture with computing and deployment resources. Such resources are the software and hardware for the purpose of service execution. The domain model in Fig. 3 shows the `Application-` and `InfrastructureArchitecture` that respectively include `Application-` and `InfrastructureFeature`. In general, a `Feature` can be accessed by `HumanActor`, be a part of another `Feature`, or be in relation with another `Feature` in the same or another architecture.

*1) Modeling of Built-in Features:* Part of the domain model captures *built-in features*, i.e., the features specific to software ecosystems and open platforms. The built-in features originate from our study on variabilities of ecosystem architectures [12,13]. As depicted in Fig. 3, the application-specific features are captured by means of `ExtensionDevelopmentKit` and `FeedbackLoopFacilitator`. `ExtensionDevelopmentKit` represents the software features that enable development on top of open platforms. This mainly includes `IDE`, `APIManagement`, and `Testing`. Android Studio is an example of `IDEs` used to develop Apps for Google Android. Android SDK is the `APIManagement` that facilitates accessing the platform APIs. Android Emulator is a `Testing` feature that is used to simulate variety of hardware for testing purposes. Moreover, `FeedbackLoopFacilitator` makes user feedback operational in the ecosystem using `Rating`, `Reviewing`, and `Ranking`. The feedback returned to the ecosystem through `Rating` and `Reviewing` is used to generate ranking lists and to improve services by service providers.

Furthermore, infrastructure-specific built-in features are grouped as `DeploymentTechnology`, `ServiceExecution`, and `Asset` (cf. Fig. 3). As the names suggest, they represent computing resources to deploy `Services` on a `DeploymentTechnology`, to execute them using `ComputingUnits`, and to deliver the execution results to an *Asset*. A `ComputingUnit` has an `OperationalEnvironment` and supports at least one `CommunicationProtocol`. For instance, Amazon.com is the provider of cloud computing services called Amazon Web Services (AWS). Figure 5 shows that `AmazonEC2` is the service to execute the `AWS1`. It uses `virtualMachine1` to execute the `AWS1` on an `AmazonLinux`. HTTPS is the `CommunicationProtocol`. The service execution is performed on `AWSSever1` and `AWSSever2`. The result of execution is sent to `userPC` [12].

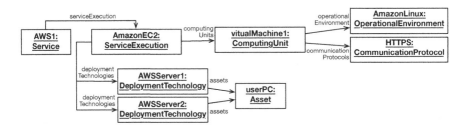

**Fig. 5.** The UML object diagram of an exemplary AWS service execution

*2) Modeling of Custom Features:* Custom features are used to design the concepts that are not part of the domain model. Such features can be a `CustomApplicationFeature` in the `ApplicationArchitecture` or a `CustomInfrastructureSoftware` and `CustomInfrastructureHardware` in the `InfrastructureArchitecture`.

### 4.2.2.1 *Application and Infrastructure Decisions of Architecture #1*
Figure 6 shows the application and infrastructure features in relation to a part of the business architecture designed using the SecoArc notations. Currently, a microservice architecture is used, where the PoC `CustomApplicationFeatures`, i.e., the `Chatbot` and `Configurator`, are deployed on `Compute Center 1` and `Compute Center 2`. To enable third-party contributions to a full extent, the team uses `Git`

as an open code repository (**v4.1**) (**v6.1**). The default way to publish is to `commit` new services into the repository. Because the services are encapsulated inside the `DockerContainers`, `Providers of ML Services` are allowed to develop both `Basic Service in Java` and `Basic Service in Python` (**v7.1**) (**v7.2**). During the service provision, the execution of basic services is handled by several docker containers. Figure 6 portraits `DockerContainer 1` that consists of two `ComputingUnits`, called `Executor 1`, `Executor 2`. The executors `register` with the `Gateway` in advance (**v8.1**). The `Gateway` is a `ResourceAllocator` that allocates each basic service to multiple executors (**v9.1**).

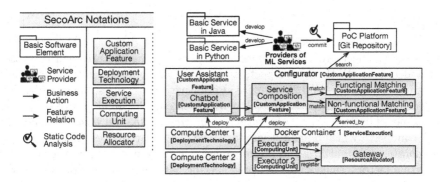

**Fig. 6.** *Architectures #1*: Application, infrastructure, and part of business architectures (Adopted from the original screenshot [14])

### 4.2.2.2 *Application and Infrastructure Decisions of Architecture #2*

Upon deciding on an own marketplace by the PoC team, related software features of the marketplaces, e.g., rating, ranking, and reviewing, are included. To create a controlled development environment, the team considers providing the service providers with an IDE and testing environment. By a drastic increase in the number of service providers, some decisions in *Architecture #1* cause scalability issues: By static resource allocation (**v8.1**), the executors are permanently waiting for jobs, thus, wasting resources if they remain idle. Furthermore, by the distributed execution (**v9.1**), if many executors become incorporated in execution of a service, the network payload will be tremendous. Therefore, the team decides that, for every basic service, a Docker container is generated that contains all the necessary environments as well as incorporated basic services (**v9.2**). A respective container is distributed in a compute center on demand and will be freed up after the execution (**v8.2**).

## 4.3 Assess Fulfillment of Business Objectives and Quality Attributes Using the SecoArc Architectural Analysis Technique

Ecosystem architecture can be further analyzed by using a pattern-matching technique in the modeling workbench. As previously mentioned, the architectural

**Table 2.** Comparison of *Architectures #1* and *#2* (The complete report of analysis can be found in the text.)

| | OSS-based Ecosystem: Innovation | | | | | | Partner-based Ecosystem: Strategic Growth | | | | | | Resale Software Ecosystem: Business Scalability | | | | | | | | |
|---|---|---|---|---|---|---|---|---|---|---|---|---|---|---|---|---|---|---|---|---|---|
| | Creativity | | | | | | Profitability | | | | | | Sustainability | | | | | | Interoperability | | |
| | Open Entrance | Open Publish | Open Platform | Free Platform | Free Licensing | Choice of Programming Language | Platform Fee | Entrance Fee | Monetized Documentation | Monetized APIs | Commercial Licensing | Closed Source Service | Rating | Reviewing | Ranking | Testing Framework | Issue Tracking | Multi-dev. Lines | BYOL | IDE | Service Execution |
| Architecture #1 | ✓ | ✓ | ✓ | ✓ | ✓ | ✓ | ✗ | ✗ | ✗ | ✗ | ✗ | ✗ | ✗ | ✗ | ✗ | ✗ | ✓ | ✓ | ✗ | ✗ | ✓ |
| Architecture #2 | ✓ | ✗ | ✓ | ✓ | ✗ | ✗ | ✗ | ✓ | ✓ | ✗ | ✓ | ✓ | ✓ | ✓ | ✓ | ✓ | ✓ | ✗ | ✓ | ✓ | ✓ |

Architectural Design Decision Realized (✓) / Not-realized (✗)

patterns in Sect. 2.1 are described using sets of design decisions. The architectural analysis checks to which extend an ecosystem architecture realizes those design decisions. With this respect, architects can 1) assess suitability of an ecosystem architecture and 2) compare alternative architectures. Specifically, the analysis has three outcomes: firstly, to which extend the architecture supports the business objectives, i.e., *innovation, strategic growth*, and *business scalability*. Secondly, to which extend it supports the quality attributes, i.e., *creativity, profitability, sustainability*, and *interoperability*. Finally, according to the value of contextual factors, suggestions to apply specific patterns and a list of exemplary real-world ecosystems are given.

### 4.3.1   Analyzing and Comparing Architectures #1 and #2

The PoC architect conducts the analysis to evaluate suitability of *Architectures #1* and *#2*. A report of the analysis is generated. Table 2 shows how the two architectures match with the patterns. Accordingly, *Architectures #1* and *#2* respectively fulfill OSS-based Ecosystem (*100%, 50%*), Partner-based Ecosystem (*0%, 66.6%*), and Resale Software Ecosystem (*33.3%, 88.8%*). This means, *Architecture #1* fulfills **innovation** the most, while *Architecture #2* enhances **business scalability** and **strategic growth**. Furthermore, the majority of decisions in *Architecture #1* contributes to **creativity** while **sustainability** and **interoperability** are partially supported. The main shift in *Architecture #2* is to include partners, who can generate revenue. Decisions like entrance fee and commercial licenses support **profitability**.

The results of analysis show that, comparing the two architectures, *Architecture #1* is a more suitable candidate with respect to the business vision in Sect. 3, as it fulfills innovation to a better extend (*100%* vs. *50%*). However, sustainability can be improved by considering the relevant design decisions, e.g., including rating and ranking. In addition, the analysis shows that existing ecosystems, with contextual factors similar to the PoC (cf. Sect. 4.1.1), conform to the OSS-based Ecosystem pattern, which confirms the suitability of this pattern for the PoC. Exemplary ecosystems provided are Mozilla, Eclipse, and Apache Cordova. The full report of analysis can be found in [14].

## 5    Evaluation

In our evaluation, we investigate on *whether SecoArc supports architects in modeling diverse design decisions and analyzing alternative ecosystem architectures with respect to the business objectives and quality attributes.* For this purpose, we design a questionnaire with which we can interview architects on the quality characteristics of SecoArc. The questionnaire is aligned with the ISO/IEC 25010 quality model [16] and serves the goal to assess the *functional suitability* of SecoArc. In this context, the functional suitability is the degree to which SecoArc satisfies the need of architects and provides value during decision-making. The questionnaire will be used to conduct a semi-structured interview with the chief architect of the PoC, who is responsible to make design decisions and to integrate the various components into one architecture.

### 5.1    Questionnaire

We design the questionnaire by referring to the sub-characteristics of functional suitability, i.e., *completeness, correctness,* and *appropriateness* [16] and casting doubt on the main elements of SecoArc, i.e., *design process, modeling language,* and *architectural analysis technique,* as well as *tool support.* As shown in Table 3, the questionnaire consists of *17* questions. The interviewee responds the questions in three scales, i.e., *No/Partially/Yes,* while reasoning about the responses. Using the semi-structured interview technique [15], we collect data on strong and weak aspects of SecoArc based on open conversations. Full responses can be found in [14].

### 5.2    Results

In summary, the interviewee expresses that the ready-to-use components of SecoArc contribute to an improved decision-making. Table 3 briefly refers to the responses. In the following, we report the results.

*1) Modeling Language & Design Process:* The architect approves that the mode ling language of SecoArc is a domain-specific language. With the design process, they help with familiarizing oneself with the novel and complex architecture of the ecosystem around the platform. The built-in features provide a correct basis to explicitly design the ecosystem-specific design decisions of PoC. Furthermore, custom features can appropriately be added. This adds flexibility

**Table 3.** Interview questionnaire and results

| | | | |
|---|---|---|---|
| **Modeling Language & Design Process** | Q1 | Does the domain knowledge of SecoArc contribute to familiarizing you with critical design decisions of the ecosystem around your platform? | + |
| | Q2 | Does the design process appropriately guide you through the ecosystem design? | + |
| | Q3 | Are the business decisions, application and infrastructure modeling features complete in terms of being sufficient for modeling your ecosystem? | + |
| | Q4 | Do you find the suggested business decisions and built-in application and infrastructure features correct (or rather contradictory or wrong)? | + |
| | Q5 | Does grouping of features help you to better understand the design space? | + |
| | Q6 | Are you able to appropriately express custom decisions of your ecosystem? | + |
| | Q7 | Are the visual notation of business decisions and application and infrastructure features appropriate? | + |
| | Q8 | Are the architectural models easy to change or reuse, so you can use them during the system evolution? | o |
| | Q9 | Can you appropriately express the relationships between the three architectures? | + |
| **Architectural Analysis** | Q10 | Is the knowledge of existing ecosystems, embedded in the patterns, beneficial for your decision-making? | + |
| | Q11 | Does the analysis help you to consider complementary business decisions and application and infrastructure features wrt. your business objectives? | + |
| | Q12 | Does the analysis make you aware of the correctness of your design decisions? E.g., by revealing the contradictory decisions to your business objectives and quality attributes? | + |
| | Q13 | Do you find the quality attributes and business objectives complete to address your needs? | o |
| | Q14 | Is the comparison of alternative architectures beneficial to your decision-making? | + |
| **Tool Support** | Q15 | Is the modeling workbench easy-to-use to design the ecosystem around your platform? | + |
| | Q16 | Are the provided specification and guide materials satisfactory to start using the tool? | + |
| | Q17 | Does the tool provide the functionality and features promised by the specification? | + |

No (-) / Partially (o) / Yes (+)

to the language, because the custom features are treated the same way as the built-in features, e.g., to group them or relate them to the human actors. Another point of appropriateness is the abstraction provided by the visual notations and the central presentation of business decisions.

*2) Architectural Analysis Technique:* The architect finds it beneficial during the decision-making to have an estimation of suitability of the PoC architecture based on the practice-proven knowledge of existing ecosystems and being able to compare different architectures. This also helps to take further actions by including complementary decisions or re-considering the ones that threaten achieving the business objectives and quality attributes.

*3) Tool Support:* Availability of the tool and guide material impact the uptake by enabling the architect to work with the ecosystem-related concepts right away. The tool is consistent with the functions described in the specification.

*4) Limitation and Future Work:* Although our approach is concerned with modeling support at design time, there is an inherent need for consistency between the models and code during the system evolution (**Q8**). A way to address this issue is to apply Aspect-Oriented Software Development to weave the decisions in the code, another way is to introduce traceability links [19]. Furthermore, future research on extensive quality models for software ecosystems is required, to address more business objectives, quality attributes, and their trade-offs (**Q13**).

## 6   Related Work

To our knowledge, there is no previous work that provides a modeling language supporting automatic analysis with respect to business, application, and infrastructure aspects, by considering the knowledge of diverse platforms. ADLs are the early approaches to describe system architecture [20]. Existing ADLs, most relevant to open platforms, support specific domains, e.g., mobile applications [6] and automotive systems [21] while business aspects are less in focus.

A body of work in literature conceptualizes economic aspects. BOUCHARAS ET AL. [22] formalize modeling ecosystems in three levels: the software ecosystem, supply network, and software vendor. YU AND DENG [23] propose a graph-based approach based on the $i*$ modeling framework for strategic buyer-supplier relationships. While this work focuses on software supply chain processes, our focus in on structure of ecosystem architecture. However, this work complements ours and can be leveraged during the business modeling activity.

Further work mainly investigates technical aspects. CHRISTENSEN ET AL. [24] present a modeling approach for the organizational, business, and software structures. However, the approach does not deal with the relation between the technical architecture and actors. SADI ET AL. contribute to a goal-oriented ecosystem design by an NFR-based specification and analysis method for openness requirements [9]. Furthermore, modeling sustainable collaborations in [25] helps clarify developers' objectives and their dependencies. In comparison to our work, SecoArc embeds the existing domain knowledge and provides automated tool support. Other work [3] surveys ecosystem variabilities. Our work is built on this work while extending them by modeling and analysis support.

## 7 Conclusion and Future Work

Opening software platforms became a novel architectural approach to enable third-party service development. Designing open platforms faces many architectural variabilities, and informed decision-making is crucial for platform providers to achieve their business objectives. However, there is a lack of comprehensive architectural guidelines that can help to tackle the variabilities while relating the design decisions to business objectives. This paper presents a pattern-driven methodological support comprising a *design process*, *modeling language*, and *architectural analysis technique*, which consolidates the knowledge of *111* open platforms and is ready-to-use as a tool. Our contributions support platform providers in informed decision-making based on the knowledge of best practices. Future work is required to enhance business modeling coupled with application and infrastructure architectures, facilitate trade-off analysis of more quality attributes, and establish consistency between architecture and code.

## References

1. Bosch, J.: Software ecosystems: taking software development beyond the boundaries of the organization. J. Syst. Softw. **7**(85), 1453–1454 (2012)
2. REVaMP² Project. www.revamp2-project.eu. Accessed 20 Mar 2020
3. Berger, T., et al.: Variability mechanisms in software ecosystems. Inf. Softw. Technol. **56**(11), 1520–1535 (2014)
4. Malavolta, I., et al.: What industry needs from architectural languages: a survey. IEEE Trans. Softw. Eng. **39**(6), 869–891 (2013)

5. Hohpe, G., et al.: The software architect's role in the digital age. IEEE Softw. **33**(6), 30–39 (2016)

6. Dörndorfer, J., Hopfensperger, F., Seel, C.: The SenSoMod-modeler-a model-driven architecture approach for mobile context-aware business applications. In: Cappiello, C., Ruiz, M. (eds.) CAiSE 2019. LNBIP, vol. 350, pp. 75–86. Springer, Cham (2019). https://doi.org/10.1007/978-3-030-21297-1_7

7. Woods, E., Bashroush, R.: Modelling large-scale information systems using ADLs–an industrial experience report. J. Syst. Softw. **99**, 97–108 (2015)

8. Zimmermann, A., et al.: Evolving Enterprise Architectures for Digital Transformations. Gesellschaft für Informatik eV (2015)

9. Sadi, M.H., Yu, E.: Accommodating openness requirements in software platforms: a goal-oriented approach. In: Dubois, E., Pohl, K. (eds.) CAiSE 2017. LNCS, vol. 10253, pp. 44–59. Springer, Cham (2017). https://doi.org/10.1007/978-3-319-59536-8_4

10. CIO Magazine: 5 Mistakes to Avoid When Deploying an Enterprise App Store. cio.com/article/2394413. Accessed 20 Mar 2020

11. Jazayeri, B., et al.: Patterns of store-oriented software ecosystems: detection, classification, and analysis of design options. In: Latin American PLOP (2018)

12. Jazayeri, B., Zimmermann, O., Engels, G., Kundisch, D.: A variability model for store-oriented software ecosystems: an enterprise perspective. In: Maximilien, M., Vallecillo, A., Wang, J., Oriol, M. (eds.) ICSOC 2017. LNCS, vol. 10601, pp. 573–588. Springer, Cham (2017). https://doi.org/10.1007/978-3-319-69035-3_42

13. Jazayeri, B., Platenius, M.C., Engels, G., Kundisch, D.: Features of IT service markets: a systematic literature review. In: Sheng, Q.Z., Stroulia, E., Tata, S., Bhiri, S. (eds.) ICSOC 2016. LNCS, vol. 9936, pp. 301–316. Springer, Cham (2016). https://doi.org/10.1007/978-3-319-46295-0_19

14. SecoArc Material & Supplementary Documents of the Case Study. sfb901.uni-paderborn.de/secoarc. Accessed 20 Mar 2020

15. Hove, S.E., Anda, B.: Experiences from conducting semi-structured interviews in empirical software engineering research. In: METRICS 2005, pp. 10–pp. IEEE (2005)

16. ISO/IEC 25010. iso.org/standard/35733.html. Accessed 20 Mar 2020

17. Hohpe, G., et al.: Twenty years of patterns' impact. IEEE Softw. **30**(6), 88–88 (2013)

18. Ben Hadj Salem, M.A.: Performance measurement practices in software ecosystem. Int. J. Prod. Perform. Manag. **62**(5), 514–533 (2013)

19. Könemann, P., Zimmermann, O.: Linking design decisions to design models in model-based software development. In: Babar, M.A., Gorton, I. (eds.) ECSA 2010. LNCS, vol. 6285, pp. 246–262. Springer, Heidelberg (2010). https://doi.org/10.1007/978-3-642-15114-9_19

20. Medvidovic, N., et al.: A classification and comparison framework for software architecture description languages. IEEE Trans. Softw. Eng. **26**(1), 70–93 (2000)

21. Kolagari, R.T., et al.: Model-based analysis and engineering of automotive architectures with EAST-ADL: revisited. Int. J. Concept. Struct. Smart Appl. **3**(2), 25–70 (2015)

22. Boucharas, V., et al.: Formalizing software ecosystem modeling. In: International Workshop on Open Component Ecosystems, pp. 41–50. ACM (2009)

23. Yu, E., Deng, S.: Understanding software ecosystems: a strategic modeling approach. In: The 3rd International Workshop on Software Ecosystems, pp. 65–76 (2011)

24. Christensen, H.B., et al.: Analysis and design of software ecosystem architectures–towards the 4S telemedicine ecosystem. Inf. Softw. Technol. **56**(11), 1476–1492 (2014)

25. Sadi, M.H., Dai, J., Yu, E.: Designing software ecosystems: how to develop sustainable collaborations? In: Persson, A., Stirna, J. (eds.) CAiSE 2015. LNBIP, vol. 215, pp. 161–173. Springer, Cham (2015). https://doi.org/10.1007/978-3-319-19243-7_17

# Co-destruction Patterns
# in Crowdsourcing
## Formal/Technical Paper

Reihaneh Bidar$^{(\boxtimes)}$ , Arthur H. M. ter Hofstede , and Renuka Sindhgatta

Queensland University of Technology, Brisbane, Australia
{r.bidar,a.terhofstede,renuka.sr}@qut.edu.au

**Abstract.** Crowdsourcing has been a successful paradigm in organising a large number of actors to work on specific tasks and contribute to knowledge collectively. However, the openness of such systems allows destructive patterns to form through actors' dynamics. As a result, the collective effort of actors may not achieve the targeted objective due to lower engagement and lower quality contributions. There are varying forms of actor dynamics that can lead to suboptimal outcomes and this paper provides a systematic analysis of these in the form of a collection of patterns, derived from both the literature and from our own experiences with crowdsourcing systems. This collection of so-called co-destruction patterns allows for an-depth analysis of corwdsourcing systems which can benefit a comparative analysis and also assist with improvements of existing systems or the set-up of new ones. A survey reveals that these patterns have been observed in practice and are perceived as worthwhile addressing.

**Keywords:** Co-destruction · Crowdsourcing · Collaboration · Patterns

## 1   Introduction

Crowdsourcing systems have become an integral medium for outsourcing tasks to a community of actors [23]. Crowdsourcing refers to the coordination of actors via online collaborative technologies to elicit their knowledge and achieve business goals [47]. The tasks involved typically include problem solving, co-creation of content, evaluating or rating ideas or products [23], and micro-tasking [9]. The integration of actors' contributions in these activities leads to improvement of innovation processes in an organisation [19] on the one hand, and provides job opportunities [32], or intrinsic and extrinsic motivation [19] on the other hand. For example, in the Figure Eight platform, actors provide solutions and receive money in exchange. However, in open source projects such as GitHub, actors contribute code and receive intrinsic rewards in return. In this paper, we focus on content creation and task-oriented crowdsourcing regardless of the type of incentives actors achieve from their contribution.

© Springer Nature Switzerland AG 2020
S. Dustdar et al. (Eds.): CAiSE 2020, LNCS 12127, pp. 54–69, 2020.
https://doi.org/10.1007/978-3-030-49435-3_4

From an economic viewpoint, the total crowdsourcing market is predicted to reach \$15–\$25 billion in 2020 from \$4.8 billion in 2016, increasing the number of people who generate income from crowdsourcing activities [29]. Despite the success of crowdsourcing systems, very little is known about the dark side and failures of crowdsourcing. Malicious workers [32], their low quality contributions, and their dishonesty [48] are examples of challenges that may cause a crowdsourcing task to fail. Collaboration among actors does not necessarily elicit valuable ideas and it is possible that actors behave counterproductively in crowdsourcing initiatives, for example through mockery or by pushing their own agenda [55]. The negative impacts on a crowdsourcing initiative, and their roots in actor behaviour, are referred to as *co-destruction* and form the focus of this paper.

In this paper, a systematic analysis of various forms of co-destruction in the context of crowdsourcing systems is conducted. As co-destruction in this context is still ill-understood, we have chosen a patterns-based approach [2], to be able to identify core recurring phenomena, their affect, their manifestation, and their detection. A patterns-based approach has the advantage of being technology-independent, sufficiently precise though not overly formalised (which would limit the range of interpretations at too early a stage), multi-faceted (allowing one to focus on different aspects of the issue), and extensible. A collection of patterns form a repository of knowledge that can be added to over time, and, in this case, form the foundation of understanding and mitigating co-destruction phenomena in a variety of crowdsourcing systems.

In the rest of the paper, relevant work related to co-destruction and crowdsourcing is discussed in Sect. 2. In Sect. 3 a set of six co-destruction patterns is proposed, each described in some depth. Section 4 analyses the potential manifestation of the co-destruction patterns across a number of crowdsourcing platforms, and Sect. 5 outlines an evaluation where occurrence and perceived importance of the patterns was assessed by users of and contributors to crowdsourcing initiatives. Section 6 discusses the findings and further work.

## 2   Related Work

The notion of co-destruction has been introduced in the Service Dominant Logic literature as a negative outcome of interactions within a service system [22] and diminished well-being of at least one of the parties involved in the collaboration [41]. Different disciplines have started to explore the dark side of participation in social media [4], and the sharing economy [38]. In a crowdsourcing context, the dark side of crowdsourcing initiatives is an emerging research area (e.g. [55]). These studies identified that technological innovation tools create adverse consequences on society that are worthy of research attention [4]. However, co-destruction resulting from actor collaboration in crowdsourcing systems is a topic that has been overlooked in the literature. It is noteworthy observing that although actors' contributions to crowdsourcing help organisations by providing diversity in ideas, knowledge, skill, and experience [14], mitigating negative consequences will make the integration of these contributions more effective and limit negative outcomes [55].

The focus of existing studies on co-destruction has mostly been on the reasons why it happens through collaboration and what its consequences are. The distinct forms of co-destruction have been ignored. Vafeas, Hughes, and Hilton [52] found inadequate communication, the absence of trust, power imbalance, inadequate coordination, and inadequate human capital to be the main reasons for failure of contribution integration. Smith [49] found co-destruction to be a failure of the integration of processes which results in unexpected resource loss (i.e., material, social, or energy), perceived misuse, and decline in actor well-being. Gatzweiler et al. [18] found violations of terms and conditions, and questioning of contributions/platform/actor-provided content as forms of deviant behaviour that occurs in crowdsourced ideation contests. Our purpose, however, is to pinpoint patterns that can emerge from actor collaboration and which may result in destructive outcomes whereas the literature has typically emphasised positive outcomes of such collaboration.

## 3   Co-destruction Patterns

We use a patterns-based approach to characterise various forms of co-destruction in crowdsourcing systems. The use of a pattern-based approach has been suggested as a systematic approach to "identifying, classifying, and documenting the available knowledge", and presenting best practices as solutions to recurring challenges [37]. More specifically, a pattern-based approach is suitable when we are dealing with understanding and characterising a reoccurring problem in a complex domain [16]. For the identification of the various co-destruction patterns we draw upon relevant literature as well as our own knowledge and experience.

Patterns collections may sometimes draw the criticism that they are not "complete". In this regard it should be pointed out that this requires a framework in which completeness can be assessed, which in turn means that we already have a solid understanding of the domain, thus obviating the need for patterns in the first place. Hence pattern collections are more appropriately referred to as comprehensive. Even here though one may argue that patterns need to be able to stand on their own and a pattern collection of valuable patterns is a worthwhile contribution to the field, which can be extended over time.

In this section we present six patterns, each of which we believe encapsulates an important fundamental problem contributing to co-destruction in crowdsourcing systems. For each of these patterns, a description and one or more real-life examples are provided as well as how the occurrence of the pattern may have a negative effect on crowdsourcing outcomes (e.g. quality, timeliness) and participants (e.g. engagement), how it manifests itself, and how it can be detected. The pattern collection provides a repository of knowledge in relation to mitigating or even preventing occurrences of co-destruction in crowdsourcing systems.

## 3.1  Collusion

**Description.** Collusion happens when groups of actors make joint decisions contrary to social rules and may result in the colluding actors having an unfair advantage over other interested actors [28]. An alternative definition refers to collusion as a situation where participants violate protocol rules by engaging in activities to gain self-benefit [57]. Collusion in crowdsourcing can result from (i) any form of vote manipulation such as intentionally biasing a rating [28], (ii) endorsing or sinking a product/service/task [3], and (iii) copying information or other people's work [28].

**Real-Life Example.** In Amazon Mechanical Turk (AMT), a task based on product reviews can be degraded by a malicious group of workers which can result in misleading feedback on or a negative review of the task [26]. Researchers found that Amazon's rating system is subject to collusion and unfair rating [20]. They also found that 35% of Amazon groups (7 out of 20 in the sample log collected by Leskovec et al. [35]) are collusive groups [3]. Collusion in the case of Amazon manifests itself as a "war of reviewers" in which a group of members are regularly corralled to write glowing reviews for themselves to increase their income or to write a negative review about competitors to increase their own reputation [20].

**Affect.** The occurrence of this pattern may result in strong biases in task outcomes (e.g. final aggregated ratings) which may mislead other actors' perceptions [28] and the "quality of future peer behaviour" [31]. Collusive behaviour results in tricking the system [11] in order to accumulate trust and achieve promotion in the system [10]. Overall, the damaging effect of such behaviour is to negatively influence the quality of outcomes (e.g. the final rating scores of products) and expected behaviour of the system [3].

**Manifestation.** This pattern manifests itself through different forms of abnormality in crowdsourcing systems such as suspicious reputation system ratings and noise caused by collusive groups. For example, one indicator of a suspicious rate is when a collusive actor gives extreme low or extreme high ratings for the target products they intend to boost or sink [28].

**Detection.** Collusion indicators have been defined for the detection of collusion for online rating tasks: (i) *Group Rating Value Similarity* helps identify groups of users posting similar ratings for similar products, (ii) *Group Rating Time Similarity* accounts for users promoting or demoting a product in a short time frame, (iii) *Group Rating Spamicity* indicates a high number of ratings posted by a single user on the same product, and (iv) *Group Members Suspiciousness* computes a metric reporting suspicious users based on their ratings as compared to computed credible ratings [3]. Collusion in crowdsourcing platforms such as AMT can be detected by computing and identifying strong inter-rater dependence across tasks especially when they diverge from the mean [28]. Another approach to detecting collusion resulting from actors using collective intelligence or indulging in group plagiarism considers the actor's ability and label repetitions. The primary assumption is that colluding actors are of lower quality or expertise and produce repeat labels or plagiarised labels [8].

### 3.2   Bias

**Description.** Humans have an inclination towards one opinion over another because of previous experiences and perceptions [5]. When this inclination is based on a contributor's subjective judgement, it may create a bias which may lead to unfair decisions toward others [13]. Personal preference can cause bias [54]. For example, bias can result in higher ranked contributors in a crowdsourcing system getting positive rates and feedback because of their reputation and not solely because of their effort and skill in completing a task.

**Real-Life Example.** In GitHub, a high correlation between reputation (technical and social), geographical location, and pull request acceptance is an example of how bias may manifest itself. Reputation positively influences a developer's decision to accept a pull request [43]. Also, the likelihood of pull-request acceptance rate is found to be 19% higher when the actors (submitter and integrator) are from the same geographical location [43].

**Affect.** Bias influences an actor's performance and decision making [5,30] and may shift the opinion of actors to an incorrect answer/solution [25]. An example of influence of bias on decision making in Kaggle is that solutions with high public scores are more likely to be selected as final solutions than solutions with high private scores during the submission phase [30]. Thus, the presence of the Bias pattern can be destructive to the functioning of the crowdsourcing platform [30].

**Manifestation.** The most common forms of the Bias pattern identified by Baeza [5] in the context of crowdsourcing systems are: i) activity bias (or wisdom of a few) "many people do only a little while few people do a lot", and ii) data bias where the content is limited to a few topics. Bias in Wikipedia can be explicit where an article supports a specific point of view. It can also be implicit where the article focuses on one aspect of the topic but omits another equally important aspect [24]. The Bias pattern can manifest itself through properties of tasks in crowdsourcing systems such as AMT, e.g. visual presentation [25].

**Detection.** Kamar et al. [25] introduced a learning model for automatic detection and correction of task-dependent biases using probabilistic modeling of crowdsourced tasks and actors. The authors address scenarios where actors (or workers) work on consensus tasks. A consensus task is a type of task where the correct answer is unknown to the task owner and the answer is derived via the aggregation of answers provided by actors. Probabilistic graphical models are used to learn and infer the relationships among actors' biases, their answers (or annotations), ground truth task answers (called the labels), and task features. In certain crowdsourcing tasks, actor biases can be detected by 'seeding' a few control questions for which the answers are known into the main task without letting the workers know which are the control questions. The number of control questions required to detect bias has been another area of research [36]. As goal of the detection mechanism is to provide quality control mechanisms, it does not distinguish biases due to lack of knowledge, actor background, or actor behavior.

### 3.3 Incompetence

**Description.** Incompetence refers to an actor's lack of sufficient capability, knowledge, experience, or skill [15,27] and reflects the quality of an actor's work on a task [27,44]. A mismatch between an actor's competence and task requirements leads to poor outcomes. For example, incompetent actors can produce low quality results because of inadequate understanding of task descriptions [17].

**Real-Life Example.** An example of incompetence concerns a labelling task in AMT, where actors were asked to label pages of digitised books. Although incompetent actors spent considerable time on task, they only provided low accuracy outcomes with low credibility due to their lack of skills, competencies, and their poor understanding of the task. Interestingly, most of the incompetent actors did not return after a not so successful first experience [27].

**Affect.** Possible consequences of incompetence are lower accuracy in task delivery [27], poor results and unsuccessful completion of the project [15], and reduced overall effectiveness of the crowdsourcing system [17]. In some cases, to maintain their reputation actors participate in tasks which are beyond their skill level, which affects the effectiveness of crowdsourcing systems [17]. The performance of an actor is an indicator of their competency [17].

**Manifestation.** Incompetence manifests as poor quality of the task being performed [17]. Actors may spend considerable amounts of time on tasks and yet yield poor results.

**Detection.** Detection mechanisms include identifying actor bias, expertise, and relationship with the task. A Bayesian Classifier Combination model is used to model the relationship of an actors' bias or competence, the output labels provided by them, and the true labels of the tasks [25]. To avoid this pattern, correctly evaluating an actors' actual competence levels is one of several methods to perform quality control in crowdsourcing systems [44].

To reduce the occurrence of this pattern in crowdsourcing systems, using a prototypical task as a pre-test and self-assessments within the pre-selection process is suggested to increase the probability of having more competent actors in task contribution. This method has been evaluated on a real-world sentiment analysis task and an image validation task [17]. The results for the sentiment analysis task revealed over 15% improvement in accuracy and 12% improvement in agreement among actors compared to the traditional performance-based method [17]. The detection of actor incompetence can lead to a competence-weighted approach with more weight given to replies from individuals with higher capabilities than from others in the crowd [44]. However, the difference between the estimated and actual competence of actors is highly related to the success or failure of competence-weighted approaches in crowdsourcing systems [44].

## 3.4 Vandalism

**Description.** Vandalism refers to "ill-intentioned contributions" to crowdsourcing tasks which are destructive in terms of the quality of "collective intelligence" [21]. Vandalism is characterised by modifications made by individual actors with bad intentions, initiating spam and producing inappropriate content [1]. For example, malicious edits in Wikis are a common form of vandalism [53]. In open-source projects such as OpenStreetMap (OSM), actors can make changes to the dataset which cause damage to the project [40].

**Real-Life Examples.** One of the most common examples of vandalism can be seen in Wikipedia. Any deletion, addition, or change of content made "in a deliberate attempt to compromise the integrity of Wikipedia" [39] is a form of vandalism. For instance, among 200,000 edits per day being conducted on average in Wikipedia, 7% are found to be vandalism [1,53]. Vandalism in OSM occurs in the form of active data corruptions. Applicability and reliability of crowd-sourced geodata, as well as the success of the whole project, are heavily affected by such cases of vandalism. During the testing phase in August 2012, the prototype marked around seven million edits as potential vandalism [40].

**Affect.** The presence of this pattern causes problems such as spending more effort on vandalism mitigation than on task contributions [1,42]. Mitigating vandalism requires time and effort of many people [42]. Furthermore, vandalism causes a crowdsourcing system to be unreliable and makes it hard to produce high-quality content [1]. Additionally, it has been found that first-time contributors have a higher potential to be affected by vandalism [53].

**Manifestation.** Depending on the nature of the crowdsourcing platform, the way this pattern manifests itself is different. In Wikipedia, vandalism manifests itself as actors participating in malicious blanking/deleting (e.g, removing significant parts of pages or even whole pages), malevolent editing, and the provision of spam links (e.g., use of disruptive, irrelevant, or inappropriate links) [39]. In OSM, this pattern manifests itself in different ways such as randomly deleting existing objects, generating fictional objects, use of automated edits (bots) in the database, and copyright infringements (e.g., use of data from Google Maps) [40].

**Detection.** The most common approach for detecting vandalism is the use of automated anti-vandalism bots [39] which utilise heuristics based on the number of edits, the size of the edit, whether the editor is anonymous or not, and many other criteria. In Wikipedia, for example, bots have been used to check every edit in real time, to spot vandalism, and revert them if necessary [39]. A similar rule-based vandalism detection method has been applied to detect common types of vandalism in the OSM database [40]. Adler et al. [1] introduced two types of vandalism detection problem: immediate vandalism (i.e., occurring in the most recent revision of an article), and historical vandalism (i.e., occurring in any revision including past ones). A machine learning classifier is used. Features include metadata elements such as the time since the article was last edited, textual features such as the use of uppercase and digit ratio, language features such as the use of biased or bad words, and reputation of the user.

## 3.5   Domination

**Description.** Domination refers to uneven power dynamics among actors in crowdsourcing systems. Through domination, a contributor who holds formal decision-making power may deliberately violate privileges and ethical rules of the platform in order to suppress, influence, or modify the contributions of others. For example, domination may present itself through a phenomenon referred to as "wisdom of few" where higher ranked or more popular actors generate most of the content [5].

**Real-Life Examples.** This pattern occurs in crowdsourcing platforms where there is some organisational structure such as Wikipedia or GitHub. In Wikipedia, dyadic dominance can occur when one user undoes edits of another user or redoes them their own way. Third-party dominance can arise when a third user restores the edits of a user which was undone by another user [33].

In crowdsourcing systems such as OpenStreetMap and Wikipedia, a small group of actors contribute very significantly, while a very large group of actors participate only occasionally [6]. In English Wikipedia for instance, the first version of half the entries was posted by only 0.04% of editors, which means only a relatively small number of actors on Wikipedia are actively contributing [5].

**Affect.** The affect of domination of small groups over others is that it creates a high risk of "elite capture" or strong demographic bias [6]. Since the dominant actor decides which other actors to hire or reward, the bargaining power balance is in favor of the dominant actor [12]. Therefore, Domination can thrive when a dominant actor possesses a superior position and other actors have limited power [12].

**Manifestation.** In privilege-based crowdsourcing systems the dynamic power of actors can be characterised as soft power or hard power. An example of soft power is actors receiving a particular label or badge (social or task-oriented) such as Guru, Expert, Deputy, based on their level of contribution to the system. Therefore, other actors rely on their opinion more because of their status. On the other hand, an editor deciding whether a contribution is accepted or not provides an example of hard power. In hard power, a dominant actor has more authority to govern contributions and this may be guided by their preferences. Hierarchies derived from edits in Wikipedia typically had anonymous users occupying the lowest positions in the hierarchy and registered users in the highest positions, confirming the intuition that registering is necessary for acquiring credibility [34].

**Detection.** A Wikipedia edit network captures three types of interactions: dyadic undo, dyadic redo, and third-party edits. From such a network a pairwise dominance ordering can be derived. The pairwise dominance ordering can be used to derive the actors' hierarchical position as a function of their editing activity [34]. In GitHub, a statistical model is used based on data from the pull requests of projects. The model shows a positive association between pull request acceptance and submitters with a higher number of followers or having a higher status (such as collaborator) [51], thus detecting manifestations of dominance based on actors' social connections.

### 3.6   Stasis

**Description.** Stasis refers to the lack of progress in a contributed task due to inaction or adversarial action by contributors. Different forms of the stasis pattern in crowdsourcing are: (i) a situation in which actions are done and undone over a period of time without reaching a resolution; (ii) a situation in which there is a lack of response to an actor's contribution to a task. For instance, a contribution remains in the submitted status because of approval not being granted by another contributor.

**Real-Life Example.** An example of the stasis pattern in Wikipedia is an "edit war" among editors of articles. In such a conflict, actors express their disagreement toward the opinion of other actors by modifying content that has been authored by them [34] and this process repeats itself ad infinitum.

**Affect.** There is a relation between the occurrence of stasis and an actor's reputation [33] and stasis may lead to vandalism. For example, actors with a higher reputation initiate most undo-redo cycles, and they are less likely the recipients of such destructive cycles [33]. Such cycles can be a manifestation of domination [34] where actors violate their privileged status to control other actors, either by not responding to their contributions or by refusing them. This behaviour is significant as actor contributions may be lost and this may negatively influence quality [7].

**Manifestation.** This pattern can manifest itself through lengthy and protracted undo-redo cycles, whose root causes are points of disagreement [34] between actors. These cycles can be found in the logs of crowdsourcing systems and are sometimes also visible to other participants (as in the case of Wikipedia). Another manifestation of stasis is the lack of contribution by actors. In GitHub, examples of lack of contributions are an owner not maintaining a project or abandoning it altogether. A study [45] found that in GitHub only 10% of users can be considered active. Hence, a lot of open source projects die from lack of contribution.

**Detection.** A controversy measure is computed for each article to detect an edit war in Wikipedia. The controversy measure considers mutual reverts made by the editors (two editors reverting each others' edits). The measure also accounts for the rank or reputation of the editors [50]. In GitHub, a linear regression model is used to identify statistically significant factors that influence the latency of a pull request. Factors such as first response time of reviewers, pull request complexity, and integrator workload are taken into consideration, and predictors among these are identified [56].

## 4   Comparative Insights

In this section, we analyse each pattern across different crowdsourcing systems to represent their existence and identify mechanisms provided by the system that impede the occurrence of the pattern. Table 1 summaries our analysis.

The ratings can take the form '+' which indicates the existence of a co-destruction pattern in the crowdsourcing system, '+/−' which suggests that some mechanisms exist that prevent the pattern's occurrence, and '−' which indicates that it is unlikely for the pattern to occur in the system.

**Wikipedia:** Collusion can manifest in Wikipedia when a group of editors can update and edit articles that can overemphasize their point of view. The process of reviewing prevents some forms of collusion (+/−). Bias can occur in the form of 'language bias' and 'reputation bias', though the core policy of Wikipedia is to provide a neutral point of view. By having many editors and reviewers the widespread presence of bias can be mitigated (+/−). Incompetence occurs when uninformed users edit articles. The review mechanism allows for correction of incompetence (+/−). Domination and deference can exist through the linear hierarchy of reviewers (+). The effects of Vandalism are not likely to be long-lasting as there are vandalism detection bots and reviewers who can block such updates (−). Stasis occurs due to constant edit wars on Wikipedia (+).

**GitHub:** Collusion in GitHub does not exist as a group of contributors define the project, different types of tasks and the task owners (−). Studies show the existence of geographical bias and reputation bias leading to a higher chance of pull request acceptance [43] (+). Incompetence occurs in GitHub as users not familiar with the source code of a project can contribute to that project. The mechanisms of review adopted by users of the system reduce this form of incompetence (+/−). Vandalism does not occur as user edits go through a review process (−). Domination can exist through the linear hierarchy controls that exist for the acceptance of source code pull-request (+). Stasis occurs due to changes made by a developer not being accepted (+).

**Waze:** Collusion in Waze can occur where a group of actors can simulate non-existent traffic jams [46]. However, the reputation ratings in Waze prevents actors from continually misreporting (+/−). Bias exists with drivers choosing specific roads and routes for reporting (+). Incompetence occurs with new users providing false or incomplete reports, but new users are initially limited with respect to the scope of the updates that they can make and some updates (e.g. road closures) have to be confirmed by other users (+/−). Very few functions require reputation thresholds, thus mitigating the occurrence of domination (−). Vandalism can occur with simulated attacks, but the actors' reputations would be impacted (−). The occurrence of Stasis is difficult as multiple users in the same location need to provide contradictory reports (−).

**OSM:** Collusion in OSM is low as the system does not provide an unfair advantage in updating the geodata. The correction by local community addresses any updates that are made [40] (+/−). Bias can occur based on the representation of a community of actors in specific geographic locations (+). Incompetence is high as mapping would require the use of the global positioning system or use of aerial imagery picture. In a study on OSM data, 76.3% of the edits by new actors were incorrect. However, in the same study, 63% of the errors were reverted within 24 h and 76.5% within 48 h [40] (+). Domination is low, with actors primarily updating local information, as there is no hierarchy $(-)$. Vandalism can exist but is corrected by the community and with the help of automated bots $(+/-)$. Statis does not exist, as all updates are immediately available $(-)$.

***AMT:*** In AMT, collusion can occur when a group of actors copy their responses with minor changes, without doing actual work [26]. Reputation mechanisms in AMT prevent actors from colluding continually $(+/-)$. Bias can occur due to actors' perceptions and inclinations. Bias can be detected by considering responses from multiple workers $(+/-)$. Incompetence occurs when actors choose to work on tasks that are not optimally suited to them [17]. The system allows the task creator to specify the skills and competencies required for the task $(+/-)$. Domination does not exist as an actor can choose to work on a task $(-)$. Vandalism is rare as it could impact reputation $(-)$. Stasis does not occur as the task has to be accepted or rejected $(-)$.

The comparative study provides us with insights into mechanisms that prevent or enable specific patterns. For example, the existence of reputation ratings of actors reduces or mitigates occurrences of collusion and vandalism. Incompetence can be high in systems that require specialized skills (e.g. OSM). Domination and Stasis occur when a small group of users claim to have superior positions in the system (reviewers or administrators). Over time, it is hoped that knowledge gained through patterns-based platform analyses can inform the configuration or construction of new platforms.

**Table 1.** Evaluating co-destruction pattern occurrence in crowdsourcing systems.

| Patterns | Wikipedia | GitHub | Waze | OSM | AMT |
|---|---|---|---|---|---|
| Collusion | $+/-$ | $-$ | $+/-$ | $+/-$ | $+/-$ |
| Bias | $+/-$ | $+$ | $+$ | $+$ | $+/-$ |
| Incompetence | $+/-$ | $+/-$ | $+/-$ | $+$ | $+/-$ |
| Domination | $+$ | $+$ | $-$ | $-$ | $-$ |
| Vandalism | $-$ | $-$ | $-$ | $+/-$ | $-$ |
| Stasis | $+$ | $+$ | $-$ | $-$ | $-$ |

## 5    Evaluation

In order to empirically assess the co-destruction patterns, we focused on two aspects: their *pervasiveness* and their *perceived importance*. To this end, we collected insights from participants that have experience with crowdsourcing initiatives and/or activities, specifically people that have contributed to or initiated crowdsourcing activities. A questionnaire was distributed through social media channels such as LinkedIn Groups and Twitter as well as by email to known contacts. The questionnaire gauged participants' experience with crowdsourcing and asked for each of the six patterns to what degree they had encountered these patterns and how important they perceived recognition and prevention of these patterns to be (both on a 1–5 Likert scale).

Of the 25 participants who started to answer the questionnaire, a total of 21 participants completed it. 14% of respondents have not contributed to a crowdsourcing platform, but have regularly used GitHub, Wikipedia or StackOverflow. Furthermore, 33% of respondents have edited an article in Wikipedia, 43% contributed source code on GitHub, 48% were owners of a project in GitHub, 38% claimed to have contributed to StackOverflow and 10% to Figure Eight (formerly CrowdFlower). Six out of 21 respondents were involved in initiating a crowdsourcing activity on GitHub, Figure Eight, or a company-specific crowdsourcing platform.

For each of the six patterns there were at least 12 respondents that have encountered that pattern. The most frequently observed patterns were Incompetence, Bias and Stasis (seen by 100%, 90% and 81% of respondents respectively). The Collusion, Vandalism and Domination patterns were least frequently observed (seen by 67%, 67% and 57% of respondents respectively). One respondent believed that the reason behind the lower frequency of some patterns such as Collusion may be that "Community is very much reactive to such events when it happens and terminates its effect quickly". Figure 1 represents the pervasiveness of the co-destruction patterns as observed by the respondents. The recognition and prevention of each of the patterns was perceived as 'Important' or 'Very Important' by at least 55% of the participants (see Fig. 2). Of particular perceived importance were the Incompetence pattern (77% found this 'Important' or 'Very Important'), the Vandalism pattern (77%) and the Stasis pattern (67%). While the sample size of 21 is small, the results are of interest as they provide an indication that these patterns have really been observed across different platforms and that their mitigation is perceived as important by many of the respondents.

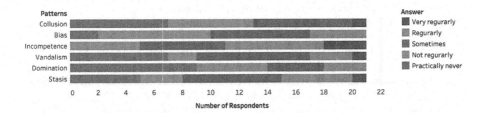

**Fig. 1.** Pervasiveness of co-destruction patterns

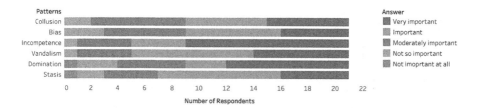

**Fig. 2.** Perceived importance of co-destruction patterns

## 6   Conclusion

There are different actor characterics and forms of dynamics in crowdsourcing systems which can lead to suboptimal outcomes and are thus ideally mitigated. In this paper, we provided a systematic analysis of destructive actor behaviour in the form of a collection of patterns, derived from both the literature and from our own experiences with crowdsourcing systems. A survey revealed that these patterns have been observed in practice and are perceived to be of significant importance to be addressed. It was also shown that a patterns-based analysis of some crowdsourcing systems provides a meaningful (comparative) insight. The patterns can be used for benchmarking purposes, for the purpose of selecting, configuring or even developing a crowdsourcing system, and for the development of new detection and mitigation methods (a potential topic for future work). Naturally, the collection of patterns can be extended and refined over time.

## References

1. Adler, B.T., de Alfaro, L., Mola-Velasco, S.M., Rosso, P., West, A.G.: Wikipedia vandalism detection: combining natural language, metadata, and reputation features. In: Gelbukh, A. (ed.) CICLing 2011. LNCS, vol. 6609, pp. 277–288. Springer, Heidelberg (2011). https://doi.org/10.1007/978-3-642-19437-5_23
2. Alexander, C.: A Pattern Language: Towns, Buildings, Construction. Oxford University Press, Oxford (1977)
3. Allahbakhsh, M., Ignjatovic, A., Benatallah, B., Beheshti, S.-M.-R., Bertino, E., Foo, N.: Collusion detection in online rating systems. In: Ishikawa, Y., Li, J., Wang, W., Zhang, R., Zhang, W. (eds.) APWeb 2013. LNCS, vol. 7808, pp. 196–207. Springer, Heidelberg (2013). https://doi.org/10.1007/978-3-642-37401-2_21
4. Baccarella, C.V., et al.: Social media? It's serious! Understanding the dark side of social media. EU Manag. J. **36**(4), 431–438 (2018)
5. Baeza-Yates, R.: Bias on the web. CACM **61**(6), 54–61 (2018)
6. Bott, M., Young, G.: The role of crowdsourcing for better governance in international development. Fletcher J. Hum. Secur. **27**(1), 47–70 (2012)
7. Brandes, U., Lerner, J.: Visual analysis of controversy in user-generated encyclopedias. Inf. Vis. **7**(1), 34–48 (2008)
8. Chen, P., et al.: Collusion-proof result inference in crowdsourcing. J. Comput. Sci. Technol. **33**(2), 351–365 (2018)

9. Chiu, C., Liang, T., Turban, E.: What can crowdsourcing do for decision support? Decis. Support Syst. **65**, 40–49 (2014)

10. Ciccarelli, G., Cigno, R.L.: Collusion in peer-to-peer systems. Comput. Netw. **55**(15), 3517–3532 (2011)

11. Daniel, F., et al.: Quality control in crowdsourcing: a survey of quality attributes, assessment techniques, and assurance actions. ACM Comput. Surv. (CSUR) **51**(1), 7 (2018)

12. Durward, D., et al.: Rags to riches-how signaling behaviour causes a power shift in crowdsourcing markets. In: ECIS (2016)

13. Eickhoff, C.: Cognitive biases in crowdsourcing. In: The Eleventh ACM International Conference on WSDM, pp. 162–170 (2018)

14. Erickson, L., Petrick, I., Trauth, E.: Hanging with the right crowd: matching crowdsourcing need to crowd characteristics (2012)

15. Estellés-Arolas, E., et al.: Towards an integrated crowdsourcing definition. J. Inf. Sci. **38**(2), 189–200 (2012)

16. Fowler, M.: Analysis Patterns: Reusable Object Models. Addison-Wesley Professional, Boston (1997)

17. Gadiraju, U., et al.: Using worker self-assessments for competence-based preselection in crowdsourcing microtasks. TOCHI **24**(4), 30 (2017)

18. Gatzweiler, A., et al.: Dark side or bright light: destructive and constructive deviant content in consumer ideation contests. J. Prod. Innov. Manag. **6**, 772–789 (2017)

19. Gebauer, J.: Crowd resistance-reasons and dynamics of user rebellions against crowdsourcing. In: ISPIM Conference Proceedings, p. 1 (2012)

20. Harmon, A.: Amazon glitch unmasks war of reviewers. The New York Times 14(8) (2004)

21. Harpalani, M., et al.: Language of vandalism: improving Wikipedia vandalism detection via stylometric analysis. In: Proceedings of the 49th Annual Meeting of the ACL: Human Language Technologies, pp. 83–88 (2011)

22. Harris, L., et al.: Not always co-creation: introducing interactional co-destruction of value in service-dominant logic. J. Serv. Mark. **24**, 430–437 (2010)

23. Howe, J.: The rise of crowdsourcing. Wired Mag. **14**(6), 1–4 (2006)

24. Hube, C.: Bias in Wikipedia. In: Proceedings of the 26th International Conference on World Wide Web Companion, pp. 717–721 (2017)

25. Kamar, E., et al.: Identifying and accounting for task-dependent bias in crowdsourcing. In: Third AAAI HCOMP (2015)

26. Kamhoua, G.A., et al.: Approach to detect non-adversarial overlapping collusion in crowdsourcing. In: 2017 IEEE 36th IPCCC, pp. 1–8 (2017)

27. Kazai, G., Kamps, J., Milic-Frayling, N.: Worker types and personality traits in crowdsourcing relevance labels. In: CIKM, pp. 1941–1944 (2011)

28. KhudaBukhsh, A.R., et al.: Detecting non-adversarial collusion in crowdsourcing. In: Second AAAI HCOMP (2014)

29. Kuek, S.C., et al.: The global opportunity in online outsourcing. World Bank (2015)

30. Lee, H.C.B., et al.: Salience bias in crowdsourcing contests. Inf. Syst. Res. **29**(2), 401–418 (2018)

31. Lee, H., Kim, J., Shin, K.: Simplified clique detection for collusion-resistant reputation management scheme in P2P networks'. In: 2010 10th International Symposium on Communications and IT, pp. 273–278. IEEE (2010)

32. Lee, K., et al.: The dark side of micro-task marketplaces: characterizing fiverr and automatically detecting crowdturfing. In: Eighth International AAAI ICWSM (2014)

33. Lerner, J., et al.: The free encyclopedia that anyone can dispute: an analysis of the micro-structural dynamics of positive and negative relations in the production of contentious Wikipedia articles. Soc. Netw. **60**, 11–25 (2018)
34. Lerner, J., Lomi, A.: The third man: hierarchy formation in Wikipedia. Appl. Netw. Sci. **2**(1), 24 (2017). https://doi.org/10.1007/s41109-017-0043-2
35. Leskovec, J., Adamic, L.A., Huberman, B.A.: The dynamics of viral marketing. ACM Trans. Web (TWEB) **1**(1), 5 (2007)
36. Liu, Q., et al.: Scoring workers in crowdsourcing: how many control questions are enough? In: NIPS 2013, pp. 1914–1922 (2013)
37. Lüdeke-Freund, F., Bohnsack, R., Breuer, H., Massa, L.: Research on sustainable business model patterns: status quo, methodological issues, and a research agenda. In: Aagaard, A. (ed.) Sustainable Business Models. PSSBIAFE, pp. 25–60. Springer, Cham (2019). https://doi.org/10.1007/978-3-319-93275-0_2
38. Malhotra, A., Van Alstyne, M.: The dark side of the sharing economy and how to lighten it. CACM **57**(11), 24–27 (2014)
39. Mola-Velasco, S.M.: Wikipedia vandalism detection. In: Proceedings of the 20th International Conference Companion on WWW, pp. 391–396. ACM (2011)
40. Neis, P., Goetz, M., Zipf, A.: Towards automatic vandalism detection in OpenStreetMap. Int. J. Geo-Inf. **1**(3), 315–332 (2012)
41. Plé, L.: Why do we need research on value co-destruction? Journal of Creating Value **3**(2), 162–169 (2017)
42. Potthast, M.: Crowdsourcing a Wikipedia vandalism corpus. In: Proceedings of the 33rd International ACM SIGIR, pp. 789–790. ACM (2010)
43. Rastogi, A.: Do biases related to geographical location influence work-related decisions in GitHub? In: Proceedings of the 38th ICSE Companion, ICSE 2016, pp. 665–667 (2016)
44. Saab, F., et al.: Modelling cognitive bias in crowdsourcing systems. Cogn. Syst. Res. **58**, 1–18 (2019)
45. Sanatinia, A., Noubir, G.: On GitHub's programming languages. arXiv preprint arXiv:1603.00431 (2016)
46. Sanchez, L., Rosas, E., Hidalgo, N.: Crowdsourcing under attack: detecting malicious behaviors in Waze. In: Gal-Oz, N., Lewis, P.R. (eds.) IFIPTM 2018. IAICT, vol. 528, pp. 91–106. Springer, Cham (2018). https://doi.org/10.1007/978-3-319-95276-5_7
47. Saxton, G.D., Oh, O., Kishore, R.: Rules of crowdsourcing: models, issues, and systems of control. IS Manag. **30**(1), 2–20 (2013)
48. Simula, H.: The rise and fall of crowdsourcing? In: 2013 46th Hawaii International Conference on System Sciences, pp. 2783–2791. IEEE (2013)
49. Smith, A.: The value co-destruction process: a customer resource perspective. Eur. J. Mark. **47**(11/12), 1889–1909 (2013)
50. Sumi, R., Yasseri, T.: Edit wars in Wikipedia. In: IEEE PASSAT-SOCIALCOM, pp. 724–727 (2011)
51. Tsay, J., et al.: Influence of social and technical factors for evaluating contribution in GitHub. In: ICSE, pp. 356–366 (2014)
52. Vafeas, M., Hughes, T., Hilton, T.: Antecedents to value diminution: a dyadic perspective. Mark. Theory **16**(4), 469–491 (2016)
53. Viégas, F.B., et al.: Studying cooperation and conflict between authors with history flow visualizations. In: Proceedings of the SIGCHI Conference ACM, pp. 575–582 (2004)
54. Wauthier, F.L., Jordan, M.I.: Bayesian bias mitigation for crowdsourcing. In: Advances in NIPS, pp. 1800–1808 (2011)

55. Wilson, M., Robson, K., Botha, E.: Crowdsourcing in a time of empowered stake-holders: lessons from crowdsourcing campaigns. Bus. Horiz. **60**(2), 247–253 (2017)
56. Yu, Y., et al.: Wait for it: determinants of pull request evaluation latency on GitHub. In: 12th IEEE/ACM MSR, pp. 367–371 (2015)
57. Zou, J., et al.: A proof-of-trust consensus protocol for enhancing accountability in crowdsourcing services. IEEE TSC **12**, 429–445 (2018)

# Information Systems Engineering with Digital Shadows: Concept and Case Studies

## An Exploratory Paper

Martin Liebenberg[(✉)] [iD] and Matthias Jarke[iD]

Computer Science Department, RWTH Aachen University, Aachen, Germany
liebenberg@kbsg.rwth-aachen.de, jarke@dbis.rwth-aachen.de

**Abstract.** The production sector has faced many difficulties in taking full advantage of opportunities found in other web application domains. Production research has focused on sophisticated mathematical models ranging from molecular materials modeling to efficient production control to inter-company supply network logistics. Often, these models have no closed-form solutions; this led to intense simulation research for individual modeling viewpoints, often labeled "Digital Twins".

However, the complexity of the overall system precludes Digital Twins covering more than just a few system perspectives, especially if near-realtime performance is required. Moreover, the wide variety of individual situations and behaviors is usually captured only as statistical uncertainty. In order to achieve better performance and more context adaptation, the interdisciplinary research cluster "Internet of Production" at RWTH Aachen University is exploring the concept of "Digital Shadows". Digital Shadows can be understood as compact views on dynamic processes, usually combining condensed measurement data with highly efficient simplified mathematical models. In this exploratory paper, we argue based on a couple of initial case studies that Digital Shadows are not just valuable carriers of deep engineering knowledge but due to their small size also help in reducing network congestion and enabling edge computing. These properties could make Digital Shadows an interesting solution to address resilience in other information-intensive dynamic systems.

**Keywords:** Digital shadows · Internet of Production (IoP) · Database views · World Wide Lab (WWL) · Collaborative information systems

## 1 Introduction

In recent years, Digital Twins became increasingly important in the research fields of production planning and controlling [25]. Digital Twins are digital

This work was funded by the Deutsche Forschungsgemeinschaft (DFG, German Research Foundation) under Germany's Excellence Strategy – EXC-2023 Internet of Production – 390621612.

S. Dustdar et al. (Eds.): CAiSE 2020, LNCS 12127, pp. 70–84, 2020.
https://doi.org/10.1007/978-3-030-49435-3_5

artefacts which represent in a production environments, for instance, a work piece or product in a production scenario. The representation is done with mathematical models or simulations which can also be regarded as models. These models are used, for example, to develop new products or improve processes [14]. Digital Twins are thought of as a digital counterpart to physical production artefacts. So they have a high resolution to be useful for every purpose in its environment. But, Digital Twins are often too slow to use them in real-time scenarios. In terms of simulations, Finite Element Method (FEM) [32] simulations are widely used in the field of production [4,18,20]. These simulations are rather expensive to be calculated because production parts are divided into hundreds to millions of discrete elements for which certain physical properties are calculated in relation of its neighbors. So that typically, a duration of one simulation run ranges from several minutes to hours or days. That is not feasible for fast reaction to defects in a production process.

Therefore, we explore the concept of Digital Shadows. The term "Digital Shadow" was first introduced about ten years ago [8] in the privacy debate on the dangers of your "Digital Footprint" where such a footprint consists of a large number of shadows or traces left by all your digital actions; since that time, there exist even companies that help you or your company against misuse of your digital shadow[1].

During the early Digital Twin debate in production engineering around 2015, Digital Shadows played only a marginal role as documented traces of the "real" production processes or its digital twin. In contrast, we want to study and treat digital shadows as "first-class citizens". In this setting, Digital Shadows are dynamic digital views or traces on a physical process or a simulation, where only those aspects are represented which are necessary for a specified purpose. This can be subsets of data from production processes, or functions mapping certain data onto subset of other data. These can then be used in scenarios where fast reaction is crucial. From a physical data management perspective, a Digital Shadow is condensed data of small size generated for a particular task in a production process so that it can be transferred in networks reducing congestion.

In the interdisciplinary research cluster "Internet of Production" at RWTH Aachen University, more than 20 institutes from mechanical engineering, material science, humanities and computer science are working on the vision of an Internet of Production (IoP) for a new level of cross-domain collaboration. In this cluster we work on systems realising the generation and usage of Digital Shadows in a global network of production facilities.

In this paper we explore Digital Shadows as a main aspect of the IoP in more detail in terms of requirements for information systems. In the next section we sketch in brief the vision of the IoP. In Sect. 3 we explore the role of Digital Shadows from two perspectives. First, we discuss in Sect. 3.1 Digital Shadows from the perspective of Database Views. Second, in Sects. 3.2 and 3.3 we present

---

[1] This is not to be confused with another stream of political economy literature concerning the "digital shadow economy" [9] related to the concept of (usually illegal) shadow economy.

two interdisciplinary use cases for very useful Digital Shadows in Plastics and Steel Engineering and demonstrate their Information Systems Engineering in a prototypical implementation. We end with a discussion on further research questions in making Digital Shadows and the IoP a reality.

## 2   IoP: Beyond Production Monitoring and Control

One core vision of the IoP is called the World Wide Lab (WWL). Here, we assume that the models can only be improved if the data is as diverse as possible. For instance, if we train a Neural Network with data coming from only one type of metal in hot rolling, it is likely that for another material the model does not work properly. So, we claim that we need to share data and models so that Digital Shadows can be improved and furthermore be shared for use in other production scenarios. We regard each experiment or even process step as part of one huge experiment in the WWL. Therefore, we want to use lightweight purpose-driven Digital Shadows to avoid, for instance, expensive simulations and network congestion [22,23]. That is, Digital Shadows are meant to be reduced models or subsets of data for certain purposes. These models should be used to calculate much faster than simulations relevant aspects of a production step so that they are enablers of important aspects of the fourth industrial revolution as mass customization of products.

With exchanging data and Digital Shadows in the IoP we go further than just monitoring processes or controlling them. We collect data from the monitoring and aggregate it to build Digital Shadows but not only from our own processes but also from others in the WWL. That means cross-domain exchange of data which can not only improve the processes in ones own company. So we can make data in its data-silos in different companies more valuable as, for example, present traffic information makes the routes in Google Maps more valuable.

## 3   Exploring the Role of Digital Shadows

Above we presented a rough idea of what we understand about a Digital Shadow in the WWL within an IoP. In this section we want to elaborate more on the meaning of Digital Shadows and how we can generate and use them.

First, we will take a look on Digital Shadows from the perspective of data base systems. Then we present two use cases, where we show the usage of Digital Shadows. Finally, we present a concept for a first prototype of a node of the IoP dealing with the generation and usage of Digital Shadows.

### 3.1   From Database Views to Digital Shadows

Our approach to formalizing the Digital Shadow concept is inspired by the highly successful 50 year old concept of database views. A view is defined as a named query on a database which can be reused in other queries or applications in the same way as a stored relation. In other words, views are Janus-faced objects which can be seen both as a mathematical model (query) and as condensed transformed data according to a specific user interest.

We are particularly interested in adapting the following roles of views to Digital Shadows:

(1) Views can be used for information hiding in conceptual schemas. In other words, data providers can employ views to determine which excerpt of their data consumers can see, and in which granularity. This makes cleverly designed views (Digital Shadows) a potentially valuable trade object and also helps privacy concerns. Research in this area dates back to the 1975 Ph.D. thesis of Mike Stonebraker on view unfolding. In the opposite direction, data mining and data-driven machine learning have been widely interpreted as detecting interesting queries/views from huge data sets, i.e. creating models from data.

(2) Conversely, recent heterogeneous data integration and exchange mechanisms make it possible for data consumers to map different data provider views to an integrated own perspective. Starting from pionieering work in IBM's CLIO project [6], recent research on mapping strategies for heterogeneous data exchange using ontologies [16] or tuple-generating dependencies across different data models [11,13] has enabled both semi-automatic generation of mappings between provider and consumer schemas, and the automated generation of code from such mappings. These recent results also enable completeness, consistency, and other data quality checks in data sharing settings – extremely important aspects that need to be linked to quality management in the production sector through the Digital Shadow concept.

(3) In many such scenarios, the Digital Shadows quickly become independent objects which must be used by the data consumers detached from their sources. The analogous research question how to maintain externally materialized views with minimal data transfer has been intensely studied in the late 1990s [30]. The equally relevant question how to answer questions only on materialized views, without access to sources has also led to useful algorithms such as MiniCon [24].

For the planned knowledge transfer from view theory to a future Digital Shadow theory, important differences must also be considered, most importantly the fact that most digital shadows will be views on processes, and that the models (analogy to the view definitions) are much more complex than simple database queries, reflecting decades on highly specialized engineering and mathematical research. In the IoP research, we have therefore decided to first get an intuition for realistic Digital Shadows relevance and challenges through a number of interdisciplinary case studies in which especially the combination of mathematical engineering theories with deep learning and related data mining techniques in Digital Shadows is explored.

## 3.2   Two Case Studies

We discuss here two highly relevant production use cases where Digital Shadows can improve processes drastically. The first is an injection moulding use case which considers the production of plastic pieces. The second is one of the most energy-intensive production steps worldwide, the hot rolling task within steel-based production where metal slaps are rolled to thinner plates. These use cases are very different. Not only the material is different but also the production process itself. The data from these processes are very different and so are the Digital Shadows.

In the following we describe the use cases in more detail and address the relation to Digital Shadows.

**Injection Moulding.** In injection moulding, an elaborate plastic piece is produced in one single complex process step using injection moulding machines. On the one hand, that makes it very efficient to produce a large number of plastic parts. On the other hand, there exists no mathematical model which describes the process as a whole. That complicates the initialization of a new process and also makes it difficult to create a Digital Shadow for the injection moulding process.

This process is executed on an injection moulding machine. A turning screw transports small plastic pellets through a long, horizontal, heated barrel. On its way through the barrel the plastic melts and is compressed in a nozzle towards the end of the barrel. For each plastic piece, the screw moves rapidly forward and forces the molten plastic through pipes into the cavity of the mold in the shape of the desired workpiece. After cooling down and hardening of the plastic, the mold opens and the workpiece is ejected with pins which are pulled out of the mold. After moving the screw back into its initial position, the next part can be produced. So, a substantial number of pieces can be produced in a short time depending on the properties of the material and the size of the cavity. There are many variations of that process, for instance, in some cases multiple pieces can be produced at once [12,27]. There exist mathematical models for some parts of that process but there are no closed-form solutions covering the whole process. Until today, the process parameters are often still determined by hand [7]. Instead of models, costly simulations such as FEM simulations, mentioned above, are used to support the parameterization. The calculation time of such simulations ranges from minutes up to hours, which is far from real-time. So it is not efficient to switch from one part to another as would be needed, for example, for mass customization. Instead, today it is more efficient to produce the same part as often as possible to save the time of reconfigure the parameters for another part.

In Fig. 1, our approach to generate Digital Shadows is depicted for predicting quality parameters of a plastic part for given parameter settings [19]. Given this Digital Shadow, it was possible to find parameters for the injection machine to attain the desired quality of the part within seconds. Because there was no closed-form mathematical models of the process which could be simplified to gain

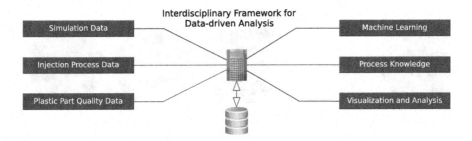

**Fig. 1.** Setup for building Digital Shadows with machine learning in the injection moulding use case.

functions representing a Digital Shadow, we used machine learning to learn these functions. Getting data from experiments takes time because the dimensions and the weight of a workpiece we needed for the quality parameters had to be measured by hand. So it was not possible to generate the amount of data which is usually needed for machine learning.

Nevertheless, it is possible to obtain Digital Shadows even from less data although data-driven machine learning approaches need a large amount of data. Experiments in our studies showed that it is possible to use the combination of simulation data and data from experiments to train Neural Networks so that data from simulations could compensate the reduced amount of data coming from the process itself. On the left in Fig. 1, is shown that for experiments in our studies two ways to get data were chosen: (a) manual experiments on the injection machine with measurements of the resulting product quality and (b) FEM simulations. The FEM simulation took about 10 min per part so that it was possible to obtain several hundred of data points. In the middle of the picture is the prototypical framework depicted we present later in this paper. It was used to store the data from the machines and the simulations. On the right-hand side in the picture is depicted that this data from the framework was used for the aforementioned machine learning. These networks learned for a range of process parameters which value a certain quality criterion, for instance weight, will be gained during the injection moulding process. Furthermore, on the right is depicted that knowledge of the process could be obtained from the framework and with visualization of the data it was possible for data analysts to select the data they needed for the machine learning approaches. For more details of the findings in this studies we refer to [19].

**Hot Rolling.** As Fig. 2 illustrates on the example of the production process of the so-called B column (the core stabilizing element in a car), hot rolling is an essential element in all steel-based production processes; moreover, it is one of the most energy-intensive production tasks world-wide (several percent of industrial energy usage), such that improvements here have a significant potential in reducing carbon footprint worldwide.

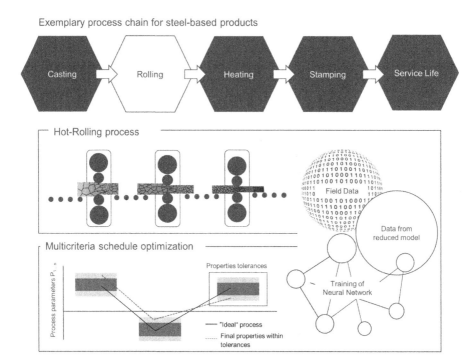

**Fig. 2.** Hot rolling within the steel production chain: schedule optimization by combining fast reduced models, field data and neural network learning in a two-layer Digital Shadow

In the hot rolling process, a hot slab of metal is pressed between a pair of rolls resulting in a reduction of the height and additional lengthening of the slab; a hot rolling mill usually comprises a series about 30 such pairs (the figure shows 3). Our study considered only reversing hot rolling mills [19], where the slab as a whole is rolled back and forth through a mill with only one pair of rolls. During one pass, with the height reduction also the microstructure within the material is changed. That microstructure influences the properties of the resulting product [15]. That is an intermediate product further processed in following production steps such as fine-blanking [1] or deep-drawing [5]. The latter is called stamping in some cases, as for the B column in Fig. 2. The core issue influencing the quality of the product and the energy consumption of the process is the combined design of the individual steps, and their overall scheduling.

In most current practice, experienced engineers manually design such a schedule, and evaluates it using FEM methods which take 30 min to 4 h in typical production processes; thus, to plan production for the next day, at most a couple of plans can be explored. In prior research, six different engineering groups from production and material science had developed reduced versions of the very complex mathematical models for the many aspects influencing the dimensions of the resulting slabs, its microstructure, the thermal condition, and energy impact of this process. Taken together, the purely model-based Digital Shadow from the clever combination of these models reduces the evaluation time to about 50 ms with little quality loss over the 30–240 min FEM computations – a speedup over 100.000 [2,29].

Unfortunately, this still does not solve the problem as there is an exponential number of possible schedules to be evaluated. To turn the fast evaluation Shadow into one that can also actively search for fast, high-quality and energy-efficient rolling schedules, given a desired combination of target parameters, a second-level Digital Shadow has been constructed. In this schedule (shown in the lower right of the figure) the reduced model evaluations are embedded in the training of a Deep Neural Network, where the training data stem both from production process and experiment data, and artificially generated schedules gained by other permutations of those schedules. The trained Neural Network can then be used to directly recommend suitable inputs (schedules) for desired outputs [19]. Note that here, the purpose of the NN-based Digital Shadow is quite different from the injection moulding use case. Even withing the hot rolling use case, a Digital Shadow could have been constructed in a similar way as for injection moulding, but without the fast models, the learning process would have been rather meaningless.

In current work, we try to demonstrate that the potential of the multi-layer Digital Shadow for improving hot rolling processes goes even further. The microstructure in the material cannot be detected during the process, but the fast models are able to calculate the inner structure of the material. That information can be used to adapt later production steps of the resulting slab. But even during the process, if it is noticed that a certain process parameter is not as expected in the rolling schedule (e.g. humidity changes due to unexpected rainfall), the Digital Shadow could re-calculate the inner structure and thus avoid regarding the slab as scrap such that the whole energy-intensive process must be repeated [26]. The in-process resilience thus achieved would additionally allow more "courageous" energy-saving schedules than the present ones which have to be extremely careful with tolerances, as they must take all likely failures into account from the start.

### 3.3   Linking Processes, Models, and Machine Learning: An Experimental Infrastructure for the IoP

Loucopoulos et al. [17] present an early requirements engineering approach to transform existing requirements for traditional production systems to requirements of cyber physical production systems. The requirements mentioned there obviously overlap with our work. However, gaining purpose-driven Digital Shadows from data out of a global multi-site WWL and share them in the multi-disciplinary IoP demands new requirements for information systems. In this regard, our ongoing IoP research also profits from the multi-year requirements engineering effort on alliance-driven data platforms within the international Industrial Data Space initiative [21] which focuses on controlled data sharing in so-called alliance driven data platforms which do not have a keystone

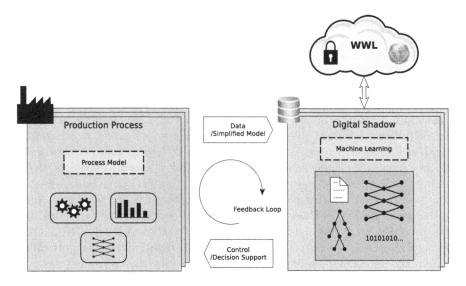

**Fig. 3.** A first concept for a node in the IoP. Digital Shadows should be exchanged securely in the WWL. The Digital Shadows are generated with data coming from different processes. A feedback loop improves Digital Shadows and processes on both sides. (Color figure online)

player – exactly the World Wide Lab setting we are envisioning for the IoP. We shall therefore not repeat this aspect here but focus on the specific aspects relevant also for the cases above.

In this section we discuss the requirements, possible solutions and a proto-typical implementation meeting important requirements of the IoP. To present these diverse requirements of information systems in the IoP, in Fig. 3, we depict the concept for an exemplary node of the IoP in a diagram. On the left-hand side the orange boxes represent the production process side. On the right-hand side the blue boxes represent the storing side for data and Digital Shadows. Above the storing part we have the connection to the WWL.

The multiple orange boxes on the left-hand side, indicate that different production processes come, for example, from one or more production facilities. A production process might have already a model but does not necessarily need to have one, which is indicated by the dashed line around the yellow box. A model can also be gained by using machine learning as shown above in our injection moulding use case. The three rounded boxes in a production process box mean that on the production process side the data should represented in visualizations of the data, the charts on the right-side, and its processes, the gears on the left, for interdisciplinary usage and understanding about the meaning of the data. Especially in a cross-domain collaboration, it is important to understand where the data comes from. The visualization should also help to decide which data can be stored and what can be used to generate purpose-drive Digital Shadows. This is similar to other data discovery approaches used in machine learning or data mining [10]. In addition, the visualization of Digital Shadows, the rounded box below, can give a better understanding of the process and can also be used for explaining decisions of an optimization system using a certain Digital Shadow.

The multiple blue boxes on the right should represent the different Digital Shadows for specific purposes stored in a database system. But to gain digital Shadows, the systems need to handle a large amount of data. But storing is only one aspect. The amount of data of a big production facility can be so high that, on the one hand, it is physically not possible to store all of it and, on the other hand, there might be no point in storing every single value of the data. However, machine learning methods need large amounts of data. Thus, we need systems which enable the analysis of sample data so that one can chose the appropriate data from a large data set for the machine learning algorithms. In addition, automatic aggregation can help to reduce the amount of data. The storage should also be able to handle data of different types. That is represented by the inner box which depicts documents, raw data and graphical models. The latter can be like Neural Networks or decision trees [28] generated by machine learning to learn models. These models should be stored for inspection or sharing. With reduced mathematical models, we do not need machine learning because we can use these models directly. Therefore, the yellow box for machine learning has a dashed line as border in the picture. Finally, in the IoP we need systems which provide Digital Shadows for application in production processes. So we think that the data and Digital Shadows should meet the FAIR principles [31] which state that data should be findable, accessible, interoperable and reusable. That encompasses, for instance, that data needs to have unique identifier, metadata describing the data and open protocols to get the data. Especially the latter is importing regarding standardized protocols so that not every machine speaks another language.

The arrow, from left to right in the middle, indicates that data and fast, simplified, mathematical models has to be transferred from the production processes to the database system to gain Digital Shadows. The lower arrow, from right to left, indicates that with Digital Shadows it should be possible to control production processes or give decision support. The latter can also incorporate other techniques from the field of artificial intelligence, for example knowledge-based approaches [3,28], which is beyond the scope of this paper.

The lock in the WWL cloud at the top indicates that we need a secure exchange of Digital Shadows and data in the WWL. Especially for data from private companies it is crucial that only trusted partners should see the data. The globe on the right in the cloud indicates that we want to use common internet technology like HTTP in the WWL. The feedback loop in the middle indicates that Digital Shadows should be improved either with more data from different production processes or with data from other facilities in the WWL. Additionally, the production processes are improved by the Digital Shadows.

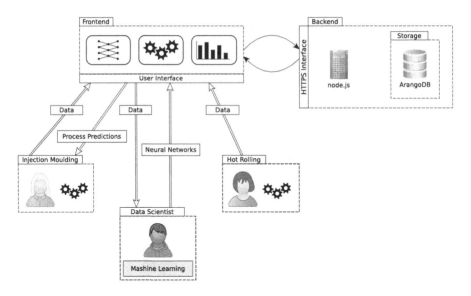

**Fig. 4.** Architecture of an early prototype of a node in the IoP. Users from different domains can upload their data and data scientists can apply machine learning on it. These models would be used to predict quality parameters of the injection moulding process, for instance.

In conclusion, we summarise the requirements for information systems in the IoP we discussed above:

1. We need data storage for storing a great number of multifarious data and models.
2. We need secure connections for transferring data from machines to a storage.
3. We need FAIR data [31].
4. We need techniques for automatic aggregating and reducing the data.
5. We need analysation methods for the data and the models.
6. The system needs to give feedback for decision support and controlling.
7. We need secure and fast protocols for the WWL.

**A Prototypical Implementation.** In an interdisciplinary subproject of our research cluster, together with data scientists, material scientists, mechanical engineers and experts in artificial intelligence, we investigated building and usage of Digital Shadows [19]. For that endeavor, we developed a prototype for a node in the IoP with a web interface working with the above described use cases of hot rolling and injection moulding. With this implementation we concentrated on meeting Requirements 1, 5, 6 from the list above. Due to the lack of a WWL we implemented only the parts below the cloud in Fig. 3 without a connection to the WWL. But, this prototype can be seen as a node in the IoP which could be connected to the WWL. For the security part of Requirement 7 we used HTTPS for the web UI.

In Fig. 4, the architecture of our prototype is depicted. It consists of a user-friendly UI in the frontend and a database and small applications on a node.js web-server in the back-end. In our project, the scientists of both use-cases could upload their data from experiments and simulation runs onto the platform. The data could be downloaded from other scientists for exploring Digital Shadows with machine learning techniques. With the results of the machine learning, we developed some applications on the platform.

In the upper right corner in Fig. 4, the backend of our prototype is depicted, where we used the schema-less database ArangoDB for storing. We chose ArangoDB to address Requirement 1 because it provides document, key/value and graph storing models and thus allows to store various sorts of data in the JSON format and is able to store huge amount of data very fast. The graph storing model was interesting for us because we wanted to store connective models such as Neural Networks representing the Digital Shadow. It is worth noting that although, we did not need to have FAIR data and, therefore, address Requirement 3 in our project it would be easy to realise it with ArangoDB and JSON. The database itself has unique identifiers and with JSON it is unproblematic to add metadata needed for FAIR.

In Fig. 4, in the upper left corner the frontend of our prototype is depicted which runs on the user's browser. As mentioned above it communicates via HTTPS with the backend to address security issues. Via the UI in the frontend, it is possible to upload data from machines and experiments which meets Requirement 2. The focus in our project was not on uploading the data directly from the machines into the database, but in principle it is possible. For the data upload, we used hand-written parsers for the different data formats of the raw data so that the users of the two use cases could upload their process data easily. In the future here one needs standardised formats so that no manual step is needed anymore.

To meet Requirement 5, one can filter, visualize and select the data for download in different formats. Because we expected confidential data from industrial partners, we restricted the view of particular data to certain registered persons only. Users can inspect the data, the models and the results of the models on the platform, which is depicted by the rounded boxes in the frontend box in Fig. 4. Among others, in the IoP, the Digital Shadow should be used to improve processes. Furthermore, the Digital Shadows should be improved in further experiments. Therefore, we visualized the learned Neural Networks so that the nodes and the weights of the connections can be inspected. That can give one interesting knowledge about the relevance of certain parameters if some connections in a Neural Network are less used then others. In the IoP a crucial aspect is to utilize the compiled Digital Shadows. Therefore, for the injection moulding use-case, we built an application to see the results of the learned Neural Networks. The user can choose two or three dimensional visualizations of the results of the Neural Network. It is possible to set the input parameters of the network with sliders. That way one can see by a range of input parameters which quality of the product is predicted. For utilizing the learned Neural Networks, we realized a micro service in a Python program. In the future we want to setup autonomous agents as micro services which should act in the WWL to find answers similar the traffic information in Google Maps but for production scenarios.

## 4    Discussion and Conclusion

In this exploratory paper, we explore the potential of establishing collections of Digital Shadows as a complement to the much-discussed Digital Twin approach in Industry 4.0 and many other settings. From a theoretical point, we argue that the enormously successful view concept in databases can serve as the starting point for a theoretical foundation of Digital Shadows, as it constituted an early combination of model-based and data-based methods which is also the core of the Digital Shadow concept.

From an empirical point of view, we explore the relevance of the idea through two initial, but rather ambitious use cases in the important industrial fields of plastics and steel-based production; the preliminary results of both case studies which combined latest advances from mathematical model-based approaches with AI-based data-driven methods illustrate the enormous potential we can expect from further pursuing this avenue.

In both the theoretical and the use case discussion, we have pointed out the strong need for intensive further research in this area not just in the production engineering, but also in the IS engineering field.

**Acknowledgments.** We thank our project partners Hasan Tercan, Richard Meyes, Julian Heinisch, Alexander Krämer for excellent collaborative work. Additionally, we thank our students Lars Scheel and Lukas Schneider for implementing our prototype.

## References

1. Altan, T., Tekkaya, A.E.: Sheet Metal Forming: Processes and Applications. ASM International (2012)
2. Bambach, M., Seuren, S.: On instabilities of force and grain size predictions in the simulation of multi-pass hot rolling processes. J. Mater. Process. Technol. **216**, 95–113 (2015)
3. Brachman, R.J., Levesque, H.J.: Knowledge Representation and Reasoning. Morgan Kaufmann, Burlington (2004)
4. Ceretti, E., Lucchi, M., Altan, T.: FEM simulation of orthogonal cutting: serrated chip formation. J. Mater. Process. Technol. **95**(1–3), 17–26 (1999)
5. Colgan, M., Monaghan, J.: Deep drawing process: analysis and experiment. J. Mater. Process. Technol. **132**(1–3), 35–41 (2003)
6. Fagin, R., Kolaitis, P.G., Miller, R.J., Popa, L.: Data exchange: semantics and query answering. Theoret. Comput. Sci. **336**(1), 89–124 (2005)
7. Fei, N.C., Mehat, N.M., Kamaruddin, S.: Practical applications of Taguchi method for optimization of processing parameters for plastic injection moulding: a retrospective review. ISRN Ind. Eng. **2013**(2013)
8. Gantz, J., Reinsel, D.: The digital universe in 2020: Big data, bigger digital shadows, and biggest growth in the far east. IDC Analyze the Future (2013)

9. Gasparenienene, L., Remeikiene, R.: Digital shadow economy: a critical review of the literature. Mediterr. J. Soc. Sci. **6**(6), 402–409 (2015)

10. Grinstein, G.G., Fayyad, U.M., Wierse, A.: Information Visualization in Data Mining and Knowledge Discovery. Morgan Kaufmann, Burlington (2002)

11. Hai, R., Quix, C., Wang, D.: Relaxed functional dependency discovery in heterogeneous data lakes. In: Laender, A.H.F., Pernici, B., Lim, E.-P., de Oliveira, J.P.M. (eds.) ER 2019. LNCS, vol. 11788, pp. 225–239. Springer, Cham (2019). https://doi.org/10.1007/978-3-030-33223-5_19

12. Kashyap, S., Datta, D.: Process parameter optimization of plastic injection molding: a review. Int. J. Plast. Technol. **19**(1), 1–18 (2015). https://doi.org/10.1007/s12588-015-9115-2

13. Kensche, D., Quix, C., Chatti, M.A., Jarke, M.: *GeRoMe*: a generic role based metamodel for model management. In: Spaccapietra, S., et al. (eds.) Journal on Data Semantics VIII. LNCS, vol. 4380, pp. 82–117. Springer, Heidelberg (2007). https://doi.org/10.1007/978-3-540-70664-9_4

14. Kritzinger, W., Karner, M., Traar, G., Henjes, J., Sihn, W.: Digital twin in manufacturing: a categorical literature review and classification. In: 16th IFAC Symposium on Information Control Problems in Manufacturing (2018). 51(11), 1016–1022

15. Lenard, J.G.: Primer on Flat Rolling. Newnes, Burlington (2013)

16. Lenzerini, M.: Direct and reverse rewriting in data interoperability. In: Giorgini, P., Weber, B. (eds.) CAiSE 2019. LNCS, vol. 11483, pp. 3–13. Springer, Cham (2019). https://doi.org/10.1007/978-3-030-21290-2_1

17. Loucopoulos, P., Kavakli, E., Chechina, N.: Requirements engineering for cyber physical production systems. In: Giorgini, P., Weber, B. (eds.) CAiSE 2019. LNCS, vol. 11483, pp. 276–291. Springer, Cham (2019). https://doi.org/10.1007/978-3-030-21290-2_18

18. Makinouchi, A., Teodosiu, C., Nakagawa, T.: Advance in FEM simulation and its related technologies in sheet metal forming. CIRP Ann. **47**(2), 641–649 (1998)

19. Meyes, R., et al.: Interdisciplinary data driven production process analysis for the internet of production. Procedia Manuf. **26**, 1065–1076 (2018)

20. Oezkaya, E., Biermann, D.: Segmented and mathematical model for 3D FEM tapping simulation to predict the relative torque before tool production. Int. J. Mech. Sci. **128**, 695–708 (2017)

21. Otto, B., Jarke, M.: Designing a multi-sided data platform: findings from the International Data Spaces case. Electron. Markets **29**(4), 561–580 (2019). https://doi.org/10.1007/s12525-019-00362-x

22. Pennekamp, J., et al.: Towards an infrastructure enabling the internet of production. In: 2019 IEEE International Conference on Industrial Cyber Physical Systems (ICPS), pp. 31–37. IEEE (2019)

23. Pennekamp, J., et al.: Dataflow challenges in an internet of production: a security & privacy perspective. In: Proceedings of the ACM Workshop on Cyber-Physical Systems Security & Privacy, pp. 27–38. ACM (2019)

24. Pottinger, R.A.: Processing queries and merging schemas in support of data integration. Ph.D. thesis, Citeseer (2004)

25. Qi, Q., Tao, F.: Digital twin and big data towards smart manufacturing and industry 4.0: 360 degree comparison. IEEE Access **6**, 3585–3593 (2018)

26. Reck, B.K., Graedel, T.E.: Challenges in metal recycling. Science **337**(6095), 690–695 (2012)

27. Rosato, D.V., Rosato, M.G.: Injection Molding Handbook. Springer Science & Business Media, New York (2012)

28. Russell, S.J., Norvig, P.: Artificial Intelligence: A Modern Approach. Pearson Education Limited, London (2010)
29. Seuren, S., Willkomm, J., Bücker, H., Bambach, M., Hirt, G.: Sensitivity analysis of a force and microstructure model for plate rolling. In: Metal Forming 2012, pp. 91–94. Wiley-VCH (2012)
30. Staudt, M., Jarke, M.: Incremental maintenance of externally materialized views. Citeseer (1996)
31. Wilkinson, M.D., et al.: The FAIR guiding principles for scientific data management and stewardship. Sci. Data **3** (2016)
32. Zienkiewicz, O.C., Taylor, R.L., Zhu, J.Z.: The Finite Element Method: Its Basis and Fundamentals. Elsevier, Amsterdam (2005)

# Model-Driven Development of a Digital Twin for Injection Molding

Pascal Bibow[2](⊠)(iD), Manuela Dalibor[1](⊠)(iD), Christian Hopmann[2],
Ben Mainz[1](iD), Bernhard Rumpe[1](iD), David Schmalzing[1](iD),
Mauritius Schmitz[2](iD), and Andreas Wortmann[1](iD)

[1] Software Engineering, RWTH Aachen University, Aachen, Germany
`dalibor@se-rwth.de`
[2] Institute for Plastics Processing in Industry and Craft at RWTH Aachen
University, Aachen, Germany
`Pascal.Bibow@ikv.rwth-aachen.de`
`http://www.se-rwth.de`, `https://www.ikv-aachen.de`

**Abstract.** Digital Twins (DTs) of Cyber-Physical Production Systems (CPPSs) enable the smart automation of production processes, collection of data, and can thus reduce manual efforts for supervising and controlling CPPSs. Realizing DTs is challenging and requires significant efforts for their conception and integration with the represented CPPS. To mitigate this, we present an approach to systematically engineering DTs for injection molding that supports domain-specific customizations and automation of essential development activities based on a model-driven reference architecture. In this approach, reactive CPPS behavior is defined in terms of a Domain-Specific Language (DSL) for specifying events that occur in the physical system. The reference architecture connects to the CPPS through a novel DSL for representing OPC-UA bindings. We have evaluated this approach with a DT of an injection molding machine that controls the machine to optimize the Design of Experiment (DoE) parameters between experiment cycles before the products are molded. Through this, our reference implementation of the DT facilitates the time-consuming setup of a DT and the subsequent injection molding activities. Overall, this facilitates to systematically engineer digital twins with reactive behavior that help to optimize machine use.

**Keywords:** Digital Twin · Injection molding · Cyber-Physical Production System · Model-driven development · Reference architecture

## 1 Introduction

DTs are an integral component of intelligent digitization [25] for smart manufacturing in Industry 4.0 [28]. Engineering DTs is time-consuming, complicated,

---

Funded by the Deutsche Forschungsgemeinschaft (DFG, German Research Foundation) under Germany's Excellence Strategy – EXC 2023 Internet of Production.

S. Dustdar et al. (Eds.): CAiSE 2020, LNCS 12127, pp. 85–100, 2020.
https://doi.org/10.1007/978-3-030-49435-3_6

and often not tightly integrated with the development of the system. The development of DTs for CPPSs requires close collaboration across the production and software domain. Misunderstandings between experts of the two domains are a frequent source of error, especially when the developed systems become increasingly complex. Model-driven engineering (MDE) bridges the gap between the production and software domain by using models that describe the DT at multiple levels of abstraction. The automated transformation of models into software implementations can improve productivity and reduce complexity [6] and opens the possibility to integrate information from other formal descriptions, *e.g.*, engineering models, into the software.

Injection molding is a manufacturing process to produce plastic parts by injecting plasticized material into a mold. Determining an ideal operation point usually requires experienced operators and extensive trials [23].

We propose a modeling method for DTs that automates engineering DTs that react to changes in the system structure and to synchronize the DT with its physical counterpart. To this end, we propose modeling the DT as a component and connector architecture with UML class diagrams specifying the data types of objects exchanged between components. Furthermore, we present a DSL to describe events that the DT of a production system reacts to. Models of this DSL are integrated into the software architecture model. From these, an integrated, reactive DT is generated that automates the execution of a DoE on an injection molding machine, learns about the current process characteristics, and optimizes setting parameters. The presented architecture thereby gets evaluated in a real CPPS. The key contributions of this paper, hence, are

1. a model-driven methodology to efficiently developing DTs for CPPSs,
2. a reference architecture for DTs evaluated in injection molding,
3. a DSL connecting digital twins to their physical counterparts, and
4. modeling techniques to specify a DT's event-driven behavior.

In the following, Sect. 2 introduces preliminaries, Sect. 3 presents a motivating example, and Sect. 4 explains the methodology. Subsequently, Sect. 5 describes the required models and the realization, Sect. 6 describes the application of the DT to the injection molding machine, and Sect. 7 discusses the reference architecture and methodology. Finally, Sect. 8 highlights related work, and Sect. 9 concludes.

## 2   Background

We realize a DT for injection molding based on our reference architecture that we implemented in MontiArc (see Sect. 2.3) [2]. The DT controls the molding machine via Open Platform Communication Unified Architecture (OPC-UA) [16].

## 2.1 Digital Shadows and Twins

The term digital twin is broadly used to describe any form of data that describes a physical system. We develop a digital twin that is partly derived from models describing the system under development. Furthermore, the DT shall provide services that allow interacting with the system or the DT itself.

**Definition** (Digital Twin (DT)). *A digital twin of a system consists of a set of models of the system, a set of digital shadows, and provides a set of services to use the data and models purposefully with respect to the original system.*

These models may be engineering models (*e.g.*, CAD, Simulink) or software models (*e.g.*, UML, SysML, MontiArc), and the services may include monitoring, optimization, projection, and visualization. Since the DT reflects a real system, it must also provide data that describes the system. As CPPSs produce immense amounts of data that often are too large to be fully processed by DTs, we introduce the concept of Digital Shadows (DSs).

**Definition** (Digital Shadow (DS)). *A digital shadow is a set of temporal data traces and/or their aggregation and abstraction collected concerning a system for a specific purpose with respect to the original system.*

Thus, DS comprise the information that DT require for fulfilling their tasks.

## 2.2 Injection Molding

Injection molding represents a highly automated, but to the same extent, complex manufacturing process to produce, *e.g.*, plastic parts without the necessity of post-processing. Different data sources, like machinery or peripheral sensors, cavity sensors, or quality control systems, enable gaining knowledge about the process. Due to complex interactions of production assets and setting parameters, determining settings of an ideal operation point at a specific machine is a challenging task. A well-experienced operator is capable of respecting the machine-specific characteristics in process setup as each machine differs in its respective process behavior. Differences in the process behavior exist even for machines of the same type or manufacturer due to wear of machine components or alternating control loops [14].

The injection molding process consists of cyclic process phases for plasticizing the granular material, injecting it into a mold according to a specific injection flow profile, and solidifying it under a set holding pressure until a molded part can be ejected. Via standardized communication protocols like OPC-UA, machine movements, and sensor data from the machine and its subordinated components are accessible. Thereby, relevant process parameters like temperatures, current volume flow, or injection pressure get monitored to build up an extensive knowledge base for a DT to use.

The machine initializes an OPC-UA server during production start and notifies the server about changes in monitored items due to machine movements. For data gathering and accessing the OPC-UA server, the OPC Foundation provides standard libraries to develop connectors. The connector acts as OPC-UA client and subscribes to the server to monitor specific parameters of consideration via so-called Node-IDs. Gathered data is then passed on to a message broker. Apache Kafka [27] is a communication platform that receives messages from a connector, acknowledges the receipt, stores the messages in a save log file, and delivers messages in case of a request.

## 2.3  MontiArc

MontiArc is an architecture description language [17]. Its principal modeling elements are component types with interfaces of typed and directed ports. The components either are atomic, and feature a behavior model or General Purpose Language implementation, or composed. Composed components contain a topology of subcomponents that exchange messages via unidirectional connectors between the ports of their typed, directed interfaces. Their behavior emerges from the behavior of their hierarchically contained subcomponents.

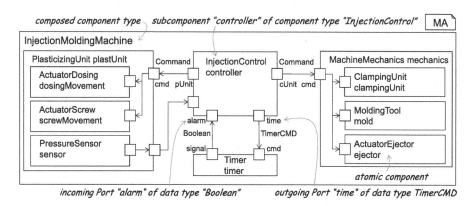

**Fig. 1.** MontiArc model of a simplified injection molding control flow showing injection molding machine components involved in the process

Figure 1 illustrates the quintessential modeling elements of MontiArc by example of an injection molding machine. The component type `InjectionMoldingMachine` hierarchically contains subcomponents of types `PlasticizingUnit`, `InjectionControl`, `Timer`, and `MachineMechanics`. The subcomponent `plastUnit` of component type `PlasticizingUnit` is composed again and features three subcomponents itself. At the core of the model is the component `controller` of type `InjectionControl` that interacts with `plastUnit` and `mechanics` and manages the injection molding process.

## 3    Example and Challenges

Several setting parameters like the volume flow profile, the ideal switchover volume for switching from the injection phase to the holding pressure phase, as well as the right processing temperatures influence the reproducibility and the profitability of the current operating point in injection molding processes. To produce plastic parts with high quality, the interdependencies of these parameters need to be respected during setup. However, a correlation of setting parameters to the final part quality is, in most cases, only possible implicitly as the settings induce a specific process behavior – represented via process models – that results in process data like a respective cavity pressure. A quality model afterward describes the correlation of process data to the final part quality [13]. To determine the ideal operating point, a well-experienced operator is necessary or an extensive DoE that uncovers correlations by statistical analysis of targeted trials. As an operator does not always have extensive knowledge in statistical analysis [5], DoE generation, conduction, and analysis need to be automated *e.g.*, by a DT.

The phases of the cyclic process require specific values that – in most cases – refer to basic estimations. The clamping force, for example, is necessary to keep the mold closed during injection and to hold against the injection pressure. Therefore, basic estimations refer, *e.g.*, to a known specific clamping force (*e.g.*, 3.0–6.5 kN/cm$^2$ for a standard polypropylene) multiplied by the projected area of the part geometry and the number of cavities inside the mold [20]. However, high values for the clamping force can lead to high energy consumption and increased wear of the mold that can be avoided by an adaption to the realized injection pressure during injection. Nevertheless, feedback of the machine data for automated adaption to current process behavior is rarely implemented.

The actual injection is one of the most crucial process phases as it determines crucial quality aspects like weld lines, incomplete filling, or burners. Therefore an operator needs to set an injection flow profile [cm$^3$/s] in accordance with the respective part geometry. Due to differences in the wall thickness of the part and the overall part geometry, the melt front velocity tends to accelerate or decelerate if the screw induces a constant volume flow. A constant melt front velocity inside the mold, on the contrary, is beneficial to realize high quality for the molded parts. Cavity pressure sensors are capable of monitoring the characteristic volume flow as a constant melt front velocity results in a linear slope of the pressure curve during the injection. A digital twin thereby might be able to analyze the incoming digital shadow from the filling process as datatrace from cavity pressure sensors and adjust the volume flow profile to realize a constant melt front velocity for high-quality parts.

## 4    Methodology

In the industry, there are DTs of products, CPPSs and their services, and complete production facilities. We present a reference architecture for DTs and a development process that facilitates adaptivity and extensibility.

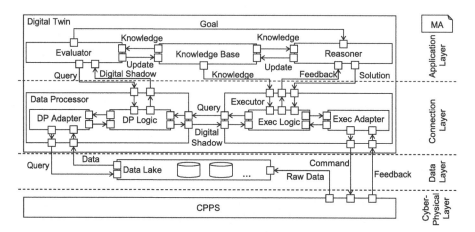

**Fig. 2.** Architecture that enables self-adaptation based on digital shadows.

### 4.1 Digital Twin Reference Architecture

We describe the reference architecture for DTs as a component and connector architecture in MontiArc to specify explicit and typed interfaces between the DT's components. MontiArc realizes the FOCUS semantic, which supports refinement along the development process from abstract requirements to very fine-grained technical specifications, and to compose existing components to new software solutions [21]. Figure 2 depicts the reference architecture and its layers: cyber-physical layer, data layer, connection layer, and application layer.

*Cyber-Physical Layer.* The cyber-physical layer describes the CPPS that the DT controls. The architecture requires the controlled system to provide at least interfaces through which data qualifying the process can be accessed and commands sent to the system. This general component representing the CPPS may be hierarchically composed of more specific components describing the physical system and its functionality.

*Data Layer.* The Data Lake [9] is an extensive data storage consisting of multiple databases or other data providers and is situated in the data layer. It stores data from a wide variety of sources, *e.g.,* sensors inside of the CPPS in a raw format or a preprocessed form. It can contain both unstructured and structured data. To support reusability, the data is annotated with metadata containing semantic information. Data Lakes also offer logic for data preparation and processing that is realized by suppliers, thus we do not model its components here, but specify that the DT can query the data within the Data Lake.

*Connection Layer.* The connection layer contains a `Data Processor` and an `Executor`. The `Data Processor` links the `Data Lake` with components at the application layer. It creates DSs that encapsulate exactly the information that is required by components at the application layer. The `Data Processor` contains two inner components. The `Data Processor Logic` receives DS queries of the application layer, transforms these into data requests, and creates DSs from the results of these requests. The `Data Processor Adapter` transforms data requests into queries for specific databases within the `Data Lake`. It receives a solution from the application layer that describes how the CPPS should behave. To realize this behavior, it requires knowledge about the system and its structure that is available in the `Knowledge Base`. The `Executor` has two inner components: the `Execution Logic` and the `Execution Adapter`. The `Execution Logic` derives a solution that shall be executed at the CPPS and its surrounding systems. The `Execution Adapter` sends commands to specific parts of the CPPS and thus controls the next actions. Feedback about the success of these commands is also processed and handed back to the application layer.

*Application Layer.* The application layer contains the smartness of the DT. The `Evaluator` analyzes DSs and detects events that occur within the system or its context. To decide on which events it must react, it refers to design-time models that describe the expected behavior of the system and also possibly erroneous behavior. The `Evaluator` also relies on knowledge from the knowledge base to decide when an event is considered negative and must be handled. Depending on the system's state and evaluation results, the `Evaluator` creates goals that it sends to the `Reasoner`. The `Reasoner` receives goals that specify what should be changed in the system's state. The `Reasoner` uses the knowledge contained in the `Knowledge Base` to create a solution that realizes these goals.

## 4.2   Model-Driven Development of a Digital Twin

We develop a model-driven methodology that facilitates the automatic generation of DTs from models describing a CPPS and its domain. Figure 3 describes the development and adaptation process for developing DTs that ground on our reference architecture. The reference architecture is implemented in MontiArc but leaves domain-specific decisions open. Thus, software engineers can adapt it to various domains by refining the components specified in the reference architecture. If the functionality of components is not required in the target domain, it is also possible to replace those components. MontiArc supports both the refinement and composition of components.

The first activity when developing the DT is to create a domain model that describes the structure of data that components of the DT exchange. As the DT monitors the system's state, the next step is to decide what kinds of events occur in the system and how the DT should react if they occur. To this end, we developed a domain-specific language that facilitates the specification of events and actions. An event describes a situation in the real system, *e.g.*, a monitored parameter reaching a threshold. Actions specify the DT's reaction to an event.

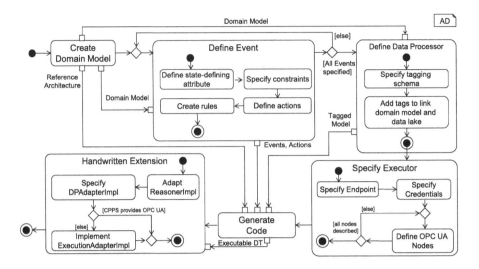

**Fig. 3.** Activity diagram of the development process of DSs based on our reference architecture and tooling.

Rules link events and actions. Thus, if an event occurs, the DT reacts with one or multiple actions. Events reference classes of the domain model that specify the structure of data that the event processes. The state-defining attribute specifies on which changes of the system's data the event should be evaluated.

The event language is developed in MontiCore and integrated with MontiArc. Thus, events and related actions describe the behavior of the DT's components. As MontiCore has a strong focus on extension, we can extend the DT in two ways: First, we can extend the model and add new events to react to situations that are domain-specific and not specified by the reference architecture. Second, we can also extend the event language and add new features to describe events and reactions for new domains. For example, we could integrate an event that requires the evaluation result of a neural network.

The next activity in designing the DT is to specify how the DT obtains DSs describing the current state of the physical system. Tagging [8] the domain model enriches it with specific data retrieval information. We developed a tagging schema that adds information for data retrieval from a Kafka broker. This schema provides tags to add information about data access via Kafka to the domain model. In case another platform is used, it is sufficient to create a new tagging schema with that facilitates the description of this platform and add respective tags to the domain model. For sending commands to the CPPS the DT relies on a specification of the machine interface. We developed the OPC-UA Description Language to specify the communication interface to the CPPS. If the production system provides an OPC-UA interface, it suffices to specify the endpoint, credentials, and nodes to realize the executor. Else the component for communication with the CPPS must be handwritten.

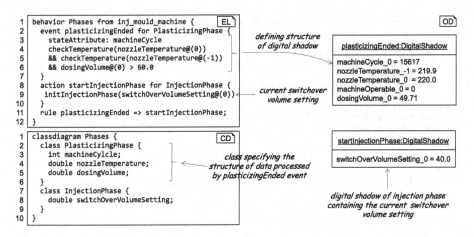

```
1  behavior Phases from inj_mould_machine {        EL
2    event plasticizingEnded for PlasticizingPhase {
3      stateAttribute: machineCycle
4      checkTemperature(nozzleTemperature@(0))
5      && checkTemperature(nozzleTemperature@(-1))
6      && dosingVolume@(0) > 60.0
7    }
8    action startInjectionPhase for InjectionPhase {
9      initInjectionPhase(switchOverVolumeSetting@(0))
10   }
11   rule plasticizingEnded => startInjectionPhase;
12 }
```

defining structure
of digital shadow

current switchover
volume setting

plasticizingEnded:DigitalShadow

machineCycle_0 = 15617
nozzleTemperature_-1 = 219.9
nozzleTemperature_0 = 220.0
machineOperable_0 = 0
dosingVolume_0 = 49.71

```
1  classdiagram Phases {                 CD
2    class PlasticizingPhase {
3      int machineCyicle;
4      double nozzleTemperature;
5      double dosingVolume;
6    }
7    class InjectionPhase {
8      double switchOverVolumeSetting;
9    }
10 }
```

class specifying the
structure of data processed
by plasticizingEnded event

startInjectionPhase:DigitalShadow

switchOverVolumeSetting_0 = 40.0

digital shadow of injection phase
containing the current switchover
volume setting

**Fig. 4.** Behavior description defining events, rules, and actions based on class diagrams. Additionally, showing that the structure of the DS is determined by the behavior definition.

We developed a generator that parses the models describing the DT MontiArc architecture, domain, data processor, and executor and creates Java code for the DT. The generation step is performed once at design time and creates the DT's logic for data retrieval, communication with the CPPS, evaluation of DSs, and reaction to these. Finally, the software engineer adapts the generated code where necessary. As the domain model centrally specifies the parameters relevant for the process and the control and the other models reference these, only one model has to be adapted when changes occur. The generator links information from all models and derives Java artifacts for the DT. This way, we can ensure that component implementations always stay consistent.

## 5   Technical Realization

The DT reference architecture presented in this paper is built to be flexible by using exchangeable components implemented in MontiArc and a model-driven approach for describing CPPS-specific properties. Our DT detects and reacts to patterns gathered from CPPS data. The Event Language (EL) supports the formulation of events based on attributes of class diagrams (CDs). A generator then produces code that comprises the logic for checking events and performing the related actions.

Figure 4 shows an excerpt of the behavior definition of the phases of an injection molding machine, which contains the event `plasticizingEnd`, and the action `startInjectionPhase`. The keyword `for` (l. 2) indicates the corresponding domain class whose information is used to check the event. A `stateAttribute` is an attribute whose value is stored, and the corresponding event is only triggered if the evaluated value of the state attribute has changed

```
 1  design of experiment VarySwitchOverVolumeAndNozzleTemp {                    DoE
 2    factorized = fully ←────────────────── fully factorial design method
 3      // injection phase
 4      param StageCountInjectionPhase = 2
 5      param SwitchOverVolume        = (min = 39, intermediate = 40.5, max= 41), 20
 6      param InjectionFlow           = 30.0, 31.0
 7      param NozzleTemperature       = (min = 220.0, max = 240.0)
 8      // dosing phase                                              second stage with
 9      param StageCountDosingPhase   = 2                            a fixed value of 20
10      param DosingVolume            = 80.0
11      param BackPressure            = 150, 145
12      // ...                                                first stage with variable
13  }                                                        values between 39 and 41
```

**Fig. 5.** Fully factorial design of experiment for varying switch-over volumes and nozzle temperatures.

compared to the last event trigger. The event definition block contains expressions about the values of the DT, such as external calls (l. 4), logical expressions ( &&, ||, !), and value comparisons (l. 6). The rule (l. 11) links the event and the corresponding action. The right side of the figure shows the corresponding DS, which are used to either check the event or perform the action. Type safety is ensured by the CD. The @-notation specifies the point in time from which the value is queried. @(0) specifies the current value, whereas @(−1) specifies the previous value of a parameter. A tagging language [8] is used to add data retrieval information to the CD while at the same time keeping it clean. Hence, the tagged values are available for the **DataProcessor**. When configuring the injection molding machine for production, the optimal values of the parameters highly depend on the wear of the machine, and environmental influences. To this end, usually, a series of experiments with varying parameter values are evaluated. The DT architecture automates the design of such experiments by providing the modeling language DoE. The language supports the fixed or variable assignment of parameter values, optionally configuring the number of adjustment and measuring cycles, and several factorial design methods, including fractional factorial designs [4]. When a DoE model is provided, the **Reasoner** manages the optimal and automated execution of the trials.

Figure 5 shows the DoE for varying the switchover volume (l. 5 first stage) and the nozzle temperature (l. 7). As the factorial design method is set to `fully` (l. 2), the plan represents $3^2 = 9$ (all combinations of three variable values for the two parameters) different parameter settings. A value can be assigned directly to a parameter or is described variably with a minimum, an intermediate value, and a maximum. The intermediate value is inferred as the average if only a minimum and maximum is specified (l. 7). Furthermore, in practice, some parameters are finely adjustable in several stages. **BackPressure** (l. 11) has a value of 150 bar in the first stage and 145 bar in the second stage. The **Reasoner** orders all resulting parameter settings such that the overall number of changes in temperature values between consecutive settings is minimized to reduce the number of cycles until the machine reaches a steady state. Closely related to the DoE is the configuration and accessibility of the parameters on the actual machine.

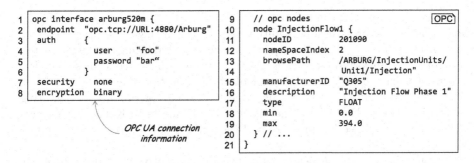

```
1   opc interface arburg520m {                    9   // opc nodes                         OPC
2     endpoint  "opc.tcp://URL:4880/Arburg"      10   node InjectionFlow1 {
3     auth      {                                 11      nodeID          201090
4              user       "foo"                   12      nameSpaceIndex  2
5              password "bar"                     13      browsePath      /ARBURG/InjectionUnits/
6              }                                   14                      Unit1/Injection"
7     security   none                             15      manufacturerID  "Q305"
8     encryption binary                           16      description     "Injection Flow Phase 1"
                                                  17      type            FLOAT
                                                  18      min             0.0
              OPC UA connection                   19      max             394.0
                 information                      20   } // ...
                                                  21 }
```

**Fig. 6.** OPC UA Description Language model describing OPC object nodes.

The provided interfaces across different machines and domains vary, but more and more machine manufacturers implement OPC-UA or a respective specification as the standard communication interface. We developed the OPC-UA Description Language that supports the definition of OPC object nodes. Additionally, the model designer has the option to specify connection information, including authentication and encryption aspects.

Figure 6 shows the parts of the OPC-UA interface of an all-electric injection molding machine of the type ARBURG ALLROUNDER 520 A 1500 that is used in the field test. Login, endpoint, and encryption information are stated to enable establishing a connection to the machine (ll. 2–8). An OPC object node is also provided (ll. 10–20). It comprises all important information about the node, such as the nodeID and the type. The min and max properties help the Reasoner and Executor to detect any invalid value before sending it to the machine. The manufacturerID is not required for communication with the machine but usually known and used as a term by the machine operator and mechanical engineers. The node InjectionFlow1 (l. 10) corresponds to the first stage of the DoE in Fig. 5 (l. 7, first value). Both models, DoE and OPC, are automatically linked in the Executor based on the names of the DoE parameters and OPC nodes.

## 6  Case Study

Injection molding requires time-consuming experiments to determine the ideal settings to run a reproducible and high-quality production process. A central composite design for three variating parameters already takes 15 operating points, each with several process cycles to run until the injection molding machine reaches a steady state and additional process cycles and parts produced for the actual measuring of data and quality criteria. Therefore, a DT is necessary that is capable of generating and executing DoEs autonomously and evaluating the resulting influences.

The proposed architecture supports the desired purpose as the developed DT is capable of performing experiments autonomously. Based on an analysis focus for specific parameters, the DT generates a DoE and suggests appropriate upper and lower values for variation. Additionally, the DT arranges the planned trials, as, *e.g.,* temperature variations require some time for balancing and, thus, should be avoided in performing the DoE. At the current proof-of-concept status, the DT implementation accesses the control of the injection molding machine by ARBURG. Via OPC-UA, it sets the respective values for running an operating point of the DoE. For data gathering, the DT connects to Kafka and gathers data about, *e.g.,* injection pressure and the volume flow in the injection phase as a digital shadow.

In our case study, the DT investigates the optimal values injection phase, where the significant parameters are the injection flow, nozzle temperature, and switchover volume. The injection flow defines how fast the machine injects plasticized material in terms of volume per time. The nozzle temperature describes the temperature at the nozzle through which the machine injects material into the mold cavity. The switchover volume specifies the volume for a phase transition from injection to holding pressure to occur. The DT automatically designs experiments variating the injection flow from $30\,cm^3/s$ to $50\,cm^3/s$, the nozzle temperature from $220\,°C$ to $260\,°C$, and the switchover volume from $10\,cm^3$ to $20\,cm^3$. In the upcoming developments, the DT will analyze the machine and process data it gets from Kafka and parameterizes a static process model (*e.g.,* regression model). The first estimation for a local optimum can thereby be derived and set as an operating point with ongoing data monitoring as a continuous digital shadow. However, further CPPS components like the linear handling robot and the weight control need, therefore, to be automated and modularly integrated into the DT architecture.

## 7    Discussion

The presented methodology and reference architecture enable the generation of a DT for setting up and executing a DoE on an injection molding machine. Currently, a parameter change within the controlled CPPS required a new generation of the DT. Future work will be operating on interpreted models such that redeploying the DT is not necessary.

The DT gathers relevant data and transmits commands to the machine to change to the machine configuration. The DT is thus capable of detecting events within the machine or its operating context and reacting to these. Unfortunately, as the machine denies starting the production process without a machine operator supervising the machine, starting the production fully automated is not possible yet. However, if the machine is already running the DT can change the settings. The current technical implementation thereby only covers a proof-of-concept state. Further integration of and interconnection with additional assets, like a tempering unit or weight control, needs to follow, as must enhance automation, to give the DT extensive control access.

Furthermore, the adaptability of the reference architecture and development process must be evaluated in other domains and for different CPPSs. The current state works on standardized communication interfaces like OPC-UA. The DT setup relies on an open communication capability to be applied to further machines or domains in production technology. As OPC-UA establishes itself to be a manufacturer-independent interface, the proposed approach is transferrable but requires the machine to provide such an OPC-UA interface. Other communication protocols are not supported yet. However, the model-driven methodology supports exchangeability and flexibility, as the components building the DT can be exchanged. For example, a new `Executor` supporting another communication technology can be added. By specifying events that the DT should react to, software engineers can adapt the DT's behavior. The DOE language focuses on requirements that are raised by the injection molding use case. In other scenarios, DTs serve other purposes; thus, this language will not be applicable.

All DSLs that we introduced are tailored to support the specification of DTs, but in other domains, different notations might be standard, and therefore, modeling relevant data elements and behaviors might be challenging. So far, no human interaction with the DT is considered. Since domain experts usually have domain knowledge that can help the DT to react appropriately to events, integrating such knowledge at runtime will be future work.

## 8   Related Work

In the field of Industry 4.0, the Internet of Things and Internet of Production, there exist various application domains of DTs. In the automotive domain, among others, [7] presents the DT approach addressing safety, maintenance, and reliability of parts or built-in systems of vehicles. Furthermore, the prediction of potential future actions of neighboring vehicles in order to increase safety is presented in [3]. [1,25,29] on the contrary address smart shopfloor management. Linking of human-based production tasks [18], geometry assurance in individualized production [24], and parallel controlling of smart workshops [15], and the integration of edge, fog and cloud computing in smart manufacturing [19] shows the diversity of DT in manufacturing. All DTs mentioned above represent specific and individualized solutions to the respective problems. Contrary to this, the DT reference architecture presented in this paper is highly flexible and supports reusability for different use case scenarios. It is adaptable to all kinds of problems and domains. The model-driven development process enables automating major parts of the development process and thus reduces the manual effort for adapting the DT for new CPPSs.

Injection molding represents a relevant use case for realizing smart production processes. Previous work in the Cluster of Excellence at RWTH Aachen University and at the Institute for Plastics Processing have already elaborated data-driven approaches for process setup [10–12,26]. Artificial Neural Networks, therefore, are trained with simulation data to learn about parameter correlations from engineering models. Each process point of the previously simulated

DoE is conducted at the real production system. The resulting data is then fed back to the Neural Network for post-training and adjusting the estimations. The methodology has already been implemented as a closed-loop system that uses autonomously conducted DoEs for targeted data gathering and post-training [22]. However, the implementation caused high effort for a single application scenario that serves now as a starting point for autonomous code generation and for developing self-adjusting DTs.

## 9 Conclusion

We have presented a reference architecture and DSLs to realize reactive DTs for CPPSs. The reference architecture is specified in MontiArc and thus facilitates the exchangeability of components of the DT. The presented method relies on models describing the DT's situations (events) and reactions. We, therefore, introduced a DSL to specify events that occur in the CPPS and how the DT reacts to these events. Furthermore, we presented a DSL for specifying the communication with the CPS via OPC-UA. We evaluated the described methodology for automating experiments that determine an ideal operating point for an injection molding machine. Thus, we showed that the DT reference architecture serves as a starting point for systematically developing DTs for injection molding. In the future, we plan to apply our reference architecture and its DSLs to different manufacturing domains to improve the usage of manufacturing equipment and resources to reduce resource consumption, manufacturing time, and cost.

## References

1. Brenner, B., Hummel, V.: Digital twin as enabler for an innovative digital shopfloor management system in the ESB logistics learning factory at Reutlingen - University. Procedia Manuf. **9**, 198–205 (2017)
2. Butting, A., Kautz, O., Rumpe, B., Wortmann, A.: Architectural programming with montiarcautomaton. In: 12th International Conference on Software Engineering Advances (ICSEA 2017), pp. 213–218. IARIA XPS Press, May 2017
3. Chen, X., Kang, E., Shiraishi, S., Preciado, V.M., Jiang, Z.: Digital behavioral twins for safe connected cars. In: Proceedings of the 21th ACM/IEEE International Conference on Model Driven Engineering Languages and Systems, pp. 144–153. ACM (2018)
4. Choudhury, I., El-Baradie, M.: Machinability assessment of inconel 718 by factorial design of experiment coupled with response surface methodology. J. Mater. Process. Technol. **95**(1–3), 30–39 (1999)
5. Fei, N.C., Mehat, N.M., Kamaruddin, S.: Practical applications of Taguchi method for optimization of processing parameters for plastic injection moulding: a retrospective review. ISRN Ind. Eng. **2013**, 1–11 (2013)
6. France, R., Rumpe, B.: Model-driven development of complex software: a research roadmap. In: 2007 Future of Software Engineering, FOSE 2007, pp. 37–54. IEEE Computer Society, Washington, DC (2007)

7. Glaessgen, E., Stargel, D.: The digital twin paradigm for future NASA and us air force vehicles. In: 53rd AIAA/ASME/ASCE/AHS/ASC Structures, Structural Dynamics and Materials Conference 20th AIAA/ASME/AHS Adaptive Structures Conference 14th AIAA, p. 1818 (2012)
8. Greifenberg, T., Look, M., Roidl, S., Rumpe, B.: Engineering tagging languages for DSLs. In: Conference on Model Driven Engineering Languages and Systems (MODELS 2015), pp. 34–43. ACM/IEEE (2015)
9. Hai, R., Geisler, S., Quix, C.: Constance: an intelligent data lake system. In: SIGMOD Conference (2016)
10. Hopmann, C., Heinisch, J., Tercan, H.: Injection molding setup by means of machine learning based on simulation and experimental data. In: ANTEC 2018 Conference and Tradeshow, Orlando, Florida, USA (2018)
11. Hopmann, C., et al.: Combined learning processes for injection moulding based on simulation and experimental data. In: Proceedings of the 33rd International Conference of the Polymer Processing Society (PPS33). Polymer Processing Society, Cancun (2017)
12. Hopmann, C., et al.: Flexibilisation of injection moulding manufacture through digitisation. In: 29th International Colloquium Plastics Technology. Shaker Verlag, Aachen (2018)
13. Klocke, F., et al.: Approaches of self-optimising systems in manufacturing. In: Brecher, C. (ed.) Advances in Production Technology. LNPE, pp. 161–173. Springer, Cham (2015). https://doi.org/10.1007/978-3-319-12304-2_12
14. Kudlik, N.: Reproducibility of the plastic injection moulding process. Dissertation, RWTH Aachen University, Verlag Mainz, Wissenschaftsverlag (1998)
15. Leng, J., Zhang, H., Yan, D., Liu, Q., Chen, X., Zhang, D.: Digital twin-driven manufacturing cyber-physical system for parallel controlling of smart workshop. J. Ambient Intell. Humaniz. Comput. 10(3), 1155–1166 (2018). https://doi.org/10.1007/s12652-018-0881-5
16. Mahnke, W., Leitner, S.H., Damm, M.: OPC Unified Architecture. Springer, Heidelberg (2009). https://doi.org/10.1007/978-3-540-68899-0
17. Medvidovic, N., Taylor, R.: A classification and comparison framework for software architecture description languages. IEEE Trans. Softw. Eng. 26, 70–93 (2000)
18. Nikolakis, N., Alexopoulos, K., Xanthakis, E., Chryssolouris, G.: The digital twin implementation for linking the virtual representation of human-based production tasks to their physical counterpart in the factory-floor. Int. J. Comput. Integr. Manuf. 32(1), 1–12 (2019)
19. Qi, Q., Zhao, D., Liao, T.W., Tao, F.: Modeling of cyber-physical systems and digital twin based on edge computing, fog computing and cloud computing towards smart manufacturing. In: ASME 2018 13th International Manufacturing Science and Engineering Conference, pp. V001T05A018–V001T05A018. American Society of Mechanical Engineers (2018)
20. Rao, N.S., Schott, N.R.: Understanding Plastics Engineering Calculations: Hands-on Examples and Case Studies. Hanser and Hanser Publications, Munich and Cincinnati (2012)
21. Rumpe, B., Wortmann, A.: Abstraction and refinement in hierarchically decomposable and underspecified CPS-architectures. In: Lohstroh, M., Derler, P., Sirjani, M. (eds.) Principles of Modeling. LNCS, vol. 10760, pp. 383–406. Springer, Cham (2018). https://doi.org/10.1007/978-3-319-95246-8_23
22. Schmitz, M., Hopmann, C., Röbig, M., Pelzer, L., Topmöller, B., Wurzbacher, S.: Jenseits menschlicher fähigkeiten. modellgestützte prozesseinrichtung durch vollvernetzte produktion im spritzgießen. Kunststoffe 109(9), 142–145 (2019)

23. Shen, C., Wang, L., Li, Q.: Optimization of injection molding process parameters using combination of artificial neural network and genetic algorithm method. J. Mater. Process. Technol. **183**(2–3), 412–418 (2007)
24. Söderberg, R., Wärmefjord, K., Carlson, J.S., Lindkvist, L.: Toward a digital twin for real-time geometry assurance in individualized production. CIRP Ann. **66**(1), 137–140 (2017)
25. Tao, F., Zhang, M.: Digital twin shop-floor: a new shop-floor paradigm towards smart manufacturing. IEEE Access **5**, 20418–20427 (2017)
26. Tercan, H., Guajardo, A., Heinisch, J., Thiele, T., Hopmann, C., Meisen, T.: Transfer-learning: bridging the gap between real and simulation data for machine learning in injection moulding. In: Wang, L. (ed.) 51st CIRP Conference on Manufacturing Systems, vol. 72, pp. 185–190. Elsevier (2018)
27. Thein, K.M.M.: Apache Kafka: next generation distributed messaging system. Int. J. Sci. Eng. Technol. Res. **3**(47), 9478–9483 (2014)
28. Wortmann, A., Barais, O., Combemale, B., Wimmer, M.: Modeling languages in industry 4.0: an extended systematic mapping study. Softw. Syst. Model. **19**(1), 67–94 (2019). https://doi.org/10.1007/s10270-019-00757-6
29. Zhang, H., Zhang, G., Yan, Q.: Digital twin-driven cyber-physical production system towards smart shop-floor. J. Ambient Intell. Humaniz. Comput. **10**(11), 4439–4453 (2018). https://doi.org/10.1007/s12652-018-1125-4

# SIoTPredict: A Framework for Predicting Relationships in the Social Internet of Things

Abdulwahab Aljubairy[1,2(✉)], Wei Emma Zhang[3], Quan Z. Sheng[1], and Ahoud Alhazmi[1,2]

[1] Department of Computing, Macquarie University, Sydney, NSW 2109, Australia
{abdulwahab.aljubairy,ahoud.alhazmi}@hdr.mq.edu.au,
michael.sheng@mq.edu.au
[2] Computer Science Department (Al.leith), Umm Al Qura University,
Makkah 21955, Saudi Arabia
[3] School of Computer Science, The University of Adelaide, Adelaide,
SA 5001, Australia
wei.e.zhang@adelaide.edu.au

**Abstract.** The Social Internet of Things (SIoT) is a new paradigm that integrates social network concepts with the Internet of Things (IoT). It boosts the discovery, selection and composition of services and information provided by distributed objects. In SIoT, searching for services is based on the utilization of the social structure resulted from the formed relationships. However, current approaches lack modelling and effective analysis of SIoT. In this work, we address this problem and specifically focus on modelling the SIoT's evolvement. As the growing number of IoT objects with heterogeneous attributes join the social network, there is an urgent need for identifying the mechanisms by which SIoT structures evolve. We model the SIoT over time and address the suitability of traditional analytical procedures to predict future relationships (links) in the dynamic and heterogeneous SIoT. Specifically, we propose a framework, namely SIoTPredict, which includes three stages: i) collection of raw movement data of IoT devices, ii) generating temporal sequence networks of the SIoT, and iii) predicting relationships among IoT devices which are likely to occur. We have conducted extensive experimental studies to evaluate the proposed framework using real SIoT datasets and the results show the better performance of our framework.

**Keywords:** Social Internet of Things (SIoT) · Link prediction · Dynamic networks · Edge exchangeability

## 1 Introduction

Crawling the Internet of Things (IoT) to discover services and information in a trusted-oriented way remains a prolonged challenge [21]. Many solutions have

© Springer Nature Switzerland AG 2020
S. Dustdar et al. (Eds.): CAiSE 2020, LNCS 12127, pp. 101–116, 2020.
https://doi.org/10.1007/978-3-030-49435-3_7

been introduced to overcome the challenge. However, due to the increasing number of IoT objects in a tremendous rate, these solutions do not scale up. Integrating social networking features into the Internet of Things (IoT) paradigm has received an unprecedented amount of attention for the purpose of overcoming issues related to IoT. There have been many attempts to integrate IoT devices in social loops such as Smart-Its friend procedure [8], Blog-jects [3], Things that Twitter [9], and Ericson Project[1]. A new paradigm has emerged from this, called *Social Internet of Things* (SIoT), and the key idea of this paradigm is to allow IoT objects to establish relationships with each other independently with respect to the heuristics set by the owners of these objects [1,2,15,18]. The perspective of SIoT is to incorporate the social behaviour of intelligent IoT objects and allow them to have their own social networks autonomously.

There are several benefits to the SIoT paradigm. First, SIoT can foster resource availability and enhance services discovery easily in a distributed manner using friends and friends of friends [1], unlike traditional IoT where search engines are employed to find services in a centralized way. Second, the centralized manner of searching IoT objects raises scalability issue, and SIoT overcomes the issue because each IoT object can navigate the network structure of SIoT to reach other objects in a distributed way [2,20,21]. Third, based on the social structure established among IoT objects, things can inquire local neighbourhood for other objects to assess the reputation of these objects. Fourth, SIoT enables objects to start new acquaintance where they can exchange information and experience.

Many research efforts have been devoted to realizing the SIoT paradigm. However, the majority of the research activities focused on identifying possible policies, methods and techniques for establishing relationships between smart devices autonomously and without any human intervention [1,2]. In addition, several SIoT architectures have been proposed [2,5,17]. In spite of the intensive research attempts on SIoT, there are insufficient considerations to model and analyze the resulted SIoT networks. The nature of SIoT is dynamic because it can grow and change quickly over time where nodes (IoT objects) and edges (relationships) appear or disappear. Therefore, there is a growing interest in developing models that allow studying and understanding this evolving network, in particular, predicting the establishment of future links (relationships) [1,15]. Predicting future relationships among IoT objects can be utilized for several applications such as service recommendation and service discovery. Thus, there is a need for identifying the mechanisms by which SIoT structures evolve. This is a fundamental research question that has not been addressed in SIoT yet, and it forms the motivation for this work.

However, the size and complexity of the SIoT network create a number of technical challenges. Firstly, the nature of the resulted network structure is *dynamic* because smart devices can appear and disappear overtime and the existed relationships may vanish and new relationships may establish. Secondly, SIoT is naturally structured as a *heterogeneous* graph with different types of entities and various relationships [2,18]. Finally, the size of SIoT network is mas-

---

[1] https://www.ericsson.com/en/blog/2012/4/a-social-web-of-things.

sive, and hence, it requires efficient and scalable methods. Therefore, this paper focuses on modelling the SIoT network and study, in particular, the problem of predicting future relationships among IoT objects. We study the possibility of relationship establishment among IoT objects when there is co-occurrence meeting in time and space. Our research question centers on how likely two IoT objects could create a relationship between each other when they have been approximately on the same geographical location at the same time on multiple occasions. In our work, we develop the SIoTPredict framework, which includes three stages: i) collecting the raw movement data of IoT devices, ii) generating temporal sequence networks of SIoT, and iii) predicting future relationships that may be established among things. The salient contributions of our study are summarized as follows:

- **Designing and implementing the SIoTPredict framework for study-ing the SIoT network.** The SIoTPredict framework consists of three main stages for i) collecting raw movement data of IoT devices, ii) generating temporal sequence networks, and iii) predicting future relationships among things. To the best of our knowledge, our framework is the first on SIoT relationship prediction.
- **Generating temporal sequence networks of SIoT.** We develop two novel algorithms in the second stage of our framework. The first algorithm identifies the stays of IoT objects and extracts the corresponding locations. The second algorithm, named Sweep Line Time Overlap, discovers when and where any two IoT objects have met.
- **Developing a Bayesian nonparametric prediction model.** We adopt the Bayesian nonparametirc learning to build our prediction model. This model can adapt the new incoming observations due to the power representation and flexibility of Bayesian nonparametric learning.
- **Conducting comprehensive experiments to assess our framework.** SIoTPredict has been evaluated by extensive experiments using real-world SIoT datasets [12]. The results demonstrate that our framework outperforms the existing methods.

The rest of this paper is organized as follows. Section 2 discusses the related works. Section 3 presents heterogeneous graph modeling for Social IoT and introduces the SIoTPredict framework. The experimental results on real SIoT datasets are presented in Sect. 4, and finally Sect. 5 concludes the paper.

## 2   Related Work

SIoT is still in the infancy stage, and several efforts have been devoted to realizing the SIoT paradigm. Most of the current research activities focused on identifying possible policies, methods and techniques for establishing relationships between smart devices autonomously and without any human intervention [2]. Atzori et al. [2] proposed several relationships that can be established between IoT objects as shown in Table 1. Some of these relationships are static such as POR and OOR, which can usually be defined in advance. Other relationships are dynamic and can be established when the conditions of the relationship are met. Roopa et al. [18] defined more relationships that may be established among IoT objects.

Nevertheless, current SIoT research lacks effective modelling and analysis of SIoT networks. However, in the context of IoT, there are a few attempts to exploiting the relationships among smart devices and users for recommending things to users. Yao et al. [23] proposed a hyper-graph based on users' social networks. They used existing relationships among users and their things to infer relationships among IoT objects. They leveraged this resulted network for recommending things of interest to users. Mashal et al. [14] modelled the relationships among users, objects, and services as a tripartite graph with hyper-edges between them. Then they explored existing recommendation algorithms to recommend third-party services. Nevertheless, these works are mainly based on users' existing relationships and the things they own. Atzori et al. [1] emphasized to modelling and analyzing the resulted social graphs (uncorrelated to human social networks) among smart objects in order to introduce proper network analysis algorithms. Therefore, our work aims to model the SIoT network in order to allow studying relationships prediction (link prediction) among IoT objects that may form in the future.

Link prediction is considered as one of the most essential problems that have received much attention in network analysis, and in particular, when anticipating the network structure at a future time. A large body of work has investigated link prediction with various aspects including similarity-based measures, algorithmic methods, and probabilistic and statistical methods [11,13]. Recently, there is a growing interest in developing probabilistic network models using Bayesian nonparametric learning. Bayesian nonparametric is capable to cap-

**Table 1.** Some main SIoT relationships [2].

| SIoT relationships | Description | Static/Dynamic |
|---|---|---|
| Parental object relationship (POR) | This relationship is established among same generation objects which are made by the same manufacturer | Static |
| Co-location object relationship (CLOR) | This relationship is established among objects that are always existed in the same place | Dynamic |
| Co-work object relationship (CWOR) | This relationship is established among objects when they collaborate to achieve a common goal or provide a particular IoT application | Dynamic |
| Ownership object relationship (OOR) | This relationship is established among objects which belong to the same user | Static |
| Social object relationship (SOR) | This relationship is established among objects when they come into contact, sporadically or continuously, because they or their owners come in touch with each other during daily routine | Dynamic |

ture the network evolution in different time steps by finding latent structure in observed data. Latent class models such as Stochastic Blockmodels (SBs) [7] and Mixed Membership Stochastic Blockmodels (MMSB) [19] depend on the vertex-exchangeability perspective where nodes are the target unit to assign into clusters. However, these models suffer from generating dense networks while most of the real-world networks tend to be sparse. To overcome this limitation, edge-exchangeable models have been proposed to deal with sparse networks [4,22]. In this perspective, edges are the main units to assign into clusters.

## 3   Bayesian Non-parametric Approach

In this section, we describe the dynamic heterogeneous SIoT graph modelling and then present the details of our SIoTPredict framework.

### 3.1   Dynamic Heterogeneous SIoT Graph Modelling

A dynamic, heterogeneous SIoT graph is composed of nodes and edges where nodes represent IoT devices, and edges represent relationships that could be of multiple different types. The formal definition is as follows.

An SIoT network can be considered as a temporal sequence of networks (as depicted in Fig. 1a) $G = \{G^{t_1}, G^{t_2}, \ldots, G^{t-n}\}$ where $G^t$ is a snapshot of the network at time $t$ and $t \in \mathbb{Z}^+$. Each snapshot of the network contains a set of nodes and edges $G^t = \{V^t, E^t, X^t\}$ where the set of edges $E^t = \{e_1^t, \ldots, e_n^t\}$ contains $N$ edges observed at time $t$ and the set of vertices $V^t$ is the set of vertices that have at least participated in one edge up to $t$ such that $V^{t-1} \subseteq V^t$. An edge $e_n^t = (v_i^t, v_j^t)$ is a tuple of two interacting nodes. $X^t = [x_1^t, x_2^t, \ldots, x_i^t]$ represents the feature matrix at time $t$ where $x_i$ is the attribute vector of node $v_n$.

Throughout the paper, we consider the dynamic relationship establishment using SIoT data as a case study. Figure 1b shows an example of the SIoT heterogeneous network. For this application, we assume that a heterogeneous SIoT graph has been obtained at time $t$ from the SIoT data. Given these data, we will predict the likelihood of a relationship (edge) creation between any two IoT devices (nodes).

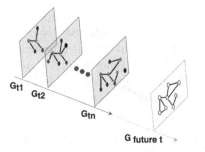

(a) Modelling SIoT heterogeneous network.

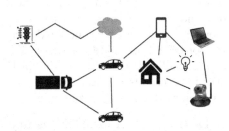

(b) An example of the SIoT heterogeneous network.

Fig. 1. The SIoT heterogeneous network.

## 3.2 The Proposed SIoTPredict Framework

This section explains our SIoTPredict framework for predicting future relationships in SIoT. Figure 2 gives an overview of the SIoTPredict framework. The framework includes three stages namely: *Stage 1:* collection of the raw movement data of IoT devices, *Stage 2:* generating the temporal sequence networks of SIoT, and *Stage 3:* prediction future relationships of the SIoT. In the following, we will provide more details on these three stages.

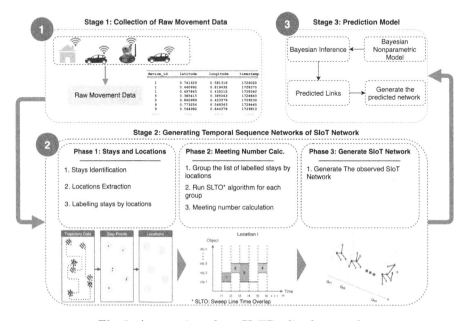

**Fig. 2.** An overview of our SIoTPredict framework.

**Stage 1. Collection of the Raw Movement Data of IoT Devices.** In the first stage of our framework, we collect the raw movement data of IoT devices. We distinguish two types of IoT devices: *mobile* and *static*. The coordinates of a static device (e.g., a light pole) are stationary and known whereas the coordinates of a mobile device (e.g., a bus) is dynamic and changing while the device is moving. We assume that mobile devices include GPS technology which provides the location coordinates of these devices along with the timestamp. We also assume mobile IoT devices send their location history records continuously (e.g., every 60 seconds). Each record contains some important fields: (`device_id`, `latitude`, `longitude`, and `timestamp`).

1. **Definition 1. A location history record** is represented by a point on the earth (`latitude`, `longitude`) and a `timestamp`. This record tells where an IoT object is at a specific time (as illustrated in Fig. 3).
2. **Definition 2. A trajectory** is a sequence of location history records of an IoT object (as illustrated in Fig. 3).

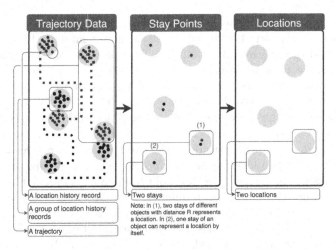

**Fig. 3.** Illustration on IoT object location, stay point, and movement trajectory

**Stage 2. Generating Temporal Sequence Networks of SIoT.** In the second stage, we generate temporal sequence networks of SIoT based on the observed raw movement data of IoT devices from *Stage 1*. Generating the temporal sequence networks of SIoT is performed in three phases as follows: *Phase 1:* identifying stays from raw movement data, extracting locations, and labelling each stay by the extracted locations, *Phase 2:* calculating the number of meetings among IoT devices using the Sweep Line Time Overlap (SLTO) algorithm, and *Phase 3:* generating temporal networks of SIoT.

*Phase 1) Identifying "stays" from the raw movement data and extracting "locations".* We are interested in knowing where objects meet. Therefore, we first need to identify the stays for all objects using their raw movement data. Then, we extract locations from these stays. This enables us to identify where and when IoT objects have stayed.

1. **Definition 3.** A **stay** is a sequence of $N$ location history records, which can be represented by ⟨longitude, latitude, Start-Time, End-Time⟩. Longitude and latitude represent the average of longitude and latitude values in the sequence. Start-Time indicates the smallest timestamp in the sequence, and End-Time represents the largest timestamp (see Fig. 3).
2. **Definition 4.** A **location** can be the latitude and longitude of one stay, or it can be the average of longitude and latitude of a group of stays. This group of stays are separated by less than or equal to a distance $R$ (see Fig. 3).

We develop Algorithm 1 for identifying stays, extracting locations and, then labelling identified stays by the extracted locations. The *input* of this algorithm is the raw movement data of IoT objects. The *output* is a list of identified stays labelled by extracted locations. The time complexity of this algorithm is quadratic since it is required to calculate the distances between each two observations in the raw movement data.

The first step focuses on stay identification (line 6–27). This step is to identify the stays for each IoT object from the given raw movement data. First, we define the time period of the stay (for example, when the value of stay period $= 10$, it means that we need to identify if an object stays at a place for 10 min). According to our assumption, each record in the raw movement data is sent every one minute, so 10 records represent 10 min. The algorithm calculates the distance among the raw movement data records according to Eq. 1, where, $d$ is the distance between the two location history records, $r$ is the radius of the sphere (earth), $\theta_1, \theta_2$ are the latitude of the two location history records, $\lambda_1, \lambda_2$ are longitude of the two location history records. Then, it groups them if their distances are less than or equal to a threshold $R$. From line (18–27), the algorithm checks each group. If a group has a number of records larger than or equal to the value of the stay period, the algorithm takes the average of the latitude and longitude of the group. It also takes the smallest timestamp of the group to be the starting time of the stay, and the largest timestamp to be the ending time of the stay.

$$distance = 2r.sin^{-1}\left(\sqrt{sin^2(\frac{(\theta_2 - \theta_1)}{2}) + cos(\theta_1).cos(\theta_2).sin^2(\frac{(\lambda_2 - \lambda_1)}{2})}\right)$$

(1)

The second step targets location extraction (line 28–40). The algorithm extracts the list of locations out of the identified stays. Since stays are represented by latitude and longitude, the algorithm calculates the distance among these stays, and groups them using a threshold $R$. The algorithm takes the average of the latitude and longitude of these stays to represent one location. If there is a stay which has not been grouped with any other stays, this stay can represent a location. Finally the third step focuses on labelling stays with locations. In this step, we label the identified stays by one of the extracted locations.

*Phase 2) Calculating the number of meetings between objects using Sweep Line Time Overlap Algorithm.* We develop Algorithm 2 to detect and report all overlapped periods occurred among the given set of stays produced by Algorithm 1. The purpose is to determine if any two IoT objects have met in a location at a particular time. This novel algorithm named as Sweep Line Time Overlap (SLTO). The SLTO algorithm is inspired by a sweep-line algorithm in geometry which finds intersections between a group of line segments. However, the SLTO algorithm identifies if there are overlapping periods among stays of the objects in a location. The idea of this algorithm is to run a virtual sweep-line parallel to y-axis and move from left to right in order to scan intervals on x-axis. When this sweep-line detects overlaps among stays (they look like line segments which represent the stay periods of objects), it starts calculating if there is an overlap and reporting these overlaps. There are two main steps.

**Algorithm 1:** Stay identification and location extraction.

**Input** : The raw movement data of IoT objects
**Output:** Stays Labelled with extracted locations

```
 1 data = raw movement data;
 2 StayPeriod = N;
 3 ASSIGN EMPTY LIST to Stay;
 4 ASSIGN EMPTY LIST to IdentifiedStays;
 5 ASSIGN EMPTY LIST to Locations;
 6 for i ← 1 to data.length − 1 do
 7 │   Stay.append(data[i]);
 8 │   for j ← i + 1 to data.length do
 9 │   │   distance ← distance(data[i], data[j]) ;                    ▷ Eq1
10 │   │   if (distance <= R) then
11 │   │   │   Stay[i].append(data[j]);
12 │   │   else
13 │   │   │   i ← j;
14 │   │   │   Break;
15 │   │   end
16 │   end
17 end
18 for i ← 1 to Stay.length do
19 │   if Stay[i].length >= StayPeriod then
20 │   │   objID ← Stay[i].objID;
21 │   │   lat ← Compute avg lat of the stay;
22 │   │   long ← Compute avg long of the stay;
23 │   │   Start-Time ← min(Stay[i].timestamp);
24 │   │   End-Time ← max(Stay[i].timestamp);
25 │   │   IdentifiedStays.append([objID,lat,long,Start-Time,End-Time]);
26 │   end
27 end
28 for i ← 1 to IdentifiedStays.length − 1 do
29 │   coords=[ ];
30 │   coords.append([IdentifiedStays[i].lat,IdentifiedStays[i].long]);
31 │   for j ← i + 1 to IdentifiedStays.length do
32 │   │   distance ← distance(IdentifiedStays[i], IdentifiedStays[j]) ; ▷ Eq1
33 │   │   if (distance <= R) then
34 │   │   │   coords.append([IdentifiedStays[j].lat,IdentifiedStays[j].long]);
35 │   │   end
36 │   end
37 │   lat ← Compute avg lat of coords;
38 │   long ← Compute avg long coords;
39 │   Locations.append([lat,long]);
40 end
```

The first step focuses on storing all the intervals of the stays (line 2–3). Since our goal is to find the overlapped periods among the set of stays, the algorithm initializes two data structures: i) a priority queue $Q$ to store all the intervals of the stays we got from Algorithm 1 in sorting order, and ii) a sweep-line status as $S$ to scan the stays from left to right.

The second step runs the sweep line $S$ (line 4–10). We get the interval end points from $Q$ one by one to allow the sweep line $S$ to scan it. The sweep line detects the start of the stay in the space, and adds it to the $S$. Also, when it detects the end of the stay (in this case, the SLTO finished from scanning the stay), the algorithm checks the last element in $S$. If it is the start of this stay, then the algorithm removes the stay form $S$ with no action. If the last element in $S$ is not the start of the finished stay, then an overlap or more have been detected between the this stay and other active stays in the $S$. Algorithm 3 reports the overlaps discovered by SLTO. It calculates the amount of the detected overlaps, and the results are reported. The time complexity of SLTO is $O(NlogN+L)$ since the stay time is only calculated when overlaps between objects exist (Fig. 4).

---

**Algorithm 2:** SLTO to find the time overlaps among the stays of objects.

| | |
|---|---|
| **Input** | : A list of stays |
| **Output:** | A list of pair of objects with the overlapped period among them |

1 **begin**
2     $Q$ = The list of stays from Algorithm 1 as [[stay endpoint value, status, interval, objeID]];
3     $S$ = Initialize the Sweep line for storing detected stays;
4     **while** $Q$ *is not empty* **do**
5         currentEvent ← $Q.get()$;
6         **if** *(currentEvent.Status == Start)* **then**
7             - Insert currentEvent into **S**;
8         **else**
9             - CheckOverlap(**S** , currentEvent);
10             - Delete currentEvent from **S**;

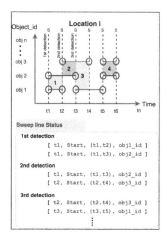

**Fig. 4.** The sweep line S moves from left to right to scan stay intervals. The 1st detection is occurred at time t1.

---

**Algorithm 3:** CheckOverlap

---

    **Input**   : S, currentEvent
    **Output:** Report the overlapping among stays
1 **begin**
2      L2 = currentEvent
3      **for** ($L1$ $in$ $S$) **do**
4          **if** $L1.start < L2.end$ & ($L2.start < L1.end$) **then**
5              OverlapPeriod $\leftarrow$ min($L1.end, L2.end$) $-$ max($L1.start, L2.start$)
6              - Report the overlap (ids of objects and OverlapPeriod)

---

*Phase 3) Generating the temporal networks of SIoT.* After obtaining the time overlapping periods of stays among IoT objects, we are able to know the count of meetings occurred between any two IoT objects. According to this, we check the rules of the targeted relationship such as how many times they have met and the length of the interval period. If the rules are met, then we build the temporal sequence of the SIoT composed from this relationship to be used in our prediction model stage.

**Stage 3. Predicting Future Relationships of the SIoT Network.** After generating the temporal sequence networks in the second stage, our next step is to model each one of them using the Bayesian non-parametric model [22]. This model allows combining structure elucidation with a predictive performance by clustering links (edges) rather than the nodes. Our aim here is to predict links (relationships) between IoT objects that are likely to occur in the subsequent snapshot of the network. Therefore, the SIoT network is modelled as an exchangeable sequence of observed links (relationships) and that allows adapting the growth of the network over time. We assume that the SIoT network clusters into groups, and for this, we model each community using a mixture of Dirichlet network distributions. The description of the model as follows:

$$
\begin{aligned}
D &:= (dk, k \in N) \sim GEM(\alpha) \\
G &:= \textstyle\sum_{\infty}^{i=1} \pi_i \delta_{\Theta_i} \sim DP(\gamma, \theta) \\
c_n &\sim D \\
u_n, v_n &\sim G
\end{aligned}
\tag{2}
$$

We model the relationships of the SIoT network using Dirichlet distribution $G$, where $\delta_{\Theta_i}$ is a delta function centered on $\Theta_i$, and $\pi_i$ is the corresponding probability of an edge to exist at $\Theta_i$, with $\sum_{\infty}^{i=1} \pi_i = 1$. The parameter $\gamma$ controls the total number of nodes in the network. To model the size and number of clusters, we use a stick-breaking distribution $GEM(\alpha)$ with concentration parameter $\alpha$ that controls the number of the clusters. The model places a distribution over all clusters, and it places per-cluster distribution over the nodes. To generate an edge, first, a cluster will be picked according to $D$. Then, two nodes (devices) will be sampled according to $G$. The probability of predicting a link between any two objects is proportional to the product of the degree of these two devices.

$$P(\theta|X, model) = \frac{P(X|\theta, model)P(\theta|model)}{\int P(\theta, X|model) \, d\theta} \qquad (3)$$

For the inference part that is based on the Bayes' rule (Eq. 3), we follow the same steps conducted in [22] to compute the distribution over the cluster assignment using the Chinese restaurant process and evaluate the predictive distribution over the $n^{th}$ link, given the previous $n-1$ links. We perform inference using an Markov chain Monte Carlo (MCMC) scheme [22].

## 4    Experiments

We evaluated the effectiveness and efficiency of the SIoTPredict framework based on comprehensive experiments. In this section, we discuss the experimental design and report the results.

### 4.1    Dataset

We used the SIoT datasets[2] to evaluate the SIoTPredict framework. These datasets are based on real IoT objects available in the city of Santander and contain a description of IoT objects. Each object is represented by fields such as (device_id, id_user, device_type, device_brand, device_model). The total number of IoT objects is 16,216. 14,600 objects are from private users and 1,616 are from public services. The dataset includes the raw movement data of devices that are owned by users and the smart city. There are two kinds of devices: static devices and mobile devices. Static devices are represented by fixed latitudes and longitudes. Mobile devices are represented by latitudes, longitudes, and timestamps. The latitude and longitude values of mobile devices are dynamic. In addition, the dataset includes an adjacency matrix for SIoT relationship produced with some defined parameters. In Table 2, we only depict SOR and SOR2 relationships and their parameters to be used in our experiments.

### 4.2    Performance Metrics and Comparison Methods

In this section, we explain the common metrics and the comparison methods.

**Performance Metrics.** Our performance metrics used in the experiments include Accuracy, Precision, Recall, and $F1$ score. Following the work of information diffusion in [6], we define the Accuracy as the ratio of correctly predicted edges to the total edges in the true network, Precision as the fraction of edges in the predicted network that are also present in the true network, Recall as the fraction of edges of the true network that are also presented in the predicted network, and finally $F1$ score as the weight average of precision and recall.

---

[2] http://www.social-iot.org/index.php?p=downloads.

**Table 2.** Parameter setting for SOR and SOR2 relationships.

| Relationship | Potential devices | Parameters |
|---|---|---|
| SOR | Private mobile devices | This relationship is based on three parameters:<br>1. Number of meetings $= 3$<br>2. Meeting duration $= 30\,\text{min}$<br>3. Interval between two consecutive meetings $= 6\,\text{h}$ |
| SOR2 | Public devices (static and mobile) and mobile private devices | This relationship is based on three parameters:<br>1. Number of meetings $= 3$<br>2. Meeting duration $= 1\,\text{min}$<br>3. Interval between two consecutive meetings $= 1\,\text{h}$ |

**Comparison Methods.** To evaluate the effectiveness of the framework, we compared the prediction model in Stage 3 with two well-known non-parametric models, namely Stochastic Bolockmodel (SB) [7] and Mixed-Membership Stochastic Blockmodel (MMBS) [19]. Although the aforementioned models are not explicitly designed for link prediction, they can be modified for the prediction task using the above procedure of selecting the $N$ highest probability edges [22]. In addition, these models suffer from the limitation of assuming a fixed number of vertices. Furthermore, we also compared our approach with common link prediction methods [10]: Resource Allocation, Adamic Adar index, Jaccard Coefficient, XGBoost, and Common Neighbor.

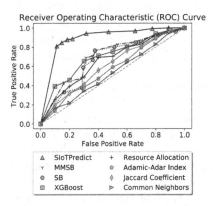

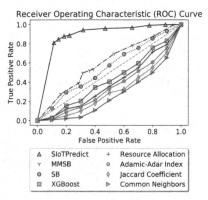

(a) ROC curve using nodes in the training set.

(b) ROC curve using nodes outside the training set.

**Fig. 5.** ROC Curves for the SIoTPredict versus the comparison methods

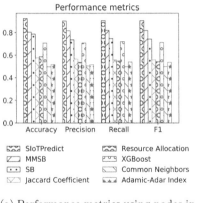

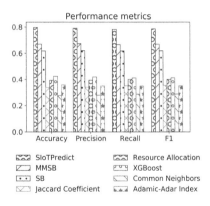

(a) Performance metrics using nodes in the training set.

(b) Performance metrics using nodes outside the training set.

**Fig. 6.** Performance of the SIoTPredict versus the comparison methods.

### 4.3  Results

We modeled the SIoT network to predict future interactions among devices, and that enabled us to have a better understanding on the resulted network. Based on the existing Bayesian models, nodes are assigned to clusters, and these clusters control the way of how these nodes establish relationships. Figure 5 and Fig. 6 show the performance of SIoTPredict against other methods. We used a small network, and the reason of that is due to the nature of SB and MMSB, which do not scale very well on large networks [16]. We experimented the performance of these models and methods in two ways. In the first experiment, we used the same nodes (i.e., IoT objects) in the training set and the test set. That means there were no nodes in the test set outside the training set. We performed experiments in this way because SB, MMSB and other methods assume nodes in the test set are not outside the training set. In the second experiment, the nodes in the test set are outside the training set.

For the overall performance, SB does not perform well against the MMSB and our model. The reason is that the assumption of SB states that nodes can only belong to one cluster whereas we see MMSB performs better than SB because it relaxes this assumption by allowing the nodes to belong to more than one clusters. However, SB, MMSB and other common methods do not perform well compared to our model on both settings as illustrated in Fig. 5 and Fig. 6. In particular, these methods perform poorly in the second setting (i.e., the nodes in the test set are outside the training set) due to their limitation on dealing with new nodes. In contrast, our model delivers the similar performance.

## 5  Conclusion

Social Internet of Things (SIoT) can foster and enhance resource availability, discovering services, assessing object reputations, composing services, exchanging information and experience. In addition, SIoT enables establishing new acquaintances, collaborating to achieve common goals, and exploiting other object capabilities. Therefore, instead of relying on centralized search engine, social structure resulted from the created relationships can be utilized in order to find the desired services. In this paper, we take the research line of SIoT to a new dimension by proposing the SIoTPredict framework that addresses the link prediction problem in the SIoT paradigm. This framework contains three stages: i) collecting raw data movement of IoT devices, ii) generating temporal sequence networks of SIoT, and iii) predicting the links that are likely form between IoT objects in the future. Ongoing work includes further assessment of the SIoTPredict framework, and enhancement of the relationship prediction by considering the features of IoT objects (e.g., services offered by the objects).

# References

1. Atzori, L., Iera, A., Morabito, G.: From smart objects to social objects: the next evolutionary step of the internet of things. IEEE Commun. Mag. **52**(1), 97–105 (2014)
2. Atzori, L., Iera, A., Morabito, G., Nitti, M.: The Social Internet of Things (SIoT) - when social networks meet the Internet of Things: concept, architecture and network characterization. Comput. Netw. **56**(16), 3594–3608 (2012)
3. Bleecker, J.: A manifesto for networked objects - cohabiting with pigeons, arphids and aibos in the Internet of Things. In: Proceedings of the 13th International Conference on Human-Computer Interaction with Mobile Devices and Services (MobileHCI), pp. 1–17 (2006)
4. Cai, D., Campbell, T., Broderick, T.: Edge-exchangeable graphs and sparsity. In: Proceedings of Advances in Neural Information Processing Systems (NIPS), pp. 4249–4257 (2016)
5. Girau, R., Martis, S., Atzori, L.: Lysis: a platform for IoT distributed applications over socially connected objects. IEEE Internet Things J. **4**(1), 40–51 (2017)
6. Gomez-Rodriguez, M., Leskovec, J., Krause, A.: Inferring networks of diffusion and influence. ACM Trans. Knowl. Discov. Data (TKDD) **5**(4), 1–37 (2012)
7. Holland, P.W., Laskey, K.B., Leinhardt, S.: Stochastic blockmodels: first steps. Soc. Netw. **5**(2), 109–137 (1983)
8. Holmquist, L.E., Mattern, F., Schiele, B., Alahuhta, P., Beigl, M., Gellersen, H.-W.: Smart-its friends: a technique for users to easily establish connections between smart artefacts. In: Abowd, G.D., Brumitt, B., Shafer, S. (eds.) UbiComp 2001. LNCS, vol. 2201, pp. 116–122. Springer, Heidelberg (2001). https://doi.org/10.1007/3-540-45427-6_10
9. Kranz, M., Roalter, L., Michahelles, F.: Things that Twitter: social networks and the Internet of Things. In: Proceedings of What Can the Internet of Things Do for the Citizen (CIoT) Workshop at the 8th International Conference on Pervasive Computing (Pervasive), pp. 1–10 (2010)
10. Liben-Nowell, D., Kleinberg, J.: The link-prediction problem for social networks. J. Am. Soc. Inform. Sci. Technol. **58**(7), 1019–1031 (2007)
11. Lü, L., Zhou, T.: Link prediction in complex networks: a survey. Physica A Stat. Mech. Appl. **390**(6), 1150–1170 (2011)

12. Marche, C., Atzori, L., Nitti, M.: A dataset for performance analysis of the social internet of things. In: Proceedings of the IEEE 29th Annual International Symposium on Personal, Indoor and Mobile Radio Communications, pp. 1–5 (2018)
13. Martínez, V., Berzal, F., Cubero, J.C.: A survey of link prediction in complex networks. ACM Comput. Surv. (CSUR) **49**(4), 1–33 (2016)
14. Mashal, I., Alsaryrah, O., Chung, T.Y.: Analysis of recommendation algorithms for Internet of Things. In: Proceedings of the IEEE Wireless Communications and Networking Conference (WCNC), pp. 1–6 (2016)
15. Nitti, M., Atzori, L., Cvijikj, I.P.: Friendship selection in the social internet of things: challenges and possible strategies. IEEE Internet Things J. **2**(3), 240–247 (2015)
16. Orbanz, P., Roy, D.M.: Bayesian models of graphs, arrays and other exchangeable random structures. IEEE Trans. Pattern Anal. Mach. Intell. **37**(2), 437–461 (2014)
17. Ortiz, A.M., Hussein, D., Park, S., Han, S.N., Crespi, N.: The cluster between internet of things and social networks: review and research challenges. IEEE Internet Things J. **1**(3), 206–215 (2014)
18. Roopa, M., Pattar, S., Buyya, R., Venugopal, K.R., Iyengar, S., Patnaik, L.: Social Internet of Things (SIoT): foundations, thrust areas, systematic review and future directions. Comput. Commun. **139**(1), 32–57 (2019)
19. Snijders, T.A., Nowicki, K.: Estimation and prediction for stochastic blockmodels for graphs with latent block structure. J. Classif. **14**(1), 75–100 (1997)
20. Tran, N.K., Sheng, Q.Z., Babar, M.A., Yao, L.: Searching the web of things: state of the art, challenges, and solutions. ACM Comput. Surv. (CSUR) **50**(4), 1–34 (2017)
21. Tran, N.K., Sheng, Q.Z., Babar, M.A., Yao, L., Zhang, W.E., Dustdar, S.: Internet of Things search engine. Commun. ACM **62**(7), 66–73 (2019)
22. Williamson, S.A.: Nonparametric network models for link prediction. J. Mach. Learn. Res. **17**(1), 7102–7121 (2016)
23. Yao, L., Sheng, Q.Z., Ngu, A.H., Li, X.: Things of interest recommendation by leveraging heterogeneous relations in the Internet of Things. ACM Trans. Internet Technol. (TOIT) **16**(2), 1–25 (2016)

# B-MERODE: A Model-Driven Engineering and Artifact-Centric Approach to Generate Blockchain-Based Information Systems

Victor Amaral de Sousa[1]([⊠]), Corentin Burnay[1], and Monique Snoeck[2]

[1] University of Namur, Namur, Belgium
{victor.amaral,corentin.burnay}@unamur.be
[2] KU Leuven, Louvain, Belgium
monique.snoeck@kuleuven.be

**Abstract.** Blockchain technology has the potential to facilitate the development and improvement of cross-organizational business processes. When it comes to developing systems relying on blockchain having this purpose, model-driven engineering is a promising approach that has been adopted by a number of solutions. This paper presents B-MERODE, a novel approach relying on model-driven engineering and artifact-centric business processes to generate blockchain-based information systems supporting cross-organizational collaborations. The feasibility of the approach is demonstrated by modeling the case of a rice supply chain. Compared to other solutions, B-MERODE provides more flexibility, more reusability and further leverages the automation potential offered by model-driven engineering.

**Keywords:** Blockchain · BPM · MDE · MERODE · Method

## 1 Introduction

With the availability of blockchain technology and its capability to run software (often referred to as smart contracts), a broad range of applications have been made possible. Among these are opportunities for the implementation, execution and monitoring of cross-organizational Business Processes (BPs), as further detailed in [1]. A blockchain can be described as "[…] a distributed database, which is shared among and agreed upon a peer-to-peer network. It consists of a linked sequence of blocks, holding timestamped transactions […] secured by public-key cryptography […]. Once an element is appended to the blockchain, it cannot be altered, turning a blockchain into an immutable record of past activity" [2, p. 3].

However, being a new technology, developing solutions relying on it remains a challenging task, for multiple reasons mentioned in [3]. These include the lack of adequate developer tools, the lack of people having the required skills and knowledge and a steep learning curve.

One of the promising approaches that can facilitate the development of Blockchain-Based Information Systems (BBISs) supporting cross-organizational collaborations is

© Springer Nature Switzerland AG 2020
S. Dustdar et al. (Eds.): CAiSE 2020, LNCS 12127, pp. 117–133, 2020.
https://doi.org/10.1007/978-3-030-49435-3_8

Model-Driven Engineering (MDE). MDE enables generating executable code from a set of models that specify the processes to be supported. For example, [4] and [5] are tool-supported methods that allow to generate Solidity BBISs respectively from BPMN diagrams and Finite State Machines (FSMs). Using MDE requires a language to create models used as input for code generation. Without insisting on MDE, authors of [6] call for the development of a shared ledger business collaboration language. This should be a language that is understood by business people and which can be used to specify cross-organizational BPs supported by blockchain technology. Such a language would foster blockchain adoption and facilitate prototyping. Furthermore, [6] argues that the language should be based on artifact-centric BP models. In the past, several approaches to model-driven blockchain-based cross-organizational BPs have been proposed. Many of those are however process-centered rather than artifact-centered. Even though a few artifact-centered approaches exist, these provide only a partial coverage of the required concepts, the code generation is not fully automated, and they impose a number of constraints to developers, hereby reducing reusability and flexibility.

As a response to the need to develop new methods for the analysis and engineering of BPs supported by blockchain (detailed in [1]), the present paper proposes B-MERODE. B-MERODE consists of a method and an artifact-centric shared ledger business collaboration language that can be used as input to generate BBISs using MDE. In the remainder of the paper, we use the term BBIS to refer to software running on the blockchain (often referred to as smart contracts). The proposed method aims to alleviate or even resolve the shortcomings of existing artifact-centered approaches. Our proposition is based on MERODE, a method for the design and implementation of intra-organizational Enterprise Information Systems (EISs). After having designed B-MERODE, we use it to model a rice supply chain case as a first validation of the feasibility of the approach.

The remainder of the paper is organized as follows. Section 2 introduces the research problem by first discussing requirements for solutions aiming at generating BBISs to support cross-organizational collaborations. Then, a review of the related work is proposed and analyzed in the light the identified requirements. Based on this, a number of improvements are suggested and the basic ingredients for a new solution allowing to realize such improvements are discussed. After that, Sect. 3 presents our solution called B-MERODE. To have a first validation of the feasibility of the proposed approach, Sect. 4 presents the case of a rice supply chain modeled using B-MERODE. Finally, Sect. 5 discusses the limitations of our approach and suggests further research leads.

## 2 Research Problem

### 2.1 Requirements

When developing blockchain-based solutions to support cross-organizational BPs, a number of requirements (both functional and non-functional) have to be met:

- Dynamic Participants Management [7]: to handle the dynamic nature of cross-organizational BPs, it is key to have the ability to change participants as the process is running (e.g. replacing a wholesaler by another in case the first becomes unavailable).

- Minimal Information Sharing [7]: considering the trust issues among collaborating organizations, which may even be competitors, minimizing the information that needs to be shared among the participants is key. This information can be about the identity of the participants, the data used in the process (e.g. details about an order) and information about the internal structure and processes of the participants.
- Formal Verification [5, 6, 8]: considering the immutable character of BBISs, it is crucial to ensure the correctness and soundness of these before deploying them. Indeed, once deployed, the code cannot be changed, and errors may be unfixable and thereby lead to unresolvable exploits.
- Reusability [8]: to avoid starting every process model from scratch, it is valuable for organizations to have the ability to reuse (parts of) models previously developed.
- Flexibility: when modeling and executing BPs, flexibility is needed for many different aspects, including management of the participants at runtime (c.f. dynamic participants management); support of variants of BPs [8]; and support for unpredictable processes (i.e. processes where the sequence of activities may vary from one case to another) [9]. We further emphasize this requirement by including, as part of the flexibility needs, the possibility for involved organizations to have as much freedom as possible in the specification and implementation of internal processes. Besides elements that are agreed upon as part of collaborations, the participants should remain free to implement their internal business processes as they want and using the technology of their choice.

## 2.2  Related Work

In the literature, a number of solutions using MDE to generate BBISs supporting cross-organizational BPs can be found. The majority of these solutions rely on process-centric BP models to specify the processes. It has been argued that artifact-centric BP models offer a better alternative to build a shared ledger business collaboration language [6]. The process-centric paradigm focuses on activities and their sequence and only skims on data-aspects. In contrast, the artifact-centric approach focuses on Business Objects (BOs) also called business artifacts, representing key tangible or conceptual entities relevant to the business. To define the different components of artifact-centric BPs and to compare different models within that paradigm, the BALSA framework can be used [10]. It describes the concerned processes as made of *Business Objects* (or *Business Artifacts*), *Lifecycles*, *Services* and *Associations*. Every BO can be related to others and is described by a number of data attributes. Furthermore, every object has a lifecycle that defines the key, business-relevant stages that it can go through. The services are used to make changes to BOs. These changes can be a modification of the value of the attributes, or the switch to a new state in the lifecycle. Finally, associations define the conditions under which services can be executed.

As detailed in [6], artifact-centric BPs have a number of advantages when it comes to creating a shared ledger business collaboration language. Indeed, the layered approach they adopt provides improved flexibility, reusability and adaptation as well as a clearer separation of concerns. On top of that, the type of models used are argued to be more intuitive, which facilitates their creation and reasoning about them. Furthermore, these models are declarative, which further improves flexibility. Finally, the proposed models support formal reasoning, which is crucial in a blockchain context. One of the important aspects of BPs which is not explicitly detailed in the BALSA framework is around permissions management. Another framework which incorporates the BALSA dimensions (in a slightly different way) as well as permissions management aspects is the Philharmonic flows framework [11]. However, artifact-centric BP models as described in the BALSA framework can incorporate the fine-grained access permission constructs defined in Artifact-Centric Service Interoperation (ACSI) hubs [6]. These constructs are argued to be well-suited for a blockchain-enabled cross-organizational context [6] and they are more flexible than the ones described in the Philharmonic flows framework.

Starting from the idea of using artifact-centric BP models and MDE, the present section focuses on solutions that, at least to some extent, belong to the artifact-centric paradigm. The solutions that were identified are *Lorikeet* [12], *FSolidM* [5] and a solution relying on *Dynamic Condition Response* (DCR) *graphs* [13]. The remainder of this section provides an overview of the coverage of the requirements identified in Sect. 2.1 in these solutions.

The dynamic management of participants is only explicitly supported by *Lorikeet*. In terms of information sharing, the solution which requires the least sharing is *Lorikeet*. *FSolidM* does not provide explicit support for data-related aspects and neither does the solution using *DCR graphs*. Furthermore, this solution requires sharing the identity of the participants. In terms of opportunities for formal verification, all the reviewed solutions can support it, to some extent. When it comes to reusability, it appears to be limited within every solution. Indeed, considering that for most solutions, only or mainly the activity sequence is effectively supported, this is the only perspective of processes that can potentially be reused. Finally, *FSolidM* and *DCR graphs* provide a lot of flexibility regarding many aspects of business processes. The reason for that is that they only or mainly support the activity sequence. The fact that aspects related to data, permissions and participants are mostly left aside by existing solutions strongly limits their reusability but also their supported flexibility. By supported flexibility we mean flexibility for aspects which are explicitly supported.

While the reviewed solutions can be associated with the artifact-centric paradigm, it appears that they do not adopt it to an extent allowing to reap the most benefits out of it. Mainly, the separation of concerns into different layers and the management of data and permissions could be further improved with a method that follows more closely the considered paradigm.

Considering this, we call for a solution which offers explicit support of BP aspects related to data, permissions, participants and activity sequences. Furthermore, we call for a solution that provides flexibility and reusability in these aspects. By supporting more aspects of BPs, the power of MDE can be further leveraged, and its return on investment further increased.

### 2.3 Ingredients for an Improved Solution

To create a solution which meets the objectives mentioned in the previous section, we rely on three foundational ingredients: MDE, artifact-centric BPs (c.f. Sect. 2.2) and MERODE. The present section introduces MERODE, motivates its choice and discusses its limitations in a context where the goal is to generate BBISs supporting cross-organizational BPs.

**Introduction to MERODE.** MERODE is a method that relies on MDE and artifact-centric BPs to design and implement intra-organizational EISs. The Platform-Independent Model (PIM) consists of a number of models that are precise and complete enough to allow for the automatic generation of an executable application from them. The method is supported by tools for creating and verifying models and for the generation of working prototypes from these models. The method also provides methodological guidelines for ensuring the quality of the EIS's design.

MERODE considers EISs as being made of three distinct layers: the domain layer, the Information System Services (ISSs) layer, and the Business Process (BP) layer. The first one describes Business Object Types (BOTs), their respective data attributes and the relationships among different object types. Examples of BOTs could be *Customer* and *Order*, with each order being related to a customer. As part of the domain layer, the lifecycles of the different BOTs are also described.

The ISSs layer describes the services offered by the software, divided in two types: input and output services. The former can affect business objects by updating their attributes' value or the current state of their lifecycle. The output services provide (reading) access to the BOs.

On top of that layer lies the BP layer. It defines the work organization and uses the defined ISSs to interact with the domain layer, which holds information about BOs.

While MERODE uses and/or suggests particular models to represent each element of the three layers, the main part whose transformation towards a working prototype is automated (by the tools developed to this date) is the domain layer[1]. The domain layer is described by means of three inter-related models. First, the Existence Dependency Graph (EDG) specifies the BOTs, the relationships among them and their respective attributes, using a subset of the Unified Modeling Language (UML) class diagram notation. Then, the Object-Event Table (OET) is used to specify the business events that can be triggered on the BOs. When an event fires, it triggers the execution of methods on the BOs, as specified in the OET. These methods are used to create, modify or end BOs. Finally, using FSMs, the lifecycles of the BOTs are specified. The FSMs define the states in which the BOTs can be and the transitions from one state to another, which happen when methods are executed. For more detailed explanations about MERODE, the reader is referred to [14] and [15]. The first source provides an overview and summary of the method while the second describes it in much more details.

**Motivations for the Use of MERODE.** In Sect. 2.2, motivations to adopt the artifact-centric paradigm to model blockchain-enabled cross-organizational collaborations have been discussed. One of the motivations for adopting MERODE as a founding approach is that it belongs to the artifact-centric paradigm and provides a good coverage of the BALSA dimensions. As suggested in artifact-centric BPs, MERODE adopts a layered approach with the domain layer, the ISSs layer and the BP layer. The EDG is used to specify business artifacts, their relationships and their attributes. The OET and the FSMs are then used to define the lifecycles of the different BOTs. Besides that, the different services defined in the ISSs layer allow to cover the services dimension. Finally, the

---

[1] A recent extension allows defining a presentation model, and generating tailored user interfaces accordingly [23]. This extension is however less relevant in a blockchain context.

BP layer allows defining the associations. This layered approach adopted by MERODE allows for more reusability and flexibility, both part of the requirements identified in Sect. 2.1. For example, while the OET and FSMs could be different from one solution to another, it would be possible to reuse a given EDG. Going further, a complete domain model could be reused for different purposes.

Overall, MERODE uses a set of layers and a set of models, and integrates all the different models in a consistent way, providing a rather holistic specification (and possible implementation) of the system being developed considering the covered BALSA dimensions.

When using multiple models that need to be integrated, consistency across the models is key to avoid undesired behaviors. The approach proposed by MERODE offers consistency by construction [14]. It does so first at a fundamental level, when defining the different models to use and their integration. On top of that, the approach includes a number of rules to be respected, and for which compliance can be checked automatically and formally. Such consistency checking across the different models is further detailed in [15, Sect. 6.3]. Still related to consistency, some of the models used in MERODE offer opportunities for formal reasoning (e.g. formal deadlocks detection [16]), which is one of the arguments in favor of artifact-centric approaches as well as one of the requirements identified in Sect. 2.1.

Overall, MERODE is a good candidate to meet the formal verification, reusability and flexibility requirements. However, the requirement of dynamic participants management is not explicitly supported. As for the minimal information sharing needs, these would depend upon the actual models built with MERODE.

As an alternative to MERODE, other approaches also offer a good coverage of the BALSA dimensions. For instance, [17] proposes to cover all the dimensions using a defined set of UML models (not especially in a blockchain context). It suggests using class diagrams for the business artifacts dimension, FSMs for lifecycles, Object Constraint Language (OCL) operation contracts for services and activity diagrams for the associations. MERODE is compatible with the proposition made in [17] but offers a better support for code generation and more flexibility in the way services and associations are specified.

In short, MERODE provides a robust basis to model information systems in a consistent, flexible, reusable and holistic way. However, this approach was not initially focused on the design of systems supporting cross-organizational BPs. Some of the limitations of MERODE for that context are discussed in the section that follows.

**Limitations of MERODE.** The first identified limitation is that there is no distinction between what needs to run on the blockchain and what can be run off the chain. However, such a distinction needs to be made in a blockchain-based setting, as discussed in [19], as it has an important impact in the way particular aspects (e.g. permissions) are managed.

A second limitation is about permissions management. Whether we are in an intra- or inter-organizational setting, it is important to define who (i.e. which role or which participant) is allowed to perform which action. However, MERODE does not specify how permissions should be handled, it has no explicit notion of neither participants not participant types and it does not explicitly support the dynamic participants management (c.f. Sect. 2.1).

These two groups of limitations call for a number of changes and extensions of MERODE to make it suitable for blockchain-enabled cross-organizational settings, which are discussed in the next section.

## 3   Contribution: B-MERODE

The present section introduces the adaptations that we propose for MERODE to make it suitable for blockchain-enabled cross-organizational settings, considering the limitations presented in the previous section. We thereby propose a new version of MERODE that we call B-MERODE. Figure 1 shows an overview of the different layers that we propose as well as their interactions. The elements that are depicted using dotted lines are the ones that have been added in B-MERODE or that were modified from MERODE. As further detailed in the remainder of this section, B-MERODE provides two new layers compared to MERODE: the permissions layer and the core information system services layer. In our approach, we also bring a number of modifications to the existence dependency graph and to the object-event table. The information system services and BP layers remain essentially the same as in MERODE. However, due to the distinction between what is managed on and off the blockchain, B-MERODE provides additional flexibility.

**Existence Dependency Graph.**  In order to support the permissions layer (described in the present section) as well as other aspects of the overall solution, a number of adaptations need to be performed at the level of the EDG. These changes are the distinction between regular and participant object types as well as the distinction between base and derived attributes.

*Regular and Participant Business Object Types.*  In the permissions layer, knowledge about the different participant types and business event types is required. Business event types have not been adapted in our approach and remain the same as in MERODE. However, to identify the different participant types, we propose an extension of the existence dependency graph. Instead of having only BOTs, a distinction is made between regular BOTs and the ones that represent participant types (as it is the case in the Philharmonic flows framework [11]). A participant type is a BOT that represents a type of entity being involved in a collaboration. For instance, in the example of [18], there were, among others, paddy batches, paddy ownerships, rice processing companies and wholesalers. The two first are regular BOTs and the two last represent different types of participants, of which multiple instances can be created (e.g. there might be multiple rice processing companies involved in a collaboration). In the end, participant object types are regular BOTs marked with a "participant" flag.

Describing the different participant types within a business network by means of the EDG provides a number of advantages. First, it allows describing the relationships among the participants, with some of them being explicitly able to influence the behavior of others. A second advantage is that it allows controlling the lifecycle of the different entities as they are involved in the collaboration. For instance, a particular process could be defined using B-MERODE models to approve a new entity to join the collaboration.

It would also be possible to dynamically add, modify and remove participants. Thereby, unlike MERODE, it allows to cover the dynamic participants management requirement identified in Sect. 2.1.

*Base, Derived OCL and Derived Complex Attributes.* A second modification that we propose to add is related to the attributes of the BOTs. In MERODE, every attribute is characterized by a name and by a value type (e.g. integer or string). A general distinction that can be made is between base attributes and derived attributes. Derived attributes have their value computed based on the value of other attributes. For instance, in the case described in [18], the overall quality score of a paddy batch is derived from the quality scores computed for the different steps in the process followed by the rice processing company. While MERODE never mentions what to do with derived attributes and therefore does not make an explicit distinction between how base versus derived attributes should be handled, in a blockchain context this distinction needs to be made explicitly. While it should be possible to modify the value of base attributes directly, it should not be possible for one of the participants to change the value of derived attributes directly. Indeed, the rules for the computation of a derived attribute should be agreed upon by the different participants, and it should not be possible to deviate from these rules (unless all concerned participants agree).

It is indeed not conceivable to let every participant decide how derived attributes are computed. This is due to the trust issues faced in the cross-organizational settings for which B-MERODE is proposed and which are not considered in MERODE.

Among the derived attributes, a distinction is also required. For some derived attributes, defining how the value should be computed is doable using OCL. In other cases, it is not possible or too complex. OCL allows defining the value of a given attribute based on other attributes of the same object/attributes of other objects to which a given object has access. However, there may be cases where external (e.g. web) services need to be used to retrieve some data, or where it is not possible or too complex to formulate the calculation rules using OCL. For instance, a web service could be consumed to retrieve the price of a stock at a given point in time. In a blockchain context, this means using an oracle to retrieve the data at hand. In this context, more flexibility should be provided. To do so, the designers creating B-MERODE models are allowed to write computation rules directly in the target programming language (i.e. the language in which BBIS code is generated).

So, three types of attributes are proposed in B-MERODE: base attributes whose value is manually set; derived OCL attributes whose value can be computed using OCL rules; and derived complex attributes that cannot be (easily) computed using OCL rules.

**Object-Event Table.** As explained in Sect. 2.3, the OET defines methods which are assigned a type of effect: creating, modifying or ending BOs. Creation and ending methods can remain defined as they are in MERODE. In MERODE no further details are given on how to specify the effects of a method. However, in a blockchain context it is required to specify at least the attributes that are (potentially) modified by the method, for two reasons.

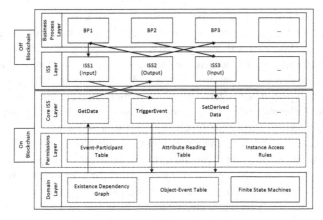

**Fig. 1.** Overview of B-MERODE layers

First, it is required to make a distinction between methods that will modify base attributes and the ones that modify derived attributes. Methods modifying derived complex attributes should be implemented as part of core information system services (more details on this later in the present section). Considering that to define which core information system services are required, it is necessary to know which derived complex attributes can indeed be modified, providing a list of modified attributes for a method allows performing this identification.

Second, in order to generate executable code for the modifying methods, it is required to know which parameters should be provided, and which attributes should get which of the parameters' value as a new value. Defining the attributes modified by a given method provides the ability to do so. B-MERODE thus further refines MERODE with defining the modified attributes for each method.

**Finite State Machines.** FSMs are defined and used in B-MERODE just as in MERODE.

**Permissions.** When modeling a collaboration, it is crucial to define the different participant types as well as their respective permissions. Apart from mentioning that authorizations are cross-cutting the three layers, the MERODE approach provides no further details as how to handle permissions. However, permissions are an essential element on which collaborating organizations need to agree, and should therefore not be left at the liberty of the respective participants. For this reason, we suggest the addition of a permissions layer (on top of the domain layer) that is executed on the blockchain and ensures that only operations allowed for a given participant are successfully executed. Furthermore, this allows controlling information sharing among the participants, which was identified as an important requirement. To model that layer, we rely on three permissions constructs of ACSI hubs that are compatible with artifact-centric BPs, as defined in [6]:

- *Views* can be used (among others) to define which BOTs and which attributes of these can be accessed by which type of participant.

- *CRUD operations* define which type of operation (create, read, update or delete) can be executed by which participant type on which BOT and/or attribute. In MERODE, the creation, modification and ending of BOs happen through the execution of methods that are triggered upon occurrence business events. Therefore, defining which participant type can create, modify or end a BO is determined by defining which business event type can be triggered by which participant type. The same goes for the modification of the attributes' values. For the reading of attributes' values, there is a need to specify which participant type can read which attribute.
- *Windows* define the conditions under which particular instances of BOTs (i.e. business objects) can be accessed (read or modified) by the different participants. For instance, in the case described in [18], a given *rice processing company* may be able to interact only with *RPCOwnership* objects that are assigned to that particular company. To define windows, we rely on the Access Control Language (ACL) used in Hyperledger Composer[2].

To represent the different permission constructs mentioned above, we propose a permissions model consisting of three components: the *Event-Participant Table* (EPT) defining which participant type can trigger which business event type (e.g. in Table 1); the *Attribute Reading Table* (ART) defining which attribute can be read by which participant type (e.g. in Table 2); and a set of *Instance Access Rules* (IARs).

For the IARs (e.g. in Sect. 4), five elements need to be defined: the type of operation (CRUD); the BOT that is concerned; the participant type for which a condition is specified; the condition itself (in OCL format); and finally, whether or not the operation should be allowed provided that the condition is met. Allowing model designers to choose whether the operation should be allowed provided that the OCL constraint is met provides the ability to specify rules either in a positive or negative formulation. For example, stating that a given customer can only see its own orders could be specified either as "a customer can see the orders that it has placed" or as "a customer cannot see the orders placed by other customers".

In the proposed permissions model, views, CRUD operations and windows are used. However, there is no one-to-one mapping between these permissions constructs and the models that we propose. The EPT contributes to the definition of a part of the CRUD operations, focusing on the create, update and delete operations. Reading permissions are mainly defined in the ART, which encompasses views and reading operations (part of CRUD operations). The IARs are used to represent the windows.

**Core Information System Services Layer.** Between the permissions layer and the ISS layer, we add another layer for *Core Information System Services* (CISSs). This layer is dedicated to the services that need to be executed on the blockchain. These include two default services: *GetData* to retrieve data from the domain layer and *TriggerEvent* to trigger events also defined in the domain layer. In addition to these services, users have to define one CISS per derived complex attribute. It will allow to modify the value of the attribute at hand, according to rules agreed upon by the different participants.

---

[2] https://hyperledger.github.io/composer/v0.19/reference/acl_language (accessed on 29/11/19).

Every call to a core ISS will check, through the permissions layer, whether or not the participant trying to create, read, modify or end a BO is allowed to do so. When one of the base attributes involved in a derived OCL attribute is updated, the derived attribute itself will have its value automatically updated. Therefore, additional core information system services are only required for derived complex attributes.

**Information System Services Layer.** In MERODE, information system services are used to interact with the domain layer. However, in B-MERODE, ISSs do not do it directly. Instead, they have to go through the CISSs layer, which will ensure that permissions are handled correctly. While the CISSs are executed and managed on the blockchain, base ISSs are not.

Using B-MERODE, collaborating organizations are free to model and implement ISSs using any technology that can interact with BBISs.

With this approach, organizations remain free to facilitate input and output in and from the domain layer as they wish and without needing to share any details about the developed services with other participants. For example, if an organization wants to combine data from the domain layer with internal data at its disposal, it can do so in an output ISS, without informing any other participant. A good example would be a service assigning tasks to individual people working for one of the participants. Indeed, the scope which is being considered in our context is the collaboration among enterprises. Therefore, while nothing prevents organizations from including details about their employees in the EDG (e.g. through an "employee" BOT), they are unlikely to be willing to share this information as part of the collaboration. Therefore, if the collaboration is kept as a scope, there is a need to manage permissions inside the organizations as well (because not every employee can do whatever he or she wants). To implement that, an ISS could be developed.

This flexibility does not come at the expense of the consistency and security of the data stored and managed on the blockchain. Indeed, every ISS needs to go through a core ISS to interact with the domain layer. Core ISSs will only execute changes/retrieve data if the operation is allowed by the permissions layer.

**Business Process Layer.** Finally, the top layer is the BP layer, as described in MERODE. Since it is also managed outside of the blockchain, participants are free to define their internal BPs using the tools, models and technologies of their choice without having to share any details with other participants. The different tasks in the process would use the services defined in the ISSs or core ISSs layer to interact with the domain layer.

### 3.1 Comparison to Related Work

Compared to other solutions, B-MERODE offers explicit support for aspects of business processes related to data, permissions, participants and activity sequence. It does so by relying on a layered approach, which allows for more flexibility and reusability. Furthermore, by explicitly covering all the aspects mentioned above, it allows to model BPs in a more holistic way. This in turn helps further leveraging the potential of MDE and thereby further increase its return on investment. Overall, B-MERODE offers a good coverage of all the requirements identified in Sect. 2.1.

Indeed, B-MERODE allows to dynamically manage participants and goes even further by allowing users to define, directly in B-MERODE, how the network of participants should be managed. In terms of information sharing, through the permissions constructs that the method incorporates, users have support and flexibility to define the information sharing needs as they wish. Regarding formal verification, the models that are used in our method to specify aspects related to data and to activity sequences can be formally verified, as discussed in [15]. On the level of reusability, by adopting a layered approach and considering the models that are used, reusability of parts of a B-MERODE model is possible. Finally, our method offers a lot of flexibility. First, the network of participants can be dynamically managed during process execution, and the way participants can evolve during the process can be specified using the provided models. Then, variants of BPs can be supported by creating new models that reuse parts of other previously developed models. On top of that, the model chosen to represent activity sequences supports unpredictable processes and variability in the process execution. Finally, with B-MERODE, organizations remain free to develop a number of services as well as their internal business processes as they wish, using the technology of their choice, and without needing to share any information about this with other participants.

## 4   Validation

In order to provide a first validation of the method that we propose, this section presents an adaptation of the rice supply chain model developed in [18] using B-MERODE. In that case, the supply chain is suffering from poor performance with issues including delayed payments, poor information access as well as fraud and tampering of information, ultimately leading to higher costs for consumers. As argued in [20], blockchain can help alleviate some of these issues. The case described in [20] is first modeled using MERODE and then with B-MERODE in [18]. The present section discusses adaptations that were made to go from the MERODE model to the B-MERODE model.

**Existence Dependency Graph.** In the EDG proposed in [18, Fig. 2], two changes need to be performed. First, we need to flag the *PaddyFarmer*, *PC* (i.e. procurement company), *RPC* (i.e. rice processing company), *WholeSaler*, *IndustrialClient* and the *Retailer* as participant types. Then, we need to make the distinction between the different types of attributes as discussed in Sect. 3. In this case, we will mark *overallQuality* as a derived OCL attribute. The EDG drawn with B-MERODE is presented in Fig. 2, in which elements in bold and italic highlight changes from the original EDG described using only MERODE constructs.

**Object-Event Table.** The OET that is proposed with B-MERODE is visually identical to the one proposed in the MERODE model [18, Sect. 2.2]. There is however a need to specify which are the attributes that are modified by modifying methods. For instance, *EV_UPDATE_TRANSP_INFO* would trigger a method on a *PCOwnership* business object, which would modify the *transportation* attribute of that object. For all the modifying methods, this information needs to be specified in B-MERODE.

**Finite State Machines.** The FSMs in B-MERODE are exactly the same as in MERODE.

**Event-Participant Table.** In the EPT shown in Table 1, a "X" in a cell means that the business event type can be triggered by the corresponding participant type. The business event types that are in the EPT are the ones found in the OET, and the participant types are the ones described in the EDG. In this EPT, one particular participant type has been added: the collaboration manager (*CollabManager*). The reason why it was added is that organizations collaborating together in a network (such as a supply chain) need to define the rules according to which new participants can join the collaboration. As this is not discussed in detail in the present paper, a simplified way of handing that is to add a dedicated participant type, the only task and permission of it is to create instances of the different participant types. In a concrete case, the collaboration manager could take different forms. It could be an actual organization (acting then as a trusted third party), or it could be a smart contract containing the rules according to which participants can be added or removed.

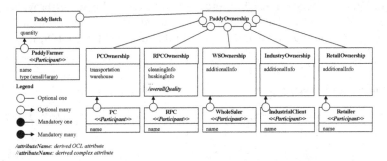

**Fig. 2.** Rice supply chain – EDG with B-MERODE

In the proposed model, every type of ownership (e.g. *PCOwnership* and *RPCOwnership*) is created by the participant type to which it corresponds (e.g. *PC* and *RPC*) when they acquire the batch. Therefore, only a procurement company (respectively, a rice processing company) can trigger the *EV_PC_TAKE_OWNERSHIP* (respectively *EV_RPC_TAKE_ OWNERSHIP*) event. Similarly, only the participant type related to a given type of ownership can mark it as finalized. Finally, the specific steps in the process that need to be executed by particular participant types and are recorded on the blockchain (e.g. cleaning step of the rice processing company) can only be recorded through the triggering of the appropriate business events (e.g. *EV_CLEAN_BATCH*) by the responsible participant type.

**Attribute Reading Table.** The second element of the permissions model that is described is the ART, available in Table 2. In that table, not all participant types are included (as BOTs from which attributes can be read). However, for all of them (except *PaddyFarmer*), the only attribute is *name* and it can be read by any participant type. For the *RPCOwnership* BOT, the scores related to the different processing steps (*cleaningInfo, huskingInfo*, etc.) are only readable by rice processing companies. However, the overall score derived from these individual scores is available to all the participants upward in the supply chain (i.e. up to the retailers and industrial clients). The remainder of the table is self-explanatory.

**Instance Access Rules.** The last element to specify in the permissions model is the set of instance access rules (IARs). An example of IAR that would apply in the rice supply chain case is the following:

```
rule OnlyOwnRPCOwnership {
    operation: [ READ, UPDATE, DELETE ],
    businessObjectType(bo): RPCOwnership,
    participantType(ptcp): RPC,
    condition: bo.creator.id != ptcp.id,
    action: DENY
}
```

The rule states that to access a *RPCOwnership* BO (reading it, updating it or deleting it), a rice processing company must be the one that created the RPCOwnership.

**(Core) Information System Services and Business Process Layer.** To provide a complete picture of the system that would be used to support the rice supply chain using B-MERODE, there are 3 layers that need to be further discussed: the CISS, ISS and BP layers.

**Table 1.** Rice supply chain – EPT

| Business Event Type | ParticipantType | | | | | | |
|---|---|---|---|---|---|---|---|
| | PaddyFarmer | PC | RPC | WholeSaler | IndustrialClient | Retailer | CollabManager |
| EV_CR_PADDY_FARMER | | | | | | | X |
| EV_CR_PADDY_BATCH | X | | | | | | |
| EV_CR_PADDY_OWNERSHIP | X | | | | | | |
| EV_CR_PC | | | | | | | X |
| EV_CR_... | ... | ... | ... | ... | ... | ... | ... |
| EV_PC_TAKE_OWNERSHIP | | X | | | | | |
| EV_PC_FINALIZE | | X | | | | | |
| EV_RPC_TAKE_OWNERSHIP | | | X | | | | |
| EV_RPC_FINALIZE | | | X | | | | |
| EV_..._TAKE_OWNERSHIP | ... | ... | ... | ... | ... | ... | ... |
| EV_..._FINALIZE | ... | ... | ... | ... | ... | ... | ... |
| EV_UPDATE_TRANSP_INFO | | | X | | | | |
| EV_CLEAN_BATCH | | | X | | | | |
| ... | ... | ... | ... | ... | ... | ... | ... |
| EV_IND_FINALIZE_ORDER | | | | | X | | |
| EV_RETAIL_FINALIZE_ORDER | | | | | | X | |

**Table 2.** Rice supply chain – ART

| Attributes | ParticipantType | | | | | |
|---|---|---|---|---|---|---|
| | PaddyFarmer | PC | RPC | WholeSaler | IndustrialClient | Retailer |
| **PaddyBatch** | | | | | | |
| quantity | ✓ | ✓ | ✓ | ✓ | ✓ | ✓ |
| **PaddyFarmer** | | | | | | |
| name | ✓ | ✓ | ✓ | ✓ | ✓ | ✓ |
| type | ✓ | ✓ | × | × | × | × |
| **PC** | | | | | | |
| name | ✓ | ✓ | ✓ | ✓ | ✓ | ✓ |
| **Retailer** | | | | | | |
| name | ✓ | ✓ | ✓ | ✓ | ✓ | ✓ |
| **PCOwnership** | | | | | | |
| transportation | ✓ | ✓ | × | × | × | × |
| warehouse | ✓ | ✓ | × | × | × | × |
| **RPCOwnership** | | | | | | |
| cleaningInfo | × | × | ✓ | × | × | × |
| ... | × | × | ✓ | × | × | × |
| /overallQuality | × | × | ✓ | ✓ | ✓ | ✓ |

In the CISSs layer, default services (as described in Sect. 3) are implemented, and no additional service needs to be defined as there are no derived complex attribute in the model. The ISSs layer describes a number of services providing reading and writing facilities for the different participants. For example, a service can be defined to read all the (accessible) information about paddy batches being processed by a given rice processing company. Such services can be developed by the different participants as they wish to do so. Finally, in the BP layer, involved participants describe the internal BPs they implement to fulfill their duties as part of the collaboration. Just as ISSs, these processes remain at the liberty and discretion of the different parties involved.

## 5  Limitations and Further Research

In the present paper, we introduced B-MERODE, a novel MDE approach to generate BBISs supporting cross-organizational BPs. B-MERODE adopts the artifact-centric BP paradigm. Unlike other comparable methods, B-MERODE has the potential to offer increased flexibility and reusability, which we identified as important requirements. Furthermore, B-MERODE can further leverage the automation potential offered by MDE. After presenting our approach, we proposed an early validation by modeling a rice supply chain.

B-MERODE is still evolving and a number of further improvements can be made. In the current proposal, B-MERODE uses six distinct models as a consequence of the layered approach, which inevitably separates a number of concerns instead of representing them into a smaller set of models. Although the separation of concerns is crucial, in a next iteration we will study whether the number of distinct models could be reduced.

Another limitation relates to the practical application of B-MERODE. Although we conceptually motivate the approach and propose an early validation by means of a practical example, a larger-scale application would be an essential next step to strengthen the validation and would allow discovering some potentially remaining weaknesses in our contribution.

Further work should also consider architectural issues related to how existing information systems would, in practice, interact with BBISs generated using B-MERODE. Those architectural aspects were beyond the scope of this paper.

Most importantly, future work will also address the transformation step required to go from the proposed models to executable code. One of the benefits of the proposed approach is that it is entirely platform independent and that it can benefit from the existing expertise on MERODE transformations. Implementations of B-MERODE could generate BBISs that can be executed on any blockchain implementation, provided that the right transformations are available. Considering the investment in time and effort that would be required for people to be able to use B-MERODE, having the ability to test the developed models onto multiple platforms could increase the return on that investment.

With B-MERODE, the present paper aims at fostering adoption of blockchain technology. An important asset is its ability to generate working software from models in a single click. Extending this to blockchain will allow creating prototypes faster and at a lower cost (as explained in [6]). Facilitating the prototyping is crucial for organizations to successfully identify and capture strategic value from blockchain technology [21]. Furthermore, prototyping is a way to improve the outcome of an organization's learning process. Such an outcome is part of the drivers of the innovation of organization's business models [22].

# References

1. Mendling, J., et al.: Blockchains for business process management - challenges and opportunities. ACM Trans. Manag. Inf. Syst. **9**(1), 1–16 (2018)
2. Seebacher, S., Schüritz, R.: Blockchain technology as an enabler of service systems: a structured literature review. In: Za, S., Drăgoicea, M., Cavallari, M. (eds.) IESS 2017. LNBIP, vol. 279, pp. 12–23. Springer, Cham (2017). https://doi.org/10.1007/978-3-319-56925-3_2
3. Amaral de Sousa, V., Burnay, C.: Towards an integrated methodology for the development of blockchain-based solutions supporting cross-organizational processes. In: IEEE 13th RCIS International Conference (2019)
4. López-Pintado, O., García-Bañuelos, L., Dumas, M., Weber, I.: Caterpillar: a blockchain-based business process management system. In: CEUR Workshop (2017)
5. Mavridou, A., Laszka, A.: Designing secure ethereum smart contracts: a finite state machine based approach. arXiv preprint arXiv:1711.09327 (2017)
6. Hull, R., Batra, V.S., Chen, Y.-M., Deutsch, A., Heath III, F.F.T., Vianu, V.: Towards a shared ledger business collaboration language based on data-aware processes. In: Sheng, Q.Z., Stroulia, E., Tata, S., Bhiri, S. (eds.) ICSOC 2016. LNCS, vol. 9936, pp. 18–36. Springer, Cham (2016). https://doi.org/10.1007/978-3-319-46295-0_2
7. Prybila, C., Schulte, S., Hochreiner, C., Weber, I.: Runtime verification for business processes utilizing the Bitcoin blockchain. FGCS **107**, 816–831 (2017)
8. van der Aalst, W.M.P.: Business process management: a comprehensive survey. ISRN Softw. Eng. **2013**, 1–37 (2013)
9. Reichert, M., Weber, B.: Enabling Flexibility in Process-Aware Information Systems: Challenges, Methods, Technologies. Springer, Heidelberg (2012). https://doi.org/10.1007/978-3-642-30409-5
10. Hull, R.: Artifact-centric business process models: brief survey of research results and challenges. In: Meersman, R., Tari, Z. (eds.) OTM 2008. LNCS, vol. 5332, pp. 1152–1163. Springer, Heidelberg (2008). https://doi.org/10.1007/978-3-540-88873-4_17
11. Chiao, C.M., Künzle, V., Reichert, M.: Integrated modeling of process- and data-centric software systems with PHILharmonicFlows. In: Workshop on CPSM (2013)
12. Tran, A.B., Lu, Q., Weber, I.: Lorikeet: a model-driven engineering tool for blockchain-based business process execution and asset management. In: CEUR Workshop (2018)
13. Madsen, M.F., Gaub, M., Høgnason, T., Kirkbro, M.E., Slaats, T., Debois, S.: Collaboration among adversaries: distributed workflow execution on a blockchain. In: Symposium on Foundations and Applications of Blockchain (2018)
14. Snoeck, M., Michiels, C., Dedene, G.: Consistency by construction: the case of MERODE. In: Jeusfeld, M.A., Pastor, Ó. (eds.) ER 2003. LNCS, vol. 2814, pp. 105–117. Springer, Heidelberg (2003). https://doi.org/10.1007/978-3-540-39597-3_11
15. Snoeck, M.: Enterprise Information Systems Engineering. TEES. Springer, Cham (2014). https://doi.org/10.1007/978-3-319-10145-3
16. Dedene, G., Snoeck, M.: Formal deadlock elimination in an object oriented conceptual schema. Data Knowl. Eng. **15**, 1–30 (1995)
17. Estañol, M., Queralt, A., Sancho, M.R., Teniente, E.: Artifact-centric business process models in UML. In: La Rosa, M., Soffer, P. (eds.) BPM 2012. LNBIP, vol. 132, pp. 292–303. Springer, Heidelberg (2013). https://doi.org/10.1007/978-3-642-36285-9_34
18. Amaral de Sousa, V., Burnay, C., Snoeck, M.: B-MERODE: Application to a Rice Supply Chain (2019). http://bit.ly/2rGeIZR. Accessed 29 Nov 2019
19. Xu, X., et al.: The blockchain as a software connector. In: Proceedings - 2016 13th Working IEEE/IFIP Conference on Software Architecture, WICSA 2016 (2016)

20. Kumar, M.V., Iyengar, N.C.S.N.: A framework for blockchain technology in rice supply chain management plantation. In: Future Generation Communication and Networking, pp. 125–130 (2017)
21. Plansky, J., O'Donnell, T., Richards, K.: A strategist's guide to blockchain. PwC report (2016)
22. Nowiński, W., Kozma, M.: How can blockchain technology disrupt the existing business models? Entrep. Bus. Econ. Rev. **5**, 173–188 (2017)
23. Ruiz, J., Sedrakyan, G., Snoeck, M.: Generating user interface from conceptual, presentation and user models with JMermaid in a learning approach. ACM International Conference Proceeding Series (2015)

# Smart Contract Invocation Protocol (SCIP): A Protocol for the Uniform Integration of Heterogeneous Blockchain Smart Contracts

Ghareeb Falazi[1]([⊠]), Uwe Breitenbücher[1], Florian Daniel[2], Andrea Lamparelli[2], Frank Leymann[1], and Vladimir Yussupov[1]

[1] IAAS, University of Stuttgart, Stuttgart, Germany
{falazi,breitenbuecher,leymann,yussupov}@iaas.uni-stuttgart.de
[2] DEIB, Politecnico di Milano, Milan, Italy
florian.daniel@polimi.it, andrea.lamparelli@mail.polimi.it

**Abstract.** Blockchains are distributed ledgers that enable the disinter-mediation of collaborative processes and, at the same time, foster trust among partners. Modern blockchains support smart contracts, i.e., software deployed on the blockchain, and guarantee their repeatable, deterministic execution. Alas, blockchains and smart contracts lack standardization. Therefore, smart contracts come with heterogeneous properties, APIs and data formats. This hinders the integration of smart contracts running in different blockchains, e.g., into enterprise business processes. This paper introduces the Smart Contract Invocation Protocol (SCIP), which unifies interacting with smart contracts of different blockchains. The protocol supports invoking smart contract functions, monitoring function executions, emitted events, and transaction finality, as well as querying a blockchain. The protocol is accompanied by a prototypical implementation of a SCIP endpoint in the form of a gateway.

**Keywords:** Blockchain · Smart Contract · Integration · SCIP

## 1 Introduction

Blockchains allow autonomous parties to engage in collaborative processes even if they have a limited degree of mutual trust. What they trust is the blockchain, which hosts exchanged data in a distributed, persistent, and immutable fashion. Blockchains thus eliminate the need for trusted third-parties, e.g., certification authorities, and lower complexity and operational costs. *Smart contracts* are user-defined applications deployed on blockchains that can be executed deterministically. They were first introduced by Ethereum [15] and later adopted by other blockchain systems. Smart contracts are usually used to model the sensitive business logic of collaborative scenarios that are governed by blockchains.

Blockchains can be categorized as permissionless and permissioned. Permissionless blockchains favor total decentralization, censorship resistance, and

© Springer Nature Switzerland AG 2020
S. Dustdar et al. (Eds.): CAiSE 2020, LNCS 12127, pp. 134–149, 2020.
https://doi.org/10.1007/978-3-030-49435-3_9

data immutability; permissioned blockchains favor data confidentiality, performance, and strong transaction processing (TP) semantics [5]. Different blockchains choose their own trade-offs at a finer degree [14]. This means that there is no "one size fits all" blockchain system, and different types of blockchains will continue to evolve and coexist. This results in the possibility that large-scale (e.g., enterprise) applications have to deal with multiple blockchains at once, each of which handling a subset of use-cases required for its own purposes [6,8].

However, blockchains lack sufficient standardization, which results in many heterogeneous APIs, different protocols and message formats. This applies to the modalities of invoking smart contract functions and monitoring their execution as well. As a result, enterprises that need to integrate the smart contracts of multiple blockchains into their processes will be faced with a tedious and error-prone task adapting to many heterogeneous interfaces.

In this work, which is a continuation of our previous research [3,4,10], we aim at providing a uniform way to interact with heterogeneous smart contracts by conceptualizing and specifying the *Smart Contract Invocation Protocol* (SCIP), which supports invoking smart contract functions and querying past and future smart contract-related events uniformly, regardless of the underlying blockchain technology. The goal is to provide an abstraction layer on top of blockchains, exposing a uniform set of operations that allow external applications to interface with smart contracts without needing to adapt to heterogeneous protocols and APIs. We also implement a prototypical gateway as a reference implementation of the protocol, and demonstrate the protocol's benefits in a case study.

## 2  Motivation

Figure 1 illustrates a collaboration setup in the domain of smart grids (from the point of view of an electrical energy provider) that requires the use of different blockchain systems: a blockchain-based energy exchange system. The management of the system is implemented using a permissioned blockchain backed by a consortium involving the various stakeholders, e.g., power plants, energy providers, and consumer households. Using a permissioned blockchain guarantees the necessary transaction processing performance and ensures confidentiality. The actual interactions between the stakeholders, e.g., selling and buying energy, is implemented using a set of smart contracts deployed on the blockchain. The scenario depicted here takes place when a power plant announces the availability of electricity at a low price. The energy provider, which monitors price changes, reacts by buying electricity in bulk from this plant and reducing the retail price of the energy it sells to households. These operations are implemented as functions of the smart contracts. To facilitate public audits, a signed digest of the previous operations is stored on a permissionless blockchain, such as Ethereum, which ensures its immutability and assigns it to a specific time instant. The digest guarantees auditors that a respective blockchain state indeed existed at that specific time instant. The necessary logic is implemented by a dedicated smart contract deployed on the permissionless blockchain.

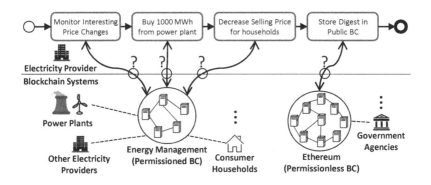

**Fig. 1.** Motivating scenario: energy management system with two blockchains.

Integrating different blockchains using traditional programming languages, such as Java or a workflow language, requires dealing with different APIs, and supporting different protocols and message formats. A typical invocation flow of a state-changing smart contract function (one that writes on the blockchain) is demonstrated in Fig. 2. Here, an external consumer application, such as our electricity provider, wants to call the function Fn1 of the smart contract SC1, so it submits a *technology-specific, signed blockchain transaction* (Tx) to one of the nodes of the desired blockchain system ❶. Then the node verifies the request and broadcasts it to the other nodes of the system ❷. Afterwards, the transaction enters the consensus process, which produces a so-called *block*, i.e., a set of agreed-upon transactions that the system has to execute next. This block is announced throughout the network and is cryptographically chained with the previous blocks at each node ❸. When the execution of the new block reaches Tx, all nodes extract the invocation parameters from its body, and use them to invoke the function Fn1 inside SC1 ❹. To this end, some form of a virtualization technology, like Docker, or Ethereum Virtual Machine (EVM) [15] is used to instantiate and run the code of the desired smart contract. During the execution, the code may read from and write to the current state causing it to deterministically change on all nodes. Although some blockchains, like Hyperledger Fabric [1], adopt a different internal flow of request processing, using blockchain smart contracts still looks similar to external consumers: they need to access a blockchain node and send *technology-specific requests* to it.

The previous scenario shows that common interactions between consumer applications and smart contracts involve: (i) invoking smart contract functions, (ii) the live monitoring of events that occur due to smart contract function invocations, and (iii) querying of past events and invocations required for data analytics and auditing. The detailed explanation of a smart contract invocation flow further shows that (iv) interacting with smart contracts involves different technologies – as a matter of fact, different networks. In addition, it is important to note that certain blockchains only support a probabilistic model of transaction durability [3,4], which (v) leaves it up to the client application to ensure that a submitted transaction has sufficient probability of being permanently stored.

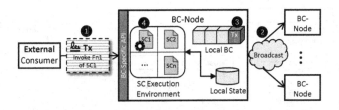

**Fig. 2.** The typical invocation process of a blockchain smart contract function.

**Problem Statement:** The previous scenario shows that participating in multiple heterogeneous blockchains requires dealing with the specificities of each blockchain system individually. This is a tedious and an error-prone task. Therefore, the problem this research approaches is *defining a set of common operations that allow smart contract clients to invoke and monitor smart contracts of heterogeneous permissioned and permissionless blockchain systems and conceptualizing and implementing a uniform protocol that supports these operations.*

## 3   Smart Contract Invocation Protocol (SCIP)

Our answer to the problem statement is the *Smart Contract Invocation Protocol* (SCIP) for the uniform interaction with heterogeneous smart contracts.

The SCIP protocol provides a homogeneous interface (roles, methods, data and message formats) for heterogeneous blockchains. The core of the interface consists of a set of *methods* that can be used by blockchain-external consumer applications, which we will refer to as *client applications*, to interact with *smart contracts*. The methods are provided to client applications via an entity, which we will refer to as the *gateway*, as this entity mediates between two or more different network technologies: the Internet and the blockchain networks. This gateway is reachable using a *Smart Contract Locator* (SCL), which is a uniform URL defined in a previous work [10], that uniquely identifies a smart contract outside the blockchain. For example, the SCL address to locate the digest-storing smart contract of the motivating scenario in Sect. 2 could look as follows: `https://gateway.com?blockchain=ethereum&blockchain-id=eth-mainnet&address =0xa0b73...0b80914`. Here, `gateway.com` is the domain of the gateway, which is thus addressable from the Internet; `ethereum` tells that the blockchain type is Ethereum; `eth-mainnet` indicates that the intended Ethereum instance is the main chain; and `0xa0b73...0b80914` is the address (shortened for brevity) at which the smart contract can be accessed within the the blockchain.

We assume that client applications *authenticate* themselves with the gateway using OAuth 2.0, and that attacks like the Man-In-The-Middle (MITM) are thus prevented. We further assume that the gateway is aware of the client's *digital*

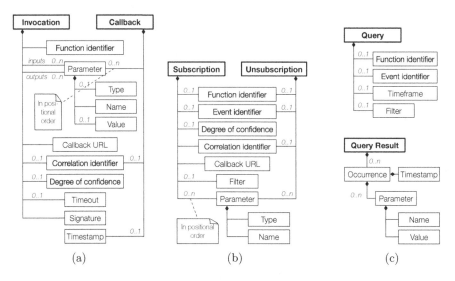

**Fig. 3.** The metamodel of SCIP messages (bold boxes) and message content fields (regular boxes). For readability, the metamodel is split into related sub-models.

*certificate(s).* These assumptions are in line with those by typical Blockchain-as-a-Service (BCaaS [11]) vendors like Amazon[1], Upvest[2] or Kaleido[3].

### 3.1 Protocol Specification

Figure 3 shows the metamodel of four request and two response messages of the protocol. Table 1 specifies the details of call constructs. The four request messages define four methods: (i) the *invocation* of a smart contract function, (ii) the *subscription* to notifications regarding function invocations or event occurrences, (iii) the *unsubscription* from live monitoring, and (iv) the *querying* of past invocations or events. All methods return a synchronous response message indicating the success or failure of the request (standard HTTP responses), and some of them additionally return one or more asynchronous responses or errors. Some methods refer to the point in time at which an event or a function invocation took place. In this context, *time* refers to the UTC timestamp of the transaction that triggered the event or invoked the function. Time is represented in SCIP using the ISO 8601-1:2019 combined date and time representation. Certain other methods have a parameter called *degree of confidence* (DoC). This refers to the likelihood that a transaction included in a block will remain persistently stored on the blockchain [4]: if a block turns out to be on a side branch of the blockchain it – including the transaction – may eventually be dropped from the blockchain. A value close to 1 means that the client application wants to receive

---

[1] https://aws.amazon.com/managed-blockchain. Visited on May 6, 2020.
[2] https://upvest.co Visited on May 6, 2020.
[3] https://kaleido.io Visited on May 6, 2020.

**Table 1.** Description of the fields used in SCIP request and response messages.

| Name | Type | Description |
|---|---|---|
| Function Identifier | string | The name of the function |
| Event Identifier | string | The name of the event |
| Inputs | Parameter[ ] | A list of function inputs |
| Outputs | Parameter[ ] | A list of function/event outputs |
| Callback URL | string | The URL to which the callback message must be sent |
| Correlation Identifier | string | A client-provided correlation identifier |
| Degree of Confidence | number | The degree of confidence required from the transaction |
| Timeout | number | The number of seconds the gateway should wait for the transaction to gain the required degree of confidence |
| Signature | string | The client's base 64-encoded signature of the contents of a request message |
| Timestamp | string | The time at which an event occurrence/function invocation happened |
| Filter | string | A C-style Boolean expression to select only certain event occurrences or function invocations |
| Timeframe | string | The timeframe in which to consider event occurrences/function invocations |
| Occurrences | Occurrence[ ] | A list of event occurrences/function invocations |
| Parameter | | |
| Name | string | The name of the parameter |
| Type | JSON schema | The abstract blockchain-agnostic type of this parameter |
| Value | any | The value of this parameter |
| Occurrence | | |
| Parameters | Parameter[ ] | A list of event/function parameters |
| Timestamp | see above | |

the result only after ruling out this possibility, whereas a value close to 0 means that it wants to receive the result as soon as it is available. It is further important to note that client messages are sent to the smart contract's SCL, which triggers the gateway. The actual SCIP endpoint is thus the gateway, which is able to extract the id of the target smart contract from the SCL and to forward incoming messages. The messages thus do not need any specific address in their body.

**The Invoke Method:** This method allows an external application to invoke a specific smart contract function. The structure of the Invocation request message, as well as the asynchronous Callback message are explained in Fig. 3a. Figure 4 shows the steps taken by the client application and the gateway when this method is triggered: The client application formulates an Invocation request message, signs it using the algorithm "SHA256withECDSA" [2] and the normative curve "secp256k1", and sends it to the gateway ❶. Then, the gateway formulates a blockchain transaction out of the request message (using the *function identifier*, and *input* fields), and signs it on behalf of the client application. Afterwards, it permanently stores the pair defined by the signed transaction (Tx) and the Signed Request Message (SRM) ❷.

The reason is that blockchain transactions are always signed by their submitters. However, the client application has no chance to do that itself since

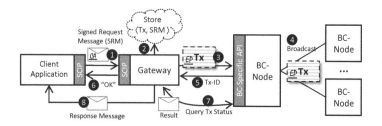

**Fig. 4.** The steps performed during the execution of an `Invoke` method.

it is unaware of the structure of the technology-specific transaction, which prevents it from formulating it in the first place. Therefore, the gateway, which knows the technical details, formulates the transaction and signs it on behalf of the client application. If the client application and the gateway are managed by two different legal entities, then the gateway might need to prove, e.g., to auditors, that the resulting transaction is indeed based on actual inputs from a unique client application request. To this end, the client application is obliged to accompany the request message with a digital signature of its content. Then, the gateway can store the pair consisting of this message along with the formulated transaction in order to prove the desired property at any time. One option for this pair to be stored is a dedicated smart contract deployed on the underlying blockchain or on a different blockchain. Another option is to store it locally by the gateway. It is left to the gateway to decide how to store it. On the other side, if the client application and the gateway are managed by the same legal entity, e.g., a gateway that manages the blockchain access for an enterprise with many internal applications, then signing the request message is not mandatory.

In the next step, the gateway sends the signed transaction to a blockchain node using its API ❸. The node, then, validates it and starts the consensus process by announcing it to the network of nodes ❹, assigning a unique id to the transaction and informing the gateway about it ❺. In response, the gateway informs the client application about the successful submission of the transaction (synchronous response to the original client request) ❻, and at the same time, starts querying the blockchain node about the status of the transaction ❼. If the transaction receives enough confidence, according to the *degree of confidence* field of the request message before the *timeout* is reached, the gateway sends an asynchronous message to the address specified by the *callback URL* field containing the execution results ❽. Note that the gateway is allowed to have its own internal timeout for such requests, which may differ from the one provided by the client. Therefore, clients should expect an asynchronous `timeout error` (wrapped as a response message) from the gateway even before the *timeout* they provided is over. To facilitate the correlation between the request message and the response message by the client application, the callback contains a copy of the *correlation identifier* provided in the request message.

**The Subscribe Method:** This method facilitates the live monitoring of smart contracts by enabling a client application to receive asynchronous notifications about the occurrences of custom or system-defined smart contract-related events or smart contract function invocations. The structure of the Subscription request message is explained in Fig. 3b. When receiving such a message, the gateway identifies the designated event/function using the fields *event identifier* or *function identifier*, respectively. The field *parameters* further helps the gateway to differentiate between overloads (functions with the same name but different parameters). Then the gateway starts monitoring the events or functions. When an occurrence is detected, the associated event outputs/function inputs are used to populate and evaluate the Boolean expression specified in the *filter*. If the expression returns true and the transaction causing the occurrence has reached the desired *degree of confidence*, a callback to the address specified in the *callback URL* field of the respective Subscription message is issued. The Callback message, described in Fig. 3c, includes details about the *parameters* associated with this occurrence as well as its *timestamp*. The *correlation identifier* of the request message is further included in the response message to enable message correlation by the client application. Note that every subscription made by a client application to the events/functions of a specific smart contract is identified by its *correlation identifier*. A new Subscription with a *correlation identifier* already in use overwrites the former one.

**The Unsubscribe Method:** This method is used to explicitly cancel subscriptions of a client created using previous invocations of the Subscribe method. The structure of the request messages is explained in Fig. 3b. It has four optional fields, which can be used in three ways: (i) if only either *function identifier* or *event identifier* plus *parameters* are present, then all respective subscriptions that belong to the target smart contract are canceled; (ii) if only the *correlation identifier* is provided, then only the subscription corresponding to the identifier is canceled; (iii) if none of the parameters is provided, then all subscriptions to the target smart contract are canceled. All other combinations are invalid. This methods only has a synchronous response that indicates its success or failure.

**The Query Method:** This method allows a client application to query the previous occurrences of events or function invocations. The structure of the Query request message, as well as the synchronous Query Result response message are explained in Fig. 3c. When receiving a Query request message, the gateway scans the history of the blockchain and searches for event occurrences/function invocations with a prototype that matches the provided *event identifier/function identifier* and *parameters*. Furthermore, *timeframe* specifies the time frame in which the search results should be considered. If the start of this timeframe is not provided, then the time of the genesis block is taken. Similarly, if the end time is not provided, then the time of the latest known block is taken. An optional *filter* can be specified similar to the Subscription message. Finally, the gateway synchronously returns a list of *occurrences*. Each occurrence indicates the corresponding event/function and which values were emitted from it or passed to it. It also indicates the *timestamp* when the occurrence took place.

```
-->  {"jsonrpc":  "2.0" , "method": "Subscribe" , "id": 1,
      "params": { "eventId": "priceChanged",
                  "params": [{"name": "newPrice",
                              "type": { "type":"integer",
                                        "minValue": 0,
                                        "maxValue": 65535 }
                             }, ...],
                  "doc": 98.9,
                  "corrId": "abcdefg12345",
                  "callback": "https://my-domain.com/callbacks",
                  "filter": "newPrice <= 500" }
     }
<--  {"jsonrpc": "2.0", "result": "OK", "id": 1}
<--  {"jsonrpc": "2.0", "method": "ReceiveCallback",
      "params": { "eventId": "priceChanged",
                  "params": [{"name": "newPrice", "value": 410}, ...],
                  "timestamp": "2019-11-06T17:08:00Z",
                  "corrId": "abcdefg12345" }
     }
```

**Fig. 5.** Example JSON-RPC message exchange for the `Subscribe` SCIP method (`-->` from client application to gateway, whereas `<--` in the other direction).

## 3.2  SCIP JSON-RPC Binding

SCIP does not prescribe SCIP endpoints which transport protocol to use to exchange its messages. That is, it does not prescribe its binding to a lower-level network protocol. In this paper, we propose a JSON-RPC [9] binding for SCIP[4]. JSON-RPC is a stateless transport-agnostic remote procedure call (RPC) protocol that uses JSON as its serialization format. It is widely used to publish the APIs of blockchains, such as Ethereum, and using it as a SCIP binding thus maintains consistency with existing blockchain conventions. Figure 5 provides an example SCIP message exchange using the JSON-RPC binding; a client application subscribes to an event and receives a synchronous confirmation and an asynchronous callback with an occurrence of the event.

## 3.3  Handling Data Types in SCIP

Generally, different blockchains support different encodings and types for parameters passed to or returned from smart contract functions or events. To hide this heterogeneity, SCIP proposes a technology-agnostic, abstract format for the data values using JSON Schema[5]. JSON Schema describes the structure of JSON data instances using basic JSON types and allows one to declare constraints on values, group values into arrays and tuples, and nest values into JSON objects. This way, native blockchain data types can be uniquely and abstractly described, and client applications can formulate function inputs in text-based JSON, without having to understand native data types.

Given the abstract specification of data inputs, the gateway can translate them into blockchain-specific formats to interact with the blockchain. For exam-

---

[4] Complete binding available at: https://github.com/lampajr/scip.
[5] JSON Schema: https://json-schema.org.

```
{"scdl_version": "1.0.1", ...        // generic smart contract properties
 "name": "SC3",                      // smart contract name
 "functions": [{                     // list of functions
    "name": "getDigest", ...         // function name and other properties
    "inputs": [{                     // function inputs
        "name": "client",            // parameter name
        "type": {                    // parameter type in JSON Schema
            "type": "string",
            "pattern": "^0x[a-fA-F0-9]{40}$"
        }}, ...],                    // other inputs of the function
    "outputs": [],                   // function outputs
    }, ...],                         // other functions of the smart contract
 "events": [{                        // event definitions
    "name": "digestStored", ...      // event name and other properties
    "outputs": [...]                 // event outputs
    }, ...]                          // other events of the smart contract
}                                    // end of SCDL descriptor
```

**Fig. 6.** Example SCDL descriptor [10] for an Ethereum smart contract.

ple, in the case of a smart contract invocation in Ethereum, the gateway will formulate a suitable *function selector* in order to invoke the intended function. This function selector is defined as the first four bytes of the SHA-3 hash of the signature of the function, which is a string composed of the function name and the parenthesised list of parameter types separated by commas, e.g., `"getDigest(address,string)"`. In order for the gateway to know which native data types to use, the request messages sent by the client application must include the abstract parameter types embedded in the *type* fields of each parameter. Then the gateway, uses 1-to-1 mapping rules predefined for each blockchain system to generate the corresponding native types out of the abstract ones[6]. This means that the gateway performs an encoding of function inputs to exactly match what the underlying blockchain expects, e.g., in terms of byte padding, arrays bracketing, serialization of complex objects, etc. The described mapping of course also applies when the client application specifies a function or event to be monitored (using the `Subscribe` method), or to be queried (using the `Query` method). Even though certain blockchains, like Hyperledger Fabric, have untyped parameters (strings), the SCIP protocol still supports abstract types to address cases like Ethereum and to enable clients to know whether a given parameter expects a numerical or textual input.

In order for a client application to learn about the abstract parameter types of functions, we assume that they have access to a *Smart Contract Description Language* (SCDL) descriptor of their target smart contracts. Such is obtained either via a dedicated *SCDL registry* or through direct contact with service providers. SCDL is a result of our previous work [10], in which we analyzed the smart contract capabilities of six prominent permissioned and permissionless blockchains, and proposed an abstract, technology-agnostic language to describe the external interfaces of smart contracts. For example, Fig. 6 shows a snippet of the SCDL descriptor of the digest-storing Ethereum smart contract presented

---

[6] Current mapping rules: https://github.com/floriandanielit/scdl#data-encoding.

in the motivating scenario of Sect. 2. The figure shows how abstract types are associated with parameter descriptions (see the `inputs` of the function).

### 3.4    Deployment Modes for SCIP Gateways

SCIP gateways represent concrete implementations of SCIP and can be deployed in a variety of configurations based on certain trade-offs. The two most immediate ones are: (a) BCaaS [11] providers, which act as intermediaries that facilitate the integration of heterogeneous blockchain smart contracts for their clients. These providers assume the responsibility of configuring the necessary SCIP gateways and managing user credentials and permissions. In addition, they are in charge of any costs incurred by accessing the underlying blockchain systems, e.g., the gas costs associated with Ethereum smart contract invocations [15]. To avoid introducing a single-point-of-failure, they may create a distributed SCIP gateway by replicating it so that it tolerates crash- or even Byzantine failures depending on the replication method used [17]. Nonetheless, such a deployment requires client applications to have a certain degree of trust in the BCaaS provider. (b) Alternatively, an enterprise may deploy its own SCIP gateway on a trusted infrastructure, e.g. on-premise, so that availability, security, and trust concerns can be controlled while still supporting its client applications with the uniform interface provided by SCIP. A disadvantage of this deployment is that the enterprise needs to manage the gateway and configure its access to the relevant blockchains itself. In future work, we will investigate the benefits and drawbacks of these and other deployments.

## 4    Validation

### 4.1    SCIP Gateway Implementation

We implemented a prototype of a SCIP gateway extending prior work intended to allow business process engines to access blockchains [3,4]. Figure 7 shows the resulting software architecture and highlights reused (light gray) and newly implemented (dark gray) components. At the top, we implemented a JSON-RPC server that exposes the SCIP methods and a JSON-RPC client that sends callback messages to client applications. Below them, the BAL (Blockchain Access Layer) core provides the logic for handling requests and sending callbacks. An *Expression Parser* supports the *filter* field of certain SCIP methods. A *Security Manager* authenticates client applications using OAuth 2.0, and handles signatures of the `Invoke` method. The core is managed by the *Blockchain Manager*, which coordinates the work of the other components and communicates with the adapter layer below it. For each supported blockchain (at the moment, Ethereum and Hyperledger Fabric), we implemented a pluggable adapter module that handles the specifics of the corresponding blockchain system. For example, it handles how smart contracts are invoked, how parameters are encoded/decoded, how events can be monitored and queried etc. Adapters communicate directly

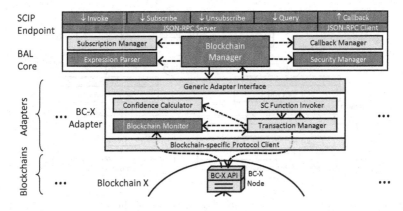

**Fig. 7.** The architecture of a prototypical SCIP gateway based on our previous work [3, 4]. Dark gray components are newly added or significantly modified.

with a blockchain node, and therefore, include a blockchain-specific protocol client to perform blockchain-specific actions, e.g., submitting a transaction. Further details and configuration instructions, e.g., on how to configure access to multiple blockchains simultaneously, can be found on Github[7].

### 4.2 Case Study Implementation

We now realize the motivating scenario of Sect. 2 using the prototypical SCIP gateway. This case study implementation logic is illustrated in Fig. 8[8].

First, we implemented a simplified energy management system via a minimal setup of the Hyperledger Fabric permissioned blockchain that contains an endorsing peer, a transaction ordering service, a certificate authority, and a CLI node, which acts as an interface to external clients. We also deployed two "chaincodes," i.e., smart contracts in Hyperledger terminology, on this setup: SC1 handles the relationship between power plants and electricity providers via the functions `changeWholesalePrice` and `buyWholesale`, and SC2 handles the relationship between electricity providers and consumer households via the function `changeRetailPrice`. The function `changeWholesalePrice` of SC1 emits the event `priceChanged` when a new price is registered by a power plant. We simulate storing digests of the operations performed on the permissioned blockchain on the Ethereum permissionless blockchain by using the Ganache[9] Etherum simulator. On this blockchain, we deploy the smart contract SC3, which contains the function `storeDigest` that is responsible for storing the digests. The access to this blockchain is provided to client applications via the *SCIP Gateway 1* and *SCIP Gateway 2* that use adapters to interface with their blockchains.

---

[7] Available at https://github.com/ghareeb-falazi/BlockchainAccessLayer/.

[8] Implementation available at: https://github.com/ghareeb-falazi/SCIP-CaseStudy.

[9] Ganache: https://www.trufflesuite.com/ganache. Visited on May 6, 2020.

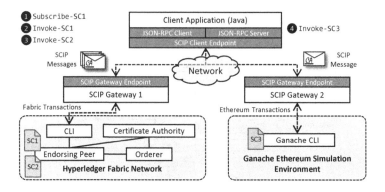

**Fig. 8.** Description of the case study showing some of the exchanged messages.

The Java application that represents the electricity provider is connected to the two gateways over a network. The client application monitors the event `priceChangedEvent` in real time by submitting a `Subscription` request message with a *filter* value of `"newPrice <= 500"`. When this condition is detected by the gateway, it sends a callback to the client. The contents of the messages exchanged during this interaction are shown in Fig. 5. In response to the event, the client application buys energy from the power plant using the `Invoke` method, which triggers the `buyWholesale` function. Afterwards, the application reduces the retail price of the energy it is selling with another call to `Invoke`, but to trigger the `changeRetailPrice` function this time. As the resulting transactions reach confidence, the client application stores the digest of the two `Invocation` messages it issued in the `SC3` smart contract of the permissionless blockchain. To this end, it issues a third `Invoke` method call, but this time to Gateway 2. This triggers the `storeDigest` function of `SC3`.

The use case shows how using the SCIP protocol to communicate with heterogeneous blockchains via gateways (that are transparent to clients) eases integration. SCIP allows a client to deal with a single protocol and to obtain a standard handling of smart contract interaction tasks, such as subscription management, event filtering, and the estimation of the degree of confidence of transactions. These would be intricate and tedious tasks if the client had to master them for each individual blockchain it needs to communicate with.

## 5    Related Work

*Blockchain interoperability* focuses on allowing blockchains to exchange data and events. It can be approached in multiple ways: notary schemes, such as Interledger [7], relay schemes, like Polkadot[10] and Cosmos[11], and hash-locking

---

[10] Polkadot: https://polkadot.network/. Visited on: May 6, 2020.
[11] Cosmos: https://cosmos.network/. Visited on: May 6, 2020.

schemes, like the Lightning Network[12]. The problem interoperability solves is enabling blockchains to communicate events though they cannot directly invoke external systems. SCIP is different in that it provides a uniform interface for external client applications to communicate with blockchains and smart contracts.

The idea of *blockchain gateways* was introduced by Thomas et al. [6]. They argue that the blockchain architecture should satisfy the same fundamental goals of the Internet architecture, and, thus, they view blockchains as autonomous systems that communicate with each other via gateways. These gateways collectively support the reachability of data stored intra-domain, and facilitate interdomain transaction mediation. However, the proposed approach does not provide a uniform entry point for external applications to blockchains.

On the other hand, *connector-based integration approaches*, like Unibright [12], introduce own platforms that communicate with blockchains on one hand and with various kinds of other, blockchain-external applications via extensible connectors on the other hand. However, unlike the SCIP protocol, these approaches can cause vendor lock-in, as they rely on proprietary platforms. In addition, they delegate the task of handling blockchain uncertainty to client applications, which requires the involvement of blockchain experts.

Xu et al. [16] take another approach on blockchain integration: they consider blockchains as *software connectors* providing external applications with communication, coordination, conversion and facilitation services. Essentially, they consider blockchains as a means to integrate applications with each other. However, they do not introduce the means that would allow client applications to communicate directly with the blockchains themselves.

Finally, the *Web Ledger Protocol* 1.0 [13] outlines a generic data model and syntax for blockchains. It also introduces the Ledger Agent HTTP API, which describes a standard mechanism to create, append, and query the blockchain. Unlike SCIP, this API does not support smart contracts and delegates too the task of handling blockchain uncertainty to client applications.

# 6  Concluding Remarks and Outlook

In this work we conceptualized and specified the Smart Contract Invocation Protocol (SCIP), a uniform protocol for the integration of heterogeneous smart contracts into enterprise applications. The protocol supports methods triggering smart contract functions, monitoring occurrences of events or function invocations in real time, and querying past occurrences. The protocol specification comes equipped with an implementation of a gateway endpoint, which we validated through a case study using it in practice. The case study shows that the benefits of SCIP are substantive in scenarios that involve multiple heterogeneous blockchains. SCIP thus advances the state of the art in blockchain integration.

---

[12] Lightning Network: https://lightning.network/. Visited on: May 6, 2020.

As future work, we plan to study alternative deployments of SCIP gateways and analyze their properties and trade-offs. We also plan to study benefits and drawbacks of alternative SCIP bindings. SCIP is available via GitHub (https://github.com/lampajr/scip) and open to contributions by the community.

More in general, SCIP paves the road for SOA-based interoperability of smart contracts and applications that transparently distribute application logic over the Internet and one or more blockchains. This may raise the need for a new wave of software engineering tools and methodologies.

# References

1. Cachin, C., Vukolic, M.: Blockchain consensus protocols in the wild (keynote talk). In: International Symposium on Distributed Computing (DISC 2017), pp. 1:1–1:16 (2017). https://doi.org/10.4230/LIPIcs.DISC.2017.1
2. Certicom Research: Standards for Efficient Cryptography 1 (SEC 1) Version 2.0. Technical report, Certicom Corp. (2009). http://www.secg.org/sec1-v2.pdf
3. Falazi, G., Hahn, M., Breitenbücher, U., Leymann, F.: Modeling andexecution of blockchain-aware business processes. SICS Softw.-Inensiv. Cyber-Phys. Syst. **34**(2–3), 105–116 (2019). https://doi.org/10.1007/s00450-019-00399-5
4. Falazi, G., Hahn, M., Breitenbücher, U., Leymann, F., Yussupov, V.: Process-based composition of permissioned and permissionless blockchain smart contracts. In: EDOC 2019 (2019). https://doi.org/10.1109/EDOC.2019.00019
5. Falazi, G., Khinchi, V., Breitenbücher, U., Leymann, F.: Transactional properties of permissioned blockchains. SICS Softw.-Inensiv. Cyber-Phys. Syst. 1–13 (2019). https://doi.org/10.1007/s00450-019-00411-y
6. Hardjono, T., Lipton, A., Pentland, A.: Towards a design philosophy for interoperable blockchain systems. CoRR (2018). http://arxiv.org/abs/1805.05934
7. Hope-Bailie, A., Thomas, S.: Interledger: creating a standard for payments. In: WWW 2016 Companion. ACM Press (2016)
8. Johnson, S., Robinson, P., Brainard, J.: Sidechains and interoperability. Preprint (2019). http://arxiv.org/abs/1903.04077
9. JSON-RPC Working Group: JSON-RPC 2.0 Specification. Technical report, JSON-RPC Working Group (2010). https://www.jsonrpc.org/specification
10. Lamparelli, A., Falazi, G., Breitenbücher, U., Daniel, F., Leymann, F.: Smart Contract Locator (SCL) and Smart Contract Description Language (SCDL). In: Yangui, S., et al. (eds.) Service-Oriented Computing, pp. 195–210. Springer, Cham (2019). https://doi.org/10.1007/978-3-030-45989-5_16
11. Samaniego, M., Deters, R.: Blockchain as a service for IoT. In: 2016 IEEE iThings/GreenCom/CPSCom/SmartData, pp. 433–436. IEEE (2016)
12. Schmidt, S., Jung, M., Schmidt, T., et al.: Unibright-the unified framework for blockchain based business integration. White paper, April 2018
13. Sporny, M., Longely, D.: The Web Ledger Protocol 1.0. Technical report, W3C Blockchain Community Group (2019). https://w3c.github.io/web-ledger/
14. Tasca, P., Tessone, C.J.: A taxonomy of blockchain technologies: principles of identification and classification. Ledger **4** (2019). https://doi.org/10.5195/ledger.2019.140
15. Wood, G.: Ethereum: a secure decentralised generalised transaction ledger - Byzantium version. Whitepaper (2018)

16. Xu, X., et al.: The blockchain as a software connector. In: 2016 13th Working IEEE/IFIP Conference on Software Architecture, WICSA 2016 (2016). https://doi.org/10.1109/WICSA.2016.21
17. Zhao, W.: Design and implementation of a Byzantine fault tolerance framework for Web services. J. Syst. Softw. **82**(6), 1004–1015 (2009). https://doi.org/10.1016/j.jss.2008.12.037

# AI and Big Data in IS

# A System Framework for Personalized and Transparent Data-Driven Decisions

Sarah Oppold[(✉)] and Melanie Herschel

University of Stuttgart, Universitätsstraße 38, 70569 Stuttgart, Germany
{Sarah.Oppold,Melanie.Herschel}@ipvs.uni-stuttgart.de

**Abstract.** Decision support systems that rely on data analytics are used in numerous applications. Their advantages are indisputable, however, they also present risks, possibly having severe impact on people's lives. Consequently, the need to support ethical or responsible behavior of such systems has recently emerged, putting an emphasis on ensuring fairness, transparency, accountability, etc. This paper presents a novel system framework that offers *transparent* and *personalized* services tailored to user profiles to serve their best interest. Our framework personalizes the choice of model for individuals or groups of users based on metadata about data sets and machine learning models. Querying and processing these metadata ensures transparency by supporting various kinds of queries by different stakeholders. We discuss our framework in detail, show why existing solutions are inadequate, and highlight research questions that need to be tackled in the future. Based on a prototypical implementation, we showcase that even a baseline implementation of our framework supports the desired transparency and personalization.

**Keywords:** Data analytics · Metadata · Model ensembles

## 1 Introduction

Data-driven *decision support systems (DSS)* are used in numerous applications today. They leverage algorithms and models of varying complexity that provide humans with predictions helpful in making decisions. While the advantages of such DSS are indisputable, they also present risks, when (inadvertently) misused or misconfigured, possibly causing severe consequences on people's lives. This has become a subject of public interest, e.g., when media divulged news on biased services. Examples include ad services that displayed ads implying a criminal record more frequently when searching for black-sounding names [24] or a system used to filter job applications that desk-rejected applicants solely because of their sex or racial origin [18]. Our vision is to provide information management solutions that facilitate the identification and avoidance of such prejudiced DSS, thereby enabling responsible DSS behavior. This paper presents a first DSS architecture with built-in capabilities that pave the way towards offering fair, transparent, and accountable services.

© Springer Nature Switzerland AG 2020
S. Dustdar et al. (Eds.): CAiSE 2020, LNCS 12127, pp. 153–168, 2020.
https://doi.org/10.1007/978-3-030-49435-3_10

Recent research, e.g., on bias in machine learning, shows that there are pitfalls everywhere in the development process of a DSS that can distort the generated predictions [2]. We believe that, despite the efforts put into developing fair [5,10], transparent [4,22], and accountable [15,23] machine learning models, we will still rely on imperfect models in many applications, including DSS. This situation reminds us of the field of medicine, where the use of drugs for the treatment of diseases poses a similar problem. For drugs, society has accepted that no perfect, side-effect free, and success-guaranteeing drug may exist. Still, they are used after they were responsibly tested and improved before going to market and transparently communicate risks and side-effects in their notice.

Analogously, we advocate that a significant step towards our vision of responsible systems would already be to devise systems that allow us to provably get as responsible as we can practically get. Two key features on this path are *personalization* and *transparency*. Here, personalization is a prerequisite for fair, best-effort, and context-aware solutions, as it allows to adapt the choice of model to a user (group) profile with some pre-defined quality criteria. This is orthogonal to research on improving models in isolation, as it takes user profiles and different optimization goals into account. Transparency, to be provided in a holistic way for the DSS, allows to improve accountability and understandability. This notion of transparency goes beyond explainable AI [22], which mostly focuses on explaining how a decision was made by a model. This ignores for instance the process of gathering training data or information on why a specific model was applied, which are integrated in our holistic notion of transparency for DSS.

This paper presents a system framework that, to the best of our knowledge, is the first holistic approach to personalized and transparent DSS. The framework optimizes the choice of model for subgroups of the population or individual persons, relying on metadata collected about data, models, and their creation processes. Optimization goals are defined based on both "classical" quality criteria such as accuracy and criteria relating to responsibility, e.g., fairness. To achieve transparency, the framework captures information to explain both choices made and results at different scales to different stakeholders in a user-friendly way. Overall, this paper contributes:

- A system framework for data-driven decision support, centered around the non-functional requirements of transparency and personalization, taking quality and usability into account. Achieving these requirements relies on several types of metadata, user profiles, and quality specifications to be met by models (Sect. 2).
- A detailed discussion on how to implement the framework components, where we describe which existing research we can build on and identify open issues that require new methods (Sect. 3).
- Using a first prototypical implementation of our framework, named LuPe [20], we showcase that even a baseline implementation of our framework supports the desired non-functional requirements of transparency and personalization on sample use cases (Sect. 4).

# 2   System Framework Overview

Our framework for personalized and transparent DSS considers different stakeholders (Sect. 2.1). Section 2.2 introduces and illustrates the framework's non-functional requirements. Section 2.3 highlights the framework components.

## 2.1   Stakeholders

A *service provider* is the legal entity that provides a specific service that incorporates a DSS. It typically employs or commissions *developers* who are responsible for the implementation and maintenance of the DSS. For the purpose of the discussion, we focus on developer tasks relating to defining models used for decision support. A *user* is an individual person that uses the service of the service provider. Finally, a *regulator* is an entity that aims at verifying the compliance of the service offered by the service provider with respect to a set of regulations. These can be internal regulations subject to audits as well as legal regulations.

## 2.2   Non-functional Requirements

Our framework considers the non-functional requirements of quality, personalization, transparency, and usability. We discuss and illustrate these using the example of a company *BestJob* that offers an online job market. *BestJob* applies a supervised learning model that recommends the most suitable job offers for each job seeking user, given their user profile.

**Quality.** We consider various quality metrics, including quality metrics to quantify model performance (e.g., accuracy) and metrics relating to fairness (e.g., bias). Given a set of quality metrics and model candidates for a specific task, the system shall determine an optimal model with respect to the quality metrics or determine a model guaranteeing certain quality bounds.

As a simple example, consider *BestJob* that aims at achieving high quality results in terms of recall while the system also has to comply with different regulations. Indeed, *BestJob* has to obey laws stating job recommendation systems must not make discriminating recommendations based on, e.g., gender. Among all available models for the task of job recommendation, suppose that one model $M_1$ obtains highest recall but is known to be gender-biased due to the training data under-representing women. Another model $M_2$ presents less gender-bias (trained on other data) but has slightly less (but still high) accuracy. Then, the latter model would be selected given the stated global optimization goals.

**Personalization.** For different individual users or user groups, the quality of a given model may vary. Thus, the system shall adapt its choice of used model depending on a user (group) profile and quality requirements. For example, reconsidering the models $M_1$ and $M_2$ previously mentioned, our framework allows to apply $M_1$ to male users while $M_2$ is applied for female users.

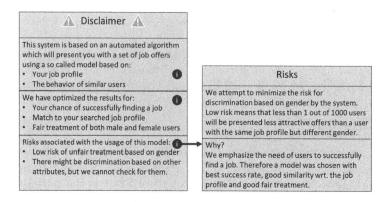

**Fig. 1.** Sample disclaimer making model behavior and risks transparent

**Transparency.** The system shall offer capabilities that easily allow different stakeholders to see what actions are performed based on which quality criteria and user profiles. In particular, the system shall be able to account for the definition and use of a model.

For instance, querying and properly processing metadata collected by our framework allows *BestJob* to communicate information that makes risks associated with their recommendations transparent. An example of a disclaimer presented to users is given in Fig. 1. It provides an overview of the data used for the recommendations, the optimization criteria the recommendations were based on, and the risks the user may be exposed to due to uncertainties and probabilities inherent in the underlying machine learning models.

**Usability.** The system shall offer tools and interfaces that allow different stakeholders to easily use the system.

Continuing the example based on Fig. 1, the initial interface provides a concise overview and allows a user to look into the details. The figure shows details for the risk assessment, focusing on gender discrimination. These details explain to users what risk of gender discrimination they are exposed to despite the effort to avoid it using an easy to understand "1 out of 1000" metaphor.

**Remarks.** While the above list is not an exhaustive list of desirable non-functional requirements for responsible DSS in general, we believe that the selected requirements are a reasonable first step in exploring solutions for responsible DSS. They are defined quite broadly to cover different aspects (including, for instance, bias as one quality dimension or diverse usability objectives) and form the foundation for further "derivable" non-functional requirements (e.g., personalization towards fairness, transparency for accountability).

Despite this limited set of non-functional requirements, many interesting research challenges lie ahead, especially given that the requirements are not independent from one another. For instance, (i) disclosing all information about the development process maximizes transparency, possibly at the cost of usability;

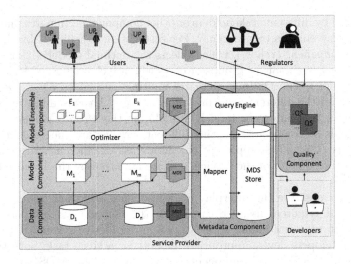

**Fig. 2.** System framework overview. (Color figure online)

(ii) global quality optimization may counter (local) personalization; (iii) multi-dimensional quality specification may reduce usability by making the system more difficult to develop. Furthermore, personalization coupled with transparency may improve the overall quality, e.g., fairness, as unfair practices of a service provider would be more easily revealed.

### 2.3  Framework Component Overview and Interplay

We now give an overview of the framework's components (colored boxes in Fig. 2) and their interplay.

The bottom layer (blue) is the *Data Component*. It manages all data sets $D_1 \ldots D_n$ relevant for models $M_1 \ldots M_m$. These models are managed by the *Model Component* (green). Each $M_i$ managed here is assumed to handle a common task $T$, providing decision support within some service offered by a service provider. We understand decision support tasks very broadly here, covering machine-learning based decision making, recommendations, etc. Apart from the fact that they share $T$, the models may differ in several ways, e.g., in the data they are trained on or in the machine learning technique used (ranging from simple supervised learning to deep learning). Therefore, both the Data and the Model Component generate so-called *Metadata Sheets (MDS)* where they store generated or collected metadata. These MDS contain metadata on quality criteria, provenance, descriptions, as well as on legal and ethical aspects. To ensure unified processing across the various system components, the MDS are stored in the *Metadata Component* (purple). The MDS received from different components are mapped to a unified format by the *Mapper* before the data is stored in the *MDS Store*. The metadata stored is then queried and processed to answer queries issued by different stakeholders or other components. In particular, metadata processing enables transparency. Personalization is achieved by the *Model Ensemble Component* (yellow), which selects the optimal model with respect to the task $T$ for individuals or groups of users who are characterized by the same *user profile (UP)*. The *Optimizer* creates multiple ensembles $E_1, \ldots, E_k$ which are intended for the different users or groups of users. The ensembles are created by selecting or combining the models available in the *Model Component*. Optimization goals or constraints for the different settings are specified in *Quality Specifications (QS)*. These represent the desiderata of different stakeholders on the performance quality of the service, and are managed by the *Quality Component* (orange).

To further describe the interplay of components and their relationships to non-functional requirements, let us discuss the components' purpose during model development and model application in a productive system, respectively.

When developers devise appropriate models for a given task, both the data component and the model component, together with their MDS, are relevant. As model appropriateness is guided by the quality component, it is equally relevant during the development stage. Overall, during model development, transparency offered via usable interfaces supports developers in testing and refining their models to best match predefined quality criteria. Personalization is only indirectly considered, as developers have to ensure that available data, models, and quality criteria are rich and diverse enough to support personalization.

An example of framework operation during the model application stage has been discussed in Sect. 2.2. Clearly, at this stage, transparency is ensured by the metadata component and targets primarily users and regulators, by offering them appropriate access and interfaces to the metadata. But also, developers have an interest in accessing metadata collected during model application, e.g., to subsequently tune their models. The optimizer, user profiles, and the quality component are the main components involved in personalization for users.

## 3    Component Details

After the overview of our framework focusing on non-functional properties and how different components relate to these, we now discuss details on the framework's individual components. Due to space constraints, we generalize the discussion of Metadata Sheets spread over several components (see Fig. 2). We also omit details on the Metadata Component because, while there certainly are interesting research questions to be solved for this component, it most readily can use existing technology for data integration of semi-structured data and possibly evolving query workloads (e.g., data lakes or RDF triple stores).

### 3.1    Metadata Sheets

Metadata Sheets (MDS) are collections of one or more metadata documents describing an object that is part of the DSS, i.e., a data set, model, or model ensemble. MDS are ideally automatically and incrementally populated alongside the development, limiting the captured metadata to pertinent information for transparency and personalization.

The scope of information to be covered by MDS in order to support personalization and transparency is quite large. Basically, every decision during development is important and should be recorded, as it may serve as evidence of responsible development or can be used by developers to improve their product. While it is fairly easy to describe the desired information to be included in MDS, it is more challenging to precisely define, model, and collect these metadata.

To define and model the desired metadata, we can leverage existing work on responsible data set metadata [9,12] and machine learning model metadata [6, 19,28]. Take for example datasheets for data sets [9], which is a question-answer based solution. It divides questions about data sets in different categories, i.e., creation motivation, composition, collection process, preprocessing, distribution, maintenance, and legal and ethical considerations. Important information, e.g., on data set quality is not included. Moreover, the free text fields leave the amount of information, level of granularity, and level of formality open to the developers. Overall, none of the existing metadata models for data sets and models provides information on all topics we consider important. More importantly, no systematic analysis of what metadata is actually needed for transparency or personalization exists, calling for research on identifying relevant metadata for our targeted transparency and personalization queries.

While it is unlikely that all metadata can be captured automatically, we aim at maximizing the automatic collection and population of the MDS to ease the burden otherwise put on developers. We can build on provenance techniques [11] that yield metadata that keep track of (data) processing. Furthermore, data profiling techniques [1], quality metrics [3], and non-discrimination metrics [5, 10] evaluated over data sets and machine learning models allow us to capture their properties and quality. However, most research in these areas results in a new, separate tool that typically does not seamlessly integrate in a software development environment. Research is necessary to instrument software that developers are already using to capture the necessary information. This includes for instance using code markup to automatically generate metadata (analogous to, e.g., JavaDoc, requiring developers to do some, but familiar work) or "piggy-backing" code on the familiar software that automatically collects metadata behind the scenes (e.g., code that automatically creates a data dependency graph from a program). Additional metadata can be automatically extracted from documents that have already been created and used for other purposes, such as requirement specifications. While natural language processing (NLP) can extract some metadata form such sources that often provide information in text form, NLP typically does not target the type of metadata required for transparency and personalization. This calls for research on information extraction techniques tailored to the metadata model used for MDS.

## 3.2  Optimizer

Intuitively, the goal of the Optimizer is to select the best model for each individual user or group of users, such that the choice of model is personalized rather than using a single model for all users that may not be able to manage complex decision boarders in the data stemming from different behavioral user profiles. What best means is encoded by a quality specification associated to user profiles, further discussed when presenting the Quality Component in Sect. 3.3. To achieve this personalization, we employ model ensembles [21]. Using model ensembles, the risk of making bad decisions is potentially reduced by reducing the risk of wrong results by a single poor performing model.

More formally, given the set of models for a task $T$ of the Model Component and associated MDS, as well as a collection of multi-dimensional optimization goals that define different model application contexts, we need model ensemble algorithms that output a minimal set of model ensembles $\{E_1, \ldots, E_k\}$ suited for the optimization goals.

A first line of relevant research towards addressing this problem are approaches for fair model ensembles. Dwork et al. [8] train a linear classifier model for each user group which they then combine using a joint loss function which can also enforce fairness constraints. Calders et al. [5] train one Bayes model for each value of the sensitive value and, on top, an overall classifier which chooses the decision of one of the separate Bayes models. These model ensemble solutions demonstrate that improving fairness is possible using model ensembles. But we need more flexible solutions that call for novel algorithms for context-aware model ensembles and the support for multi-dimensional, possibly conflicting optimization goals, e.g., accuracy vs fairness. That is, we aim at creating a model ensemble based on the model quality with respect to the feature space matching a user profile. Existing algorithms in a second line of research, in particular for dynamic ensemble generation [7,14,25–27] can neither incorporate the context information nor go beyond one optimization criterion (typically accuracy).

We plan to extend the dynamic ensemble generation algorithms in order to enable personalized decision support system. First, we have to incorporate new metrics such as bias metrics, and allow for optimization of different quality goals, e.g., using skyline algorithms for pareto optimal solutions. In Sect. 4.1 we present a baseline algorithm for dynamic ensemble selection.

Of course, the performance gained by using model ensembles heavily relies on the set of input models. Within the Model Component, no model has to be of good quality for all quality metrics and all possible data objects. It suffices to achieve good quality results with respect to some quality metrics for some of the data space. In this setting, developers face the challenging problem to learn a diverse set of models that is able to cover the optimization for all quality metrics and the whole data space.

While there is research on machine learning and diversity, most of it focuses on either creating models to produce diverse results [17] or are learned to determine appropriate diversity, or distance metrics [16]. To the best of our knowledge, no research on diversity of models has been conducted so far.

The set of multi-dimensional optimization goals stems from different application requirements on multiple dimensions by different stakeholders. When combined, these may present some goals that simply cannot be met (their score being maximized) simultaneously. It is then crucial that the set of models available in the Model Component holds at least one model that is "good enough" in at least one dimension, to achieve a partial optimization goal. However, the set of models should not be too specific or large. Thus, in devising algorithms that determine a finite set of models, future research needs to find the "sweet spot" between minimizing size of the finite set of models vs maximizing the coverage of models with respect to optimization goals, while ensuring diversity of models.

## 3.3 Quality Component

The Quality Component encapsulates quality specifications (QS) that specify the optimization goals mentioned above. These can relate to user preferences and profiles, be imposed by regulators, or translate the optimization goals developers aim at when devising the decision support system.

The QS are separated from the actual models as they should not be part of the application itself. The developers should not be the ones to single-handedly decide which responsibility criterion is more important than others or which fairness metric to use. That is, our framework aims for a separation of concerns regarding the development of the DSS and the decision on which optimization goals the system should strive for (given the different stakeholders with different interests in mind). After careful consideration, we opt to place the Quality Component in the service provider space (see Fig. 2) because this is where it is used and no user wants to store multiple of these files for multiple systems on their different computers. However, the service provider should allow transparent access to QS (to stakeholders with legitimate interest) and should provide means to add or update QS.

For users, we want to use user-specific information to obtain a personalized model ensemble. This requires users to provide some personal information through their user profile. We are aware of the discussion on including protected attributes in decision making. In this work, we follow the path to explore how to improve the decision making process in terms of diversity or fairness by leveraging protected attributes that allow to detect and eliminate discrimination. Nevertheless, this should comply with legal and ethical rules. When not stored at the level of a single person, i.e., when using user profiles as a generic description of a group of persons, our framework could still achieve its goal without requiring protected attributes from individuals.

Overall, QS define how a DSS should behave, in general along multiple dimensions (accuracy, runtime, bias, etc.). This resembles policies that are formal guidelines for behavior of information systems. They are for example used in the context of autonomic computing [13]. In particular Goal Policies, where a predefined desired state of the system is reached automatically if respective conditions are met by the current state, may be used to implement QS. However, we are not aware of any techniques that deal with multiple QS with possibly conflicting desired behaviors. We have already raised this issue previously when discussing the components taking such possibly conflicting QS as input.

Given a collection of possibly conflicting QS that take multiple dimensions into account, we need an efficient algorithm to determine the minimal set of QS that is representative of the full collection. Otherwise, the other components relying on the QS would have to deal with an "unclean" input possibly yielding higher runtime or lower output quality. Clearly, the notions of minimal and representative first have to be formalized. Based on these foundations, research on algorithms to find this core set of QS or, alternatively, to enumerate possible alternative solutions can be explored.

## 4    Framework Implementation and Validation

Above, we have discussed how to possibly implement the different framework components, leveraging existing research and identifying open research questions. Clearly, our system framework is in its exploratory stage and it may take years to investigate all open research questions fully, especially as there is room for a variety of approaches. In order to demonstrate the framework's pertinence to filling the gap in providing personalized and transparent DSS, this section presents a first prototypical implementation, called LuPe [20]. We discuss in Sect. 4.1 how we developed the critical parts of the system framework to produce a proof of concept of our system framework. Further details on LuPe can be found in a demonstration description [20]. Section 4.2 then uses LuPe in a use case based validation of achieved personalization and transparency, respectively.

### 4.1    The LuPe System Prototype

So far, LuPe focuses on binary classification tasks. For illustration and also in the following evaluation, we refer to a classification problem that arises in a credit allocation scenario, where a bank employee uses LuPe to help her decide whether a customer should receive a loan or not. For our implementation, we rely on open source tools, i.e., Apache Spark ML library[1] or Angular IO[2]. We also use the publicly available German Credit Data[3] data set.

While deciding on the metadata to model within the MDS processed by LuPe, we simply settled for metadata that could be captured easily and that trivially combine existing methods. That is, we manually derived data to form MDS templates and included information on general characteristics, provenance information, variable descriptions for data sets, and model specific details for machine learning models (similar to data set nutrition labels [12]). We enriched

---

[1] https://spark.apache.org/docs/latest/api/python/pyspark.ml.html.

[2] https://angular.io.

[3] https://archive.ics.uci.edu/ml/datasets/statlog+(german+credit+data).

the templates with automatically, collected metadata e.g., using simple data profiling methods provided by Apache Spark and bias metrics that we implemented ourselves. All MDS can be viewed online[4].

In order to create a diverse set of models in LuPe, we chose to optimize models for accuracy because this option was available out-of-the-box in Apache Spark ML. We introduced model diversity by using used different types of Apache Spark ML learners and different subsets of the training data set to learn multiple binary classification models.

In LuPe, the quality specifications define for a given state (i.e., of user group feature characteristics) the desired state in form of a quality metric that has to be optimized by the system. More formally, we define a quality specification $QS$ as a 3-tuple $QS = (og, c, s)$, with a set $og$ of optimization goals (e.g, minimize false positives), a set of constraints $c$ that the model should satisfy, and an optional corresponding action if the constraint cannot be met, e.g.,

$$\text{apply if } \frac{p(label = positive|gender = female)}{p(label = positive|gender = male)} \geq 0.8$$
$$\text{discard } otherwise$$

An example of a quality specification in JSON format is given below. The optimization goal of $q1$ is "maximize accuracy metric" and the expression in the user group determines that $q1$ applies to women. Apart from optimizing the system for all users, this Quality Profile allows to specifically aim at maximizing the accuracy for women.

```
{''id'': ''q1'',
 ''description'': ''Maximize accuracy for women'',
 ''optimizationGoal'': {
     ''qualityMetric'': ''accuracy'',
     ''direction'': ''max''},
 ''userGroup'': ''sexAndStatusclassVec_A92 = 1.0''}
```

To implement an Optimizer for the Model Ensemble Component of LuPe, we extend dynamic ensemble generation as existing algorithms [7,14,25–27] cannot take multi-dimensional optimization goals into account.

Algorithm 1 shows pseudocode for a baseline Optimizer implementation for dynamic model selection. More formally, given a quality specification $QS = (og, c, s)$, a set of models $\mathcal{M}$, and respective metadata $MDS_i^M$ for model $M_i \in \mathcal{M}$, find the model $M \in \mathcal{M}$ which fulfils the set of constraints $c$ and optimizes the optimization goal $og$. Given a quality specification $QS$, we first compare the available models to the constraints in order to eliminate all invalid models, i.e., all models whose quality profile does not qualify them to be used. Next, we apply Dynamic Classifier Selection by Local Accuracy [26] on the valid set of models. To explain our model decision in detail, we use the ranked list of models with

---

[4] LuPe website: https://www.ipvs.uni-stuttgart.de/departments/de/research/projects/fat_dss/.

**Algorithm 1:** Dynamic model selection implementation on quality specifications.

---

**Input:** $QS = (og, c, s)$, $\mathcal{M} = \{M_1, ..., M_n\}$
**Output:** $\mathcal{M}_{sorted}$: list of models ranked by their quality
$\mathcal{M}_{sorted} \leftarrow \emptyset$                    //new List of models
$\mathcal{M}_{valid} \leftarrow \emptyset$                    //new List of models
**forall the** $M \in \mathcal{M}$ **do**
    **forall the** $c \in QS.c$ **do**
        **if** $M.getMDS.qualityprofile$ $satisifes$ $c \wedge c.event \neq$ '$discard$' **then**
            $\mathcal{M}_{valid} \leftarrow \mathcal{M}_{valid} \cup M$

$\mathcal{M}_{sorted} \leftarrow DCSLA(og, \mathcal{M}_{valid})$
$MDS \leftarrow generateMetadata(\mathcal{M}_{sorted}, QS)$
$MDSStore.add(MDS)$
**return** $\mathcal{M}_{sorted}$

---

respect to the accuracy for $og$ in the feature space next to $s$. As we described earlier, we also store a $MDS^E$ for each model ensemble, which is why we collect the necessary information and store it in the MDS store.

The Metadata Component is, at its essence, a data integration system, for which a large body of research and practical solutions exist. However, since we opted to create all MDS in a similar fashion and we only created one MDS for each model or data set in our prototype, we do not need to integrate the MDS to illustrate the power of our system framework idea. We simply store the JSON files locally without making use of bigger storage system solutions.

In general, implementations of our framework need sophisticated querying capabilities to satisfy the different needs of the various stakeholders. This can be achieved using visualizations, query languages, chatbots or a combination of all approaches. To keep it simple in our first framework implementation, we opt to rely on simple functions which can be called to access the stored MDS data, which obviously restricts the flexibility of the query engine. LuPe provides access to lists of models and data sets, as well as all MDS details for other components. In accordance with the implementation description of the Model Ensemble Component, the optimizer queries and uses this information to identify personalized model ensembles. We also provide human stakeholders with access to the MDS Store through visualizations. Screenshots of these visualizations, in particular informed consent forms provided for users and component overview and component details provided for developers and regulators are shown in Fig. 3.

Given the above description of the LuPe framework implementation, we validate that it achieves personalization and transparency through two use cases.

### 4.2   Use Case Based Validation of Personalization and Transparency

**Personalization.** Our first study focuses on personalized decision support, with the intention of reducing gender bias. In order to assess whether the quality has indeed improved when personalizing for the user group gender, we perform a quantitative evaluation. For evaluation purposes, the data set needs to be split into two data sets $D1$ and $D2$, the former being used to train and evaluate the

**Table 1.** Accuracy of individual models during training (a) and model ensemble (b)

| Model | Accuracy (All) | Accuracy (sex='Female') | Accuracy (sex='Male') |
|---|---|---|---|
| $m1$ | 0.8283 | 0.9255 | 0.7796 |
| $m2$ | 0.8310 | 0.9247 | 0.7841 |
| $m3$ | 0.7633 | 0.9059 | 0.6918 |
| $m4$ | 0.7731 | 0.9116 | 0.7036 |
| $m5$ | 0.7771 | 0.9056 | 0.7127 |
| $m6$ | 0.8402 | 0.9101 | 0.8052 |
| $m7$ | 0.8397 | 0.9140 | 0.8025 |
| $m8$ | 0.8141 | 0.8910 | 0.7756 |
| $m9$ | 0.7977 | 0.8959 | 0.7484 |
| $m10$ | 0.7650 | 0.8756 | 0.7096 |

| Number of users | 9792 |
|---|---|

| Accuracy | |
|---|---|
| Without personalization | 0.8509 |
| With personalization | 0.8531 |

(a) Accuracy of different models for all users and for gender user groups

(b) Accuracy of model ensemble

Informed consent:

General disclaimer

This application is based on data analysis predictions using machine learning algorithms. We used the publicly availble German Credit Dataset and Apache Spark ml libraries to train machine learning models. For additional information, please contact us via e-mail.
People are different and the decision making process should reflect this. Therefore, we have trained a diverse set of models which perform differently for different users. To follow our paradigm offering a fair service, we select the best available model for the chosen level of personalization and quality metric.

Personalized performance information

| model ID | accuracy for all | accuracy for female | accuracy for similar users |
|---|---|---|---|
| m2 | 0.739 | 0.738 | 0.9 |
| m3 | 0.616 | 0.659 | 0.8 |
| m4 | 0.717 | 0.596 | 0.75 |
| m6 | 0.732 | 0.706 | 0.85 |
| m7 | 0.751 | 0.651 | 0.8 |
| m5 | 0.688 | 0.647 | 0.95 |

(a) Alice's informed consent sheet

(b) Backend overview

**Fig. 3.** Screenshots of the credit classification scenario LuPe frontend [20].

models and the latter to evaluate the model ensembles. Since the previously mentioned German Credit data set is too small to be further split, we apply LuPe for a second scenario. In this scenario, we classify users with respect to their wage using the publicly available Adult[5] data set. The respective MDS for this second scenario are available at the LuPe website as well. Accuracy results for ten individual models $m1$ through $m10$ during the training phase are shown in Table 1(a), while Table 1(b) reports results of the model ensembles.

Using the overall best model $m6$ during training for all users in the test data set achieves an accuracy of 0.8509. When opting for the best model for different user groups, i.e., $m1$ for female and $m6$ for male users, we achieve a slightly higher accuracy of 0.8531. While LuPe performs slightly better on this very low personalization level that merely distinguishes users according to gender, this is

---

[5] https://archive.ics.uci.edu/ml/datasets/adult.

not yet satisfactory. Having used LuPe, we can study the metadata sheets. We uncover that the data shows class imbalance with about two thirds of the data in the bad outcome class. We assume as a result that several models present high false negative rates and that the models' overall quality might not be sufficient. This insight is gained by leveraging the transparency feature of LuPe, further discussed below. Clearly, the results we obtain show that further research is needed on diversifying the set of trained models as discussed in Sect. 3.2. Also, for better results, we have explored more fine grained personalization levels, i.e., based on profiles similar to a user profile (see Fig. 3(a)). While accuracy results are promising, the algorithm does not scale to the larger Adult data set. This emphasizes the importance of future research on more fine grained model quality profiles and more efficient personalization algorithms.

**Transparency.** For regulators and developers, LuPe offers a glimpse behind the scenes which is depicted in Fig. 3(b). This visualization provides these stakeholders with an overview of the ingredients forming the system, including all data sets, models, and model ensembles. Additionally, in this simplistic visualization we provide all metadata information for each ingredient on demand. Using the metadata stored by LuPe we are already able to give an overview on possibly complex systems and to answer various audit questions such as *"Has the data been normalized before model training?"* or *"What data was the model trained on?"*. But clearly, a lot of additional metadata is necessary to support the wide range of possible queries. While this emphasizes the need to model and collect additional metadata for various types of queries, these queries need to be efficiently executed and the results presented to users in an understandable way.

For a user, LuPe offers a visual interface that displays an informed consent sheet (see Fig. 3(a)). It textually points out the intention of using personalization and the impact that different personalization levels may have on the accuracy experienced by the user. Determining if, how, and to what extent such information (and its presentation) affect users needs to be systematically studied, e.g., through user studies.

## 5 Conclusion and Outlook

This paper presented a system framework for personalized and transparent decision support systems. Exploring such systems is essential in addressing the challenges that arise with the increasing demand to devise fair, accountable, and transparent data-driven decision support systems.

After a system framework overview, we discussed individual components in detail, highlighting the current state of the art and discussing why existing solutions are not adequate. We then presented a first implementation of our framework, incorporating first baseline solutions that address the more general research challenges that need to be further explored. Based on two use cases, we validated that our solutions to enable personalized and transparent decision support systems are promising, and are worth investigating in the future.

Exploring and optimizing the technical feasibility and aspects of supporting personalization and transparency is only the first step in quickening the adoption of responsible decision support systems in practice. further research is necessary in many different directions. To name just a few, these include aspects of security and privacy, reduction of ramp-up costs of setting up and maintaining such systems to continue to allow start-ups to be profitable, or resolving the tension between transparency and intellectual property, as proprietary models are at the heart of many modern business models.

# References

1. Abedjan, Z., Golab, L., Naumann, F.: Profiling relational data: a survey. VLDB J. **24**(4), 557–581 (2015). https://doi.org/10.1007/s00778-015-0389-y
2. Barocas, S., Selbst, A.D.: Big data's disparate impact. Calif. L. Rev. **104**, 671 (2016)
3. Batini, C., Scannapieco, M.: Data Quality: Concepts Methodologies and Techniques. Data-Centric Systems and Applications. Springer, Heidelberg (2006). https://doi.org/10.1007/3-540-33173-5
4. Burrell, J.: How the machine 'thinks': understanding opacity in machine learning algorithms. Big Data Soc. **3**(1), 1–12 (2016)
5. Calders, T., Verwer, S.: Three naive Bayes approaches for discrimination-free classification. Data Min. Knowl. Discov. **21**(2), 277–292 (2010)
6. Data Mining Group: Portable format for analytics (PFA). http://dmg.org/pfa/index.html. Accessed 11 Oct 2019
7. Dos Santos, E.M., Sabourin, R., Maupin, P.: A dynamic overproduce-and-choose strategy for the selection of classifier ensembles. Pattern Recogn. **41**(10), 2993–3009 (2008)
8. Dwork, C., Immorlica, N., Kalai, A.T., Leiserson, M.: Decoupled classifiers for group-fair and efficient machine learning. In: FAT* (2018)
9. Gebru, T., et al.: Datasheets for datasets. In: FAT ML (2018)
10. Hajian, S., Domingo-Ferrer, J.: Direct and indirect discrimination prevention methods. In: Custers, B., Calders, T., Schermer, B., Zarsky, T. (eds.) Discrimination and Privacy in the Information Society: Data Mining and Profiling in Large Databases, vol. 3. Springer, Heidelberg (2013). https://doi.org/10.1007/978-3-642-30487-3_13
11. Herschel, M., Diestelkämper, R., Ben Lahmar, H.: A survey on provenance: What for? What form? What from? VLDB J. **26**(6), 881–906 (2017). https://doi.org/10.1007/s00778-017-0486-1
12. Holland, S., Hosny, A., Newman, S., Joseph, J., Chmielinski, K.: The dataset nutrition label: a framework to drive higher data quality standards. Draft (2018)
13. Kephart, J.O., Walsh, W.E.: An artificial intelligence perspective on autonomic computing policies. In: POLICY (2004)
14. Ko, A.H., Sabourin, R., de Souza Britto Jr., A.: From dynamic classifier selection to dynamic ensemble selection. Pattern Recogn. **41**(5), 1718–1731 (2008)
15. Kroll, J.A., Barocas, S., Felten, E.W., Reidenberg, J.R., Robinson, D.G., Yu, H.: Accountable algorithms. Univ. PA Law Rev. **165**, 633–705 (2016)
16. Kulis, B.: Metric learning: a survey. Found. Trends® Mach. Learn. **5**(4), 287–364 (2013)
17. Li, J., Galley, M., Brockett, C., Gao, J., Dolan, B.: A diversity-promoting objective function for neural conversation models. In: NAACL-HLT (2016)

18. Lowry, S., Macpherson, G.: A blot on the profession. Br. Med. J. (Clin. Res. Ed.) **296**(6623), 657–658 (1988)
19. Mitchell, M., et al.: Model cards for model reporting. In: FAT* (2019)
20. Oppold, S., Herschel, M.: LuPe: a system for personalized and transparent data-driven decisions. In: CIKM (2019)
21. Polikar, R.: Ensemble based systems in decision making. IEEE Circ. Syst. Mag. **6**(3), 21–45 (2006)
22. Ribeiro, M.T., Singh, S., Guestrin, C.: "Why should I trust you?": explaining the predictions of any classifier. In: KDD (2016)
23. Singh, J., Cobbe, J., Norval, C.: Decision provenance: harnessing data flow for accountable systems. IEEE Access **7**, 6562–6574 (2019)
24. Sweeney, L.: Discrimination in online ad delivery. Queue **11**(3), 1–19 (2013)
25. Woloszynski, T., Kurzynski, M.: A probabilistic model of classifier competence for dynamic ensemble selection. Pattern Recogn. **44**, 2656–2668 (2011)
26. Woods, K., Kegelmeyer, W.P., Bowyer, K.: Combination of multiple classifiers using local accuracy estimates. TPAMI **19**(4), 405–410 (1997)
27. Woźniak, M., Graña, M., Corchado, E.: A survey of multiple classifier systems as hybrid systems. Inf. Fusion **16**, 3–17 (2014)
28. Yang, K., Stoyanovich, J., Asudeh, A., Howe, B., Jagadish, H.V., Miklau, G.: A nutritional label for rankings. In: SIGMOD (2018)

# Online Reinforcement Learning for Self-adaptive Information Systems

Alexander Palm(✉)[iD], Andreas Metzger[iD], and Klaus Pohl[iD]

paluno – The Ruhr Institute for Software Technology, University of Duisburg-Essen,
Essen, Germany
{alexander.palm,andreas.metzger,klaus.pohl}@paluno.uni-due.de

**Abstract.** A self-adaptive information system is capable of maintaining its quality requirements in the presence of dynamic environment changes. To develop a self-adaptive information system, information system engineers have to create self-adaptation logic that encodes when and how the system should adapt itself. However, developing self-adaptation logic may be difficult due to design time uncertainty; e.g., anticipating all potential environment changes at design time is in most cases infeasible. Online reinforcement learning (RL) addresses design time uncertainty by learning the effectiveness of adaptation actions through interactions with the system's environment at run time, thereby automating the development of self-adaptation logic. Existing online RL approaches for self-adaptive information systems exhibit two shortcomings that limit the degree of automation: they require manually fine-tuning the exploration rate and may require manually quantizing environment states to foster scalability. We introduce an approach to automate the aforementioned manual activities by employing policy-based RL as a fundamentally different type of RL. We demonstrate the feasibility and applicability of our approach using two self-adaptive information system exemplars.

**Keywords:** Self-adaptation · Reinforcement learning · Information system engineering

## 1 Introduction

The concept of *self-adaptation* facilitates developing information systems that are capable of maintaining their quality requirements even if the systems' environment changes dynamically [3,25]. Self-adaptation thereby helps developing systems that can operate in a resilient way at run time. To this end, a self-adaptive information system can modify its own structure, parameters and behavior at run time based on its perception of the environment, of itself and of its requirements. An example is a self-adaptive online store that must maintain its performance requirements under changing workloads. Faced with a sudden increase in workload, the online store may adapt itself by deactivating optional system features to use less resources; e.g., it may deactivate its resource-intensive

© Springer Nature Switzerland AG 2020
S. Dustdar et al. (Eds.): CAiSE 2020, LNCS 12127, pp. 169–184, 2020.
https://doi.org/10.1007/978-3-030-49435-3_11

recommendation engine [17]. Another example is a predictive business process monitoring system that generates alarms for triggering proactive process adaptations [12,21]. If a violation of a process performance objective is predicted, the system may trigger an adaptation of the running process to use more or different resources to speed up the execution of the remaining process steps.

To develop a self-adaptive information system, information system engineers have to develop *self-adaptation logic* that encodes when and how the system should adapt itself. Information system engineers, for instance, may specify event-condition-action rules that define which adaptation action is executed in response to a given environment change. Developing self-adaptation logic requires an intricate understanding of the information system and its environment, and how adaptations impact on system quality [7,8]. Among other concerns, it requires anticipating the potential environment changes the system may encounter at run time to define how the system should adapt itself in response to these environment changes. However, anticipating all potential environment changes at design time is in most cases infeasible due to *design time uncertainty* [8,24]. In addition, while the principle effects of an adaptation on the system may be known, accurately anticipating the effect of a concrete adaptation is difficult; e.g., due to simplifying assumptions made during design time [8,15].

One emerging way to address design time uncertainty is to employ *online* reinforcement learning (RL) [1,2,4,10,19,22,31,32,35]. RL can learn the effectiveness of adaptation actions through interactions with the system's environment. This means that instead of information system engineers having to manually develop the self-adaptation logic, the system automatically learns the self-adaptation logic via machine learning at run time. The information system engineer expresses the learning problem in a declarative fashion, in terms of the learning goals the system should achieve. In the online store example, they may express maintaining system performance as a learning goal. Online RL thereby automates the manual engineering task of developing the self-adaptation logic.

Existing online RL approaches for self-adaptive information systems exhibit two shortcomings that limit the degree of automation that may be achieved. First, to facilitate convergence of learning, information system engineers have to manually fine-tune the rate of exploration versus exploitation, i.e., how often adaptation actions are selected that were not selected before. Second, most existing approaches use a lookup table to represent the learned knowledge, which requires information system engineers to manually quantize environment states to facilitate scalability if the environment has a high number of states. These two manual activities may be expensive and potentially unreliable [15] and may require information not available at design time due to design time uncertainty.

Our main idea is to automate the aforementioned manual activities by employing *policy-based RL* as a fundamentally different type of RL [23,29]. In simple terms, policy-based RL represents the learned knowledge as a an artificial neural network [29]. Our approach conceptually, formally and technically integrates policy-based RL into a well-known self-adaptive system reference model. Our approach thereby facilitates online RL for self-adaptive information systems without having to (1) manually quantize environment states and (2) manually fine-tune the exploration rate. We demonstrate the feasibility and applicability of our policy-based approach using two information system exemplars: a self-adaptive web application and a predictive process monitoring system.

In the remainder of the paper, we provide a more detailed problem description in Sect. 2, introduce our approach in Sect. 3, present our experimental evaluation in Sect. 4, discuss limitations in Sect. 5, and analyze related work in Sect. 6.

## 2   Problem Statement

As motivated above, RL helps to effectively automate the engineering of an information system's self-adaptation logic. In general, RL learns the effectiveness of an agent's actions through the agent's interactions with its environment [28]. At time step $t$ the agent executes an action $a_t$ in environment state $s_t$. As a result, the environment transitions to $s_{t+1}$ at time step $t + 1$ and the agent receives a reward $r_{t+1}$ for executing the action. The goal of RL is to optimize cumulative rewards. When RL is used for self-adaptive information systems, "action" means the concrete adaptation action (such modifying the structure, parameters or behavior of the system), "agent" takes the role of the self-adaptation logic, and "environment" includes the information system to be adapted at run time.

Existing approaches that use RL for building self-adaptive information systems utilize some variant of *value-based* RL (see Sect. 6). Value-based RL is a model-free RL technique that employs a so called value function for representing the learned knowledge. The value function gives the expected cumulative reward when performing a particular action in a given state [28]. A concrete action may be selected by choosing the action that has the highest value in a given state. Typical variants of value-based RL are Q-Learning and SARSA [28], which differ in how they update the value function. Existing RL approaches for self-adaptive information systems use two different ways to represent the value function:

**Value Function as Lookup Table.** Most existing approaches store the value function in a lookup table (see Sect. 6). Even though such tabular solution techniques are straightforward to implement and well understood [31], they exhibit two key shortcomings. First, due to the discrete nature of the lookup table, tabular solution techniques are limited to discrete state and action spaces and cannot cope with continuous state and action spaces. Specifically, this means that environment states have to be enumerable and cannot be represented by continuous (e.g., real-valued) variables [22,31]. Second, the size of the lookup table directly depends on the number of environment states that have to be stored, and thus the size increases exponentially with the number of state variables. As a result, tabular solution techniques suffer from poor scalability, because the learning process has to collect data for all entries of the table to learn effectively [22,31].

A common way to address these limitations is to quantize continuous environment states by defining a sufficiently small number of discrete environment states [28]. Such quantization is a manual activity performed by information system engineers, and thus may be expensive and potentially unreliable. The environment states may be quantized too coarse-grained to reflect reality, or they may be quantized too fine-grained, which may lead to poor scalability due to a too large size of the lookup table. Also, the extent of the state space (i.e., set of all states) may be unknown due to design time uncertainty, and thus defining lower and upper bounds of discrete states may not be possible. To know the extent of the state space would mean that developers at design time can anticipate all potential environment changes the system may encounter at run time.

**Value Function Approximation.** An alternative approach to avoid quantization of the state space is to approximate the value function; e.g., using linear or non-linear techniques (such as artificial neural networks). This allows coping with large state spaces by generalizing over unseen states [28]. Despite such function approximation, value-based RL in general faces the exploration-exploitation dilemma [28]. To optimize rewards, actions should be selected that have shown to be effective (aka. exploitation). However, to discover such actions in the first place, actions that were not selected before should be selected (aka. exploration). One typical solution to the exploration-exploitation dilemma is the $\epsilon$-greedy mechanism. During learning, the $\epsilon$-greedy mechanism randomly chooses an action with probability $\epsilon$. The challenge for an information system engineer is to fine-tune the balance between exploitation and exploration in order to ensure convergence of the learning process [28]. As an example, the information system engineer may implement a mechanism that decreases $\epsilon$ over time, thereby reducing the amount of exploration in order to facilitate convergence. However, for online learning this poses the challenge of when and how to increase $\epsilon$ again in order to capture non-stationary environments, i.e., environments in which the results of adaptation actions change over time [28].

Summarizing, the degree of automation of existing approaches is limited. Information system engineers have to perform manual activities that may require effort or may be difficult to perform due to design time uncertainty.

## 3  Policy-Based Online Reinforcement Learning Approach

**Self-adaptive System Reference Model as Basis.** Our approach enhances the MAPE-K model, a well-known reference model for self-adaptive systems [14,16,18]. As shown in Fig. 1 this model suggests conceptually structuring a self-adaptive system into two main elements: *system logic* and *self-adaptation logic*. The self-adaptation logic is further structured into four main conceptual activities that leverage a common *knowledge* base. The knowledge base includes information about the managed system and its environment (e.g., encoded

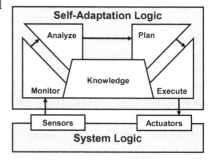

**Fig. 1.** MAPE-K reference model [16]

in the form of models at run time), as well as adaptation goals (requirements) and adaptation strategies or rules. The four activities are concerned with *monitoring* the system logic and the system's environment via *sensors*, *analyzing* the monitoring data to determine the need for an adaptation, *planning* adaptation actions, and *executing* these adaptation actions via *actuators*, thereby modifying the system logic at run time.

**Policy-Based Reinforcement Learning Foundations.** The fundamental idea behind policy-based RL is to directly use and optimize a parametrized stochastic *action selection policy* [23,29]. The action selection policy maps states to a probability distribution over the action space (i.e., set of possible actions). This means that actions are selected by sampling from this probability distribution. A *learning cycle* consists of a predefined number of $n$ time steps. At the end of each learning cycle, the trajectory of $n$ actions, states and rewards are used for a policy update. During a policy update, the policy parameters are perturbed based on the rewards received, such that the resulting probability distribution is shifted towards a direction which increases the likelihood of selecting actions which led to a higher cumulative reward.

**Conceptual Overview of Approach.** Figure 2 depicts the conceptual architecture of our approach, showing how the elements of policy-based RL are integrated into the MAPE-K loop. The dark-gray area indicates where the *action selection* of RL takes the place of the *analyze* and *plan* activities of MAPE-K. The learned *stochastic policy* takes the role of the self-adaptive system's *knowledge* base.

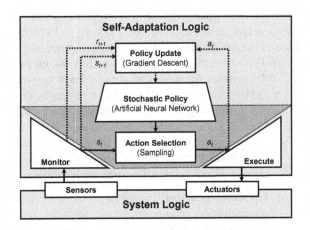

**Fig. 2.** Conceptual architecture of policy-based approach

At run time the policy is used by the self-adaptation logic to select (via sampling) an adaptation action $a_t$ based on the current state $s_t$ determined by the *monitoring* activity. Action selection determines whether there is a need for an adaptation (given the current state) and plans (i.e., selects) the respective adaptation action to *execute*. A *policy update* utilizes the trajectory of actions $a_t$, states $s_{t+1}$, and rewards $r_{t+1}$ to update the policy. In our approach, policy updates are performed via so-called policy gradient methods [28,29], because the policy is represented as an artificial neural network. In our architecture, rewards are computed by the monitoring activity, as this activity has access to all sensor information collected from the system and its environment.

**Formalization of Approach.** As mentioned above, the learning problem is stated in a declarative fashion. Typically, it can be formalized as a Markov decision process $MDP = (S, A, T, R)$, with

- $S$ being the state space composed of a set of environment and system states $s \in S$ observable by monitoring via the system logic's sensors (e.g., system workload and performance of the system),
- $A$ being the action space with a set of possible adaptation actions $a \in A$, i.e., possible ways the system may be adapted using the system logic's actuators (e.g., turning off or on different system features),
- $T : S \times A \times S \rightarrow [0, 1]$ being the transition probability among states with $T(s_t, a_t, s_{t+1}) = \Pr(s_{t+1}|s_t, a_t)$, which gives the probability that adaptation action $a_t$ in state $s_t$ will lead to a state $s_{t+1}$, and
- $R : S \rightarrow \mathbb{R}$, being a reward function which specifies the numerical reward the system receives in state $s_t$. The reward function expresses the learning goal to achieve, which in our case expresses maintaining the quality requirements of the system (e.g., performance should not fall below a given threshold).

Policy-based reinforcement learning finds a solution to the MDP in the form of a parametrized stochastic policy $\pi_\theta : S \times A \rightarrow [0, 1]$, giving the probability of taking adaptation action $a$ in state $s$, i.e., $\pi_\theta(s, a) = \Pr(a|s)$. The policy's parameters (weights of the artificial neural network) are given as a vector $\theta \in \mathbb{R}^d$.

Regarding design time uncertainty, we assume that we know $A$, $S$, and $R$, but do not know $T$. More precisely, even if we do not know the exact states and thus state space $S$, we know the state variables. As an example, even if we do not know exact workloads of a web application (and maybe not even the maximum workload), we can express a state variable workload $w \in \mathbb{N}^+$. We assume that we do not know $T$ due to design time uncertainty about how adaptation impacts on system quality. As an example, we may not have an exact understanding of how different configurations of the system perform under different workloads.

**Proof-of-Concept Implementation** To select a concrete policy-based RL algorithm for the implementation of our approach, we took into account two main considerations. First, as we assume we do not know the transition function $T$, we need to use a model-free variant of policy-based RL. Second, to facilitate online learning, we need an algorithm that continuously updates the policy without waiting for a final outcome, i.e., without waiting for reaching a terminal state. Actor-critic algorithms are a model-free variant of policy-based RL algorithms that use bootstrapping (i.e., knowledge is updated continuously without waiting for a final outcome). We use proximal policy optimization (PPO [26]) as a state-of-the-art actor-critic algorithm. PPO is rather robust for what concerns hyper-parameter settings. Thereby, we avoid extensive hyper-parameter tuning compared to other actor-critic algorithms. In addition, PPO avoids too large policy updates by using a so called clipping function. A too large policy update may mean that RL misses the global optimum and remains stuck in a local optimum. To represent the actor and critic models of PPO, we used multi-layer perceptrons with two hidden layers of 64 neurons each (neurons in the input and output layers depended on the respective number of action and state variables).

## 4    Experimental Evaluation

To demonstrate the feasibility and applicability of our approach, the scope of our experiments is to analyze whether the system is able to learn and improve its self-adaptation logic at run time. We did not perform a comparative analysis with existing value-based approaches at this stage, because such comparison would be beyond the scope of the current paper. Such comparison would require the careful variation and analysis of a range of parameters for the value-based approach, including the setting of different exploration rates, as well as different levels and forms of quantization of the state space. In particular, one has to be careful not to perform unfair comparisons. As an example, the comparison may be strongly influenced by the chosen quantization (see Sect. 2). A too fine-grained quantization may mean the value-based approach exhibits extremely slow convergence. A too coarse-grained quantization may mean the value-based approach will not be able to distinguish between different states and thereby will not be able to optimize cumulative rewards.

### 4.1    Self-adaptive Web Application

**Subject System.** We use the auction web application *Brownout-RUBiS* as a subject system [17]. When a user requests a specific item, the application's recommendation engine provides a list of recommended items based on past auctions. Due to the resource needs of the recommendation engine, Brownout-RUBiS has to balance two quality requirements: maximizing the user experience by providing many recommendations, while minimizing the user-perceived latency. Therefore, the recommendation engine can be adapted by setting a so-called dimmer value $\delta \in [0, 1]$, which represents the per-request probability that the recommendation engine is activated. The dimmer value thus impacts on both quality requirements: A high rate of recommendations increases user experience, but at the same time also increases resource needs and thus may increase latency.

**MDP of Subject System.** We express the learning problem as input for our approach as shown in Table 1. We define the reward function $r_t \in R$ such that learning may find a good balance between low latency and high recommendation rates. We define the reward function such that a greater $r_t$ is better and aim at *maximizing* the cumulative reward. We assume that user satisfaction will decrease for latencies higher than $\lambda_{\max}$ and thus penalize latencies above $\lambda_{\max}$.

**Table 1.** MDP of self-adaptive web application

| State $s_t = (u_t, \alpha_t, \lambda_t)$ | $u_t \in \mathbb{N}^+$: | monitored number of user requests |
|---|---|---|
| | $\alpha_t \in [0,1]$: | monitored recommendation ratio |
| | $\lambda_t \in \mathbb{R}^+$: | monitored latency |
| Action $a_t \in A$ | $A = \delta \in [0,1]$: | adapt the dimmer value |
| Reward $r_t = \alpha_t \cdot f(\lambda_t)$ | $\alpha_t \in [0,1]$: | monitored recommendation ratio |
| | $\lambda_t \in \mathbb{R}^+$: | monitored latency |
| | $f(\lambda_t)$: | utility function, $f(\lambda_t) = 1$ if $\lambda_t \leq \lambda_{\max}$; $= 0$ if $\lambda_t > 2 \cdot \lambda_{\max}$; $= -\lambda_t/\lambda_{\max} + 2$ else *(= linearly decreasing reward)* |

**Experimental Setup.** We deployed Brownout-RUBiS on a virtual machine with 64 GB RAM running Ubuntu 16.04.5. We used *httpmon* [17] as workload generator deployed on a separate virtual machine to generate different kinds of workloads. We synthesized workloads using different, representative workload patterns from the literature [19]: stable (constant number of requests), off/on (reflecting periodic batch processing), and cyclic (workload increases and decreases in periods). We also replayed an excerpt of a real-world workload trace [20].

We used ca. 4,600 learning cycles for each kind of workload, as this was a sufficiently high number to observe convergence. Each learning cycle used monitoring data from 128 consecutive time steps (the default setting of the PPO algorithm we use in our implementation, see Sect. 3). We set $\lambda_{\max} = 20$ ms as latency threshold, because it is low enough to require a dimmer value below 1.

**Experimental Results.** Figure 3 shows the results for each kind of workload. The diagrams show the state, action and reward at each learning cycle averaged over the observations of 128 time steps.

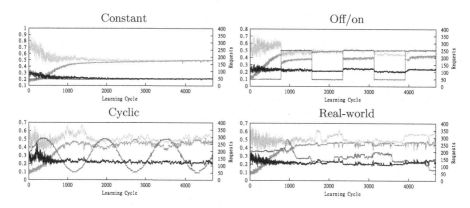

**Fig. 3.** Learning behavior for self-adaptive web application; **blue** = workload, **black** = latency;  green = dimmer value; red = reward (Color figure online)

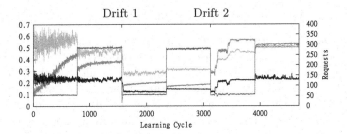

**Fig. 4.** Learning behavior in non-stationary environment; **blue** = workload, **black** = latency; green = dimmer value; red = reward (Color figure online)

The results show how our approach enables the system to adapt itself. The system automatically adapts the dimmer value depending on the workload, thereby optimizing the balance between latency and user experience (as visible in the increase of cumulative rewards). While at the beginning of the learning process, the adaptation of the dimmer value shows a high variance for all workload patterns, after some time the variance of adaptation actions becomes visibly lower. For the **constant workload**, the reward converges towards a value of around 0.47 after ca. 1,950 learning cycles and stabilizes at a dimmer value around 0.5, which leads to the highest recommendation ratio without violating the latency threshold. For the **off/on workload**, the reward increases over time for the off as well as the on workload settings. From the second iteration onwards, convergence can be observed. When comparing learning for the off and on periods separately, one can observe that learning is able to reuse knowledge about similar workloads over time. The **cyclic workload**, similar to the off/on workload, indicates how learning may generalize from already acquired knowledge. The overall observations are very much comparable to those of the off/on workload, except that the average reward increases and decreases more slowly, because the workload changes more smoothly. For the **real-world workload**, our approach is able to learn from previously experienced states and is able to keep the reward roughly at the same level by adjusting the dimmer value even though the workload changes over time. Especially if a similar workload reoccurs, our approach is able to quickly determine an effective adaptation action.

Figure 4 shows how our approach automatically captures non-stationary environments. After learning cycle 1562 ("Drift 1"), we reduced the virtual machine compute resources by half. This means that for the same dimmer value the system experiences a higher latency, because less compute resources are available. Our approach learns to decrease the dimmer value such that the latency threshold is not violated. After learning cycle 3125 ("Drift 2"), we increased the resources by 1.5. Again, the dimmer values are set accordingly. Note that our approach is able to capture this non-stationarity without explicitly monitoring the changes in compute resources and without explicitly changing the exploration rate.

## 4.2   Self-adaptive Process Monitoring System

**Subject System.** We use a predictive process monitoring system introduced in our earlier work [21]. The system uses neural network ensembles to predict process outcomes. In addition, the system computes so called reliability estimates, which give the probability that predictions are accurate. Only when the reliability is above a given threshold, the system issues an alarm in order to trigger a proactive process adaptation. Thereby the system aims to find a good trade-off between prediction accuracy and prediction earliness (later predictions are more accurate, but leave less time for adaptations). Experimental results show that lower thresholds may lead to higher savings in process costs, whilst posing the risk that such savings may not be achieved in all situations. Higher thresholds may capture more situations but can lead to lower savings. However, a good threshold is not known a priori. One solution is to determine the threshold using a sub-set of the training data [30]. Here, we use online RL as an alternative to learn when to trigger an alarm based on the predictions and their reliability.

**MDP of Subject System.** We express the learning problem as shown in Table 2. For defining $r_t \in R$, we penalize the system for late predictions (thereby incentivizing earliness) as well as for high process execution costs (following the cost model from [30]). Like above, we aim at *maximizing* the cumulative reward, and thus express the reward function such that a greater $r_t$ is better.

**Table 2.** MDP of self-adaptive process monitoring system

| State $s_t = (\pi_t, \rho_t)$ | $\pi_t \in [0,1]$: | relative prefix-length (*smaller values mean earlier in the process*) |
|---|---|---|
| | $\hat{o}_t \in \mathbb{R}$: | predicted numeric process outcome |
| | $\rho_t \in [0,1]$: | prediction reliability |
| Action $a_t \in A$ | $A = \{1,0\}$: | 1 = trigger alarm; 0 = do not trigger alarm |
| Reward $r_t = -(e_t + c_t)$ | $e_t = 1.5$: | Penalization of late predictions |
| | $c_t \in \mathbb{N}$: | Process execution costs = 100 if false negative prediction (*contractual penalty*) = 50 if true positive prediction (*adapt. costs*) = 100 if false positive prediction (*adapt. + compensation costs*) |

**Experimental Setup.** We use the implementation of the predictive process monitoring system presented in [21]. We selected the BPIC 2017 data set[1], because the process instances covered by the data set are sufficiently long to observe the effect of earliness. Also, the data set has a sufficient number of process instances and predictions to allow us to observe convergence of learning.

---

[1] https://www.win.tue.nl/bpi/doku.php?id=2017:challenge.

**Experimental Results.** Figure 5 shows the results by depicting how the rate of adaptations, earliness (in terms of relative prefix-length when an adaptation was made), process execution costs, and overall rewards evolve. Other than in the web application case, we do not show the development of the state variables, because the state variables do not change smoothly over time, but may be quite different between each consecutive time step.

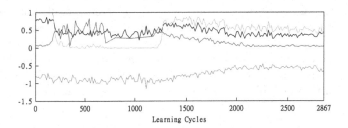

**Fig. 5.** Learning behavior for self-adaptive process monitoring system; green = rate of adaptations; **blue** = earliness; **black** = costs/100; red = overall reward/100 (Color figure online)

Like for the self-adaptive web application, the results show how our approach enables the system to adapt itself. It can be seen that the approach indeed is able to learn when to adapt in order to maximize rewards. The reward begins to increase after around 1,100 learning cycles and converges to a value of around −60 after 2,000 cycles. Also, the results show how the system learns the trade-off between accuracy and earliness. Up to learning cycle 250, the system always adapts as early as possible. However, this entails high costs due to low prediction accuracy at the beginning of process execution. Then, between learning cycles 250 and 1,250 the system learns that a very low rate of adaptations may lead to low costs. However, this does not help increase rewards, because many adaptations happen rather late (earliness around 0.5 on average). After learning cycle 1,250 the system starts learning that earlier predictions deliver higher rewards and thereby finds a trade-off between accuracy and earliness.

## 5  Discussion

### 5.1  Threats to Validity

**Internal Validity.** To observe whether policy-based RL in principle has the expected effect, we used a multi-layer perceptron as a simple neural network to represent the policy. In order not to trade the problem of finding a good quantization of the state space and a suitable setting of the exploration rate in value-based RL for hyper-parameter tuning in policy-based RL, we used only default hyper-parameter settings. Also, we repeated each of the experiments multiple times in order to assess potential random effects due to the stochastic nature of the neural networks. Even though there were some differences in the speed of convergence, the learning behavior was consistent across these repetitions.

**External Validity.** We used two different kinds of self-adaptive information systems in our experiments. For the web application, we used state-of-the-art computer infrastructure and different workloads (both synthetic and real) to get realistic measurements. For the business process monitoring system, we used a large, public real-world data set. The learning problems for both systems differ in terms of the action variable (continuous vs. discrete). Still, both problems only consider a single action variable. For discrete action variables, this is due to the current limitations of our approach for what concerns the size of the action space (see below). For continuous action variables, our approach in principle is applicable to more than one action variable, because the used PPO algorithm can cope with that. We plan further experiments to confirm this.

## 5.2    Limitations

**Handling Large Discrete Adaptation Spaces.** The policy-based RL algorithms we use can handle a large action space during online learning, provided the action space is continuous. However, these algorithms do not naturally generalize over a set of non-continuous, i.e., discrete, actions and thus cannot extend to previously unseen actions [9]. Typically, self-adaptive information systems have large discrete action spaces, such as feature-oriented or architecture-based self-adaptive systems. As an example, take a system that offers ten optional system features that may be dynamically activated and deactivated in any combination. Its adaptation space thus contains $2^{10} = 1024$ adaptation actions. These 1024 adaptation actions cannot be represented as a continuous variable. For such self-adaptive systems with large discrete action spaces, our approach currently is not applicable. One solution may be to embed the discrete actions in a continuous space and use nearest-neighbor search to find the closest discrete actions [9].

**Convergence of Reinforcement Learning.** Performance of machine learning depends, to a large degree, on the amount of data available for learning. When used for self-adaptive systems, RL may require quite many learning cycles until the learning process converges [22]. In our experiments, learning for both subject systems required around 2,000 learning cycles (with data from 256,000 time steps) to converge. Until RL has converged, the system most likely executes inefficient adaptations, because not enough observations have yet been made. Inefficient adaptations may lead to negative effects, because they are executed in the live system [11]. To speed up convergence, one may aim to find good initial estimates for the learned knowledge [10, 28, 34] or perform offline learning via simulations of the system [31]. Still, online RL may not be applicable for systems that operate in an environment where the effects of the "trial-and-error" nature of RL may not be tolerable; e.g., if adaptation actions may harm the environment or if an adversary in the environment may maliciously manipulate input data.

# 6   Related Work

Existing approaches that use RL for online learning in self-adaptive information systems resort to value-based RL. We structure the discussion into how they represent the value function (also see Sect. 2).

**Value Function as Lookup Table.** Amoui et al. use SARSA to learn effective adaptation actions for a self-adaptive web application [1]. They radically quantize environment states by defining only two values for each of the state variables. To this end, thresholds defined by domain experts are employed. Huang et al. employ Q-Learning for the dynamic optimization of resource allocation in operational business processes [13]. In addition to optimizing the resource allocation for a single process instance, they propose an optimization across process instances by considering the global resource costs when updating the value table. Dutreilh et al. employ Q-Learning for autonomic cloud resource management [10]. They assume upper bounds for the state variables can be given; e.g., based on experimental observation. Bu et al. employ Q-Learning for the self-configuration of cloud virtual machines and applications [5]. To facilitate scalability, they define three discrete states, representing high, medium and low ranges of the respective state variable. Arabnejad et al. apply fuzzy Q-Learning and SARSA for cloud auto-scaling [2]. Environment states are quantized and thereby limited to small sets of states expressed in fuzzy logic. The benefit of fuzzy logic is that many states can be represented by only a few fuzzy states. However, their approach still requires identifying "discrete" fuzzy elements in the fuzzy set based on which RL operates. Caporuscio et al. propose using value-based RL for multi-agent service assembly [6]. The agents share state monitoring information and use Q-Learning with a tabular representation of the value function. Zhao et al. use Q-Learning in combination with case-based reasoning to generate and update adaptation rules [35]. They quantize continuous environment states using equidistant points. Wang et al. use multi-agent Q-Learning for adaptive service compositions [32]. They assume that the environment can be represented by a finite, discrete set of states. In contrast to the above approaches, our policy-based approach does not require discrete states or manual quantization, but it can directly handle large and continuous environments.

**Value Function Approximation.** Tesauro et al. [31] use Q-Learning with nonlinear function approximation for autonomic cloud resource allocation. They use a neural network (multi-layer perceptron) for approximating the value function. They suggest using softmax or $\epsilon$-greedy as exploration mechanism and observe that – for their specific subject system –, they can learn good policies without requiring exploration. Yet, they do not analyze whether this observation may generalize to other kinds of systems. Xu et al. use Q-Learning together with function approximation (via artificial neural networks) for autonomic cloud management [34]. Moustafa and Zhang use Q-Learning with linear function approximation (via linear regression) for QoS-aware web service composition [22]. Wang et al. use Q-Learning with function approximation via deep neural networks (recurrent neural networks) for adaptive service composition [33]. Silvander propose using Q-Learning with function approximation via a deep neural network (DQN) for the optimization of business processes [27]. All these approaches use $\epsilon$-greedy as exploration mechanism, requiring fine-tuning of the exploration rate. In contrast, our approach does not require explicitly controlling the exploration rate, but exploration is done automatically via probabilistic action selection.

## 7   Conclusion

We introduced and experimentally evaluated an online reinforcement learning approach to facilitate engineering of self-adaptive information systems. Our approach contributes to information system engineering by increasing the degree of automation. Concretely, our approach does neither require manually quantizing environment states nor manually having to determine suitable exploration parameters for the reinforcement learning algorithm to work. As future work, we will extend our approach to handle large discrete action spaces in order to capture additional types of self-adaptive systems. We will also investigate whether deep learning models facilitate better representation of the learned knowledge.

**Acknowledgments.** We cordially thank Claas Keller, Tristan Kley and Jan Löber for supporting us in carrying out the experiments, Zoltan Mann for comments on earlier versions of the paper, as well as the anonymous reviewers for their constructive comments. Research leading to these results received funding from the EU's Horizon 2020 research and innovation programme under grant agreements no. 780351 (ENACT), 731932 (TransformingTransport), and 871493 (DataPorts).

## References

1. Amoui, M., Salehie, M., Mirarab, S., Tahvildari, L.: Adaptive action selection in autonomic software using reinforcement learning. In: 4th International Conference on Autonomic and Autonomous Systems (ICAS 2008), pp. 175–181. IEEE (2008)
2. Arabnejad, H., Pahl, C., Jamshidi, P., Estrada, G.: A comparison of reinforcement learning techniques for fuzzy cloud auto-scaling. In: 17th International Symposium on Cluster, Cloud and Grid Computing (CCGRID 2017), pp. 64–73. ACM (2017)
3. Aschoff, R., Zisman, A.: QoS-driven proactive adaptation of service composition. In: Kappel, G., Maamar, Z., Motahari-Nezhad, H.R. (eds.) ICSOC 2011. LNCS, vol. 7084, pp. 421–435. Springer, Heidelberg (2011). https://doi.org/10.1007/978-3-642-25535-9_28
4. Barrett, E., Howley, E., Duggan, J.: Applying reinforcement learning towards automating resource allocation and application scalability in the cloud. Concurrency Comput. Pract. Exp. **25**(12), 1656–1674 (2013)
5. Bu, X., Rao, J., Xu, C.: Coordinated self-configuration of virtual machines and appliances using a model-free learning approach. IEEE Trans. Parallel Distrib. Syst. **24**(4), 681–690 (2013)
6. Caporuscio, M., D'Angelo, M., Grassi, V., Mirandola, R.: Reinforcement learning techniques for decentralized self-adaptive service assembly. In: Aiello, M., Johnsen, E.B., Dustdar, S., Georgievski, I. (eds.) ESOCC 2016. LNCS, vol. 9846, pp. 53–68. Springer, Cham (2016). https://doi.org/10.1007/978-3-319-44482-6_4

7. Chen, T., Bahsoon, R.: Self-adaptive and online QoS modeling for cloud-based software services. IEEE Trans. Software Eng. **43**(5), 453–475 (2017)
8. D'Ippolito, N., Braberman, V.A., Kramer, J., Magee, J., Sykes, D., Uchitel, S.: Hope for the best, prepare for the worst: multi-tier control for adaptive systems. In: 36th International Conference on Software Engineering (ICSE 2014), pp. 688–699. ACM (2014)
9. Dulac-Arnold, G., Evans, R., Sunehag, P., Coppin, B.: Reinforcement learning in large discrete action spaces. CoRR abs/1512.07679 (2015)
10. Dutreilh, X., Kirgizov, S., Melekhova, O., Malenfant, J., Rivierre, N., Truck, I.: Using reinforcement learning for autonomic resource allocation in clouds: towards a fully automated workflow. In: 7th International Conference on Autonomic and Autonomous Systems (ICAS 2011), pp. 67–74 (2011)
11. Filho, R.V.R., Porter, B.: Defining emergent software using continuous self-assembly, perception, and learning. TAAS **12**(3), 16:1–16:25 (2017)
12. Franco, J.M., Correia, F., Barbosa, R., Rela, M.Z., Schmerl, B.R., Garlan, D.: Improving self-adaptation planning through software architecture-based stochastic modeling. J. Syst. Softw. **115**, 42–60 (2016)
13. Huang, Z., van der Aalst, W.M.P., Lu, X., Duan, H.: Reinforcement learning based resource allocation in business process management. Data Knowl. Eng. **70**(1), 127–145 (2011)
14. de la Iglesia, D.G., Weyns, D.: MAPE-K formal templates to rigorously design behaviors for self-adaptive systems. TAAS **10**(3), 15:1–15:31 (2015)
15. Jamshidi, P., Camara, J., Schmerl, B., Kästner, C., Garlan, D.: Machine learning meets quantitative planning: Enabling self-adaptation in autonomous robots. In: 14th Symposium on Software Engineering for Adaptive and Self-Managing Systems (SEAMS 2019). ACM (2019)
16. Kephart, J.O., Chess, D.M.: The vision of autonomic computing. IEEE Comput. **36**(1), 41–50 (2003)
17. Klein, C., Maggio, M., Arzén, K.E., Hernández-Rodriguez, F.: Brownout: building more robust cloud applications. In: 36th International Confernce on Software Engineering (ICSE 2014), pp. 700–711. ACM (2014)
18. de Lemos, R., et al.: Software Engineering for self-adaptive systems: a second research roadmap. In: de Lemos, R., Giese, H., Müller, H.A., Shaw, M. (eds.) Software Engineering for Self-Adaptive Systems II. LNCS, vol. 7475, pp. 1–32. Springer, Heidelberg (2013). https://doi.org/10.1007/978-3-642-35813-5_1
19. Lorido-Botran, T., Miguel-Alonso, J., Lozano, J.A.: A review of auto-scaling techniques for elastic applications in cloud environments. J. Grid Comput. **12**(4), 559–592 (2014)
20. Mann, Z.Á.: Resource optimization across the cloud stack. IEEE Trans. Parallel Distrib. Syst. **29**(1), 169–182 (2018)
21. Metzger, A., Neubauer, A., Bohn, P., Pohl, K.: Proactive process adaptation using deep learning ensembles. In: Giorgini, P., Weber, B. (eds.) CAiSE 2019. LNCS, vol. 11483, pp. 547–562. Springer, Cham (2019). https://doi.org/10.1007/978-3-030-21290-2_34
22. Moustafa, A., Zhang, M.: Learning efficient compositions for QoS-aware service provisioning. In: International Conference Conference on Web Services (ICWS 2014), pp. 185–192. IEEE Computer Society (2014)
23. Nachum, O., Norouzi, M., Xu, K., Schuurmans, D.: Bridging the gap between value and policy based reinforcement learning. In: Advances in Neural Information Processing Systems (NIPS 2017), vol. 12, pp. 2772–2782 (2017)

24. Ramirez, A.J., Jensen, A.C., Cheng, B.H.C.: A taxonomy of uncertainty for dynamically adaptive systems. In: 7th International Symposium on Software Engineering for Adaptive and Self-Managing Systems (SEAMS 2012), pp. 99–108 (2012)

25. Salehie, M., Tahvildari, L.: Self-adaptive software: landscape and research challenges. TAAS **4**(2), 1–42 (2009)

26. Schulman, J., Wolski, F., Dhariwal, P., Radford, A., Klimov, O.: Proximal policy optimization algorithms. CoRR abs/1707.06347 (2017)

27. Silvander, J.: Business process optimization with reinforcement learning. In: Shishkov, B. (ed.) BMSD 2019. LNBIP, vol. 356, pp. 203–212. Springer, Cham (2019). https://doi.org/10.1007/978-3-030-24854-3_13

28. Sutton, R.S., Barto, A.G.: Reinforcement Learning: An Introduction. MIT Press, Cambridge (2018)

29. Sutton, R.S., McAllester, D.A., Singh, S.P., Mansour, Y.: Policy gradient methods for reinforcement learning with function approximation. In: Advances in Neural Information Processing Systems 12 (NIPS 1999), pp. 1057–1063 (2000)

30. Teinemaa, I., Tax, N., de Leoni, M., Dumas, M., Maggi, F.M.: Alarm-based prescriptive process monitoring. In: Weske, M., Montali, M., Weber, I., vom Brocke, J. (eds.) BPM 2018. LNBIP, vol. 329, pp. 91–107. Springer, Cham (2018). https://doi.org/10.1007/978-3-319-98651-7_6

31. Tesauro, G., Jong, N.K., Das, R., Bennani, M.N.: On the use of hybrid reinforcement learning for autonomic resource allocation. Cluster Comput. **10**(3), 287–299 (2007)

32. Wang, H., et al.: Integrating reinforcement learning with multi-agent techniques for adaptive service composition. TAAS **12**(2), 8:1–8:42 (2017)

33. Wang, H., Gu, M., Yu, Q., Fei, H., Li, J., Tao, Y.: Large-scale and adaptive service composition using deep reinforcement learning. In: Maximilien, M., Vallecillo, A., Wang, J., Oriol, M. (eds.) ICSOC 2017. LNCS, vol. 10601, pp. 383–391. Springer, Cham (2017). https://doi.org/10.1007/978-3-319-69035-3_27

34. Xu, C., Rao, J., Bu, X.: URL: a unified reinforcement learning approach for autonomic cloud management. J. Parallel Distrib. Comput. **72**(2), 95–105 (2012)

35. Zhao, T., Zhang, W., Zhao, H., Jin, Z.: A reinforcement learning-based framework for the generation and evolution of adaptation rules. In: International Conference on Autonomic Computing (ICAC 2017), pp. 103–112. IEEE Computer Society (2017)

# Aspect Term Extraction Using Deep Learning Model with Minimal Feature Engineering

Felipe Zschornack Rodrigues Saraiva, Ticiana Linhares Coelho da Silva[✉],
and José Antônio Fernandes de Macêdo

Insight Data Science Lab, Federal University of Ceará, Fortaleza, Brazil
{felipezrs,ticianalc}@insightlab.ufc.br, jose.macedo@dc.ufc.br

**Abstract.** With the explosive growth of social media on the Web, opinion mining has been extensively investigated and consists of the automatic identification and extraction of opinions, emotions, and sentiments from text and multimedia data. One of the tasks involved in opinion mining is Aspect Term Extraction (ATE) which aims at identifying aspects (attributes or characteristics) that have been explicitly evaluated in a sentence or a document. For example, in the sentence *"The picture quality of this camera is amazing"*, the aspect term is *"picture quality"*. This work proposes POS-AttWD-BLSTM-CRF, a neural network architecture using a deep learning model, and minimal feature engineering, to solve the problem of ATE in opinionated documents. The proposed architecture consists of a BLSTM-CRF classifier that uses the part-of-speech tag (POS tags) as an additional feature, along with a BLSTM encoder with an attention mechanism to allow the incorporation of another relevant feature: the grammatical relations between words. The experiments show that the proposed architecture achieves promising results with minimal feature engineering comparing to the state-of-the-art solutions.

**Keywords:** Aspect term extraction · Encoder · Attention mechanism · Word dependencies · Bidirectional long short-term memory · Conditional random fields

## 1 Introduction

With the explosive growth of social media on the Web, opinion mining has been extensively investigated and consists of the automatic identification and extraction of opinions, emotions, and sentiments from text and multimedia data. [15] defines opinion mining as five different tasks. The first one is the extraction of all entity expression. The second task is the extraction of all aspect expressions of the entities, and the third consists of extracting the opinion holder and time. The fourth comprises the aspect sentiment classification that determines whether each opinion on an aspect is positive, negative or neutral. And the last task consists of generating the tuples based on the results of the previous tasks.

© Springer Nature Switzerland AG 2020
S. Dustdar et al. (Eds.): CAiSE 2020, LNCS 12127, pp. 185–198, 2020.
https://doi.org/10.1007/978-3-030-49435-3_12

For example, in the sentence from a blog poster *"The picture quality of my Motorola camera phone is amazing"*. The task 1 should extract the entity ORG expression, "Motorola". Task 2 should extract aspect expression, "picture quality". Task 3 should find the holder of the opinions in the sentence, the blog author. Task 4 should find that the sentence gives positive opinion on the picture quality.

In this work, we focus on the second task and we tackle the aspect term extraction task as a classification problem, where each word in the sentence is tagged using the IOB2 format (short for Inside, Out and Begin). The words that are aspect terms are labeled with "B". In case an aspect term consists of multiple words, the first word receives the "B" label and the remaining aspect words receive the "I" label. The words that are not aspect terms are labeled with "O". The Fig. 1 illustrates the IOB2 tagging format described.

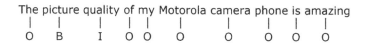

**Fig. 1.** Aspect extraction example using the IOB2 tagging format.

Companies of products and services usually spend increasing amounts of money in knowledge-based systems or expert systems to track consumer complaints online. For instance, the e-commerce applications as Amazon, Booking, among others encourage buyers to review the products or services they like and dislike to let the customers make informed decisions about the products or services they purchase. These applications can benefit from the Tasks 2 and 4 to extract all aspect expressions (products or services) and if each aspect is positive, negative or neutral. Considering the sentence *"The picture quality of my Motorola camera phone is amazing, however, the battery drains in just a few hours."* from a buyer complaint, an information system that integrates our proposed solution (aspect extraction classifier) and an aspect sentiment classifier can provide knowledge to help Motorola to improve the phone's battery life.

Different approaches, either supervised, unsupervised or semi-supervised, have been proposed to perform the task of aspect extraction [21] and, more recently, deep neural networks achieved promising results [20]. However, state-of-the-art techniques present some drawbacks. Usually, these proposals require a huge set of training examples [22], compelling some authors to compensate for the low accuracy obtained from models trained using a few examples with post-processing tasks, auxiliary lexicons, and language rules.

This work proposes a neural network architecture POS-AttWD-BLSTM-CRF model using a deep learning model, however with minimal feature engineering, to solve the problem of ATE in opinionated documents, like reviews of products or restaurants. We propose an encoder structure, similar to the one presented in [24], with an attention mechanism [1] that allows the use of a new additional feature: grammatical relation between words (word dependencies).

The word dependencies feature is important to the problem of aspect extraction because aspect terms are usually nominal subjects (syntactic subjects) with an adjective associated. It also helps to identify multiple word aspect terms, using the compound dependency between nouns in a noun phrase. We also use the Part-of-speech tag (POS tags) as another feature, because most of the aspect terms present in the sentences are nouns associated with one or more adjectives [20], thus the POS tagging information can help to identify which words are aspect terms. Another reason to use these two additional features is to mitigate the problem of out of vocabulary (OOV) words when there is no pre-trained word embedding to use as input to the model.

The experiments show that the proposed architecture achieves promising results with minimal feature engineering comparing to the state-of-the-art solutions. This is also the first work, to the best of our knowledge, to use an attention mechanism to harness the information of word dependencies to address the problem of aspect term extraction.

The remaining of this paper is organized as follows. Section 2 describes our proposed deep neural network architecture. Section 3 discusses the related works. Section 4 presents the conducted experiments and the results. Section 5 draws the final conclusions and the future works.

## 2   POS-AttWD-BLSTM-CRF Model

In this section, we describe some important word features used to train the proposed model. Then, we explain the proposed model architecture to perform aspect term extraction.

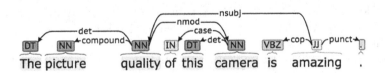

**Fig. 2.** Example of the word dependencies generated by the Stanford Dependencies [6].

### 2.1   Feature Selection

We sought two main goals while determining which features to use to train our model. First, to retain original information of each word. And second, to obtain a structural representation of the sentence that shows the importance of each word and the role it plays in the sentence. Following, we discuss the input features to our model: the word itself and the word dependency.

The word itself is the main input feature of the model. It contains all relevant information that has not been manually extracted from other features, and, of course, it is still useful for classifying whether or not it is an aspect term. It is represented by a pre-trained embedding vector.

Another feature is the word dependency that is a position related feature, in which all words in the sentence can be associated with each other. Figure 2 shows an example of word dependencies for the sentence *"The picture quality of this camera is amazing."*. However, it is not practical to incorporate this feature on the data by just concatenating it to the input words (as usually performed by other approaches when considered other features, like the POS tag [20]), because the word dependency feature vector has the same size of the sentence and, as the input sentences might have different lengths, then the input vectors would have different lengths. However, the neural network should receive vectors with a fixed length as input.

To solve this problem, we could limit the size of the sentences to a maximum number of words $\gamma$, and pad the input vectors with less than $\gamma$ words. But this limits the model to not accept input sentences with size greater than $\gamma$ without missing information. Another solution is the attention mechanism used in the encoder structure that will be explained in the next subsection. It allows the incorporation of word dependency, so the model can take advantage of the grammatical dependency between the words to regard to certain parts of the sentence, i.e. to the most relevant ones, improving the identification of aspect terms.

### 2.2 Model Architecture

As mentioned before, the trained model is capable of, given a sentence, $W = (w_0, w_1, ..., w_N)$ where each $w_i$ represents a word of the sentence, classify such word $w_i$ if it corresponds to an aspect term using IOB2 format. To this end, our proposed model was designed based on the encoder-decoder architecture proposed in [5] and [24]. This architecture has two main modules: an encoder, responsible for learning a vector representation for a sequence of tokens and a decoder, responsible for generating a sequence of tokens from a vector that represents an encoded sequence.

In general, this architecture is used to build models that can learn how to transform a sequence of tokens into another one. Our model is based on encoder-decoder architecture, however, its modules do not necessarily have the same roles. In this paper, the encoder is responsible for generating a vector representation of an entire sentence, and then provides information about the whole sentence as input for the classifier. This is similar to the original encoder purpose. But, instead of a decoder, we have a classifier that receives as input a sequence of words (represented by its features), and the vector that represents the full sentence encoded, as we can see in the Fig. 3.

LSTM (stands for Long Short-Term Memory) is a variant of recurrent neural networks (RNNs), capable to capture time dynamics in series via cycles in the network, designed to deal with the problem of gradient vanishing inherent to RNNs [17]. Because of these characteristics, they proved to be very useful in sequential labeling tasks like the ATE [13]. The encoder of our proposal is implemented using a BLSTM (stands for Bidirectional LSTM) stack architecture [9]. In BLSTMs, one LSTM layer (forward) receives the input sequence as input and

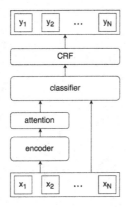

**Fig. 3.** Overview of the proposed model.

another LSTM layer (backward) receives the inverted sentence as input. All in all, BLSTM can capture both past and future information. As you can see in Fig. 4, our proposed architecture has two stacks of LSTM networks.

The layer above the encoder (Fig. 4) is the attention mechanism. It allows a model to automatically captures the parts of a source sentence that are most relevant than the others to predict a target word [1]. Instead of using the same context vector, or sentence representation, generated by the encoder for all words, it computes a different context vector for each word based on the grammatical relation between the words in the sentence. Thus, when performing the classification, every word has its own specific context vector.

The context vector is a weighted sum of the hidden outputs generated by the encoder. The attention weights (denoted by $\alpha_{i,j}$) are calculated, for each word, based on the word dependencies between the word being classified and the word representation of each word in the sentence given by the encoder. Figures 5 and 6 illustrate the word dependencies matrix for the sentence *"The picture quality of this camera is amazing."* and the calculation of the attention weights $\alpha_{i,j}$ for the word *quality* respectively.

All in all, the encoder consists of a BLSTM, with an attention mechanism, to map the input sentence, along with its POS tags, to context vectors of fixed dimensionality. The classifier is a BLSTM with a CRF layer on top. The CRF considers the correlations between the neighbors' labels, making a global choice instead of decoding each label independently. In ATE problem it is specifically useful to correctly label multiple word aspect terms [13]. As shown in Fig. 4, for each word in the input sentence, the classifier uses the word embedding (from GloVe [19]), the POS tag vector and the context vector obtained from the encoder with an attention mechanism to compute representations that are passed to a CRF layer to evaluate the output labels. Both encoder and the classifier are trained jointly to maximize the conditional probability of the sentence labels given an input sentence.

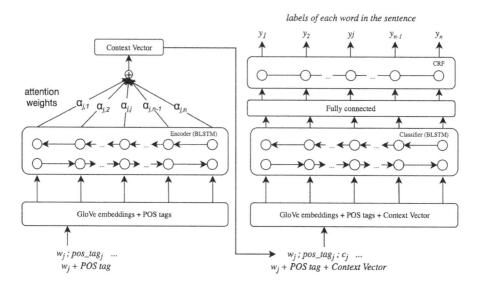

**Fig. 4.** The neural network architecture proposed. The attention mechanism uses the word dependencies information to weight the encoder hidden states and combines them to generate a different context vector for each word in the sentence.

It is worth to mention that we handle the words for which there is no pre-trained embedding vector, our approach sets the word embedding vector to zero. Moreover, in this paper, we use GloVe as a pre-trained embedding model, however, our approach is flexible to use any other model.

## 3   Related Work

Some deep learning models have been proposed to solve the problem of aspect extraction. The paper [12] proposed a hierarchical deep learning structure to learn representations for words (embeddings) which aim to explain the aspect-sentiment relationship at the phrase level. Their model used the dependency parse of the phrase to compute the embeddings, where each level of the tree was represented by an embedding. The embeddings learned were then used to the joint modeling of aspects and sentiments, for the posterior aspect and sentiment extraction.

The paper [20] proposes PORIA, a 7-layer Convolutional Neural Network along with a set of linguistic rules to tag each word in sentences as being aspects or not. [20] used pre-trained embeddings as input features and a sentiment lexicon, beyond that part of speech vectors as handcrafted features to improve the model performance, filtering 6 basic parts of speech (noun, verb, adjective, adverb, preposition, conjunction) and encoding it as a 6-dimensional binary vector for each input word.

|          | The | picture  | quality  | of   | this | camera | is   | amazing | .     |
|----------|-----|----------|----------|------|------|--------|------|---------|-------|
| The      | -   | -        | det      | -    | -    | -      | -    | -       | -     |
| picture  | -   | -        | compound | -    | -    | -      | -    | -       | -     |
| quality  | det | compound | -        | -    | -    | nmod   | -    | nsubj   | -     |
| of       | -   | -        | -        | -    | -    | case   | -    | -       | -     |
| this     | -   | -        | -        | -    | -    | det    | -    | -       | -     |
| camera   | -   | -        | nmod     | case | det  | -      | -    | -       | -     |
| is       | -   | -        | -        | -    | -    | -      | -    | cop     | -     |
| amazing  | -   | -        | nsubj    | -    | -    | cop    | -    | -       | punct |
| .        | -   | -        | -        | -    | -    | -      | -    | punct   | -     |

**Fig. 5.** Word dependencies matrix for the sentence *"The picture quality of this camera is amazing."*

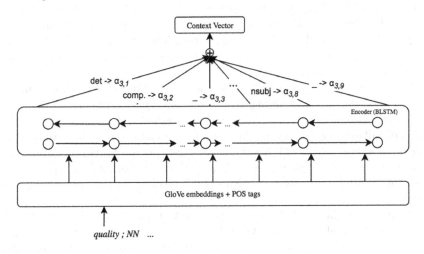

**Fig. 6.** Illustration of how the attention weights are computed for the word *quality*.

The paper [8] proposed a two-layer BLSTM-CRF model, trained on automatically labeled datasets, to extract aspects. [8] created an unsupervised algorithm to automatically label the datasets used as the training set. [29] uses a dependency-tree RNN (DT-RNN) with CRF and three hand-crafted features: POS tags, name-list, and sentiment lexicon to perform the tasks of aspect term extraction and opinion term extraction at the same time. The motivation of using the DT-RNN to encode grammatical dependency between words for feature learning was because it is infeasible or difficult to incorporate the dependency structure explicitly as input features.

[30] uses an attention mechanism to identify both aspect and opinion terms in a sentence: one attention layer to identify aspect terms and another attention layer to identify opinion terms. The goal is to avoid using engineered features, like word dependencies. In [30], each attention layer learns a prototype vector, a general feature representation for aspect terms and opinion terms. The attention weights measure the extent of correlation between each input token and the prototype using a tensor operator. Tokens with high weight values are labeled as an aspect or opinion terms. The attention layers were coupled to fully exploit the relations between aspect terms and opinion terms.

The framework proposed by [14] for ATE problem and uses truncated history attention and a selective transformation network to incorporate opinion information. $IHS\_RD$ [4] is a model that uses the IHS Goldfire linguistic processor and a CRF. Such model won the competition SEMEVAL 2014, which was an ATE subtask on the Laptop domain. The paper [27] proposes a CRF classifier with manually engineered features. [27] was the winner of the SEMEVAL 2014 challenge, ATE subtask on the Restaurant domain. [26] is an RNN-CRF classifier with manually engineered features, the winner of the SEMEVAL 2016 challenge, ATE subtask on the Restaurant domain.

The paper [18] addresses the problem of aspect-based sentiment analysis, that is quite different comparing to our approach since [18] extracts the aspect category. The proposed approach is a hierarchical attention model combined with LSTM. The paper [18] also incorporates affective commonsense knowledge into the deep neural network.

[32] proposes the use of a CNN model with two types of pre-trained embeddings: general-purpose embeddings and domain-specific embeddings, to improve the aspect extraction task. The general purpose embeddings are trained on a corpus of billions tokens e.g., GloVe [19]. The domain-specific embeddings are trained using the fastText [3] library on a review corpus restricted to the same domain of the reviews where the aspect extraction task is being performed, which can be seen as a drawback because in some domains this data may not be available.

[23] improves the DE-CNN model proposed in [32] introducing control layers between the embedding and CNN layers to add noise on each CNN layer's input. The control layers and CNN layers are trained separately, in an asynchronous fashion, to avoid over-fit training data. As the model uses the same double embedding layer of the previous DE-CNN model, it also presents its same limitations.

The paper [7] provides a summary of different approaches for aspect term extraction. Most of them include standard and variants of Convolutional Neural Networks (CNN), Long-Short Term Memory (LSTM) and Gated Recurrent Unit (GRU). They also investigated pre-trained and fine-tuned word embeddings and part-of-speech as our approach. However, none of them proposed the same model architecture as ours with minimal feature engineering.

Other works on natural language processing tasks, like Named Entity Recognition (NER), have been using attention mechanisms to obtain state-of-the-art results. As the paper [16] which proposed a BLSTM-CRF with an attention mechanism to perform chemical NER. [2] and [31] use a self-attention mechanism to the neural architecture aiming at solving the NER problem in a cross-lingual setting by transferring knowledge from a source language to a target language with few or no labels. To the best of authors' knowledge, this is the first work that uses an attention mechanism combined with information of word dependencies to tackle the problem of aspect term extraction.

## 4   Experimental Evaluation

In this section, we present the experimental evaluation conducted to assess our proposed POS-AttWD-BLSTM-CRF model.

### 4.1   Datasets

The aspect datasets used for training the model were the Laptop and Restaurant domain training sets from the SemEval 2014 competition[1] and the Restaurant domain training set, Subtask 2, from the SemEval 2016 competition[2]. Both datasets are tagged using the IOB2 tags and their statistics are described in Table 1.

The datasets were pre-processed and annotated with POS tags generated using the Stanford POS tagger [28] and word dependencies generated by the Stanford Dependencies [6]. In total, there were 41 different types of POS tags and 39 different types of word dependencies in the datasets. It is worth to emphasize that we did not manually select a subset of those features, we used all the existent POS tags and word dependencies, and let the model select those that are most relevant during the training phase.

### 4.2   Evaluation Metrics

To evaluate the model, we calculated the precision, recall and F1 score of the sentences from the test set against the ground truth. The precision measures the proportion of words that were correctly classified as an aspect term over all the aspect terms retrieved from the model. The recall is the proportion of detected true aspect terms over the ground truth. The F1 score is a metric derived from the other two metrics, precision, and recall.

---

[1] http://alt.qcri.org/semeval2014/task4/index.php?id=data-and-tools.
[2] http://alt.qcri.org/semeval2016/task5/index.php?id=data-and-tools.

**Table 1.** Number of training sentences, test sentences, and aspect terms present in the SEMEVAL 2014 and 2016 datasets.

| Domain | Training | Test | Total | Number of aspect terms |
|---|---|---|---|---|
| Laptop (2014) | 3,041 | 800 | 3,841 | 2,373 |
| Restaurant (2014) | 3,045 | 800 | 3,845 | 3,699 |
| Restaurant (2016) | 2,000 | 676 | 2,676 | 2,530 |

### 4.3   Competitors

We assessed three different models based on POS-AttWD-BLSTM-CRF model to study the importance of the POS tag feature and the attention mechanism using word dependencies for the problem of aspect term extraction:

- **Enc-BLSTM-CRF**: the encoder and the BLSTM-CRF classifier using no additional features.
- **Enc-BLSTM-CRF+POS**: the encoder and the BLSTM-CRF classifier with the POS tag feature.
- **POS-AttWD-BLSTM-CRF**: our proposal, the encoder with the attention mechanism on word dependencies, and the BLSTM-CRF classifier, along with the POS tag feature.

We also compare our proposed (AttWD-BLSTM-CRF+POS) with state-of-the-art models for the ATE task:

- **BLSTM-CRF**: a BLSTM-CRF classifier from [8].
- **Poria**: a deep convolutional neural network combined with language rules, that uses filtered POS tags and a lexicon as additional features, from [20].
- **Li**: a framework for ATE that uses truncated history attention and a selective transformation network to incorporate opinion information, from [14].
- **IHS_RD**: a model that uses the IHS Goldfire linguistic processor and a CRF [4].
- **DLIREC**: a CRF classifier with manually engineered features [27].
- **NLANGP**: a RNN-CRF classifier with manually engineered features [26].
- **DE-CNN**: a CNN model using general-purpose and domain-specific pre-trained word embeddings [32].
- **Ctrl**: the DE-CNN model using control layers between the embedding and CNN layers [23].

### 4.4   Experimental Setup

Table 2 reports the list of parameters used by our model POS-AttWD-BLSTM-CRF and its variations during the evaluation. For what concerns the parameters used by POS-AttWD-BLSTM-CRF, we remind that we need to define the number of LSTM cell units used on the encoder and classifier, the ideal number of epochs to train the model, and the dropout rate. We randomly sampled 10% of the datasets for validation and we select the values that achieved the best results. The models were trained using Adam algorithm [11] with a learning rate of 0.01 and a dropout rate of 20% [10] on LSTM layers.

To represent each word in a sentence by its embedding, we used the 300d GloVe embeddings [19] trained on 6B tokens. Word embeddings are distributed representations of text, which encode semantic and syntactic properties of words.

For the other competitors discussed in the last section, we avoid studying the best configuration for each of their parameters. Instead, we present in the next section the results reported in their papers and the comparison with our results.

**Table 2.** The hyperparameters used for each model and dataset.

| Domain | Model | # Epochs | # Cells (Enc.) | # Cells (Class.) |
|---|---|---|---|---|
| Laptop (2014) | Enc-BLSTM-CRF | 30 | 128 | 256 |
| | Enc-BLSTM-CRF+POS | 32 | 128 | 256 |
| | POS-AttWD-BLSTM-CRF | 56 | 128 | 256 |
| Restaurant (2014) | Enc-BLSTM-CRF | 22 | 128 | 256 |
| | Enc-BLSTM-CRF+POS | 16 | 128 | 256 |
| | POS-AttWD-BLSTM-CRF | 46 | 128 | 256 |
| Restaurant (2016) | Enc-BLSTM-CRF | 58 | 256 | 256 |
| | Enc-BLSTM-CRF+POS | 37 | 256 | 256 |
| | POS-AttWD-BLSTM-CRF | 31 | 256 | 256 |

## 4.5 Experimental Results

Table 3 shows the evaluation metric values obtained for each model on the test sets. The results show the average performance after 10 runs.

From the results presented in Table 3, we claim that both the POS tag feature and the attention mechanism with word dependencies are important to improve the recall metric, increasing the model capability of identifying aspect terms in the sentences, reducing the number of false negatives.

Table 4 shows the F1 scores obtained using our proposed architecture and the state-of-the-art methods. The results reported for our competitors were copied from their papers. Our model achieved competitive results when compared with other state-of-the-art models, but using only the POS tag and word dependencies feature, and without manually selecting a subset of them or other features as those approaches. We believe our model is a promising alternative baseline with minimal feature engineering effort.

**Table 3.** Results obtained using the three different models. P stands for precision, R for recall and F1 for F1 score.

| Domain | Model | P | R | F1 |
|---|---|---|---|---|
| Laptop (2014) | Enc-BLSTM-CRF | 89.31% | 73.59% | 80.69% |
| | Enc-BLSTM-CRF+POS | 88.50% | **74.90%** | 81.12% |
| | POS-AttWD-BLSTM-CRF | **89.51%** | 74.78% | **81.47%** |
| Restaurant (2014) | Enc-BLSTM-CRF | 89.52% | 85.50% | 87.46% |
| | Enc-BLSTM-CRF+POS | 88.97% | **86.61%** | 87.75% |
| | POS-AttWD-BLSTM-CRF | **89.81%** | 86.00% | **87.86%** |
| Restaurant (2016) | Enc-BLSTM-CRF | 72.35% | 70.07% | 71.15% |
| | Enc-BLSTM-CRF+POS | 72.15% | 72.23% | 72.13% |
| | POS-AttWD-BLSTM-CRF | **73.05%** | **73.15%** | **73.04%** |

**Table 4.** Comparison between the F1 scores obtained using our architecture and state-of-the-art methods. The symbol '-' indicates the results were not available in the paper.

| Model | Laptop (2014) | Restaurant (2014) | Restaurant (2016) |
|---|---|---|---|
| IHS_RD | 74.55% | 79.62% | - |
| DLIREC | 73.78% | 84.01% | - |
| NLANGP | - | - | 72.34% |
| BLSTM-CRF | 77.96% | 84.12% | - |
| Li | 79.52% | 85.61% | 73.61% |
| Poria | 82.32% | 87.17% | - |
| DE-CNN | 81.59% | - | 74.37% |
| Ctrl | **82.73%** | - | **75.64%** |
| POS-AttWD-BLSTM-CRF (our) | 81.47% | **87.86%** | 73.04% |

## 5    Conclusion and Future Work

In this work, we have addressed the problem of aspect term extraction. We used an encoder structure with an attention mechanism that allowed the use of an important feature: grammatical dependencies between words. We also used POS tags as another feature, but unlike other works, we did not manually select a subset of those features, we let the model select those that are most relevant. Our proposed architecture compared to the state-of-the-art models shows very promising results without resorting to manual inputs like dictionaries or linguistic rules, only minimal feature engineering.

Analyzing product reviews increasingly becomes a research practice of great value to e-commerce, with the explosive growth of user-generated content on the Web. As the number of reviews is increasing to thousands or even millions, it is challenging for the potential buyers and the manufacturers to read through them to make a wise decision. Consider an e-commerce system architecture, in the web interface, the buyer can review the products or services he/she likes and dislikes. As a future research line, we aim at extending our proposed deep learning model (POS-AttWD-BLSTM-CRF) as a component of the e-commerce architecture with a module to continuously consume the product and service reviews as stream data (using the Apache Kafka framework [25], for instance), and another module with a microservice that can consume each fired stream and extract the aspect term and aspect sentiment using our deep learning model. The results outputted by the model can be stored in the e-commerce application database and show when required by the potential buyers or the manufacturers.

# References

1. Bahdanau, D., Cho, K., Bengio, Y.: Neural machine translation by jointly learning to align and translate. arXiv preprint arXiv:1409.0473 (2014)
2. Bharadwaj, A., Mortensen, D., Dyer, C., Carbonell, J.: Phonologically aware neural model for named entity recognition in low resource transfer settings. In: Proceedings of the 2016 Conference on Empirical Methods in Natural Language Processing, pp. 1462–1472 (2016)
3. Bojanowski, P., Grave, E., Joulin, A., Mikolov, T.: Enriching word vectors with subword information. Trans. Assoc. Comput. Linguist. **5**, 135–146 (2017)
4. Chernyshevich, M.: IHS R&D belarus: cross-domain extraction of product features using CRF. In: Proceedings of the 8th International Workshop on Semantic Evaluation (SemEval 2014), pp. 309–313 (2014)
5. Cho, K., et al.: Learning phrase representations using RNN encoder-decoder for statistical machine translation. arXiv preprint arXiv:1406.1078 (2014)
6. De Marneffe, M.C., Manning, C.D.: Stanford typed dependencies manual. Technical report, Stanford University (2008)
7. Do, H.H., Prasad, P., Maag, A., Alsadoon, A.: Deep learning for aspect-based sentiment analysis: a comparative review. Expert Syst. Appl. **118**, 272–299 (2019)
8. Giannakopoulos, A., Musat, C., Hossmann, A., Baeriswyl, M.: Unsupervised aspect term extraction with B-LSTM & CRF using automatically labelled datasets. arXiv preprint arXiv:1709.05094 (2017)
9. Graves, A., Fernández, S., Schmidhuber, J.: Bidirectional LSTM networks for improved phoneme classification and recognition. In: Duch, W., Kacprzyk, J., Oja, E., Zadrożny, S. (eds.) ICANN 2005. LNCS, vol. 3697, pp. 799–804. Springer, Heidelberg (2005). https://doi.org/10.1007/11550907_126
10. Hinton, G.E., Srivastava, N., Krizhevsky, A., Sutskever, I., Salakhutdinov, R.R.: Improving neural networks by preventing co-adaptation of feature detectors. arXiv preprint arXiv:1207.0580 (2012)
11. Kingma, D.P., Ba, J.: Adam: a method for stochastic optimization. arXiv preprint arXiv:1412.6980 (2014)
12. Lakkaraju, H., Socher, R., Manning, C.: Aspect specific sentiment analysis using hierarchical deep learning. In: NIPS Workshop on Deep Learning and Representation Learning (2014)
13. Lample, G., Ballesteros, M., Subramanian, S., Kawakami, K., Dyer, C.: Neural architectures for named entity recognition. arXiv preprint arXiv:1603.01360 (2016)
14. Li, X., Bing, L., Li, P., Lam, W., Yang, Z.: Aspect term extraction with history attention and selective transformation. arXiv preprint arXiv:1805.00760 (2018)

15. Liu, B., Zhang, L.: A survey of opinion mining and sentiment analysis. In: Aggarwal, C., Zhai, C. (eds.) Mining Text Data, pp. 415–463. Springer, Boston (2012). https://doi.org/10.1007/978-1-4614-3223-4_13
16. Luo, L., et al.: An attention-based BiLSTM-CRF approach to document-level chemical named entity recognition. Bioinformatics **34**(8), 1381–1388 (2017)
17. Ma, X., Hovy, E.: End-to-end sequence labeling via bi-directional LSTM-CNNs-CRF. arXiv preprint arXiv:1603.01354 (2016)
18. Ma, Y., Peng, H., Cambria, E.: Targeted aspect-based sentiment analysis via embedding commonsense knowledge into an attentive LSTM. In: Thirty-Second AAAI Conference on Artificial Intelligence (2018)
19. Pennington, J., Socher, R., Manning, C.D.: GloVe: global vectors for word representation. In: Empirical Methods in Natural Language Processing (EMNLP), pp. 1532–1543 (2014). http://www.aclweb.org/anthology/D14-1162
20. Poria, S., Cambria, E., Gelbukh, A.: Aspect extraction for opinion mining with a deep convolutional neural network. Knowl.-Based Syst. **108**, 42–49 (2016)
21. Rana, T.A., Cheah, Y.N.: Aspect extraction in sentiment analysis: comparative analysis and survey. Artif. Intell. Rev. **46**(4), 459–483 (2016)
22. Ravi, S., Larochelle, H.: Optimization as a model for few-shot learning (2016)
23. Shu, L., Xu, H., Liu, B.: Controlled CNN-based sequence labeling for aspect extraction. arXiv preprint arXiv:1905.06407 (2019)
24. Sutskever, I., Vinyals, O., Le, Q.V.: Sequence to sequence learning with neural networks. In: Advances in Neural Information Processing Systems, pp. 3104–3112 (2014)
25. Thein, K.M.M., Nyunt, T.T.S.: Apache Kafka: a high-throughput distributed messaging system. In: Thirteenth International Conference On Computer Applications (ICCA 2015) (2015)
26. Toh, Z., Su, J.: NLANGP at SemEval-2016 task 5: improving aspect based sentiment analysis using neural network features. In: Proceedings of the 10th International Workshop on Semantic Evaluation (SemEval 2016), pp. 282–288 (2016)
27. Toh, Z., Wang, W.: DLIREC: aspect term extraction and term polarity classification system. In: Proceedings of the 8th International Workshop on Semantic Evaluation (SemEval 2014), pp. 235–240 (2014)
28. Toutanova, K., Klein, D., Manning, C.D., Singer, Y.: Feature-rich part-of-speech tagging with a cyclic dependency network. In: Proceedings of the 2003 Conference of the North American Chapter of the Association for Computational Linguistics on Human Language Technology, vol. 1, pp. 173–180. Association for Computational Linguistics (2003)
29. Wang, W., Pan, S.J., Dahlmeier, D., Xiao, X.: Recursive neural conditional random fields for aspect-based sentiment analysis. arXiv preprint arXiv:1603.06679 (2016)
30. Wang, W., Pan, S.J., Dahlmeier, D., Xiao, X.: Coupled multi-layer attentions for co-extraction of aspect and opinion terms. In: Thirty-First AAAI Conference on Artificial Intelligence (2017)
31. Xie, J., Yang, Z., Neubig, G., Smith, N.A., Carbonell, J.: Neural cross-lingual named entity recognition with minimal resources. arXiv preprint arXiv:1808.09861 (2018)
32. Xu, H., Liu, B., Shu, L., Yu, P.S.: Double embeddings and CNN-based sequence labeling for aspect extraction. arXiv preprint arXiv:1805.04601 (2018)

# State Machine Based Human-Bot Conversation Model and Services

Shayan Zamanirad[1(✉)], Boualem Benatallah[1,2], Carlos Rodriguez[1],
Mohammadali Yaghoubzadehfard[1], Sara Bouguelia[2], and Hayet Brabra[2]

[1] University of New South Wales (UNSW), Sydney, Australia
{shayanz,boualem,crodriguez,m.yaghoubzadehfard}@cse.unsw.edu.au
[2] LIRIS – University of Claude Bernard Lyon 1, Villeurbanne, France
{sara.bouguelia,hayet.brabra}@univ-lyon1.fr

**Abstract.** Task-oriented virtual assistants (or simply *chatbots*) are in very high demand these days. They employ third-party APIs to serve end-users via natural language interactions. Chatbots are famed for their easy-to-use interface and gentle learning curve (it only requires one of humans' most innate ability, the use of *natural language*). Studies on human conversation patterns show, however, that day-to-day dialogues are of *multi-turn* and *multi-intent* nature, which pushes the need for chatbots that are more resilient and flexible to this style of conversations. In this paper, we propose the idea of leveraging Conversational State Machine to make it a core part of chatbots' *conversation engine* by formulating conversations as a sequence of *states*. Here, each state covers an *intent* and contains a nested state machine to help manage tasks associated to the conversation *intent*. Such enhanced *conversation engine*, together with a novel technique to spot implicit information from dialogues (by exploiting *Dialog Acts*), allows chatbots to manage tangled conversation situations where most existing chatbot technologies fail.

**Keywords:** Conversational chatbot · State machine · Natural language processing · REST API

## 1 Introduction

Messaging bots, software robots, and virtual assistants (hereafter for simplicity called *chatbots*), are used by millions of people every day [9]. Applications such as Siri, Google Now, Amazon Alexa, Baidu and Cortana have a presence in our living rooms and are with us all the time. New chatbots are developed continuously, from those providing psychological counseling to task-oriented chatbots that help book flights and hotels. They use human-friendly interfaces, using natural language (e.g., text or voice), to access complex cognitive backend, which tries to understand user needs and serve them by invoking the proper services. Despite the interest and usage of chatbots, their interactions with users are still in primitive stage.

© Springer Nature Switzerland AG 2020
S. Dustdar et al. (Eds.): CAiSE 2020, LNCS 12127, pp. 199–214, 2020.
https://doi.org/10.1007/978-3-030-49435-3_13

Studies on human-chatbot conversation patterns (e.g. [21]) reveal that, in practice, conversations are *multi-turn*, where there may exist missing information (e.g. "location") in users' utterances (e.g. *"what will the weather be like tomorrow?"*) that needs to be fulfilled by the chatbot before an actual API call be invoked. Other examples include an invocation of an API by the chatbot to resolve the value of a missing parameter, a question by a chatbot to a user to confirm an inferred intent value or make a choice among several options, extracting an intent parameter value from the history of user and chatbot interactions. In addition, according to studies on human-chatbot dialogue patterns (e.g. [25]), switching between different intents is a natural behaviour for users. Thus, there is a need for more dynamic and rich abstractions to represent and reason about multi-turn and multi-intent conversational patterns. The main challenge of achieving this objective arise from variations in open-end interactions and the large space of APIs that are potentially unknown to developers.

In this paper, we propose a multi-turn and multi-intent conversational model that leverages Hierarchical State Machines (HSMs) [7,27]. HSMs are a well-known model suited to describing reactive behaviours, which are very relevant for conversations but other specific users-bot-API conversation behaviours must be modelled too. More specifically, HSMs reduce complexity that may be caused by the number of states that are needed to specify interactions between users, chatbots and services.

In this approach, conversations are represented as a sequence of *states* each covering an *intent*. A state relies on a *nested state machine* to manage required tasks towards handling an *intent* to completion. Transitions between states are triggered when certain conditions are satisfied (e.g., detection of new intent, detection of missing required parameter). The proposed *conversational model and engine*, together with new techniques to identify implicit information from dialogues (by exploiting *Dialog Acts* [25]), enable chatbots to manage tangled and multi-turn conversational situations. In summary, our contribution is three-folded:

- We propose the concept of conversation state machines as an abstraction to represent and reason about dialog patterns. Conversational state machines represent multi-turn and multi-intent conversations where state represent intents, their parameters and actions to realise them. Transitions automatically trigger actions to perform desired intent fulfillment operations. The proposed model extends hierarchical state machine model, to effectively support complex user intents through conversations among users, chatbots services and API invocations.
- We propose a *dialog act* recognition technique to identify state transition conditions. We use dialog acts to specify interaction styles between users, chatbots and APIs (e.g., user submit utterance, chatbot detect missing slot value, chatbot ask user to provide missing slot value, user submit a new utterance to supply missing value).
- We develop a conversation management engine that is used to initiate, monitor and control the run-time interactions between users, chatbots and APIs.

The knowledge required at runtime by the conversation management engine is extracted from chatbot specification (i.e., developer supplied user intents) and user utterances. In this way, the conversation manager automates the generation of run-time nested conversation state machines that are used to deploy, monitor and control conversations with respect to user intents and utterances.

## 2 Related Work

**Conversational Bots.** Bots are computer programs that provide natural language conversations between users and software systems. The input of such systems is natural language utterances (text/voice). The system also generates an appropriate response (in form of text/voice) back to the user. Bots are generally categorized into two classes [5,15]: (i) Non-task oriented, and (ii) Task oriented.

*Non-task* oriented bots focus on open domain conversations with users (i.e., non predefined goal of conversations). Examples for this type of bots include DBpediabot [1], Cleverbot[1] and Mitsuku[2]. This type of bots handle open-domain conversations and hardly keep track of conversation states and are therefore not designed to perform specific user tasks (e.g., task management).

*Task-oriented* bots, on the other hand, allow users to accomplish a goal (e.g. maintain schedules [6]) using information provided by users during conversations. Since the focus of this paper is on task-oriented bots, the word *"chatbot"* refers to this type of bots for simplicity. Task-oriented bots are classified into two categories [5]: *pipeline* and *end-to-end*. A *pipeline-based* chatbot is built with a set of components, each responsible for a specific task [5]. Research in this area mainly focuses on such tasks, including user intents classification [26], finding slot/value pairs [8] and controlling dialog states [9]. Interested readers are referred to [10] for a comprehensive discussion. On the other hand, *end-to-end* chatbots leverage the idea of generative models and apply neural-based approaches [18] to train and build a model that can decide what the next system action should be by looking at the dialog history [24]. Such chatbots take in user utterances (as sequences of input tokens [10]) and generates actions (such as API invocations, database queries) as sequences of output tokens. Research in this context includes the work by Rastogi et al. Li et al. [18] tackled the problem of building an end-to-end model by considering it as a task completion system, where its final goal is to complete a task (e.g. booking ticket), Furthermore, using memory networks [28], and query reduction networks [23] are other approaches that have been proposed to tackle the challenge of having end-to-end conversational chatbots.

---

[1] https://www.cleverbot.com/.

[2] https://www.pandorabots.com/mitsuku/.

1. **User**      *Book a table at Time for Thai please*
2. **Chatbot** *What is the date?*
3. **User**      *hmmm... never mind! Do I have any appointment on Saturday*
4. **Chatbot** *I cannot see anything on your calendar, you look free for Saturday.*
5. **User**      *Ok, thanks!*

**Fig. 1.** User changes the intent to know about her calendar schedule

**Dialogue Management.** Controlling the conversation flow, known as *dialogue management*, is one of the key tasks in conversational chatbots. Dialogue management includes keep tracking of information that is entered implicitly or explicitly by users, managing complex interactions with users, and choosing appropriate actions based on the history of interactions [13]. Research in this context includes the work by Lopez et al. [19], who leveraged the concept of workflows by proposing a system that takes a business process model and generates a list of dialog management rules to deploy/run the chatbot.

Henderson et al. [11] formalized interactions as hidden states with random sequences and transition probabilities using Markov decision processes (MDP) trained on example conversations. More advanced techniques that build on NLP provide rule- and template-based conversations for data science tasks [14], pattern-matching over context-aware conversations for DevOps processes [2], nested and sequence conversations to accomplish complex data science tasks [9], integration of state machines and re-enforcement learning for dialog optimization [7], state and slot tracking during conversations [16]. However, these efforts do not focus on augmenting conversations with knowledge that is essential for the superimposition natural language interactions over large number of evolving APIs.

We identified two main limitations in the works above: First, they heavily rely on the availability of massive amounts of annotated data, structured knowledge base and conversation data. Collecting domain-specific dialog data is laborious [26] and hinders scalability in the context of larger and multi-domain systems. Second, existing end-to-end systems are hard to trace: They can be considered "black-boxes" that accept user utterances in input and return new system states/actions as output. Since in this paper we are addressing the issue of supporting *multi-intent* conversations in chatbots, the use of existing probabilistic approaches such as memory networks and MDPs becomes prohibitive due to the need for collecting huge training datasets for the intents that the chatbot aims to support. We therefore opt for pipeline-based chatbots, built with a set of key components designed to perform specific tasks (e.g. intent recognition). As we will discuss in the following sections, the main difference between our approach and existing pipeline-based ones is the clear separation between the *conversation logic* and *actual implementation* of such logic. At the center of our approach, we utilize the concept of HSMs [7,27] by formulating user-chatbot interaction as a sequence of states. Such abstraction helps bot developers seamlessly define/choose user intent(s) they would like their chatbot to support.

# 3    Human-Chatbot Conversations

A conversation between user and chatbot can be formulated as a sequence of utterances. For example, to answer user utterance *"Please remind @Sarah that we have meeting tomorrow by 1:30PM"*, after performing the task (e.g. reminder) chatbot replies with, e.g., *"Ok, reminder sent to Sarah"*. Studies on human conversation patterns [12,20,22] reveal that human-chatbot dialogue can be divided into three categories:

- **Single Intent**[3]**- Single Turn**: Interaction between user and chatbot is in the form of <*Question, Answer*> pairs. The assumption here is that user provides all the required information (e.g. slots[4]/values) at once, in one single utterance [30]. Thus, each utterance from user (e.g. *"Please text Bob that we are in meeting room 401K"*) has a reply from chatbot (*"We are in meeting room 401K' is sent to Bob"*). This type of conversation is *stateless*, i.e., each user utterance is treated separately without using any knowledge from past conversations or context. Thus, if any information is missing in user utterance (e.g. location, date), chatbot is not able to perform the required task (e.g. *book a flight ticket*). Finally, in this type of conversation, parties talk about only about one specific intent (e.g. *schedule meetings* [6]) during the whole conversation.
- **Single Intent - Multi Turn**: Providing missing information (e.g. location, date) to generate a complete intent is a common behaviour that people follow in their daily conversations [12,15]. For example, while talking to a friend on the phone we may ask, "I'm going to have lunch, do you you have any suggestion?" to get some ideas for lunch. However, without specifying the place where we are at (e.g. "UNSW") or our preference for today (e.g. "Thai food", "Sandwich", "noodle"), our friend is less likely able to give us concrete suggestions. Thus, she asks questions to get more details (e.g. "Where are you?", "What do you prefer", "Do you like something soupy?"). Similar to this example, information (e.g. "departureDate", "destinationCity") that chatbot needs to perform a task (e.g. *call Expedia API to book a flight ticket*) is scattered across multiple user utterances.
- **Multi Intent - Multi Turn**: In this type of conversation, the intent continuously changes. Figure 1 exemplifies a dialogue where user changes the intent by asking about *"her appointment on the weekend"*. Changing intent is something usual that people do in their day-to-day conversations [12]. However, participating in a multi-intent conversation where conversation information is scattered into multiple utterances, is a challenging task for chatbots [24]. Such difficulty stems mainly from the challenges of identifying user intent changes [21], and tracking slots information for each intent in a conversation. In the following sections, we explain our approach to empower chatbots in handling this type of conversations by utilising Hierarchical State Machines (HSMs).

---

[3] An *intent* refers to users' purposes, which a chatbot should be able to respond to (e.g. *"find restaurant"* or *"book table"*).

[4] A *slot* is an important information that is necessary for a chatbot to understand in order to be able to serve the correct answer (e.g. location, data, time).

# 4    Conversation State Machines

We propose to represent User-Chatbot-API conversations using an extended hierarchical state machine model. In this model, a state machine contains a set of states representing user intents. We call these states, "intent-states". An intent-state characterizes the fulfillment of specific user intent. In the following, we describe different types of states and transitions between states:

**Basic Intent State:** When user utterance carries all the required information to fulfill the user intent, chatbot does not need to communicate with user to get any further information. We call this state a *basic* intent state, where chatbot has everything needed to perform required action (e.g., API call). For example, given a user utterance (e.g. *"What is the weather forecast in Sydney?"*) with an intent (e.g. "GetWeather"), chatbot invokes an API (e.g. *OpenWeatherMap* to get weather condition) and returns a message to user (e.g. *"We have Scattered showers in Sydney."*). The interaction between user and chatbot is straight forward, without any further question from chatbot.

**Nested State:** If user utterance has missing information, then the chatbot needs to communicate with user to get missing values before it perform further actions to fulfill the intent. In this situation, the intent-state relies on other nested states [9] to complete the intent. More specifically, a *nested state* is used by chatbot to ask user for missing values of intent slots. Based on user response a nested state is divided into two categories: (i) *nested slot-value state*, and (ii) *nested slot-intent state*.

   *Nested slot-value state* represents a situation where user explicitly provides "value" for the slot-filling question asked by chatbot. For example, in *restaurant booking* chatbot, given the chatbot question *"What is the date?"* (to fulfill *bookingDate* slot), user answers with *"This Sunday"*. This answer does not require any further processing as it provides the missing slot (e.g. *bookingDate*) value.

   *Nested slot-intent state* represents a situation where user does not provide slot "value" directly, but provides an utterance with a new request (i.e., new intent) that the chatbot needs to process to obtain the missing value. For example, considering the *restaurant booking* chatbot, given the chatbot question *"What is the date?"*, user replies with *"Which day of the weekend am I free?"*. The answer from the user is another utterance whose processing identifies another intent which is represented by another intent-state e.g. "CheckCalendar". In order to obtain the slot value in this case, the parent intent-state ("BookRestaurant") triggers a transition to a nested slot-intent state ("CheckCalendar").

## 4.1    Transitions Between States

Transitions between states are triggered when actions are performed (e.g., asking a clarification question to a user to resolve an intent parameter value) or upon the detecting intent switch in conversations (i.e., detecting a new intent). We identify three types of transitions: (i) *new intent*, (ii) *nested slot.value*, and (iii) *nested slot.intent* transitions.

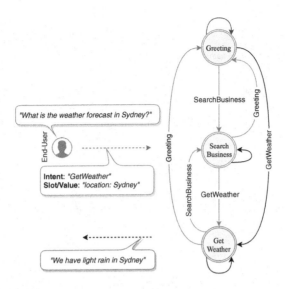

**Fig. 2.** Transition between intent-states based on user intent - current intent-state is denoted by *blue* color, "new intent" transition is highlighted in *orange* (Color figure online)

**New intent** transitions refer to the movements between intent-states. The state machine transits to an a new intent-state if the processing of a new user utterance identifies a new intent (an intent is that is not handled by the current conversation state). Figure 2 shows an example of *"new intent"* transition between two intent-states (*SearchBusiness, GetWeather*). For example, assuming that state machine is in "Greeting" intent-state, user asks for restaurant suggestions. User utterance i.e. *"Any Italian restaurant near Kingsford"* triggers a transition to move from the state "Greeting" (current intent-state) to the state "SearchBusiness" (new intent-state). Then after, user utters another request, e.g. *"What is the weather forecast in Sydney?"*). This new user utterance has a different intent (e.g. "GetWeather"). Thus, it triggers a transition to move from "SearchBusiness" to "GetWeather" intent-state (blue colored state in Fig. 2).

**Nested slot.value** transition represents the movement of state machine to nested slot-value state. The state machine moves to a slot-value state if user provides a "value" for the missing slot upon a bot request for such value. Figure 3 shows an example of *"nested slot.value"* transition within "GetWeather" intent-state. For example, to fill a missing slot (e.g. *location*), state machine moves from parent state "GetWeather" (current intent-state) to the nested slot-value state "location" (depicted with red colour in Fig. 3) where chatbot asks user to provide information (e.g. *"Where are you?"*). User replies with a value (e.g. "I'm in Sydney"). The state machine moves back from nested slot-value state "location" to the parent state "GetWeather" to continue the conversation with user.

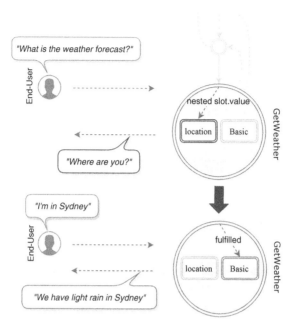

**Fig. 3.** Transition to nested slot-value state denoted by red color (Color figure online)

**Nested slot.intent** transitions indicate the movements of state machine to nested slot-intent states. For example, to fill a missing slot (e.g. *location*), chatbot asks user to provide information (e.g. *"Where are you?"*). User's answer (e.g. *"Where is my home town?"*) carries another intent (e.g. "GetUserDetails") to obtain the missing value. This new intent is handled by a nested state in which the value of the missing value is obtained (e.g., by invoking an API).

## 5    Generating State Machines

We devise *"State Machine Generater"* (SMG), a service that is used to generate a state machine that allows chatbot to manage conversations at run-time. SMG takes as input (i) user utterances, and (ii) bot specification which is a set of intents (e.g. *Greeting, SearchBusiness, GetWeather, GoodBye*). In the following, we explain the steps taken by SMG to generate a state machine.

### 5.1    Generating Intent States from Bot Specification

When SMG receives a bot specification (i.e., a set of user intents), it creates an intent-state per user intent. For example, an intent-state, namely *SearchBusiness* state is created to represents the user intent "SearchBusiness" (i.e., get list of restaurants and cafes).

**Table 1.** Examples of *Dialog Acts* in a conversation between user and chatbot.

| User | Chatbot |
|------|---------|
| Is there any Italian restaurant around?<br>[*New Intent*] | Where are you?<br>[*Request Information*] |
| I'm in Kingsford.<br>[*Provide Information*] | I found *Mamma Teresa* in "412 Anzac Pde..."<br>[*Provide Information*] |

SMG creates intent-states for two types of user intents. The first type of user intent is general communication intent (e.g. *Greeting, GoodBye*). These intents are fulfilled using *(question, answer)* pairs that do not require any API invocation. The second type of user intent requires the invocation of an API method to be completed. For example, in "GetWeather" user intent, the chatbot needs to invoke *OpenWeatherMap* API to retrieve weather conditions and fulfills user intent.

### 5.2   Generating Transitions Between States

At run time, the bot generates three types of transitions namely "new intent state", "intent state to nested slot.value state", "intent state to nested slot.intent state". To generate these transitions, we leverage dialog acts [25]. In this section, we first describe dialog acts and then we explain how SMG generates transitions using dialog acts.

**Dialog Acts.** Understanding user needs and engaging in natural language conversations requires chatbot to identify hidden actions in user utterances, called *dialog acts*. Whether the user is making a statement, or asking a question, or negotiating on suggestions, are all hidden acts in user utterances [4].

In a nutshell, dialog acts convey the meaning of utterances at the level of illocutionary force [15]. For instance, 42 dialog acts were identified in [25]. Inspired by this work and empirical studies on human-chatbot conversations [12], we adapted dialog acts to the requirements of *multi intent - multi turn* chatbots that leverage APIs. Table 1 shows examples of these dialog acts.

More specifically, we focus on the following dialog acts:

- *U-New Intent*: this act indicates that user has a new intent. For example, when user says *"Which day of this weekend am I free?"*), her intention is to know about her availability time for the weekend (intent is e.g. *CheckCalendar*).
- *C-Request Information*: This act indicates that chatbot asks user to provide missing slot value. For example, chatbot asks the user (e.g. *"Where are you?"*) to provide her location.

- **U-Provide Information**: This act indicates that user provides an information (e.g. *"15 March"*) for a former question asked by the chatbot (e.g. *"What is the date?"*).
- **U-Provide Nested Intent**: This act indicates that user provides utterance (e.g. *"When is my birthday?"*) to answer a former question asked by chatbot (e.g. *"What is the date?"*). The completion of this utterance requires transition to a nested intent state.
- **C-Provide Information**: This act indicates that chatbot replies to user request by providing an answer. For example, chatbot answer (e.g. *"I found Mamma Teresa, it's in 412 Anzac Parade..."*) to the question asked by user (e.g. *"Is there an Italian restaurant around?"*).

**Generating Transitions.** We annotate user-chatbot conversation messages using dialog acts. Thus, sequences of dialog acts (e.g. <*C-request info, U-provides info, ...*>) can be inferred from conversations. We call these sequences dialog act patterns. Dialog act patterns are used by the SMG to generate state transitions.

*New Intent-State* - The SMG generates this type of transition upon identifying the dialog act patterns:

- <*U-new intent*>: It describes a situation where user starts a conversation by uttering a request (e.g. *What is the weather forecast for Sydney today?*) which is annotated with *U-New Intent* dialog act. This triggers a "new intent-state" transition from "Greeting" (current intent-state) to the "GetWeather" intent-state (as shown in Fig. 2 with blue color).
- <*..., C-provide info, U-new intent*>: It represents a situation where user utters another request (annotated with *U-New Intent* dialog act) right after an answer from chatbot. The chatbot answer is related to a request asked by user in previous conversation turns. For example, when chatbot answers user request with e.g. *"The weather in Sydney is sunny today"*, the user asks a new utterance i.e. *"I want to drink slushy, is there any McDonald's around?"*. The new user utterance carries a new intent (e.g. *SearchRestaurant*). This triggers a "new intent-state" transition from "GetWeather" intent-state to "SearchRestaurant" intent-state.

*Intent State to Nested slot.value State* - The SMG generates this type of transition upon identifying the following pattern: <*..., C-request info, U-provide info*>. This pattern describes a situation where user utters a request with missing information that the chatbot needs before it can fulfills the user intent. Thus, chatbot asks user to provide the missing information. In this case the user answer provides the missing value. Figure 3 shows an example of *"nested slot.value"* transition within "GetWeather" intent-state. For example, when user asks for weather condition (*"What is the weather forecast?"*), a "nested slot.value" transition from "GetWeather" intent-state (current state) to "location" nested slot-value state is created. Chatbot then asks *"Where are you?"* and user replies with *"I'm in Sydney"*. The state machine then goes back to the parent intent-state "GetWeather".

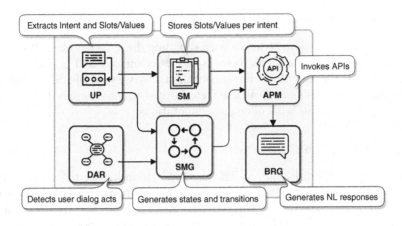

**Fig. 4.** Conversation manager architecture

*Nested slot.value State to Nested slot.intent State* - SMG generates this type of transition upon identifying the following pattern: $<..., C\text{-}request\ info, U\text{-}provide$ *nested intent>*. This pattern describes a situation where a chatbot asks user to provide a value for a missing slot value (e.g. *location*). The user answers with another request with an intent to compute this value using another service. For example, when chatbot asks *"Where are you?"*, the user answers with the utterance *"Where is my home town?"* which is annotated with *U-Provide Nested Intent* dialog act. This pattern triggers a "nested slot.intent" transition from "location" nested slot-value state (current state) to "GetUserDetails" nested intent-state. In this state, chatbot invokes an API to get the "user home town". The result (e.g. "Sydney") is the value for missing slot (e.g. location).

## 6 Conversation Manager Service

In order to support *multi-intent and multi-turn* conversations, chatbots need we devise a service that initiates, monitors and controls conversations. This service is called *conversation manager*. It utilises a set of components to communicate with users, manages the hierarchical state machine, and invoke APIs.

### 6.1 Conversation Manager Architecture

Figure 4 shows the architecture of conversation manager service. In terms of software architecture, the *conversation manager* relies on the following components namely *Utterance Parser (UP), Dialog Act Recogniser (DAR), State Machine Generator (SMG), Slot Memory (SM), API Manager (APM)* and *Bot Response Generator* (BRG). While *UP, APM* and *BRG* are general components that exist in every chatbot and we refer interested readers to [5,13] for details about such components. In this section, we describe *DAR, SMG, and SM* implementation details.

## 6.2 Dialog Act Recogniser

DAR classifies user utterance into a corresponding dialogue act class. It can use any classification model such as Naive Bayes, MaxEntropy and Support Vector Machine (SVM). In the current implementation, DAR uses a Bi-LSTM classifier [17] trained on Switchboard Dialogue Act Corpus[5] which contains 1155 human to human conversations with dialog act annotations.

## 6.3 State Machine Generator

SMG leverages pyTransitions[6], an off-the-shelf python library to generate state machines. To generate intent-states for general user intents, SMG initialises the *Machine* class from the library with intent-state (e.g. *Greeting, GoodBye*) along with an initial state (e.g. Greeting). To generate intent-states for intents with API invocations, SMG uses an extension module in the library. It imports *NestedState* class from the library with initialization arguments as "name" and "children". "name" refers to the name of intent (e.g. *SearchBusiness*) and "children" refers to required slots of the API (e.g. *type, location*). To generate transitions, SMG uses the "add_transition" operation in *Machine* class of pyTransitions library. A transition is generated by passing the "source" (e.g. *GetWeather*) and "destination" (e.g. *SearchBusiness*) states as arguments to the operation.

## 6.4 Slot Memory Service

"Remembering" the information that user provides in each turn is an essential feature for chatbots. This feature is indispensable when it comes to *multi-intent* conversations, where conversations involve several intents and slot values might be missing in some conversation turns [9]. Having a component that helps recall such information from user utterances throughout the conversation is therefore necessary. This is where the *Slot Memory* (SM) service comes into play. SM stores extracted information from user utterances (e.g. intents, slots/values) sourced from *utterance parser* component in each turn of conversation. In the current version of SM, it uses Redis[7] to store, update and fetch slots/values (e.g. "location": "Barker street") information per intent (e.g. *SearchBusiness*).

# 7    Validation

In order to explore how our proposed conversational model effectively empowers chatbots to handle *multi-intent multi-turn* conversations we run a user study. To exploit this model within chatbots, we create two services for bot developers: (i) *API-KG*, an API Knowledge Graph which contains information about APIs, their methods and annotated training dataset associated to them.

---

[5] https://web.stanford.edu/jurafsky/swb1_dialogact_annot.tar.gz.

[6] https://github.com/pytransitions/transitions.

[7] https://redis.io/.

(ii) *Bot Builder*, a service that semi-automates chatbot development and deployment. *Bot Builder* takes any intent of interest from bot developer and deploys a trained chatbot (with our conversation model embedded inside) over third-party platforms (such as *DialogFlow*). We refer the interested reader to our work [29] for more explanation of these services.

**Participants.** We involved PhD students in Computer Science with experience in cloud services as participants for this user study.

**Study Scenario.** Participants were asked to build a devops chatbot to interact with Amazon Elastic Compute Cloud (EC2)[8]. We chose *devops* domain because of its multiple intents nature. It is a challenging domain for chatbots to handle many intents in conversations. All chatbots in this study should support the following intents: {*Run, Stop, Start, Terminate, Describe*}*Instances*, {*Create, Describe*}*Volumes*, {*Create, Describe*}*Snapshots* and *DescribeImages*. These intents are chosen based on daily basis devops tasks for cloud infrastructure admins; therefore, a devops chatbot is expected to handle such intents for end-users (e.g. cloud admins). Each participant was asked to build four versions of his/her chatbot using the following setups:

- Wit.ai: Participants were asked to use this platform in their chatbots to recognise intents/slots. However, this platform does not have any dialogue management mechanism [3]. Therefore, chatbots that leverage this platform are only able to handle single-turn conversations. The aim of this setup is to emphasize the need for multi-turn conversations.
- Wit.ai + iConverse[9]: In this setup, participants were asked to leverage our proposed conversational model along with Wit.ai in their chatbots. Thus, chatbots are able to manage multi-turn conversations.
- DialogFlow: This platform not only offers intent/slot recognition feature, but it also provides a simple conversational model for chatbots. Thus, chatbots can handle multi-turn conversations. We consider this conversational model as the baseline.
- DialogFlow + iConverse: For this setup, participants used our proposed model instead of the baseline model (provided by DialogFlow). The aim is to see if there is any performance boost in chatbots in handling complex and ambiguous interactions.

**Results and Findings.** We collected a gold standard dataset of 100 utterances for mentioned 10 intents, on average 10 utterance per intent, from Amazon EC2 CLI guideline[10]. We use this dataset to analyse the performance of chatbots by considering the following criteria: (RQ1) *"how many messaging rounds, including both user and chatbot messages, needed to complete all intents?"*, (RQ2) *how many times, on average, chatbot asks user to fulfill missing information*

---

[8] https://aws.amazon.com/ec2/.

[9] For simplicity, we call our conversational model as iConverse in this section.

[10] https://docs.aws.amazon.com/cli/latest/userguide/cli-services-ec2.html.

**Table 2.** Evaluation results. We report on average values for RQs on the settings, Wit baseline (WA-B), DialogFlow baseline (DF-B), Wit + iConverse (WA-I), DialogFlow + iConverse (DF-I)

| Criteria | Settings | | | | Performance upgrades | |
|---|---|---|---|---|---|---|
|  | WA-B | WA-I | DF-B | DF-I | WA-B ->WA-I | DF-B ->DF-I |
| RQ1 | 120.5 | **34.1** | 78.6 | 39 | **56.61%** | 50.38 |
| RQ2 | NA | **6.4** | 40.1 | 8.5 | **84.03%** | 78.80% |
| RQ3 | NA | 0.7 | 17.2 | **0.3** | 95.93% | **98.25%** |
| RQ4 | NA | **0** | 26.1 | 0 | **100%** | **100%** |

for all intent?, (RQ3) "how many times chatbot forgets the topic of conversation (user intent) due to filling a missing information?", and (RQ4) how many times, on average, chatbot forgets user provided values for missing information in all intents? (due to intent changes). As we leveraged on third-party NLU platforms (Wit.ai and DialogFlow) for the Utterance Parser (UP) component in our conversational model, we could no measure the intent/slot recognition accuracy of chatbots in this study.

The evaluation results (Table 2) shows that leveraging Wit.ai (without no dialogue management mechanism) leads to have low performance in user intent accomplishment metric (RQ1) when interactions are in the form of multi-turn. This supports the need for leveraging a conversation engine within the body of chatbots. Combining Wit.ai (as NLU model) with our proposed conversational engine, however, delivers promising performance upgrades in RQ1 and RQ2 metrics comparing to the baseline model (conversation model provided by Wit.ai) by 56.61% and 84.03%, respectively. Moreover, chatbots that benefit from our conversation engine along with DialogFlow (as NLU model only), experienced a boost in performance for RQ3 and RQ4 by 98.25% and 100%. This elevation in performance for RQ4, compare to the baseline model, is because of exploiting the Slot Manager (SM) component inside our proposed model. Due to space limits, gold dataset along with evaluation results in-depth details are available to interested reader[11].

# 8    Conclusions and Future Work

In this paper we proposed a novel approach for the management of *multi-intent multi-turn* conversations based an extended HSM model. We proposed state machine generation techniques to support the automated initiation, monitoring and control of conversations. Our work also comes with its own limitations and space for possible improvements. For instance, we plan to extend our current study to involve qualitative studies by exploring how chatbots with our conversation model perform compare to the chatbots using conversation models provided by third-party platforms.

---

[11] https://tinyurl.com/t9hqyx4.

**Acknowledgement.** We acknowledge Data to Decisions CRC (D2D-CRC) and LIRIS Laboratory for funding this research.

# References

1. Athreya, R.G., Ngomo, A.C.N., Usbeck, R.: Enhancing community interactions with data-driven chatbots - the DBpedia chatbot. In: WWW 2018 (2018)
2. Bradley, N.C., Fritz, T., Holmes, R.: Context-aware conversational developer assistants. In: ICSE 2018 (2018)
3. Braun, D., et al.: Evaluating natural language understanding services for conversational question answering systems. In: ACL 2017 (2017)
4. Bunt, H.: The semantics of dialogue acts. In: IWCS 2011 (2011)
5. Chen, H., Liu, X., Yin, D., Tang, J.: A survey on dialogue systems: recent advances and new frontiers. arXiv preprint arXiv:1711.01731 (2017)
6. Cranshaw, J., et al.: Calendar. help: designing a workflow-based scheduling agent with humans in the loop. In: CHI 2017 (2017)
7. Cuayahuitl, H., Renals, S., Lemon, O., Shimodaira, H.: Reinforcement learning of dialogue strategies with hierarchical abstract machines. In: SLT 2006 (2006)
8. Deoras, A., Sarikaya, R.: Deep belief network based semantic taggers for spoken language understanding. In: Interspeech 2013 (2013)
9. Fast, E., Chen, B., Mendelsohn, J., Bassen, J., Bernstein, M.S.: Iris: a conversational agent for complex tasks. In: CHI 2018 (2018)
10. Gao, J., Galley, M., Li, L., et al.: Neural approaches to conversational AI. Found. Trends® Inf. Retrieval **13**(2–3), 127–298 (2019)
11. Henderson, M.S.: Discriminative methods for statistical spoken dialogue systems. Ph.D. thesis, University of Cambridge (2015)
12. Hutchby, I., Wooffitt, R.: Conversation Analysis. Polity, Cambridge (2008)
13. Ilievski, V., Musat, C., Hossmann, A., Baeriswyl, M.: Goal-oriented chatbot dialog management bootstrapping with transfer learning. arXiv:1802.00500 (2018)
14. John, R. J. L., Potti, N., Patel, J. M.: Ava: from data to insights through conversations (2017)
15. Jurafsky, D., Martin, J.H.: Speech and Language Processing, vol. 3. Pearson, London (2017)
16. Kim, A., et al.: A two-step neural dialog state tracker for task-oriented dialog processing. Comput. Intell. Neurosci. **2018**, 11 (2018)
17. Kumar, H., Agarwal, A., Dasgupta, R., Joshi, S.: Dialogue act sequence labeling using hierarchical encoder with CRF. In: AAAI 2018 (2018)
18. Li, X., Chen, Y.N., Li, L., Gao, J., Celikyilmaz, A.: End-to-end task-completion neural dialogue systems. arXiv preprint arXiv:1703.01008 (2017)
19. López, A., Sànchez-Ferreres, J., Carmona, J., Padró, L.: From process models to chatbots. In: Giorgini, P., Weber, B. (eds.) CAiSE 2019. LNCS, vol. 11483, pp. 383–398. Springer, Cham (2019). https://doi.org/10.1007/978-3-030-21290-2_24
20. Łupkowski, P., Ginz, J.: A corpus-based taxonomy of question responses. In: IWCS 2013 (2013)
21. Mensio, M., et al.: Multi-turn QA: A RNN contextual approach to intent classification for goal-oriented systems. In: WWW 2018 (2018)
22. Raux, A., Eskenazi, M.: A finite-state turn-taking model for spoken dialog systems. In: NAACL 2009 (2009)
23. Seo, M., Min, S., Farhadi, A., Hajishirzi, H.: Query-reduction networks for question answering. arXiv preprint arXiv:1606.04582 (2016)

24. Shah, P., et al.: Building a conversational agent overnight with dialogue self-play. arXiv:1801.04871 (2018)
25. Stolcke, A., et al.: Dialogue act modeling for automatic tagging and recognition of conversational speech. Comput. Linguist. **26**(3), 339–373 (2000)
26. Yan, Z., Duan, N., Chen, P., Zhou, M., Zhou, J., Li, Z.: Building task-oriented dialogue systems for online shopping. In: AAAI 2017 (2017)
27. Yannakakis, M.: Hierarchical state machines. In: van Leeuwen, J., Watanabe, O., Hagiya, M., Mosses, P.D., Ito, T. (eds.) TCS 2000. LNCS, vol. 1872, pp. 315–330. Springer, Heidelberg (2000). https://doi.org/10.1007/3-540-44929-9_24
28. Yoshino, K., Hiraoka, T., Neubig, G., Nakamura, S.: Dialogue state tracking using long short term memory neural networks. In: IWSDS 2016 (2016)
29. Zamanirad, S.: Superimposition of natural language conversations over software enabled services. Ph.D. thesis, University of New South Wales, Sydney, Australia (2019). http://handle.unsw.edu.au/1959.4/65005
30. Zamanirad, S., et al.: Programming bots by synthesizing natural language expressions into API invocations. In: ASE 2017 (2017)

# Process Mining and Analysis

# Stochastic-Aware Conformance Checking: An Entropy-Based Approach

Sander J.J. Leemans[1]([✉]) [iD] and Artem Polyvyanyy[2] [iD]

[1] Queensland University of Technology, Brisbane, QLD 4000, Australia
s.leemans@qut.edu.au
[2] The University of Melbourne, Parkville, VIC 3010, Australia
artem.polyvyanyy@unimelb.edu.au

**Abstract.** Business process management (BPM) aims to support changes and innovations in organizations' processes. Process mining complements BPM with methods, techniques, and tools that provide insights based on observed executions of business processes recorded in event logs of information systems. State-of-the-art discovery and conformance techniques completely ignore or only implicitly consider the information about the likelihood of processes, which is readily available in event logs, even though such stochastic information is necessary for simulation, prediction and recommendation in models. Furthermore, stochastic information can provide business analysts with further actionable insights on frequent and rare conformance issues.

In this paper, we propose precision and recall conformance measures based on the notion of entropy of stochastic automata that are capable of quantifying, and thus differentiating, frequent and rare deviations between an event log and a process model. The feasibility of using the proposed precision and recall measures in industrial settings is demonstrated by an evaluation over several real-world datasets supported by our open-source implementation.

**Keywords:** Process mining · Information theory · Stochastic conformance checking · Entropy · Precision · Recall · Fitness

## 1 Introduction

A business process is an orchestration of activities and resources in an organisation, aiming to achieve a business objective. Business process management (BPM) is an interdisciplinary field that studies concepts and methods that support and improve the way business processes are designed, performed, and analyzed in organizations, with the ultimate goal of reducing their costs, execution times, and failure rates through incremental changes and radical innovations [1,2]. Research in BPM has resulted in a range of methods, tools and techniques for identifying, designing, enacting, monitoring and innovating operational business processes [3,4].

© Springer Nature Switzerland AG 2020
S. Dustdar et al. (Eds.): CAiSE 2020, LNCS 12127, pp. 217–233, 2020.
https://doi.org/10.1007/978-3-030-49435-3_14

Process mining aims to discover, monitor and improve real-world processes using the knowledge accumulated in event logs produced by modern information systems [5], where an event log is a collection of traces, each representing executed events of a customer, order, claim, etc. traversing the business process. As multiple traces might share the same sequence of steps through the process, event logs are inherently stochastic: by accumulating information about business process executions observed over extended periods of time, event logs encode the true likelihood of executing the various sequences of steps through the process. This knowledge about the frequencies attached to real-world processes is invaluable for business process redesign and analysis practices [6], as it can inform flexible performance management [7] and generation of novel business models and processes, both incremental [8] and radical [9,10]. For instance, consider the following event logs, each consisting of 2 distinct traces, with 1,000 traces in total:

$$L_1 = [\langle \text{x-ray}, \text{treat}\rangle^{999}, \qquad \qquad L_2 = [\langle \text{x-ray}, \text{treat}\rangle^1,$$
$$\text{vs}$$
$$\langle \text{MRI}, \text{treat}\rangle^1] \qquad \qquad \langle \text{MRI}, \text{treat}\rangle^{999}]$$

Even though these event logs consist of the same distinct traces, they are very different. In $L_1$, the $\langle \text{MRI}, \text{treat}\rangle$ trace is the exception, while in $L_2$ it is the rule, which likely will influence optimisation strategies.

Some examples of advanced uses of process mining are prediction, recommendation and simulation. In a running trace, using a process model, prediction techniques aim to estimate certain properties of the trace's future steps towards completion, for instance its outcome, its risk of being delayed, its cost, etc. Based on these predictions, recommendation techniques automatically suggest mitigation or optimisation steps for the future of the trace. As different paths through the process model might lead to different properties, prediction and recommendation techniques inherently need to be aware of the stochastic perspective of the process model.

In process optimisation projects, simulation can be used to measure the impact of proposed process changes before they are implemented, and thus before the implementation costs are incurred. That is, several process models with proposed changes are simulated and key performance indicators (for instance, throughput, trace duration characteristics, etc.) are measured, such that a favourable model can be chosen. Key performance indicators such as throughput and trace duration largely depend on the paths taken through the model and, hence, the outcome of the simulations depends on the stochastic perspective of the model.

Even though simulation, prediction and recommendation depend heavily on the stochastic perspective of process models (*stochastic process models*), few techniques have been proposed to construct such models automatically (*stochastic process discovery* techniques) [11]. Typically, the stochastic perspective is constructed by hand as an extension of an existing process model.

However, to truly treat the stochastic perspective of process models as a first-class citizen, it is also necessary to evaluate it. That is, the stochastic perspectives, as modelled manually or discovered by stochastic discovery techniques, might differ substantially from the stochastic perspective of the event log. Thus, stochastic process models risk not being true representations of the actual real-life business process and predictions, recommendations and simulations might return misleading results [12]. Few techniques have been proposed that can be used to verify or assess the quality of stochastic process models with respect to event logs, that is, to perform *stochastic conformance checking* [13], however with the limitation of not supporting loops.

In classical (non-stochastic) conformance checking, typically four dimensions are considered to compare a log to a (non-stochastic) process model: (1) fitness, which expresses the part of behaviour of the event log that is supported by the model, (2) precision, which expresses the part of the model's behaviour that is also in the event log, (3) generalisation, which expresses the likelihood that future behaviour is captured in the model, and (4) simplicity, which expresses whether the model expresses its behaviour in a clear and concise way [14,15]. However, in these existing measures the stochastic perspective of models is not taken into account, and thus they are not suitable to fully evaluate models for, e.g., prediction, recommendation and simulation.

For instance, in [16], we reported on a project with a major German health insurance company that aimed to analyse and simplify about 4,000 of their stochastic process models captured using the EPC notation annotated with probabilities of taking various decisions. The insurer relied on these stochastic models to estimate the number of employees to hire to enact all the operational processes in a calendar year. Given logs of executed processes at the end of the year, the measures proposed in this paper can be used to assess the correctness of the estimates. In Sect. 4, we further illustrate the applicability of our measures in this scenario.

In this paper, we lift two quality measures used in process mining, namely fitness and precision, to consider the stochastic perspectives of event logs (which are inherently stochastic due to the multiplicities of traces occurring) and stochastic process models. That is, we propose two stochastic conformance checking measures, which compare an event log to a stochastic process model. The measures consider both log and model as stochastic automata, and compare the entropy [17] of these automata with the entropy of a third automaton that represents the conjunctive stochastic behaviour of the log and the model. While the measures support any stochastic process model whose behaviour can be represented in a finite stochastic deterministic automaton (see Sect. 2), we illustrate and implemented the measures for Stochastic Petri nets (see Sect. 2). Concretely, this paper contributes:

o Stochastic-aware recall and precision conformance measures for event logs and process models grounded in the entropy of stochastic languages [17,18];
o Eight properties for stochastic-aware conformance measures that aim at establishing the usefulness of measures that satisfy them;
o A publicly available implementation of the proposed conformance measures; and

o An evaluation that demonstrates the applicability and feasibility of the measures in real-life industrial settings.

The remainder of the paper is structured as follows: The next section introduces notions used to support subsequent discussions. Section 3 presents our stochastic-aware precision and recall measures. After that, the measures are evaluated in Sect. 4, and related work is discussed in Sect. 5. Finally, Sect. 6 concludes the paper.

## 2    Stochastic Languages, Petri Nets and Automata

This section introduces notions used in the discussions in the subsequent sections.

Let $\Sigma$ be an alphabet of activities, then $\Sigma^*$ is the set of all possible sequences of activities (*traces*) over $\Sigma$. Let $\epsilon$ denote the empty trace. A *language* $\subseteq \Sigma^*$ is a, possibly infinite, set of traces.

**Definition 1 (Stochastic language).** *A stochastic language $L$ is a function $L: \Sigma^* \to [0,1]$, denoting a probability for each trace, such that $\sum_{t \in \Sigma^*} L(t) = 1$.*

An *event log* is a multiset of traces. For instance, the event log $L_e = [\epsilon, \langle a \rangle^2, \langle a, a \rangle^4, \langle a, a, a \rangle, \langle a, a, a, a \rangle^2]$ consists of 10 traces. Its corresponding stochastic language is $[\epsilon^{0.1}, \langle a \rangle^{0.2}, \langle a, a \rangle^{0.4}, \langle a, a, a \rangle^{0.1}, \langle a, a, a, a \rangle^{0.2}]$ and its corresponding language is $\{\epsilon, \langle a \rangle, \langle a, a \rangle, \langle a, a, a \rangle, \langle a, a, a, a \rangle\}$.

**Definition 2 (Stochastic deterministic finite automaton, adapted from [18]).** *A stochastic deterministic finite automaton (SDFA) is a tuple $(S, \Sigma, \delta, p, s_0)$, where $S$ is a set of states, $\Sigma$ is an alphabet of activities, $\delta : S \times \Sigma \to S$ is a transition function, $p : S \times \Sigma \to [0,1]$ is a probability function, and $s_0 \in S$ is the initial state.*

The probability to terminate in a particular state $s$ is denoted by $p(s, \lambda)$, $\lambda \notin \Sigma$, and is equal to $1 - \sum_{a \in \Sigma} p(s, a)$. Consequently, for each state, the probabilities of leaving the state or terminating at it should sum to 1, i.e., $\forall s \in S : p(s, \lambda) + \sum_{a \in \Sigma} p(s, a) = 1$.

The stochastic languages that can be represented by SDFAs are called *stochastic deterministic regular languages* [18]. For instance, all event logs can be represented by SDFAs (we included a translation in an accompanying technical report [19]). Figure 1a shows the SDFA of our example event log $L_e$. Notice that SDFAs do not inherit all the properties of deterministic finite automata. For instance, SDFAs are not closed under union, that is, the union of two stochastic languages represented by SDFAs is not necessarily expressible by an SDFA [20]. Therefore, we did not attempt to find valid reduction strategies for SDFAs, but leave this as future work.

**Definition 3 (Petri net).** *A Petri net (PN) is a tuple $(P, T, A, M_0, l)$ in which $P$ is a set of places, $T$ is a set of transitions $(T \cap P = \varnothing)$, $A \subseteq (P \times T) \cup (T \times P)$ is an arc relation, $M_0$ (multiset over $P$) is the initial marking and $l: T \to \Sigma$ is a partial labelling function.*

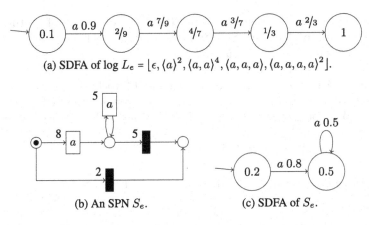

(a) SDFA of log $L_e = \lfloor \epsilon, \langle a \rangle^2, \langle a, a \rangle^4, \langle a, a, a \rangle, \langle a, a, a, a \rangle^2 \rfloor$.

(b) An SPN $S_e$.    (c) SDFA of $S_e$.

**Fig. 1.** Examples of an event log and a Stochastic Petri net, and their corresponding stochastic deterministic finite automata. For convenience, the numbers in the states denote the probability of termination.

A *marking* is a multiset over $P$, capturing the state of the net by indicating tokens on the places in $P$. A transition $t \in T$ is *enabled* in a marking $M$ if for each place $p'$ such that $(p', t) \in A$ it holds that $p' \in M$. If $t$ fires, then all these places $p'$ are removed from $M$, and to each $p''$ such that $(t, p'') \in A$ a token is added to the new marking, and if $l(t)$ exists, it indicates this activity $l(t)$ being executed. A *path* in a Petri net is an alternating sequence of markings and transitions such that the markings can be traversed by firing the immediately preceding transitions, and such that in the last marking no transition is enabled. The trace corresponding to a path is the sequence of transitions projected to activities using $l$, excluding transitions that are not mapped by $l$. The language of the net is the set of all possible traces for which there exist corresponding paths in the net.

A *stochastic Petri net* (SPN) is a Petri net that expresses a stochastic language. Several ways to enrich a Petri net with stochastic information have been proposed (refer to [21] for an overview). The techniques presented in this paper apply to any type of SPN that can be translated to an SDFA. Nevertheless, for illustrative purposes, we consider a type of SPN in which transitions are annotated with weights:

**Definition 4 (Stochastic Petri net).** *A Stochastic Petri net (SPN) is a tuple* $(P, T, A, M_0, l, w)$ *such that* $(P, T, A, M_0, l)$ *is a Petri net and* $w : T \to \mathbb{R}^+$ *is a function that assigns weights to transitions.*

Given a marking $M$, the probability that an enabled transition $t$ fires in $M$, denoted by $p(M, t)$, is proportional to $t$'s weight compared to the weight of all enabled transitions: $p(M, t) = w(t) / \sum_{t' \text{ enabled in } M} w(t')$. Then, the probability of a path consisting of transitions $t_1 \ldots t_n$ and markings $M_0 \ldots M_n$ in an SPN is the product of the transitions' probabilities: $\Pi_{1 \le i \le n} p(M_i, t_i)$. The probability of a trace in an SPN is the sum of the probabilities over all paths that induce the trace, and the stochastic language of an SPN is the collection of all the traces induced by all the paths in the SPN (and all other traces having probability 0). Figure 1b shows an example of an SPN $S_e$.

If an SPN can be translated to an SDFA, then the SPN must have a finite state space (which still might include loops), and its stochastic perspective needs to be describable by an SDFA. For instance, Fig. 1c shows the SDFA of SPN $S_e$ in Fig. 1b. We characterise the class of SPNs that express stochastic regular languages and discuss some particularities that arise when translating SPNs to SDFAs in an accompanying technical report [19].

## 3 Stochastic-Aware Conformance Checking

This section presents our new technique for stochastic-aware precision and recall measures, which computes these measures by considering the SDFAs of an event log and a stochastic process model. It first creates a projection of both SDFAs to obtain the behaviour that is common to both. Then, precision and recall are obtained by considering the entropy of the SDFAs and their projections.

Our technique can be applied to any stochastic process modelling formalism, as long as the stochastic language of a model can be expressed as an SDFA. We first introduce the projection, second we describe how we compute entropy, and finally we explain how we compute precision and recall. We then discuss practical considerations of our implementation of the measures, and introduce desirable properties for stochastic conformance checking measures.

**Projection.** A *projection* of two SDFAs $L$ and $M$, denoted by $\mathcal{P}(L, M)$, is an SDFA that contains the behaviour that is present in both $L$ and $M$. For non-stochastic deterministic finite automata, there are well-known algorithms to establish a projection [22].[1] These algorithms typically construct synchronous walks in both automata, taking a step only when it is allowed in both $L$ and $M$. We use a similar strategy: whenever both automata are able to take a step, this step is added to the projection. The probability of such a step is the probability of the corresponding step in $L$.

For instance, consider the two SDFAs shown in Figs. 1a and 1c. Their projections are shown in Figs. 2a and 2b. Notice that if from a particular state an outgoing edge is removed, then the probability of this edge is added to the termination probability at that state.

**Entropy.** Intuitively, the *entropy* of an SDFA describes the number of yes/no questions (bits) that would on average be required to guess an unknown random trace supported by the SDFA. For any stochastic language $L$, the entropy $H$ can be defined as follows, using a convention that $0 \log 0 = 0$, cf. [17]:

$$H(L) = - \sum_{t \in \Sigma^*} p(t \in L) \log_2 p(t \in L). \tag{1}$$

---

[1] For non-stochastic DFAs, a projection is often called a conjunction. We do not use this term here to avoid confusion with the "stochastic" conjunction of two SDFAs, as this "stochastic" conjunction may not necessarily yield an SDFA again.

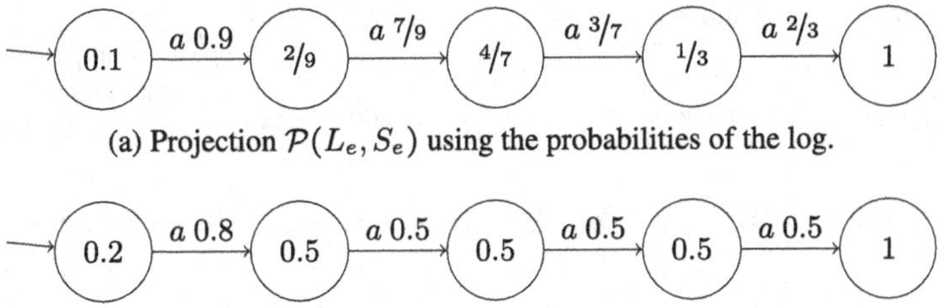

(a) Projection $\mathcal{P}(L_e, S_e)$ using the probabilities of the log.

(b) Projection $\mathcal{P}(S_e, L_e)$ using the probabilities of the model.

**Fig. 2.** Projections of the SDFAs shown in Fig. 1.

As $\Sigma^*$ is infinite, $H$ cannot be computed by iterating over $\Sigma^*$. Therefore, we compute the entropy using a procedure adapted from [18]. Given an SDFA $A = (S, \Sigma, \delta, p, s_0)$ that describes a stochastic language, the entropy of the stochastic language of $A$ is:

$$H(A) = - \sum_{\delta(s,a)} c_s p(s, a) \log_2 p(s, a) - \sum_{s \in S} c_s p(s, \lambda) \log_2 p(s, \lambda), \tag{2}$$

where each state $s \in S$ uses a constant $c_s$, which can be obtained iteratively [18]:

$$c_s^0 = 0 \tag{3}$$

$$c_s^{t+1} = \left( \sum_{\delta(s',a)=s} c_{s'}^t \cdot p(s', a) \right) + \begin{cases} 1 & s = s_0 \\ 0 & s \neq s_0 \end{cases} \tag{4}$$

For instance, for the automaton shown in Fig. 1c, the iterative steps are as follows: $c^0 = [0,0]$, $c^1 = [1,0]$, $c^2 = [1, c_0^1 \cdot 0.8 + c_1^1 \cdot 0.5] = [1, 0.8]$, $c^3 = [1, c_0^2 \cdot 0.8 + c_1^2 \cdot 0.5] = [1, 1.2]$, $c^4 = [1, 1.4]$, $c^5 = [1, 1.5]$, $c^6 = [1, 1.55]$, $c^7 = [1, 1.575]$, $\ldots c = [1, 1.6]$ and $H = -(c_0 0.8 \log_2 0.8 + c_1 0.5 \log_2 0.5) \approx 1.05$. This method converges deterministically to the correct value [18].

**Computing Precision & Recall.** Finally, to compute precision and recall for a log $L$ and a model $M$ (both translated to SDFAs), our technique uses the entropy of the projection $\mathcal{P}$ and compares it to the entropy of $L$ and $M$:

$$recall(L, M) = \frac{H(\mathcal{P}(L, M))}{H(L)} \qquad precision(L, M) = \frac{H(\mathcal{P}(M, L))}{H(M)} \tag{5}$$

For these measures to work, the entropy of the log and the model cannot be 0. Furthermore, in an accompanying technical report [19] we show that $H(\mathcal{P})$ is always lower than both $H(L)$ and $H(M)$, thus our measures return values between 0 and 1.

For our example log $L_e$ and model $S_e$ (Fig. 1), recall is 1 and precision is 0.914.

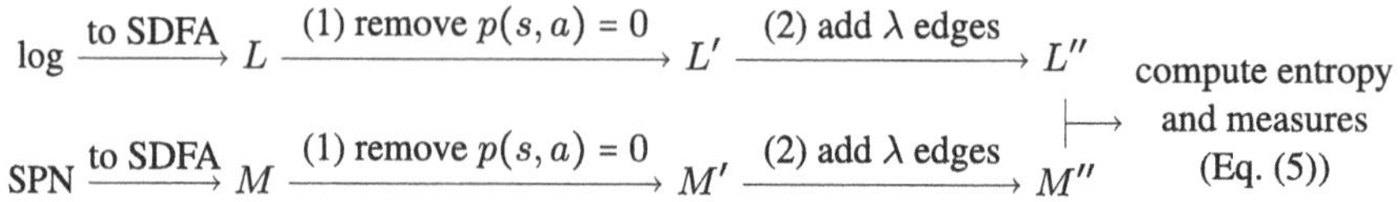

$$\log \xrightarrow{\text{to SDFA}} L \xrightarrow{(1) \text{ remove } p(s,a) = 0} L' \xrightarrow{(2) \text{ add } \lambda \text{ edges}} L''$$

compute entropy and measures (Eq. (5))

$$\text{SPN} \xrightarrow{\text{to SDFA}} M \xrightarrow{(1) \text{ remove } p(s,a) = 0} M' \xrightarrow{(2) \text{ add } \lambda \text{ edges}} M''$$

**Fig. 3.** Overview of the steps taken to increase the applicability of our measures.

**Practical Considerations.** Next, we discuss some practical considerations that accompany our new measures, and additional steps to increase their applicability, using the overview shown in Fig. 3.

Step (1): Equation (2) requires that every edge in the two input SDFAs has a non-zero probability, as $\log 0$ is undefined (i.e., if $\delta(s,a) = b$ then $p(s,a) > 0$). This is easily ensured using a pre-processing step on the SDFAs, which filters out these edges.

Step (2): Model and log cannot have zero entropies, i.e., they must contain more than one trace with non-zero probability (be deterministic). In our implementation, we pre-process each SDFA before projecting and measuring entropy: from each terminating state $s$, we add one step out of $s$ with a small probability $\lambda$ towards a fresh state. This transition has a fresh label, and this label is reused for the pre-processing of both SDFAs. This influences entropy in both SDFAs, but only by $0 \sim 0.15$ entropy.

In [18], it is shown that Eq. (4) converges for SDFAs as long as from each state it is possible to eventually terminate. This corresponds with our definition of stochastic languages (Definition 1), which requires that the sum of probabilities over all traces should be 1. In case an SDFA has a livelock which can be reached with non-zero probability, the probabilities of its traces do not sum to 1 and hence such an SDFA has no stochastic language. This is inherently satisfied by event logs, and ensured with a check in our implementation of the translation of SPNs to SDFAs.

Empty event logs or stochastic process models that do not support any traces do not describe stochastic languages and are hence not supported by our technique. This is a common restriction in process mining: sound workflow nets and process trees have the same limitation and cannot express the empty language either.

**Implementation.** The proposed measures have been implemented as a plug-in of the ProM framework [23]: "Compute relative entropy of a log and a stochastic Petri net". The measures themselves are deterministic. However, due to the order in which transitions are read from a Petri net and double-precision arithmetic, small differences might occur between runs.

**Properties of Stochastic Precision and Recall.** A measure that is not known to satisfy any property can be considered to return "magic" numbers. In [12,14,15,24], several properties for classical conformance measures are proposed. Next, we adapt some existing properties to the realm of stochastic-aware measures, introduce new stochastic-specific properties, and justify that our measures indeed possess these properties.

**P1** A stochastic-aware conformance measure should be deterministic;

**P2** A stochastic-aware conformance measure should depend on the stochastic languages of logs and models and not on their representations;

Properties P1 and P2 hold for our conformance-aware precision and recall measures, as both the projection and the entropy are computed using deterministic procedures with only stochastic languages as inputs.

**P3** Stochastic-aware conformance measures should return values greater than or equal to 0 and less than or equal to 1;

Our precision and recall measures satisfy Property P3: as shown in an accompanying technical report [19]. A conformance value of 1 signifies a perfect conformance, which for the stochastic-aware measures can be instantiated as follows:

**P4** If an event log and a model express the same stochastic language, then they should have a perfect stochastic-aware precision, i.e., a precision of 1;

**P5** If an event log and a model express the same stochastic language, then they should have a perfect stochastic-aware recall, i.e., a recall of 1;

Properties P4 and P5 hold for our precision and recall measures, because if the log and model express the same stochastic language, then the projection will have the same stochastic language as well. Then, the entropy of all three stochastic languages is obviously equal, hence the numerator and denominator in Eq. (5) are equal.

**P6** If a log $L_1$ assigns to each trace from a model $M$ a higher probability than another log $L_2$, then the precision of $L_1$ should be higher than of $L_2$:
If $\forall_{t \in \Sigma^*} M(t) > 0 \Rightarrow (L_1(t) \geq L_2(t))$ then $precision(L_1, M) \geq precision(L_2, M)$;
Furthermore, if there is a trace of $M$ in $L_1$ and not in $L_2$, then the precision of $L_1$ should be strictly higher than of $L_2$:
If $\forall_{t \in \Sigma^*} M(t) > 0 \Rightarrow L_1(t) \geq L_2(t)$ and $\exists_{t \in \Sigma^*} M(t) > 0 \wedge L_1(t) > 0 \wedge L_2(t) = 0$,
then $precision(L_1, M) > precision(L_2, M)$;

**P7** If a model $M_1$ assigns to each trace from an event log $L$ a higher probability than another model $M_2$, then the recall of $M_1$ should be higher than of $M_2$:
If $\forall_{t \in \Sigma^*} L(t) > 0 \Rightarrow M_1(t) \geq M_2(t)$ then $recall(L, M_1) \geq recall(L, M_2)$;
Furthermore, if there is a trace of $L$ in $M_1$ and not in $M_2$, then the recall of $M_1$ should be strictly higher than of $M_2$:
If $\forall_{t \in \Sigma^*} L(t) > 0 \Rightarrow M_1(t) \geq M_2(t)$ and $\exists_{t \in \Sigma^*} L(t) > 0 \wedge M_1(t) > 0 \wedge M_2(t) = 0$,
then $recall(L, M_1) > recall(L, M_2)$;

The first parts of P6 and P7 hold for our measures: for recall (resp. precision), the projection $P(L, M_1)$ is a super-graph of the projection $P(L, M_2)$, and as for recall (resp. precision) all the probabilities are derived from $L$ (resp $M$), the probabilities on the edges common to these SDFAs are equivalent. Then, the properties follow using reasoning similar to P3. The second part of the properties then holds by extension.

Finally, similar to the precision and recall measures in information retrieval, we argue that stochastic-aware precision should be equal to recall with the arguments flipped:

**P8** Given two stochastic languages $A$ and $B$ and stochastic-aware precision (*precision*) and recall (*recall*) measures, it should hold that $precision(A, B) = recall(B, A)$.

Property P8 holds for our measures by definition.

## 4    Evaluation

In this section, we evaluate the measures introduced in this paper. First, we investigate whether the measures are true reflections of differences in stochastic languages. Second, we show that the measures are feasible to compute on real-life event logs and stochastic models. Third, we illustrate the practical relevance of our measures on a repository of real-life industrial stochastic process models.

**Real Reflections of Differences: Ranking of Synthetic Models.** Consider an event log $L$ containing 6 distinct traces: $[\langle a, b, c\rangle^{10}, \langle a, c, b\rangle^{15}, \langle a, d\rangle^{30}, \langle a, d, e, d\rangle^{20}, \langle a, d, e, d, e, d\rangle^{15}, \langle a, d, e, d, e, d, e, d\rangle^{10}]$. In this example, we consider four different stochastic process models (SPNs, see Fig. 4) that a user might consider to represent this event log and use to gain insights about the process that generated the event log. Model $S_1$ was discovered by a stochastic process discovery technique [11] from $L$. Model $S_2$ is a manually created SPN that is similar to $S_1$ but has different probabilities. That is, the stochastic perspective differs. Model $S_3$ enumerates $L$'s traces having corresponding probabilities: a *trace model*. Model $S_4$ represents all behaviour and is a *flower model*, with probabilities derived from $L$ based on the frequencies of the activities. Table 1 shows (fragments of) the stochastic languages of these models.

We applied the measures presented in this paper (S), the Earth Movers' (EMSC) [13] measure, as well as the non-stochastic alignment-based (A) [25] and projected (P) [26] precision measures. The results are shown in Table 2 (recall of S is 1 for all models).

All measures, corresponding to intuition, consider the trace model $S_3$ to be perfectly representing the event log, and agree on the flower model $S_4$ having the lowest precision. Second, intuitively, the probabilities that $S_1$ attaches to the traces in $L$ are *closer* to those in $L$ than the probabilities that $S_2$ attaches to these traces. Thus, we would argue that $S_1$ represents $L$ better than $S_2$, which both stochastic conformance checking measures confirm (S, EMSC). A and P do not see any difference between these models. Finally, it is remarkable that EMSC's values for $S_2$ and $S_4$ are very close, which may be due to EMSC having to unfold the loop in the flower model, which is bounded and brings the compared

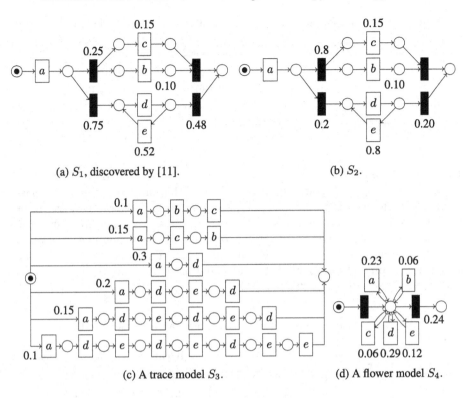

(a) $S_1$, discovered by [11].

(b) $S_2$.

(c) A trace model $S_3$.

(d) A flower model $S_4$.

**Fig. 4.** Four Stochastic Petri nets that could represent our event log $L$.

**Table 1.** Stochastic languages of $L$ and the SPNs in Fig. 4 ($p$ is probability).

| Trace | $p$ in $L$ | $p$ in $S_1$ | $p$ in $S_2$ | $p$ in $S_3$ | $p$ in $S_4$ |
|---|---|---|---|---|---|
| $\langle a, b, c \rangle$ | 0.1 | 0.1 | 0.32 | 0.1 | 0.000199 |
| $\langle a, c, b \rangle$ | 0.15 | 0.15 | 0.48 | 0.15 | 0.000199 |
| $\langle a, d \rangle$ | 0.3 | 0.36 | 0.05 | 0.3 | 0.016008 |
| $\langle a, d, e, d \rangle$ | 0.2 | 0.19 | 0.03 | 0.2 | 0.000557 |
| $\langle a, d, e, d, e, d \rangle$ | 0.15 | 0.1 | 0.03 | 0.15 | 0.000019 |
| $\langle a, d, e, d, e, d, e, d \rangle$ | 0.1 | 0.05 | 0.02 | 0.1 | 0.000001 |
| Other traces | 0 | 0.05 | 0.08 | 0 | 0.983017 |

language falsely closer to $L$. Our measures support loops, which is reflected in the low precision score for $S_4$.

This illustrates that conformance techniques that are not stochastic-aware cannot fully grasp the differences between the stochastic perspective in these process models.

**Table 2.** Stochastic measures compared to regular conformance checking techniques.

| Rank | This paper (S) | EMSC [13] | Alignment-based (A) [25] | Projected (P) [26] |
|------|----------------|-----------|--------------------------|--------------------|
| 1 | $S_3$ (1) | $S_3$ (1) | $S_3$ (1) | $S_3$ (1) |
| 2 | $S_1$ (0.918) | $S_1$ (0.908) | $S_1, S_2$ (0.846) | $S_1, S_2$ (0.934) |
| 3 | $S_2$ (0.834) | $S_2$ (0.570) | | |
| 4 | $S_4$ (0.096) | $S_4$ (0.509) | $S_4$ (0.292) | $S_4$ (0.551) |

**Practical Feasibility.** Next, we report on the feasibility of the proposed stochastic-aware precision and recall measures. To this end, we applied a stochastic discovery technique proposed in [11] to 13 publicly available real-life event logs[2] to obtain stochastic block-structured Petri nets.[3] We then measured the precision and recall values for the event logs and the corresponding discovered nets, as well as the times spent to compute them. The code used to run the evaluation is publicly available.[4] The machine used to compute the measures had an E5-1620 CPU with 32 GB RAM.

**Table 3.** Precision and recall values and times taken to compute them.

| Log | Traces | Events | Activities | Recall | Precision | Time (ms) |
|-----|--------|--------|------------|--------|-----------|-----------|
| BPIC11 | 1,143 | 150,291 | 624 | 0.000 | 0.000 | 6,747,782 |
| BPIC12 | 13,087 | 262,200 | 36 | 0.770 | 0.080 | 147,497 |
| BPIC13-closed | 1,487 | 6,660 | 7 | 0.677 | 0.888 | 22 |
| BPIC13-open | 7,554 | 65,533 | 13 | 1.000 | 0.605 | 11 |
| BPIC13-incidents | 819 | 2,351 | 5 | 1.000 | 0.630 | 13,427 |
| BPIC15-1 to 5 | Discovery out of memory | | | | | |
| BPIC17 | 31,509 | 1,202,267 | 66 | 0.111 | 0.011 | 2,919,223 |
| Road Fines | 150,370 | 561,470 | 11 | 0.772 | 0.497 | 245 |
| Sepsis | 1,050 | 15,214 | 16 | 0.939 | 0.109 | 3,210 |

Table 3 summarises the results. Some results could not be obtained: for the BPIC15 logs, the discovery technique ran out of memory, thus our measures could not be applied. For BPIC11, discovery returned a model in which all transitions were silent. Hence, this model expressed the stochastic language $[\epsilon^1]$ and thus recall and precision are both 0, as the log did not have the empty trace. One

---

[2] The event logs are accessible via https://data.4tu.nl/repository/collection:event_logs_real.

[3] The source code of the discovery technique is accessible via https://svn.win.tue.nl/repos/prom/Packages/StochasticPetriNets/Trunk (svn revision 39823).

[4] The source code used in the evaluation is accessible via https://svn.win.tue.nl/repos/prom/Packages/StochasticAwareConformanceChecking/Trunk (revision 41855).

could argue that our measures are strict as both the traces and their probabilities captured in the log and model should match well for high scores. However, one could also argue that the tested discovery technique is, apparently, unable to discover models that represent the likelihood of traces in the event logs well, indicating the need for further research in such techniques.

The reported computation times show that the computation of the stochastic-aware precision and recall measures is feasible on real-life logs, even on complex event logs like BPIC11, taking at most two hours, but much less time for the other tested event logs. Further analysis showed that for SDFAs with large cycles, Eq. (4) might need a quadratic number of steps (in the size of the state space $S$) to converge, and that this is indeed the most expensive step of our measures. However, run time was not infeasible in our evaluation: at most two hours for the largest logs of most complex processes we tested, but generally much less. Nevertheless, as future work, this step might be optimised using the SDFA's structure.

**Practical Usefulness: German Health Insurance Company.** In this section, we demonstrate the practical usefulness of our measures in the context of the case study with the German health insurance company [16]. As the company used the hand-crafted stochastic process models for resource planning, it is important that they do not describe the same traces. Otherwise, there is a risk of double resource allocation and, consequently, financial loss to the company. Due to a high number of models, i.e., approximately 4 000 models, manual analysis is intractable.[5]

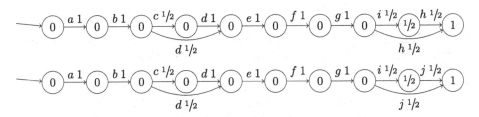

**Fig. 5.** Two slightly different SDFAs from a German insurer ($h \leftrightarrow j$).

To identify models that describe identical (and frequent) traces, we performed their pairwise comparisons using our stochastic-aware conformance measures. Models that do not describe a proper stochastic language were discarded. Furthermore, only models with a single start node and a single end node were considered. This filtering step resulted in the collection of 3 090 models. The average time of computing a stochastic conformance measure between a pair of models using our tool, either precision or recall, was 69 ms. As a result, we discovered 48 pairs of distinct models that describe, among others, some identical traces. Two anonymised

---

[5] The models are not publicly available, as per the terms of the agreement with the company.

models from the collection, for which both stochastic recall and precision values are equal to 0.4, are shown in Fig. 5. Business analysts of the insurance company should assess these two models for potential double allocation of resources for support of the corresponding business operations. As these models capture identical frequent traces, the analysts may further consider to combine them into a single model.

# 5  Discussion and Related Work

A dozen of conformance checking measures have been proposed to date. For a comprehensive overview of the conformance checking field, we refer the reader to [5,14,27]. The vast majority of the existing conformance measures address nondeterministic models and logs. Nondeterminism, as a concept in computer science, was introduced in [28] in the context of nondeterministic finite automata. Nondeterminism, as used in automata theory, states that a choice of the next step in a computation does not necessarily determine its future. This interpretation differs from the one employed in the context of distributed systems, which says that there is no preference among the computations of a system. As such, the latter interpretation provides an abstraction mechanism that allows treating all the computations of a system as being equally good, or equally likely to be induced by the system. Similar to nondeterminism, probabilities can be used to abstract from unimportant or unknown aspects of a system. However, by associating different probabilities with different computations of a system one can encode that certain computations are more likely to be induced by the system than others [20]. In [12], van der Aalst stressed the need to consider probabilities in conformance checking.

Some conformance checking techniques use stochastic elements, however without targeting stochastic models. For instance, Hidden Markov Models (HMMs) have been used to model business processes and to check conformance. In [29], recall and precision are computed by translating Petri nets and event logs to HMMs. However, the stochastic perspective of HMMs is not used, as all the events in a particular state are treated as being equally likely. Another limitation is that parallelism is not supported.

In [14], a precision measure and a recall measure were proposed for process mining founded in the notion of the topological entropy of a regular language. In [14], a framework for conformance checking approaches is proposed, which is instantiated using cardinalities and entropy. The measures proposed in this paper can be seen as extensions of the entropy-based technique for stochastic languages.

Alignments [30] search for a least-cost path through event log and model, thereby being robust to slight deviations between traces. As recall takes the frequency of traces into account, the stochastic perspective of logs is taken into account. However, alignment-based precision measures [25] do not consider the stochastic perspective of the model. Alignment-based precision measures might be extended to support stochastic process models, for instance by searching for a most-likely path. Projected conformance checking [26] addresses long run times of conformance checking techniques by projecting behavior onto subsets of activities of a certain size. The measures presented in this paper can be extended in a similar fashion. Generalised conformance checking [31] compares an event log and model based on a given trust level for each, derived, for instance, from identified data quality issues [32]. In stochastic conformance checking, one could consider the probability attached to each trace in log and model to be an indication of trust, yielding an alternative, possibly more fine-grained, view on their differences.

To the best of our knowledge, the Earth Movers' Stochastic Conformance checking technique [13] is the only stochastic conformance checking technique proposed today. In this technique, the log and model's stochastic languages are seen as distributions of traces, and the Wasserstein metric is applied. While intuitive, it does not support infinite languages (that is, models with loops), while our measure supports such languages. Furthermore, our work contributes to the ongoing discussion on ideal conformance checking measures by proposing properties that this measure should have [12,14,15,24], by extending these to the stochastic context.

Finally, to compare SDFAs, the Kullback-Leibler (KL) divergence [18] could be used. However, KL-divergence does not exist if one SDFA supports a trace that the other SDFA does not support, making it unsuitable for conformance checking purposes.

## 6   Conclusion

In process mining, the stochastic perspective of event logs and process models is essential to inform process optimisation efforts and techniques, such as simulation, prediction, recommendation, and to inform staffing decisions: without a stochastic perspective, efforts spent on optimisation are at risk of being spent on rare, exceptional behavior, and lead to misinformed decisions.

In this paper, we contributed to making the stochastic perspective a first-class citizen of process mining techniques, by introducing a stochastic-aware conformance checking technique for two measures: fitness and precision. The proposed precision and recall measures are applicable to an arbitrary event log and a model that describes a finite or infinite number of traces using a finite number of reachable states. Eight desirable properties of stochastic conformance checking measures were identified, and the adherence of our measures to these properties was shown.

An evaluation based on our publicly available implementation confirmed the feasibility of using the measures in real-life industrial settings. We acknowledge that our measures have limitations, which give rise to future work: Various notions of correctness for process models, like boundedness or soundness, classify a process model that can induce an infinite number of states as incorrect. However, as such models can appear in practice due to modelling errors, it is relevant to extend the proposes measures to account for infinite-state models.

Our measures address (to some extent) the problem of partial trace matches [15]: common prefixes of traces are considered and contribute to the measures, however common postfixes are not. Thus, a model and a log that have their first activity different will be considered to be completely disjoint. This limitation can be addressed by considering both the original SDFA and its edge-reversed version during construction of the projection. Finally, our measures consider the stochastic perspective of either log or model, but not both. In future work, this could be addressed.

**Acknowledgment.** Artem Polyvyanyy was partly supported by the Australian Research Council Discovery Project DP180102839.

# References

1. Weske, M.: Business Process Management. Concepts, Languages, Architectures. Springer, Heidelberg (2012). https://doi.org/10.1007/978-3-642-28616-2
2. Dumas, M., La Rosa, M., Mendling, J., Reijers, H.A.: Fundamentals of Business Process Management. Springer, Heidelberg (2018). https://doi.org/10.1007/978-3-662-56509-4_9
3. van der Aalst, W.M.P.: Business process management: a comprehensive survey. ISRN Softw. Eng. **2013**, 1–37 (2013)
4. Rosemann, M., vom Brocke, J.: The six core elements of business process management. In: vom Brocke, J., Rosemann, M. (eds.) Handbook on Business Process Management 1. IHIS, pp. 105–122. Springer, Heidelberg (2015). https://doi.org/10.1007/978-3-642-45100-3_5
5. van der Aalst, W.M.P.: Process Mining-Data Science in Action, 2nd edn. Springer, Heidelberg (2016). https://doi.org/10.1007/978-3-662-49851-4
6. Feldman, M.S., Pentland, B.T.: Reconceptualizing organizational routines as a source of flexibility and change. Adm. Sci. Q. **48**(1), 94–118 (2003)
7. LeBaron, C., Christianson, M.K., Garrett, L., Ilan, R.: Coordinating flexible performance during everyday work: an ethnomethodological study of handoff routines. Organ. Sci. **27**(3), 514–534 (2016)
8. Yi, S., Knudsen, T., Becker, M.C.: Inertia in routines: a hidden source of organizational variation. Organ. Sci. **27**(3), 782–800 (2016)
9. Deken, F., Carlile, P.R., Berends, H., Lauche, K.: Generating novelty through interdependent routines: a process model of routine work. Organ. Sci. **27**(3), 659–677 (2016)
10. Sonenshein, S.: Routines and creativity: from dualism to duality. Organ. Sci. **27**(3), 739–758 (2016)
11. Rogge-Solti, A., van der Aalst, W.M.P., Weske, M.: Discovering stochastic petri nets with arbitrary delay distributions from event logs. In: Lohmann, N., Song, M., Wohed, P. (eds.) BPM 2013. LNBIP, vol. 171, pp. 15–27. Springer, Cham (2014). https://doi.org/10.1007/978-3-319-06257-0_2
12. van der Aalst, W.M.P.: Relating process models and event logs-21 conformance propositions. In: ATAED, CEUR, vol. 2115, pp. 56–74 (2018)
13. Leemans, S.J.J., Syring, A.F., van der Aalst, W.M.P.: Earth movers' stochastic conformance checking. In: Hildebrandt, T., van Dongen, B.F., Röglinger, M., Mendling, J. (eds.) BPM 2019. LNBIP, vol. 360, pp. 127–143. Springer, Cham (2019). https://doi.org/10.1007/978-3-030-26643-1_8

14. Polyvyanyy, A., Solti, A., Weidlich, M., Ciccio, C.D., Mendling, J.: Monotone precision and recall measures for comparing executions and specifications of dynamic systems. ACM TOSEM (2020, in press)

15. Polyvyanyy, A., Kalenkova, A.A.: Monotone conformance checking for partially matching designed and observed processes. In: ICPM, pp. 81–88 (2019)

16. Polyvyanyy, A., Smirnov, S., Weske, M.: Reducing complexity of large EPCs. In: MobIS, GfI, vol. 141, pp. 195–207 (2008)

17. Cover, T.M., Thomas, J.A.: Elements of Information Theory, 2nd edn. Wiley, Hoboken (2006)

18. Carrasco, R.C.: Accurate computation of the relative entropy between stochastic regular grammars. ITA 31(5), 437–444 (1997)

19. Leemans, S.J., Polyvyanyy, A.: Proofs with stochastic-aware conformance checking: an entropy-based approach (2019). https://eprints.qut.edu.au/129860/

20. Vidal, E., Thollard, F., de la Higuera, C., Casacuberta, F., Carrasco, R.C.: Probabilistic finite-state machines-part I. IEEE Trans. Pattern Anal. Mach. Intell. 27(7), 1013–1025 (2005)

21. Marsan, M.A., et al.: The effect of execution policies on the semantics and analysis of stochastic petri nets. IEEE Trans. Software Eng. 15(7), 832–846 (1989)

22. Linz, P.: An Introduction to Formal Languages and Automata, 4th edn. JBP, Burlington (2006)

23. van Dongen, B.F., de Medeiros, A.K.A., Verbeek, H.M.W., Weijters, A.J.M.M., van der Aalst, W.M.P.: The ProM framework: a new era in process mining tool support. In: Ciardo, G., Darondeau, P. (eds.) ICATPN 2005. LNCS, vol. 3536, pp. 444–454. Springer, Heidelberg (2005). https://doi.org/10.1007/11494744_25

24. Tax, N., Lu, X., Sidorova, N., Fahland, D., van der Aalst, W.M.P.: The imprecisions of precision measures in process mining. Inf. Process. Lett. 135, 1–8 (2018)

25. Muñoz-Gama, J., Carmona, J.: A fresh look at precision in process conformance. In: Hull, R., Mendling, J., Tai, S. (eds.) BPM 2010. LNCS, vol. 6336, pp. 211–226. Springer, Heidelberg (2010). https://doi.org/10.1007/978-3-642-15618-2_16

26. Leemans, S.J.J., Fahland, D., van der Aalst, W.M.P.: Scalable process discovery and conformance checking. Softw. Syst. Model. 17(2), 599–631 (2016). https://doi.org/10.1007/s10270-016-0545-x

27. Carmona, J., van Dongen, B.F., Solti, A., Weidlich, M.: Conformance Checking-Relating Processes and Models. Springer, Cham (2018)

28. Rabin, M.O., Scott, D.S.: Finite automata and their decision problems. IBM J. Res. Dev. 3(2), 114–125 (1959)

29. Rozinat, A.: Process mining: conformance and extension. Ph.D. thesis, Eindhoven University of Technology (2010)

30. van der Aalst, W.M.P., Adriansyah, A., van Dongen, B.F.: Replaying history on process models for conformance checking and performance analysis. DMKD 2(2), 182–192 (2012)

31. Rogge-Solti, A., Senderovich, A., Weidlich, M., Mendling, J., Gal, A.: In log and model we trust? A generalized conformance checking framework. In: La Rosa, M., Loos, P., Pastor, O. (eds.) BPM 2016. LNCS, vol. 9850, pp. 179–196. Springer, Cham (2016). https://doi.org/10.1007/978-3-319-45348-4_11

32. Suriadi, S., Andrews, R., ter Hofstede, A., Wynn, M.: Event log imperfection patterns for process mining: towards a systematic approach to cleaning event logs. IS 64, 132–150 (2017)

# Conformance Checking Approximation Using Subset Selection and Edit Distance

Mohammadreza Fani Sani[1(✉)], Sebastiaan J. van Zelst[1,2],
and Wil M.P. van der Aalst[1,2]

[1] Process and Data Science Chair, RWTH Aachen University, Aachen, Germany
{fanisani,s.j.v.zelst,wvdaalst}@pads.rwth-aachen.de
[2] Fraunhofer FIT, Birlinghoven Castle, Sankt Augustin, Germany

**Abstract.** Conformance checking techniques let us find out to what degree a process model and real execution data correspond to each other. In recent years, alignments have proven extremely useful in calculating conformance statistics. Most techniques to compute alignments provide an exact solution. However, in many applications, it is enough to have an approximation of the conformance value. Specifically, for large event data, the computation time for alignments is considerably long using current techniques which makes them inapplicable in reality. Also, it is no longer feasible to use standard hardware for complex process models. This paper, proposes new approximation techniques to compute approximated conformance checking values close to exact solution values in less time. These methods also provide upper and lower bounds for the approximated alignment value. Our experiments on real event data show that it is possible to improve the performance of conformance checking by using the proposed methods compared to using the state-of-the-art alignment approximation technique. Results show that in most of the cases, we provide tight bounds, accurate approximated alignment values, and similar deviation statistics.

**Keywords:** Process mining · Conformance checking approximation · Alignment · Subset selection · Edit distance · Simulation

## 1 Introduction

One of the main branches of process mining is conformance checking, aiming at investigating conformity of a discovered/designed process model w.r.t, real process executions [1]. This branch of techniques is beneficial to detect deviations and to measure how accurate a discovered model is. In particular, the techniques in this branch are able to check conformance based on process modeling formalisms that allow for describing concurrency, i.e., the possibility to specify order-independent execution of activities. Early conformance checking

© Springer Nature Switzerland AG 2020
S. Dustdar et al. (Eds.): CAiSE 2020, LNCS 12127, pp. 234–251, 2020.
https://doi.org/10.1007/978-3-030-49435-3_15

techniques, e.g., '"token-based replay" [2], often lead to ambiguous and/or unpredictable results. Hence, alignments [3] were developed with the specific goal to explain and quantify deviations in a non-ambiguous manner. Alignments have rapidly turned into the de facto standard conformance checking technique [4]. Moreover, alignments serve as a basis for techniques that link event data to process models, e.g., they support performance analysis, decision mining [5], business process model repair [6] and prediction techniques. However, computing alignments is time consuming on real large event data, which makes it unusable in reality.

In many applications, we need to compute alignment values several times, e.g., if we want to have a suitable process model for an event log, we need to discover many process models using various process discovery algorithms with different settings, and, measure how each process model fits with the event log using alignment techniques. As normal alignment methods require considerable time for large event data, analyzing many candidate process models is impractical. Consequently, by decreasing the alignment computation time, we can consider more candidate models in a limited time. Moreover, in several cases, we do not need to have accurate alignment values, i.e., it is sufficient to have a quick approximated value or a close lower/upper bound for it.

In this paper, we propose several conformance checking approximation methods that provide approximated alignment values plus lower and upper bounds for the actual alignment value. The underlying core idea, is to consider just a subset of the process model behavior, instead of its all behavior. The methods additionally return problematic activities, based on their deviation rates. Using these methods, users are able to adjust the amount of process model behaviors considered in the approximation, which affects the computation time and the accuracy of alignment values and their bounds.

We implemented the methods in two open-source process mining tools and applied them on several large real event data and compared them with the state-of-the-art alignment approximation method. The results show that using some of proposed methods, we are able to approximate alignment values faster and at the same time the approximated values are very close to actual alignment values.

The remainder of this paper is structured as follows. In Sect. 2, we discuss related work. Section 3 defines preliminary notation. We explain the main method in Sect. 4 and evaluate it in Sect. 5. Section 6 concludes the paper.

## 2   Related Work

Several process mining techniques exists, ranging from process discovery to prediction. We limit related work to the field of conformance checking and sampling techniques in the process mining domain. We refer to [1] for an overview of process mining.

In [7], the authors review the conformance checking techniques in process mining domain. In [8] different methods for conformance checking and its

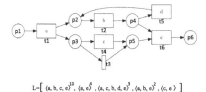

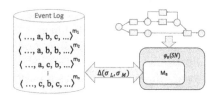

**Fig. 1.** An example Petri net and an event log in a multiset view.

**Fig. 2.** Overview of the proposed approach. It uses $M_B \subseteq \phi_v(SN)$ to approximate alignment costs.

applications are covered. Early work in conformance checking uses token-based replay [2]. The techniques replay a trace of executed events in a Petri net and add missing tokens if transitions are not able to fire. After replay, a conformance statistic is computed based on missing and remaining tokens. Alignments were introduced in [9] and have rapidly developed into the standard conformance checking technique. In [10,11], decomposition techniques are proposed for alignment computation. Moreover, [12] proposes a decomposition method to find an approximation of the alignment in a faster time. Applying decomposition techniques improves computation time, i.e., the techniques successfully use the divide-and-conquer paradigm, however, these techniques are primarily beneficial when there are too many unique activities in the process [13]. Recently, general approximation schemes for alignments, i.e., computation of near-optimal alignments, have been proposed [14]. Finally, the authors in [4] propose to incrementally compute prefix-alignments, i.e., enabling real-time conformance checking for event data streams.

A relatively limited amount of work has been done to use sampling approaches in process mining domain. In [15], the authors proposed a sampling approach based on Parikh vectors of traces to detect the behavior in the event log. In [16], the authors recommend a trace-based sampling method to decrease the discovery time and memory footprint that assumes the process instances have different behavior if they have different sets of directly follows relations. Furthermore, [17] recommends a trace-based sampling method specifically for the Heuristic miner [18]. In both of these sampling methods, we have no control on the size of the final sampled event data. Also, depend on the defined behavioral abstraction,the methods may select almost all the process instances. Finally, all these sampling methods are unbiased and consequently they leads to non-deterministic results. In [19], we analyze random and biased sampling methods with which we are able to adjust the size of the sampled data for process discovery. Moreover, [36] shows that using a clustering-based instance selection method will provide more precise and simpler process models.

Some research focuses on alignment value approximation. [20] proposes sampling the event log and applying conformance checking on the sampled data. The method increases the sample size until the approximated value is accurate enough. However, the method does not guarantee the accuracy of the approximation, e.g., by providing bounds for it. In Sect. 5, we show that if there is lot of unique behavior in the event log, using this method, the approximation time exceeds the computation time for finding the alignment value. The authors of [21] propose a conformance approximation method that applies relaxation labeling methods on a partial order representation of a process model. Similar to the previous method, it does not provide any guarantee for the approximated value. Furthermore, it needs to preprocess the process model each time. In this paper, we propose multiple alignment approximation methods that increase the conformance checking performance. The methods also provide bounds for alignment values and a deviation ratio of problematic activities.

## 3   Preliminaries

In this section, we briefly introduce basic process mining and, specifically, conformance checking terminology and notations that ease the readability of this paper.[1]

Given a set $X$, a multiset $\mathcal{B}$ over $X$ is a function $\mathcal{B} \colon X \to \mathbb{N}_{\geq 0}$ that allows certain elements of $X$ appear multiple times. $\overline{\mathcal{B}} = \{e \in X \mid \mathcal{B}(e) > 0\}$ is the set of elements present in the multiset. The set of all multisets over a set $X$ is written as $\mathcal{B}(X)$.

Given a system net $SN$, $\phi_f(SN)$ is the set of all complete firing sequences of $SN$ and $\phi_v(SN)$ is the set of all possible *visible* traces, i.e., complete firing sequences starting its initial marking and ending in its final marking projected onto the set of observable activities (not silent transitions, e.g., $t_3$ in Fig. 1). To measure how a trace aligns to a process model, we need to define the notation of moves. A *move* is a pair $(x, t)$ where the first element refers to the log and the second element refers to the corresponding transition in the model.

**Definition 1 (Legal Moves).** *Let $L \in \mathcal{B}(\mathcal{A}^*)$ be an event log, where $\mathcal{A}$ is the set of activities and let $T$ be the set of transitions in the model. Moreover, let $l$ be a function that returns the label of each transition. $A_{LM} = \{(x, (x, t)) \mid x \in \mathcal{A} \wedge t \in T \wedge l(t) = x\} \cup \{(\gg, (x, t)) \mid t \in T \wedge l(t) = x\} \cup \{(x, \gg) \mid x \in \mathcal{A}\}$ is the set of* legal moves.

For example, $(a, t_1)$ means that both log and model make an "$a$ move" and the move in the model is caused by the occurrence of transition $t_1$ (as the label of $t_1$ is $a$). Note that $\gg$ indicates "no move" in log/model trace. Now, we define Alignment as follows [10].

**Definition 2 (Alignment).** *Let $\sigma_L \in L$ be a log trace and $\sigma_M \in \phi_f(SN)$ a complete firing sequence of a system net $SN$. An alignment of $\sigma_L$ and $\sigma_M$ is a sequence of pairs $\gamma \in A_{LM}^*$ such that the projection on the first element (ignoring $\gg$) yields $\sigma_L$ and the projection on the second element (ignoring $\gg$ and transition labels) yields $\sigma_M$.*

---

[1] For some concepts, e.g., labeled Petri net and System net please use the definitions in [10].

An alignment is a sequence of legal moves such that after removing all $\gg$ symbols, the top row corresponds to a trace in the event log and the bottom row corresponds to a complete firing sequence in $\phi_f(SN)$. The middle row corresponds to a visible path when ignoring the $\tau$ steps, i.e., corresponding to silent transitions (e.g., $t_3$ in Fig. 1). For silent transitions, there is no corresponding recorded event in the log. The following alignments relate to $\sigma_L = \langle a, c, b, d, e\rangle$ and the Petri net in Fig. 1.

$$\gamma_1 = \begin{array}{|c|c|c|c|c|c|} \hline a & \gg & c & b & d & e \\ \hline a & \tau & \gg & b & \gg & e \\ \hline t_1 & t_3 & & t_2 & & t_6 \\ \hline \end{array} \quad \gamma_2 = \begin{array}{|c|c|c|c|c|} \hline a & c & b & d & e \\ \hline a & c & b & \gg & e \\ \hline t_1 & t_4 & t_2 & & t_6 \\ \hline \end{array}$$

By considering the label of visible transitions of an alignment, we find the corresponding model trace, e.g., the model trace of $\gamma_1$ is $\langle a, b, e\rangle$. To quantify the costs of misalignments we introduce a move cost function $\delta$. *Synchronous moves*, i.e., moves that are similar in the trace and the model, have no costs, i.e., for all $x \in \mathcal{A}$, $\delta((x, (x, t)) = 0$. Moves in model only have no costs if the transition is invisible, i.e., $\delta(\gg, t) = 0$ if $l(t) = \tau$.

**Definition 3 (Cost of Alignment).** *Cost function $\delta \in A_{LM} \to \mathbb{R} \geq 0$ assigns costs to legal moves. The cost of an alignment $\gamma \in A_{LM}^*$ is $\delta(\gamma) = \Sigma_{(x,y)\in\gamma}\delta(x,y)$.*

In this paper, we use a standard cost function $\delta_S$ that assigns unit costs: $\delta_S(\gg, t) = \delta_S(x, \gg) = 1$ if $l(t) \neq \tau$. In the above example alignments, $\delta_S(\gamma_1) = 2$ and $\delta_S(\gamma_2) = 1$. Given a log trace and a system net, we may have many alignments. To select the most appropriate one, we select an alignment with the lowest total costs.

**Definition 4 (Optimal Alignment).** *Let $L \in \mathcal{B}(\mathcal{A}^*)$ be an event log and let $SN$ be a system net with $\phi_v(SN) \neq \emptyset$.*

- *For $\sigma_L \in L$, $\Gamma_{\sigma_L,SN} = \{\gamma \in A_{LM}^* | \exists_{\sigma_M \in \phi_f(SN)}$ is an alignment of $\sigma_L$ and $\sigma_M\}$.*
- *An alignment $\gamma \in \Gamma_{\sigma_L,SN}$ is optimal for trace $\sigma_L \in L$ and system net $SN$ if for any alignment $\gamma' \in \Gamma_{\sigma_L,SN} : \delta(\gamma') \geq \delta(\gamma)$.*
- *$\gamma_{SN} \in \mathcal{A}^* \to A_{LM}^*$ is a mapping that assigns any log trace $\sigma_L$ to an optimal alignment, i.e., $\gamma_{SN}(\sigma_L) \in \Gamma_{\sigma_L,SN}$ and $\gamma_{SN}(\sigma_L)$ is an optimal alignment.*
- *$\lambda_{SN} \in \mathcal{A}^* \to \mathcal{A}^*$ is a mapping that assigns any log trace $\sigma_L$ to visible activities of the model trace of the optimal alignment.*

In the running example, $\gamma_{SN}(\langle a, c, b, d, e\rangle) = \gamma_2$ ($\gamma_2$ is optimal), and $\lambda(\langle a, c, b, d, e\rangle) = \langle a, c, b, e\rangle$ is the corresponding model trace for the optimal alignment.

We can compute the distance of two traces (or two sequences) faster using the adapted version of Levenshtein distance [22]. Suppose that $\sigma, \sigma' \in \mathcal{A}^*$, Edit Distance function $\triangle(\sigma, \sigma') \to \mathbb{N}$ returns the minimum number of edits that are needed to transform $\sigma$ to $\sigma'$. As edit operations, we allow deletion/insertion of an activity (or a transition label) in a trace, e.g., $\triangle(\langle a, c, f, e\rangle, \langle a, f, c, a\rangle) = 4$, corresponds to two deletions and two insertions. This measure is symmetric, i.e.,

$\triangle(\sigma, \sigma') = \triangle(\sigma', \sigma)$. It is possible to use the $\triangle$ function instead of the standard cost function. Thus, $\triangle$ and $\delta_S$ return same distance values. The $\triangle$ function is expendable from unit cost (i.e., $\delta_S$) to another cost by giving different weights to insertion and deletion of different activities.

In [23], it is explained that the Levenshtein metric before normalization satisfies the triangle inequality. In other words, $\triangle(\sigma, \sigma') \leq \triangle(\sigma, \sigma'') + \triangle(\sigma'', \sigma')$. Moreover, suppose that $S$ is a set of sequences, $\Phi(\sigma_L, S) = \min_{\sigma_M \in S} \triangle(\sigma_L, \sigma_M)$ returns the distance of the most similar sequence in $S$ for $\sigma_L$.

Let $\phi_v(SN)$ is a set of all visible firing sequences in $SN$, and $\gamma_{SN}(\sigma)$ is an optimal alignment for sequence $\sigma$. It is possible to use $\Phi(\sigma, \phi_v(SN))$ instead of $\delta_S(\gamma_{SN}(\sigma))$ [2]. Using the edit distance function, we are able to find which activities are required to be deleted or inserted. So, not only the cost of alignment; but, the deviated parts of the process model (except invisible transitions) are also detectable using this function.

It is possible to convert misalignment costs into the fitness value using Eq. 1. It normalizes the cost of optimal alignment by one deletion for each activity in the trace and one insertion for each visible transition in the shortest path of model (SPM). The fitness between an event log $L$ and a system net $SN$ (i.e., $Fitness(L, SN)$) is a weighted average of traces' fitness.

$$fitness(\sigma_L, SN) = 1 - \frac{\delta(\gamma_{SN}(\sigma))}{|\sigma_L| + \min_{\sigma_M \in \phi_f} (|\sigma_M|)} \tag{1}$$

## 4    Approximating Alignments Using Subset of Model Behavior

As computational complexity of computing alignment is exponential in the number of states and the number of transitions, it is impractical for larger petri nets and event logs [24]. Considering that the most time consuming part in the conformance checking procedure is finding an optimal alignment for each $\sigma_L \in L$ and the system net $SN$ leads us to propose an approximation approach that requires fewer alignment computations. The overview of the proposed approach is presented in Fig. 2. We suggest to use $M_B \subseteq \phi_v(SN)$ instead of the whole $\phi_v(SN)$ and apply the edit distance function instead of $\delta_S$. In the following lemma, we show that using this approach, we have an upper bound for the cost of alignment (i.e., a lower bound for the fitness value).

**Lemma 1 (Alignment Cost Upper Bound).** *Let $\sigma_L \in \mathcal{A}^*$ is a log trace, and $\sigma_M \in \phi_v(SN)$ is a visible firing sequence of SN. We have $\delta_S(\gamma_{SN}(\sigma_L)) \leq \triangle(\sigma_L, \sigma_M)$ where $\gamma_{SN}(\sigma_L)$ is the optimal alignment.*

**Proof:** We shown that $\triangle(\sigma_L, \sigma_M) = \delta_S(\gamma)$, so we have $\triangle(\sigma_L, \sigma_M) \geq \delta_S(\gamma_{SN}(\sigma_L))$. Therefore, if $\delta_S(\gamma_{SN}(\sigma_L)) > \triangle(\sigma_L, \sigma_M)$, $\gamma_{SN}(\sigma_L)$ is not an optimal alignment. Consequently, if we use any $M_B \subseteq \phi_v(SN)$, $\Phi(\sigma_L, M_B)$ returns an upper bound for the cost of optimal alignment.

---

[2] Because of the page limit, we do not provide the proof of this statement here.

Here, we explain the main components of our proposed approach, i.e., constructing a subset of model behavior ($M_B$) and computing the approximation.

### 4.1  Constructing Model Behavior ($M_B$)

As explained, we propose to use $M_B$ i.e., a subset of visible model traces to have an approximated alignment. An important question is how to construct $M_B$. In this regard, we propose two approaches, i.e., *simulation* and *candidate selection*.

**1) Simulation:** The subset of model traces can be constructed by simulating the process model. In this regard, having a system net and the initial and final markings, we simulate some complete firing sequences. Note that we keep only the visible firing sequences in $M_B$. It is possible to replay the Petri net randomly or by using more advanced methods, e.g., stochastic petri net simulation techniques. This approach is fast; but, we are not able to guarantee that by increasing the size of $M_B$ we will obtain the perfect alignment (or fitness) value, because the model traces are able to be infinite. Another potential problem of this method is that the generated subset may be far from traces in the event log that leads to have an inaccurate approximation.

**2) Candidate Selection:** The second method to construct $M_B$ is computing the optimal alignments of selected traces in the event log and finding the corresponding model traces for these alignments. In this regard, we first select some traces (i.e., candidates) from the event log $L$ and put them in $L_C$. Then for each $\sigma_L \in L_C$ we find the optimal alignment and insert $\lambda_{SN}(\sigma_L)$ to $M_B$. Thereafter, for other traces $\sigma'_L \in L'_C$ (i.e., $L'_C = L - L_C$), we will use $M_B$ and compute $\Phi(\sigma'_L, M_B)$.

As the triangle inequality property holds for the edit distance function, it is better to insert $\lambda_{SN}(\sigma_L)$ in $M_B$ instead of considering $\sigma_L$. To make it more clear, let $\sigma_L$ be a log trace, $SN$ is a system net, and $\sigma_M = \lambda_{SN}(\sigma_L)$ is the corresponding visible model trace for an optimal alignment of $\sigma_L$ and $SN$. According to the triangle inequality property, for any trace $\sigma \in L$, we have $\triangle(\sigma, \sigma_M) \leq \triangle(\sigma, \sigma_L) + \triangle(\sigma_L, \sigma_M)$. So, the cost of transforming $\sigma_L$ to $\sigma_M$ is less than the cost of transforming it to $\sigma_L$ and then to $\sigma_M$. As $\Phi(\sigma_L, M_B)$ returns the minimum cost of the most similar sequence in $M_B$ to $\sigma_L$, putting directly the alignments of traces $M_B$ causes to have a smaller upper bound for alignment cost. Moreover, it is possible to have $\lambda_{SN}(\gamma_{SN}(\sigma_1)) = \lambda_{SN}(\gamma_{SN}(\sigma_2))$ for $\sigma_1 \neq \sigma_2$. Therefore, by inserting $\lambda_{SN}(\sigma_1)$ instead of $\sigma_1$ in $M_B$, we will have $M_B$ with fewer members that increases the performance of the approximation.

To select the candidate traces in $L_C$, we propose three different methods. We can select these traces *randomly* or based on their *frequency* in the event log (i.e, $L(\sigma_L)$). The third possible method is to apply a *clustering* algorithm on the event log and put the traces in $K$ different clusters based on their control flow information. We then select one trace, i.e., medoid for each cluster that represents all cluster's members. It is expected that by using this approach, the detected bounds will be more accurate.

**Table 1.** Result of using the proposed approximation method for the event log that is given in Fig. 1 considering that $M_B = \{\langle a, b, e \rangle, \langle a, b, c, e \rangle\}$.

| Trace | $\delta_S(\gamma_{SN})$ | Min $\triangle$ | Actual Fitness | LBoundFitness | UBoundFitness | AppxFitness | Freq |
|---|---|---|---|---|---|---|---|
| $\langle a, b, c, e \rangle$ | 0 | 0 | 1 | 1 | 1 | 1 | 10 |
| $\langle a, e \rangle$ | 1 | 1 | 0.8 | 0.8 | 0.8 | 0.8 | 4 |
| $\langle a, c, b, d, e \rangle$ | 1 | 2 | 0.875 | 0.75 | 1 | 0.857 | 3 |
| $\langle a, b, e \rangle$ | 0 | 0 | 1 | 1 | 1 | 1 | 2 |
| $\langle c, e \rangle$ | 2 | 2 | 0.6 | 0.5 | 0.8 | 0.8 | 1 |
| $L$ | $\sim$ | $\sim$ | 0.921 | 0.898 | 0.95 | 0.929 | $\sim$ |

## 4.2   Computing Alignment Approximation

After constructing $M_B$, we use it for all traces in the $L'_C$. Note that for the *simulation* method, $L_C = \emptyset$ and $L'_C = L$. Moreover, for the *candidate selection* method, we use the alignment values that already computed by in constructing $M_B$. To compute the lower bound for the fitness value, we compute the fitness value of all of the $\sigma \in L'_C$ using $\Phi(\sigma, M_B)$. Afterwards, based on the weighted average of this fitness and alignments that are computed in the previous part, the lower bound for the fitness value is computed.

For the upper bound of fitness value, we compare the length of each trace in $L'_C$ with the shortest path in the model (i.e., $SPM$). To find $SPM$, we compute the cost of the optimal alignment for an empty trace (i.e., $\langle \rangle$) and the system net. In the example that is given in Fig. 1, $SPM = 3$. If the length of a trace is shorter than the $SPM$, we know that it needs at least $SPM - \sigma_L$ insertions to transform to one of model traces in $\phi_v(SN)$. Otherwise, we consider at least 0 edit operation for that trace. Because, it is possible that there is a model trace s.t. $\sigma_M \in \phi_v(SN)$ and $\sigma_M \notin M_B$ and it perfectly fits to the log trace. After computing the upper bound values for all traces in $L'_C$, based on the weighted average of them and the computed fitness values of traces in $L_C$, we compute the upper bound value for fitness.

To compute the approximation values, for each trace in $\sigma \in L'_C$, we compute the $\Phi(\sigma, M_B)$ and compare it to the average fitness value of $L_C$. If the fitness value of the new trace is higher than $Fitness(L_C, SN)$, we consider $\Phi(\sigma, M_B)$ as the approximated fitness value; otherwise, $Fitness(L_C, SN)$ will be considered for the approximation. Similar to the bounds, we use the weighted averages of fitness values of $L_C$ and $L'_C$ to compute the approximated fitness value of whole event log. Note that for the simulation method that $L_C = \emptyset$, the approximated fitness value for each trace (and for the whole event log) is equal to the lower bound.

Finally, the proposed method returns the number of asynchronous (i.e., deletions and insertions) and synchronous moves for each activity in the event log. This information helps the data analyst to find out the source of deviations.

The computed bounds and the approximated fitness value for each trace and the overall event log in Fig. 1 based on $M_B = \{\langle a, b, e \rangle, \langle a, b, c, e \rangle\}$ is given in Table 1. This $M_B$ is possible to gained by computing the alignment of the two most frequent traces in the event log or by simulation. The approximated fitness will be 0.929 that its accuracy equals to 0.008. The proposed bounds are 0.95 and 0.898. Moreover, the method returns the number of insertion and deletions that are 1 insertion for $a$, 5 insertion for $b$, 3 deletions for $c$, 3 deletions for $d$, and nothing for $e$.

By increasing $|M_B|$, we expect to have more accurate approximations and bounds. But, increasing the $|M_B|$ for the candidate selection approach increases the number of required alignments computations and consequently increases the computation time.

## 5   Evaluation

In this section, we aim to explore the accuracy and the performance of our methods. We first explain the implementation, and, subsequently, we explain the experimental setting. Finally, the experimental results and some discussions will be provided.

### 5.1   Implementation

To apply the proposed conformance approximation method, we implemented the *Conformance Approximation* plug-in in the ProM [25] framework[3]. It takes an event log and a Petri net as inputs and returns the conformance approximation, its bounds, and the deviation rates of different activities. In this implementation, we let the user adjusts the size of $M_B$ and the method to select and insert model traces in it (i.e., *simulation* and alignment of selected candidates). If the user decides to use alignments for creating model behavior, she can select candidates based on their *frequency*, *random*, or using the *clustering* algorithm. For finding the distance of a log trace and a model trace, we used the *edit distance* function, which is an adapted version of the Levenshtein distance [22]. To cluster traces, we implement the K-Medoids algorithm that returns one trace as a candidate for each cluster [26] based on their edit distance.

To apply the methods on various event logs with different parameters, we ported the developed plug-in to RapidProM, i.e., an extension of RapidMiner and combines scientific work-flows with a several process mining algorithms [27].

### 5.2   Experimental Setup

We applied the proposed methods on eight different real event logs. Some information about these event logs is given in Table 2. Here, *uniqueness* refers to $\frac{Variant\#}{Trace\#}$.

For process discovery, we used the Inductive Miner [34] with infrequent thresholds equal to 0.3, 0.5, and 0.7. We applied conformance approximation methods with different settings. In this regard, an approximation parameter is

---

[3] https://svn.win.tue.nl/repos/prom/Packages/LogFiltering.

**Table 2.** Statistics regarding the real event logs that are used in the experiment.

| Event log | Activities# | Traces# | Variants# | DF# | Uniqueness |
|---|---|---|---|---|---|
| BPIC-2012 [28] | 23 | 13087 | 4336 | 138 | 0.33 |
| BPIC-2018-Department [29] | 6 | 29297 | 349 | 19 | 0.01 |
| BPIC-2018-Inspection [29] | 15 | 5485 | 3190 | 67 | 0.58 |
| BPIC-2018-Reference [29] | 6 | 43802 | 515 | 15 | 0.01 |
| BPIC-2019 [30] | 42 | 251734 | 11973 | 498 | 0.05 |
| Hospital-Billing [31] | 18 | 100000 | 1020 | 143 | 0.01 |
| Road [32] | 11 | 150370 | 231 | 70 | $\sim$0 |
| Sepsis [33] | 16 | 1050 | 846 | 115 | 0.81 |

used with values equal to $1, 2, 3, 5, 10, 15, 20, 25$ and $30$. This value for the *Simulation* method is the number of simulated traces times $|L|$, and for the *candidate selection* methods (i.e., *clustering*, *frequency*, and *random*), it shows the relative number of selected candidates, i.e., $\frac{|L_C|}{|L|}$. We also compared our proposed method with the *statistical* sampling method [20]. The approximation parameter for this method determines the size and the accuracy of sampling and we consider $\epsilon = \delta =$ approximation parameter $\times 0.001$. We did not consider [12] in the experiments, as it does not improve the performance of normal computation of alignment [35] for event logs which have few unique activities using the default setting. Even for some event logs with lots of unique activities in [12], the performance improvement of our methods is higher. Because of the page limit, we do not show results of this experiment here.

In all experiments and for all methods, we used eight threads of CPU. Moreover, each experiment was repeated four times, since the conformance checking time is not deterministic, and the average values are shown.

To evaluate how the conformance approximation is able to improve the performance of the conformance checking process, we used the $PI = \frac{Normal\ Conformance\ Time}{Approximated\ Conformance\ Time}$. In this formula, a higher $PI$ value means conformance is computed in less time. As all our proposed methods need a preprocessing phase (e.g., for clustering the traces), we compute the $PI$ with and without the preprocessing phase.

The accuracy of the approximation, i.e., the difference between approximated conformance value and the actual fitness value shows how close is the approximated fitness to the actual fitness value that is computed by $Accuracy = |AccFitness - AppxFitness|$. Also, we measure the distance of the provided upper and lower bounds. The bound width of an approximation is computed by $BoundWidth = UBFitness - LBFitness$. Tighter bound widths means that we have more accurate bounds.

## 5.3    Experimental Result and Discussion

In Fig. 3, we show how different approximation methods improve the performance of conformance checking. For most of the cases, the improvement is higher for the *simulation* method. It is because, the most time consuming part in conformance checking is computing the optimal alignment. As in the *simulation* method, there is no need to do any alignment computation, it is faster than any other method. For some event logs, the *statistical* sampling method [20] is not able to provide the approximation faster than the normal conformance checking (i.e., $PI < 1$). It happens because, this method is not able to benefit from the parallel computing of alignment and after each alignment computation it needs to check if it needs to do more alignment or not. For the *statistical* method, decreasing approximation parameter leads to more precise approximations; however, it causes to have less $PI$ value. Among the *candidate selection* methods, using the *frequency* method usually leads to a higher $PI$ value.

For some event logs, e.g., *Road*, none of the method has a high $PI$ value. It happens because in Fig. 3, we consider the preprocessing time. The preprocessing time corresponds to choosing the candidate traces and simulating the process model behaviors that needs to be done once per each event log or process model. For the candidate selection methods, this phase is independent of process models and for doing that we do not need to consider any process model. For the simulation method, this phase is independent of the given event log. Thus, we are able to do the preprocessing step before conformance approximation. If we use some event log standards such as MXML and Parquet, we do not need to preprocess the event log for the *frequency* and *random* method because we know the number of variants and their frequency beforehand.

In Fig. 4, we show the performance improvement without considering the preprocessing time. As the *statistical* sampling method does not have preprocessing phase, it is not shown in this figure. It is shown that there is a linear decrement in improvement of the *candidate selection* methods by increasing the approximation parameter. It is expectable, as increasing in this parameter for candidate selection methods means more optimal alignment computations that requires more time. For example, by considering 5 for this parameter, means that we need to compute 5% of all optimal alignments of the normal conformance checking. Therefore, it is expected that the approximated conformance value will be computed in 20 times faster than using normal alignment.

After analyzing the performance improvement capabilities of the proposed methods, in Table 3, we compare the accuracy of their approximations. In this regard, the average accuracy values of the approximated conformance values are shown in this table. The lower value means a higher accuracy or in other words, the approximated fitness value is closer to the actual fitness value. In this table, *Fitness* shows the actual fitness value when the normal conformance checking method is used. We used different values for the approximation parameter as explained in Sect. 5.2. The results show that for most of the event logs the accuracy of the *simulation* method is not good enough. However, for *BPIC*-2018-*Reference* and *BPIC*-2018-*Department*, that have simpler process models, using

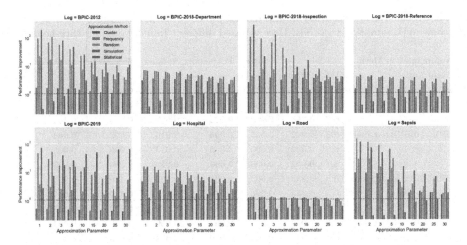

**Fig. 3.** Performance improvement with consideration of preprocessing time.

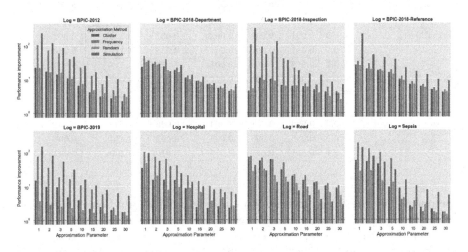

**Fig. 4.** Performance improvement without consideration of preprocessing time.

this method, we generated almost all the model behavior (i.e., $M_B = \phi_v$) and obtain perfect accuracy. Results show that if we use the *statistical*, and *frequency* methods, we usually obtain accuracy value below 0.01 which is acceptable for many applications. Among the above methods, results of the statistical sampling method are more stable and accurate. However, the accuracy of candidate selection methods is usually improved by using a higher approximation parameter.

In the next experiment, we aim to evaluate the provided bounds for the approximation. Figure 5 shows how increasing the value of the approximation parameter increases the accuracy of the provided lower and upper bounds. As the *statistical* method does not provide any bounds, we do not consider it in this

**Table 3.** The average accuracy of approximation for conformance values when we use different approximation methods. Here we used different Inductive miner thresholds.

| Approximation Method | | | Cluster | Frequency | Random | Simulation | Statistical |
|---|---|---|---|---|---|---|---|
| Event Log | IMi | Fitness | | | | | |
| BPIC-2012 | 0.3 | 0.874 | 0.001 | 0.001 | 0.073 | 0.360 | 0.002 |
| | 0.5 | 0.813 | 0.006 | 0.022 | 0.011 | 0.302 | 0.004 |
| | 0.7 | 0.755 | 0.008 | 0.032 | 0.037 | 0.271 | 0.005 |
| BPIC-2018-Department | 0.3 | 0.962 | 0.005 | 0.006 | 0.016 | 0.000 | 0.004 |
| | 0.5 | 0.962 | 0.005 | 0.006 | 0.013 | 0.000 | 0.005 |
| | 0.7 | 0.962 | 0.005 | 0.006 | 0.018 | 0.000 | 0.003 |
| BPIC-2018-Inspection | 0.3 | 0.886 | 0.003 | 0.008 | 0.007 | 0.446 | 0.008 |
| | 0.5 | 0.853 | 0.006 | 0.012 | 0.013 | 0.429 | 0.005 |
| | 0.7 | 0.800 | 0.007 | 0.021 | 0.027 | 0.370 | 0.003 |
| BPIC-2018-Reference | 0.3 | 0.943 | 0.006 | 0.006 | 0.059 | 0.000 | 0.004 |
| | 0.5 | 0.943 | 0.006 | 0.006 | 0.051 | 0.000 | 0.003 |
| | 0.7 | 0.943 | 0.006 | 0.006 | 0.048 | 0.000 | 0.005 |
| BPIC-2019 | 0.3 | 0.905 | 0.014 | 0.001 | 0.031 | 0.408 | 0.004 |
| | 0.5 | 0.930 | 0.015 | 0.001 | 0.018 | 0.419 | 0.003 |
| | 0.7 | 0.930 | 0.015 | 0.001 | 0.016 | 0.418 | 0.002 |
| Hospital | 0.3 | 0.991 | 0.002 | 0.002 | 0.031 | 0.324 | 0.002 |
| | 0.5 | 0.747 | 0.001 | 0.001 | 0.055 | 0.117 | 0.003 |
| | 0.7 | 0.573 | 0.003 | 0.001 | 0.017 | 0.013 | 0.002 |
| Road | 0.3 | 0.992 | 0.003 | 0.002 | 0.069 | 0.082 | 0.003 |
| | 0.5 | 0.758 | 0.002 | 0.002 | 0.023 | 0.046 | 0.007 |
| | 0.7 | 0.717 | 0.001 | 0.002 | 0.004 | 0.069 | 0.005 |
| Sepsis | 0.3 | 0.993 | 0.001 | 0.004 | 0.006 | 0.456 | 0.001 |
| | 0.5 | 0.988 | 0.003 | 0.006 | 0.003 | 0.414 | 0.003 |
| | 0.7 | 0.891 | 0.011 | 0.015 | 0.010 | 0.260 | 0.003 |

experiment. The *simulation* method is not able to provide tight bound widths for most of the event logs. For most of the event logs, the *frequency* method results in tighter bounds. However, for event logs like *Sepsis* which there is no high frequent trace-variant, the *clustering* method provides more accurate bounds. If there are high frequent variants in the event log, it is recommended to use the *frequency* approximation method. Note that, for all methods, by increasing the value of approximation parameter, we decrease the bound width.

Considering both Fig. 4 and Fig. 5, we observe that there is a trade-off between the performance and the accuracy of the approximation methods. By increasing the number of visible traces in $M_B$, we need more time to approximate the fitness value; but, we will provide more accurate bounds. In the case that we set the approximation parameter to 100, the bound width will be zero; however, there will not any improvement in performance of the conformance checking. By adjusting the approximation parameter, the end user is able to specify the performance improvement.

Figure 5 shows that for some event logs like *Sepsis* and *BPIC-2018-Inspection*, none of the approximation methods are able to provide tight bounds. That hap-

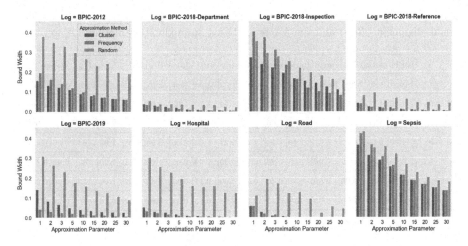

**Fig. 5.** The average of bound width using different approximation methods.

**Table 4.** The average similarity of traces in different event logs.

| BPIC-2012 | Department | Inspection | References | BPIC-2019 | Hospital | Road | Sepsis |
|---|---|---|---|---|---|---|---|
| 3.686 | 1.224 | 3.269 | 1.481 | 5.108 | 1.745 | 1.113 | 3.956 |

pens because in these event logs not only do we have lots of unique traces; but, also these traces are not close to each other. In Table 4, we show the average of edit distance of the most similar trace in the event logs that equals to $Average_{\sigma \in L} \Phi(\sigma, L - \sigma)$. If the traces in an event log are similar to each other, we are able to provide tight bounds by the approximation methods. This characteristic of the event log can be analyzed without any process model before the approximation. Therefore, it is expected to use more traces in $M_B$ when the traces are not similar. Using this preprocessing step, user is able to adjust the approximation parameter easier.

Finally, we analyze the accuracy of the provided information about deviations. We first analyze the normal alignments of event logs and process models. Thereafter, for each alignment, we determine the six most problematic activities based on their deviation ratio that is computed based on the following formula.

$$DeviationRatio = \frac{AsynchronousMoves}{AsynchronousMoves + SynchronousMoves} \quad (2)$$

Afterwards, we compare the deviation ratio of these problematic activities with the case that the approximation method was used. The result of this experiment is given in Table 5. Here, we used the *frequency* selection method with an approximation parameter equal to 10. We did not compare the result with the *statistical* method as the goal of this method is either the fitness value or the number of asynchronous moves; but, could not return both of them at the same

**Table 5.** Comparison of deviation ratio of the six most problematic activities using normal alignment (*Real*) and the *frequency* based approximation method (*Appx*).

| | BPIC-2012 | | Department | | Inspection | | References | | BPIC-2019 | | Hospital | | Road | | Sepsis | |
|---|---|---|---|---|---|---|---|---|---|---|---|---|---|---|---|---|
| | Appx | Real | Appx | Real | Appx | Real | Appx | Real | Appx | Real | Appx | Real | Appx | Real | Appx | Real |
| Activity 1 | 1.00 | 1.00 | 1.00 | 1.00 | 1.00 | 1.00 | 1.00 | 1.00 | 1.00 | 1.00 | 1.00 | 0.99 | 1.00 | 0.96 | 1.00 | 1.00 |
| Activity 2 | 1.00 | 1.00 | 0.53 | 0.53 | 1.00 | 1.00 | 1.00 | 0.50 | 1.00 | 1.00 | 1.00 | 0.95 | 1.00 | 0.96 | 1.00 | 1.00 |
| Activity 3 | 1.00 | 0.94 | 0.37 | 0.37 | 1.00 | 1.00 | 0.31 | 0.28 | 1.00 | 0.98 | 0.96 | 0.95 | 1.00 | 0.83 | 0.59 | 0.48 |
| Activity 4 | 0.64 | 0.45 | 0.06 | 0.06 | 1.00 | 0.85 | 0.00 | 0.00 | 1.00 | 0.91 | 1.00 | 0.88 | 1.00 | 0.82 | 0.43 | 0.32 |
| Activity 5 | 0.16 | 0.01 | 0.00 | 0.00 | 0.58 | 0.40 | 0.00 | 0.00 | 0.13 | 0.11 | 0.83 | 0.82 | 1.00 | 0.72 | 0.20 | 0.25 |
| Activity 6 | 0.67 | 0.00 | 1.00 | 0.00 | 0.29 | 0.16 | 0.01 | 0.00 | 0.13 | 0.11 | 0.82 | 0.82 | 0.10 | 0.10 | 0.27 | 0.22 |

time[4]. Results show that using the *frequency* method, we find the problematic activities that have high deviation rates.

Considering all the experiments, we conclude that using frequency of traces for selecting candidates is more practical. Moreover, the candidate selection methods give more flexibility to users to trade off between the performance and the accuracy of approximations compared to the *statistical* method that sometimes could not improve the performance and has nondeterministic results. In addition, the proposed methods provide bounds for the approximated alignment value and deviation rates for activities that is useful for many diagnostic applications. Finally, the proposed methods are able to use parallel computation and benefit from adjusted computational resources.

## 6    Conclusion

In this paper, we proposed approximation methods for conformance value including providing upper and lower bounds. Instead of computing the accurate alignment between the process model and all the traces available in the event log, we propose to just consider a subset of possible behavior in the process model and use it for approximating the conformance value using the edit distance function. We can find this subset by computing the optimal alignments of some candidate traces in the event log or by simulating the process model. To evaluate our proposed methods, we developed them in ProM framework and also imported them to RapidProM and applied them on several real event logs. Results show that these methods decrease the conformance checking time and at the same time find approximated values close to the actual alignment value. We found that the *simulation* method is suitable to be used when the given process model is simple. We also show that using the *frequency* method is more applicable to select the candidate traces and have accurate results. Results also indicate that although

---

[4] Approximating deviations is required much more time using the *statistical* method.

the *statistical* method [20] is able to approximate accurately, it takes more time and for some event logs, it is slower than the normal conformance checking.

As future work, we aim to find out what the best subset selection method is due to the available time and event data. Also, it is possible to provide an incremental approximation tool that increases the $M_B$ during the time and let the end user decide when the accuracy is enough. Here, we did not use the probabilities for the simulation method, we think that by using the distribution in the event log, we enhance the *simulation* method.

# References

1. van der Aalst, W.M.P.: Process Mining - Data Science in Action, 2nd edn. Springer, Heidelberg (2016). https://doi.org/10.1007/978-3-662-49851-4
2. Rozinat, A., Van der Aalst, W.M.: Conformance checking of processes based on monitoring real behavior. Inf. Syst. **33**(1), 64–95 (2008)
3. Adriansyah, A., Munoz-Gama, J., Carmona, J., van Dongen, B.F., van der Aalst, W.M.P.: Alignment based precision checking. In: La Rosa, M., Soffer, P. (eds.) BPM 2012. LNBIP, vol. 132, pp. 137–149. Springer, Heidelberg (2013). https://doi.org/10.1007/978-3-642-36285-9_15
4. van Zelst, S.J., Bolt, A., Hassani, M., van Dongen, B.F., van der Aalst, W.M.P.: Online conformance checking: relating event streams to process models using prefix-alignments. Int. J. Data Sci. Anal. **8**(3), 269–284 (2017). https://doi.org/10.1007/s41060-017-0078-6
5. De Leoni, M., van der Aalst, W.M.: Data-aware process mining: discovering decisions in processes using alignments. In: Proceedings of the 28th Annual ACM Symposium on Applied Computing, pp. 1454–1461. ACM (2013)
6. Fahland, D., van der Aalst, W.M.P.: Model repair-aligning process models to reality. Inf. Syst. **47**, 220–243 (2015)
7. Elhagaly, M., Drvoderić, K., Kippers, R.G., Bukhsh, F.A.: Evolution of compliance checking in process mining discipline. In: 2nd International Conference on Computing, Mathematics and Engineering Technologies (iCoMET), pp. 1–6. IEEE (2019)
8. Carmona, J., van Dongen, B., Solti, A., Weidlich, M.: Epilogue. Conformance Checking, pp. 261–263. Springer, Cham (2018). https://doi.org/10.1007/978-3-319-99414-7_13
9. van der Aalst, W.M.P., Adriansyah, A., van Dongen, B.F.: Replaying history on process models for conformance checking and performance analysis. Wiley Interdiscip. Rev. Data Min. Knowl. Discov. **2**(2), 182–192 (2012)
10. Van der Aalst, W.M.: Decomposing petri nets for process mining: a generic approach. Distrib. Parallel Databases **31**(4), 471–507 (2013). https://doi.org/10.1007/s10619-013-7127-5
11. Munoz-Gama, J., Carmona, J., Van Der Aalst, W.M.: Single-entry single-exit decomposed conformance checking. Inf. Syst. **46**, 102–122 (2014)
12. Lee, W.L.J., Verbeek, H.M.W., Munoz-Gama, J., van der Aalst, W.M.P., Sepúlveda, M.: Recomposing conformance: closing the circle on decomposed alignment-based conformance checking in process mining. Inf. Sci. **466**, 55–91 (2018)
13. Verbeek, H.M.W., van der Aalst, W.M.P., Munoz-Gama, J.: Divide and conquer: a tool framework for supporting decomposed discovery in process mining. Comput. J. **60**(11), 1649–1674 (2017)

14. Taymouri, F., Carmona, J.: A recursive paradigm for aligning observed behavior of large structured process models. In: La Rosa, M., Loos, P., Pastor, O. (eds.) BPM 2016. LNCS, vol. 9850, pp. 197–214. Springer, Cham (2016). https://doi.org/10.1007/978-3-319-45348-4_12

15. Carmona, J., Cortadella, J.: Process mining meets abstract interpretation. In: Balcázar, J.L., Bonchi, F., Gionis, A., Sebag, M. (eds.) ECML PKDD 2010. LNCS (LNAI), vol. 6321, pp. 184–199. Springer, Heidelberg (2010). https://doi.org/10.1007/978-3-642-15880-3_18

16. Bauer, M., Senderovich, A., Gal, A., Grunske, L., Weidlich, M.: How much event data is enough? A statistical framework for process discovery. In: Krogstie, J., Reijers, H.A. (eds.) CAiSE 2018. LNCS, vol. 10816, pp. 239–256. Springer, Cham (2018). https://doi.org/10.1007/978-3-319-91563-0_15

17. Berti, A.: Statistical sampling in process mining discovery. In: The 9th International Conference on Information, Process, and Knowledge Management, pp. 41–43 (2017)

18. Weijters, A.J.M.M., Ribeiro, J.T.S.: Flexible heuristics miner (FHM). In: CIDM (2011)

19. Sani, M.F., van Zelst, S.J., van der Aalst, W.M.P.: The Impact of Event Log Subset Selection on the Performance of Process Discovery Algorithms. In: Proceedings of New Trends in Databases and Information Systems, ADBIS 2019 Short Papers, Workshops BBIGAP, QAUCA, SemBDM, SIMPDA, M2P, MADEISD, and Doctoral Consortium, Bled, Slovenia, September 8–11, 2019, pp. 391–404 (2019). https://doi.org/10.1007/978-3-030-30278-8_39

20. Bauer, M., van der Aa, H., Weidlich, M.: Estimating process conformance by trace sampling and result approximation. In: Hildebrandt, T., van Dongen, B.F., Röglinger, M., Mendling, J. (eds.) BPM 2019. LNCS, vol. 11675, pp. 179–197. Springer, Cham (2019). https://doi.org/10.1007/978-3-030-26619-6_13

21. Padró, L., Carmona, J.: Approximate computation of alignments of business processes through relaxation labelling. In: Hildebrandt, T., van Dongen, B.F., Röglinger, M., Mendling, J. (eds.) BPM 2019. LNCS, vol. 11675, pp. 250–267. Springer, Cham (2019). https://doi.org/10.1007/978-3-030-26619-6_17

22. Sellers, P.H.: On the theory and computation of evolutionary distances. SIAM J. Appl. Math. 26(4), 787–793 (1974)

23. Marzal, A., Vidal, E.: Computation of normalized edit distance and applications. IEEE Trans. Pattern Anal. Mach. Intell. 15(9), 926–932 (1993)

24. Adriansyah, A., Munoz-Gama, J., Carmona, J., van Dongen, B.F., van der Aalst, W.M.: Measuring precision of modeled behavior. Inf. Syst. E-Bus. Manage. 13(1), 37–67 (2015). https://doi.org/10.1007/s10257-014-0234-7

25. van der Aalst, W.M.P., van Dongen, B., Günther, C.W., Rozinat, A., Verbeek, E., Weijters, T.: Prom: The process mining toolkit. BPM (Demos), 489(31), 9–13 (2009). http://ceur-ws.org/Vol-489/

26. De Amorim, R.C., Zampieri, M.: Effective spell checking methods using clustering algorithms. In: Proceedings of the International Conference Recent Advances in Natural Language Processing RANLP, pp. 172–178 (2013)

27. van der Aalst, W.M.P., Bolt, A., van Zelst, S.: RapidProM: Mine your processes and not just your data. CoRR abs/1703.03740 (2017)

28. Van Dongen, B.F. (Boudewijn): BPI challenge 2012 (2012)

29. Van Dongen, B.F. (Boudewijn), Borchert, F. (Florian): BPI challenge 2018 (2018)

30. Van Dongen, B.F. (Boudewijn): BPI challenge 2019 (2019)

31. Mannhardt, F.: Hospital billing-event log. Eindhoven University of Technology. Dataset, pp. 326–347 (2017)

32. De Leoni, M., Mannhardt, F.: Road traffic fine management process. Eindhoven University of Technology, Dataset (2015)
33. Mannhardt, F.: Sepsis cases-event log. Eindhoven University of Technology (2016)
34. Leemans, S.J.J., Fahland, D., van der Aalst, W.M.P.: Discovering block-structured process models from event logs containing infrequent behaviour. In: Lohmann, N., Song, M., Wohed, P. (eds.) BPM 2013. LNBIP, vol. 171, pp. 66–78. Springer, Cham (2014). https://doi.org/10.1007/978-3-319-06257-0_6
35. Dongen, B.F.: Efficiently computing alignments. In: Weske, M., Montali, M., Weber, I., vom Brocke, J. (eds.) BPM 2018. LNCS, vol. 11080, pp. 197–214. Springer, Cham (2018). https://doi.org/10.1007/978-3-319-98648-7_12
36. Sani, M.F., Boltenhagen, M., van der Aalst, W.M.P: Prototype selection based on clustering and conformance metrics for model discovery. CoRR (2019). http://arxiv.org/abs/1912.00736. arXiv:1912.00736

# Quantifying the Re-identification Risk of Event Logs for Process Mining
## Empiricial Evaluation Paper

Saskia Nuñez von Voigt[1]([⊠]), Stephan A. Fahrenkrog-Petersen[2],
Dominik Janssen[3], Agnes Koschmider[3], Florian Tschorsch[1],
Felix Mannhardt[4,5], Olaf Landsiedel[3], and Matthias Weidlich[2]

[1] Technische Universität Berlin, Berlin, Germany
{saskia.nunezvonvoigt,florian.tschorsch}@tu-berlin.de
[2] Humboldt-Universität zu Berlin, Berlin, Germany
{stephan.fahrenkrog-petersen,matthias.weidlich}@hu-berlin.de
[3] Kiel University, Kiel, Germany
{doj,ak,ol}@informatik.uni-kiel.de
[4] SINTEF Digital, Trondheim, Norway
felix.mannhardt@sintef.no
[5] NTNU Norwegian University of Science and Technology, Trondheim, Norway

**Abstract.** Event logs recorded during the execution of business processes constitute a valuable source of information. Applying process mining techniques to them, event logs may reveal the actual process execution and enable reasoning on quantitative or qualitative process properties. However, event logs often contain sensitive information that could be related to individual process stakeholders through background information and cross-correlation. We therefore argue that, when publishing event logs, the risk of such re-identification attacks must be considered. In this paper, we show how to quantify the re-identification risk with measures for the individual uniqueness in event logs. We also report on a large-scale study that explored the individual uniqueness in a collection of publicly available event logs. Our results suggest that potentially up to all of the cases in an event log may be re-identified, which highlights the importance of privacy-preserving techniques in process mining.

## 1 Introduction

Process mining uses data recorded in the form of event logs by information systems to, for example, reveal the actual execution of business processes [1]. Since most activities in modern organization are supported by technology, each process execution produces a digital footprint indicating the occurrence and timing of activities. Consequentially, event logs may contain sensitive information and are vulnerable to adversarial attacks. Unfortunately, there is no general method

© Springer Nature Switzerland AG 2020
S. Dustdar et al. (Eds.): CAiSE 2020, LNCS 12127, pp. 252–267, 2020.
https://doi.org/10.1007/978-3-030-49435-3_16

on how to safely remove personal and sensitive references. Since the existence of privacy threats are generally known, the willingness to publish event logs is low. Publicly available event logs, however, are necessary to evaluate process mining models [2–4] and therefore discussions are needed on how to safely publish event logs. Against this background, we argue that it is crucial to understand the risk of data re-identification in event logs and process mining. With this insight, we can balance how much information of an event log can be shared and how much should be anonymized to preserve privacy. While many examples confirm the general risk of data re-identification [5–7], the re-identification risk of event logs has not received much attention yet.

The intention of this paper is to raise awareness to the re-identification risk of event logs and therefore provide measures to quantify this risk. To this end, we provide an approach to express the *uniqueness* of data, which is derived from models that are commonly adopted by process mining techniques. Each event recorded in an event log consists of specific data types, such as the activity name of the respective process step, the timestamp of its execution, and event attributes that capture the context and the parameters of the activity. Additionally, sequences of events that relate to the same case of a process, also known as traces, come with data attributes, so-called case attributes that contain general information about the case. To extract sensitive information, an adversary uses background knowledge to link a target's attributes with the case/event attributes in the event log, e.g., by cross-correlating publicly-available sources. The higher the uniqueness of an event log, the higher an adversary's chances to identify the target. Our approach therefore explores the number of cases that are uniquely identifiable by the set of case attributes or the set of event attributes. We use this information to derive a measure of uniqueness for an event log, which serves as a basis for estimating how likely a case can be re-identified.

To demonstrate the importance of uniqueness considerations for event logs, we conducted a large-scale study with 12 publicly available event logs from the 4TU.Centre for Research Data repository.[1] We categorized the records and assessed the uniqueness where cases refer to a natural person. Our results for these logs suggest that an adversary can potentially re-identify up to all of the cases, depending on prior knowledge. We show that an adversary needs only a few attributes of a trace to successfully mount such an attack.

The contributions of this paper can be summarized as follows:

– We present an approach to quantify the privacy risk associated to event logs. In this way, we support the identification of information that should be suppressed when publishing an event log, thereby fostering the responsible use of logs and paving the way for novel use cases based on event log analysis.
– By reporting the results of a large-scale evaluation study, we highlight the need to develop privacy-preserving techniques for event logs with high utility for process analytics. Our notions of individual uniqueness may serve as a catalyst for such efforts, since they make the inherent privacy risks explicit.

---

[1] https://data.4tu.nl/repository/collection:event_logs_real.

This paper is structured as follows. Section 2 illustrates privacy threats in process mining. Section 3 presents our approach for quantifying the re-identification risk. We analyze publicly available event logs and discuss the results in Sect. 4. We review related work in Sect. 5, before Sect. 6 concludes this paper.

**Table 1.** Event log example

| case id | activity | timestamp | case attributes | event attributes |
|---------|----------|-----------|-----------------|------------------|
| 1000 | registration | 03/03/19 23:40:32 | {age: 26, sex: m} | {arrival: check-in} |
| 1000 | triage | 03/04/19 00:27:12 | {age: 26, sex: m} | {status: uncritical} |
| 1000 | liquid | 03/04/19 00:47:44 | {age: 26, sex: m} | {liquid: NaCl} |
| ... | ... | ... | ... | ... |
| 1001 | registration | 03/04/19 00:01:24 | {age: 78, sex: f} | {arrival: ambulance} |
| 1001 | antibiotics | 03/04/19 00:09:06 | {age: 78, sex: f} | {drug: penicillin} |
| ... | ... | ... | ... | ... |

## 2   Privacy Threats in Process Mining

Process mining uses event logs to discover and analyze business processes. Event logs capture the execution of activities as events. A finite sequence of such events forms a trace, representing a single process instance (aka case). For example, the treatment of patients in an emergency room includes a number of events, such as blood sampling and analysis, which together follow a certain structure as determined by the process. Accordingly, the events related to an individual patient form a case. In addition, case attributes provide general information about a case, e.g., place of birth of a patient. Each event consists of various data types, such as the name of the respective *activity*, the *timestamp* of the execution, and *event attributes*. Event attributes are event-specific and may be changing over time, e.g., a temperature or the department performing a treatment. The key difference between case attributes and event attributes is that case attributes do *not* change their value for a case during the observed period of time. We show a synthetic event log example capturing an emergency room process in Table 1.

Considering the structure of an event log, several privacy threats are identified. Linking a case to an individual can reveal sensitive information, e.g., in an emergency room process, certain events can indicate that a patient is in a certain condition. In general, case attributes can contain various kinds of sensitive data, revealing racial or ethnic origin, political opinions, religious or philosophical beliefs, as well as financial or health information. Likewise, an event log can reveal information about the productivity [8] or the work schedule of hospital staff. Such kind of staff surveillance is a critical privacy threat. Clearly, it is essential to include privacy considerations in process mining projects. We assume that an adversary's goal is to identify an individual in an event log linking external information. Depending on the type of background information, different adversary models are possible. We assume a targeted re-identification, i.e., an adversary has information about specific individuals, which includes a subset of the attribute values. Based thereon, the adversary aims to reveal sensitive information, e.g., a diagnosis. Here, we assume that an adversary knows that an individual is present in the event log. In this paper, we consider the uniqueness measure to quantify the re-identification risk of sensitive information, thereby providing a basis for managing privacy considerations.

**Table 2.** Preparation of event log

| case id | sex | age | activity | timestamp | arrival channel |
|---------|-----|-----|----------|-----------|-----------------|
| 10 | male | 26 | [reg., liquid, . . .] | [3/3/19, 3/4/19, . . .] | [check-in, none, . . .] |
| 11 | female | 78 | [reg., antibiotics] | [3/4/19, 3/4/19] | [ambulance, none] |
| 12 | female | 26 | [reg., liquid, . . .] | [3/5/19, 3/7/19, . . .] | [check-in, none, . . .] |
| . . . | . . . | . . . | . . . | . . . | . . . |

## 3  Re-identifications of Event Logs

To apply our uniqueness measure to cases, we summarize all occurring event data to its corresponding case. This assumption eases handling multiple events belonging to the same case. Since case attributes are invariant over time, they only need to be taken into consideration once, whereas event attributes may be different for every event and therefore their temporal change needs to be considered. Table 2 provides a respective example. Each row in this table belongs to one case. The case attributes "sex" and "age" are listed in separate columns. The columns "activity", "timestamp", and "arrival channel" contain an ordered list of the respective attributes. For example, the case id 11 has only two events and therefore two activities. The second activity "antibiotics" on March 04, 2019 has no "arrival channel" (i.e., it is "none").

The uniqueness of an event log serves as a basis for estimating how likely a case can be re-identified. We investigate a number of so-called projections that can be considered as a data minimization technique, effectively reducing the potential risks of re-identification in an event log. Projections refer to a subset of attributes in the event log. They can easily be adopted to assess the risk in different scenarios. Table 3 summarizes the projections for event logs and their potential usage in process mining. Projection A contains the sequence of all executed activities with their timestamps, while projection F only contains the case attributes. It has been shown that even sparse projections of event logs hold privacy risks [4]. Therefore, in our evaluation, we will consider the re-identification risk for various projections.

### 3.1   Uniqueness Based on Case Attributes

In addition to unique identifiers (UID), so-called quasi-identifiers are information that can be linked to individuals as well. A combination of quasi-identifiers may be sufficient to create a UID. In event logs, the case attributes can be seen as quasi-identifier. For example, in the event log of the BPI Challenge 2018 [9], the area of all parcels and the ID of the local department can be considered as case attributes. Measuring the uniqueness based on case attributes is a common way to quantify the re-identification risk [10]. Case uniqueness and thus an individual uniqueness highly increases the risk of re-identification. A single value of a case attribute does not lead to identification. The combination with other attributes, however, may lead to a unique case. In particular, when linking attributes to other sources of information, it may result in successful re-identification.

**Table 3.** Projections of event logs

| projection | data included | exemplary usage in process mining |
|---|---|---|
| A | activities, timestamps | analysis of bottlenecks |
| B | activities, event and case attributes | predictive process monitoring |
| C | activities, event attributes | decision mining |
| D | activities, case attributes | trace clustering |
| E | activities | process discovery |
| F | case attributes | traditional data mining |

We define uniqueness as the fraction of unique cases in a event log. Let $f_k$ be the frequency of the $k$th combination of case attributes values in a sample. One case is unique if $f_k = 1$, i.e., there is no other case with the same values of case attributes. Accordingly, uniqueness for case attributes is defined as

$$U_{\text{case}} = \frac{\sum I(f_k = 1)}{N}, \tag{1}$$

where the indicator function $I(f_k = 1)$ is 1, if the $k$th combination is unique, and $N$ is the total number of cases in the event log. Referring to our data in Table 2, the attribute value "sex: female" leads to two possible case candidates (id:10 and id:11), i.e., $f_k = 2$, which implies that the combination is not unique. Taking "age" as an additional quasi-identifier into account, makes all three listed cases unique, i.e., $U_{\text{case}} = 1$. Since often a sample of the event log is published, we distinguish between sample uniqueness and population uniqueness. The number of unique cases in the sample is called sample uniqueness. With population uniqueness, we refer to the amount of unique cases in the complete event log (i.e., population). Based on the disclosed event log we can measure the sample uniqueness. The population uniqueness is the number of cases that are unique within the sample and are also unique in the underlying population from which the data has been sampled. Usually the event log is a sample from a population and the original event log is not available. Therefore, the population uniqueness cannot be measured and must be estimated.

There are several models to estimate the population uniqueness from a sample. These methods model the population uniqueness based on extrapolations of the contingency table to fit specific distributions to frequency counts [10]. We adopt the method of Rocher and Hendrickx [7] to estimate the population uniqueness.[2] The authors use Gaussian copulas to model population uniqueness, approximate the marginals from the sample, and estimate the likelihood for a sample unique being a population unique. For this analysis, we assume that the event log is a published sample. By applying the method, we estimate the population uniqueness of cases in terms of their case attributes.

### 3.2   Uniqueness Based on Traces

Most of the published event logs for process mining do not have many case attributes, only event attributes. For example, the Sepsis event log [11] has only one case attribute ("age"). However, a case can also be unique based on the events. We measure the uniqueness using the traces. A trace consists of an ordered set of activities $a_1, a_2, \ldots a_n$, their timestamps $t_1, t_2, \ldots t_n$ and $l$ event attributes $e_{11}, \ldots e_{ln}$. A tuple $p_j = (a_j, t_j, e_{1j}, \ldots, e_{lj})$ represents a point from the trace $[(a_1, t_1, e_{11}, \ldots, e_{l1}), (a_2, t_2, e_{12}, \ldots, e_{l2}), \ldots, (a_n, t_n, e_{1n}, \ldots, e_{ln})]$. We assume that an adversary's main goal is to re-identify an individual given a number of points and to reveal other sensitive points. We argue that an adversary has a certain knowledge and knows some points, which she is able to link with the event log. In particular, we assume that an adversary knows that a certain person is contained in the event log. In other words, we consider the published event log as population. As our example in Table 2 shows, even without considering the case attributes, all cases are unique: Case 11 is uniquely identifiable by its second activity "antibiotics". The Cases 10 and 12 are uniquely identified by combining the activity with the respective timestamp. An adversary for example might have information about a patient's arrival (e.g., "check-in: 3/5/19"). Given this information as a point from the trace it is sufficient for an adversary to identify the patient and reveal additional information from the event log.

Accordingly, we express the re-identification risk as the ratio of unique cases. The uniqueness of a trace can be measured similarly to location trajectories [12,13]. In location trajectories, points consist only of a location and a timestamp. In contrast, we have not only two-dimensional but multi-dimensional points with i.a. an activity, a resource, and a timestamp. Let $\{c_i\}_{i=1,\ldots,N}$ be the event consisting of a set of $N$ traces. Given a set of $m$ random points, called $M_p$ we compute the number of traces that include the set of points. A trace is unique if the set of points $M_p$ is only contained in a single trace. The uniqueness of traces given $M_p$ is defined as

$$U_{\text{trace}} = \frac{\sum \delta_i}{N}, \qquad (2)$$

where $\delta_i = 1$, if a trace is unique $|\{c_i | M_p \subseteq c_i\}| = 1$, otherwise $\delta_i = 0$.

---

[2] Code available at https://github.com/computationalprivacy.

## 4    Results

For our evaluation we used the publicly available event logs from the 4TU.Centre for Research Data. We classified the event logs into real-life-individuals (R) and software (S) event logs. The case identifier of real-life-individuals refers to a natural person, e.g., the ADL event log [14] includes activities of daily living activities of individuals. In event logs referring to software activities, events do not directly refer to a natural person, but to technical components. For instance, the BPI Challenge 2013 event log [15] consists of events from an incident management system. Some of the software related event logs even consist of a single case, which makes measuring uniqueness of cases more difficult. However, if a suitable identifier can be linked to the cases, it will also be possible to measure the uniqueness for software related event logs. For example, the incidents in the BPI Challenge 2013 event log are processed by a natural person. By using an appropriate transformation, this natural person could serve as a case identifier.

In the following, we apply our methods to estimate the uniqueness of the real-life-individuals event logs (R) only. We measure the uniqueness of case attributes for event logs with more than one case attribute only. Table 4 summarizes the results of our classification, provides some basic metrics on the number of cases and activities, and indicates the applied uniqueness measures.

For improved readability and for ethical considerations (see Sect. 4.3 for details), we will apply our methods and discuss intermediate results in detail only for the BPI Challenge 2018 [9] and the Sepsis [11] event logs. For all other event logs, we provide condensed and pseudonymized results. Note that the pseudonymized event logs in the following sections have not the same order as in Table 4, but the pseudonymization is consistent across the evaluation.

### 4.1    Uniqueness Results Based on Case Attributes

The BPI Challenge 2018 event log is provided by the German company "data experts". It contains events related to application of payments process of EU's Agricultural Guarantee Fund. The event log consists of 43,809 cases, each representing a farmer's direct payments application over a period of three years. We identified "payment_actual" (PYMT), "area" (ARA), "department" (DPT), "number_parcels" (#PCL), "smallfarmer" (SF), "young-farmer" (YF), "year" (Y) and "amount_applied" (AMT) as case attributes. The data contributor generalized the attributes PYMT, #PCL, and AMT by grouping the values in 100 bins, where the bins are identified by the minimum value [9].

To determine the impact of case attributes, we evaluate their uniqueness using various combinations. Specifically, we investigate which combinations of attribute values make cases more distinct and thus unique. The more extensive an adversary's background knowledge is, the more likely it is that this individual

**Table 4.** Classification of event logs

| event log | category | #cases | #activities | uniqueness | |
|---|---|---|---|---|---|
| | | | | case attr | traces |
| ADL [14] | R | 75 | 34 | no | yes |
| BPIC 2012 [16] | R | 13,087 | 24 | yes | yes |
| BPIC 2015 [17] | R | 1,199 | 398 | yes | yes |
| BPIC 2017 [18] | R | 31,509 | 26 | yes | yes |
| BPIC 2018 [9] | R | 43,809 | 14 | yes | yes |
| CCC 2019 [19] | R | 10,035 | 8 | no | yes |
| Credit [20] | R | 20 | 29 | no | yes |
| HB [21] | R | 100,000 | 18 | no | yes |
| RlH [22] | R | 1,143 | 624 | no | yes |
| WABO [23] | R | 1,434 | 27 | yes | yes |
| RTFM [24] | R | 150,370 | 11 | no | yes |
| Sepsis [11] | R | 1,049 | 16 | no | yes |
| Apache [25] | S | 3 | 74 | – | – |
| BPIC 2013 [15] | S | 1,487 | 4 | – | – |
| BPIC 2014 [26] | S | 46,616 | 39 | – | – |
| BPIC 2016 [27] | S | 25,647 | 600 | – | – |
| BPIC 2019 [28] | S | 251,734 | 42 | – | – |
| JUnit [29] | S | 1 | 182 | – | – |
| NASA [30] | S | 2,566 | 47 | – | – |
| SWA [31] | S | 1 | 106 | – | – |

becomes unique and thus identifiable. For each combination, we count the number of unique cases. As expected, the more case attributes are known, the more unique the cases become. Table 5 (left) shows that when considering PYMT only, there are 40.9% unique cases. In combination with #PCL, uniqueness increases to 69.8%. With all case attributes, 84.5% of the cases are unique in the sample.

However, the sample uniqueness alone does not lead to a high re-identification risk. Therefore we also have to consider the population uniqueness We used the method described in Sect. 3.1 to estimate the population uniqueness and approximate the marginals from the published event log. In Table 5 (left), we present the average estimated population uniqueness of five runs. Interestingly, the population uniqueness with a single case attribute (PYMT) is already 16.1%. Considering all case attributes, a population uniqueness of around 97% is observed. We measure the sample uniqueness and estimate the population uniqueness for all event logs with more than one case attribute resulting in four event logs for the analysis. We do not consider case attributes that contain activities of the event log (i.e., the first executed activity), since we assume that an adversary does not know the exact order of executed activities. Table 5 (right) lists the average

**Table 5.** Sample uniqueness and population uniqueness (estimated) based on case attributes (left for BPI Challenge 2018; right for all event logs)

| combination | sample | population | event log | sample | population |
|---|---|---|---|---|---|
| PYMT | 0.409 | 0.161 | 3. | 0.011 | 0.005 |
| PYMT, ARA | 0.476 | 0.164 | 6. | 0.035 | 0.071 |
| PYMT, DPT | 0.528 | 0.419 | 7. | 0.152 | 0.146 |
| PYMT, #PCL | 0.698 | 0.594 | 8. | 1.000 | 0.952 |
| PYMT, ARA, #PCL | 0.747 | 0.649 | | | |
| PYMT, DPT, #PCL | 0.788 | 0.718 | | | |
| PYMT, DPT, #PCL, ARA, SF | 0.845 | 0.971 | | | |

sample uniqueness and the average estimated population uniqueness after five runs. We notice that not all event logs show a high uniqueness based on the case attributes. In case of the BPI Challenge 2018 event log, it can be observed that even a small number of case attributes produces a high uniqueness and thus a high re-identification risk.

### 4.2 Uniqueness Results Based on Traces

The Sepsis event log is obtained from the information system of a Dutch hospital. It contains events related to logistics and treatment of patients that enter the emergency room and are suspected to suffer from sepsis, which is a life-threatening condition that warrants immediate treatment. Originally, the event log was analyzed regarding the adherence to guidelines on timely administration of antibiotics and, more generally, related to the overall trajectory of patients [32]. The data was made publicly available for research purposes [11]. Several measures were taken to prevent identification, including:

- randomization of timestamps by perturbing the start of cases and adjusting timestamps of respective subsequent events accordingly
- pseudonymization of discharge related activities, e.g., "Release A"
- generalization of employee information by stating the department only
- pseudonymization of the working diagnosis
- generalization of age to groups of 5 years and at least 10 people.

The event log consists of 1,049 cases with 16 different activities. Each case represents the pathway through the hospital of a natural person. The traces have an average length of 14 points (min = 3, max = 185). In contrast to the BPI Challenge 2018 event log, the Sepsis event log has only one attribute that can be used as a case attribute.

To estimate the uniqueness of traces, we use the method described in Sect. 3.2. The points in the Sepsis event log consist of activities, timestamps, and departments that are currently responsible for a patient's treatment. The "age" serves as case attribute. Since patients are treated in different departments, the "department" does not satisfy the time-invariant criteria of a case attribute (cf. Sect. 2).

For each case, we randomly select $m$ points of the trace and count the number of traces with identical points. In other words, we look for other traces that for example include the same activities by the same department. We opt for a random point selection to avoid making assumptions on the adversary's knowledge. We are aware that this may underestimate the re-identification risk. As a consequence, a high uniqueness in our results emphasizes the re-identification risk as a more sophisticated and optimized point selection would likely lead to an even higher uniqueness.

In Fig. 1, we show the uniqueness of traces for different values of $m$ points and different projections.[3] As expected, we generally observe that more points lead to a higher uniqueness. Assuming that timestamps are correct (which they are not), projection A shows that four points including the activity and the timestamp are sufficient to identify all traces. By generalizing timestamps, i.e., reducing the resolution to days, only 31% of traces are unique when considering four points and 70% when considering all points of a trace. Hence, the results clearly show the impact of generalization on the re-identification risk.

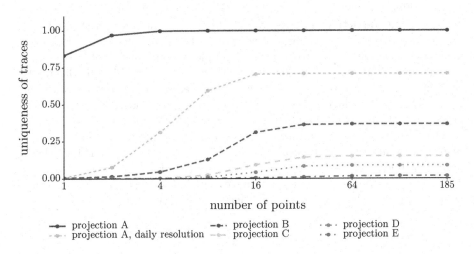

**Fig. 1.** Uniqueness based on traces for Sepsis event log.

The privacy-enhancing effect of removing values from the event log becomes apparent, when considering the other projections. Projection B, for example, omits timestamps but otherwise assumes that an adversary has background knowledge on all activities, case and event attributes. Yet, it is able to significantly limit the uniqueness to approximately 37%. Projection D, where case attributes and activities are still included, is even able to limit the uniqueness of traces to a maximum of 9%. The uniqueness of traces remains stable for more than 64 points since only 2% of the traces have more than 64 points.

---

[3] Code available at https://github.com/d-o-m-i-n-i-k/re-identification-risk

Our method of estimating the uniqueness based on traces can be applied to all event logs categorized as real-life-individuals (R). Figure 2 presents the uniqueness for all event logs for different projections. We evaluate the uniqueness given 10%, 50%, and 90% of possible points per trace, i.e., an adversary knows this number of points per case. Grey fields without numbers imply that this projection could not be evaluated due to missing attributes.

In Fig. 2 we observe a similar trend as before for the Sepsis event log: Projection A generally leads to a high uniqueness. By omitting information, expressed by the various projections, the uniqueness decreases. This becomes apparent when comparing projection B to C, where the case attributes are removed. Projection E, i.e., considering the activities only, leads to a small uniqueness, with the exception of event log 5 and 9. We explain this by the fact that these event logs have many different activities and have a varying trace length per case. For event log 10, we can already see a clear reduction of the uniqueness for projection B. This can be explained by the small number of case attributes and small number of unique activities.

The most surprising event log is 11. It has no unique cases. The prime reason for this difference is the result of a timestamp in daily resolution and the small number of unique activities. It is worth adding that increasing the number of points from 10% to 50% is significant with respect to uniqueness compared to the number of points from 50% to 90%. For example, the uniqueness of projection A for event log 10 increases from 62.4% in Fig. 2a to 73.7% in Fig. 2b. Given 90% of points of the trace, we cannot observe an increase of the uniqueness for event log 10. This can also be observed for other event logs and other projections. The prime cause of this is the high variance of the trace length.

Overall in our study, we find that the uniqueness based on traces is higher than on case attributes (cf. results in Table 5). For example, event log 3 has a sample uniqueness based on case attributes of 1.1%. Based on traces, however, it reaches for projection C a case uniqueness of 84.4%. We conclude that traces are particularly vulnerable to data re-identification attacks.

## 4.3  Discussion

Our results demonstrate that 11 of 12 evaluated event logs have a uniqueness greater than 62%, even for a random selection of trace points. More specific information, e.g., the order of individual activities, can lead to a greater uniqueness with fewer points. Additional knowledge about the process in general could be used by an adversary to predict certain activities, which was also confirmed in [33]. The random selection, however, clearly shows that little background knowledge is sufficient and already induces a considerable re-identification risk for event logs. In contrast, generalization of attributes helps to reduce the risk [34]. The results, however, show that combining several attributes, such as case attributes and activities, still yields unique cases. In combination with lowering the resolution of values, e.g., publishing only the year of birth instead of the full birthday, reduces the re-identification risk. Such generalization techniques can also be applied to timestamps, activities, or case attributes.

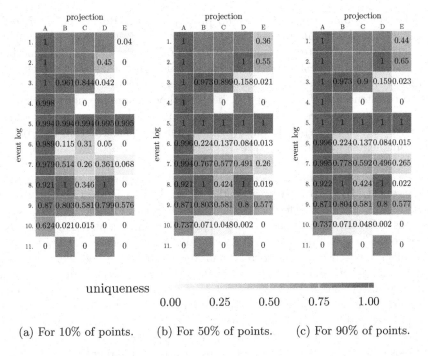

(a) For 10% of points.     (b) For 50% of points.     (c) For 90% of points.

**Fig. 2.** Uniqueness based on traces for all event logs.

Along the lines of the data minimization principle, i.e., limiting the amount of personal data, omitting data is simply the most profound way to reduce the risk, which we clearly see when taking our projections into account. Consequently, the projections can be used to reduce the re-identification risk.

We apply our methods to already published event logs to point out the risk of re-identification in the domain of process mining. To this end, we only quantify the risk and refrain from cross-correlating other event logs, which might re-identify individuals. In addition, we take measures such as pseudonymizing event logs in our evaluation to neither expose nor blame specific event logs.

## 5   Related Work

*Re-identification Attacks.* Re-identification attacks were addressed and successfully carried out in the past by a large number of researchers [6,7,12,13,35,36]. Narayanan and Shmatikov [35] de-anonymize a data set from Netflix containing movie ratings by cross-correlating multiple data sets. In [36], they modified their approach to apply it to social networks. In contrast, our adversary's goal is to re-identify an individual (also known as singling out) and not reconstruct all attribute values of an individual. We therefore measure the uniqueness. We base our uniqueness measures on two well-known approaches [7,12,13] and adapt them for the domain of event logs and process mining. Rocher et al. [7] estimate the population uniqueness based on given attribute values. We employ their method to estimate the uniqueness based on case attributes. Our method to estimate the uniqueness based on traces relies on the approach presented in [12,13], where uniqueness in mobility traces with location data is estimated. Due to the structure of an event log, both methods alone are not sufficient to determine the uniqueness in event logs and require data preparation. For example, event logs have a specific format that requires transformation in order to apply uniqueness measures on traces.

*Privacy in Process Mining.* Awareness of privacy issues in process mining has increased [37], particularly since the General Data Protection Regulation (GDPR) was put into effect. Although the Process Mining Manifesto [38] demands to balance utility and privacy in process mining applications, the number of related contributions is still rather small. To preserve privacy in event logs while still discovering the correct main process behavior has been addressed by Fahrenkrog-Petersen et al. [4]. Their algorithm guarantees $k$-anonymity and $t$-closeness while maximizing the utility of the sanitized event log. In general, $k$-anonymity aggregates the data in such a way that each individual cannot be distinguished based on its values from at least $k - 1$ other individuals of the data set [39,40]. Yet, it has been shown in the past that neither $k$-anonymity, nor $t$-closeness are sufficient to provide strong privacy guarantees [41].

The strongest privacy model available to date, which provides provable privacy guarantees, is differential privacy. It was recently incorporated in a first privacy-preserving technique for process mining [2]. The approach presents a privacy engine capable of keeping personal data private by adding noise to queries. The privacy techniques of [2,4] have been combined in a web-based tool [3]. Pseudonymization of data sets related to process mining has been discussed in [42,43]. Values of the original data set is replaced with pseudonyms. However, the encryption still allows for a potential re-identification by an adversary with knowledge about the domain and the statistical distribution of the encrypted data. Beside technological privacy challenges for process mining, the approach of [44] also discuss organizational privacy challenges by means of a framework. Although, the approach points to several privacy concerns in process mining, no technical solution is presented. Pika et al. [33] assess the suitability of existing privacy-preserving approaches for process mining data. They propose a framework to support privacy-preserving process mining analysis. While Pika et al. analyze the suitability of existing data transformation approaches to anonymize process data, they do not provide an approach to support the identification of information, e.g., atypical process behavior, that should be suppressed to reduce the re-identification risk of subjects. Our metric fills this gap and helps data owners to identify the unique cases with atypical process behavior.

In comparison to existing related works on privacy-aware approaches for process mining, this paper makes an attempt to quantify the re-identification risk. Data publishers can determine which information should be suppressed before releasing an event log for process mining. If a high re-identification risk is detected, the approaches mentioned above might be able to lower the risk of re-identification and therefore to provide higher privacy guarantees.

## 6   Conclusion

This paper identifies and evaluates the risk of re-identification in event logs for process mining. We reveal that there is a serious privacy leakage in the vast majority of the event logs used widely in the community. To address this issue, we argue for the use of methods to estimate the uniqueness that allow event log publishers to carefully evaluate their event logs before release and if need to suppress certain information. Overall, real-world data traces are an essential means to evaluate and compare algorithms. This paper shows that we as a community have to act more carefully, though, when releasing event logs, while also highlighting the need to develop privacy-preserving techniques for event logs. We believe that this work will foster the trust and increases the willingness for sharing event logs while providing privacy guarantees.

**Acknowledgement.** We thank Yves-Alexandre de Montjoye for providing his code to estimate data uniqueness, which we used in our evaluation.

## References

1. van der Aalst, W.M.P.: Process Mining - Data Science in Action, 2nd edn. Springer, Heidelberg (2016). https://doi.org/10.1007/978-3-662-49851-4
2. Mannhardt, F., Koschmider, A., Baracaldo, N., Weidlich, M., Michael, J.: Privacy-preserving process mining. Bus. Inf. Syst. Eng. **61**(5), 595–614 (2019). https://doi.org/10.1007/s12599-019-00613-3
3. Bauer, M., Fahrenkrog-Petersen, S.A., Koschmider, A., Mannhardt, F.: ELPaaS: event Log Privacy as a service. In: Proceedings of the Dissertation Award, 17th International Conference on Business Process Management, BPM 2019, p. 5 (2019)
4. Fahrenkrog-Petersen, S.A., van der Aa, H., Weidlich, M.: PRETSA: event log sanitization for privacy-aware process discovery. In: Proceedings of the International Conference on Process Mining, ICPM 2019, pp. 1–8 (2019)
5. Lavrenovs, A., Podins, K.: Privacy violations in Riga open data public transport system. In: Proceedings of the IEEE 4th Workshop on Advances in Information, Electronic and Electrical Engineering, AIEEE 2016, pp. 1–6 (2016)
6. Douriez, M., Doraiswamy, H., Freire, J., Silva, C.T.: Anonymizing NYC taxi data: does it matter? In: Proceedings of the IEEE International Conference on Data Science and Advanced Analytics, DSAA 2016, pp. 140–148 (2016)
7. Rocher, L., Hendrickx, J., Montjoye, Y.A.: Estimating the success of re-identifications in incomplete datasets using generative models. Nat. Commun. **10**, 1–9 (2019)
8. Pika, A., Leyer, M., Wynn, M.T., Fidge, C.J., Ter Hofstede, A.H., van der Aalst, W.M.: Mining resource profiles from event logs. In: Proceedings of ACM Transactions on Management Information Systems, TMIS 2017, vol. 8, no. 1, p. 1 (2017)
9. van Dongen, B., Borchert, F.: BPI Challenge 2018. TU Eindhoven, Dataset (2018)

10. Dankar, F.K., El Emam, K., Neisa, A., Roffey, T.: Estimating the re-identification risk of clinical data sets. BMC Med. Inform. Decis. Mak. **12**(1), 66 (2012)
11. Mannhardt, F.: Sepsis Cases - Event Log. TU Eindhoven, Dataset (2016)
12. Song, Y., Dahlmeier, D., Bressan, S.: Not so unique in the crowd: a simple and effective algorithm for anonymizing location data. In: Proceeding of the 1st International Workshop on Privacy-Preserving IR, PIR@SIGIR 2014, vol. 2014, pp. 19–24 (2014)
13. de Montjoye, Y.A., Hidalgo, C.A., Verleysen, M., Blondel, V.D.: Unique in the crowd: the privacy bounds of human mobility. Sci. Rep. **3**, 1376 (2013)
14. Sztyler, T., Carmona, J.: Activities of Daily Living of Several Individuals. University of Mannheim, Germany. Dataset (2015)
15. Steeman, W.: BPI Challenge 2013. Ghent University, Dataset (2013)
16. van Dongen, B.: BPI Challenge 2012. 4TU.Centre for Research Data. Dataset (2012)
17. van Dongen, B.: BPI Challenge 2015. 4TU.Centre for Research Data. Dataset (2015)
18. van Dongen, B.: BPI Challenge 2017. TU Eindhoven, Dataset (2017)
19. Munoz-Gama, J., de la Fuente, R., Sepúlveda, M., Fuentes, R.: Conformance Checking Challenge 2019 (CCC19). 4TU.Centre for Research Data. Dataset (2019)
20. Djedović, A.: Credit Requirement Event Logs. 4TU.Centre for Research Data. Dataset (2017)
21. Mannhardt, F.: Hospital Billing - Event Log. TU Eindhoven, Dataset (2017)
22. van Dongen, B.: Real-life Event Logs - Hospital log. TU Eindhoven, Dataset (2011)
23. Buijs, J.: Receipt Phase of an Environmental Permit Application Process ('WABO'). Eindhoven University of Technology, Dataset (2014)
24. de Leoni, M., Mannhardt, F.: Road Traffic Fine Management Process. TU Eindhoven, Dataset (2015)
25. Leemans, M.: Apache Commons Crypto 1.0.0 - Stream CbcNopad Unit Test Software Event Log. TU Eindhoven. Dataset (2017)
26. van Dongen, B.: BPI Challenge 2014. 4TU.Centre for Research Data. Dataset (2014)
27. Dees, M., van Dongen, B.: BPI Challenge 2016. 4TU.Centre for Research Data. Dataset (2016)
28. van Dongen, B.: BPI Challenge 2019. 4TU.Centre for Research Data. Dataset (2019)
29. Leemans, M.: JUnit 4.12 Software Event Log. TU Eindhoven. Dataset (2016)
30. Leemans, M.: NASA Crew Exploration Vehicle (CEV) Software Event Log. TU Eindhoven, Dataset (2017)
31. Leemans, M.: Statechart Workbench and Alignments Software Event Log. TU Eindhoven, Dataset (2018)
32. Mannhardt, F., Blinde, D.: Analyzing the trajectories of patients with sepsis using process mining. In: Joint Proceedings. Volume 1859 of CEUR Workshop Proceedings, RADAR+EMISA 2017, pp. 72–80. CEUR-WS.org (2017)
33. Pika, A., Wynn, M.T., Budiono, S.: Towards privacy-preserving process mining in healthcare. Proceedings of International Workshop on Process-Oriented Data Science for Healthcare, PODS4H 2019, p. 12 (2019)
34. Zook, M., et al.: Ten simple rules for responsible big data research (2017)
35. Narayanan, A., Shmatikov, V.: Robust de-anonymization of large sparse datasets. In: Proceedings of the 29th IEEE Symposium on Security and Privacy, S&P 2008, pp. 111–125 (2008)

36. Narayanan, A., Shmatikov, V.: De-anonymizing Social Networks. In: Proceedings of the 30th IEEE Symposium on Security and Privacy, S&P 2009, pp. 173–187 (2009)
37. Spiekermann, S., Cranor, L.: Engineering privacy. IEEE Trans. Softw. Eng. **35**(1), 67–82 (2009)
38. van der Aalst, W., et al.: Process mining manifesto. In: Daniel, F., Barkaoui, K., Dustdar, S. (eds.) BPM 2011. LNBIP, vol. 99, pp. 169–194. Springer, Heidelberg (2012). https://doi.org/10.1007/978-3-642-28108-2_19
39. Sweeney, L.: k-anonymity: a model for protecting privacy. Int. J. Uncertainty Fuzziness Knowl. Based Syst. **10**(05), 557–570 (2002)
40. Samarati, P., Sweeney, L.: Protecting privacy when disclosing information: k-anonymity and its enforcement through generalization and suppression. SRI International (1998)
41. Dwork, C., McSherry, F., Nissim, K., Smith, A.: Calibrating noise to sensitivity in private data analysis. In: Theory of Cryptography, Third Theory of Cryptography Conference, TCC 2006, pp. 265–284 (2006)
42. Rafiei, M., von Waldthausen, L., van der Aalst, W.M.P.: Ensuring confidentiality in process mining. In: Proceedings of the 8th International Symposium on Data-driven Process Discovery and Analysis, SIMPDA 2018, pp. 3–17 (2018)
43. Burattin, A., Conti, M., Turato, D.: Toward an anonymous process mining. In: Proceedings of the 3rd International Conference on Future Internet of Things and Cloud, FiCloud 2015, Rome, Italy, pp. 58–63 (2015)
44. Mannhardt, F., Petersen, S.A., Oliveira, M.F.: Privacy challenges for process mining in human-centered industrial environments. In: Proceedings of the 14th International Conference on Intelligent Environments, IE 2018, pp. 64–71 (2018)

# An Approach for Process Model Extraction by Multi-grained Text Classification

Chen Qian[1], Lijie Wen[1(✉)], Akhil Kumar[2], Leilei Lin[1], Li Lin[1], Zan Zong[1], Shu'ang Li[1], and Jianmin Wang[1]

[1] School of Software, Tsinghua University, Beijing 100084, China
qc16@mails.tsinghua.edu.cn, wenlj@tsinghua.edu.cn
[2] Smeal College of Business, Penn State University, State College 16802, USA

**Abstract.** Process model extraction (PME) is a recently emerged inter-discipline between natural language processing (NLP) and business process management (BPM), which aims to extract process models from textual descriptions. Previous process extractors heavily depend on manual features and ignore the potential relations between clues of different text granularities. In this paper, we formalize the PME task into the multi-grained text classification problem, and propose a hierarchical neural network to effectively model and extract multi-grained information without manually-defined procedural features. Under this structure, we accordingly propose the coarse-to-fine (grained) learning mechanism, training multi-grained tasks in coarse-to-fine grained order to share the high-level knowledge for the low-level tasks. To evaluate our approach, we construct two multi-grained datasets from two different domains and conduct extensive experiments from different dimensions. The experimental results demonstrate that our approach outperforms the state-of-the-art methods with statistical significance and further investigations demonstrate its effectiveness.

**Keywords:** Process model extraction · Multi-grained text classification · Coarse-to-fine learning · Convolutional neural network

## 1 Introduction

The widespread adoption of conversational agents such as Alexa, Siri and Google Home demonstrates the natural demand for such assistive agents. To go beyond supporting the simplistic queries such as *"what should I do next?"*, these agents need domain-specific procedural knowledge [9]. Procedural knowledge, also called *"how-to-do-it"* knowledge, is the knowledge related to the execution of a series of interrelated tasks [26]. A major source of procedural knowledge is contained in natural textual instructions [34], such as cooking recipes that describe cooking procedures and maintenance manuals that describe repair procedures for various devices and gadgets. While it is possible to manually understand, extract and

© Springer Nature Switzerland AG 2020
S. Dustdar et al. (Eds.): CAiSE 2020, LNCS 12127, pp. 268–282, 2020.
https://doi.org/10.1007/978-3-030-49435-3_17

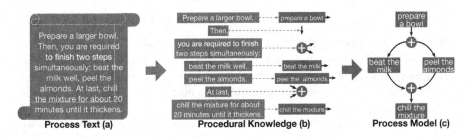

**Fig. 1.** Illustration of the PME problem.

reuse such knowledge from texts, ultimately that is a very labor-intensive option [20]. To facilitate reuse and repurpose of procedural knowledge, **process model extraction (PME)** is emerging to automatically extract underlying **process models** from **process texts**. As Fig. 1 illustrates, PME extracts and presents the main actions (nodes) and their ordering relations (sequence flows) expressed in the cooking recipe as a process model. This task can liberate humans from the manual efforts of creating and visualizing procedural knowledge by making assistive agents understand process texts intelligently [9].

However, PME is challenging as it requires agents to understand complex descriptions of actions and involves multi-grained information mining. For example, in Fig. 1, to extract the whole process model, the process extractor has to recognize *whether a sentence is describing an action?* (sentence-level information) and *who does what in a sentence describing an action?* (word-level information). Recent research efforts have been made to extract the main procedural knowledge. For example, language-rule based extractors [12] used pre-defined language rules to extract procedural knowledge. Pattern-matching based extractors [26] used NLP tagging or parsing tools to analyze sentences and extract corresponding information from triggered patterns. Knowledge-based extractors employed pre-defined ontology [12] or world model [8] to help extract that information. However, traditional methods suffer from weak generalizability when applied in open-domain or open-topic scenarios since they: 1) require much large-scale and domain-specific procedural features; and 2) ignore the relations between sentence-level and word-level subtasks.

In this paper, we propose a new framework to extract process models from process texts. Specifically, we first formalize the PME task into the multi-grained text classification problem, and then propose a hierarchical neural network to effectively model and extract multi-grained information without manually defined procedural features. Under this hierarchical structure, we accordingly propose the coarse-to-fine (grained) learning mechanism, training multi-grained tasks in coarse-to-fine grained order, to share the high-level knowledge for the low-level tasks. To train and evaluate our model, we construct two multi-grained datasets from two different domains and conduct extensive experiments from different dimensions. Experimental results demonstrate that our approach outperforms state-of-the-art methods with statistical significance.

In summary, this paper makes the following contributions:

- We first formalize the PME task into the multi-grained text classification problem and design a new hierarchical network to model the conditional relation among multi-grained tasks. Supported by automatic feature extraction, it can extract procedural knowledge without employing manual features and defining procedural knowledge.
- We propose the coarse-to-fine learning mechanism that trains multi-grained tasks in coarse-to-fine (grained) order to apply the sentence-level knowledge for the word-level tasks.
- We construct two multi-grained datasets from two different domains to train and evaluate multi-grained text classifiers. The results demonstrate that our approach outperforms the state-of-the-art methods.

## 2   Related Work

Several **language-rule based** methods have been originally applied to process extraction [18, 29, 32, 34]. Specifically, [34] introduced a generic semantic representation of procedures for analyzing instructions, using Stanford Parser to automatically extract structured procedures from instructions. [32] described an approach for the automatic extraction of workflows from cooking recipes resulting in a formal description of cooking instructions. A chain of standard information extraction pipeline was applied with the help of GATE. They were dedicated to the special characteristics of textual cooking instructions (verb centric, restricted vocabulary of ingredients, relatively independent sentences). Although they are easy to develop and interpret, they require a large number of linguistic rules created by domain experts.

Along this line, **pattern-matching based** methods [7, 8, 26–28, 31] designed various language patterns, considering basic language patterns [27], syntactic tree [7, 31] and anaphora resolution [26, 28]. For example, [27] presented on the step of anaphora resolution to enrich the process models extracted by introducing a lexical approach and two further approaches based on a set of association rules which were created during a statistical analysis of a corpus of workflows. However, these studies are to some extent limited by domain-specific knowledge bases, making them not applicable for open-domain or open-topic scenarios.

Recently, some **knowledge based** methods [10, 12, 13] have been applied to this problem and they were shown to perform well. For example, [12] proposed an ontology-based workflow extraction framework that extended classic NLP techniques to extract and disambiguate tasks in texts. Using a model-based representation of workflows and a domain ontology, the extraction process used a context-based approach to recognize workflow components such as data and control elements in a flow. However, they also require a large quantity of cognition-level knowledge, such as a world model [8, 10] or an ontology [12, 13], which would be time-consuming and labor-intensive to build.

There also exist some **machine-learning based** studies which incorporated traditional machine learning techniques into process extraction [20, 23].

[20] leveraged support vector machine to automatically identify whether a task described in a textual process description is manual or automated. [23] used semi-supervised conditional random fields and support vector machine to label process texts and recognize main information.

Other process-related works include process state tracing, action extraction and process search. For example, [3,4,30] proposed neural machine-reading models that constructed dynamic knowledge graphs from procedural text. [2] introduced a network to understand the procedural text through simulation of action dynamics. [24,25] set out to generate the textual descriptions from process models. [15] proposed a probabilistic model to incorporate aspects of procedural semantics and world knowledge. [1] aimed to answer biological questions by predicting a rich process structure and mapping the question to a formal query.

## 3   Methodology

We first formalize the PME task into the multi-grained text classification problem. Given a process text $T = \langle S^1, S^2, \cdots, S^n \rangle$ where $S^i = \langle W_1^i, W_2^i, \cdots, W_{|S^i|}^i \rangle$ is a sequence of words, $\forall i = 1, 2, \cdots, n$. For each $S^i \in T$, the key of PME ($\alpha$) is to predict a corresponding set of labels that describe the type of the sentence and its corresponding word-level arguments, $\alpha(S^i) = (sType, sSemantic, sArgs)$. $sType$ indicates the type of sentence $S^i$, which can be *Action* or *Statement*. The *Action* indicates that $S^i$ is an action mention and *Statement* refers to a non-action sentence. If $S^i$ is categorized into *Action* type, then $sSemantic$ is $\varnothing$ (empty marker) and $sArgs = [aRole, aName, aObject]$ denotes the action's executor, action name and direct object respectively. Otherwise, $sArgs$ is $\varnothing$ and $sSemantic$ can be one of $\{\triangleright, \triangleleft, \bullet, \times, +\}$ relation symbols that determine how actions are coordinated. The five relations refer to the beginning of a block of actions (*block begins*), the ending of a block of actions (*block ends*), a successive relation, an optional relation and a concurrent relation, respectively.

*Example 1.* Consider the two sentences in Fig. 1: $S^i$ = "you are required to finish two steps" and $S^j$ = "chill the mixture for about 20 min until it thickens". $S^i$ means that two following actions should be chosen and done concurrently, thus it is labeled as a *concurrency relation*, $\alpha(S^i) = (Statement, +, \varnothing)$. $S^j$ is an *action mention*, thus it is labeled with its role, action name and object, $\alpha(S^j) = (Action, \varnothing, [\varnothing, chill, mixture])$.

We argue that PME involves three main text classification subtasks:

**ST1 Sentence Classification** (Sentence-level): identifying whether a sentence is describing an action or a statement.
**ST2 Sentence Semantics Recognition** (Sentence-level): recognizing the semantics of a *Statement* sentence to control the execution of following actions, i.e., *block begins*, *block ends*, *successive relation*, *optional relation* and *concurrency relation*.

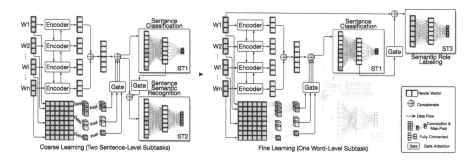

**Fig. 2.** High-level overview of the proposed method MGTC, which consists of two stages: a) The coarse-grained learning phase combines the bi-directional encoding layer and convolutional neural networks to *pre-train* two sentence-level tasks. b) The fine-grained learning phase utilizes the learned sentence-level knowledge to *fine-tune* the word-level task.

**ST3 Semantic Role Labeling** (Word-level): assigning semantic roles (*aRole*, *aName*, *aObject*) to words or phrases in an *Action* sentence.

Note that these three tasks are not independent because ST2 and ST3 are conditioned on ST1, i.e., for a single sentence, the result of ST1 determines whether the sentence is passed to ST2 or ST3.

### 3.1   Overall Framework

To mine sentence-level and word-level information effectively, we propose a deep-learning-based network to effectively avoid manually defining domain-specific procedural features, called Multi-Grained Text Classifier (MGTC). Figure 2 shows the framework of our proposed approach. Specifically, we design a hierarchical structure to model the conditional relations between three subtasks and to effectively extract textual clues from different granularities. Under this framework, we accordingly propose the coarse-to-fine (grained) learning mechanism, training coarse tasks in advance before training fine-grained tasks to share the learned high-level knowledge to the low-level tasks, which conforms with the procedure of human learning more than those methods without the consideration of different granularities. By problem mapping, the output of our model is the sentence-level and word-level labels (see Fig. 1(b) and Example 1), which could be further easily visualized (i.e., from Fig. 1(b) to Fig. 1(c)) as a specific/general process model or a process structure tree [25] via intuitively creating nodes and building sequence flows from the extracted procedural knowledge [8].

### 3.2   Coarse-Grained Learning of the Sentence-Level Knowledge.

The goal of this phase is to learn sentence-level knowledge in advance. First, it takes a sequence of embedded words $S^i = \langle W_1^i, W_2^i, \cdots \rangle$ as input. Then, the word vectors are bidirectionally encoded to capture inherent clues in a sentence. Meanwhile, a convolutional neural network (CNN) is used to capture local $n$gram features in a sentence. After concatenating $n$gram features and sentence embedding, two sentence-level tasks are trained jointly, using a weight-sharing multitask learning framework, to share learned high-level knowledge between two tasks and improve the generalization ability.

**Embedding Layer.** We use BERT [5] or Word2Vec to obtain word vectors. BERT is an autoencoding language model, which has been the currently state-of-the-art pre-training approach. Given the input token sequence, a certain portion of tokens are replaced by a special symbol [MASK], and the model is trained to recover the original tokens from the corrupted version. Since density estimation is not part of the objective, BERT is allowed to utilize bidirectional contexts for reconstruction. This can close the aforementioned bidirectional information gap in autoencoding language modeling, leading to improved performance.

**Encoding Layer.** As a special type of recurrent neural network (RNN), LSTM [14] is particularly suitable for modeling the sequential property of text data. At each step, LSTM combines the current input and knowledge from the previous steps to update the states of the hidden layer. To tackle the gradient vanishing problem of traditional RNNs, LSTM incorporates a gating mechanism to determine when and how the states of hidden layers can be updated. Each LSTM unit contains a memory cell and three gates (i.e., an input gate, a forget gate, and an output gate). The input and output gates control the input activations into the memory cell and the output flow of cell activations into the rest of the network, respectively. The memory cells in LSTM store the sequential states of the network, and each memory cell has a self-loop whose weight is controlled by the forget gate. Let us denote each sentence as $(S_i, L_i)$, where $S_i = [W_i^1, W_i^2, \cdots, W_i^n]$ as a sequence of word vectors representing the plain text and $L_i$ as its label; and $[d^1, d^2, \cdots, d^n]$ denotes the sequence of word vectors of $S_i$. At step $t$, LSTM computes unit states of the network as follows:

$$i^{(t)} = \sigma(U_i d^t + W_i h^{(t-1)} + b_i) \tag{1}$$

$$f(t) = \sigma(U_f d^t + W_f h^{(t-1)} + b_f) \tag{2}$$

$$o(t) = \sigma(U_o d^t + W_o h^{(t-1)} + b_o) \tag{3}$$

$$c(t) = f_t \odot c^{(t-1)} + i^{(t)} \odot \tanh(U_c d^t + W_c h^{(t-1)} + b_c) \tag{4}$$

$$h^{(t)} = o^{(t)} \odot \tanh(c^{(t)}) \tag{5}$$

where $i^{(t)}$, $f^{(t)}$, $o^{(t)}$, $c^{(t)}$, and $h^{(t)}$ denote the state of the input gate, forget gate, output gate, memory cell, and hidden layer at step $t$. $W$, $U$, $b$ respectively denote the recurrent weights, input weights, and biases. $\odot$ is the element-wise product. We can extract the latent vector for each step $T$ from LSTM. In order to capture the information from the context both preceding and following a word, we use the bi-directional LSTM (Bi-LSTM) [21]. We concatenate the latent vectors from both directions to construct a bi-directional encoded vector $h_i$ for every single word vector $W_i^j$, which is:

$$\overrightarrow{h_i} = \overrightarrow{LSTM}(W_i^j), i \in [1, |S_i|] \tag{6}$$

$$\overleftarrow{h_i} = \overleftarrow{LSTM}(W_i^j), i \in [1, |S_i|] \tag{7}$$

$$h_i = [\overrightarrow{h_i}, \overleftarrow{h_i}] \tag{8}$$

**Convolution Layer.** We also employ multiscale filters to capture local $n$gram information in a sentence. Let $x_1^n$ refer to the concatenation of vectors $x_1, x_2, \cdots, x_n$. The convolution layer involves a set of filters $w \in \mathbb{R}^{h \times k}$, which is solely applied to a window of $h$ to produce a new feature map $v =:$

$$\left[ \begin{bmatrix} \sigma(w_i x_1^h + b_1) \\ \sigma(w_i x_2^{h+1} + b_1) \\ \cdots \\ \sigma(w_i x_{n-h+1}^n + b_1) \end{bmatrix}, \begin{bmatrix} \sigma(w_i x_1^h + b_2) \\ \sigma(w_i x_2^{h+1} + b_2) \\ \cdots \\ \sigma(w_i x_{n-h+1}^n + b_2) \end{bmatrix} \cdots \right] \tag{9}$$

where $\sigma(\cdot)$ is the sigmoid function and $b_i$ is a bias term. Meanwhile, we use the max-pooling operation: $\hat{v} = max(v_i)$ to extract the most important features within each feature map.

**Multi-task Learning.** The goal of this module is to incorporate the multiple features for final sentence-level predictions. Since not all features contribute equally to the final task, we employ the gate attention mechanism to weight each concept information. For a feature representation $z$, we define the gate-attention as follows: $g = \sigma(Wz + b)$, where $\sigma$ denotes the sigmoid activation function, which guarantees the values of $g$ in the range $[0, 1]$. $W$ and $b$ are a weight and a bias term which need to be learned. Then, all convoluted representations are injected into the sentence representation by weighted fusing: $z_c = z_T \oplus (g \otimes z)$, where $\otimes$ denotes element-wise multiplication, $\oplus$ denotes concatenation and $z_T$ is the BiLSTM representation. The effect of gate attention is similar to that of feature selection. It is a "soft" feature selection which assigns a larger weight to a vital feature, and a small weight to a trivial feature. Note that we additionally incorporate the hidden feature of ST1 into the input representations of ST2 via a self-attention gate to model the conditional relation between the two sentence-level tasks.

After concatenating all features, it is input into two fully connected multi-layer perceptron (MLP) networks to realize feature fusion:

$$o_i = softmax(W_2 \cdot (W_1 \cdot V + b_1) + b_2) \tag{10}$$

where $W_1$, $W_2$, $b_1$ and $b_2$ are parameters of a network. To obtain the probability distribution on each type $t \in [1, T]$, the *softmax* operation is computed by: $p_k = \frac{\exp(o_t)}{\sum_{i=1}^{T} \exp(o_i)}$, where $T$ is the class number of a classification task.

**Model Training (The Coarse-Grained Learning Phase).** We use cross-entropy loss function to train the coarse-grained learning phase, when given a set of training data $x_t, y_t, e_t$, where $x_t$ is the $t$-th training example to be predicted, $y_t$ is one-hot representation of the ground-truth type and $e_t$ is the model's output. The goal of training is to minimize the loss function:

$$J(\theta_1, \theta_2) = -\lambda_1\Big(\sum_{i=1}^{M}\sum_{t_1=1}^{t_1=T_1} y_t^{t_1} \cdot \log(e_t^{t_1})\Big) - \lambda_2\Big(\sum_{i=1}^{M}\sum_{t_2=T_1+1}^{t_2=T_1+T_2} y_t^{t_2} \cdot \log(e_t^{t_2})\Big) \tag{11}$$

$$\lambda_1 + \lambda_2 = 1, \lambda_1, \lambda_2 \geq 0$$

where $M$ is the number of training samples; $T_{1/2}$ is the category number of each subtask; $\lambda_{1/2}$ is a linear balance parameter. The multi-task learning phase can be further decomposed into learning two single tasks successively.

### 3.3   Fine-Grained Learning of the Word-Level Knowledge

Note that the features of a small-scale classification task may be higher quality than the features of a large-scale classification tasks since the small-scale classification task has relatively sufficient training data [16]. Based on that, compared with sentence-level tasks, we regard the word-level tasks as relatively "large-scale" classification tasks, initializing parameters of the word-level task from the sentence-level tasks and later fine-tuning it. The transfer of parameters can provide a better starting point for the latter than training from scratch using randomly initialized parameters [11].

As the right part of Fig. 2 shows, we extract the last-hidden features $z_s$ in ST1 as learned sentence-level knowledge and concatenate it with word-level embedding $z_w$ via the gate-attention mechanism. The fused representation $[z_s, g(z_w) \odot z_w]$ is fed into a MLP module to perform the word-level prediction. In this phase, we freeze ST2 (the light gray part) since ST2 and ST3 are independent.

**Model Training (The Fine-Grained Learning Phase).** Similarly, we use cross-entropy loss function to train the fine-grained learning phase, when given a set of training data $x_t, y_t, e_t$, where $x_t$ is the $t$-th training example to be predicted, $y_t$ is one-hot representation of the ground-truth type and $e_t$ is the model's output. The goal of training is to minimize the loss function:

$$J(\theta_3) = -\sum_{i=1}^{M}\sum_{t_3=1}^{t_3=T_3} y_t^{t_3} \cdot \log(e_t^{t_3}) \tag{12}$$

where $M$ is the number of training samples; $T_3$ is the category number of ST3.

## 4   Experiments

In this section, we first introduce the experimental setup (datasets, baselines and implementation details). The experimental results are then demonstrated to validate the effectiveness of our approach on different datasets.

## 4.1    Datasets

Since traditional methods mainly use off-the-shelf NLP tools to analyze sentences and extract corresponding information under the pre-defined features or patterns; thus, there was no directly available multi-grained corpus for the PME task. To this end, we constructed two multi-grained PME corpora for the task of extracting process models from texts:

- **Cooking Recipes (COR).** We collected cooking recipes from the world's largest food-focused social network[1]. This corpora has a large and diverse collection of more than 200 cooking recipes and covers every kind of meal type including appetizers, breakfast, desserts, drinks, etc.
- **Maintenance Manuals (MAM).** We collected raw maintenance manuals from a wiki-based site[2] that teaches people how to fix almost all devices. This corpora contains more than 160 maintenance descriptions and covers almost all devices including computer hardware, phones, cars, game consoles, etc.

In the two raw corpora, we first split all documents into sentences and manually assigned labels to them. The sentence-level tags denote whether a sentence is describing cooking ingredients or maintenance tools, performing main actions, or executing conditions. Furthermore, we split all sentences into words and manually assign labels to them to denote the executor, action name and ingredients/tools of actions, i.e., the semantic roles. The statistics of those datasets is given in Table 1.

**Table 1.** Statistics of the two multi-grained datasets.

| Domain | COR | MAM |
|---|---|---|
|  | Recipe | Maintenance |
| # Labeled sentences | 2,636 | 2,172 |
| # Labeled words | 14,260 | 20,612 |
| # Sentence-level categories | 5 | 5 |
| # Word-level categories | 4 | 4 |

## 4.2    Baselines

We chose several representative baselines:

- A pattern-matching based method (PBSW) [27], which uses NLP tagging tools to extract important linguistic patterns and adopts a set of heuristic anaphora resolution mechanisms to extract corresponding procedural knowledge.

---

[1]  https://www.recipe.com.
[2]  https://www.ifixit.com.

- A language-rule based method (ARWE) [28], which introduces a lexical approach and two further approaches based on a set of association rules created during a statistical analysis of a corpus of workflows.
- A traditional-learning based method (RPASVM) [20], which leverages SVM to automatically identify whether a task described in a textual description is manual, an interaction of a human with an information system or automated.

### 4.3   Implementation Details

We used BERT [5] with text representations of size 100 (also can use Word2Vec [22] in our architecture). In training, we used a Rectified Linear Unit (ReLU) as an activation function [19] and the Adam optimizer [17]. The network was run for 1,000 iterations with a mini-batch size of 32 at the coarse and the fine training. The learning rate is $10^{-4}$. We implement MGTC using Python 3.7.3[3] and Tensorflow 1.0.1[4]. All of our experiments were run on a single machine equipped with an Intel Core i7 processor, 32 GB of RAM, and an NVIDIA GeForce-GTX-1080-Ti GPU. For comparison, all methods have been evaluated with the same training and test data. We divide datasets into train/test sets using an 8:2 ratio. The statistical significance between all baseline methods and MGTC is tested using a two-tailed paired t-test [6]. Our code and data are available at https://github.com/qianc62/MGTC.

### 4.4   Overall Performance

We compare all baseline methods, MGTC and its variants in terms of *classification accuracy*. Besides, we extract corresponding process models from the classification results and compare the *behavior similarity* between extracted models and the gold models using existing behavior evaluation methods [33]. The overall results (accuracy of predicted labels) are summarized in Table 2. From the evaluation results, we can make several key observations:

1) Our proposed model MGTC consistently outperforms all methods on all subtasks with statistical significance. On ST1 (single sentence classification), MGTC improves the accuracy by 7.97% and 7.24% on COR and MAM against the strongest competitor, respectively. On ST2 (sentence semantics recognition), MGTC improves the accuracy by 3.92% and 13.94% on COR and MAM, respectively. On ST3 (semantic role labeling), MGTC still outperforms all methods, improving accuracy by 9.75% and 2.18%, respectively. We believe that this is promising as word-level tasks face the problem of sparseness and ambiguity compared with sentence-level tasks, i.e., words have not relatively enough contextual information, which poses a great challenge for ST3. Moreover, in terms of behavior similarity between the extracted models and the gold models, employing the deep-learning-based framework improves

---

[3] https://www.python.org.
[4] https://www.tensorflow.org.

**Table 2.** Experimental results (accuracy; %) of all baselines, MGTC and its variants. *DOP, PPP, TVC, OPM, ARM* and *FMS* denote mechanisms applied in reference papers. ▲ and △ indicate the best and the second-best performing methods among all the baselines, respectively. The best performance among all methods is highlighted in boldface. The * denotes statistical significance ($p \leq 0.05$) compared to MGTC.

| Method | Task & Dataset | | | | | | | |
|---|---|---|---|---|---|---|---|---|
| | ST1 | | ST2 | | ST3 | | PME | |
| | COR | MAM | COR | MAM | COR | MAM | COR | MAM |
| **PBSW**+*DOP* | 47.63* | 47.58* | 43.66* | 39.49* | 34.38* | 35.60* | 30.35* | 30.27* |
| **PBSW**+*DOP*+*PPP* | 51.52* | 52.55* | 45.40* | 45.67* | 48.58* | 47.36* | 38.04* | 37.17* |
| **PBSW**+*DOP*+*PPP*+*TVC* | 66.53* | 47.42* | 55.48* | 46.65* | 50.28* | 49.62* | 46.27* | 36.07* |
| **ARWE**+*OPM* | 70.66* | 60.46* | 62.43* | 62.45* | 58.46* | 61.62* | 52.46* | 51.09* |
| **ARWE**+*OPM*+*ARM* | 76.39* | 69.51* | 56.52* | 72.53△ | 71.38△ | 77.62△ | 65.21△ | 59.50* |
| **ARWE**+*OPM*+*ARM*+*FMS* | 71.63* | 69.60* | 61.37* | 64.48* | 72.64▲ | 78.26▲ | 69.57▲ | 66.11▲ |
| **RPASVM**+*1* gram | 82.53△ | 81.65△ | 84.44△ | 71.55* | 63.39* | 60.39* | 57.76* | 60.23* |
| **RPASVM**+*1* gram+*2* gram | 85.37▲ | 84.50▲ | 87.61▲ | 72.55▲ | 67.33* | 64.53* | 56.59* | 61.23△ |
| **MGTC** | **93.34** | **91.74** | **91.53** | **86.49** | **82.39** | **80.44** | **77.40** | **75.77** |
| **MGTC**\ Gate Mechanism | 90.37* | 88.58* | 89.40* | 84.57* | 77.62* | 76.42* | 67.39* | 71.64* |
| **MGTC**\ Coarse-to-Fine | 91.55* | 89.45* | 88.31* | 84.53* | 79.44* | 76.22* | 74.46* | 72.29* |

behavior accuracy by 7.83% and 12.66% respectively, which further verifies that MGTC can extract procedural knowledge without employing manual features and complex procedural knowledge.

2) From ablation studies, we can see that the performance improves after employing the gate-attention mechanism and coarse-to-fine learning. For example, employing coarse-to-fine learning improves the behavior similarity by 2.94% and 3.48% on COR and MAM. That is to say, both the gate-attention mechanism and coarse-to-fine learning can improve accuracy, which shows the effectiveness of the two mechanisms. This is consistent with our intuition that training coarse tasks in advance before fine-grained tasks can learn to better learning procedural knowledge.

3) The experimental results also demonstrate the disadvantages of the manual-feature-based methods. First, since traditional methods employ diverse manual mechanisms or features, they suffer from the problems of poor quality and lack of adaptability. In contrast, deep-learning-based methods learn hidden contextual features automatically and always maintain their superior performance. Second, by considering the long-term language changes, the framework with mixture of multiscale filters can understand texts' semantics better and extract more accurate information. Third, over all subtasks and datasets, we can see that MGTC can maintain more stable results, which suggests that MGTC is more robust on different subtasks and datasets.

### 4.5   Further Investigation

To further investigate the independent effect of the key parameters or components in our framework, we compare our method with those replacing with

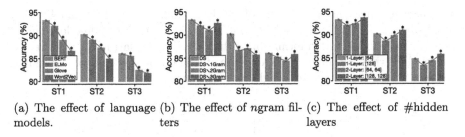

(a) The effect of language models. (b) The effect of $n$gram filters (c) The effect of #hidden layers

**Fig. 3.** Ablation analysis of different components (language models, $n$gram filters, the number of hidden layers) on three subtasks. DS denotes the default settings. \ is the removing operation. * denotes statistical significance ($p \leq 0.05$) compared to MGTC.

other standard components, using the default settings described in Sect. 4.3. The results are shown in Fig. 3.

**Effect of Language Models.** Fig. 3(a) shows the performance of those variants employing different language models (BERT, ELMo, GloVe and Word2Vec). It can be observed that, when the default BERT is replaced with ELMo, GloVe or Word2Vec, the performance consistently decreases. Particularly, on ST3, using Word2Vec decreases the accuracy about 4.58 points, which shows that pretraining on large-scale corpora can better capture linguistic information.

**Effect of Multi-scale $n$gram.** Fig. 3(b) shows the performance of the variants after removing $n$gram ($n = 1,2,3$) filters from MGTC. It can be observed that, when $n$gram filters are removed from the network, it decreases performance of on average by $3.18\%/4.02\%/1.06\%$ on the three tasks respectively. This demonstrates that $n$gram filters make a contribution to the promising scores. In particular, removing $3$ gram filters obviously influences the performance of ST2, suggesting that $3$ gram features play an important role in ST2.

**Effect of the Number of Hidden Layers.** From Fig. 3(c), we can observe that the performance of two-layer MLP indicates that imposing some more nonlinearity is useful, and that the one-layer networks seem slightly weak for certain subtasks. However, further increasing the number of layers may degrade the performance because the model becomes too complicated to train. Using a two-layer architecture seems like a good trade-off between speed and accuracy.

We also conducted more experiments to further investigate the performance of traditional learning (TRAL) and our proposed coarse-to-fine learning method (C2FL). From Fig. 4(a) we can observe that ST1 first converges after a $1.8e$ average duration ($1e = 10^5$ ms), followed by ST2 ($4.1e$) and ST3 ($8.2e$). Moreover, comparing the results of TRAL and C2FL, one can see that C2FL consistently magnifies and scatters the time consumption on three subtasks. The main reason for this is that coarse-to-fine learning architecture would leverage learned features from sentence-level tasks to word-level tasks in a gradual manner; thus, word-level tasks (ST3) would consume more time than sentence-level tasks (ST1 and ST2). From Fig. 4(b), the N-fold cross-validation results show that the generalization performance of C2FL is remarkably higher than TRAL's on all subtasks. This further indicates that employing coarse-to-fine learning is more useful in extracting information with different granularities. Therefore, we can conclude that, although at the expense of longer running time, coarse-to-fine learning tends to converge to a higher performance.

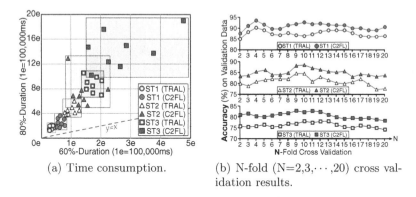

(a) Time consumption.          (b) N-fold (N=2,3,···,20) cross validation results.

**Fig. 4.** Further investigation of the traditional learning (TRAL) and our proposed coarse-to-fine learning (C2FL).

## 5   Discussion

Note that many publicly-available model-text pairs (e.g., [8]) are not considered as our datasets, because our supervised method inevitably needs **much-larger** scale of **labeled** (both sentence- and word-level) training data than traditional rule-based ones. Both requirements (data scale and label) are not fully satisfied on previous datasets which are almost uniformly small or unlabeled.

Moreover, the datasets used in this paper consist of relatively general process texts. Thus, a classic pattern-matching based method [8] is not considered in this version because it mainly focuses on extracting Business Process Model and Notation (BPMN) that contains many **specific** elements, such as swimlanes and artifacts, whose attributes currently have no corresponding specifically-defined labels to perform procedural knowledge extraction via our "relatively general" model. Adding such features is a possible extension of our work.

It is also worth mentioning that although we aim to extract from general process texts, our model might suffer from low external validity. One main reason is that both recipes and manuals are rather sequential by nature, which means that we can expect a rather small number of concurrent streams of actions and complex choices. However, note that deep-learning-based methods, to some extent, tend to be more generalized than pattern-based ones, due to their ability for "adaptive knowledge learning" (rather than those that work with a fixed human-defined knowledge). This limitation further motivates us to design more general and robust models in future work.

# 6  Conclusion

In this paper, we formalize the PME task into the multi-grained text classification problem and propose a hierarchical multi-grained network to model and extract multi-grained information without manually defined procedural features. Under this structure, we accordingly propose the coarse-to-fine learning mechanism, training multi-grained tasks in coarse-to-fine grained order, to apply the high-level knowledge for the low-level tasks. The results demonstrate that our approach outperforms the state-of-the-art methods with statistical significance and the further investigations demonstrate its effectiveness. Therefore, we draw two main conclusions as follows: 1) The deep-learning-based process extractor can effectively capture procedural knowledge without the need for defining domain-specific procedural features; and 2) Our proposed hierarchical network and the coarse-to-fine learning mechanism can better learn the word-level clues based on pre-learned sentence-level knowledge.

**Acknowledgement.** The work was supported by the National Key Research and Development Program of China (No. 2019YFB1704003), the National Nature Science Foundation of China (No. 71690231) and Tsinghua BNRist. Lijie Wen is the corresponding author.

# References

1. Berant, J., Srikumar, V., Chen, P.C., et al.: Modeling biological processes for reading comprehension. In: EMNLP (2014)
2. Bosselut, A., Levy, O., Holtzman, A., et al.: Simulating action dynamics with neural process networks. In: ICLR (2018)
3. Dalvi, B.B., Huang, L., Tandon, N., et al.: Tracking state changes in procedural text: a challenge dataset and models for process paragraph comprehension. In: NAACL (2018)
4. Das, R., Munkhdalai, T., Yuan, X., et al.: Building dynamic knowledge graphs from text using machine reading comprehension. arXiv:1810.05682 (2018)
5. Devlin, J., Chang, M.W., Lee, K., et al.: BERT: pre-training of deep bidirectional transformers for language understanding. In: NAACL (2019)
6. Dror, R., Baumer, G., Shlomov, S., Reichart, R.: The Hitchhiker's guide to testing statistical significance in natural language processing. In: ACL (2018)
7. Epure, E.V., Martín-Rodilla, P., Hug, C., et al.: Automatic process model discovery from textual methodologies. In: RCIS, pp. 19–30 (2015)
8. Fabian, F., Jan, M., Frank, P.: Process model generation from natural language text. In: CAiSE (2011)
9. Feng, W., Zhuo, H.H., Kambhampati, S.: Extracting action sequences from texts based on deep reinforcement learning. In: IJCAI (2018)
10. Friedrich, F.: Automated generation of business process models from natural language input (2010)
11. Haj-Yahia, Z., Deleris, L.A., Sieg, A.: Towards unsupervised text classification leveraging experts and word embeddings. In: ACL (2019)
12. Halioui, A., Valtchev, P., Diallo, A.B.: Ontology-based workflow extraction from texts using word sense disambiguation. bioRxiv (2016)

13. Halioui, A., Valtchev, P., Diallo, A.B.: Bioinformatic workflow extraction from scientific texts based on word sense disambiguation and relation extraction. IEEE/ACM Trans. Comput. Biol. Bioinform. **15**(6), 1979–1990 (2018)

14. Hochreiter, S., Schmidhuber, J.: Long short-term memory. In: Neural Computation (1997)

15. Kiddon, C., Ponnuraj, G.T., Zettlemoyer, L., et al.: Mise en place: unsupervised interpretation of instructional recipes. In: EMNLP (2015)

16. Kim, K.M., Kim, Y., Lee, J., et al.: From small-scale to large-scale text classification. In: WWW (2019)

17. Kingma, D.P., Ba, J.L.: Adam: a method for stochastic optimization. In: ICLR (2015)

18. Kolb, J., Leopold, H., Mendling, J., et al.: Creating and updating personalized and verbalized business process descriptions. In: The Practice of Enterprise Modeling, pp. 191–205 (2013)

19. Krizhevsky, A., Sutskever, I., Hinton, G.E.: ImageNet classification with deep convolutional neural networks. In: NeurIPS, pp. 1097–1105 (2012)

20. Leopold, H., van der Aa, H., Reijers, H.A.: Identifying candidate tasks for robotic process automation in textual process descriptions. In: Enterprise, Business-Process and Information Systems Modeling (2018)

21. Melamud, O., Goldberger, J., Dagan, I.: Learning generic context embedding with bidirectional LSTM. In: CoNLL (2016)

22. Mikolov, T., Sutskever, I., Chen, K., et al.: Distributed representations of words and phrases and their compositionality. In: NeurIPS (2013)

23. Ni, W., Wei, Z., Zeng, Q., Liu, T.: Case information extraction from natural procedure text. CIMS **24**(7), 1680–1689 (2018)

24. Qian, C., Wen, L., Kumar, A.: BePT: a behavior-based process translator for interpreting and understanding process models. In: CIKM, pp. 1873–1882 (2019)

25. Qian, C., Wen, L., Wang, J., Kumar, A., Li, H.: Structural descriptions of process models based on goal-oriented unfolding. In: CAiSE, pp. 397–412 (2017)

26. Schumacher, P., Minor, M.: Extracting control-flow from text. In: IRI, pp. 203–210, August 2014. https://doi.org/10.1109/IRI.2014.7051891

27. Schumacher, P., Minor, M., Schulte-Zurhausen, E.: Extracting and enriching workflows from text. In: IRI, pp. 285–292, August 2013

28. Schumacher, P., Minor, M., Schulte-Zurhausen, E.: On the use of anaphora resolution for workflow extraction. In: Bouabana-Tebibel, T., Rubin, S.H. (eds.) Integration of Reusable Systems. AISC, vol. 263, pp. 151–170. Springer, Cham (2014). https://doi.org/10.1007/978-3-319-04717-1_7

29. Schumacher, P., Minor, M., Walter, K.: Extraction of procedural knowledge from the web: a comparison of two workflow extraction approaches. In: WWW (2012)

30. Tandon, N., Mishra, B.D., Grus, J., et al.: Reasoning about actions and state changes by injecting commonsense knowledge. In: EMNLP (2018)

31. Vakulenko, S.: Extraction of process models from business process descriptions (2011)

32. Walter, Kirstin, Minor, M., Bergmann, R.: Workflow extraction from cooking recipes. In: ICCBR (2011)

33. Weidlich, M., Mendling, J., Weske, M.: Efficient consistency measurement based on behavioral profiles of process models. In: TSE (2014)

34. Zhang, Z., Webster, P., Uren, V., et al.: Automatically extracting procedural knowledge from instructional texts using natural language processing. In: LREC (2012)

# LoGo: Combining Local and Global Techniques for Predictive Business Process Monitoring

Kristof Böhmer[✉] and Stefanie Rinderle-Ma

Faculty of Computer Science, University of Vienna, Vienna, Austria
{kristof.boehmer,stefanie.rinderle-ma}@univie.ac.at

**Abstract.** Predicting process behavior in terms of the next activity to be executed and/or its timestamp can be crucial, e.g., to avoid impeding compliance violations or performance problems. Basically, two prediction techniques are conceivable, i.e., global and local techniques. Global techniques consider all process behavior at once, but might suffer from noise. Local techniques consider a certain subset of the behavior, but might loose the "big picture". A combination of both techniques is promising to balance out each others drawbacks, but exists so far only in an implicit and unsystematic way. We propose LoGo as a systematic combined approach based on a novel global technique and an extended local one. LoGo is evaluated based on real life execution logs from multiple domains, outperforming nine comparison approaches. Overall, LoGo results in explainable prediction models and high prediction quality.

**Keywords:** Predictive process monitoring · Sequential rule mining · Local prediction · Global prediction · Explainable prediction models

## 1 Introduction

Predictive process monitoring provides insights into the future of ongoing process executions, i.e., process instances that are currently executed. For this historic process executions are analyzed to, for example, predict the next execution event's activity and timestamp. With this, resource utilization can be optimized or impending Service-Level Agreement *violations* can be *averted*, cf. [22,23].

Related work typically applies a fuzzy and implicit mixture of *global* and *local* prediction techniques. *Global* techniques take all historic process behaviour into account at once [23]. On the one side, they exploit significant global behaviour, but on the other side require to handle possibly large noisy data collections. In comparison, *local* prediction techniques focus on a certain subset of the historic process behaviour, for example, those traces that are most similar to a ongoing trace which is predicted upon [5]. Local techniques, on the one side, enable data and noise reduction in early stages of the prediction by taking only a subset of the data into account. But on the other side hinder the identification of significant global behaviour reflecting the "big picture" of the process execution behavior.

© Springer Nature Switzerland AG 2020
S. Dustdar et al. (Eds.): CAiSE 2020, LNCS 12127, pp. 283–298, 2020.
https://doi.org/10.1007/978-3-030-49435-3_18

Hence, it seems promising to combine local and global techniques as they compensate each others drawbacks. However, the currently applied unsystematic or implicit combination of local and global techniques forces the applied machine learning techniques (e.g., recurrent neural networks, cf. [19]) into covering both (local *and* global) in a *single* prediction model at once, and determining if local *or* global prediction and data should be preferred for each prediction task. Given, such learning techniques are not aware of any logical separation between local and global prediction, they struggle to "learn' and represent this separation during their prediction model training phase; with varying success, cf. [2,19,23].

Overall, this might result in complex prediction models, high model training times, reduced flexibility, and diminished prediction results, cf. [5,19,23]. Accordingly, we propose an explicit combination of specialized local and global prediction techniques instead of an unsystematic or implicit one. Here, both techniques are shallow ones [2] as they are designed for either local or global prediction and yield explainable prediction models. In detail, we propose a novel global prediction technique which could be applied in a stand-alone fashion. To demonstrate and exploit the outlined advantages of combining global and local techniques, the global technique is complemented with a local one that is extended based on previous work in [5].

Specifically, the combined approach works as follows: first, the global technique is applied to exploit global significant process execution behaviour if possible. If no significant behaviour can be exploited the local technique is applied as a fallback, cf. [5], as it is less affected by noise.

Formally: Let $p$ be an execution trace of process $P$ for which the next activity execution should be predicted. Further let $L$ hold all historic execution traces $t$ of $P$. The key idea is to mine Sequential Prediction Rules (SPR) from $L$ to identify significant global behaviour in the historic data (global prediction). Behaviour is assumed as significant if the related SPRs have a high confidence. Rules have been used in existing data analysis formalisms and mining approaches [26]. This work extends them into SPRs in order to become capable of predicting future behaviour, i.e., upcoming activities and their execution timestamps. Such SPRs form the prediction model $M$, enabling to predict the next activity in a majority of prediction scenarios, i.e. in about 60% of all predictions as shown in Sect. 4.

The proposed global prediction technique is not able to yield any predictions based on $M$ if none of the SPRs contained in $M$ match to $p$'s behaviour. In other words, if no significant execution behaviour was identified in $L$ by the global prediction technique which is relevant for $p$'s current execution state. In this case, the proposed combined approach LoGo employs a local prediction technique, i.e., extended based on [5], as a fallback. The work in [5] relies on the similarity between $p$ and $t \in L$ to identify the most relevant behaviour (traces, resp.) to form a probability based prediction model. Accordingly, even if the similarity between $p$ and $t \in L$ is low there will always be some traces which are the "most" similar ones. These most similar traces serve as a basis to predict future behaviour even if a global, e.g., SPR based, technique is unable to do so.

This paper is organized as follows: Prerequisites and the proposed approach are introduced in Sect. 2. Details on prediction model generation and its application are given in Sect. 2 and 3. Section 4 covers the evaluation (real life data, multiple comparison approaches) while Sect. 5 discusses related work. Finally, conclusions, discussions, and future work are outlined in Sect. 6.

## 2 Prerequisites and General Approach

The presented approach enables to predict process instance execution behaviour (e.g., in the form of an process execution event) to be observed next, based on a given ongoing process instance trace $p$. However, this section, for the sake of simplicity, focuses on the prediction of next event activities. Details on temporal behaviour prediction (execution event timestamps, resp.) are given in Sect. 3.

Overall, the prediction is based on a prediction model $M$ which is generated from a bag of historic process execution traces $L$, i.e., an execution log. The latter is beneficial as $L$ can be $a$) automatically generated by process engines; $b$) represents real behaviour (including noise and ad-hoc changes); and $c$) it is independent of outdated documentation, cf. [5,18]. Formally, log $L$ is defined as:

**Definition 1 (Execution Log).** *Let $L$ be a finite bag of **execution traces** $t \in L$. Let further $t := \langle e_1, \cdots, e_n \rangle$ be an ordered list of execution **events** $e_i := (ea, et)$. Hereby, $e_i$ represents the execution of **activity** $e_i.ea$ which was started at **timestamp** $e_i.et \in \mathbb{R}_{>0}$. The **order** of $e_i \in t$ is determined by $e_i.et$.*

Definition 1 enables the identification of global activity orders and related temporal information. Hence, it it is sufficient for next event prediction. Further Definition 1 is generic. Thus it enables the representation of standardized log data formats, such as, the eXtensible Event Stream[1] or custom organization dependent formats (cf. Sect. 4). In the running example provided in Table 1, the event $e_2$ for trace $t_2$ (i.e., $t_2.e_2$) represents the execution of activity E at timestamp 54.

**Table 1.** Running example log $L$ as excerpt of the Helpdesk-Log used in Sect. 4

| Process $P$ | Trace $t$ | Event $e_i := (ea, et)$ where $ea$ = activity, $et$ = timestamp | | | | | |
|---|---|---|---|---|---|---|---|
| | | $e_1$ | $e_2$ | $e_3$ | $e_4$ | $e_5$ | $e_6$ |
| $P_1$ | $t_1$ | (A,23) $\rightarrow$ | (E,32) $\rightarrow$ | (E,37) $\rightarrow$ | (F,40) $\rightarrow$ | (C,47) $\rightarrow$ | (W,53) |
| $P_1$ | $t_2$ | (A,49) $\rightarrow$ | (E,54) $\rightarrow$ | (F,61) $\rightarrow$ | (F,68) $\rightarrow$ | (C,69) $\rightarrow$ | (R,78) |
| $P_1$ | $t_3$ | (A,40) $\rightarrow$ | (F,45) $\rightarrow$ | (E,49) $\rightarrow$ | (F,51) $\rightarrow$ | (C,57) $\rightarrow$ | (W,63) |
| $P_1$ | $t_4$ | (E,17) $\rightarrow$ | (F,21) $\rightarrow$ | (D,22) $\rightarrow$ | (F,25) $\rightarrow$ | (C,30) $\rightarrow$ | (R,38) |

---

[1] http://xes-standard.org/ – IEEE 1849-2016 XES Standard.

Further, similar to [5], the following *auxiliary* functions are applied:

- $\{S\}^0$ returns the element in the set/bag $S$, given that $S$ is a singleton.
- $C := A \oplus b$ appends $b$ to a copy $C$ of the collection given by $A$.
- $\langle \cdot \rangle^l$ retains the last element of a list.
- $\langle \cdot \rangle_i$ retains the list item with index $i \in \mathbb{N}_{>0}$.

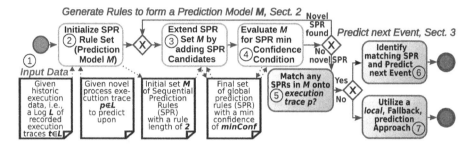

**Fig. 1.** Proposed SPR based prediction approach – overview

Figure 1 gives an overview on the proposed prediction approach. Its expected *input data* ① comprises historic execution traces $t \in L$ (log, resp.) of a process $P$ to create a prediction model $M$; and an ongoing execution $p \notin L$ of $P$ for which the next event should be predicted. Hereby, $M$ can be created, even before $p$'s execution starts. Further, the same $M$ can be reused for different traces of $P$.

Here the *prediction model* $M$ consists of a set of Sequential Prediction Rules (SPR). SPRs expand upon *sequential rules* which have been proposed in sequential rule mining approaches, e.g., [25]. There, a sequential rule $s$ is defined as $s := \langle E, F, F \rangle$ where $E$ and $F$ refer to process activity executions. The order of the "entries" in $s$ expresses in which order the activities must be observed in a trace $t$ to conclude that $s$ *matches* $t$. Regarding activity execution orders, existing work names the following patterns that are of interest for this: "A *followed by* B" means that if A is executed eventually B must be executed [21]. "A *immediately followed by* B" requires that as soon A has been executed B must follow next [21].

This work extends existing sequential rule formalisms, in order to increase their predictive capabilities, into SPRs. In the following a SPR $r$ is defined as

$$r := (pas = \langle pas_1, \cdots, pas_m \rangle, pre, fut) \tag{1}$$

where $pas_1, \ldots, pas_m$, $pre$, and $fut$ refer to activity executions. The order of these "entries" in $r$ imposes requirements on the expected activity execution order over a corresponding execution trace $t$. These are, in detail, $pas_m$ *followed by* $pre$; $pre$ *immediately followed by* $fut$ while for the activities in $pas$ a *followed by* order is expected (similar to sequential rules). Obviously, this constitutes an extension when compared to existing sequential rules which commonly utilize only a single relation pattern. Further, the rule "entries" $pas$ (historic execution behaviour), *pre* (most recently executed activity), and *fut* (the activity to be executed next) become assigned a specific semantic meaning. This is another difference to existing sequential rules as they treat each of the "entries" equally.

Overall these extensions give SPRs their prediction capabilities, increases their flexibility and reduce over- *and* underfitting. For example, *pas* enables to consider global behaviour when creating $M$ or predicting – reducing underfitting. In comparison, overfitting is reduced based on the relaxed *followed by relation* implied on *pas* (and its "entries") and *pre*. The latter, combined with the *immediately followed by* relation between *pre* and *fut* enables to represent in $M$ and subsequently exploit while predicting that, given, *pas* and *pre* was observed for $p$ the to be predicted next (i.e., immediately following) activity is, likely, *fut*.

Hereby, all SPR entries combined with the expected activity orders provide a foundation to predict $p$'s next activity based on SPRs. For the running example in Table 1, the SPR $r := (\langle E \rangle, F, F)$ matches to $t_3$ while a similar sequential rule $s := (\langle E, F, F \rangle)$ matches to $t_2$ and $t_3$; illustrating that the made extensions increase the focus of SPRs over sequential rules. In the following we will also denote SPRs as `pas | pre ⇒ fut` in order to be more illustrative – when appropriate.

How to mine SPRs as defined in Eq. 1 from an execution log $L$? As depicted in Fig. 1, the mining approach comprises three interconnected steps. First, the prediction model $M$ is *initialized* ② with the set of all *minimal* SPRs over a log $L$. Here, a SPR $r := (pas, pre, fut)$ is called minimal if $pas = \emptyset$. Formally, the initial prediction model $M_{init}$ is defined and generated as follows:

$$M_{init} := \{(\emptyset, e.ea, e'.ea) | e, e' \in t, t \in L\} \tag{2}$$

Assuming that $L$ solely holds $t_1$, see Table 1, then $M_{init} := \{(\langle \rangle, A, A), (\langle \rangle, A, E), (\langle \rangle, A, F), (\langle \rangle, A, C), (\langle \rangle, A, W), (\langle \rangle, E, A), \cdots \}$, i.e., all possible *pre/fut* combinations (similar to a Cartesian product). For the sake of brevity, $M_{init}$ is given in parts.

Subsequently, iterative SPR *extension* ③ and *evaluation* ④ steps are performed (cf. Fig. 1). *Extension:* For each SPR $r := (pas, pre, fut) \in M_{init}$ all possible extensions of $r.pas$ are explored (i.e., by adding one activity in $L$'s activities to it) as potential SPRs for an extended prediction model $M_{ext}$. For this, the first iteration exploits $M_{init}$ while later utilize the most recent $M_{ext}$. Formally: $\forall r \in M_{init}, a \in A := \{e.ea | e \in t, t \in L\}$ an extended SPR set is built:

$$M_{ext} := \{(r.pas \oplus a, r.pre, r.fut) | a \in A\} \tag{3}$$

$M_{ext} := \{(r.pas \oplus a, r.pre, r.fut) | a \in A\}$.

*Evaluation:* All rules in $M_{ext}$ are then evaluated based on their *confidence* (cf. Definition 2) [26]. The confidence reflects the "likelihood" that a given combination of activity observations, as defined in $r.pas$, results in the future behaviour represented in $r$ to be observed. In other words, the most recently executed activity $r.pre$ will be directly succeeded by $r.fut$. Here we exploit the common confidence metric [26] to measure global behaviour (and thus SPR) significance.

**Definition 2 (SPR Confidence).** *Let SPR $r := (pas, pre, fut)$ be a sequential rule and $L$ be a log. The confidence $conf(L, r) \in [0, 1]$ of $r$ is defined as:*

$$conf(L, r) := \frac{count(pas \mid pre \Rightarrow fut, L)}{count(pas \mid pre \Rightarrow \cdot, L)}$$

*where count determines the number of traces in $L$ which $r$ matches to. The numerator considers all "entries" of $r$ (**full match**) while the denominator ignores $r.fut$ (**partial match**), cf. Sect. 3.1. This follows commonly applied association rule confidence calculation techniques, as described in [25].*

An example for the confidence calculation is given in Sect. 3.1. We found alternatives to the confidence metric such as lift or support [26] to have no or even a negative impact as the use of even low support values (e.g., a minimal support of 0.001) frequently results in generating underfitted prediction models.

The evaluation of each rule is performed based on a user configurable minimal confidence threshold $minc \in [0, 1]$. Accordingly, only SPRs with a confidence above $minc$, i.e., $conf(L, r) > minc$, will be retained from $M_{ext}$ to form this iterations version of $M$. The assumption behind that is: the higher the confidence, the higher the significance of a given rule and, in return, the global execution behaviour it represents. Finally, the resulting prediction model $M$ turns out as:

$$M := \{r \in \bigcup_{M_{ext}} \mid conf(r) > minc\} \tag{4}$$

Rule extension ④ and evaluation ③ cycles (cf., Fig. 1) are repeated until no additional novel SPRs can be identified. Altogether, the repeated extension and evaluation of rules in $M$ aims at identifying and extracting global significant execution behaviour. For this work this means that a specific unique combination of activity observations (see $pas$) results in a high likelihood that the next occurrence of $pre$ will directly be followed by the activity $fut$, cf. Sect. 3.

Finally, the SPRs in prediction model $M$ are exploited to predict the activity to be executed next for an ongoing process execution trace $p \notin L$. For this, it must first be determined if *appropriate* SPRs are available in $M$ for the prediction task at hand (⑤, Fig. 1). A SPR $r := (pas, pre, fut)$ is appropriate if $pas$ matches $p$ and $r.pre = p^l.ea$, i.e., the present activity $r.pre$ is equal to the most recently executed process activity in $p$. Out of these rules $r$, the appropriate SPR with the highest confidence is assumed as the most relevant one such that its $r.fut$ becomes the expected (predicted, resp.) activity to be executed next for $p$ ⑥.

If appropriate SPRs (global behaviour, resp.) cannot be identified we propose to *fall back* to a local prediction technique (⑦, Fig. 1). Such techniques, typically, are not solely relying on matching specific global behaviour and hence can be applied in a more flexible manner. Throughout the evaluation, a local prediction technique [5] was chosen and extended for this. Further details on the outlined prediction algorithms, their application and SPR matching are given in Sect. 3.

# 3   SPR Based Predictive Monitoring

This section discusses details on SPR mining including the exploitation of existing sequential rule mining optimization strategies and the relation between and prediction of control and temporal execution behaviour.

## 3.1   SPR Mining and Optimizations

Creating the prediction model and mining the related SPRs requires to apply the proposed *extension* and *evaluation cycle*, cf. Fig. 1. The latter requires to determine if and how recorded execution traces $t \in L$ match to a given SPR $r$. We assume that a SPR can be matched to $t$ either *partly* and/or *fully*, specifically:

**Full Match**: Given a trace $t$, it is *fully* matched by $r$ if all activity executions specified by $r$ (i.e., past $r.pas$, present $r.pre$, and future $r.fut$ behaviour) can be observed in $t$ in the specified order. Hereby, the activities in $r.pas$ must occur in the orders specified by their indexes $r.pas_i$ (i.e., activity $r.pas_2$ must occur *after* activity $r.pas_1$ was observed, i.e., a *followed by relation* is used). To increase the flexibility of this matching technique arbitrary gaps, i.e., $n \in \mathbb{N}_0$ activity executions, in $t$ are permitted between each matching occurrence of $r.pas_i$. The latter results in less strict prediction models which are less prone to overfitting.

For example, an assumed $r.pas := \langle A, E \rangle$ would match to $t_1$, $t_2$, *and* $t_3$ in the running example, cf. Table 1. Hereby, A and E are only direct successors in $t_1$ and $t_2$. In comparison an unrelated activity execution (i.e., F) takes place between A and E in $t_3$. In future work more complex SPR representations will be explored which, inter alia, restrict the maximum gap between matches for $r.pas$.

In addition, each SPR $r$ consists of $r.pre$ and $r.fut$, cf. Definition 1. Hereby, $r.fut$ is required to be a *direct* successor to $r.pre$ in a given trace $t$ to conclude that $r$ matches to $t$ (i.e., an *immediately followed by* relation is used). This is because here we are interested in predicting the direct successive activity execution (i.e., $r.fut$) for a given most recently executed activity (i.e., $r.pre$).

**Partial Match:** In comparison a *partial* match is already given when $r.pas$ and $r.pre$ can be observed in a given trace $t$ (i.e., $r.fut$ is ignored). Similarly to a full match gaps of arbitrary length are permitted between activity observations (*followed by relation*, resp.). Overall, the described full and partial match concept pave the ground for the SPR confidence calculation outlined previously in Definition 2. Hereby, the full match is implemented accordingly for $count(pas \mid pre \Rightarrow fut, L)$ while a partial match is utilized for $count(pas \mid pre \Rightarrow \cdot, L)$ on the traces in $L$.

For example, given SPRs $r_1 := (\langle E \rangle \mid C \Rightarrow R)$ and $r_2 := (\langle E, F, F \rangle \mid C \Rightarrow R)$ along with the traces in the running example Table 1 following matching results would be observed. While $r_1$ results in a full match for $t_1, t_4$ and a partial match for $t_1, t_2, t_3, t_4$; $r_2$ fully matches $t_1, t_4$ and partially also matches $t_1, t_4$. Accordingly the confidence of $r_1$ is $2/4 = 0.5$ while for $r_2$ it becomes $2/2 = 1$ such that $r_2$ is assumed as representing more significant behaviour/predictions.

Finally, the outlined SPR matching (evaluation, resp.) and expansion steps are combined to mine SPRs and create the prediction model $M$, cf. Algorithm 1. For this, first an initial preliminary prediction model with minimal SPRs is created. Subsequently, the preliminary rules in $M$ are expanded in an iterative manner to increase, iteration by iteration, their respective confidence. Finally, all identified potential SPRs are evaluated based on a final confidence evaluation step. The latter ensures that each $r \in M$ complies to the minimal user chosen confidence threshold $minc \in [0,1]$. Hereby, a prediction model $M$ is created which can in return be utilized to predict upcoming activity executions for novel ongoing execution traces $p$ of $P$ based on significant historic behaviour in $L$.

---

**Algorithm** sprMine(*historic traces* $t \in L$, *minimum SPR confidence* $minc \in [0,1]$)
  **Result:** final prediction model $M$ (SPR collection, resp.)
  $A := \{e.ea | e \in t; t \in L\}$ // all activities in L
  $M_{init} := \{(\varnothing, a, a') | a, a' \in A\}$ // initial set of minimal SPRs to expand, Fig. 1 ②
  $M_{ext} := M_{init}$ // SPR set for the expansion process, start with $M_{init}$
  $M := \varnothing$ // the prediction model, a set of SPRs; initially empty
  do
      // create all possible SPR expansions, exploit previous iteration, Fig. 1 ③
      $M_{ext} := \{(r.pre \oplus a, r.pre, r.fut) | r \in M_{ext}, a \in A\}$
      // stop condition, $M_{ext}$'s SPRs shall full match to at least a single $t \in L$
      $M_{ext} := \{r \in M_{ext} | count(r, L) > 0\}$
      $M := M \cup \{r \in M_{ext} | conf(r, L) > minc\}$ // evaluating $M_{ext}$ to enforce the
        min. confidence requirement, Fig. 1 ④, cf. Def. 2
  while $|M_{ext}| > 0$ // expand SPRs till no new behaviour can be learned
  return $M$

**Algorithm 1:** Mines SPRs for a given log $L$ of historic executions.

---

**Optimization:** For the sake of understandability and simplicity the outlined Algorithm 1 and concepts, cf. Sect. 2, do not reflect a number of optimization strategies which were applied by its public prototypical implementation used throughout the evaluation, cf. Sect. 4. For example, instead of iterating over all traces in $L$ throughout each iterative step the implementation holds a list of relevant (i.e., fully matching traces) for each rule. When extending a rule solely this list is analyzed and updated. Further optimizations are applied when generation the initial ($M_{init}$) and extended ($M_{ext}$) version of the SPRs. For example, instead of generating all possible (potential) rules only direct successors in $L$ taken into consideration to restrict the generated rules to behaviour which is at least once observed in $L$ – reducing the SPR evaluation efforts. Hereby, this work builds upon optimization strategies proposed for association rules by [25], enabling to reduce the impact of a potential state explosions.

## 3.2  SPR Based Predictions and Fallbacks

After finalizing the prediction model $M$ the activity to be executed next can be predicted for novel ongoing execution traces $p$ where $p \notin L$, cf. Algorithm 2. For this the most recently executed activity ($p^l.ea$) is utilized to identify all *relevant* SPRs in $M$ based on a *rough* and a *fine* filter. The *rough* filter assumes a SPR as relevant if its present activity value (i.e., $r.pre$) is equal to the most recently executed activity in $p$ (i.e., $p^l.ea$) *and* if $r.pas$ could be observed beforehand (i.e., before $p^l$) in $p$'s execution events. We assume that under this circumstances a rule is most likely related to the current execution state of $p$ and its direct future.

Finally, the confidence of each SPR in the roughly filtered representation of $M$ is determined to identify the SPR (rule resp.) with maximum confidence, resulting in a *fine* filter. Hereby, the assumption is that the most confident applicable rule has the highest probability to represent global significant behaviour relevant for $p$'s current execution state and its to be predicted future. If the rough filter removes all rules from $M$ the proposed technique is found to be not applicable for $p$'s current state. The latter can occur if the behaviour in $p$ is too novel, unique, or varying (concept drift) and such could not be mined from $L$.

Throughout the evaluation we found that about 40% of all activity predictions were affected by this, see Sect. 4 for a detailed discussion. Accordingly, we propose to apply an alternative local prediction technique in such cases which is not or less affected by such execution behaviour, such as, the technique presented in [5]. Given such a unique execution behaviour the latter technique can still be applied as it solely relies on trace similarities and probability distributions. Such similarities might become low or the probability distributions become less significant but nevertheless some future can and will still be predictable.

---

**Algorithm** sprPredictAct(*ongoing trace p, SPR prediction model M, historic traces L*)
  **Result:** predicted activity to be executed next $a$ for the ongoing trace $p$
  $a := \varnothing$ // by default no activity could be predicted
  $M' := \{r \in M | r.pre = p^l.ea\}$ // filter for relevance by recently executed activity
  if $M' \neq \varnothing$ // only if relevant SPRs are available then
    $mcr := \{r \in M' | conf(r, L) > conf(r', L), r' \in M\}^0$ // filter, max confidence
    $a := mcr.fut$ // r.fut is the most probable activity
  else
    | // get $a$ by applying a fallback technique, such as, [5]
  return $a$ // the activity to be predicted next (SPR or fallback)

**Algorithm 2:** Prediction for trace $p$ and prediction model $M$.

---

For example, imagine that $L$ consists of the traces $t_1$ to $t_3$ given in the running example, cf. Table 1. When assuming $t_4$ as the currently ongoing trace $p$ which should be predicted upon and that $p$'s most recently observed execution event is $t_4.e_5$ (i.e., the execution of activity C). Firstly, a number of rules will be generated and stored in $M$. Hereby, $M$ will, inter alia, contain, $r_1 := (\langle A \rangle \mid E \Rightarrow E)$ with a confidence $c$ of $0.\dot{3}$, $r_2 := (\langle E, F \rangle \mid C \Rightarrow W)$ with $c := 0.\dot{6}$ and $r_3 := (\langle E, F, F \rangle \mid C \Rightarrow R)$ with $c := 1$. Secondly, the rules in $M$ are roughly filtered based on $r.pre$ (which should be equal to $p$'s most recent activity C) and $r.pas$ which should be observed in $p$'s execution events before $p^l$. Accordingly, only $r_2$ and $r_3$ will be taken into consideration for the next fine granular filtering step.

Fine granular filtering identifies the SPR in $M$ with the highest confidence. Given that $r_2$ has a confidence of $c := 0.\dot{6}$ while $r_3$ has a confidence of $c := 1$ it is determined that $r_3$ should be applied for the final prediction step. That final step exploits the information given in $r_3$ on the related future behaviour (i.e., $r_3.fut$) to predict the direct successor activity for $p^l$ (cf., $t_4.e_5$) correctly as R, cf. Table 1.

Demonstrating an advantage of the proposed significant global behaviour based prediction technique over local techniques. Hence, a local prediction technique, such as, [5], could come to the conclusion that, based on $L$, C is followed by W with a likelihood of $0.\dot{6}$ while R follows on C with a likelihood of $0.\dot{3}$. In return *incorrectly* predicting W as $t_4.e_5$'s most likely direct successor, cf. Table 1.

The proposed global technique predicts based on the SPR with the highest confidence. Alternatives, which were inspired by *bagging* and *boosting* were also explored, cf. [3]. These include, for example, to take the activity with has, on average, the highest relative confidence based on all appropriate SPRs or to choose the future activity which is backed up by the most SPRs. However, throughout the evaluation no consistent tendencies towards one of the explored alternatives were recognized. Hence, the described most simple approach was applied.

### 3.3 Prediction of Temporal Behaviour

The proposed prediction technique is capable of predicting upcoming activities based on unique global execution behaviour. This also paves a foundation to improve the temporal behaviour prediction technique presented in [5]. The latter is capable of predicting the occurrence timestamp of the next activity execution.

For this, [5] is extended by adding a preliminary filtering step. It filters the traces in $L$ such that $LC \subseteq L$ only retains traces $t \in L$ for which an immediately followed by relation between the most recently executed activity in the ongoing trace $p$, i.e., $p^l$, and its predicted successive activity, cf. Algorithm 3, can be observed. Overall, this reduces the noise in $LC \subseteq L$ which the local prediction technique has to cope with – improving the achieved temporal behaviour (i.e., next execution event timestamp) prediction quality, as shown in Sect. 4.

---

**Algorithm** tempHistFilter(*ongoing trace p, predicted activity a, historic traces L*)
   **Result**: $L\check{C}$, a less noisy representation of $L$, cleaned based on the predicted activity $a$
   $LC := \varnothing$ // cleaned representation of $L$
   **foreach** $t \in L$ // each trace is independently analyzed **do**
      **for** $histTraceIndex = 0$ **to** $|t| - 1$ // check each activity **do**
         // $t$'s events to evaluate for their direct successive activity relation
         $a_1 := t_{histTraceIndex}.ea$, $a_2 := t_{histTraceIndex+1}.ea$
         // between the most recent activity in $p$ and its predicted next activity **if**
         $a_1 = p^l.ea \wedge a_2 = a$ **then**
            $LC := LC \cup \{t\}$ **break** // preserve $t \in L$ only if deemed relevant
   **return** $LC$

**Algorithm 3:** Preparing $L$ for temporal behaviour prediction.

---

This is achieved by the proposed flexible combination of two specialized techniques. Enabling that improvements and advantages gained in one technique can be integrated into existing alternative solutions to improve their prediction quality as well. For example, assume the first three traces in the running example, cf. Table 1, as $L$ and also assume the most recently executed activity as C for the ongoing trace $p$ ($t_4.e_5$, resp.). Without the proposed noise reduction approach the next activity execution timespan between $t_4.e_5$ and $t_4.e_6$ would be predicted based on all three traces in $L$ as 6 (resulting in a timestamp of 36) by [5].

This is because 6 is the most frequently observed timespan for $C$ and an arbitrary successive activity execution based on the non filtered $L$. When applying the proposed filtering approach, cf. Algorithm 3, $LC \subseteq L$ is reduced to only hold trace $t_2$ as it is the only trace for which C is directly followed by R. Hereby, the predicted timestamp becomes 39 as the timespan between C and R based on $t_2$ is 9; reducing the timestamp prediction error for this example from 2 to 1.

## 4    Evaluation

The evaluation utilizes real life process execution logs from multiple domains in order to assess the prediction quality and feasibility of the proposed approach LoGo, namely: BPI Challenge 2012[2] (BPIC) and Helpdesk[3]. Both were chosen as they are the *primary evaluation data source* for a range of existing state-of-the-art approaches: [1,2,5–7,13,23]. This enables to compare the proposed approach[4] with diverse alternative techniques, such as, neural network or probability based prediction approaches with varying focus on local/global behaviour.

**BPIC 2012 Log:** The BPIC 2012 log is provided by the Business Process Intelligence Challenge (BPIC) 2012. It contains traces generated by the execution of a finance product application process. This process consists of one manually and two automatically executed subprocesses: 1) application state tracking (automatic); 2) handling of application related work items (*manual*); and 3) offer state tracking (automatic). The comparison approaches, such as, [5,7,23], are only interested in the prediction of manually performed events. Accordingly, this and the comparison work narrow down the events in the log to become comparable. Overall 9,657 traces with 72,410 execution events were retained.

**Helpdesk Log:** This log is provided by a software company and contains execution traces generated by a support-ticket management process. The log holds 3,804 traces which consist of 13,710 execution events. We assume the helpdesk log as being more *challenging* than the BPIC log. This is because the structural and temporal fluctuation along with the number of activities is higher while the amount of traces, from which behaviour can be learned, is lower.

**Comparison Approaches:** The proposed approach is compared with nine alternative process execution behaviour prediction approaches, see [1,5–7,13,23]. These apply a number of techniques, such as, finite state automata, histogram like prediction models or neural networks. The latter, either use Recurrent Neural Networks (RNN) – which incorporate feedback channels between the neurons a network is composed of – or Long Short-Term Memory (LSTM) based neural

---

[2] DOI: https://doi.org/10.4121/uuid:3926db30-f712-4394-aebc-75976070e91f.

[3] DOI: https://doi.org/10.17632/39bp3vv62t.1.

[4] Public prototypical implementation: https://github.com/KristofGit/LoGo.

networks. LSTM based neural networks were found to deliver consistent high quality results by adding the capability to "memorize" previous states, cf. [23].

## 4.1 Metrics and Evaluation

This work applies the same metrics and evaluation concepts as *previous work*, such as, [5,23], to archive *comparability*. First, the *Mean Absolute Error* (MAE) measure enables to analyze the temporal behaviour prediction quality. For this, the difference between the real observed temporal behaviour in the logs and the predicted timestamps is aggregated. Here, MAE was chosen as it is less affected by unusual short/large inter event timespans (outliers), than alternatives, such as, Mean Square Error, cf. [23]. Secondly, we apply the activity prediction *accuracy*; using the percentage of correctly predicted next activity executions.

Before each evaluation run the log traces were chronologically ordered based on their first event's timestamp (ascending). Enabling to separate them into training (first 2/3 of the traces) and test data (remaining 1/3). Subsequently, all possible sub traces, $t_{[1,n]}$ where $2 \leq n < |t| - 1$, are generated from the test data and the $(n+1)$th event (activity and timestamp) is predicted. The minimal sub traces length of $\geq 2$ provides a sufficient behaviour base for each prediction task. We are aware that this can potentially result in using information from the *future*, if the training data contains long running traces. However, for the sake of *comparability* with existing work the described approach was applied.

## 4.2 Evaluation Results

Primary tests were applied to identify an appropriate minimum SPR confidence *minc* value for each log and prediction task. For this, potential confidence values, ranging between 0.7 to 0.9, were analyzed. Lower/higher values were not taken into consideration as significant overfitting/underfitting was observed for them.

The achieved evaluation results are summarized in Table 2 (event timestamp prediction) and 3 (activity prediction) – the best result is marked in bold. Overall, the proposed SPR based prediction approach outperforms the state-of-the-art comparison approaches. Throughout the evaluation 64% (BPIC 2012) and 58% (Helpdesk) of the events could be predicted based on SPRs alone, without the need of applying the proposed fallback mechanism. In addition, we compared the correctness of the local prediction approach (fallback, resp. [5]) when the SPR based prediction was applicable. In such cases the SPR based approach predicted 84% of all activities correctly while the fallback approach only achieved 77%.

Accordingly, it can be concluded that the exploitation of global behaviour improves the quality of the prediction results compared to approaches which mainly focus on local behaviour. Nevertheless, given that the proposed fallback mechanism was required regularly it can be assumed that the recorded execution behaviour fluctuates significantly, e.g., because of process drift, cf. [7]. A manual and process mining based inspection of the logs confirmed this observations – which are likely intensified by the long time spans recorded in each log. Future work will explore advanced means to represent global behaviour to address this situation based on clustering, filtering techniques, and extended rule formalisms.

**Table 2.** Evaluation results: Execution event timestamp prediction MAE

| | Timestamp, Mean Absolute Error (MAE) in days | | | | | | |
|---|---|---|---|---|---|---|---|
| | Proposed SPR | Similarity histogram probability [5] | Set abstraction probability [1] | Bag abstraction probability [1] | Sequence abstraction probability [1] | LSTM Neural network [23] | Recurring neural network [23] |
| Helpdesk | 3.37 | 3.54 | 5.83 | 5.74 | 5.67 | 3.75 | 3.98 |
| BPIC 2012 | 1.53 | 1.54 | 1.97 | 1.97 | 1.91 | 1.56 | N.A.[a] |

[a] Results denoted as N.A. are not available as the compared work does not cover the respective log or prediction task during its respective evaluation.

**Table 3.** Evaluation results: Execution event activity prediction accuracy

| | Activity, Prediction Accuracy | | | | | | |
|---|---|---|---|---|---|---|---|
| | Proposed SPR | LSTM neural network [7] | Similarity histogram probability [5] | LSTM neural network [13] | Finite automaton probability [6] | LSTM neural network [23] | Recurring neural network [23] |
| Helpdesk | 0.80 | 0.78 | 0.77 | N.A.[a] | N.A.[a] | 0.71 | 0.66 |
| BPIC 2012 | 0.78 | 0.77 | 0.77 | 0.62 | 0.72 | 0.76 | N.A.[a] |

[a] Results denoted as N.A. are not available as the compared work does not cover the respective log or prediction task during its respective evaluation.

The evaluation shows that the proposed approach is feasible and outperforms a range of comparison approaches. In addition, we found that the generated prediction model can easily be updated if new traces become available or the process model is changed. This is because the prediction model is composed of independent rules which have no relation to each other, such that, existing (e.g., outdated) rules can easily be removed while new rules can be added. This property also results in $M$ becoming more transparent and explainable.

**Baseline:** An additional baseline approach was evaluated. For activity prediction it determines and predicts the most frequent activity for each trace index. Event timestamps are predicted based on the average execution duration between two successive activity executions. The baseline approach achieved an activity accuracy of 0.49 along with a MAE of 1.61 for the BPIC 2012 log.

## 5   Related Work

Existing prediction work can be assigned into four main categories: $a$) predicting the next event [23]; $b$) estimating remaining execution times [23]; $c$) classifying and predicting instance outcomes [9]; and $d$)predicting risks which could hinder successful instance completions [4]. For this work, we assume $a$) as most relevant.

Related work seems not to take the differences between local vs. global prediction techniques into account *explicitly*. When analyzing the applied fundamental techniques, such as, neural networks, (hidden) markov models, support vector machines, and state automata they, by design, apply a fuzzy mixture of local/global prediction techniques/models [8,12,14,15,15,16,23,24]. Hence, they aggregate all behaviour in $L$ into a single prediction model using a single technique which is neither specifically optimized for local nor global prediction. This results in requiring the underling core technology to determine which kind of local/global execution behaviour is relevant for each individual event prediction task.

For this, recent work [7,23], seems to apply a distinct focus on neural network based techniques. Hereby, commonly advanced LSTM networks with multiple hidden layers and up to hundreds of neurons are applied. Such approaches achieve top end prediction quality, see Sect. 4, but imply significant hardware and computation time requirements throughout the prediction model generation/learning phase. For example, [19] used servers with 128GB of memory and multiple high end GPUs. While [23] stated the individual timespan required for a single training iteration as between *"15 and 90 seconds per training iteration"* [23, p. 483] – while frequently hundreds to thousands of iterations are required.

Such lengthy and computation intense training cycles can harden a prediction approaches' application. Especially for flexible, changing (concept drift), and non centralized application scenarios, cf. [11,27]. Such are, for example, observed throughout the application of processes in the Internet of Things [27] or during process executions in the Cloud [11]. Given that each change can result in the need to update all prediction models such volatile scenarios can trigger frequent and lengthy training phases for the neural network based approaches.

Accordingly, we assume LoGos capability to train explainable prediction models within minutes on single-core processors, as advantageous. LoGo gains these advantages by being highly specialized on the data (process execution traces) and the task at hand (activity and temporal prediction). In comparison alternative techniques, such as, neural networks have broader applications (e.g., they support also failure prediction) while these flexibility seems to be connected with higher computational requirements and less explainable models, cf. [2,17].

## 6    Discussion and Outlook

This paper focuses on two challenges $a$) to provide a global prediction approach; $b$) which can be combined with existing local prediction approaches. We conclude that the proposed approach LoGo was able to meet both challenges. Further, this work evaluates the impact of global behaviour on predictions and compares with and even outperforms a number of related state-of-the-art prediction approaches.

Applying the proposed separation of local and global prediction capabilities into two distinct mixable techniques/models enables to choose the most appropriate one for each upcoming prediction task (similar to ensemble learning, cf. [10]). Compared to alternative prediction approaches these separation also results in simpler prediction models, enabling to gain explainable model capabilities, cf. [20]. As prediction models can have a significant impact on an organization we see this as a significant aspect to leverage a decision maker's trust into such predictions and prediction results, cf. [17]. Finally, the task specialization (i.e., process instance activity and timestamp prediction) of the proposed techniques reduces its hardware requirements and complexity in comparison to general purpose techniques, such as, neural networks [2]. Overall, we assume that this eases the proposed approaches' application on today's fluctuating processes.

Future work will *a*) explore advanced representations of global behaviour; and *b*) widen the global behaviour which is taken into account. Hereby, especially the representation of the past behaviour is of relevance as it can become more or less precise. In this work we applied sequential rules for this, as they are well known and generic such that SPRs will less likely struggle with *overfitting*.

# References

1. Van der Aalst, W.M., Schonenberg, M.H., Song, M.: Time prediction based on process mining. Inf. Syst. **36**(2), 450–475 (2011)
2. Appice, A., Mauro, N.D., Malerba, D.: Leveraging shallow machine learning to predict business process behavior. In: Services Computing, SCC 2019, Milan, Italy, 8–13 July 2019, pp. 184–188 (2019)
3. Bauer, E., Kohavi, R.: An empirical comparison of voting classification algorithms: Bagging, boosting, and variants. Mach. Learn. **36**(1–2), 105–139 (1999)
4. van Beest, N.R.T.P., Weber, I.: Behavioral classification of business process executions at runtime. In: Dumas, M., Fantinato, M. (eds.) BPM 2016. LNBIP, vol. 281, pp. 339–353. Springer, Cham (2017). https://doi.org/10.1007/978-3-319-58457-7_25
5. Böhmer, K., Rinderle-Ma, S.: Probability based heuristic for predictive business process monitoring. In: Panetto, H., Debruyne, C., Proper, H.A., Ardagna, C.A., Roman, D., Meersman, R. (eds.) OTM 2018. LNCS, vol. 11229, pp. 78–96. Springer, Cham (2018). https://doi.org/10.1007/978-3-030-02610-3_5
6. Breuker, D., Matzner, M., Delfmann, P., Becker, J.: Comprehensible predictive models for business processes. MIS Q. **40**(4), 1009–1034 (2016)
7. Camargo, M., Dumas, M., González-Rojas, O.: Learning accurate LSTM models of business processes. In: Hildebrandt, T., van Dongen, B.F., Röglinger, M., Mendling, J. (eds.) BPM 2019. LNCS, vol. 11675, pp. 286–302. Springer, Cham (2019). https://doi.org/10.1007/978-3-030-26619-6_19
8. Ceci, M., Lanotte, P.F., Fumarola, F., Cavallo, D.P., Malerba, D.: Completion time and next activity prediction of processes using sequential pattern mining. In: Džeroski, S., Panov, P., Kocev, D., Todorovski, L. (eds.) DS 2014. LNCS (LNAI), vol. 8777, pp. 49–61. Springer, Cham (2014). https://doi.org/10.1007/978-3-319-11812-3_5
9. Conforti, R., Fink, S., Manderscheid, J., Röglinger, M.: PRISM – a predictive risk monitoring approach for business processes. In: La Rosa, M., Loos, P., Pastor, O. (eds.) BPM 2016. LNCS, vol. 9850, pp. 383–400. Springer, Cham (2016). https://doi.org/10.1007/978-3-319-45348-4_22
10. Dietterich, T.G.: Ensemble methods in machine learning. In: Kittler, J., Roli, F. (eds.) MCS 2000. LNCS, vol. 1857, pp. 1–15. Springer, Heidelberg (2000). https://doi.org/10.1007/3-540-45014-9_1
11. Euting, S., Janiesch, C., Fischer, R., Tai, S., Weber, I.: Scalable business process execution in the cloud. In: Cloud Engineering, pp. 175–184. IEEE (2014)

12. Evermann, J., Rehse, J.R., Fettke, P.: Predicting process behaviour using deep learning. Decis. Support Syst. **100**, 129–140 (2017)
13. Evermann, J., Rehse, J.-R., Fettke, P.: A deep learning approach for predicting process behaviour at runtime. In: Dumas, M., Fantinato, M. (eds.) BPM 2016. LNBIP, vol. 281, pp. 327–338. Springer, Cham (2017). https://doi.org/10.1007/978-3-319-58457-7_24
14. Ferilli, S., Esposito, F., Redavid, D., Angelastro, S.: Extended process models for activity prediction. In: Kryszkiewicz, M., Appice, A., Ślęzak, D., Rybinski, H., Skowron, A., Raś, Z.W. (eds.) ISMIS 2017. LNCS (LNAI), vol. 10352, pp. 368–377. Springer, Cham (2017). https://doi.org/10.1007/978-3-319-60438-1_36
15. Francescomarino, C.D., et al.: Predictive process monitoring methods: which one suits me best? In: Business Process Management, pp. 77–93 (2018)
16. Di Francescomarino, C., Ghidini, C., Maggi, F.M., Petrucci, G., Yeshchenko, A.: An eye into the future: leveraging a-priori knowledge in predictive business process monitoring. In: Carmona, J., Engels, G., Kumar, A. (eds.) BPM 2017. LNCS, vol. 10445, pp. 252–268. Springer, Cham (2017). https://doi.org/10.1007/978-3-319-65000-5_15
17. Ghorbani, A., Abid, A., Zou, J.: Interpretation of neural networks is fragile. Artif. Intell. **33**, 3681–3688 (2019)
18. Greco, G., Guzzo, A., Pontieri, L.: Mining taxonomies of process models. Data Knowl. Eng. **67**(1), 74–102 (2008)
19. Lin, L., Wen, L., Wang, J.: Mm-Pred: a deep predictive model for multi-attribute event sequence. In: Data Mining, pp. 118–126. SIAM (2019)
20. Lipton, Z.C.: The mythos of model interpretability. Queue **16**(3), 30:31–30:57 (2018)
21. Ly, L.T., Maggi, F.M., et al.: Compliance monitoring in business processes: Functionalities, application, and tool-support. Inf. Syst. **54**, 209–234 (2015)
22. Mehdiyev, N., et al.: A multi-stage deep learning approach for business process event prediction. In: Business Informatics, vol. 1, pp. 119–128. IEEE (2017)
23. Tax, N., Verenich, I., La Rosa, M., Dumas, M.: Predictive business process monitoring with LSTM neural networks. In: Dubois, E., Pohl, K. (eds.) CAiSE 2017. LNCS, vol. 10253, pp. 477–492. Springer, Cham (2017). https://doi.org/10.1007/978-3-319-59536-8_30
24. Pandey, S., Nepal, S., Chen, S.: A test-bed for the evaluation of business process prediction techniques. In: Collaborative Computing, pp. 382–391. IEEE (2011)
25. Pei, J., et al.: Mining sequential patterns by pattern-growth: the prefixspan approach. Knowl. Data Eng. **16**(11), 1424–1440 (2004)
26. Sheikh, L.M., Tanveer, B., Hamdani, M.: Interesting measures for mining association rules. In: Multitopic Conference, pp. 641–644. IEEE (2004)
27. Žliobaitė, I., Pechenizkiy, M., Gama, J.: An overview of concept drift applications. In: Japkowicz, N., Stefanowski, J. (eds.) Big Data Analysis: New Algorithms for a New Society. SBD, vol. 16, pp. 91–114. Springer, Cham (2016). https://doi.org/10.1007/978-3-319-26989-4_4

# Business Process Variant Analysis Based on Mutual Fingerprints of Event Logs

Farbod Taymouri[1(✉)], Marcello La Rosa[1], and Josep Carmona[2]

[1] The University of Melbourne, Melbourne, Australia
{farbod.taymouri,marcello.larosa}@unimelb.edu.au
[2] Universitat Politècnica de Catalunya, Barcelona, Spain
jcarmona@cs.upc.edu

**Abstract.** Comparing business process variants using event logs is a common use case in process mining. Existing techniques for process variant analysis detect statistically-significant differences between variants at the level of individual entities (such as process activities) and their relationships (e.g. directly-follows relations between activities). This may lead to a proliferation of differences due to the low level of granularity in which such differences are captured. This paper presents a novel approach to detect statistically-significant differences between variants at the level of entire process traces (i.e. sequences of directly-follows relations). The cornerstone of this approach is a technique to learn a directly-follows graph called *mutual fingerprint* from the event logs of the two variants. A mutual fingerprint is a lossless encoding of a set of traces and their duration using discrete wavelet transformation. This structure facilitates the understanding of statistical differences along the control-flow and performance dimensions. The approach has been evaluated using real-life event logs against two baselines. The results show that at a trace level, the baselines cannot always reveal the differences discovered by our approach, or can detect spurious differences.

## 1 Introduction

The complexity of modern organizations leads to the co-existence of different *variants* of the same business process. Process variants may be determined based on different logical drivers, such as brand, product, type of customer, geographic location, as well as performance drivers, e.g. cases that complete on-time vs. cases that are slow.

Identifying and explaining differences between process variants can help not only in the context of process standardization initiatives, but also to identify root causes for performance deviations or compliance violations. For example, in the healthcare domain, two patients with similar diseases might experience different care pathways, even if they are supposed to be treated alike [1,2]. Moreover, even if the care pathways are the same in terms of sequences of activities, they could have different performance, e.g. one patient may be discharged in a much shorter timeframe than the other [3].

© Springer Nature Switzerland AG 2020
S. Dustdar et al. (Eds.): CAiSE 2020, LNCS 12127, pp. 299–318, 2020.
https://doi.org/10.1007/978-3-030-49435-3_19

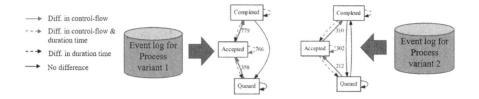

**Fig. 1.** Example of mutual fingerprints for an IT service desk process

Comparing business process variants using process execution data (a.k.a. event logs) recorded by information systems, is a common use case in process mining [4]. Existing techniques for process variant analysis [5,6] detect statistically-significant differences between variants at the level of individual entities (such as process activities) and their relationships (e.g. directly-follows relations between activities). However, these techniques often lead to a proliferation of differences due to the low level of granularity in which such differences are captured.

This paper presents a statistically sound approach for process variant analysis, that examines both the order in which process activities are executed (a.k.a. control-flow) and their duration (a.k.a. performance), using the event logs of two process variants as input. The cornerstone feature of this approach is the ability to provide statistically significant control-flow differences between process variants, via the use of a novel graph-based representation of a process, namely *mutual fingerprint*. The fingerprint of a process variant is a directly-follows graph that only shows the behavior of that variant that is statistically significantly different from that of another process variant, hence the term "mutual". This lossless encoding of differences can be seen as the latent representation of a process variant that provides a considerably simplified representation of the underlying behavior, focusing only on differences. For example, Fig. 1 shows the discovered mutual fingerprints for two example process variants. One can see that the fingerprint of process variant 2 has an extra edge, i.e., *(Queued, Completed)*, that does not appear in the other fingerprint. In a mutual fingerprint graph, different edge types are used to capture differences in the control-flow and activity duration.

The approach to construct mutual fingerprints consists of three steps: i) feature generation, ii) feature selection, and iii) filtering. Given the event log of the two variants, the first step exploits *Discrete Wavelet Transformation* to obtain a lossless encoding of the two variants (along the control-flow and activity duration dimensions) into a set of vectors. The second step adopts a machine learning strategy combined with statistical tests to determine what subset of features, i.e. events, discriminates the two process variants at a given significant level. The third step filters traces of each process variant that do not carry any discriminatory events.

The approach has been evaluated using process variants from four real-life event logs, against two baseline techniques. The comparison includes a quantitative assessment of the results and a discussion on execution time.

The paper is organized as follows. Related work and preliminaries are presented in Sect. 2, and 3 respectively. The approach is presented in Sect. 4, followed by the evaluation in Sect. 5. Finally, Sect. 6 concludes the paper and discusses some avenues for future work.

## 2  Related Work

We report only the most recent approaches related to our contribution. The interested reader can find a complete analysis in [7]. The work by van Beest et al. [8] relies on the product automaton of two event structures to distill all the behavioral differences between two process variants from the respective event logs, and render these differences to end users via textual explanations. Cordes et al. [9] discover two process models and their differences are defined as the minimum number of operations that transform on model to the other. This work was extended in [10] to compare process variants using annotated transition systems. Similarly, [11] creates a difference model between two input process models to represent differences. Pini et al. [12] contribute a visualization technique that compares two discovered process models in terms of performance data. The work in [13] proposes an extension of this work, by considering a normative process model alongside with event logs as inputs, and adding more data preparation facilities. Similarly, [14] develops visualisation techniques to provide targeted analysis of resource reallocation and activity rescheduling.

Particularly relevant to our approach are the works by Bolt et al. and Nguyen et al., because they are grounded on statistical significance. Bolt et al. [15] use an annotated transition system to highlight the differences between process variants. The highlighted parts only show different dominant behaviors that are statistically significant with respect to edge frequencies. This work was later extended in [5], by inducting decision trees for performance data among process variants. Nguyen et al. [6] encode process variants into *Perspective Graphs*. The comparison of perspective graphs results in a *Differential Graph*, which is a graph that contains common nodes and edges, and also nodes and edges that appear in one perspective graph only. As shown in the evaluation carried out in this paper, these two works, while relying on statistical tests, may lead to a proliferation of differences due to the low level in which such differences are captured (individual activities or activity relations). Our approach lifts these limitations by extracting entire control-flow paths or performance differences that constitute statistically significant differences between the two process variants.

## 3  Preliminaries

In this section we introduce preliminary definitions required to describe our approach such as event, trace, event log and process variant. Next, we provide some basic linear algebra definitions that will be specifically used for our featuring encoding.

**Definition 1 (Event, Trace, Event Log).** *An event is a tuple* $(a, c, t, (d_1, v_1),$ $\ldots, (d_m, v_m))$ *where* $a$ *is the activity name,* $c$ *is the case id,* $t$ *is the timestamp and* $(d_1, v_1), \ldots, (d_m, v_m)$ *(where* $m \geq 0$*) are the event or case attributes and their values. A trace is a non-empty sequence* $\sigma = e_1, \ldots, e_n$ *of events such that* $\forall i, j \in [1..n]\ e_i.c = e_j.c$. *An event log* $L$ *is a set* $\sigma_1, \ldots \sigma_n$ *of traces.*

**Definition 2 (Process variant).** *An event log* $L$ *can be partitioned into a finite set of groups called process variants* $\varsigma_1, \varsigma_2, \ldots, \varsigma_n$, *such that* $\exists d$ *such that* $\forall$ $\varsigma_k$ *and* $\forall \sigma_i, \sigma_j \in \varsigma_k$, $\sigma_i.d = \sigma_j.d$.

The above definition of a process variant emphasizes that process executions in the same group must have the same value for a given attribute, and each process execution belongs only to one process variant[1].

**Definition 3 (Vector).** *A vector,* $\mathbf{x} = (x_1, x_2, \ldots, x_n)^T$, *is a column array of elements where the ith element is shown by* $x_i$. *If each element is in* $\mathbb{R}$ *and vector contains* $n$ *elements, then the vector lies in* $\mathbb{R}^{n \times 1}$, *and the dimension of* $\mathbf{x}$, *dim*$(\mathbf{x})$, *is* $n \times 1$.

We represent a set of $d$ vectors as $\mathbf{x}^{(1)}, \mathbf{x}^{(2)}, \ldots, \mathbf{x}^{(d)}$, where $x^{(i)} \in \mathbb{R}^{n \times 1}$. Also, they can be represented by a matrix $\mathbf{M} = (\mathbf{x}^{(1)}, \mathbf{x}^{(2)}, \ldots, \mathbf{x}^{(d)})$ where $\mathbf{M} \in \mathbb{R}^{n \times d}$. We denote the *ith* row of a matrix by $\mathbf{M}_{i,:}$, and likewise the *ith* column by $\mathbf{M}_{:,i}$. The previous definitions can be extended for a set of columns or rows, for example if $R = \{3, 5, 9\}$ and $C = \{1, 4, 6, 12\}$, then $\mathbf{M}_{R,C}$ returns the indicated rows and columns.

**Definition 4 (Vector space).** *A vector space consists of a set* $V$ *of vectors, a field* $\mathbb{F}$ *(*$\mathbb{R}$ *for real numbers), and two operations* $+, \times$ *with the following properties,* $\forall \mathbf{u}, \mathbf{v} \in V, \mathbf{u} + \mathbf{v} \in V$, *and* $\forall c \in F, \forall \mathbf{v} \in V, c \times \mathbf{v} \in V$.

**Definition 5 (Basis vectors).** *A set* $B$ *of vectors in a vector space* $V$ *is called a basis, if every element of* $V$ *can be written as a finite linear combination of elements of* $B$. *The coefficients of this linear combination are referred to as coordinates on* $B$ *of the vector.*

A set $B$ of basis vectors is called *orthonormal*, if $\forall \mathbf{u}, \mathbf{v} \in B, < \mathbf{u}^T, \mathbf{v} >= 0$, and $\|\mathbf{u}\|_2 = 1$, $\|\mathbf{v}\|_2 = 1$. A *basis matrix* is a matrix whose columns are basis vectors.

For example, the set of $\mathbf{e}^{(1)} = (0, 0, 0, 1)^T$, $\mathbf{e}^{(2)} = (0, 0, 1, 0)^T$, $\mathbf{e}^{(3)} = (0, 1, 0, 0)^T$, and $\mathbf{e}^{(4)} = (1, 0, 0, 0)^T$ constitutes a vector space in $\mathbb{R}^4$. Also, they are orthonormal basis vectors in $\mathbb{R}^4$, since every vector in that space can be represented by finite combination of them, for example, $(1, 2, -3, 4)^T = 1 \times \mathbf{e}^{(4)} + 2 \times \mathbf{e}^{(3)} - 3 \times \mathbf{e}^{(2)} + 4 \times \mathbf{e}^{(1)}$. The set of $\mathbf{e}^{(1)}, \mathbf{e}^{(2)}, \mathbf{e}^{(3)}$, and $\mathbf{e}^{(4)}$ are linearly independent. The corresponding basis matrix, called *canonical basis matrix*, is $\mathbf{E} = (\mathbf{e}^{(1)}, \mathbf{e}^{(2)}, \mathbf{e}^{(3)}, \mathbf{e}^{(4)})$.

---

[1] Definition 2 can be easily generalized to more than one attribute, and arbitrary comparisons.

# 4  Proposed Approach

Process variant analysis can help business analysts to find *why* and *how* two business process variants, each represented by a set of process executions, differ from each other. In this paper we focus on statistically identifying the differences of two process variants, either in the control flow or in the performance dimension. For instance, we are interested in identifying which sequences of activities occur more frequently in one process variant, or which activity has a statistically significant difference in duration between the two process variants.

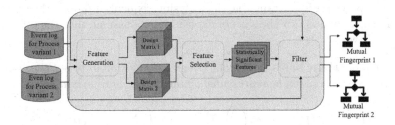

**Fig. 2.** Approach for constructing mutual fingerprints

Given the event logs of two process variants, our approach revolves around the construction of a representative directly-follows graph from each variant, called *mutual fingerprint*. A fingerprint highlights the statistically-significant differences between the two variants, along the control-flow and activity duration dimensions. To construct such mutual fingerprints, we perform the following three steps, as shown in Fig. 2:

1. **Feature generation:** This step encodes every single trace of the input event log of each of the two process variants, into a set of vectors of the same length for every event. Each vector contains the respective wavelet coefficients for a specific event. Essentially, a wavelet coefficient is an encoding of the time series behind each trace. For a trace, these vectors are stacked into a single vector. This way allows the encoding of a process variant as a matrix, called *design matrix*, which is used in the next step.
2. **Feature selection:** In this step, the wavelet coefficients are used to build features to train a binary classifier. This procedure can be repeated several times for cross-validation purposes, and a statistical test is performed on top of the results of cross-validation, to ensure that the selected features (events classes in the log) provide enough information to discriminate the two classes arising from the two process variants.
3. **Filtering:** This last step filters the log of each process variant by keeping only those traces that contain discriminatory events discovered from the previous stage. A mutual fingerprint is then built from the traces left for each process variant log.

In the rest of this section, we first formally define the notion of discrete wavelet transformation and then use this to illustrate the above three steps in detail.

## 4.1  Discrete Wavelet Transformation and Time-Series Encoding

In Sect. 3 we defined a vector space, however, it must be noted that for an arbitrary vector space, there are infinitely number of basis matrices where one can be obtained from the others by a linear transformation [16]. Among several basis matrices, *Haar basis* matrix is one of the most important set of basis matrix in $\mathbb{R}^n$ that plays an important role in analysing sequential data [17]. Formally, it is defined as follows (for the sake of exposition lets assume that the dimension is power of two):

**Definition 6 (Haar basis matrix).** *Given a dimension of power two, i.e., $2^n$, the Haar basis matrix can be represented by the following recurrent equation [18]:*

$$\mathbf{H}(n) = \left( \mathbf{H}(n-1) \otimes \begin{pmatrix} 1 \\ 1 \end{pmatrix}, \mathbf{I}(n-1) \otimes \begin{pmatrix} 1 \\ -1 \end{pmatrix} \right), \quad \mathbf{H}(0) = 1 \qquad (1)$$

*where $\mathbf{H}(n)$ is the matrix of Haar vectors of degree $2^n$, $\mathbf{I}(n)$ is an identity matrix of size $2^n$, and $\otimes$ is the outer-product operator.*

Haar basis vectors can be derived for dimensions of arbitrary lengths that are not necessarily to be power of two, however, the recurrent formula becomes more complicated [19]. A few examples of Haar basis matrices are as follows:

$$\mathbf{H}(1) = \begin{pmatrix} 1 & 1 \\ 1 & -1 \end{pmatrix}, \quad \mathbf{H}(2) = \begin{pmatrix} 1 & 1 & 1 & 0 \\ 1 & 1 & -1 & 0 \\ 1 & -1 & 0 & 1 \\ 1 & -1 & 0 & -1 \end{pmatrix}$$

From now on, we show a Haar basis matrix by $\mathbf{H}$ whenever the corresponding dimension is understood from the context.

**Definition 7 (Time-series data [20]).** *A time series $\{x_t\}$, is a sequence of observations on a variable taken at discrete intervals in time. We index the time periods as $1, 2, ..., k$. Given a set of time periods, $\{x_t\}$ is shown as a column vector $\mathbf{x} = (x_1, ..., x_k)^T$ or a sequence $x_1 x_2 ... x_k$.*

Every time-series data can be decomposed into a set of basis time-series called *Haar Wavelet* [21]. A Haar wavelet time-series represents the temporal range of variation in the form of a simple step function. For a given time-series, $\{x_i\}$, of length $n$, the corresponding Haar wavelet basis time-series are shown by Haar basis vectors in $\mathbb{R}^n$ [19], see Definition 6. For example, consider a time-series like $\mathbf{x} = (3, 5, 9, 1)^T$, then it can be decomposed into the sets of Haar wavelet time-series shown in Fig. 3.

In the above example, one sees that each Haar wavelet time-series has a corresponding Haar basis vector. Thus, the input time-series, $\mathbf{x}$, can be represented as the sum of Haar basis vectors with corresponding coefficients. More compactly, it can be easily represented by the following matrix operation, called *Discrete Wavelet Transformation* (DWT):

$$\mathbf{x} = \mathbf{Hw} \tag{2}$$

where $\mathbf{w}$ is a column vector that contains wavelet coefficients. For the above example, Eq. 2 is as follow:

$$\begin{pmatrix} 3 \\ 5 \\ 9 \\ 1 \end{pmatrix} = \begin{pmatrix} 1 & 1 & 1 & 0 \\ 1 & 1 & -1 & 0 \\ 1 & -1 & 0 & 1 \\ 1 & -1 & 0 & -1 \end{pmatrix} \begin{pmatrix} 4.5 \\ -0.5 \\ -1 \\ 4 \end{pmatrix}$$

The crucial observation, is that for a given time-series, the set of Wavelet coefficients show available variations in the time-series at different resolutions. The first coefficient is the global average value of time-series, i.e., $w_1 = \frac{3+5+9+1}{4} = 4.5$. The second coefficient shows the difference in average between the average of the first half and the average of the second half, i.e., $\frac{(5+3)/2 - (1+9)/2}{2} = -0.5$. This process can be applied recursively until reaching a single element. Hence, one can use Wavelet coefficients as a sound way to encode time-series that inherit variability information.

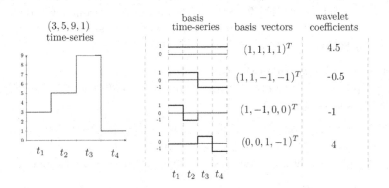

**Fig. 3.** Decomposition of a time-series into a set of Haar Wavelet series

## 4.2   Feature Generation

The technique in this section generates a sets of multidimensional features, $\mathbf{x}$, for every trace $\sigma$. The procedure can be seen as an encoding task that maps a trace into a multidimensional vector space. This encoding is used to identify both control-flow and performance differences between two process variants. For the sake of simplicity we present it for control-flow dimension.

The technique in this section provides numerous advantages for analysing sequential data. It is a *lossless* encoding such that the input time-series can be recovered by the Haar basis matrix for that vector space, see Eq. (2). Second, by DWT-encoding the time-series before analysing it, well-known problems of *auto-correlation* and *cross-correlation* are significantly alleviated, since the generated features are almost uncorrelated [21,22]. Thus, without losing information one can safely work only with wavelet coefficients rather than over the raw data.

Given an input trace, the proposed technique contains three parts, i.e., *binarization*, *vectorization*, and *stacking*. Binarization is a procedure to generate a set of time-series from an input trace. Vectorization encodes every time-series into a vector representation with the help of DWT. Finally, to have a consolidated representation for the generated vectors, they are stacked into a single vector.

The starting point for generating a set of features in a vector space is to represent an input trace as several $\{0,1\}$ time-series that are called binarization. Formally:

**Definition 8 (Binarization).** *Given a universal set of activity names $\mathcal{E}$, and trace $\sigma$, function $f()$ maps $\sigma$ into a set of $|\mathcal{E}|$ time-series of length $|\sigma|$, i.e., $\forall e_i \in \mathcal{E}, f : (e_i, \sigma) \rightarrow \{0,1\}^{|\sigma|}$.*

The above definition provides time-series of zeros for an event that does not exist in an input trace. This way one can represent all traces in a unique vector space[2]. For example, consider a trace like $\sigma = e_1 e_2 e_1 e_1$, with $\mathcal{E} = \{e_1, e_2, e_3\}$, then, $f(e_1, \sigma) = 1011$, $f(e_2, \sigma) = 0100$, and $f(e_3, \sigma) = 0000$.

Binarization of a given trace provides a time-series for each event of it. Vectorization based on DWT, see Eq. 2, captures simultaneously frequency and location in time information, and embeds auto-correlation and cross-correlation information in the generated features. Formally:

**Definition 9 (Vectorization).** *Given a time-series $\mathbf{x} = (x_1, x_2, \ldots, x_n)^T$ where $x_i \in \{0,1\}$, function $g()$, computes the corresponding wavelet coefficients, $\mathbf{w}$, for $\mathbf{x}$, i.e., $g(\mathbf{x}) = \mathbf{w} = \mathbf{H}^{-1}\mathbf{x}$.*

In the above definition, $\mathbf{H}^{-1}$ is the inverse of Haar basis matrix for $\mathbb{R}^n$. For example, for time-series $\mathbf{x}^{(1)} = (1,0,1,1)^T$, $\mathbf{x}^{(2)} = (0,1,0,0)^T$, and $\mathbf{x}^{(3)} = (0,0,0,0)^T$ the corresponding wavelet coefficients $\mathbf{w}^{(1)}$, $\mathbf{w}^{(2)}$, and $\mathbf{w}^{(3)}$ are as follows:

$$\underbrace{\begin{pmatrix} 0.75 \\ -0.25 \\ 0.5 \\ 0 \end{pmatrix}}_{\mathbf{w}^{(1)}} = \underbrace{\begin{pmatrix} 0.25 & 0.25 & 0.25 & 0.25 \\ 0.25 & 0.25 & -0.25 & -0.25 \\ 0.5 & -0.5 & 0 & 0 \\ 0 & 0 & 0.5 & -0.5 \end{pmatrix}}_{\mathbf{H}^{-1}} \underbrace{\begin{pmatrix} 1 \\ 0 \\ 1 \\ 1 \end{pmatrix}}_{\mathbf{x}^{(1)}}, \underbrace{\begin{pmatrix} 0.25 \\ -0.25 \\ -0.5 \\ 0 \end{pmatrix}}_{\mathbf{w}^{(2)}}, \underbrace{\begin{pmatrix} 0 \\ 0 \\ 0 \\ 0 \end{pmatrix}}_{\mathbf{w}^{(3)}}$$

---

[2] In practice we keep only non-zero elements in the implementation.

According to the above example, for a trace like $\sigma = e_1 e_2 e_1 e_1$, to have a consolidate representation we stack together the coefficient vectors into a single vector, formally:

**Definition 10 (Vector stacking).** *For an input trace $\sigma$, and universal of activities $\mathcal{E}$, with $|\mathcal{E}| = k$, lets assume that $\mathbf{w}^{(1)}, \mathbf{w}^{(2)}, \ldots, \mathbf{w}^{(k)}$ show the corresponding wavelet coefficients vectors, then the stacked vector is defined as $\mathbf{w}^{(\sigma)} = (\mathbf{w}^{(1)^T}, \mathbf{w}^{(2)^T}, \ldots, \mathbf{w}^{(k)^T})$.*

Regarding to the above definition, a design matrix $\mathbf{D}$ for a process variant is defined to be a matrix whose rows are the stacked vectors of the corresponding traces. As an example for a process variant containing only two traces, i.e., $\sigma_1 = e_1 e_2 e_1 e_1$, and $\sigma_2 = e_1 e_2 e_3 e_1$, the respective design matrix after binarization, vectorization, and stacking is as follow:

$$\mathbf{D} = \begin{array}{c} \\ \mathbf{w}^{(\sigma_1)} \\ \mathbf{w}^{(\sigma_2)} \end{array} \begin{array}{cccccccccccc} e_1 & e_1 & e_1 & e_1 & e_2 & e_2 & e_2 & e_2 & e_3 & e_3 & e_3 & e_3 \\ \left( \begin{array}{cccccccccccc} 0.75 & -0.25 & 0.5 & 0 & 0.25 & -0.25 & -0.5 & 0 & 0 & 0 & 0 & 0 \\ 0.5 & -0.25 & 0 & 0 & 0.25 & -0.25 & -0.5 & 0 & 0.25 & -0.25 & 0 & 0.5 \end{array} \right) \end{array}$$

One can see that the first four columns show the wavelet coefficients for event $e_1$, the second four columns show the wavelet coefficients for event $e_2$, and so on. It is easy to see that wavelet coefficients for $e_2$ are the same for $\sigma_1$ and $\sigma_2$; however for $e_1$ only three out of four coefficients are equal which shows different frequency and location of this event between $\sigma_1$ and $\sigma_2$.

In practice, to have a unique and common vector space for the encoding of two process variants, we set the dimension of the vector space to the length of the longest trace for both variants. If the alphabet of process variants are different then the union of them is considered as the universal alphabet. Also, an analyst can generate different kind of features; for example one can create a design matrix for adjacent events in traces, where the features are like $e_i e_j$, with $j = i + 1$, instead of only single events.

**Time Complexity.** The time complexity of the proposed approach is cubic on the length of the longest trace in the worst-case. However, in practice it is much less than this amount: lets assume that there are two process variants $\varsigma_1, \varsigma_2$ with $n_1, n_2$ number of traces respectively, $\mathcal{E}$, is the universal activity names, and $d = \max|\sigma|, \forall \sigma \in \varsigma_1, \varsigma_2$, is the length of the longest trace between variants. Thus, computing the Haar basis matrix and its inverse for $\mathbb{R}^d$ require $\mathcal{O}(log_2 d)$, and $\mathcal{O}(d^3)^3$ operations respectively. It must be mentioned that [23] proposed $\mathcal{O}(d^2)$ for computing the inverse of a matrix in an incremental way. To create the design matrix $\mathbf{D}^{(i)}$, for $i = 1, 2$, the number of required operations is $\mathcal{O}(n_i * (d * \mathcal{E}))$. However, this matrix is very sparse since for an input trace $\sigma$, only the entries related to $e_i \in \sigma$ are non-zero. Another possibility to alleviate significantly the overall complexity is by precomputing and storing Haar matrices.

---

[3] Note that the cubic complexity is the required time for computing the inverse matrix from scratch. To this end, there are much more efficient approaches like Coppersmith–Winograd algorithm with $\mathcal{O}(d^{2.37})$.

## 4.3   Feature Selection

This section presents a novel feature selection method, grounded on machine learning, that captures the statistically significant features between two design matrices, i.e., $\mathbf{D}^{(i)}$, for $i = 1, 2$. Generally speaking, the representation of an entity in an arbitrary vector space contains a set of *relevant* and *irrelevant* features. Though, it is unknown as prior knowledge. Thus, a feature selection algorithm is the process of selecting a subset of relevant features that are the most informative ones with respect to the class label.

Though feature selection procedures have numerous advantages for machine learning algorithms, in this paper, we leverage the idea of feature selection to highlight the existing differences between two process variants (class 1 and class 2). It must be stressed that every events $e_i \in \mathcal{E}$ is represented by a set of features (columns) in the designed matrices, see Definition 10, and each row is called an instance. The feature selection technique in this paper is a *wrapper* method, where a classifier is trained on a subset of features. If the trained classifier provides acceptable performance according to some criteria for unseen instances, i.e., test instances, then the subset of features is selected and called *discriminatory* features.

Before proceeding, and for the sake of exposition we stack the design matrices $\mathbf{D}^{(1)}, \mathbf{D}^{(2)}$, with the corresponding class labels into a matrix called *augmented design matrix* as follow:

$$\mathbf{X} = \begin{pmatrix} \mathbf{D}^{(1)} & \mathbf{1} \\ \mathbf{D}^{(2)} & \mathbf{2} \end{pmatrix} \tag{3}$$

Where $\mathbf{1}, \mathbf{2}$ are column vectors showing the class labels. It is clear that $\mathbf{X}$ has $d \times \mathcal{E} + 1$ features or columns. From $\mathbf{X}$, and for a subset of features, $\mathcal{S} \subseteq \mathcal{E}$, we split $\mathbf{X}$ into training and test datasets and denote them by $\mathbf{X}^{(train)}_{:,\mathcal{S}}$, and $\mathbf{X}^{(test)}_{:,\mathcal{S}}$. It must be mentioned that, to create training and test datasets we use *stratified sampling* method which keeps the proportion of classes similar in either datasets [24]. Stratified sampling helps to create sub-samples that are representative of the initial dataset.

**Definition 11 (Discriminatory feature).** *A subset of features, $\mathcal{S}$, with $|\mathcal{S}| \leq d \times \mathcal{E} + 1$ is discriminatory if a binary classification function $f : \mathbb{R}^{|\mathcal{S}|} \rightarrow \{1, 2\}$ that is trained on $\mathbf{X}^{(train)}_{:,\mathcal{S}}$, provides acceptable performance according to some criteria for unseen instances in $\mathbf{X}^{(test)}_{:,\mathcal{S}}$.*

Definition 11 does not pose any restrictions on the shape or the number of parameters for $f()$, indeed, according to *universal approximation theorem* there exist such a mapping function between any two finite-dimensional vector spaces given enough data [25].

There are several ways to measure the performance of a classifier on unseen instances. An appropriate metric for imbalanced classes is $F_1$ score. It measures the performance of a classifier for one of classes only, e.g., class 1 or positive class, and does not take into account the true negatives, i.e., correct predictions for the other class into account, hence some information are missed [26]. Since in our setting two classes (i.e., process variants) are equally important, and for each subset of features the proportion of class labels varies, and probably imbalanced, we propose *weighted* $F_1$ score as follow:

$$\bar{F}_1 = \gamma_1 F_1^{(1)} + \gamma_2 F_1^{(2)} \tag{4}$$

Where $F_1^{(i)}$, for $i = 1, 2$ shows the $F_1$ obtained by the classifier for classes (i.e., 1, 2) on $\mathbf{X}_{:,S}^{(test)}$. The coefficients $\gamma_1$, $\gamma_2$ shows the proportion of class labels in the test dataset. It must be noted that the values of $\gamma_1$ and $\gamma_2$ varies for different subset of features. For example, assume that $\mathbf{X}^{(test)}$ contains three instances as shown below:

$$\mathbf{X}^{(test)} = \begin{array}{c} \\ \mathbf{w}^{(\sigma_1)} \\ \mathbf{w}^{(\sigma_2)} \\ \mathbf{w}^{(\sigma_3)} \end{array} \begin{pmatrix} \begin{array}{ccccccccccc|c} e_1 & \cdots & \cdots & e_1 & e_2 & \cdots & \cdots & e_2 & e_3 & \cdots & \cdots & e_3 & class \\ 0.75 & -0.25 & 0.5 & 0 & 0.25 & -0.25 & -0.5 & 0 & 0 & 0 & 0 & 0 & 1 \\ 0.5 & -0.25 & 0 & 0 & 0.25 & -0.25 & -0.5 & 0 & 0.25 & -0.25 & 0 & 0.5 & 1 \\ 0.25 & -0.25 & -0.5 & 0 & 0 & 0 & 0 & 0 & 0.75 & -0.25 & 0.5 & 0 & 2 \end{array} \end{pmatrix}$$

The test dataset corresponds to the wavelet coefficients for three traces $\sigma_1 = e_1 e_2 e_1 e_1$, $\sigma_2 = e_1 e_2 e_3 e_1$, and $\sigma_3 = e_3 e_1 e_3 e_3$, where the first two traces belong to one process variant (class 1), and the last trace comes from another process variant (class 2). One can see that if we consider $S$ as the columns related to $e_1$, then the proportion of classes are $\frac{2}{3}$ and $\frac{1}{3}$, however for columns related to $e_3$ both numbers are $\frac{1}{2}$. The reason is, an arbitrary trace $\sigma_i$ contains portion of alphabet $\mathcal{E}$, hence the coefficients $\gamma$ vary from subset to subset, and must be adjusted dynamically.

For a subset of features, $S$, the worst performance of a classifier, $f()$, happens when it provides a single label for all test instances. It takes place when there is not enough information in $S$ for the classifier to discriminate classes (process variants). In more details, if $n_1$, and $n_2$ show the number of instances for each class in $\mathbf{X}_{:,S}^{(test)}$, then the worst performance happens when $f()$ labels all test instances as class 1 ($F_1^{(1)} = \frac{2n_1}{n_2 + 2n_1}$), or as class 2 ($F_1^{(2)} = \frac{2n_2}{n_1 + 2n_2}$), therefore we denote the worst performance of classifier $f()$ by $\bar{F}_1^{(0)}$, that is defined as the weighted average of worst cases as follows:

$$\bar{F}_1^{(0)} = \underbrace{\frac{n_1}{n_1 + n_2}}_{\gamma_1} \times \underbrace{\frac{2n_1}{n_2 + 2n_1}}_{F_1^{(1)}} + \underbrace{\frac{n_2}{n_1 + n_2}}_{\gamma_2} \times \underbrace{\frac{2n_2}{n_1 + 2n_2}}_{F_1^{(2)}} \tag{5}$$

One must note that the value of $\bar{F}_1^{(0)}$ like coefficients $\gamma_1$ and $\gamma_2$ varies for different $S$; thus it is adjusted dynamically.

Regarding Eq. 5, for a subset of features, $S$, we define acceptable performance for a classification function $f()$ if its performance measured by $\bar{F}_1$ score, is statistically greater than the corresponding $\bar{F}_1^{(0)}$ score at some significant level $\alpha$. Formally, we formulate a statistical test containing the following hypotheses:

$$\underbrace{H_0 : \bar{F}_1 = \bar{F}_1^{(0)}}_{\text{Null-hypothesis}}, \qquad \underbrace{H_1 : \bar{F}_1 > \bar{F}_1^{(0)}}_{\text{Alternative-hypothesis}} \tag{6}$$

The null-hypothesis ($H_0$) in Eq. 6 assumes that for a subset of features $\mathcal{S}$, the classifier $f()$ is unable to discriminate test instances; in other words if $\mathcal{S}$ represents columns relating to a set of events, then, it claims that the control-flows containing these events are not statistically different between process variants, whereas the alternative-hypothesis ($H_1$) claims they differ.

To make the statistical test in Eq. 6 work, we invoke *stratified k-fold cross-validation* procedure to measure the performance of the classifier $k$ times for $\mathcal{S}$. In each round of cross-validation, different training and test datasets, $\mathbf{X}_{:,\mathcal{S}}^{(train)}$, and $\mathbf{X}_{:,\mathcal{S}}^{(test)}$ are obtained via stratified sampling method, and the corresponding $\bar{F}_1$ score is calculated. Based on *Central Limit Theorem* (CLT), the average of $\bar{F}_1$ scores ($k$ times) approximates a normal distribution for $k > 30$ or a $t-$distribution for small $k$ numbers [27].

**Complexity.** In practice, a feature selection algorithm has to do an exhaustive search to obtain subsets of features that are representative of the input dataset. In general, given $n$ features there could be $2^n$ candidates for selecting subset of features; however in our setting, the search space is limited to subsets of adjacent features available in process variants. Therefore the respective search space reduces drastically.

### 4.4 Filtering

This section elucidates the findings of the previous step. In fact, identifying discriminatory events, though statistically significant, does not provide enough insights for the analyst to understand the existing differences. To bring this information into a human-readable form, one can create a directly-follows graph for each process variant by only considering those traces that carry information about discriminatory parts. Technically, assume $\mathcal{S}$ contains features relating to event $e_i$, and it was found to be statistically significant between two process variants, then all traces containing $e_i$ are kept. This procedure continues for all discriminatory elements (an event or a set of them). A *mutual fingerprint* is a directly-follows graph created based on these sets of traces for each process variant separately.

## 5    Evaluation

We implemented our approach in Python 2.7 and used this prototype tool to evaluate the approach over different real-life datasets, against two baselines [5,6]. As discussed in Sect. 4.3, the proposed feature selection approach can be coupled with any classifier. We trained a Support Vector Machine (SVM) with Radial Basis Function (RBF) kernel and ten times stratified cross validation of the results. We used SVM with RBF because it has been shown that this machine learning method deals well with sparse design matrices [21], like those that we build for the process variants in our datasets (a great portion of entries in these matrices are zero). The experiments were conducted on a machine with an Intel Core i7 CPU, 16 GB of RAM and MS Windows 10.

## 5.1  Setup and Datasets

Table 1 provides descriptive statistics for the four real-life event logs that we used in our experiments. We obtained these datasets from the "4TU Data Center" public repository [28]. The logs cover different processes: road traffic fine management process at an Italian municipality (RTFM log), flow of patients affected by sepsis infection (SEPSIS), IT incident and problem management at Volvo (BPIC13), and permit request at different Dutch municipalities (BPIC15). For each log, we established two process variants on the basis of the value of an attribute (e.g. in the case of the RTFM log, this is the amount of the fine, while in the case of SEPSIS this is the patient's age), in line with [6]. The attributes used to determine the variants, and their values, are also reported in Table 1. As we can see from the table, each log has class imbalance (one variant is much more frequent than the other). Due to lack of space, in the rest of this section we focus on the RFTM log only. The interested reader can find the results for all four logs online.[4]

**Table 1.** Datasets and corresponding process variants [28]

| Event log | | | | | | |
|---|---|---|---|---|---|---|
| Event log | Process Variant | Cases (uni.) | $|\sigma|_{min}$ | $|\sigma|_{max}$ | $|\sigma|_{avg}$ | $|Events|$ (uni.) |
| RTFM | 1) Fine's amount $\geq 50$ | 21243 (159) | 2 | 20 | 4 | 91499 (11) |
| | 2) Fine's amount $< 50$ | 129127 (169) | 2 | 11 | 4 | 469971 (11) |
| SEPSIS | 1) Patient's age $\geq 70$ | 678 (581) | 3 | 185 | 15 | 10243 (16) |
| | 2) Patient's age $\leq 35$ | 76 (51) | 3 | 52 | 9 | 701 (12) |
| BPIC13 | 1) Organization $= A_2$ | 553 (141) | 2 | 53 | 8 | 4221 (3) |
| | 2) Organization $= C$ | 4417 (611) | 1 | 50 | 7 | 29122 (4) |
| BPIC15 | 1) Municipality $= 1$ | 1199 (1170) | 2 | 62 | 33.1 | 36705 (146) |
| | 2) Municipality $= 2$ | 831 (828) | 1 | 96 | 38.6 | 32017 (134) |

Figure 4 shows the directly-follows graph (a.k.a. process map) for the two process variants of the RTFM log: the first one, obtained from the sublog relative to fines greater than or equal to 50 EUR, the other obtained from the sublog relative to fines lower than 50 EUR. Process maps are the common output of automated process discovery techniques. To aid the comparison between process variants, the arcs of process maps can be enhanced with frequency or duration statistics, such as case frequency or average duration. Yet, even with such enhancements, when the graphs are dense like those in Fig. 4, identifying control-flow or duration differences between the two variants becomes impracticable. Accordingly, the main objective of our evaluation is to use our approach and the two baselines to answer the following research question:

– *RQ1: What are the key differences in the control flow of the two process variants?*

---

[4] https://doi.org/10.6084/m9.figshare.10732556.v1.

After we have identified these key differences, we can enrich the results with an analysis of the differences in activity duration, leading to our second research question:

– *RQ2: What are the key differences in the activity durations of the two process variants?*

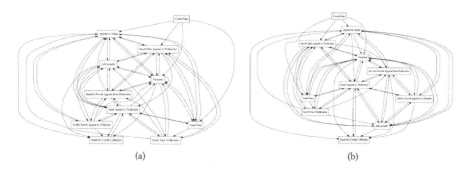

**Fig. 4.** Directly-follows graph of the two process variants of the RFTM log: (a) Fine's amount $\geq 50$; (b) Fine's amount $< 50$

To answer RQ1, we apply our approach by considering which pair of adjacent events, called an edge, i.e., $e_i e_{i+1}$ is selected as a discriminatory edge. We consider only edges that are available in process variants. An edge shows the finest control-flow unit. Next, to answer RQ2, we include an additional analysis to examine whether the average duration time for an edge varies significantly between process variants. Essentially RQ2 boils down to running a statistical test between the corresponding average duration times of the same edge in the two variants.

### 5.2    Results

Table 2 shows the edges in the two directly-follows graphs of Fig. 4 that are statistically significantly different both in frequency and in time (i.e. the temporal order of execution within a path of the graph), as obtained by our approach.

Table 2 also contains the classifier's performance, measured by $\bar{F}_1$. For each edge, this score is statistically greater (averaged from ten times cross-validation) than the corresponding worst case, $\bar{F}_1^{\,0}$, see Eq. 5. Besides, we note that the coefficients $\gamma_1$ and $\gamma_2$ vary for each edge. This shows that the proportion of class labels vary for each edge. The two baselines [5,6] cannot provide such results. It is because they only consider the relative frequency of an edge in each process variant, and apply a statistical test on such frequencies, and neglect the *order* in which such edge occurs within a path of the directly-follows graph. Thereby, they miss to capture the backward and forward information in a trace (or path in the directly-follows graph) containing that edge.

**Table 2.** Significantly-different edges in frequency and order, between the directly-follows graphs of Fig. 4, obtained with our approach

| Edge | $\gamma_1$ | $\gamma_2$ | $\bar{F_1}^0$ | $\bar{F_1}$ | P-value |
|------|-----------|-----------|---------------|-------------|---------|
| ('Add penalty', 'Payment') | 0.17 | 0.83 | 0.18 | 0.35 | 0.009 |
| ('Payment', 'Payment') | 0.19 | 0.81 | 0.20 | 0.38 | 0.006 |
| ('Payment', 'Send for Credit Collection') | 0.23 | 0.77 | 0.22 | 0.34 | 0.006 |

Figure 5 shows the mutual fingerprints resulting from the edges in Table 2. For comparison purposes, Fig. 6 shows two annotated directly-follows graphs obtained with the baseline in [5].[5]

For ease of discussion, let us neglect the type of edge (solid, dashed) in Fig. 5. The edges in Table 2 are highlighted in red in Fig. 5. In effect, traces that contain a discriminatory edge, like *(Payment, Send for Credit Collection)* differ between process variants. An offender whose fine's amount is greater than or equal to 50 Euros goes through more steps, i.e. through a different control flow as shown in Fig. 5(a). In contrast, an offender whose fine's amount is below 50 Euros, goes to less steps, as in Fig. 5(b).

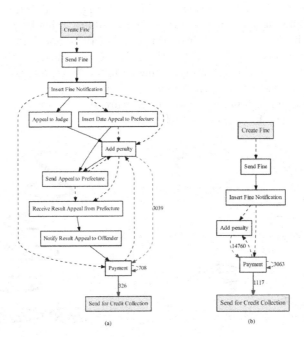

**Fig. 5.** Answer to RQ1: Discovered mutual fingerprints for the RFTM variants in Table 1; (a) Fingerprint for variant Fine's amount $\geq$ 50, (b) Fingerprint for variant Fine's amount < 50 (Color figure online)

---

[5] Obtained using the default settings in ProM 6.9.

In contrast, the baseline in [5] comes up with a single directly-follows graph for both process variants (Fig. 6). We note that the approach in [6] produces similar results, which we did not show due to lack of space. The baselines are unable to identify control-flow differences completely. Rather, they show (statistically-significant) differences at the level of individual edges. For example, in [5], the thickness of each edge shows the frequency of that edge. Even if a statistical test is applied for each edge to determine whether the corresponding frequency varies between process variants, this information is not sufficient to identify differences in paths. The problem is exacerbated by the fact that a directly-follows graph generalises process behavior since the combination of the various edges give rise to more paths than the traces in the event log. Indeed the baselines [5,6] consider only the edge's frequency, whereas our approach considers both frequency and location of an edge simultaneously. For example, the approach in [5] identifies that the frequency of *(Create Fine, Payment)* (the orange edge) is different between process variants. In contrast, in our approach it was found that this particular edge does not discriminate the two process variants from a control-flow perspective. In fact, the paths containing this edge, though having different frequencies, are very similar in the two variants.

Also, "Insert fine notification → Appeal to Judge" is not depicted in Fig. 5(b), since it does not contribute to any statistically-significant control-flow difference between the two variants. However, it appears in Fig. 5(a) because it is in any path that contains at least one of the edges in Table 2. This is a good feature of our approach, since the edge in question itself does not contribute to any differences, but its occurrence and location affect other edges for the respective variant, giving rise to different mutual fingerprints. That said, as a side effect, sometimes the resulting fingerprints might contain a large number of edges. In contrast, the baselines [5,6] are unable to capture such correlation because the frequency of an edge is considered in their analysis.

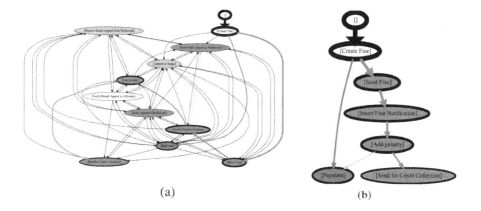

(a)                              (b)

**Fig. 6.** Answer to RQ1: Directly-follows graph obtained for the two variants in the RFTM log according to [5]. The frequency of an edge is shown by its thickness while the color shows the difference between the edge frequencies in the two variants: (a) all edges shown; (b) edges with frequency ≤ %5 are cut (Color figure online)

**Table 3.** Answer to RQ2: comparing edge durations between the two variants

| Edge | $\overline{\Delta t_1}$ (day) | $\overline{\Delta t_2}$ (day) | P-value |
|---|---|---|---|
| ('Create Fine', 'Send Fine') | 72.48 | 92.98 | 0 |
| ('Create Fine', 'Payment') | 11.52 | 10.38 | 0.0089 |
| ('Send Appeal to Prefecture', 'Add penalty') | 26.13 | 20.00 | 0.0004 |
| ('Add penalty', 'Payment') | 152.38 | 169.43 | 0 |
| ('Add penalty', 'Receive Result Appeal from Prefecture') | 58.17 | 46.39 | 0.0151 |
| ('Payment', 'Payment') | 77.60 | 101.97 | 0 |
| ('Payment', 'Add penalty') | 30.94 | 33.27 | 0.0086 |
| ('Insert Fine Notification', 'Payment') | 28.83 | 26.48 | 0.0083 |
| ('Insert Fine Notification', 'Insert Date Appeal to Prefecture') | 34.24 | 35.50 | 0.0069 |
| ('Insert Date Appeal to Prefecture', 'Add penalty') | 22.94 | 24.96 | 0.0016 |
| ('Send Appeal to Prefecture', 'Receive Result Appeal from Prefecture') | 49.25 | 56.19 | 0.0354 |

**Table 4.** Performance of the proposed approach

| Dataset | Execution time (s) | Memory usage (MB) 95% C.I |
|---|---|---|
| RTFM | 2340 | (473–608) |
| SEPSIS | 217 | (170–218) |
| BPIC13 | 152 | (380–410) |
| BPIC15 | 3470 | (980–1040) |

To answer RQ2, we compared the average duration time $\Delta t$ for each edge of the two process variants (capturing the activity duration), and then applied $t$-tests with unequal variances. The results are shown in Table 3. We superimposed those edges with statistically significant differences in duration, over the corresponding fingerprints by using dashed edges, as shown in Fig. 5. Both baseline [5,6] provide the same results for the duration time.

*Execution Time.* Table 4 shows the execution time of our approach for each dataset. Time performance is affected by the size and complexity of the event log. For example, in the table we can observe longer times for the RFTM log (39 min), where the number of cases is high, and for BPIC15 (58 min), where the number of unique events is relatively high. Yet, the approach performs within reasonable bounds on a standard laptop configuration. Comparatively, the two baseline techniques are much faster, namely in the order of a few minutes.

Table 4 also shows RAM occupancy. This is monitored every 10 s, and next, the 95% confidence interval is computed. One can see that the amount of memory for BPIC15 is larger than the other datasets. This can be attributed to many unique events available in each process variant, which give rise to an augmented matrix with a high number of columns. Yet, memory use is quite reasonable (ranging from 473MB min for RFTM to 1.04 GB max for BPIC15).

## 6    Conclusion

In this paper, we presented a novel approach to identify statistically-significant differences in the control-flow and activity durations of two business process variants, each captured as an event log. The cornerstone technique of this approach is the construction of a novel encoding of discriminatory features from an event log, called mutual fingerprint, based on a discrete wavelet transformation of time series extracted from the traces of the event log. The approach was evaluated using four real-life logs against two baselines for process variant analysis. The results show that at trace level, our approach reveals significant statistical discrepancies between the two variants, whereas the baselines used in our evaluation are unable to detect these differences. Furthermore, the presented approach performs within reasonable execution times, despite the more involving computations.

We foresee the applicability of the devised encoding technique based on discrete wavelet transformation to a range of process mining problems. These range from predictive process monitoring through to trace clustering, outlier detection, and process drift identification and characterization.

**Reproducibility.** The source code required to reproduce the reported experiments can be found at https://github.com/farbodtaymouri/RuleDeviance.

**Acknowledgments.** This research is partly funded by the Australian Research Council (DP180102839) and Spanish funds MINECO and FEDER (TIN2017-86727-C2-1-R).

## References

1. Suriadi, S., Mans, R.S., Wynn, M.T., Partington, A., Karnon, J.: Measuring patient flow variations: a cross-organisational process mining approach. In: Ouyang, C., Jung, J.-Y. (eds.) AP-BPM 2014. LNBIP, vol. 181, pp. 43–58. Springer, Cham (2014). https://doi.org/10.1007/978-3-319-08222-6_4
2. Swinnen, J., Depaire, B., Jans, M.J., Vanhoof, K.: A process deviation analysis – a case study. In: Daniel, F., Barkaoui, K., Dustdar, S. (eds.) BPM 2011. LNBIP, vol. 99, pp. 87–98. Springer, Heidelberg (2012). https://doi.org/10.1007/978-3-642-28108-2_8
3. Poelmans, J., Dedene, G., Verheyden, G., Van der Mussele, H., Viaene, S., Peters, E.: Combining business process and data discovery techniques for analyzing and improving integrated care pathways. In: Perner, P. (ed.) ICDM 2010. LNCS (LNAI), vol. 6171, pp. 505–517. Springer, Heidelberg (2010). https://doi.org/10.1007/978-3-642-14400-4_39
4. van der Aalst, W.: Process Mining: Data Science in Action, 2nd edn. Springer, Heidelberg (2016). https://doi.org/10.1007/978-3-662-49851-4
5. Bolt, A., de Leoni, M., van der Aalst, W.M.: Process variant comparison: using event logs to detect differences in behavior and business rules. Inf. Syst. **74**, 53–66 (2018)

6. Nguyen, H., Dumas, M., La Rosa, M., ter Hofstede, A.H.M.: Multi-perspective comparison of business process variants based on event logs. In: Trujillo, J.C., et al. (eds.) ER 2018. LNCS, vol. 11157, pp. 449–459. Springer, Cham (2018). https://doi.org/10.1007/978-3-030-00847-5_32

7. Taymouri, F., Rosa, M.L., Dumas, M., Maggi, F.M.: Business process variant analysis: survey and classification (2019). arXiv:1911.07582

8. van Beest, N.R.T.P., Dumas, M., García-Bañuelos, L., La Rosa, M.: Log delta analysis: interpretable differencing of business process event logs. In: Motahari-Nezhad, H.R., Recker, J., Weidlich, M. (eds.) BPM 2015. LNCS, vol. 9253, pp. 386–405. Springer, Cham (2015). https://doi.org/10.1007/978-3-319-23063-4_26

9. Cordes, C., Vogelgesang, T., Appelrath, H.-J.: A generic approach for calculating and visualizing differences between process models in multidimensional process mining. In: Fournier, F., Mendling, J. (eds.) BPM 2014. LNBIP, vol. 202, pp. 383–394. Springer, Cham (2015). https://doi.org/10.1007/978-3-319-15895-2_32

10. Ballambettu, N.P., Suresh, M.A., Bose, R.P.J.C.: Analyzing process variants to understand differences in key performance indices. In: Dubois, E., Pohl, K. (eds.) CAiSE 2017. LNCS, vol. 10253, pp. 298–313. Springer, Cham (2017). https://doi.org/10.1007/978-3-319-59536-8_19

11. Kriglstein, S., Wallner, G., Rinderle-Ma, S.: A visualization approach for difference analysis of process models and instance traffic. In: Daniel, F., Wang, J., Weber, B. (eds.) BPM 2013. LNCS, vol. 8094, pp. 219–226. Springer, Heidelberg (2013). https://doi.org/10.1007/978-3-642-40176-3_18

12. Pini, A., Brown, R., Wynn, M.T.: Process visualization techniques for multi-perspective process comparisons. In: Bae, J., Suriadi, S., Wen, L. (eds.) AP-BPM 2015. LNBIP, vol. 219, pp. 183–197. Springer, Cham (2015). https://doi.org/10.1007/978-3-319-19509-4_14

13. Wynn, M., et al.: ProcessProfiler3D: a visualisation framework for log-based process performance comparison. DSS **100**, 93–108 (2017)

14. Low, W., van der Aalst, W., ter Hofstede, A., Wynn, M., Weerdt, J.D.: Change visualisation: analysing the resource and timing differences between two event logs. Inf. Syst. **65**, 106–123 (2017)

15. Bolt, A., de Leoni, M., van der Aalst, W.M.P.: A visual approach to spot statistically-significant differences in event logs based on process metrics. In: Nurcan, S., Soffer, P., Bajec, M., Eder, J. (eds.) CAiSE 2016. LNCS, vol. 9694, pp. 151–166. Springer, Cham (2016). https://doi.org/10.1007/978-3-319-39696-5_10

16. Strang, G.: Introduction to Linear Algebra, 5th edn. Wellesley-Cambridge Press, Cambridge (2016)

17. Santoso, S., Powers, E.J., Grady, W.M.: Power quality disturbance data compression using wavelet transform methods. IEEE Trans. Power Delivery **12**(3), 1250–1257 (1997)

18. Rao, K., Ahmed, N.: Orthogonal transforms for digital signal processing. In: IEEE ICASSP 1976, vol. 1, pp. 136–140 (1976)

19. Gallier, J., Quaintance, J.: Linear Algebra and Optimization with Applications to Machine Learning: Volume I (2019)

20. Shumway, R.H., Stoffer, D.S.: Time Series Analysis and Its Applications: with R Examples. Springer Texts in Statistics, 4th edn. Springer, Cham (2017). https://doi.org/10.1007/978-3-319-52452-8

21. Aggarwal, C.C.: Data Mining. Springer, Cham (2015). https://doi.org/10.1007/978-3-319-14142-8

22. Bakshi, B.R.: Multiscale analysis and modeling using wavelets (1999)

23. Yi, B., Sidiropoulos, N.D., Johnson, T., Jagadish, H.V., Faloutsos, C., Biliris, A.: Online data mining for co-evolving time sequences. In: Proceedings of 16th IEEE, ICDE (2000)
24. Liu, H., Motoda, H.: Computational Methods of Feature Selection (2007)
25. Hornik, K., Stinchcombe, M., White, H.: Multilayer feedforward networks are universal approximators. Neural Netw. **2**(5), 359–366 (1989)
26. Powers, D.M.W.: Evaluation: from precision, recall and f-measure to ROC, informedness, markedness and correlation (2011)
27. Wackerly, D.D., Mendenhall, W., Scheaffer, R.L.: Mathematical Statistics with Applications, 7th edn. Duxbury Advanced Series (2008)
28. 4TU: Centre for Research Data (2019). https://data.4tu.nl/repository

# DeepAlign: Alignment-Based Process Anomaly Correction Using Recurrent Neural Networks

Timo Nolle[(⊠)], Alexander Seeliger, Nils Thoma, and Max Mühlhäuser

Telecooperation Lab, Technische Universität Darmstadt, Darmstadt, Germany
{nolle,seeliger,thoma,max}@tk.tu-darmstadt.de

**Abstract.** In this paper, we propose DeepAlign, a novel approach to multi-perspective process anomaly correction, based on recurrent neural networks and bidirectional beam search. At the core of the DeepAlign algorithm are two recurrent neural networks trained to predict the next event. One is reading sequences of process executions from left to right, while the other is reading the sequences from right to left. By combining the predictive capabilities of both neural networks, we show that it is possible to calculate sequence alignments, which are used to detect and correct anomalies. DeepAlign utilizes the case-level and event-level attributes to closely model the decisions within a process. We evaluate the performance of our approach on an elaborate data corpus of 252 realistic synthetic event logs and compare it to three state-of-the-art conformance checking methods. DeepAlign produces better corrections than the rest of the field reaching an overall $F_1$ score of 0.9572 across all datasets, whereas the best comparable state-of-the-art method reaches 0.6411.

**Keywords:** Business process management · Anomaly detection · Deep learning · Sequence alignments

## 1 Introduction

Process anomaly detection can be used to automatically detect deviations in process execution data. This technique infers the process solely based on distributions of the execution data, without relying on an abstract definition of the process itself. While these approaches can accurately pinpoint an anomaly in a process, they do not provide information about what should have been done instead. Although, the knowledge about the occurrence of an anomaly is valuable, much more value lies in the knowledge of what was supposed to happen and how to avoid this behavior in the future.

Process mining techniques are centered around the notion of a process model that describes the correct behavior of a process. Conformance checking techniques can be utilized to analyze process executions for their conformance with a process model. This method has the benefit of not only detecting deviations from the defined process but also of providing the closest conforming path through the process, thereby correcting it.

© Springer Nature Switzerland AG 2020
S. Dustdar et al. (Eds.): CAiSE 2020, LNCS 12127, pp. 319–333, 2020.
https://doi.org/10.1007/978-3-030-49435-3_20

The correctness of the conformance checking result depends on the quality of the process model. Furthermore, a correct execution of a process is not necessarily defined by a correct order of process steps but can depend on a variety of other parameters. For example, it might not be allowed that the same person executes two consecutive process steps or a process might differ depending on the country it is being executed in. All these possibilities have to be accounted for both in the process model and the conformance checking algorithm to ensure a correct result. If no process model is available, conformance checking cannot be used and the creation of a good reference model is a time-consuming task.

An automatic process anomaly correction is therefore desirable, combining the autonomy of an anomaly detection algorithm with the descriptive results from conformance checking. Against this background, we propose the DeepAlign[1] algorithm, which combines these two benefits. It borrows from the field of anomaly detection and employs two recurrent neural networks (RNN), trained on the task of next event prediction, as an approximate process model [18]. Inspired by the alignment concept from conformance checking, we show that a bidirectional beam search [17] can be used to align a process execution with the process model as approximated by the two RNNs.

DeepAlign can not only detect that process steps have been skipped, but it can also predict which process steps should have been executed instead. Furthermore, it does not rely on a reference model of the process, nor any prior knowledge about it. It can be used to automatically detect anomalies and to automatically correct them.

## 2   Background

Before we describe the DeepAlign algorithm, we must first introduce some concepts from the field of process mining and deep learning.

### 2.1   Process Mining

Process mining is centered around the idea of human-readable representations of processes called process models. Process models are widely used in business process management as a tool for defining, documenting, and controlling business processes inside companies.

During the execution of a digital business process, each process step is stored in a database. This includes information on when the process step was executed (timestamp), what process step was executed (activity), and to which business case it belongs (case identifier). These three fundamental bits of event information are the basis for every process mining algorithm and are usually combined into a single data structure called event log.

A log consists of cases, each of which consists of events executed within a process, and some attributes connected to the case (case attributes). Each event is defined by an activity name and its attributes (e.g., a user who executed the event).

---

[1] Available on GitHub https://github.com/tnolle/deepalign.

**Definition 1.** *Case, Event, and Log. Let $\mathcal{E}$ be the set of all events. A case is a sequence of events $c \in \mathcal{E}^*$, where $\mathcal{E}^*$ is the set of all sequences over $\mathcal{E}$ Let $\mathcal{C}$ be the set of all cases. An event log is a set of cases $\mathcal{L} \subseteq \mathcal{C}$.*

Event logs can be used to automatically discover a process model. Discovery algorithms analyze the event logs for process patterns and aim to produce a human-readable process model that likely produced the event log. Multiple discovery algorithms exist, such as the Heuristics Miner [20] and the Inductive Visual Miner [9].

## 2.2 Alignments

In process analytics, it is desirable to relate the behavior observed in an event log to the behavior defined in a process model. This discipline is called conformance checking. The goal of conformance checking is to find an alignment between an event log and a reference process model. The reference model can be manually designed or be discovered by a process discovery algorithm.

**Definition 2.** *Alignment. An alignment [5] is a bidirectional mapping of an event sequence $\sigma_l$ from the event log to a possible execution sequence $\sigma_m$ of the process model. It is represented by a sequence of tuples $(s_l, s_m) \in (\mathcal{E}^{\gg} \times \mathcal{E}^{\gg}) \backslash \{(\gg, \gg)\}$, where $\gg$ is an empty move and $\mathcal{E}^{\gg} = \mathcal{E} \cup \{\gg\}$. We say that a tuple represents a synchronous move if $s_l \in \mathcal{E}$ and $s_m \in \mathcal{E}$, a model move if $s_l = \gg$ and $s_m \in \mathcal{E}$, and a log move if $s_l \in \mathcal{E}$ and $s_m = \gg$. An alignment is optimal if the number of empty moves is minimal.*

For $\sigma_l = \langle a, b, c, x, e \rangle$ and $\sigma_m = \langle a, b, c, d, e \rangle$, the two optimal alignments are

$$\begin{array}{|c|c|c|c|c|c|} \hline a & b & c & x & \gg & e \\ \hline a & b & c & \gg & d & e \\ \hline \end{array} \quad \text{and} \quad \begin{array}{|c|c|c|c|c|c|} \hline a & b & c & \gg & x & e \\ \hline a & b & c & d & \gg & e \\ \hline \end{array}$$

where the top row corresponds to $\sigma_l$ and the bottom row corresponds to $\sigma_m$, mapping moves in the log to moves in the model and vice versa.

## 2.3 Recurrent Neural Network (RNN)

Recurrent neural networks (RNN) have been designed to handle sequential data such as sentences. An RNN is a special kind of neural network that makes use of an internal state (memory) to retain information about already seen words in a sentence. It is processing a sentence word for word, and with each new word, it will approximate the probability distribution over all possible next words. Neural networks can be efficiently trained using a gradient descent learning procedure, minimizing the error in the prediction by tuning its internal parameters (weights). The error can be computed as the difference between the output of the neural network and the desired output.

After the training procedure, the neural network can approximate the probability distribution over all possible next words, given an arbitrary length input sequence. With slight alterations, RNNs can be applied to event logs, which we will explain further in Sect. 3.

## 2.4   Beam Search

In natural language processing, it is common to search for the best continuation of a sentence under a given RNN model. To find the most probable continuation, every possible combination of words has to be considered which, for a length of $L$ and a vocabulary size of $V$, amounts to $V^L$ possible combinations. Due to the exponential growth of the search space, this problem is NP-hard.

Instead, a greedy approach can be taken, producing always the most likely next word given a start of a sentence, based on probability under the RNN. However, this approach does not yield good results because it approximates the total probability of the sentence continuation based only on the probability of the next word. A more probable sentence might be found when expanding the search to the second most probable next word, or the third, and so on.

Beam search (BS) is a greedy algorithm that finds a trade-off between traversing all possible combinations and only the most probable next word. For every prediction, the BS algorithm expands only the $K$ most probable sentence continuations (beams). In the next step, the best $K$ probable continuations over all $K$ beams from the previous step are chosen, and so on. For $K = 1$, BS is equivalent to the greedy 1-best approach explained above. BS has the advantage of pruning the search space to feasible sizes, while still traversing a sufficient part of the search space to produce a good approximation of the most likely sentence continuation.

The BS algorithm is iteratively applied, inserting new words with each step, until convergence, i.e., the end of a sentence is reached, indicated by the end of sentence symbol.

## 2.5   Bidirectional Beam Search

The BS algorithm continues a sentence until a special end of sentence symbol is predicted. However, if the sentence has a defined beginning and end, this approach cannot be used because a unidirectional RNN only knows about the beginning of the sentence and not the end. This has been demonstrated and been addressed in [17] with a novel bidirectional beam search (BiBS) approach. Instead of using a single unidirectional RNN, the authors propose to use two separate unidirectional RNNs, one reading the input sentences forwards, and one reading them backwards.

The problem that arises with a gap in the middle of a sentence is that the probability of the resulting sentence, after the insertion of a new word, cannot be computed by a single RNN without re-computation of the remainder of the sentence. In BiBS, this probability is approximated by the product of the probability of the beginning of the sentence (by the forward RNN), the end of the sentence (by the backward RNN), and the joint probability of inserting the new word (according to both RNNs). The original BS algorithm is extended to expand the search space based on this joint probability, ensuring a proper fit both for the beginning and the end of the sentence.

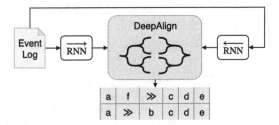

**Fig. 1.** The DeepAlign algorithm makes use of two next event prediction RNNs and an extended bidirectional beam search (green) to produce alignments (Color figure online)

The BiBS algorithm is iteratively applied to the original sentence, updating it with each step, until convergence, i.e., no insertions would yield a higher probability in any of the $K$ beams.

## 3  DeepAlign

In this section we describe the DeepAlign algorithm and all its components. An overview of the algorithm is shown in Fig. 1. Two neural networks are trained to predict the next event, one reading cases from left to right (forwards), the other reading them from right to left (backwards). An extended BiBS is then used to transform the input case to the most probable case under the two RNN models. Lastly, an alignment is calculated based on the search history of the algorithm.

### 3.1  Next Event Prediction

Next event prediction aims to accurately model the decisions being made in a process. These decisions are based on multiple parameters, such as the history of a case, the attributes connected to past events, and the case level attributes. To succeed, a machine learning model must take into account all of these parameters.

In this paper, we propose a new neural architecture for next event prediction. It has been designed to model the sequence of activities (control-flow), the attributes connected to these activities (event attributes), and the global attributes connected to the case (case attributes). Figure 2 shows the architecture in detail.

At the heart of the network is a Gated Recurrent Unit (GRU) [7], a type of RNN. This GRU is iteratively fed an event, consisting of its activity and its event attributes, and must predict the corresponding next event. Each categorical attribute is fed through an embedding layer to map the values into a lower-dimensional embedding space. To include the case attributes, we make use of the internal state of the GRU. Instead of initializing the state with zeros (the default), we initialize it based on a representation of the case attributes. All case attributes are transformed by a case attribute network, consisting of two fully-connected layers (FC), to produce a real-valued representation of the

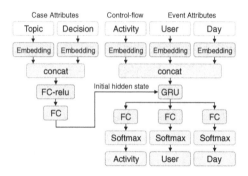

**Fig. 2.** RNN architecture for an event log with two case attributes (*Topic* and *Decision*) and two event attributes (*User* and *Day*)

case attributes. In other words, we initialize the next event prediction with a representation of the case attributes, thereby conditioning it to predict events according to these case attributes. Finally, the GRU output is fed into separate FC layers with Softmax activations to produce a probability distribution over all possible attributes of the next event (i.e., the prediction of the next event).

We train the networks with a GRU size equal to two times the maximum case length on mini-batches of size 100 for 50 epochs using the Adam optimizer with standard parameters [8]. The first layer of the case attribute network has an output size of the GRU size divided by 8 and the second layer output is equal to the hidden state size of the GRU. These parameters were chosen following an exhaustive grid search, however, we found that any reasonable setting generally worked.

### 3.2 The DeepAlign Algorithm

In the context of processes, the sentences of words from above will become the cases of events from the event log. By replacing the next word prediction RNNs with next event prediction RNNs in the BiBS algorithm we can apply it to event logs. Instead of only predicting the next word, the RNNs will predict the next event, including the most likely event attributes.

Our goal is to utilize the two RNNs as the reference model for conformance checking and produce an alignment between log and the RNNs. Alignments can be interpreted as a sequence of *skip* (synchronous move), *insertion* (model move), or *deletion* (log move) operations. The BiBS algorithm already covers the first two operations, but not the last. To allow for deletions, we have to extend the BiBS algorithm.

Let $\overrightarrow{\text{RNN}}$ be the forward event prediction RNN and $\overleftarrow{\text{RNN}}$ be the backward RNN. Let further $\text{RNN}(h, c)$ be the probability of case $c$ under RNN, initialized with the hidden state $h$.

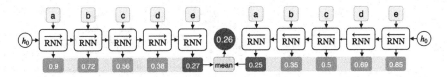

**Fig. 3.** The probability of a case $c = \langle a, b, c, d, e \rangle$ is computed by the average probability of the case under both the forward and the backward RNN

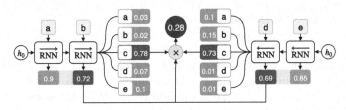

**Fig. 4.** The probability of a case $c = \langle a, b, d, e \rangle$ after the insertion of an event $c$ after $b$ is computed by the joint probability $\langle a, b \rangle$ under the forward RNN, $\langle d, e \rangle$ under the backward RNN, and the probabilities of continuing the case with $c$ under both RNNs

The probability of a case $c$ under the two RNNs can be computed by

$$P(c) = \frac{1}{2} \left( \overrightarrow{\mathrm{RNN}} (h_0, c) + \overleftarrow{\mathrm{RNN}} (h_0, c) \right),$$

where $h_0$ is the output of the case attribute network. If no case attributes are available, the initial state is set to zeros. An example is shown in Fig. 3.

For an insertion of an event $e$ at time $t$ in a case $c$, the probability under the two RNNs can be approximated by

$$P_{\mathrm{ins}}(c, e, t) = \overrightarrow{\mathrm{RNN}} (h_0, c_{[1:t]}) \cdot \overrightarrow{\mathrm{RNN}} \left( \overrightarrow{h}_t, e \right)$$
$$\cdot \overleftarrow{\mathrm{RNN}} \left( \overleftarrow{h}_{t+1}, e \right) \cdot \overleftarrow{\mathrm{RNN}} (h_0, c_{[t+1:T]}),$$

where $T$ is the total case length, $c_{[1:t]}$ is the index notation to retrieve all events from $c$ until time t, and $\overrightarrow{h}_t$ is the hidden state of $\overrightarrow{\mathrm{RNN}}$ after reading $c_{[1:t]}$. Similarly, $\overleftarrow{h}_{t+1}$ is the hidden state of $\overleftarrow{\mathrm{RNN}}$ after reading $c_{[t+1:T]}$. An example is shown in Fig. 4.

The probability of deleting $n$ events at time $t$ in a case $c$ can be approximated by

$$P_{\mathrm{del}}(c, n, t) = \overrightarrow{\mathrm{RNN}} (h_0, c_{[1:t]}) \cdot \overrightarrow{\mathrm{RNN}} \left( \overrightarrow{h}_t, c_{[t+n]} \right)$$
$$\cdot \overleftarrow{\mathrm{RNN}} \left( \overleftarrow{h}_{t+n}, c_{[t]} \right) \cdot \overleftarrow{\mathrm{RNN}} (h_0, c_{[t+n:T]}).$$

An example is shown in Fig. 5.

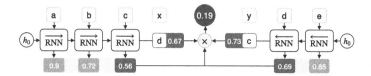

**Fig. 5.** The probability of a case $c = \langle a, b, c, x, y, d, e \rangle$ after the deletion of $x$ and $y$ is computed by the joint probability of $\langle a, b, c \rangle$ under the forward RNN, $\langle d, e \rangle$ under the backward RNN, and the probabilities of continuing the case with $d$ and $c$ under the forward and backward RNN, respectively

Algorithm 1 shows the full DeepAlign process of aligning a case $c$ with the two RNNs. The algorithm is initialized with an initial set of beams $B = \{c\}$, i.e., the original case. For each possible operation, the probabilities are computed using the aforementioned equations, and the top-K beams are returned. For simplicity, we assume that top-K always returns the updated cases according to the operations with the highest probability. The number of events that can be deleted in one step can be controlled with the parameter $N$. This is necessary because successively deleting single events does not necessarily generate higher probabilities than removing multiple events at once.

---

**Algorithm 1:** DeepAlign algorithm

**Data**: Given a set of beams $B$, maximum number of beams $K$, and a maximum deletion size $N$

**while** *not converged* **do**

    $B' = \emptyset$;

    **for** $b \in B$ **do**

        $B' = B' \cup P(b)$;

        **for** $t = 1, ..., T$ **do**

           $B' = B' \cup \{P_{\text{del}}(b, n, t) \mid n \in 1, ..., N\} \cup \{P_{\text{ins}}(b, e, t) \mid e \in \mathcal{E}\}$

        **end**

    **end**

    $B = \text{top-K}\,(B')$

**end**

**Result**: $B$, the top-K beams after convergence

---

Algorithm 1 does not yet return alignments, but the top-K updated cases. By keeping a history of the top-K operations (*skip*, *deletion*, and *insertion*) in every iteration, we can obtain the alignment directly from the history of operations. A *deletion* corresponds to an empty move on the model, whereas an *insertion* corresponds to an empty move in the log.

The top-K selection in Algorithm 1 will select the top K beams based on the probability under the RNN models. In case of ties, we break the tie by choosing the beam with fewer empty moves (insertions and deletions).

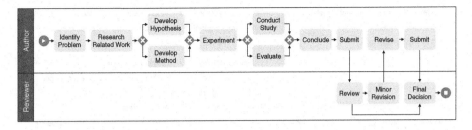

**Fig. 6.** A simple paper submission process which is used as an example in the evaluation

## 4    Experiments

We evaluate the DeepAlign algorithm for the task of anomaly correction. Given an event log consisting of normal and anomalous cases, an anomaly correction algorithm is expected to align each case in the event log with a correct activity sequence according to the process (without anomalies) that produced the event log.

We use a simple paper submission process as a running example throughout the remainder of this paper. The process model in Fig. 6 describes the creation of a scientific paper. It includes the peer review process, which is executed by a reviewer, whereas the paper is written by an author.

To evaluate the accuracy of the corrections, we generated six random process models using PLG2 [6]. The models vary in complexity with respect to the number of activities, breadth, and width. Additionally, we use a handmade procurement process model called P2P as in [15].

To generate event attributes, we create a likelihood graph [4] from the process models which includes probabilities for event attributes connected to each step in the process. This method has been proposed in [14]. A likelihood graph for the paper process from Fig. 6 is shown in Fig. 7.

For each process step, the probability of the resource executing it is shown in yellow. Depending on the resource, the probabilities of the next process steps are shown in blue. Note that there is a long-term dependency between the steps *Develop Hypothesis* and *Conduct Study*, and, similarly, between *Develop Method* and *Evaluate*. That is, *Conduct Study* never eventually follows *Develop Method*, and, likewise, *Evaluate* never eventually follows *Develop Hypothesis*.

We can generate event logs by using a random-walk through the likelihood graph, complying with the transition probabilities, and generating activities and attributes along the way. In addition to the event attributes, we also generate case attributes, as well as, dependencies between the case attributes and the output probabilities in the likelihood graph. For the paper process, we generate two case attributes, *Decision* and *Topic*.

If the topic is *Theory*, this implies that *Develop Hypothesis* will occur in a case, whereas if the topic is *Engineering*, it implies *Develop Method* will occur. The decision can be *Accept*, *Weak Accept*, *Borderline*, *Weak Reject*, or *Reject*. For simplicity, we define that there will only be a *Minor Revision* if the *Decision*

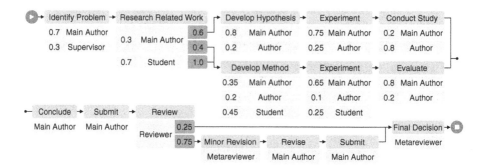

**Fig. 7.** A likelihood graph with user attribute; 1.0 probabilities omitted for simplicity

is either *Accept* or *Weak Accept*. There will be no *Minor Revision* otherwise. We have generated an event log that follows these rules that we use as an example throughout the remainder of the paper. The paper process was not used in the evaluation because of its simplicity.

For each of the 7 other process models, we generate 4 random event logs with varying numbers of event and case attributes. Additionally, we introduce noise to the event logs by randomly applying one of 7 anomalies to a fixed percentage of the cases in the event log. We generate datasets for noise levels between 10% and 90% with a step size of 10% (9 in total). We gather a ground truth dataset for the anomaly correction problem by retaining the original cases before alteration. The 7 anomalies are defined as follows.

- *Skip*: A sequence of up to 2 necessary events has been skipped
- *Insert*: Up to 2 random activities have been inserted
- *Rework*: A sequence of up to 3 events has been executed a second time
- *Early*: A sequence of up to 2 events has been executed too early, and hence is skipped later in the case
- *Late*: A sequence of up to 2 events has been executed too late, and hence is skipped earlier in the case
- *Attribute*: An incorrect attribute value has been set in up to 3 events

To analyze the impact of the case and event attributes, we evaluate four different implementations of DeepAlign: one that does not use any attributes (DeepAlign∅), one that only uses case attributes (DeepAlignC), one that only uses event attributes (DeepAlignE), and one that uses both (DeepAlignCE).

Additionally, we evaluate baseline approaches that first discover a process model using a discovery algorithm and then calculate the alignments [1]. We chose the Heuristics Miner [20] and the Inductive Miner [9] using the implementations of the PM4Py library [2]. For completeness, we also evaluate the conformance checking algorithm using a perfect Reference Model, i.e., the one used to generate the event logs.

We run the DeepAlign algorithm for a maximum number of 10 iterations with a beam size of $K = 5$ and a maximum deletion size of $N = 3$, and consider the top-1 beam for the evaluation. The Inductive Miner and the Heuristics Miner are used as implemented in PM4Py. For the Heuristics Miner, we use a dependency threshold of 0.99, and for the Inductive Miner, we use a noise threshold of 0.2.

## 5   Evaluation

The overall results are shown in Table 1. For each dataset we run the algorithms and evaluate the correction accuracy, that is, an alignment is regarded as correct if the model sequence is exactly equal to the ground truth sequence. For correct alignments, we calculate the optimality of the alignment (i.e., if the number of empty moves is minimal). For incorrect alignments, we calculate the distance from the ground truth sequence with Levenshtein's algorithm. Accuracy is measured as the macro average $F_1$ score of normal $(F_1^N)$ and anomalous $(F_1^A)$ cases across all datasets and noise levels.

**Table 1.** Correction accuracy, average error for incorrect alignments (based on the Levenshtein distance), and alignment optimality for correct alignments; best results are shown in bold typeface

| | CF | CA | EA | $F_1^N$ | $F_1^A$ | $F_1$ | Error | Optimal |
|---|---|---|---|---|---|---|---|---|
| Reference Model | ✓ | – | – | 0.9011 | 0.9331 | 0.9171 | **1.46** | – |
| Heuristics Miner | ✓ | – | – | 0.6678 | 0.6144 | 0.6411 | 3.33 | – |
| Inductive Miner | ✓ | – | – | 0.6007 | 0.2438 | 0.4222 | 2.18 | – |
| DeepAlign∅ | ✓ | – | – | 0.7950 | 0.8111 | 0.8030 | 2.52 | 99.8% |
| DeepAlignC | ✓ | ✓ | – | 0.8918 | 0.9290 | 0.9104 | 2.41 | **99.9%** |
| DeepAlignE | ✓ | – | ✓ | 0.9261 | 0.9582 | 0.9421 | 1.65 | 86.9% |
| DeepAlignCE | ✓ | ✓ | ✓ | **0.9442** | **0.9702** | **0.9572** | 1.84 | 86.6% |

Interestingly, DeepAlignE, and DeepAlignCE both outperform the perfect Reference Model approach. This is because the Reference Model does not contain any information about the case and event attributes. The Heuristics Miner yields much better results in the anomaly correction task than the Inductive Miner, however, DeepAlign∅ outperforms both, without relying on case or event attributes.

Reference Model, Heuristics Miner, and Inductive Miner all produce optimal alignments because the alignment algorithm guarantees it. The DeepAlign algorithm shows a significant drop in alignment optimality when including the event attributes. The drop in optimality can be attributed to the fact that we always predict the top-1 attribute value for inserted events in the DeepAlign algorithm. Furthermore, it might be connected to the attribute level anomalies that we introduced as part of the generation. The best results are achieved when

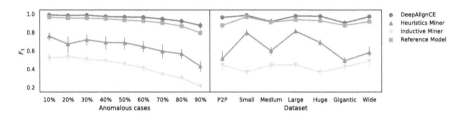

**Fig. 8.** $F_1$ score for each algorithm per noise ratio (left) and per dataset (right); error bars indicate variance across all runs

including both the case and the event attributes. Figure 8 shows the $F_1$ score for each algorithm per noise level and per dataset. DeepAlignCE always performs better than the Reference Model, and significantly better than the two mining approaches.

We want to finish the evaluation with examples from the paper dataset to illustrate the results of the DeepAlign algorithm. This is the resulting alignment for a case with a *Skip* anomaly,

| Identify Problem | ≫ | ≫ | Experiment | Evaluate | Conclude | Submit | Review | ... |
|---|---|---|---|---|---|---|---|---|
| Identify Problem | Research Related Work | Develop Method | Experiment | Evaluate | Conclude | Submit | Review | ... |

this is the result for a case with a *Late* anomaly,

| Identify Problem | ≫ | ≫ | Experiment | Research Related Work | Develop Method | Evaluate | Conclude | Submit | ... |
|---|---|---|---|---|---|---|---|---|---|
| Identify Problem | Research Related Work | Develop Method | Experiment | ≫ | ≫ | Evaluate | Conclude | Submit | ... |

and this is the result for a case with an *Insert anomaly.*

| Identify Problem | Research Related Work | Random activity 10 | Develop Method | Experiment | Evaluate | Conclude | Random activity 12 | Submit | ... |
|---|---|---|---|---|---|---|---|---|---|
| Identify Problem | Research Related Work | ≫ | Develop Method | Experiment | Evaluate | Conclude | ≫ | Submit | ... |

The DeepAlign method can also be utilized to generate sequences from nothing, that is, to align the empty case with the most likely case according to the model. Depending on the case attributes that are used to initialize the RNNs, the results will be different.

For Decision = Reject and Topic = Engineering the resulting sequence is ⟨ Identify Problem, Research Related Work, Develop Method, Experiment, Evaluate, Conclude, Submit, Review, Final Decision ⟩, whereas if we set Topic = Theory the resulting sequence is ⟨ Identify Problem, Research Related Work, Develop Hypothesis, Experiment, Conduct Study, Conclude, Submit, Review, Final Decision ⟩. The DeepAlign algorithm correctly generates a sequence including the *Develop Method* and *Develop Hypothesis* activities according to the setting of the *Topic* case attribute. It also does not generate the *Minor Revision* activity because the *Decision* is *Reject*. When setting Decision = Accept, DeepAlign will generate the sequence including the *Minor Revision* branch. A similar effect can be observed when altering the event attributes.

This demonstrates that the RNNs are indeed capable of learning the rules behind the decisions in the paper process (cf. [18]). Although the paper dataset contains unambiguous dependencies between the case attributes and the resulting correct sequences, the overall results on the randomly generated datasets indicate that case and event attributes ought not to be neglected.

## 6   Related Work

Anomaly detection in business processes is frequently researched. Many approaches exist that aim to detect anomalies in a noisy event log (i.e., an event log that contains anomalous cases).

Bezerra et al. have proposed multiple approaches utilizing discovery algorithms to mine a process model and then use conformance checking to infer the anomalies [3]. Böhmer et al. proposed a technique based on an extended likelihood graph that is utilizing event-level attributes to further enhance the detection [4]. The approach from [4] requires a clean event log (i.e., no anomalies in the log), but it has been shown that the same technique can be applied to noisy logs as well [14]. Recently, Pauwels et al. presented an approach based on Bayesian Networks [16]. Deep learning based approaches are presented in [13] and [14]. However, none of these approaches can be utilized to correct an anomalous case or to produce an alignment.

Since Bezerra et al. presented their approach based on discovery algorithms in 2013, Mannhardt et al. have proposed both a data-aware discovery algorithm [11] and a data-aware conformance checking algorithm [12]. The conformance checking algorithm relies on a configurable cost function for alignments that must be manually defined to include the case and event attributes. Our approach does not rely on a manual definition of the cost function, it traverses the search space based on learned probabilities instead.

Although alignments represent the current state-of-the-art in conformance checking [1], they often pose a significant challenge because they are computationally expensive. Van Dongen et al. address this issue in [19], compromising between computational complexity and quality of the alignments. Very recently, Leemans et al. have presented a stochastic approach to conformance checking [10], which can speed up the computation.

All of these approaches either rely on a non-data-aware discovery technique, require a manual effort to create a proper cost function, or they cannot generate alignments. To the best of our knowledge, DeepAlign is the first fully autonomous anomaly correction method.

## 7   Conclusion

We have demonstrated a novel approach to calculate alignments based on the DeepAlign algorithm. When no reference model is available, two recurrent neural networks can be used to approximate the underlying process based on execution data, including case and event attributes. The empirical results obtained in the experiments indicate that RNNs are indeed capable of modeling the behavior of a process solely based on an event log event if it contains anomalous behavior.

To the best of our knowledge, this is the first time that deep learning has been employed to calculate alignments in the field of process mining. Although we evaluate DeepAlign in the context of anomaly correction, many other applications are conceivable. For example, instead of training on a log that contains anomalies, a clean log could be used. Furthermore, a clean log can be obtained from an existing reference model, and DeepAlign could be used to find alignments. In other words, it might be possible to convert a manually created process model into a DeepAlign model. A discovery algorithm based on DeepAlign is also imaginable since DeepAlign can also be utilized to generate sequences from scratch. Depending on the case attributes the resulting predicted sequences will be different. We think that this idea lends itself to further research.

We further believe that the DeepAlign algorithm could be employed to reduce the memory consumption of an alignment algorithm since the search space is efficiently pruned during the bidirectional beam search. However, on the downside, DeepAlign does not guarantee optimal alignments. This weakness can be addressed by employing an optimal alignment algorithm between the input sequence and the corrected sequence, albeit at the expense of efficiency.

In summary, DeepAlign is a novel and flexible approach with great application potential in many research areas within the field of process mining.

**Acknowledgments.** This work is funded by the German Federal Ministry of Education and Research (BMBF) Software Campus project "R2PA" [01IS17050], Software Campus project "KADet" [01IS17050], and the research project "KI.RPA" [01IS18022D].

## References

1. Adriansyah, A., van Dongen, B.F., van der Aalst, W.M.: Memory-efficient alignment of observed and modeled behavior. BPM Center Report 3 (2013)
2. Berti, A., van Zelst, S.J., van der Aalst, W.: Process Mining for Python (PM4Py): bridging the gap between process-and data science, pp. 13–16 (2019)
3. Bezerra, F., Wainer, J.: Algorithms for anomaly detection of traces in logs of process aware information systems. Inf. Syst. **38**(1), 33–44 (2013)

4. Böhmer, K., Rinderle-Ma, S.: Multi-perspective anomaly detection in business process execution events. In: Debruyne, C., et al. (eds.) OTM 2016. LNCS, vol. 10033, pp. 80–98. Springer, Cham (2016). https://doi.org/10.1007/978-3-319-48472-3_5

5. Jagadeesh Chandra Bose, R.P., van der Aalst, W.: Trace alignment in process mining: opportunities for process diagnostics. In: Hull, R., Mendling, J., Tai, S. (eds.) BPM 2010. LNCS, vol. 6336, pp. 227–242. Springer, Heidelberg (2010). https://doi.org/10.1007/978-3-642-15618-2_17

6. Burattin, A.: PLG2: multiperspective process randomization with online and offline simulations. In: BPM 2016 (Demos), pp. 1–6 (2016)

7. Cho, K., et al.: Learning phrase representations using RNN encoder-decoder for statistical machine translation. arXiv preprint arXiv:1406.1078 (2014)

8. Kingma, D., Ba, J.: Adam: a method for stochastic optimization. arXiv preprint arXiv:1412.6980 (2014)

9. Leemans, S.J., Fahland, D., Van Der Aalst, W.M.: Process and deviation exploration with inductive visual miner. In: BPM 2014 (Demos), vol. 1295, no. 46, 8 (2014)

10. Leemans, S.J.J., Syring, A.F., van der Aalst, W.M.P.: Earth movers' stochastic conformance checking. In: Hildebrandt, T., van Dongen, B.F., Röglinger, M., Mendling, J. (eds.) BPM 2019. LNBIP, vol. 360, pp. 127–143. Springer, Cham (2019). https://doi.org/10.1007/978-3-030-26643-1_8

11. Mannhardt, F., De Leoni, M., Reijers, H.A.: The multi-perspective process explorer. In: BPM 2015 (Demos), vol. 1418, pp. 130–134 (2015)

12. Mannhardt, F., de Leoni, M., Reijers, H.A., van der Aalst, W.M.P.: Balanced multi-perspective checking of process conformance. Computing **98**(4), 407–437 (2015). https://doi.org/10.1007/s00607-015-0441-1

13. Nolle, T., Luettgen, S., Seeliger, A., Mühlhäuser, M.: Analyzing business process anomalies using autoencoders. Mach. Learn. **107**(11), 1875–1893 (2018)

14. Nolle, T., Luettgen, S., Seeliger, A., Mühlhäuser, M.: BINet: multi-perspective business process anomaly classification. Inf. Syst., 101458 (2019)

15. Nolle, T., Seeliger, A., Mühlhäuser, M.: BINet: multivariate business process anomaly detection using deep learning. In: Proceedings of the 16th International Conference on Business Process Management - BPM 2018, pp. 271–287 (2018)

16. Pauwels, S., Calders, T.: An anomaly detection technique for business processes based on extended dynamic Bayesian networks. In: Proceedings of the 34th ACM/SIGAPP Symposium on Applied Computing, pp. 494–501. ACM (2019)

17. Sun, Q., Lee, S., Batra, D.: Bidirectional beam search: forward-backward inference in neural sequence models for fill-in-the-blank image captioning. In: Proceedings of the IEEE Conference on Computer Vision and Pattern Recognition - CVPR 2017, pp. 6961–6969 (2017)

18. Tax, N., van Zelst, S.J., Teinemaa, I.: An experimental evaluation of the generalizing capabilities of process discovery techniques and black-box sequence models. In: Gulden, J., Reinhartz-Berger, I., Schmidt, R., Guerreiro, S., Guédria, W., Bera, P. (eds.) BPMDS/EMMSAD -2018. LNBIP, vol. 318, pp. 165–180. Springer, Cham (2018). https://doi.org/10.1007/978-3-319-91704-7_11

19. van Dongen, B., Carmona, J., Chatain, T., Taymouri, F.: Aligning modeled and observed behavior: a compromise between computation complexity and quality. In: Dubois, E., Pohl, K. (eds.) CAiSE 2017. LNCS, vol. 10253, pp. 94–109. Springer, Cham (2017). https://doi.org/10.1007/978-3-319-59536-8_7

20. Weijters, A., Ribeiro, J.: Flexible heuristics miner (FHM). In: Proceedings of the 2011 IEEE Symposium on Computational Intelligence and Data Mining - CIDM 2011, pp. 310–317. IEEE (2011)

# Workforce Upskilling: A History-Based Approach for Recommending Unfamiliar Process Activities

Anastasiia Pika$^{(\boxtimes)}$ and Moe T. Wynn

Queensland University of Technology, Brisbane, Australia
{a.pika,m.wynn}@qut.edu.au

**Abstract.** Human resource allocation decisions have a direct impact on the performance of a business process. Many approaches to optimal resource allocation have been proposed in the Business Process Management community. The majority of these approaches aim to optimise process performance; hence, recommend activities to experienced employees. To remain competitive, modern organisations also need to grow the capabilities of their employees and offer them upskilling opportunities. In this article, we propose an approach for recommending unfamiliar activities to employees by comparing their work histories with work histories of other similar employees. The aim of the proposed approach is to put employees on a gradual path of multi-skilling whereby they are provided with an opportunity to perform unfamiliar process activities and thus gain their experience through learning-by-doing. The approach is based on the analysis of process execution data and has been implemented. In the evaluation, we compared recommendations provided by the approach with actual activity executions of different employees recorded in process data. The evaluation demonstrated the effectiveness of the approach for different publicly available event logs and configuration settings.

**Keywords:** Multi-skilling · Resource allocation · Recommendation · Collaborative filtering · Process execution data

## 1  Introduction

Organisations are constantly striving to balance the amount of work they need to perform in their business operations with the capacity of their workforce to complete said work. Their goal is to allocate the 'right' kind of work to the 'right' person so that the work is completed in time and is of high quality.

Many approaches to efficiently allocate human resources to work activities have been proposed within the Business Process Management community [3]. Existing resource allocation approaches recommend that a number of criteria are considered; for example, resource experience, preferences, availability, previous performance or compatibility [2]. The majority of resource allocation approaches

© Springer Nature Switzerland AG 2020
S. Dustdar et al. (Eds.): CAiSE 2020, LNCS 12127, pp. 334–349, 2020.
https://doi.org/10.1007/978-3-030-49435-3_21

aim to optimise process performance; hence, they recommend activities to experienced resources. While such approaches may improve the performance of processes, they do not necessarily align with the capability development needs of an organisation and its employees. To maintain its competitive edge, modern organisations need to grow the capabilities of their employees over time [21] and offer them learning and development opportunities on the job [5,10]. In this article, we target the following research question: *how can we recommend process activities that are unfamiliar to employees by analysing their work history recorded in process execution data?*

Our proposed approach is based on the assumption that groups of employees (e.g., in the same role or performing similar activities) follow similar learning paths. These learning paths can be discovered from event logs and can guide the allocation of unfamiliar activities. The approach consists of two main parts: (1) find employees with similar work histories to the employee under consideration; and (2) recommend unfamiliar activities to the employee based on the work histories of similar employees. The approach was implemented and evaluated using multiple event logs. The evaluation demonstrated the performance of the approach for different configurations and data sets.

The proposed approach complements other approaches for resource allocation in the literature. In addition to utilising this approach to grow organisational capacity and enrich the skillsets of employees, the approach can be useful for identifying suitable employees for an activity when experienced employees are not available. Thus, the approach is also applicable in the operational support setting for process-aware information systems.

The rest of the paper is organised as follows. In Sect. 2, we present the preliminaries for the proposed approach. Section 3 details the proposed approach for recommending unfamiliar process activities to employees. Section 4 presents the results from the evaluation conducted with multiple real-life event logs. Section 5 discusses assumptions, limitations and directions for further research. Section 6 summarises the related work and Sect. 7 concludes the paper.

## 2   Preliminaries

Organisations often use information systems to support execution of their business processes and these systems often record information about process executions in event logs [1]. Such logs may contain information about process instance identifiers, activities performed in the process, timestamps of these activities, resources (i.e., employees) who performed the activities and various data attributes related to the process (e.g., customer type). Our approach is based on the analysis of such event logs. Below, we provide a definition of the event log and specify minimum data required by our approach.

**Event Log.** Let $\mathcal{E}$ be the set of all events, an *event log* $EL \subseteq \mathcal{E}$ is a set of events. Events can have different attributes and we assume that at least the following attributes are recorded for each event: *activity*, *resource* and *time*. The value of attribute $a$ of event $e$ is denoted as $e_a$. For example, $e_{time}$ is the timestamp of event $e \in EL$. Let $R$ denote the set of all resources, $A$ denote the set of all activities and $T$ denote the set of all timestamps in event log $EL$. The sets $\mathcal{E}$, $EL$, $A$, $R$ and $T$ are finite and non-empty.

## 3   Approach

The overall idea of our approach is inspired by collaborative filtering (CF) recommender systems which are widely used in e-commerce to recommend new products or services to users. Collaborative filtering is "the process of filtering or evaluating items through the opinions of other people" [15]. CF recommender systems analyse ratings provided by users to items (e.g., movies or books) and recommend new items to users with similar tastes (e.g., to those who liked similar movies or bought similar books). A recommendation cannot be provided if a user has "tastes so unique that they are not shared by anybody else" [15].

An underlying assumption of our approach is that groups of employees follow similar learning paths in an organisation. Employees learn new activities gradually (e.g., new employees first perform a small set of simple activities and over time they start performing activities that require more experience). Information about activities performed by employees at different times is typically recorded in event logs. The main idea of the approach is to analyse such event log data to identify employees with similar work histories and recommend unfamiliar activities to an employee based on the work histories of similar employees.

Figure 1 depicts an illustrative example which we will use to explain the proposed approach. The figure shows activity executions of seven resources who were active during different periods of time before time $t$. Let us assume that we would like to recommend a new activity to resource $r$. In order to recommend a new activity to resource $r$, we first compare activity execution history of $r$ with histories of other resources ($r_1$–$r_6$) to identify similar resources (Algorithm 1). We then analyse activity execution histories of similar resources to recommend

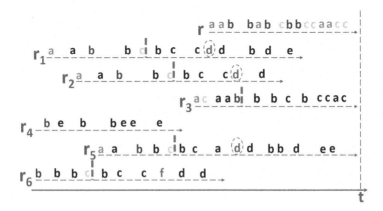

**Fig. 1.** An illustrative example with activity execution history of seven resources. (Color figure online)

a suitable new activity for resource $r$ (Algorithm 2). Table 1 provides a summary of main steps of Algorithm 1 (Step 1.1–Step 1.3) and Algorithm 2 (Step 2.1–Step 2.2) and shows the output values returned by each step.

**Table 1.** Output values from Algorithm 1 and Algorithm 2 for the example in Fig. 1.

| Algorithm step | Output value |
| --- | --- |
| 1.1. Extract past activities $A_{past}^r$ for resource $r$ | $A_{past}^r = \{a, b, c\}$ |
| 1.2. Identify all similar resources $R_{sim}$ | $R_{sim} = \{r_1, r_2, r_3, r_5, r_6\}$ |
| 1.3. Identify similar resources $R_{sim}^{new}$ who performed a new activity | $R_{sim}^{new} = \{r_1, r_2, r_5, r_6\}$ |
| 2.1. Identify new activities $A_{new}$ performed by similar resources | $A_{new} = \{d, f\}$ |
| 2.2. Recommend new activities $A_{rec}$ | $A_{rec} = \{d\}$ |

Below, we describe the two algorithms and explain how the values in Table 1 are calculated. The approach takes as input four thresholds:

- $min_{PastActivities}$ – the minimum number of activities that must be performed by a given resource before a recommendation can be provided to the resource.
- $min_{ResourceSimilarity}$ – the minimum resource similarity ($[0,1]$).
- $min_{SimilarResources}$ – the minimum number of similar resources.
- $min_{ActivitySupport}$ – the minimum fraction of similar resources who must perform a given activity for it to be considered for a recommendation. (For example, if the value of $min_{ActivitySupport}$ is 1 then an activity is only recommended if it was the next new activity performed by all similar resources.)

The value of threshold $min_{PastActivities}$ can be determined based on the knowledge of the process (e.g., a fraction of all activities in the process). The effect of other thresholds on the performance of the approach is evaluated in Sect. 4.

**Algorithm 1.** Algorithm 1 specifies how we identify similar resources. To identify similar resources, we compare sets of activities performed by different resources. One could also consider other aspects of work history (e.g., activity frequencies or outcomes), we discuss this direction for future work in Sect. 5.

The algorithm takes as input an event log $EL$, a given resource $r$ (for whom we would like to recommend a new activity), a given time point $t$ (when a recommendation is needed) and thresholds $min_{PastActivities}$, $min_{ResourceSimilarity}$ and $min_{SimilarResources}$. Algorithm 1 consists of three main steps.

In step 1.1, we extract a set of activities $A_{past}^r$ performed by resource $r$ before time $t$. For the example depicted in Fig. 1, $A_{past}^r = \{a, b, c\}$. If the number of activities in $A_{past}^r$ is lower than the threshold $min_{PastActivities}$, then we cannot provide a recommendation for resource $r$ at time $t$. The rationale behind this is that if the work history of a resource is very short (e.g., for an employee who just joined an organisation), then there is not enough information to identify similar resources (sufficient information about user history is a requirement of CF recommender systems). Let us assume that $min_{PastActivities} = 2$ for the example in Fig. 1, then the algorithm can proceed (as $|A^r_{past}| > 2$).

In step 1.2, we identify all similar resources $R_{sim}$. Measuring the similarity of resources based on their complete work histories (e.g., using sequence clustering) would not be appropriate, as the similarity of new employees and experienced employees would be low. Therefore, the similarity $sim^{r'}_r$ of resource $r$ and a given resource $r'$ is measured as the fraction of activities in $A^r_{past}$ that were also performed by $r'$. For example, $sim^{r_1}_r = 1$ as resource $r_1$ performed all activities in $A^r_{past}$ (i.e., $a$, $b$ and $c$); while similarity $sim^{r_6}_r = 2/3$ as resource $r_6$ only performed activities $b$ and $c$. A set of similar resources $R_{sim}$ comprises all resources whose similarity with resource $r$ is not lower than threshold $min_{ResourceSimilarity}$. Let us assume that $min_{ResourceSimilarity} = 0.6$ for the example in Fig. 1, then $R_{sim} = \{r_1, r_2, r_3, r_5, r_6\}$ (resource $r_4$ is not included as $sim^{r_4}_r$ (1/3) is lower than $min_{ResourceSimilarity}$ (0.6)). If the number of similar resources is lower than threshold $min_{SimilarResources}$, then a recommendation cannot be provided. Let us assume that for the example in Fig. 1, $min_{SimilarResources} = 3$, then the algorithm can proceed (as $|R_{sim}| > 3$).

In step 1.3, we identify those similar resources $R^{new}_{sim}$ who performed a new activity after execution of activities in $A^r_{past}$ and before $t$. First, we identify the earliest time $t^{r'}_a$ when all activities from $A^r_{past}$ were performed by a given resource $r'$ (the earliest times for similar resources are marked by vertical red dashed lines in Fig. 1). $R^{new}_{sim}$ comprises all similar resources who performed a new activity after time $t^{r'}_a$ and before time $t$. For the example in Fig. 1, $R^{new}_{sim} = \{r_1, r_2, r_5, r_6\}$ (resource $r_3$ did not perform any new activities). If the number of resources in $R^{new}_{sim}$ is below threshold $min_{SimilarResources}$, then a recommendation is not provided. For the example in Fig. 1, the algorithm can proceed (as $|R^{new}_{sim}| > 3$). Similar resources who did not perform new activities are likely to be at the same stage of their careers as resource $r$; therefore, we cannot learn from their work histories and they are not further considered.

**Algorithm 2.** Algorithm 2 recommends the next new activity for resource $r$ at time $t$. Recommending the next new activity can be challenging for processes in which employees follow similar but not exactly the same learning paths. To better accommodate such scenarios, we also implemented the second version of the approach which recommends a set of new activities (we discuss the second version of the approach at the end of this section). In this paper, we focus on recommending the next new activity or a set of activities; one could also consider recommending activity sequences (i.e., learning paths) or time periods during which a resource should start performing new activities (these directions for future work are discussed in Sect. 5).

The algorithm takes as input event log $EL$, resource $r$, time $t$, threshold $min_{ActivitySupport}$ and outputs of Algorithm 1 ($R^{new}_{sim}$, $t^{r'}_a$ and $A_{t^{r'}_a}$ for all $r' \in$

**Algorithm 1:** Find similar resources

**Input:** event log $EL$, resource $r$, time $t$, given thresholds $min_{PastActivities}$, $min_{ResourceSimilarity}$ and $min_{SimilarResources}$

**Output:** $R_{sim}^{new}$, $t_a^{r\prime}$ and $A_{t_a^{r\prime}}$ for all $r\prime \in R_{sim}^{new}$

/* **Step 1.1. Extract work history** $A_{past}^r$ **of resource** $r$ **at time** $t$      */
$A_{past}^r := \{a \in A \mid \exists e \in EL[e_{activity} = a \wedge e_{resource} = r \wedge e_{time} < t]\}$
**if** $|A_{past}^r| < min_{PastActivities}$ **then**
  |  *no recommendation*
**end**

/* **Step 1.2. Find similar resources** $R_{sim}$                                     */
$R_{sim} := \emptyset$
**for** *each* $r\prime \in R$ **do**
  |  $A_{past}^{r\prime} := \{a \in A \mid \exists e \in EL[e_{activity} = a \wedge e_{resource} = r\prime \wedge e_{time} < t]\}$
  |  $sim_r^{r\prime} := |A_{past}^r \cap A_{past}^{r\prime}| / |A_{past}^r|$
  |  **if** $r\prime \neq r \wedge sim_r^{r\prime} \geq min_{ResourceSimilarity}$ **then**
  |    |  $R_{sim} := R_{sim} \cup \{r\prime\}$
  |  **end**
**end**
**if** $|R_{sim}| < min_{SimilarResources}$ **then**
  |  *no recommendation*
**end**

/* **Step 1.3. Find similar resources** $R_{sim}^{new}$ **who performed a new**
   **activity after executing all activities in** $A_{past}^r$ **and before** $t$     */
$R_{sim}^{new} := \emptyset$
**for** *each* $r\prime \in R_{sim}$ **do**
  |  $T_{start} := \emptyset$
  |  **for** *each* $a \in A_{past}^r \cap A_{past}^{r\prime}$ **do**
  |    |  $T_a^{r\prime} := \{t\prime \in T \mid \exists e \in EL[e_{time} = t\prime \wedge e_{resource} = r\prime \wedge e_{activity} = a]\}$
  |    |  $T_{start} := T_{start} \cup \{ \min_{t\prime \in T_a^{r\prime}} t\prime \}$
  |  **end**
  |  $t_a^{r\prime} := \max_{t\prime \in T_{start}} t\prime$
  |  $A_{t_a^{r\prime}} := \{a \in A \mid \exists e \in EL[e_{activity} = a \wedge e_{resource} = r\prime \wedge e_{time} < t_a^{r\prime}]\}$
  |  **if** $\exists e \in EL[e_{activity} \notin A_{t_a^{r\prime}} \wedge e_{resource} = r\prime \wedge e_{time} > t_a^{r\prime} \wedge e_{time} < t]$ **then**
  |    |  $R_{sim}^{new} := R_{sim}^{new} \cup \{r\prime\}$
  |  **end**
**end**
**if** $|R_{sim}^{new}| < min_{SimilarResources}$ **then**
  |  *no recommendation*
**end**

$R_{sim}^{new}$). Our assumption is that the next new activity that will be likely performed by resource $r$ after time $t$ is the next new activity that was frequently performed by similar resources when they were at the same career stage as is resource $r$ at time $t$. Algorithm 2 consists of two main steps.

In step 2.1, we identify the first new activity performed by each resource $r\prime \in R_{sim}^{new}$ after $t_a^{r\prime}$, a set $A_{new}$ comprises all such activities. In Fig. 1 such activities are highlighted with red color ($A_{new} = \{d, f\}$).

In step 2.2, we recommend new activities $A_{rec}$. For each activity $a\prime \in A_{new}$, we get activity frequency $freq_{a\prime}$ (the fraction of resources in $R_{sim}^{new}$ who performed the activity); $freq_{max}$ is the maximum activity frequency. In the example in Fig. 1, $freq_d = 0.75$ (as it was the first new activity for three out of four resources), $freq_f = 0.25$ and $freq_{max} = 0.75$. If $freq_{max} < min_{ActivitySupport}$ then a recommendation is not provided (if similar resources perform different new activities then a recommendation is not reliable). Let us assume that for the example in Fig. 1 $min_{ActivitySupport} = 0.6$; hence, a recommendation can be provided (as $freq_{max} > 0.6$). The algorithm returns the set of recommended activities $A_{rec}$ which comprises all activities whose frequency is equal to $freq_{max}$ (in Fig. 1, $A_{rec} = \{d\}$). In practice, $A_{rec}$ usually consists of only one activity, it is possible that $A_{rec}$ includes more than one activity if the process includes activities that are completed at the same time or if $min_{ActivitySupport} \le 0.5$.

### Algorithm 2: RECOMMEND NEW ACTIVITIES

**Input**: event log $EL$, resource $r$, time $t$, threshold $min_{ActivitySupport}$, $R_{sim}^{new}$, $t_a^{r\prime}$
and $A_{t_a^{r\prime}}$ for all $r\prime \in R_{sim}^{new}$

**Output**: recommended activities $A_{rec}$

```
/* Step 2.1. Extract new activities A_new from similar resources    */
```
$A_{new} := \emptyset$

**for** *each* $r\prime \in R_{sim}^{new}$ **do**

$\quad E_{new}^{r\prime} := \{e \in EL \mid e_{time} > t_a^{r\prime} \wedge e_{time} < t \wedge e_{resource} = r\prime \wedge e_{activity} \notin A_{t_a^{r\prime}}\}$

$\quad T_{new}^{r\prime} := \{t\prime \in T \mid \exists e \in E_{new}^{r\prime}[e_{time} = t\prime]\}$

$\quad A_{new}^{r\prime} := \{a \in A \mid \exists e \in E_{new}^{r\prime}[e_{activity} = a \wedge e_{time} = \min_{t\prime \in T_{new}^{r\prime}} t\prime]\}$

$\quad A_{new} := A_{new} \cup A_{new}^{r\prime}$

**end**

```
/* Step 2.2. Extract recommended activities A_rec                    */
```
**for** *each* $a \in A_{new}$ **do**

$\quad freq_a := |\{r\prime \in R_{sim}^{new} \mid a \in A_{new}^{r\prime}\}|/|R_{sim}^{new}|$

**end**

$freq_{max} := \max_{a \in A_{new}} freq_a$

**if** $freq_{max} < min_{ActivitySupport}$ **then**

$\quad$ *no recommendation*

**end**

$A_{rec} := \{a \in A_{new} \mid freq_a = freq_{max}\}$

The algorithms described above recommend the next new activity. In the second version of the approach, we consider for a recommendation all new activities performed by a similar resource within a given time period (e.g., within a week or month) from the first new activity performed by the resource. We then recommend all activities whose frequency is higher than or equal to threshold $min_{ActivitySupport}$ (rather than an activity with the maximum frequency).

## 4   Evaluation

### 4.1   Data Sets and Experimental Setup

The performance of the approach was evaluated using three real event logs (Table 2). Two logs, referred to here as BPIC12[1] and BPIC17[2], contain events from a loan application process in a Dutch financial institution recorded during two different time periods. The third log, referred to here as WABO[3], contains information about a receipt phase of an environmental permit application process.

Table 2. Characteristics of event logs used in the evaluation.

| Log | Events | Cases | Activities | Resources | Generalists[a] | Log duration |
|---|---|---|---|---|---|---|
| BPIC12 | 244,190 | 13,087 | 24 | 68 | 59 | 166 days |
| BPIC17 | 238,481 | 14,254 | 25 | 107 | 88 | 6 months[b] |
| WABO | 8,577 | 1,434 | 27 | 48 | 22 | 479 days |

[a] We refer to resources who perform at least 1/3 of all process activities as generalists.
[b] We used events from the period 1/01/2016–30/06/2016 due to slow performance.

We conducted leave-one-out cross-validation and compared recommendations provided by the approach with actual activity executions recorded in the logs[4]. For a given resource $r$ and for a given point in time $t_{split}$, a recommendation is learned from events recorded before time $t_{split}$ and compared with the first new activity (or activities for the second version of the approach) recorded for resource $r$ after time $t_{split}$. This was repeated for all resources in each log. For each resource, time $t_{split}$ was set to the midway between the time of the first activity and the time of the first occurrence of the last new activity recorded for the resource in the log (such split ensures that for each resource at time $t_{split}$ there is at least one activity recorded before and after time $t_{split}$).

---

[1] https://data.4tu.nl/repository/uuid:3926db30-f712-4394-aebc-75976070e91f.
[2] https://data.4tu.nl/repository/uuid:5f3067df-f10b-45da-b98b-86ae4c7a310b.
[3] https://data.4tu.nl/repository/uuid:a07386a5-7be3-4367-9535-70bc9e77dbe6.
[4] The source code is available at https://github.com/a-pika/TaskRecommender.

In the evaluation, we used two performance measures. We measured the fraction of resources for whom a recommendation was provided (referred to here as 'recommendations') and the average accuracy of the recommendations. The first version of our approach recommends the next new activity and the second version of the approach recommends all new activities to be performed within a given time period $t_{period}$ from the first new activity. For the first version, the accuracy of a recommendation provided to a resource at time $t_{split}$ is *1* if the recommended activity is the next new activity recorded for the resource after time $t_{split}$; otherwise, the accuracy is *0*. For the second version, the accuracy of a recommendation provided to a resource at time $t_{split}$ was measured as the fraction of recommended activities that were performed by the resource after time $t_{split}$ within time $t_{period}$ from the first new activity.

## 4.2   Results

To evaluate various factors affecting the performance of the approach, we conducted three experiments using the three event logs described in Sect. 4.1. In Experiment 1, we evaluated the effect of different threshold values on the approach performance. In Experiment 2, we compared the performance of the two versions of the approach. In Experiment 3, we compared the performance of the approach for all resources with the performance for generalists only.

**Experiment 1: The Impact of Threshold Values on the Performance.**
In the first experiment, we evaluated the impact of different values of thresholds $min_{ResourceSimilarity}$, $min_{SimilarResources}$ and $min_{ActivitySupport}$ on the performance of the approach. The value of threshold $min_{PastActivities}$ was set to 5 for all event logs and for all experiments[5]. In this experiment, we applied the first version of the approach (i.e., recommending the next new activity). We varied the values of one threshold at a time and fixed the values of two other thresholds. The fixed values used in the experiment were as follows: $min_{ResourceSimilarity} = 0.7$, $min_{SimilarResources} = 3$ and $min_{ActivitySupport} = 0.7$.

Figures 2a–2c show the recommendations and the accuracy for different values of threshold $min_{ResourceSimilarity}$ (ranging from 0.1 to 0.9) for the three logs. We can observe that for log WABO (Fig. 2a), no recommendations were provided for values 0.1 and 0.3 and starting from the minimum resource similarity of 0.5 the accuracy is 1 and the number of recommendations does not change much. For log BPIC12 (Fig. 2b), there are no big differences in the accuracy and the number of recommendations for threshold values 0.1–0.7, while for value 0.9 the accuracy increases and the number of recommendations decreases. For log BPIC17 (Fig. 2c), the accuracy gradually increases, while the number of recommendations does not change much. The charts show that higher values of the minimum resource similarity threshold yield better accuracy; however, the number of recommendations may decrease (due to a smaller number of similar resources). We can also observe that the effect is more pronounced for log

---

[5] Reliable recommendations cannot be provided to resources with short work histories.

WABO (Fig. 2a) and is less significant for the other two logs. It is possible that there are more similar resources in these two logs; hence, the effect of the minimum resource similarity threshold is less pronounced for them.

Figures 2d–2f demonstrate the effect of threshold $min_{SimilarResources}$ and Figs. 2g–2i show the effect of threshold $min_{ActivitySupport}$ on the approach performance for the three logs. For both thresholds, we can observe similar trends for the three logs: higher values of a threshold ($min_{SimilarResources}$ or $min_{ActivitySupport}$) yield better accuracy and reduce the number of recommendations. Figure 2 shows that threshold $min_{ActivitySupport}$ has the biggest impact on the performance for all logs. It is expected that the accuracy is poor for values of $min_{ActivitySupport}$ that are below 0.5 as in such scenarios more than one activity can be included in the recommendation (when similar resources perform different unfamiliar activities), and hence, the recommendation is not reliable.

Experiment 1 showed the trade-off between the accuracy and the number of recommendations. For example, in Fig. 2h, recommendations are provided to 41% of resources with the average accuracy of 0.61; however, they could only be provided to 3% of resources with the accuracy of 1. The experiment also showed that the impact of the thresholds on the performance is similar for all logs (higher values yield better performance); however, specific values that could achieve a

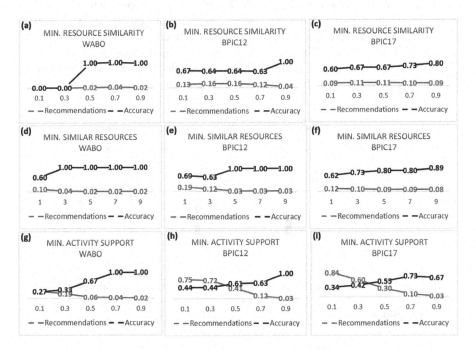

**Fig. 2.** Experiment 1: the impact of threshold values on the approach performance (Recommendations – the fraction of resources for whom a recommendation was provided; accuracy – the average accuracy of the recommendations).

given level of performance are different for different logs. In future work, we plan to use machine learning to configure the thresholds.

**Experiment 2: The Performance of Different Versions of the Approach.** In Experiment 1, we evaluated the first version of our approach which recommends the next new activity. In Experiment 2, we evaluated the second version of the approach which recommends a set of new activities to be performed within a given period of time from the next new activity. We evaluated two time periods: 7 days and 30 days. We used the following values of the thresholds: $min_{ResourceSimilarity} = \{0.6, 0.7, 0.8\}$, $min_{SimilarResources} = \{2, 3, 4\}$ and $min_{ActivitySupport} = \{0.6, 0.7, 0.8\}$ (the values were selected based on the results of Experiment 1 as they yielded optimal performance for the three logs). The experiment was performed for all combinations of these values (i.e., 27 times) and we report the average values in Fig. 3. Figure 3a shows the average fraction of resources for whom a recommendation was provided (by two versions of the approach) and Fig. 3b shows the average accuracy of the recommendations. We can see that for all logs the number of recommendations is higher for the second version of the approach and is higher for the longer time period (i.e., 30 days). The accuracy does not change much for log WABO and for the other two logs it is higher for the second version of the approach. The experiment shows that predicting the next new activity is more challenging than predicting a set of new activities and the longer the time period that is considered, the better the performance of the approach. This outcome is expected as the number of employees who follow similar learning paths will be usually higher than the number of employees who follow the exact same learning path in an organisation.

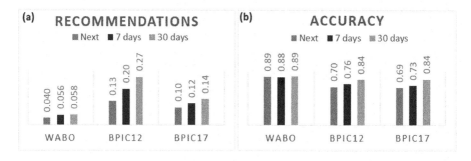

**Fig. 3.** Experiment 2: the performance of different versions of the approach (Next – recommending the next new activity; 7 days and 30 days – recommending new activities to be performed within 7 days and 30 days from the next new activity).

**Experiment 3: The Performance of the Approach for Generalists.** Experiments 1 and 2 were conducted using information about all resources recorded in the event logs. This approach may not be suitable for resources who only perform very few activity types in the process (i.e., specialists). In Experiment 3, we compared the performance of the approach for all resources with the performance for generalists. We set the threshold that generalists perform at least 1/3 of all activity types in the process. Table 2 shows the number of all resources and the number of generalists in each log. We used the same threshold values as in Experiment 2 and we show the average performance values in Fig. 4. We evaluated the performance of both versions of the approach (denoted as 'Next' and '30 days' in Fig. 4). As expected, the number of recommendations is higher for generalists than for all resources (Fig. 4a) for both versions of the approach for all event logs, while the average accuracy does not change much (Fig. 4b).

The experiments demonstrated the performance of the approach for different configurations and real event logs. They showed that the approach can provide recommendations to multiple resources with the accuracy ranging from 0.6 to 0.9 (depending on the configuration and the log, see Figs. 2–4), while few recommendations can be provided with the accuracy close to 1.

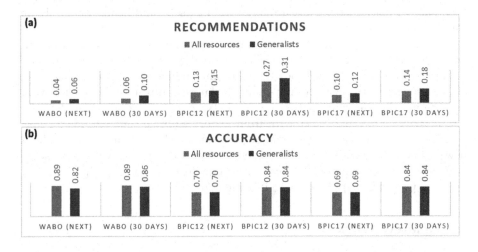

**Fig. 4.** Experiment 3: the performance of the approach for all resources and generalists.

## 5    Assumptions, Limitations and Future Work

An assumption of our approach is that groups of employees follow similar learning paths; the proposed approach is not suitable for organisations in which employees have unique career trajectories. We assume that there are no dependencies between recommended activities and activities previously performed by a resource; an investigation of activity pre-requisites is a direction for future work. We also assume that the process is in a steady state (i.e., it is not changing over time); one could investigate the possibility to only use recent work history.

A limitation of our approach is the use of a simple resource similarity measure which compares sets of activities performed by different employees. A direction for future work is to devise resource similarity measures that consider additional factors (e.g., the order of activities, activity frequencies, durations or activity outcomes [13]). A richer notion of resource similarity could help to improve the performance of the approach (it could be possible to provide more accurate recommendations with fewer similar resources). Another limitation of the approach is the need to specify the values of the four thresholds which are input to the approach; in future work we plan to configure the thresholds (e.g., by using hyperparameter optimisation techniques). The performance of the approach was evaluated by comparing activity recommendations with actual activity executions recorded in event logs; a direction for future work is an evaluation of the effect of the approach on organisational capacity and employee development.

The approach presented in this article is algorithmic; one could also consider the possibility to use machine learning techniques. For example, an application of clustering algorithms to identify similar resources could be investigated; a challenge is that learning paths of new and experienced employees may not be considered similar by such algorithms. One could also apply machine learning algorithms (e.g., deep neural networks) to learn activity recommendations; however, such algorithms often require large training sets, and hence, may only be suitable for large organisations.

In this work, we focused on recommending unfamiliar activities to potential generalists; the approach could be extended for specialists to recommend unfamiliar case or activity types (e.g., recommending more complex cases or activities related to new product groups). Another direction for future work is recommending learning paths (i.e., activity sequences rather than the next new activity). One could also learn from history suitable time periods for new activities (e.g., a new activity should be performed no later than six months from now). Finally, the possibility to combine the proposed approach with approaches that consider other resource allocation criteria (e.g., resource compatibility or previous performance) [2] could be investigated.

## 6  Related Work

Business Process Management is concerned with the development of new methods and techniques for design, implementation, execution and analysis of business processes. Employees and their skill sets play a crucial role in running efficient and cost effective business operations and organisations are always exploring ways to grow the capabilities of their employees over time (e.g., a learning organisation [5]). Process-aware information systems allocate resources to process activities at run time according to some pre-defined criteria (e.g., based on roles); however, "current systems provide limited support for resource allocation" and "actual resource allocation is delegated to people to some extent" [7]. Systems that support flexible business processes allow employees to select methods suitable for a particular process instance (rather than allocating specific tasks to resources) [4,6]; however, resources who can handle the process instance are still selected based on pre-defined criteria (e.g., roles or qualifications [4]).

Russell et al. [14] proposed a set of resource patterns that describe how a resource interacts with a process-aware information system. A role-based allocation pattern, for example, offers the work to a resource with a specific role while a round-robin allocation pattern offers a fair and equitable allocation by sharing work equally among resources. Other patterns utilise the knowledge of previous performance of resources (e.g., in the case of the retain familiar pattern and the history-based distribution pattern). Although these resource patterns do not explicitly consider workforce upskilling concerns, the proposed approach can be seen as an advanced form of the history-based distribution pattern [14].

Organisational mining is an area of process-oriented data mining which is concerned with extracting insights about various aspects of resource behaviour from event logs [13, 19] and includes history-based resource allocation approaches [2, 3]. A recent systematic mapping study [3] identified 95 approaches which tackle the problem of human resource allocation in business processes. A taxonomy of human resource allocation criteria was proposed by Arias et al. [2] based on an extensive literature review of existing approaches. The proposed taxonomy captures the following resource allocation criteria: the number of required resources, resource experience and expertise, resource preferences, previous performance, role, social context (e.g., collaboration or compatibility), trustworthiness ("notion of trust degree that a resource may have to execute activities") and resource workload [2]. These works [2, 3] provide an extensive overview of resource allocation approaches; however, *the capability development needs of employees (i.e., workforce upskilling) are not explicitly considered by the taxonomy.*

Existing resource allocation approaches can discover resource assignment rules from event logs (e.g., Schönig et al. [16, 17]); optimise resource allocation in order to improve process performance (e.g., an approach proposed by Park and Song [12] optimises resource allocation for "a maximum flow with the smallest possible cost"; an approach proposed by Huang et al. [9] optimises resource allocation "by trying to minimize long-term cost" using reinforcement learning; and an approach proposed by Havur et al. [8] derives "an optimal schedule for work items that have dependencies"); or they provide support for resource allocation decisions (e.g., a recommender system proposed by Sindhgatta et al. [18] "uses information on the performance of similar resources in similar contexts to predict a resource's suitability for a task"). *All these approaches are process-centric (i.e., they aim to improve the performance of a process) and they disregard skill development needs of employees.*

The need to take human-centric approach in resource allocation was raised by Kabicher-Fuchs and Rinderle-Ma [11] who proposed a collection of work experience measures. Kabicher-Fuchs et al. [10] proposed a resource allocation algorithm which considers experience development goals explicitly specified by employees. A genetic algorithm based approach by Starkey et al. [20] optimises team moves and upskilling specifically for engineers; "the next logical skill set for any given engineer" is an input to the algorithm. Similar to these works, we argue that resource development needs should be considered by resource allocation methods; however, unlike these works, *our approach recommends new activities to employees by analysing their work history recorded in event logs.*

# 7    Conclusion

Human resource allocation decisions have a direct impact on the performance of business processes. The problem of assigning suitable employees to process activities has got a lot of attention in the Business Process Management community; however, the majority of resource allocation approaches do not consider the capacity development needs of organisations and individual employees. In this article, we proposed an approach for recommending unfamiliar process activities to employees by analysing work histories recorded in process execution data. The approach was implemented and evaluated using three real event logs. The evaluation demonstrated the effectiveness of the approach for different event logs and configuration settings. The proposed approach is the first attempt to provide history-based recommendations of unfamiliar process activities to employees using process execution data and it opens an array of opportunities for further research, which we discussed in this article.

# References

1. van der Aalst, W.: Process Mining: Data Science in Action. Springer, Berlin (2016). https://doi.org/10.1007/978-3-662-49851-4_1
2. Arias, M., Munoz-Gama, J., Sepúlveda, M.: Towards a taxonomy of human resource allocation criteria. In: Teniente, E., Weidlich, M. (eds.) BPM 2017. LNBIP, vol. 308, pp. 475–483. Springer, Cham (2018). https://doi.org/10.1007/978-3-319-74030-0_37
3. Arias, M., Saavedra, R., Marques, M.R., Munoz-Gama, J., Sepúlveda, M.: Human resource allocation in business process management and process mining: a systematic mapping study. Manag. Decis. **56**(2), 376–405 (2018)
4. Dellen, B., Maurer, F., Pews, G.: Knowledge-based techniques to increase the flexibility of workflow management. Data Knowl. Eng. **23**(3), 269–295 (1997)
5. Dymock, D., McCarthy, C.: Towards a learning organization? employee perceptions. Learn. Organ. **13**(5), 525–537 (2006)
6. Faustmann, G.: Enforcement vs freedom of action an integrated approach to flexible workflow enactment. ACM SIGGROUP Bull. **20**(3), 5–6 (1999)
7. Havur, G., Cabanillas, C.: History-aware dynamic process fragmentation for risk-aware resource allocation. In: Panetto, H., Debruyne, C., Hepp, M., Lewis, D., Ardagna, C.A., Meersman, R. (eds.) OTM 2019. LNCS, vol. 11877, pp. 533–551. Springer, Cham (2019). https://doi.org/10.1007/978-3-030-33246-4_33
8. Havur, G., Cabanillas, C., Mendling, J., Polleres, A.: Resource allocation with dependencies in business process management systems. In: La Rosa, M., Loos, P., Pastor, O. (eds.) BPM 2016. LNBIP, vol. 260, pp. 3–19. Springer, Cham (2016). https://doi.org/10.1007/978-3-319-45468-9_1
9. Huang, Z., van der Aalst, W.M., Lu, X., Duan, H.: Reinforcement learning based resource allocation in business process management. Data Knowl. Eng. **70**(1), 127–145 (2011)
10. Kabicher-Fuchs, S., Mangler, J., Rinderle-Ma, S.: Experience breeding in process-aware information systems. In: Salinesi, C., Norrie, M.C., Pastor, Ó. (eds.) CAiSE 2013. LNCS, vol. 7908, pp. 594–609. Springer, Heidelberg (2013). https://doi.org/10.1007/978-3-642-38709-8_38

11. Kabicher-Fuchs, S., Rinderle-Ma, S.: Work experience in PAIS – concepts, measurements and potentials. In: Ralyté, J., Franch, X., Brinkkemper, S., Wrycza, S. (eds.) CAiSE 2012. LNCS, vol. 7328, pp. 678–694. Springer, Heidelberg (2012). https://doi.org/10.1007/978-3-642-31095-9_44

12. Park, G., Song, M.: Prediction-based resource allocation using LSTM and minimum cost and maximum flow algorithm. In: ICPM 2019, pp. 121–128. IEEE (2019)

13. Pika, A., Leyer, M., Wynn, M.T., Fidge, C.J., ter Hofstede, A., van der Aalst, W.: Mining resource profiles from event logs. ACM TMIS 8(1), 1 (2017)

14. Russell, N., Van Der Aalst, W.M., Ter Hofstede, A.H.: Workflow Patterns: The Definitive Guide. MIT Press, Cambridge (2016)

15. Schafer, J.B., Frankowski, D., Herlocker, J., Sen, S.: Collaborative filtering recommender systems. In: Brusilovsky, P., Kobsa, A., Nejdl, W. (eds.) The Adaptive Web. LNCS, vol. 4321, pp. 291–324. Springer, Heidelberg (2007). https://doi.org/10.1007/978-3-540-72079-9_9

16. Schönig, S., Cabanillas, C., Di Ciccio, C., Jablonski, S., Mendling, J.: Mining team compositions for collaborative work in business processes. Softw. Syst. Model. 17(2), 675–693 (2016). https://doi.org/10.1007/s10270-016-0567-4

17. Schönig, S., Cabanillas, C., Jablonski, S., Mendling, J.: A framework for efficiently mining the organisational perspective of business processes. Decis. Support Syst. 89, 87–97 (2016)

18. Sindhgatta, R., Ghose, A., Dam, H.K.: Context-aware recommendation of task allocations in service systems. In: Sheng, Q.Z., Stroulia, E., Tata, S., Bhiri, S. (eds.) ICSOC 2016. LNCS, vol. 9936, pp. 402–416. Springer, Cham (2016). https://doi.org/10.1007/978-3-319-46295-0_25

19. Song, M., van der Aalst, W.: Towards comprehensive support for organizational mining. Decis. Support Syst. 46(1), 300–317 (2008)

20. Starkey, A.J., Hagras, H., Shakya, S., Owusu, G.: A genetic algorithm based approach for the simultaneous optimisation of workforce skill sets and team allocation. In: Bramer, M., Petridis, M. (eds.) Research and Development in Intelligent Systems XXXIII, pp. 253–266. Springer, Cham (2016). https://doi.org/10.1007/978-3-319-47175-4_19

21. Ulrich, D., Lake, D.: Organizational capability: creating competitive advantage. Acad. Manag. Perspect. 5(1), 77–92 (1991)

# Requirements and Modeling

# Evaluating the Benefits of Model-Driven Development

## Empirical Evaluation Paper

África Domingo[1]([⊠]), Jorge Echeverría[1]([⊠]), Óscar Pastor[2]([⊠]),
and Carlos Cetina[1]([⊠])

[1] Universidad San Jorge, SVIT Research Group, Zaragoza, Spain
{adomingo,jecheverria,ccetina}@usj.es
[2] Universidad Politecnica de Valencia, PROS Research Center, Valencia, Spain
opastor@dsi.upv.es

**Abstract.** Researchers have been evaluating the benefits of Model-Driven Development (MDD) for more than a decade now. Although some works suggest that MDD decreases development time, other works limit MDD benefits to academic exercises and to developers without experience. To clarify the benefits of MDD, we present the results of our experiment, which compares MDD and Code-centric Development (CcD) in terms of correctness, efficiency, and satisfaction. Our experiment achieves fidelity to real-world settings because the tasks are taken from real-world video game development, and the subjects use domain frameworks as they are used in real-world developments. Our results challenge previous ideas that limit the benefits of MDD to academic exercises and to developers without experience. Furthermore, our results also suggest that understanding the benefits of MDD might require researchers to rethink their experiments to include the social part of software development.

**Keywords:** Model-Driven Development · Code-centric development · Empirical evaluation · Experiment

## 1 Introduction

Model-Driven Development (MDD) [19] promotes software models as the cornerstone of software development. In comparison to popular programming languages, these software models are less bound to the underlying implementation and are closer to the problem domain. Model transformation is at the heart of MDD since MDD aims to generate the software code from the models. This generation ranges from skeleton code to fully functional code systems.

For more than a decade, researchers have been evaluating the benefits of MDD [1,2,6–8,11–13,16–18]. Some works [6,11,18] conclude that MDD decreases development time (up to 89% ) relative to Code-centric Development

Partially supported by MINECO under the Project ALPS (RTI2018-096411-B-I00).

S. Dustdar et al. (Eds.): CAiSE 2020, LNCS 12127, pp. 353–367, 2020.
https://doi.org/10.1007/978-3-030-49435-3_22

(CcD) [11]. Other works [8,17] suggest that gains might only be achieved in academic exercises. Furthermore, other works [8,12] assert that only developers without experience benefit from MDD. Therefore, more experimentation is needed to clarify the benefits of MDD.

In the context of MDD, domain frameworks (bodies of prewritten code) help model transformations to fill the abstraction gap between models and code (see Fig. 1 left). These frameworks are not exclusive of MDD. In the context of CcD, developers also use frameworks to accelerate development (see Fig. 1 right). However, previous experiments neglect the use of domain frameworks. This triggers the question of whether MDD benefits would hold when frameworks are considered.

In this work, we present our experiment, which compares MDD and CcD in terms of correctness, efficiency, and satisfaction. The tasks of our experiment are extracted from the real-world software development tasks of a commercial video game (Kromaia[1] released on PlayStation 4 and Steam). A total of 44 subjects (classified in two groups based on development experience) performed the tasks of the experiment. In our experiment, both MDD and CcD leverage a domain framework (see Fig. 1).

Our results challenge previous ideas that suggest that MDD gains are only achieved in academic settings. In our experiment with tasks from real-world development, MDD improved correctness and efficiency by 41% and 54% respectively. The results also contradict the previous claim that MDD benefits are limited to developers without experience. In the experiment, developers without experience (49% and 69%) as well as developers with experience (39% and 54%) significantly improved their results with MDD.

Furthermore, the results also uncover a paradox. Despite the significant improvements in correctness and efficiency, the intention of use of MDD did not achieve maximum values. We think this should influence future experiments to go beyond the technical facet and explore the cultural aspect of software development.

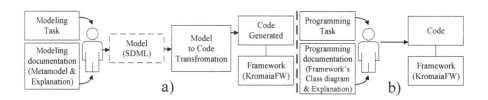

**Fig. 1.** a) Artifacts in the MDD task b) Artifacts in the CcD task

The rest of the paper is organized as follows: Sect. 2 reviews the related work. Section 3 describes our experiment, and Sect. 4 shows the results. Section 5 describes the threats to validity. Finally, Sect. 6 concludes the paper.

---

[1] https://youtu.be/EhsejJBp8Go.

## 2   Related Work

In the Motorola Case Study, Baker et al. [2] present their experiences deploying a top-down approach to MDD for more than 15 years in a large industrial context, resulting in a set of high-level strategies to enhance MDD deployment and success. Anda and Hansen [1] analyze the use of MDD with UML in software development companies. They show that developers who applied UML in modelling and enhancing legacy software experienced more challenges than those who modelled and developed new software from scratch. They propose a need for better methodological support in applying UML in legacy development.

Krogmann and Becker [11] present one of the first comparisons between MDD and CcD software development with respect to effort. Despite its limitations (it is not as a controlled experiment), their case study compares two software development projects, each of which was developed using a different method. They conclude that the model-driven approach could be carried out in only 11% of the time that of the code-centric approach. Another comparative case study of model-driven development with code-centric development by Kapteijns et al. [8] claims that MDD can be successfully applied to small-scale development projects under easy conditions. Heijstek and Chaudron [6] focused their case study on report specific metrics to analyze model size, complexity, quality, and effort. They analyze an industrial MDD project that was developed for the equivalent of 28 full-time team members. They showed that an increase in productivity, a reduction in complexity, and benefits from a consistent implementation are attributed to the use of MDD techniques. Mellegård and Staron [13] analyze the main modelling artefacts in the analysis and design phase of projects with respect to required effort and perceived importance. They conclude that the distribution of effort between models and other artefacts is similar in code-centric development to that of model-driven development. The factors for a successful adoption of MDD in a company were analyzed later by Hutchinson et al. [7] through interviews of 20 subjects from three different companies. They claim that a progressive and iterative approach, transparent organizational commitment and motivation, integration with existing organizational processes, and a clear business focus are required to guarantee success in the adoption of MDD techniques.

The experiment conducted by Martínez et al. [12] with undergraduate students compares three methods: Model-driven, Model-Based, and Code-Centric, regarding perceived usefulness, ease of use, intention of use, and compatibility. They conclude that the Model-Driven method is considered to be the most useful one, although it is also considered to be the least compatible with previous developers' experiences. Pappoti et al. [18] also present an experiment with a group of students in which an MDD based approach using code generation from models is compared with manual coding. When code generation was applied, the development time was consistently shorter than with manual coding. The participants also indicated that they had fewer difficulties when applying code generation. For Panach et al. [17], the benefits of developing software with MDD depend on the development context characteristics, such as problem complexity and the developers' background experience with MDD. However, in a later work [16], where they report the results of six replications of the same experiment, they confirm that MDD yields better quality independently of problem complexity, and that the effect is bigger when the problems are more complex.

**Table 1.** Empirical studies on MDD

| Work | Modelling Language | Domain Framework | Sample size | Context | Type of Study | Variables |
|------|------|------|------|------|------|------|
| [2] | UML | No | Not given | Industry | Case Study | Quality—Productivity |
| [1] | UML | No | 28 | Industry | Experiment | Difficulty—Use—Utility |
| [11] | DSL (GMFML) | No | 11 | Academia | Case Study | Quality—Efficiency Time effort |
| [6] | UML | No | 4 | Industry | Case Study | Quality—Effort Size—Complexity |
| [8] | UML | No | 1 | Industry | Case Study | Quality—Productivity Maintainability |
| [13] | UML | No | 3 | Industry | Case Study | Effort |
| [7] | UML | No | 20 | Industry | Case Study | Factors for a successful adoption of MDD |
| [12] | UML DSL (OOH4RIA) | No | 26 | Academia | Experiment | Perceived usefulness Perceived ease of use Intention to adopt Compatibility |
| [18] | UML | No | 29 | Academia | Experiment | Efficiency—Effort Participants' opinion |
| [17, 16] | UML | No | 26 | Academia | Experiment | Quality—Effort Satisfaction—Productivity |
| This work | DSL(SDML) | Yes | 44 | Academia[a] | Experiment | Correctness—Efficiency Satisfaction |

[a] The tasks in our experiment are based on a real-world video game, but all participants involved are still students. Also, an experiment outside a company setting is by nature artificial.

Table 1 summarizes the related work. In contrast to previous works, we address the use of a domain framework as part of both MDD and CcD. This dimension has not been explored before. This contributes to achieving fidelity to real-world development since domain frameworks are fairly popular in both MDD and CcD contexts.

## 3  Experiment Design

### 3.1  Objectives

According to the guidelines for reporting software engineering experiments [22], we have organized our research objectives using the Goal Question Metric template for goal definition, which was originally presented by Basili and Rombach [3]. Our goal is to:

**Analyze** software development methods, **for the purpose of** comparison, **with respect to** correctness of the software developed, efficiency, and user satisfaction; **from the point of view of** novice and professional developers, **in the context of** developing software for a video game company.

## 3.2 Variables

In this study, the independent variable is the software development method (*Method*). It has two values, MDD and CcD, which are the methods used by subjects to solve the tasks.

Given that our experiment evaluates the benefits of MDD, and the most reported benefit of MDD is decreased development time, we consider two dependent variables, *Correctness* and *Efficiency*, which are related to the software that is developed. *Correctness* was measured using a correction template, which was applied to the programming artifacts developed by the participants after the experiment. *Correctness* was calculated as the percentage of passing assert statements with respect to the total number of assert statements. To calculate *Efficiency*, we measured the time employed by each subject to finish the task. *Efficiency* is the ratio of *Correctness* to time spent (in minutes) to perform a task.

We measured users satisfaction using a 5-point Likert-scale questionnaire based on the Technology Acceptance Model (TAM) [14], wich is used for validating Information System Design Methods. We decompose satisfaction into three dependent variables as follows: *Perceived Ease of Use* (PEOU), the degree to which a person believes that learning and using a particular method would require less effort. *Perceived Usefulness* (PU), the degree to which a person believes that using a particular method will increase performance, and *Intention to Use* (ITU), the degree to which a person intents to use a method. Each of these variables corresponds to specific items in the TAM questionnaire. We averaged the scores obtained for these items to obtain the value for each variable.

## 3.3 Design

Since the factor under investigation in this experiment is the software development method, we compared MDD and CcD. In order to improve experiment robustness regarding variation among subjects [21], we chose a repeated measurement using the largest possible sample size. To avoid the order effect, we chose a crossover design and we used two different tasks, T1 and T2. All of the subjects used the two development methods, each one of which was used in a different task.

The subjects had been randomly divided into two groups (G1 and G2). In the first part of the experiment, all of the subjects solved T1 with G1 using CcD and G2 using MDD. Afterwards, all of the subjects solved T2, G1 using MDD and G2 using CcD.

## 3.4    Participants

The subjects were selected according to convenience sampling [22]. A total of 44 subjects performed the experiment. There were 35 second-year undergraduate students from a technological program and 9 masters students in a subject about advanced software modelling currently employed as professional developers. The undergraduate students were novice developers and the master students were professional developers.

The subjects filled out a demographic questionnaire that was used for characterizing the sample. Table 2 shows the mean and standard deviation of age, experience, hours per day developing software (Code Time) and hours per day working with models (Model Time). On average, all of the masters students had worked four years developing software. They worked on software development six hours per day while the undergraduate students, on average, dedicated less than 1.5 h to developing software each day. We used a Likert scale form 1 to 8 to measure the subjects' knowledge about domain-specific languages (DSL know) and programming languages (PL know). The mean and standard deviation of their answers are also in Table 2. All of them evaluated higher their programming language knowledge than their ability with models.

**Table 2.** Results of the demographic questionnaire

| | Age $\pm\sigma$ | Experience $\pm\sigma$ | Code time $\pm\sigma$ | Model time $\pm\sigma$ | DSL Know $\pm\sigma$ | PL Know $\pm\sigma$ |
|---|---|---|---|---|---|---|
| Undergraduate | $22.2\pm0.4$ | $0.6\pm1.4$ | $1.4\pm0.8$ | $1.0\pm0.4$ | $3\pm1.7$ | $4.2\pm1.8$ |
| Masters | $27\pm2.6$ | $4.3\pm3.2$ | $6.2\pm2.0$ | $0.9\pm0.3$ | $3.4\pm1.0$ | $6.2\pm1.2$ |
| Total | $21.6\pm3.2$ | $1.4\pm2.4$ | $2.4\pm2.3$ | $1\pm0.4$ | $3.1\pm1.7$ | $4.6\pm1.9$ |

The experiment was conducted by two instructors and one video game software engineer (the expert), who designed the tasks, prepared the correction template, and corrected the tasks. The expert provided information about both the domain-specific language and the domain framework. During the experiment, one of the instructors gave the instructions and managed the focus groups. The other instructor clarified doubts about the experiment and took notes during the focus group.

## 3.5    Research Questions and Hypotheses

We seek to answer the following three research questions:

**RQ1.** Does the method used for developing software impact the *Correctness* of code? The corresponding null hypotheses is $H_{C0}$: The software development method does not have an effect on *Correctness*.

**RQ2.** Does the method used for developing software impact the *Efficiency* of developers to develop software? The null hypotheses for *Efficiency* is $H_{E0}$: The software development method does not have an effect on *Efficiency*.

**RQ3.** Is the user satisfaction different when developers use different methods of software development? To answer this question we formulated three hypotheses based on the variables *Perceived Ease of Use*, *Perceived Usefulness*, and *Intention to Use*:$H_{PEOU}$, $H_{PU}$ and $H_{ITU}$ respectively. The corresponding null hypotheses are:

$H_{PEOU0}$: The software development method does not have an effect on *Perceived Ease of Use*.

$H_{PU0}$: The software development method does not have an effect on *Perceived Usefulness*

$H_{ITU0}$: The software development method does not have an effect on *Intention to Use*.

The hypotheses are formulated as two-tailed hypotheses since not all of the empirical or theoretical studies support the same direction for the effect.

## 3.6   Experiment Procedure

The diagram in Fig. 2 shows the experiment procedure that can be summarises as follows:

1. The subjects received information about the experiment. An instructor explained the parts in the session, and he advised that it was not a test of their abilities.
2. A video game software engineer explained to the subjects the problem context and how to develop game characters on a video game with the domain framework to be used later in the experiment. The average time spent on this tutorial was 30 min.
3. The subjects completed a demographic questionnaire. One of the instructors distributed and collected the questionnaires, verifying that all of the fields had been answered and that the subject had signed the voluntary participation form in the experiment.
4. The subjects received clear instructions on where to find the statements for each task, how to submit their work, and how to complete the task sheet and the satisfaction questionnaire at the end of each task.
5. The subjects performed the first task. The subjects were randomly divided into two groups (G1 and G2) to perform the tasks with the domain framework. The subjects from G1 developed the first task coding with C++, and the subjects from G2 developed the task using MDD. The instructors used the distribution in the room to distinguish one group from another and to give specific guidance to each subject if requested.
6. The subjects completed a satisfaction questionnaire about the method used to perform the task.
7. The subjects answered an open-ended questionnaire about the method used to perform the task.
8. An instructor checked that each subject had filled in all of the fields on the task sheet and on the satisfaction questionnaire.

9. The subjects performed the second task exchanging methods. In other words, the subjects from G1 performed the second task using MDD, and the subjects from G2 performed the task using C++. Then, the subjects filled out the satisfaction questionnaire and the open-ended questionnaire that were related to the method used.
10. A focus group interview about the tasks was conducted by one instructor while the other instructor took notes.
11. Finally, the video game software engineer corrected the tasks and an instructor analyzed the results.

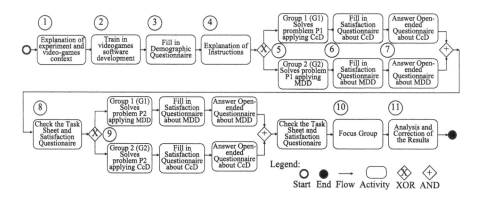

**Fig. 2.** Experimental procedure

In the tasks, the subjects were requested to develop the code of a part of the Kromaia video game, specifically a different game boss for each task. On average, the tasks took about 50 model elements of Shooter Definition Model Language (MDD), and about 300 lines of code (CcD). Learn more about developing the game bosses at https://youtu.be/Vp3Zt4qXkoY. The materials used in this experiment (the training material, the consent to process the data, the demographic questionnaire, the satisfaction questionnaire, the open-ended questionnaire, the task sheet and the materials used in the focus group) are available at http://svit.usj.es/MDD-experiment.

The experiment was conducted on two different days at *Universidad San Jorge* (Zaragoza, Spain) by the same instructors and a video game software engineer. On the first day, the experiment was performed by the masters students. On the second day, the undergraduate students performed the experiment. The masters and undergraduate students did not know each other. Their schedules at the university were completely different and the programs they followed are aimed at different types of student profiles.

## 4    Results

For the data analysis we have chosen the Linear Mixed Model (LMM) test [20] also used in others crossover experiments in software engineering [9]. LMM handles correlated data resulting from repeated measurements. The dependent variables for this test are *Correctness, Efficiency, Perceived Ease of Use, Perceived Usefulness,* and *Intention to Use.* In our study, the subjects are random factors and the *Method* used to develop software (MDD or CcD) is a fixed factor (the primary focus of our investigation). The statistical model (Model 1) used in this case is described as:

$$DV \sim Method + (1|\,subject) \tag{1}$$

Additionally, the subjects experience is also consider to be a fixed effect. We consider the variables *Experience* and the sequence *Method* and *Experience* to be fixed effects to account for their potential effects in determining the main effect of *Method* [9]. The statistical model (Model 2) used in this case is described in the following formula:

$$DV \sim Method + Experience + Method * Experience + (1|\,Subjec) \tag{2}$$

The statistical model fit for each variable has been evaluated based on goodness of fit measures such as Akaike's information criterion (AIC) and Schwarz's Bayesian information criterion (BIC). The model with the smaller AIC or BIC is considered to be the better fitting model. Additionally, the variance explained in the dependent variables by the statistical models is evaluated in terms of $R^2$ [9, 15].

To quantify the difference between MDD and CcD, we have calculated the effect size using the means and standard deviations of the dependent variables of each method to obtain the standardized difference between the two means, Cohen's d Value [4]. Values of Cohen d between 0.2 and 0.3 indicate a small effect, values around 0.5 indicate a medium effect, and values greater than 0.8 indicate a large effect. This value also allows us to measure the percentage of overlaps between the distributions of the variables for each method.

We have selected box plots and histograms to describe the data and the results.

## 4.1   Hypothesis Testing

The results of the Type III test of fixed effects for the fixed factors for each one of the statistical models used in the data analysis are shown in Table 3.

For all of the variables, *Method* obtained p-values less than 0.05, regardless of the statistical model used for its calculation. Therefore, all the null hypotheses are rejected. Thus, the answers to the research questions **RQ1**, **RQ2** and **RQ3** are affirmative. The method used for developing software has a significant impact on the correctness of code, efficiency, and the satisfaction of developers.

However, the fixed factors *Experience* and *Method\*Experience* obtained p-values greater than 0.05, which implies that neither the developers experience nor the combination of both fixed factors had a significant influence on the changes in correctness of code, or the efficiency and the satisfaction of the developers.

**Table 3.** Results of test of fixed effects for each variable and each model

|  | Model 1 | Model 2 | | |
| --- | --- | --- | --- | --- |
|  | *Method* | *Method* | *Experience* | *Method\*Experience* |
| *Correctness* | (F = 643.3, p = .000) | (F = 137.7, p = .000) | (F = 2.5, p = .120) | (F = 1.9, p = .175) |
| *Efficiency* | (F = 1084.4, p = .000) | (F = 83.8, p = .000) | (F = 1.9, p = .171) | (F = .6, p = .447) |
| *Ease of use* | (F = 451.7, p = .000) | (F = 14.2, p = .001) | (F = .4, p = .508) | (F = .12, p = .730) |
| *Usefulness* | (F = 545.7, p = .000) | (F = 9.97, p = .003) | (F = 2.0, p = .168) | (F = 0.0, p = .965) |
| *Intention to Use* | (F = 341.4, p = .000) | (F = 5.3, p = .026) | (F = .2, p = .689) | (F = 1.1, p = .965) |

## 4.2 Statistical Model Validity and Fit

The use of the Linear Mixed Model test assumed that residuals must be normally distributed. The normality of the errors had been verified by the Shapiro-Wilk test and visual inspections of the histogram and normal Q-Q plot. All of the residuals, except the ones carried out for *Efficiency*, obtained a p-value greater than 0.05 with the normality test. We obtained normally distributed residuals for *Efficiency* by using square root transformation. For the statistical analysis of the variable *Efficiency* with LMM, we used $DV = sqrt(Efficiency)$ in formulas (1) and (2). For the rest of the variables, $DV$ is equal to their value.

**Table 4.** Comparison of alternative models for each variable

|  | Variance explained | | Model fit | | | |
| --- | --- | --- | --- | --- | --- | --- |
|  | $R^2$ | | AIC | | BIC | |
|  | Model 1 | Model 2 | Model 1 | Model 2 | Model 1 | Model 2 |
| *Correctness* | 63.8% | 65.7% | −59.617 | −56.313 | −49.847 | −46.638 |
| *Efficiency* | 57.9% | 58.6% | −412.078 | −398.820 | −402.261 | −398.097 |
| *Ease of use* | 4.8% | 14.1% | 232.593 | 232.281 | 241.917 | 244.004 |
| *Usefulness* | 10.9% | 13.7% | 218.295 | 217.452 | 228.113 | 227.176 |
| *Intention to use* | 4.8% | 6.2% | 270.298 | 268.847 | 280.115 | 278.570 |

The assessment of statistical model fit is summarized in Table 4. The values of the fit statistics $R^2$, AIC and BIC for each one of the statistical models are listed for each dependent variable. The fraction of total variance explained by both statistical models is similar. Model 2 obtained slightly better values of $R^2$, but the difference is not big. The AIC and BIC criteria were smaller for Model 1 in *Correctness* and *Efficiency*, and the difference was small for the other variables in favour of Model 2. This suggests that the *Method* factor explains much of the variance in the dependent variables. The factors incorporated in Model 2 with respect to Model 1 did not have a significant influence on the changes in the correctness of code, or the efficiency and satisfaction of the developers, as we have reported in Sect. 4.1.

## 4.3   Effect Size

The effect size of a Cohen d value of 2.63 for *Correctness* indicates that the magnitude of the difference is large. The mean of *Correctness* for MDD is 2.63 standard deviations bigger than the mean of *Correctness* for CcD. The mean for MDD is the 99.5 percentile of the mean for CcD. The box plots in Fig. 3(a) illustrate this result. This means that the distributions only have 9.7% of their areas on common, as shows Fig. 3(c).

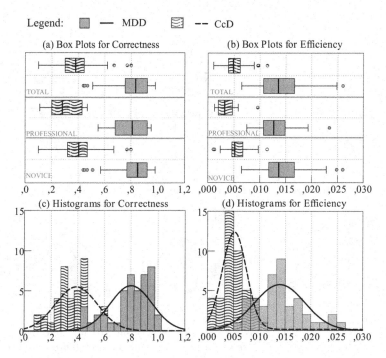

**Fig. 3.** Box plots and histograms for *Correctness* and *Efficiency*: (a) and (b) for *Correctness*; (c) and (d) for *Efficiency*

There is also a large effect size with a Cohen d value of 2.33 for *Efficiency*. The magnitude of the difference is also large. The mean for *Efficiency* for MDD, is 2.33 standard deviations bigger than the mean for efficiency for CcD. Again the mean for MDD is the 99.5 percentile of the mean for CcD (Fig. 3(b)) and the distributions of efficiency are different for 88% of their areas (Fig. 3(d)). The effect size of the differences based on using MDD or CcD for *Perceived Ease of Use* is medium-high, with a Cohen d value of 0.78. The box plots of Fig. 4(a) and the histograms of Fig. 4(d) illustrate how the differences in *Perceived Ease of Use* are not as great as the ones for *Correctness* or *Efficiency*. The magnitude of the difference between methods of development decreases to medium in the case of *Perceived Usefulness* with a Cohen d value of 0.69. Both the box plots of

Fig. 4(b) and the histograms of Fig. 4(e) illustrate a similar distribution to the one for *Perceived Ease of Use*. Again there is not a big difference in the diagrams corresponding to each subject group (professionals or novices)

*Intention to Use* obtained the lowest Cohen's d value (0.445), which means that the effect size of the method in this case is small to medium: the histograms of Fig. 4(f) shows that the distributions have much in common. The box plots of Fig. 4(c) shows that, in this case, the difference in the mean scores of *intention of use* (in favor of MDD versus CcD), is greater for the group of professionals than for the group of novices or the total group.

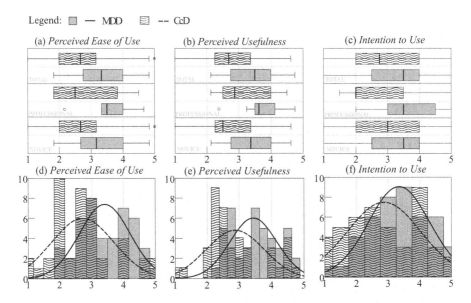

**Fig. 4.** Box plots and histograms for satisfaction: (a) and (d) for *Perceived Ease of Use*; (b) and (e) for *Perceived Ease of Use*; and (c) and (f) for *Intention to Use*

These data allow us to give more precise answers to **RQ1**, **RQ2**, and **RQ3**: for *Correctness* and *Efficiency*, the impact of the method used for development is very large, while, for satisfaction, the magnitude of the difference is medium.

### 4.4   Interpretation of the Results

Nowadays, domain frameworks are widely used in software development. The pre-implemented frameworks save developers time by using implementations that had been developed previously. In previous comparisons between MDD and CcD, one may argue that the benefits of MDD might come from the lack of a domain framework for CcD. This was not the case in our experiment.

Benefits must come from the software model itself and the model transformation (from model to code) that MDD adds to the framework. We still do not know if the key lies on the abstraction of models, the automation of transformations, or a combination of these. However, it turns out that a framework on its own is not enough to achieve the benefits of MDD.

In our focus group interviews, both the professionals and the novices agreed that the abstraction of models is a double-edged sword. On the one hand, the subjects stated that models empower them to focus on the task at hand. On the other hand, the subjects stated that they lose control of the code generated. The subjects acknowledge that this loss of control negatively influences their intention of use. A few subjects stated that this loss of control would be alleviated if the model transformation were considered as another developer of the team. This triggers an interesting new direction of research, exploring the social implications of MDD on development teams.

## 5    Threats to Validity

To describe the threats of validity of our work, we use the classification of [22].

**Conclusion Validity.** The *low statistical power* was minimized because the confidence interval is 95%. To minimize the *fishing and the error rate* threat, the tasks and corrections were designed by a video game software engineer. Furthermore, this engineer corrected the tasks. The *Reliability of measures* threat was mitigated because the measurements were obtained from the digital artefacts generated by the subjects when they performed the tasks. The *reliability of treatment implementation* threat was alleviated because the treatment implementation was identical in the two sessions. Also, the tasks were designed with similar difficulty. Finally, the experiment was affected by the *random heterogeneity of subjects* threat. The heterogeneity of subjects allowed us to increase the number of subjects in the experiment.

**Internal Validity.** The *interactions with selection* threat affected the experiment because there were subjects who had different levels of experience in software development. To mitigate this threat, the treatment was applied randomly. Other threat was *compensatory rivalry*: the subjects may have been motivated to perform the task with a higher level of quality by using the treatment that was more familiar to them.

**Construct Validity.** *Mono-method bias* occurs due to the use of a single type of measure [17]. All of the measurements were affected by this threat. To mitigate this threat for the correctness and efficiency measurements, an instructor checked that the subjects performed the tasks, and we mechanized these measurements as much as possible by means of correction templates. We mitigated the threat to satisfaction by using a widely applied model (TAM) [5]. The *hypothesis guessing* threat appears when the subject thinks about the objective and the results of the experiment. To mitigate this threat, we did not explain the research questions or the experiment design to the subjects. The *evaluation apprehension* threat appears when the subjects are afraid of being evaluated. To weaken this threat, at the beginning of the experiment the instructor explained to the subjects that the experiment was not a test about their abilities. *Author* *bias* occurs when the people involved in the process of creating the experiment artifacts subjectively influence the results. In order to mitigate this threat, the tasks were balanced, i.e., their sizes and difficulty were the same for all treatments. Furthermore, the tasks were extracted from a commercial video game. Finally, the *mono-operation bias* threat occurs when the treatments depend on a single operationalization. The experiment was affected by this threat since we worked with a single treatment.

**External Validity.** The *interaction of selection and treatment* threat is an effect of having a subject that is not representative of the population that we want to generalize. However, using students as subjects instead of software engineers is not a major issue as long as the research questions are not specifically focused on experts [10]. It would be necessary to replicate the experiment with different subject roles in order to mitigate this threat. The *domain* threat appears because the experiment has been conducted in a specific domain, i.e., video games development. We think that the generalizability of findings should be undertaken with caution. Other experiments in different domains should be performed to validate our findings.

## 6    Conclusion

In this work, we present an experiment that compares MDD and CcD in terms of correctness, efficiency, and satisfaction. Our experiment goes beyond the state of the art in terms of real-world fidelity and statistical power. A higher fidelity to real-world software development is achieved by means of the use of domain frameworks as they are used in real-world developments. Statistical power is enhanced by increasing the sample size. Our results challenge previous ideas that limit the benefits of MDD to academic exercises and to developers without experience. Furthermore, our results also suggest a new research direction that should include the social aspect of software development in order to better understand the benefits of MDD.

## References

1. Anda, B., Hansen, K.: A case study on the application of uml in legacy development. In: ISESE 2006 - Proceedings of the 5th ACM-IEEE International Symposium on Empirical Software Engineering (2006)
2. Baker, P., Loh, S., Weil, F.: Model-driven engineering in a large industrial context—motorola case study. In: Briand, L., Williams, C. (eds.) MODELS 2005. LNCS, vol. 3713, pp. 476–491. Springer, Heidelberg (2005). https://doi.org/10.1007/11557432_36
3. Basili, V.R., Rombach, H.D.: The tame project: towards improvement-oriented software environments. IEEE Trans. Softw. Eng. **14**(6), 758–773 (1988)
4. Cohen, J.: Statistical Power for the Social Sciences. Laurence Erlbaum and Associates, Hillsdale (1988)
5. Davis, F.D.: Perceived usefulness, perceived ease of use, and user acceptance of information technology. MIS Q. **13**(3), 319–340 (1989)

6. Heijstek, W., Chaudron, M.R.V.: Empirical investigations of model size, complexity and effort in a large scale, distributed model driven development process. In: Conference Proceedings of the EUROMICRO (2009)
7. Hutchinson, J., Rouncefield, M., Whittle, J.: Model-driven engineering practices in industry. In: Proceedings - International Conference on Software Engineering (2011)
8. Kapteijns, T., Jansen, S., Brinkkemper, S., Houet, H., Barendse, R.: A comparative case study of model driven development vs traditional development: the tortoise or the hare. From Code Centric to Model Centric Software Engineering Practices Implications and ROI (2009)
9. Karac, E.I., Turhan, B., Juristo, N.: A controlled experiment with novice developers on the impact of task description granularity on software quality in test-driven development. IEEE Trans. Softw. Eng. (2019)
10. Kitchenham, B.A., et al.: Preliminary guidelines for empirical research in software engineering. IEEE Trans. Softw. Eng. $28(8)$, 721–734 (2002)
11. Krogmann, K., Becker, S.: A case study on model-driven and conventional software development : the palladio editor. In: Software Engineering (2007)
12. Martínez, Y., Cachero, C., Meliá, S.: MDD vs. traditional software development: a practitioner's subjective perspective. In: Information and Software Technology (2013)
13. Mellegård, N., Staron, M.: Distribution of effort among software development artefacts: an initial case study. In: Bider, I., et al. (eds.) BPMDS/EMMSAD -2010. LNBIP, vol. 50, pp. 234–246. Springer, Heidelberg (2010). https://doi.org/10.1007/978-3-642-13051-9_20
14. Moody, D.L.: The method evaluation model: a theoretical model for validating information systems design methods. In: ECIS 2003 Proceedings. p. 79 (2003)
15. Nakagawa, S., Schielzeth, H.: A general and simple method for obtaining r2 from generalized linear mixed-effects models. Meth. Ecol. Evol. $4(2)$, 133–142 (2013)
16. Navarrete, J.I.P., et al.: Evaluating model-driven development claims with respect to quality: a family of experiments. IEEE Trans. Softw. Eng. (2018)
17. Panach, J.I., España, S., Dieste, Ó., Pastor, Ó., Juristo, N.: In search of evidence for model-driven development claims: an experiment on quality, effort, productivity and satisfaction. Inf. Softw. Technol. $62$, 164–186 (2015)
18. Papotti, P.E., do Prado, A.F., de Souza, W.L., Cirilo, C.E., Pires, L.F.: A quantitative analysis of model-driven code generation through software experimentation. In: Salinesi, C., Norrie, M.C., Pastor, Ó. (eds.) CAiSE 2013. LNCS, vol. 7908, pp. 321–337. Springer, Heidelberg (2013). https://doi.org/10.1007/978-3-642-38709-8_21
19. Selic, B.: The pragmatics of model-driven development. IEEE Softw. $20(5)$, 19–25 (2003)
20. West, B.T., Welch, K.B., Galecki, A.T.: Linear Mixed Models: A Practical Guide Using Statistical Software. Chapman and Hall/CRC, Boca Raton (2014)
21. Wilde, N., Buckellew, M., Page, H., Rajilich, V., Pounds, L.T.: A comparison of methods for locating features in legacy software. J. Syst. Softw. $65(2)$, 105–114 (2003)
22. Wohlin, C., Runeson, P., Höst, M., Ohlsson, M.C., Regnell, B., Wesslén, A.: Experimentation in Software Engineering. Springer, Heidelberg (2012). https://doi.org/10.1007/978-3-642-29044-2

# Workarounds in Business Processes:
# A Goal-Based Analysis

Nesi Outmazgin[(✉)], Pnina Soffer[(✉)], and Irit Hadar[(✉)]

University of Haifa, Mount Carmel, 3498838 Haifa, Israel
nesi@zefat.ac.il, {spnina,hadari}@is.haifa.ac.il

**Abstract.** Workarounds in business processes and information systems (IS) have attracted research attention in recent years. Deviating from official processes, workarounds are goal-driven adaptations. Understanding the underlying problems or perceived barriers that motivate workarounds is essential for suggesting appropriate solutions which would lead to process and IS improvement. The premise taken in this paper is that workarounds are often motivated by misalignments between organizational goals, goals of local-units and actors, and the business process that should realize these goals. With this premise, we propose an i*-based analysis for identifying such misalignments that are associated to workarounds. We report an industrial case study that demonstrates the analysis and associates workarounds with the underlying misalignments. Improvement recommendations that were made following the analysis have been accepted by the organization and are currently being implemented.

**Keywords:** Business process workarounds · Improvement opportunities · Goal misalignment analysis · Case study · I*

## 1 Introduction

Workarounds in business processes and information systems are a common phenomenon in practice, which has recently received considerable research attention. According to Alter [1], a workaround is "a goal-driven adaptation, improvisation, or other change to one or more aspects of an existing work system in order to overcome, bypass, or minimize the impact of obstacles, exceptions, anomalies, mishaps, established practices, management expectations, or structural constraints that are perceived as preventing that work system or its participants from achieving a desired level of efficiency, effectiveness, or other organizational or personal goals." This definition, however, is very broad, tying together quick fixes of technology mishaps, shadow IT systems, and deviations from the required course of action in business processes.

In this paper we specifically address workarounds in business processes. While generally adopting Alter's definition of workarounds, we focus on workarounds in business processes that deviate from the official process specification, but are nonetheless performed while pursuing the process goal. As an example, consider a purchasing process where an order is issued before all the required approvals are obtained. This is

© Springer Nature Switzerland AG 2020
S. Dustdar et al. (Eds.): CAiSE 2020, LNCS 12127, pp. 368–383, 2020.
https://doi.org/10.1007/978-3-030-49435-3_23

clearly a deviation from the official process, requiring an order to be issued only once all approvals have been given. Yet, the goal of the process (purchasing required goods) is pursued. Nevertheless, while technology-oriented workarounds (quick fixes, shadow IT) are often considered positively as creative and innovative solutions to existing problems, workarounds in business processes, even when promoting process goals, are typically considered negatively, as a form of intentional non-compliance, which can also harm achieving other important organizational goals as a result of focusing exclusively on one particular goal.

Business processes are designed and practiced for the purpose of standardizing, streamlining, and managing collaborative work across different units in an organizational system, thus promoting the achievement of business goals [7, 8]. Compliance with the required process is important for several reasons. First, since business processes often apply to different organizational units, standardization is an enabler of collaboration. When a process participant does not act as expected, the work of others along the process may be hampered. Second, processes frequently reflect obligations to external parties that must be met, regulations that must be complied with, and standards the organization is committed to. Last, business processes are designed to support the organization's goals, and non-compliance may impose risks and negatively impact business performance.

Our premise, which follows Alter's definition of workarounds, is that workarounds are performed for a reason, and are driven by underlying problems and limitations in the process or in the information system, the perceptions of employees, or that of their management. Analyzing and understanding the motivation behind workaround decisions may hence reveal their root causes and lead to targeted improvement solutions.

Process improvement based on workarounds has been suggested in the past (e.g., [6, 20]), but these suggestions focused on adopting the workarounds as part of the formal procedures. Evidently, when workarounds are associated with risks and other negative consequences, such adoption is not desirable. Our approach differs from previous ones in proposing a systematic goal-based analysis with the aim of revealing the problems that motivate workarounds. Improvement should be achieved by addressing these problems rather than by adopting the workarounds. Our proposed analysis is anchored in motivational theories and based on previous empirical findings. We demonstrate the analysis through an industrial case study.

The remainder of the paper is organized as follows: Sect. 2 provides background and related work about workarounds and relevant motivational theories. Section 3 describes our proposed analysis approach using i* models, which is demonstrated in a case study reported in Sect. 4. Section 5 provides a concluding discussion concerning the approach and the case study.

## 2  Workarounds and Goal Misalignment

### 2.1  Related Work on Workarounds

Workarounds have been studied quite extensively in recent years, in different contexts and from different point of views. Ferneley and Sobreperez [5] suggested classifying workarounds as "harmless," "hindrance," or "essential." Determining which class is suitable, however, might differ depending on one's perspective and also reflects local considerations rather than organizational ones. Wilkin and Davern [20] show examples of workarounds that solve problems at an operational perspective but have harmful results at a managerial one. Recognizing this, Röder et al. [10] investigated the factors that managers weigh when deciding whether to tolerate workarounds. The findings reveal that managers consider the trade-off between possible benefits and risks resulting from the workarounds, before deciding whether to tolerate them.

Specific attention has been given to workarounds in healthcare and nursing processes, where rigid processes are sometimes impossible to follow [6]. For example, Beerepoot et al. [3] suggests criteria for accepting workarounds in healthcare processes as the formal practice or rejecting them. Still, workarounds have been observed in processes of various domains. Outmazgin and Soffer [13, 14] identified generic mechanisms by which workarounds are performed in business processes and derived patterns for detecting workarounds using process mining techniques.

In general, workarounds have been described in the literature as a goal-seeking behavior, motivated by perceived obstacles on the way to some desired goal [1]. Specifically concerning business processes, researchers (e.g., [15]) indicated that workarounds may occur when the prescribed procedures require additional effort of users and this effort is perceived as extraneous to their perceived goals. A related theme is of misfit or misalignment. Goal misalignment is mentioned as a possible source in the theory of workarounds [1]. Malaurent and Avison [9] describe workarounds in an internationally distributed organization, motivated by misalignment between headquarter intentions and the needs of local branches and subsidiary companies. Misfit as a source of workarounds, specifically in the context of ERP systems and the processes they support, was highlighted by [17, 18], and others.

## 2.2   Organizational vs. Local-Unit Goals

Business process management emphasizes a cross-organizational perception, guided by the aim to standardize and prescribe end-to-end procedures, as opposed to local functional "silos" [7]. Transforming employees' "siloed" perception into a cross-organizational one is considered one of the challenges associated with BPM implementation in an organization [7], while naturally the main and immediate commitment of employees is to their local unit [16]. Ideally, the goals of each local unit in the organization should be derived from global organizational goals, and realized through the corresponding business processes, all aligned with each other, as illustrated in Fig. 1.

However, very often misalignment among these elements exists or is perceived to exist for various reasons. Misalignment between organizational and local unit goals may occur when trade-off relations exist among goals, and goals set for specific local units are not highly weighed in the overall organizational perspective. For example, a specific local unit may have a goal to quickly respond and fulfill its tasks as fast as possible, while an overall consideration would also take costs into account, thus limit overtime work. Employees are typically well aware of and committed to the immediate goals of their local unit, and might not be aware of the full scope of considerations at the organizational level.

Misalignment between local goals and the process is inevitable when the goals of the local unit and of the organization are not aligned, and the process is designed to

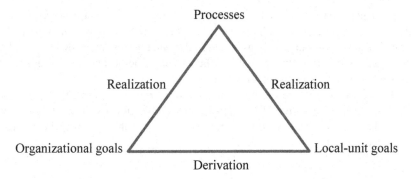

**Fig. 1.** An aligned goal-process triangle.

realize organizational goals. With the local goals in mind, the process is perceived as an obstacle, and this motivates a workaround. A different case would be when the process is not aligned with the local unit goals nor with organizational goals, leading to the conclusion that it is simply not well designed. We note, however, that employees act upon their perceptions, and might not be aware of the full rationale of the processes. A case where the process is aligned with the local unit goal but not with organizational goals is also possible, although less prevalent.

Our premise in this paper is that the misalignments between the elements presented in Fig. 1 drive workaround intentions. In what follows, we propose to systematically analyze goals and processes and thereby reveal misalignments using goal models.

## 3 Using Goal Models for Misalignment Detection

The three elements of the goal-process triangle can be captured using i* models [4, 21], and conflicts among elements as potential drivers of workarounds can be analyzed. However, to accomplish a consistent representation, some adjustments of the modeling are needed. In i*, the Strategic Dependency (SD) model provides a high-level representation of the actor interactions in the process, and enables understanding their dependency connections and the high-level goals that drive them. This understanding can support an examination of where the Strategic Rationale (SR) model should focus. The SR model focuses on specific actors and enables analyzing their goals and tasks, as well as positive and negative contributions among these elements. In our terms, the actors stand for local units. Since our aim is to capture conflicts between organizational goals, local unit goals, and prescribed processes, we propose the following modeling guidelines to ensure these elements are captured in the model in a consistent manner.

(1) Organizational goals and derived (local) goals: For each actor, we consider the root goal(s) as organizational goals, assigned to the actors by virtue of their role in the organization. Local-unit goals are derived from the root goal of the actor and are presented inside its boundaries. In i* SR models, these goals can appear as intentional goals or quality goals (ovals and clouds, respectively), as shown in Fig. 2.

(2) Dependency goals: Each actor can have additional goals that emerge from the dependency connections with other actors. These goals support or help to achieve organizational goals primarily assigned to the other actors. In i* SR models, these goals are related to tasks or goals of the dependee actor, and are represented as derived dependency goals, as shown in Fig. 2.

(3) Tasks: All tasks presented in the i* model are intended to realize the actor goals, both goals that are derived from dependency connections with other actors, and those that are directly derived from higher-level goals of the actor and can thus be viewed as "local".

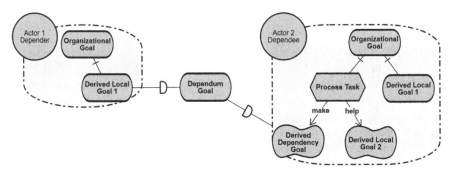

**Fig. 2.** Example of an i* model showing derivation of goals.

Since some of the derived goals and tasks of each actor stem from the actor's "own" goals (derived from organizational goals assigned to the actor), while other goals and tasks are derived from dependency relations, they are not necessarily well aligned with each other. For detecting and analyzing goal misalignment in the model, the focus should be on the negative contributions (e.g., Break or Hurt) of the goals and tasks. In fact, dependency connections with other actors create "pulling forces" on the actor in conflicting directions. The example in Fig. 3 illustrates goal misalignment detection.

As shown in the example presented in Fig. 3, the faculty head (actor 1) depends on the lecturer (actor 2), who needs to perform a task for realizing this goal. However, the lecturer has a quality goal "Flexibility with syllabus building" that is hampered by this task. The quality goal is likely derived from other goals (e.g., organizational goal – the root goal) or from dependency relations with other actors. In this example, the task creates a negative contribution (break) to the quality goal, so there is a misalignment between the dependency goal, realized by the task, and the local quality goal.

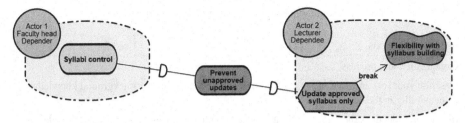

**Fig. 3.** Example of misalignment due to dependency relations between actors.

## 4 Case Study

### 4.1 Setting and Method

We demonstrate the proposed analysis approach through a case study, following the guidelines of interpretive case study research for understanding phenomena through the research participants' interpretation [12]. The case study was performed in a large organization operating in the domains of telecommunication, IT services, and information security. This organization employs approximately 1500 employees and is a part of a globally operating corporation that has 5300 employees. The process on which we focus is sales forecast based on price proposals, which is a cross-organizational process, involving many actors and departments, and is essential for the ongoing operations of the organization. It deals with creation, management and approval of price proposals before they can be sent to the customers. The main considerations include the profitability rate, business rules, and solution building for the customers. In addition to creation and approval of price proposals, the process deals with a variety of pre-sales activities. Ultimately, it serves for communicating opportunities and expected business deals as an operational forecast the management uses for long-term planning. The process is supported by a dedicated information system that was locally developed. It is related to other processes, such as customers sales management and purchase ordering.

We collected data through semi-structured interviews [19] with eight stakeholders of different operational and managerial roles, whose experience in the organization ranged from three to 21 years. The interviews focused on the processes as viewed by the interviewees, related goals and tasks, improvement opportunities, and workarounds that are performed (see interview guide in Table 1). We complemented the interviews by collecting documents regarding formal procedures and processes, ISO work procedures and reports, and by carefully studying the information system, its user interface, functionality, and database schema.

The interviews took 45–90 min each, and were conducted in the offices of the organization. All the interviews were audio recorded and transcribed, and in addition, phone calls and emails were exchanged after the interviews to obtain additional explanations and further validation of the interview transcripts. Following the interviews, we created a BPMN model of the process for gaining a comprehensive understanding of its flow and rules, and presented the model to the interviewees for approval. The BPMN served as an input for the detailed analysis.

**Table 1.** Guiding questions for the semi-structured interviews.

| Interview questions | Goal | Used for |
|---|---|---|
| Organization and process | | |
| Describe your role and area of responsibility in the organization | Background and introduction | Background knowledge |
| In your opinion, does the organization follow clear work procedures and standards like ISO, SOX, JCI? Are they implemented as expected? | To understand commitments to legal and external procedures, policies, and regulations | Background knowledge |
| In your opinion, how are organizational and procedural changes managed and accepted? | To uncover change management issues, fixed paradigms and resistance to changes | Background knowledge |
| What are the organization's core processes? For each process state: is it departmental, cross-organizational or global? | To assess the studied process and examine its scope and boundaries | Background knowledge |
| Describe the process from your viewpoint. What would you suggest in order to improve the process? Do you think the IS contributes to the effectiveness and efficiency of the process? Please elaborate | To learn the process To elicit goals sought by improvement ideas To uncover misalignments between the as-is process and the perceived goals | - BPMN model - i* model - Conflict identification |
| What is your role in the process? Do you think your areas of responsibility in the process fit your area of expertise? How so? | To elicit Actor boundaries, tasks, goals and dependencies To elicit workarounds, possibly those related to expertise | - BPMN model - i* model - Workarounds list |
| Do you think that other process participants exceed their responsibility areas? How so? | To uncover workarounds performed by others | Workarounds list |
| Is there manual work in the process? Where? | To uncover difficulties in the process and workarounds | Workarounds list |
| Participant's perceptions of goals and possible misalignments | | |
| From your point of view, what are the organizational goals the process is intended to achieve? Were the process goals presented or explained to you? | To uncover perceived organizational goals Possibly, to elicit related workarounds | - i* model - Workarounds list |

(*continued*)

**Table 1.** (*continued*)

| Participant's perceptions of goals and possible misalignments | | |
|---|---|---|
| What are the main goals you are expected to achieve as part of your role? In what ways are others involved and contribute to achieving these goals? | To uncover perceived local-unit goals<br>To learn the dependency relations among the actors | - i* model<br>- Conflict identification |
| What are the tasks you need to perform although they do not contribute directly to the goals you are expected to accomplish? Why do you need to perform them? | To elicit perceived misalignments between goals and tasks<br>To uncover motivation for workarounds | - i* model<br>- Conflict identification |
| Are there known and defined KPIs for the process? Are they measured on a personal or organizational level? | To elicit quality goals | i* model |
| Are there certain situations that justify performing actions other than what is required in the process? | To examine and learn goal misalignment situations in a detailed manner<br>To elicit workarounds | - Conflict identification<br>- Workarounds list |
| In your opinion, does the official process include all the tasks required to accomplish your goals? If not, what do you think is missing? | To uncover perceived obstacles, gaps and technological barriers in the process<br>To identify process improvement opportunities | - Workarounds list<br>- Conflict identification |
| In general, are you satisfied with the process? Would you suggest other ways of achieving the relevant goals? | To examine improvement ideas, including those already performed informally (as workarounds) | Workarounds list |
| Workarounds in the process | | |
| In your opinion, what is a business process workaround? Do you think management would define it similarly? If not, how do you think they would define it? | To assess perceptions about management view of workarounds | Background knowledge |
| Are you familiar with workarounds that are performed in the process? If so, in which situations and how often? How are they identified? | To examine and learn workarounds in a detailed manner, their frequencies and the impact to the organization | Workarounds list |

(*continued*)

**Table 1.** (*continued*)

| Workarounds in the process | | |
| --- | --- | --- |
| Why, in your opinion, are these workarounds performed? Do these workarounds help participants in accomplishing their goals? Do you think that these workarounds help to accomplish organizational goals? | To learn the motivation for process workarounds<br>To relate the misalignment situations to specific workarounds | - Workarounds list<br>- Conflict identification |
| What do you think are the consequences of these workarounds? What would happen if they cannot be performed? | To elicit perceived impacts of workarounds | Conflict identification |
| Do you think that the process workarounds are related to obstacles of any kind? Do you think that with a more flexible process they would still be performed? | To understand the motivation for performing workarounds<br>To examine process improvements\opportunities | Conflict identification |
| In your opinion, are workarounds performed regularly? Do they require skills or deep familiarity with the process? | To clarify the motivation and the effort involved in workarounds | Workarounds list |

Text analysis and interpretation of the transcribed interviews were performed to identify the process goals as perceived by the interviewees, gradually constructing goal and dependency diagrams. In particular, conflicts and misalignments were sought between the identified goals and between the goals and the process, as depicted in the validated BPMN. This was done following the guidelines outlined in Sect. 3. In parallel, we listed the workarounds reported in the interviews. Following our assumption of correlation between workarounds and misalignments, we used the list of workarounds as triangulation for the identified misalignments, and iterated to reveal additional misalignments that could be related to the reported workarounds. Last, we proposed solution directions for the identified misalignments and presented them for evaluation to the director of procedures and methods, pre-sale department manager, and sales department manager.

## 4.2  Goal Misalignment Detection

According to the approach presented in Sect. 3, we first created the SD model of the sales forecast process for understanding the dependencies between the actors and the main organizational goal pursued by each of them, and then we zoomed into the SR model to examine and focus on the misalignment detection.

As shown in the SD model in Fig. 4, the customer manager is the main actor of the sales forecast process, and hence a detailed SR model was created for this actor. The main goal of this actor is to promote sales according to the sales targets. This is done while creating the price proposal, gradually building the solution offering with the related part numbers and specification, service agreement, and a full "proposal kit." Every detail needs to be approved through an approval round by several role holders, until a customer commitment to purchase the content of the price proposal is received.

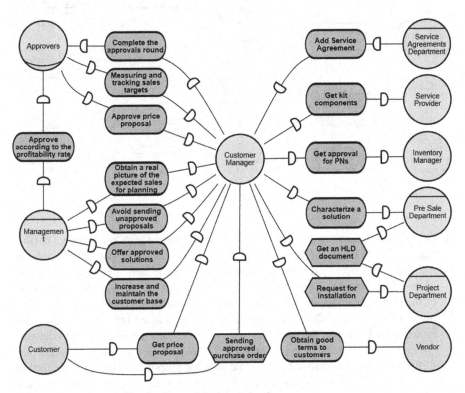

**Fig. 4.** SD model of the sales forecast process.

To execute this process, the customer manager has two directions of dependencies with other actors. In one direction, the customer manager depends on other actors (e.g., the approvers, the service provider). The second direction is where other actors depend on the customer manager (e.g., management, service agreements department).

Due to space limitations, we cannot show and discuss the details of the entire SR model. Rather, we focus here on two relatively simple examples to illustrate the analysis approach. The first example illustrates a goal misalignment related to local goals derived from the dependencies with external actors, and the second example illustrates a goal misalignment related to local goals derived from their root goal. In both examples the misalignment is between those goals and the goals of the external actor through the dependencies, as follows:

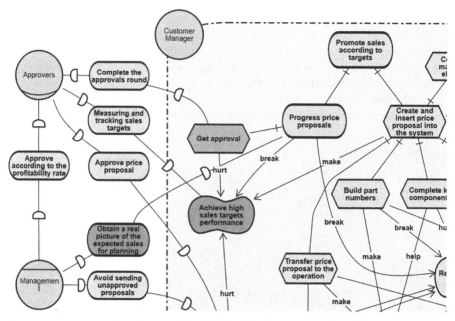

**Fig. 5.** Example A.

(1) Goal misalignment was detected between the "Achieve high sales targets performance" and "Obtain a real picture of the expected sales for planning" goals. In Fig. 5, the dependency of the management actor for the goal "Obtain a real picture of the expected sales for planning" relates to the goal "Progress price proposals" of the customer manager, since when price proposals are entered and progressed in the IS, they are visible to management and serve as an indication of expected future sales. However, the model shows a negative contribution (break) to the goal "Achieve high sales target performance". The explanation is that sales target performance is measured based on the rate of price proposals, which are realized as sales orders. To achieve high sales target performance, the customer manager needs to enter price proposals only towards the closing of a deal, when they are almost certain to lead to an actual sale. In addition, the regular approval rounds associated with progressing price proposals may delay the process, and reduce sales performance, as seen by the hurt relation between "Get approval" and "Achieve high sales target performance".

(2) Goal misalignment was detected between the goal "Avoid sending unapproved proposals" and the goals "Respond quickly and flexibly" and "Satisfy the customer" goals. In Fig. 6, the dependency of the management actor for the goal "Avoid sending unapproved price proposals" relates to the task "Send the approved price proposal to the customer" of the customer manager. This leads to a negative contribution to two goals: it hurts the "Satisfy the customer" goal and breaks the "Respond quickly and flexibly" goal. This is because of the requirement of management to only send to the customers price proposals that completed the approval round, both for new

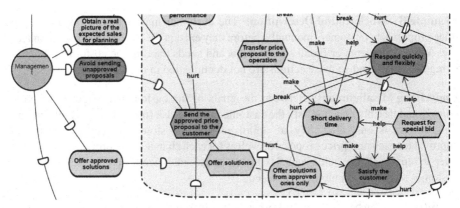

**Fig. 6.** Example B.

price proposals and for each change in the proposal introduced after its approval. As a result, the customer manager cannot respond quickly and the satisfaction of the customers can be reduced.

### 4.3 Workarounds

As described in Sect. 4.1, we collected workarounds independent of the misalignment analysis, and looked for connections between workarounds and misalignments. Eventually we could associate each of the workarounds with one or more of the identified misalignments, and vice versa. We demonstrate this for the misalignment examples presented above:

**Example A - Workaround Description:** The customer manager creates a new price proposal in the IS only after closing the deal with the customer. Specifically, all negotiations with the customers are done unofficially without any record in the IS. Only after receiving a signed purchase order from the customer does the customer manager start the process of creating a price proposal and getting all the required approvals. Evidently, the customer manager works around the process and gets a post-factum approval for the price proposal.

**Underlying Misalignment:** Between the goals to achieve high sales target performance measures and to manage and progress the price proposals, which, in turn, supports the management goal to have a forecast of potential sales ahead of time in order to plan for it. The sales target performance is based on the price proposals which actually materialize into a sales order. Hence, the customer manager is not motivated to report unclosed deals.

**Result:** Price proposals that are still in process, before closure, do not exist in the IS and so they cannot be considered by management for planning, i.e., management actor's goal to obtain a real picture of the expected sales for planning purposes is hampered.

**Example B - Workaround Description:** The customer manager prepares and sends price proposals to customers manually, before they exist in the IS. The customer manager uses Word documents or Excel spreadsheets and sends them to the customers directly in regular email, and so these actions are not documented in the IS.

**Underlying Misalignment:** Between the goals of the customer manager to respond quickly and flexibly and to satisfy the customer and the task (official process) of sending price proposals only after they are approved. If the customer manager waits for an approval for each new price proposal as well as for each change in the proposal introduced after its approval, the quick and flexible response goals would not be achieved, and customer's satisfaction might be reduced.

**Result:** Harm can be caused for the organization by sending unapproved price proposals that might create commitment to unprofitable or risky deals.

### 4.4  Improvement Opportunities

Using the goal models and identifying their correspondence to reported workarounds, we were able to reveal various misalignments and understand how they drive workaround situations. This understanding can be leveraged and yield improvement opportunities for the business process. Based on the examples above, the following improvements were suggested to the organization:

(1) Changing the measures used for assessment of the sales performance – as the customer managers are currently evaluated for sales target performance in a way that motivates them to avoid entering price proposals to the IS until closure of all the details of the deal. Therefore, the suggestion is to change the measures of the sales target performance to ones that would eliminate the conflict between high sales performance (calculated based on the percentage of materialized price proposals) and managing the price proposals in the IS. For example, changing the measure to reflect the number of sales opportunities, sales activities or potential sales income can motivate the customer managers to enter price proposals as soon as possible and manage them through the IS, resulting in alignment between the sales performance goal and that of documenting and progressing price proposals in the IS. In addition, the measure can also consider customers' billing rate, to motivate the customer managers to supervise price proposals all the way down to ordering and payment.

(2) Reducing the strictness of the procedure of approvals and approval rounds. We propose to do this in two ways. First, by introducing threshold conditions for the amount and the profitability rate of the price proposals that require approval. This would increase the degree of freedom for the customer managers and enable a quick processing of small price proposals. Second, by introducing several different approval trails that can be selected according to price proposal amounts and the profitability rate, and considering whether this is a new price proposal or a change in an existing one. Currently, each price proposal for any amount requires the same approval round and the same approvals hierarchy. Our suggestion is to offer a shorter and

quicker route for proposals or changes that are of relatively low risk (new proposals of small amounts or small changes of approved proposals). These suggestions can significantly increase the flexibility of the customer managers in the negotiation with the customers and shorten response times, thus increasing the customer satisfaction level. The task would change to sending prices proposals according to the approval policy, and this would still be aligned with the management goal of avoiding sending unapproved proposals while introducing minimal delay to this process.

The suggested improvement ideas and the relevant goal misalignment situations were presented in the case study organization to the director of procedures and methods, the pre-sale department manager, and the sales department manager. The suggestions were discussed in the organization and approved as an improvement plan. Currently these improvements are being implemented in the organization.

## 5   Concluding Discussion

In this paper, we have shown how workarounds in business processes can be analyzed systematically using goal models, and how this analysis can reveal the underlying problems that motivate workarounds. Thus, this analysis can lead to targeted and ongoing process improvement.

Earlier suggestions have been made to utilize workaround information for process improvement (e.g., [6, 20]). These, however, mostly suggested to adopt the workaround as a formal procedure when appropriate. In contrast, we aim to reveal the problems and, specifically, the perceived misalignments that drive the workaround intention, and to solve them. Addressing the problems directly may yield other solutions, which may be more beneficial or less risky than the workarounds that are taken.

Our analysis differs from previously suggested analysis approaches, which typically focused on the workarounds themselves. Examples include [2] and [3], where workarounds are studied and analyzed for determining whether they are acceptable as an official process, and [10], where responses of managers to workarounds are considered. In [11] workarounds are represented as designated parts in process models so they can be visualized and recognized, but not in relation to their sources.

In contrast, we focus on the conflicts and misalignments underlying existing workarounds, using the well-established i* model. With this we gain another advantage – the information needed for constructing a goal model is easier to obtain than information concerning workarounds. Employees are likely to be much more cooperative regarding their goals and actions than regarding workarounds they perform.

The reported case study demonstrates how misalignment of goals and processes can be recognized in an i* model and associated with workarounds that are performed in the process. The guidelines we suggested for the creation of the i* model are intended to enable a consistent representation of how local goals and tasks are derived from organizational goals and from dependencies among actors for realizing these goals. The interview guide that was used is generic and can be used in similar projects. We further demonstrate how improvement suggestions can be made when specifically addressing the revealed misalignments. The specific suggestions we made have been evaluated in the case study organization and found adequate to the extent that they are currently being implemented. This indicates the potential of our approach, whose main idea is to leverage workarounds for process improvement by addressing their sources rather than the workarounds themselves, which are rather a symptom than a solution.

Toward using this analysis method in industry, it is important to consider and address the following challenges: (1) properly build and use i* models – the analysis should be performed by professional analysts, who are familiar with i* modeling; (2) implement i* according to the proposed analysis guidance, in the context of capturing global and local goals – analysts should understand and follow the guidance, which could possibly require some training; and, (3) rely on openness of employees in interviews – different questions posed around central topics allow for some triangulation of the elicited information, in order to mitigate risks of social-serving bias and other biases potentially affecting employees' responses.

Several limitations need to be acknowledged. The approach proposed in this paper was thus far implemented in a single case study. Additional implementations in different organizations would provide a more generalizable view of the benefits of this approach. The approach uses interviews as a central means for eliciting data, which is subject to report and self-serving biases. This limitation is mitigated, to some extent, by triangulation with data elicited from complementary sources (see Sect. 4.1).

Future research can focus further on the complementary data sources and search for ways to extract some of the information in automatic ways, for example, based on log events analysis, reducing human effort required for the workaround analysis process.

**Acknowledgement.** The research is supported by the Israel Science Foundation under grant agreement 669/17.

# References

1. Alter, S.: Theory of workarounds. Commun. Assoc. Inf. Syst. **34**(1), 1041–1066 (2014)
2. Alter, S.: A workaround design system for anticipating, designing, and/or preventing workarounds. In: Gaaloul, K., Schmidt, R., Nurcan, S., Guerreiro, S., Ma, Q. (eds.) CAISE 2015. LNBIP, vol. 214, pp. 489–498. Springer, Cham (2015). https://doi.org/10.1007/978-3-319-19237-6_31
3. Beerepoot, I., Ouali, A., van de Weerd, I., Reijers, H.A.: Working around health information systems: to accept or not to accept? In: Proceedings of the 27th European Conference on Information Systems (ECIS 2019) (2019)
4. Dalpiaz, F., Franch, X., Horkoff, J.: istar 2.0 language guide (2016). arXiv preprint arXiv: 1605.07767
5. Ferneley, E.H., Sobreperez, P.: Resist, comply or workaround? an examination of different facets of user engagement with information systems. Eur. J. Inf. Syst. **15**(4), 345–356 (2006)
6. Friedman, A., et al.: A typology of electronic health record workarounds in small-to-medium size primary care practices. J. Am. Med. Inf. Assoc. **21**, 78–83 (2014)
7. Hammer, M.: What is business process management? In: vom Brocke, J., Rosemann, M. (eds.) Handbook on Business Process Management 1. IHIS, pp. 3–16. Springer, Heidelberg (2015). https://doi.org/10.1007/978-3-642-45100-3_1

8. Harmon, P.: Business Process Change: A Guide for Business Managers and BPM and Six Sigma Professionals. Morgan Kaufmann, Burlington (2010)
9. Malaurent, J., Avison, D.: Reconciling global and local needs: a canonical action research project to deal with workarounds. Inf. Syst. J. **26**(3), 227–257 (2016)
10. Röder, N., Wiesche, M., Schermann, M., Krcmar, H.: Why managers tolerate workarounds– the role of information systems (2014)
11. Röder, N., Wiesche, M., Schermann, M., Krcmar, H.: Workaround aware business process modeling. In: Wirtschaftsinformatik, pp. 482–496 (2015)
12. Runeson, P., Höst, M.: Guidelines for conducting and reporting case study research in software engineering. Empirical Softw. Eng. **14**(2), 131 (2009). https://doi.org/10.1007/s10664-008-9102-8
13. Outmazgin, N., Soffer, P.: Business process workarounds: what can and cannot be detected by process mining. In: Nurcan, S., et al. (eds.) BPMDS/EMMSAD -2013. LNBIP, vol. 147, pp. 48–62. Springer, Heidelberg (2013). https://doi.org/10.1007/978-3-642-38484-4_5
14. Outmazgin, N., Soffer, P.: A process mining-based analysis of business process workarounds. Softw. Syst. Model. **15**(2), 309 (2016). https://doi.org/10.1007/s10270-014-0420-6
15. Poelmans, S.: Workarounds and distributed viscosity in a workflow system: a case study. ACM SIGGROUP Bull. **20**(3), 11–12 (1999)
16. Sobreperez, P.: Technological frame incongruence, diffusion, and noncompliance. In: León, G., Bernardos, A.M., Casar, J.R., Kautz, K., De Gross, J.I. (eds.) TDIT 2008. ITIFIP, vol. 287, pp. 179–196. Springer, Boston, MA (2008). https://doi.org/10.1007/978-0-387-87503-3_10
17. Strong, D.M., Volkoff, O.: Understanding organization-enterprise system fit: a path to theorizing the information technology artifact. MIS Q. **34**(4), 731–756 (2010)
18. van Beijsterveld, J.A., Van Groenendaal, J.H.: Solving misfits in ERP implementations by SMEs. Inf. Syst. J. **26**(4), 369–393 (2016)
19. Walsham, G.: Doing interpretive research. Eur. J. Inf. Syst. **15**(3), 320–330 (2006)
20. Wilkin, C.L., Davern, M.: Acceptance of post-adoption unanticipated IS usage: towards a taxonomy. Data Base Adv. Inf. Syst. **43**(3), 9–25 (2012)
21. Yu, E.: Modelling strategic relationships for process reengineering. Soc. Model. Requirements Eng. **11**, 2011 (2011)

# Digging into Business Process Meta-models: A First Ontological Analysis

Greta Adamo[1,2], Chiara Di Francescomarino[1], and Chiara Ghidini[1(✉)]

[1] Fondazione Bruno Kessler, Trento, Italy
{adamo,ghidini,dfmchiara}@fbk.eu
[2] DIBRIS, University of Genoa, Genoa, Italy

**Abstract.** While modern definitions of business processes exist and are shared in the Business Process Management community, a commonly agreed meta-model is still missing. Nonetheless, several different business process meta-models have been recently proposed and discussed in the literature, which look at business process models from different perspectives, focusing on different aspects and often using different labels for denoting the same element or element relation.

In this paper, we start from elements and relations discovered inspecting the literature on business process meta-models through a systematic literature review. We then combine these elements and relations to build a business process meta-model. The obtained *literature-based business process meta-model*, which is on purpose built to disclose criticalities, is then inspected and discussed. The analysis reveals, besides the lack of attention to some crucial business process elements, issues and inconsistencies in the literature meta-models. An ontological analysis is finally carried out and possible solutions to the discovered issues are proposed.

**Keywords:** Business process modelling · Ontological analysis · Meta-models

## 1 Introduction

Modern textual definitions of business processes such as [30] go beyond the classical control-flow dimensions, by taking into account also other important perspectives related to organisational, data, and goal-oriented aspects. The increased attention towards other dimensions than the behavioural one, has recently brought to a rapid growth of approaches and tools in the stream of multi-perspective business process modeling and mining [15], where other perspectives such as resources, data, time, and so on are exploited to augment the basic control-flow one. Such a hype on multiple aspects of business processes shows that the time is now ripe to focus on an investigation of multi-perspective process constructs and relations also at the conceptual level. A commonly agreed broad view on business processes, with clear and shared definitions of business

© Springer Nature Switzerland AG 2020
S. Dustdar et al. (Eds.): CAiSE 2020, LNCS 12127, pp. 384–400, 2020.
https://doi.org/10.1007/978-3-030-49435-3_24

process entities such as resources, data needed and produced by activities, different types of events, an so on, already at the conceptual level, would be crucial for instance to foster the communication and the data compatibility among information system procedures and data structures designed and described using different modeling paradigms and notations.

By looking at the business process meta-model literature, a number of different meta-models have been proposed. These meta-models vary greatly ranging from very general ones to meta-models tailored to a specific business process modeling language and, as such, characterised by the language specificities. Despite the differences and the disalignments between these meta-models, such a literature can be leveraged in order to investigate commonalities, differences and especially criticalities emerging from them.

In this paper we start from such an existing literature on business process meta-models and we analyse it through a systematic literature review in order to discover the business process elements and relations most investigated in state-of-the-art business process meta-models (Sect. 2). We then combine the discovered elements and relations in a *literature-based meta-model* of business processes (Sect. 3), which is on purpose built by simply joining discovered elements and relations, so as to disclose problems and inconsistencies. A number of criticalities arise from the analysis of the meta-model (Sect. 4): besides the under-investigation and under-specification of some of the relevant business process elements (e.g., the goal of a process), unclear relations and recursive subsumption cycles have been identified in the organisational and data components of the emerging meta-model. In order to deal with such criticalities, an ontological analysis has been carried out and possible solutions for the identified issues proposed in Sect. 5. Finally, related and future works are presented (Sect. 6 and 7).

## 2   Discovering Meta-model Components from the Literature

In this section we describe the elements and relations extracted through a *Systematic Literature Review* (SLR) on business process meta-models reported in [4]. First we provide few details about the SLR; in Sect. 2.1 we summarise the analysis of the elements reported in the SLR [4]; and in Sect. 2.2 we focus on a novel part related to the analysis of relations among elements emerged from the SLR.

*Systematic Literature Review Setting.* In the SLR we collected papers (up to 2018) from three paper repositories - DBLP, Scopus, and Web of Science (WoS) - and two reference conference venues, i.e., the *Business Process Management* (BPM) conference series and the *Conference on Advanced Information Systems Engineering* (CAiSE) series. We retrieved 1306 papers from the three repositories (without considering collections) using the following query:

```
metamodel OR meta-model AND business process OR process model
```
$$(1)$$

The conference venues were manually searched and we selected 452 works from BPM proceedings and 1065 from CAiSE proceedings for a total of 2463 papers (without duplicates). We identified and applied 3 *inclusion criteria* and 8 *exclusion criteria*, as well as four quality assessment criteria in order to filter the extracted papers, and we reduced the 2463 works to 36 papers that constitued our primary studies.

## 2.1   Literature-Based Elements

From the meta-models contained in the 36 primary studies we identified the recurrent business process (modelling) *elements*. Specifically, we extracted 374 single elements[1] grouped in 12 macro elements: *activity, event, state, sequence flow, time, data flow, data object, actor, resource, value, goal, context*. Out of the 374 single elements we kept only the ones appearing in at least two meta-models, thus reducing the number to 91.

Table 1 reports the 91 elements, organised according to the 12 macro-elements. The table also reports the number of meta-models in which the element occurred (reported in round brackets). For instance, the element time point occurred in (2) meta-models. Elements with the same (very similar) meaning but with different names, i.e., syntactic variables, have been all classified under a single name. The table also reports in round brackets, for each macro-element, the number of elements per category together with the total number of occurrences of macro-category elements. For example, the macro-element *state* includes 5 different elements for a total of 27 occurrences of those elements. Elements labelled as *events* have been classified either as events with a BPMN-like semantics, i.e., "something that happens during the course of a process" [21] (event-BPMN) or as events à-la EPC, i.e., in terms of pre-postconditions (event-EPC).

From the analysis we identified four main groups of macro-elements: *activity, sequence flow, data object,* and *actor*. The *sequence flow* macro-element is the most articulated one with its 18 elements and 91 occurrences. An interesting group is the one of *data object*, showing different types of knowledge (17 in total) that can appear in business process model elements, even though their appearance is not as common as the one of the other three groups. The second largest group is *activity* with its 64 occurrences. Also this group is very diversified including many kinds of "activities" and especially the most recurrent element in the meta-models, i.e., activity (27). Another key area of business processes is the *actor*/organisational aspect. Indeed, also in the meta-models, we found several occurrences of organisational-related elements (72). We also surprisingly found that other groups of elements appearing in existing business definitions, as for instance *goal* and *value*, do not occur in the meta-models. In particular *goal* is considered as central in one of the more recent business process definition proposed by Weske in [30], however the element goal appears

---

[1] We considered as single elements only those that are not collections of other elements. For instance "business process", "process" and "control flow" were not included in this analysis.

**Table 1.** Recurring elements in meta-models.

| Macro-element | Element |
|---|---|
| *activity* (9/64) | **activity** (27), **atomic activity** (9), **compound activity** (13), activity instance (4), manual activity (2), automatic activity (2), collaborative organisational activity (2), critical organizational activity (2), cancel activity (3) |
| *event* (10/41) | **event-EPC** (4), **event-BPMN** (9), event sub-process (3), throw event (2), interrupting (2), start event (6), intermediate event (3), end event (8), message event (2), event location (2) |
| *state* (5/27) | state (4), **precondition** (9), postcondition (8), data input (3), data output (3) |
| *sequence flow* (18/91) | conditional control flow (4), sequence (3), multimerge (2), multi choice (2), syncronisation point (2), connecting object (7), sequence flow (7), condition (2), merge (2), join (2), fork (2), **gateway** (16), complex gateway (2), event-based gateway (2), **parallel gateway** (12), **inclusive gateway** (9), **exclusive gateway** (11), flow operator (4) |
| *time* (3/6) | time point (2), cycle time duration (2), temporal dependency (2) |
| *data flow* (6/19) | message flow (5), data flow (5), association (3), conversational link (2), knowledge flow (2), assignment to an actor (2) |
| *data object* (17/48) | **artifact** (9), physical artifact (2), data object (5), message (3), conversation (3), call conversation (2), information (3), physical knowledge support (2), internal knowledge (2), tacit knowledge (2), external knowledge (2), explicit knowledge (2), procedural knowledge (2), knowledge (3), document (2), artifact instance (2), data store (2) |
| *actor* (14/72) | **actor** (14), collective agent (4), organisation (6), organisation unit (6), human expert (2), internal agent (2), external agent (2), client (4), position (4), application (4), **role** (15), process owner (2), process participant (4), person (3) |
| *resource* (8/50) | **resource** (13), material resource (3), immaterial resource (3), information (4), position (4), **role** (15), application (4), process participant (4) |
| *value* (2/5) | measure (3), cost (2) |
| *goal* (2/8) | organisational objective (2), goal (6) |
| *context* (2/4) | context (2), business area (2) |

only few times in the meta-models. Yet, also some time-related elements are not very represented. For instance only five elements are considered in the macro-element *state* and also the element state itself appears in only 4 meta-models. We also observed that five elements are considered as members of more than one group, such as `information`, `position`, `role`, `application`, and `process participant`. In this sense, the macro-element *resource* is the most interconnected having elements in common with the group *actor* and *data object*. This aspect is mainly due to the fact that some elements could play several roles in a business process (model). For instance `information` could be conceived as a resource but also as a data object.

Overall, only 14 elements of the extracted ones occurred in at least the 25% of the meta-models. These elements are reported in bold in Table 1. The only element that appeared in more than half of the meta-models is `activity`.

## 2.2 Literature-Based Relations

For the identification of the relations among meta-model elements, we decided to focus on the elements that: (i) either occurred in at least the 25% of the primary studies (i.e., the ones in bold in Table 1)[2]; or (ii) occurred at least 6 times in the macro-categories without any representative element (i.e., `goal`). These criteria guarantee that most of the macro-elements include their most recurrent components. In total 15 elements were considered: `activity`, `atomic activity`, `compound activity`, `event-BPMN`, `event-EPC`, `gateway`, parallel gateway (`AND`), inclusive gateway (`OR`), exclusive gateway (`XOR`), `precondition`, `artifact`, `actor`, `role`, `resource` and `goal`.

Among these elements, we identified 89 relations, which were reduced to 57 after merging the ones with similar semantics, and removing others that were scarcely significant (e.g., *is_related_with*), unless they were the only representative relation between a pair of elements. Table 2 reports the resulting 57 relations among pairs of elements and the number of meta-models in which the relation occurred (among round brackets)[3]. Specifically, in Table 2, we grouped business process modelling elements acting as domain and codomain of the relations into the three basic business process modeling language categories (BEHAVIOURAL, ORGANISATIONAL and DATA) and a fourth GOAL category characterizing the elements related to the goal of the process. Relations are organized such that each block collects the list of relations having as domain an element belonging to the catetgory in the row and as codomain an element belonging to the category in the column[4]. For instance, the relation *involves* between `activity` and `actor` lies at the cross between the BEHAVIOURAL row (as `activity` is a BEHAVIOURAL element) and the ORGANISATIONAL column (as `actor` is an ORGANISATIONAL element).

---

[2] For *event* we considered the sum of the frequencies of `event-BPMN` and `event-EPC`.

[3] The list of the 57 relations with cardinalities and references is available at https://drive.google.com/file/d/1Yzftl3ZCfGiMz9cZmFAcoevb0agmWDh6/view?usp=sharing. When two or more relations overlap, we keep the less restrictive cardinality.

[4] The element `resource` is used both in terms of human resource, i.e., ORGANISATIONAL resource and in terms of DATA resource, so the relations having `resource` as domain or codomain are duplicated in the table.

**Table 2.** Recurring relations in meta-models.

| | BEHAVIOURAL | | | ORGANISATIONAL | | | DATA | | | GOAL | | |
|---|---|---|---|---|---|---|---|---|---|---|---|---|
| | Domain | Codomain | Relation | Domain | Codomain | Relation | Domain | Codomain | Relation | Domain | Codomain | Relation |
| BEHAVIOURAL | activity | activity | composed_of, transition(CF) | activity | actor | involves, performed_by | activity | artifact | invokes, manipulates, is_performed on | activity | goal | supports |
| | | event-EPC | creates, predecessor, successor, | | role | under_the_ responsibility | | | requires, input, output | | | |
| | | event-BPMN | initiated_by | | resource | requires, input, output | | resource | requires, input, output | | | |
| | | precondition | requires | | | | | | | | | |
| | atomic activity | activity | is_a(7) | atomic activity | resource | produces_or consumes | atomic activity | artifact | is_related_to | | | |
| | | compound activity | belongs_to | | actor | performed_by | | resource | produces_or_ consumes | | | |
| | compound activity | activity | is_a(7) composed_of refined_by | compound activity | actor | performed_by | | | | | | |
| | | atomic activity | composed_of | | | | | | | | | |
| | | compound activity | composed_of | | | | | | | | | |
| | event-EPC | activity | activates successor predecessor | | | | | | | | | |
| | gateway | activity | is_a | | | | | | | | | |
| | | compound activity | is_related_ with | | | | | | | | | |
| | AND | gateway | is_a(9) | | | | | | | | | |
| | OR | gateway | is_a(9) | | | | | | | | | |
| | XOR | gateway | is_a(11) | | | | | | | | | |
| | precondition | activity | is_required_by enables | | | | | | | | | |
| ORGANISATIONAL | actor | activity | carries_out(2) | actor | actor | is_associated_ with | actor resource | resource artifact | uses/owns is_a | actor | goal | achieves |
| | | | | | role | inherited_role, is_a | | | | | | |
| | role | activity | enacts, inherited_task, responsible, temporal_ relationship | | resource | uses/owns | | | | | | |
| | | | | resource- | role | is_a | | | | | | |
| | | | | | actor | satisfies | | | | | | |
| | resource | activity | assigned_to | role | actor | is_a | | | | | | |
| | | precondition | is_a (data/action) | | role | subordinated _of | | | | | | |
| | | | | | resource | is_a | | | | | | |
| DATA | resource | activity | assigned_to | resource- | actor | satisfies | resource | artifact | is_a | | | |
| | | precondition | is_a (data/action) | | role | is_a | | | | | | |
| GOAL | | | | | | | | | | goal | goal | composed_of |

The analysis of Table 2 shows that relations among elements in existing meta-models are relatively few considering the number of the retrieved elements. Most of the relations appear in only one meta-model, as for instance the relation assigned_to between resource and activity. In contrast, a very small collection of relations occur in more than one meta-model, as for instance the is_a relation between atomic activity and activity as well as compound activity and activity.

By looking at the table, we can observe that the BEHAVIOURAL elements are mostly disjoint from the ORGANISATIONAL/DATA and GOAL categories. We can indeed identify two main clusters of relations: the one having domain and codomain elements in the BEHAVIOURAL category (top left cell of Table 2); and the one with domain and codomain elements in the ORGANISATIONAL\DATA categories (central cells in Table 2). Besides these two main clusters, we can identify few relations at the cross between the BEHAVIOURAL and ORGANISATIONAL/DATA categories and very few relations involving the GOAL category (and corresponding goal element).

Focusing on the elements, we can also observe that some of them are scarcely connected through relations. For instance, the element goal acts as the domain of only one reflexive relation (goal composed_of goal) and as codomain of only two further relations (achieves and supports). Elements such as artifact, AND, XOR, OR and event-BPMN, EPC are other examples of elements that are poorly connected to other elements. In contrast activity is shown to be the most interconnected element: it is the domain of 17 types of relations and the codomain of 19 types of relations. In the group of ORGAN- ISATIONAL elements, the element acting as domain for most of the relations is instead actor, having as codomain mainly ORGANISATIONAL and DATA elements. By looking at the number of different relations between pairs of elements, we can observe that, also in this case, while most of the pairs of elements have at most one relation, the highest number of different relations can be found between activity and event-EPC and event-BPMN as well as between role and activity. Finally, a handful of elements display a finer level of granularity being composed of simpler entities, e.g., activity, compound activity and goal.

Summing up, more than 10% of the types relations occurred more than once in state-of-the-art meta-models: the is_a relation between atomic activity and activity, between compound activity and activity, between AND and gateway as well as between OR, XOR and gateway; and the relation carries_out between actor and activity. Slightly more than 63% of the relations included the element activity either as domain or codomain. Around 42% of the relations have both domain and codomain in the BEHAVIOURAL elements, more than 17% involve ORGANISATIONAL/DATA domains and codomains, while out of the remaining of the relations, 35% is at the intersection of the two and roughly 5% of the relations deals with the GOAL elements.

*Limitations of the SRL.* The limitations of the SRL may mainly concern flaws in selection of the papers, imprecisions introduced in the extraction of data from the selected works, and potential inaccuracies due to the subjectivity of the analysis carried out. To mitigate them we did follow the guidelines reported in [13]. A further limitation of this study lies in the facts that only one researcher selected the candidate primary studies, and one researcher worked on the data extraction. Both aspects have been mitigated by the fact that another researcher checked the inclusion and the exclusion of the studies, and another researcher checked the data extraction, as suggested in [6].

## 3    The Literature-Based Meta-model

The extraction of the elements and the relations allows us to outline those characteristics of business processes (models) deemed most important by the number of scholars who have proposed business process meta-models in the literature. In this section we combine the extracted elements and relations, by merging all of them in a unique meta-model, the so called *literature-based business process meta-model* (*LB meta-model*).

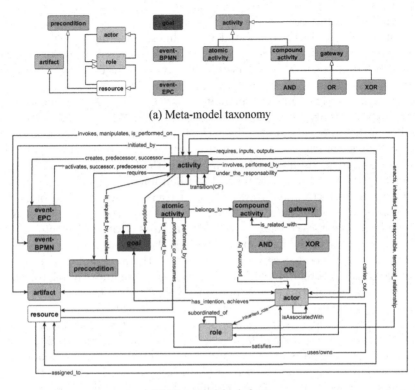

(a) Meta-model taxonomy

(b) Meta-model relations

**Fig. 1.** Literature-based meta-model

We are aware of the problems arising from a study in which the information from different sources is blindly brought together. However, as a provocation, in order to better investigate the criticalities that can arise, we build such as *LB meta-model*, which allows us to see how business process model views can be rich but also conflicting. Having said so, a further problem we had to overcome in creating the meta-model was the establishment of the semantics of its components (i.e., the labels' semantics) or, at the very least, the clarification of their intended meaning. In fact, only few authors did include explicit semantics, while for most of the cases it was either lacking or provided in terms of commonsense descriptions. Since our overarching meta-model is generated from the ones present in the surveyed papers, in order to avoid bias, we also opted to use a commonsense semantics of business process (modelling) elements.

Figure 1 depicts the literature-based meta-model in UML. In the meta-model gray is used for the BEHAVIOURAL elements, pink for ORGANISATIONAL elements, yellow for the DATA elements and red box for the unique GOAL element. Finally, the resource element, which is shared by the ORGANISATIONAL and DATA components, is depicted in white.

Observing Fig. 1, it is immediately clear that `activity` is the most important element. It is directly connected with almost all other elements, that is
reasonable given its centrality for business processes. Moreover, most of the elements of the BEHAVIOURAL component (e.g., `atomic activity`, `compound
activity`, `gateway`) are related through *is_a* relations to `activity`. In
contrast to `activity`, more than half of the BEHAVIOURAL elements (e.g.,
`event-BPMN`, `event-EPC`, `gateway`, `AND`, `OR` and `XOR`) are almost disconnected from the other categories. This lack of connection with other components
is particularly surprising for `gateways` that we would have expected to be connected not only with BEHAVIOURAL but also with DATA elements, considering
the fact that they deal with control and decision flow.

Looking at the DATA and ORGANISATIONAL elements, we can also notice that,
despite the importance of data and organisational aspects in business processes, a
unique DATA element - `artifact` - and two ORGANISATIONAL elements - `actor`
and `role` - appear in the meta-model, besides the shared `resource` element.
The `artifact`, which has several relations with the `activity` (and its sub-
classes) and an *is_a* relation with `resource`, is only indirectly related to the
other elements. For instance, it is indirectly connected to the `actor`, through
the `activity` element: the `actor` *carries_out* an `activity`, which, in turn
*manipulates* an `artifact`. An `actor`, besides *performing* `activities`,
has also other *agentive capabilities*, e.g., it *uses and owns* `resources`, as
well as *achieves* `goals`. The `resource` element also presents a number of
relations, many of which are *is_a* relationships. Lying at the cross between the
DATA and ORGANISATIONAL boundaries, indeed, it has been classified in different
terms, e.g, as a *precondition*, as an *artifact* and as a *role*.

Last but not least, the meta-model in Fig. 1 reveals the marginal role of the
GOAL category and of the `goal` element, which appears as an auxiliary element
that *is_composed_of* other `goals`, *supports* `activities` and is achieved
by `actors`.

To conclude this section we provide a brief description of the taxonomy of
the *LB meta-model* (Fig. 1a). Looking at the BEHAVIOURAL component, we can
observe two main subsumption blocks, where an element is specialised into elements with a finer level of granularity: `atomic` and `compound activity`
are sub-classes of `activity`, and parallel (`AND`) inclusive (`OR`) and exclusive (`XOR`) gateways are sub-classes of `gateway`. Instead, `event-BPMN`, `EPC`
are floating within the taxonomy. Moreover, besides reconfirming the centrality of the `activity`, we can also notice that all the BEHAVIOURAL elements -
except for the `event-BPMN`, `EPC` and `precondition` - are subsumed directly
or indirectly from the `activity` element. Here we expected that al least the
`event-BPMN` element could also be classified as a "dynamic" (with a duration)
entity.

Considering the ORGANISATIONAL and DATA components, these are not integrated with the BEHAVIOURAL part. The *is_a* relations are intricately articulated: `resource` *is_a* sub-class of `role`, `artifact` and `precondition`;
moreover `role` is an `actor` and viceversa. As a consequence, a `resource` is a

sub-class of `actor`. Finally, looking at the GOAL component, the `goal` element is completely disconnected from any other element in the taxonomy.

## 4 Discussion

The analysis carried out in the previous section reveals that the extracted meta-model is not very well balanced: some parts and elements have richer descriptions, while others are only roughly specified. The elements and relations extracted from the primary studies reveal a good level of maturity in the BEHAVIOURAL component both in terms of elements and relations among elements. Also some of the ORGANISATIONAL and DATA elements, such as `actor`, `resource` and `artifact`, are quite well investigated although their semantics and relations are still quite unclear. The GOAL component, instead, is under-investigated and represented both in terms of elements and relations. The relations between elements across different categories are also rather limited, thus leaving the BEHAVIOURAL, the DATA/ORGANISATIONAL and the GOAL components poorly connected the one to the other. Also within the same category, we can find a disproportion among elements: for instance, in the BEHAVIOURAL category, `activity` has been largely studied and is well connected to almost all the other elements, while elements as `event-BPMN` and `event-EPC` are less investigated and connected to the other elements.

The imbalance among elements and categories in the *LB meta-model* is even more critical when taking into account their importance in business processes. For instance, according to Weske, a business process is "a set of activities that are performed in coordination in an organizational and technical environment. These activities jointly realize a business *goal*." [30]. By looking at the *LB meta-model* and at its taxonomy, however, we can clearly notice that the `goal` element, besides being under-investigated in the literature, is also scarcely connected. This can be due to the lack of a graphical element for representing goals in most of the business process modelling graphical notations. Indeed, only few notations include an explicit symbol for the representation of goals as described in [1]. Similarly, *value*, which appears in several business process definitions, does not appear at all in the *LB meta-model*.

A second criticality that we can observe in the *LB meta-model* revolves around event (and its two semantics) and `precondition`. The same label, indeed, is used in the literature for denoting two different concepts. The `event-BPMN` is commonly understood as "something that happens during the course of a process" [21], that is, as an exogenous activity. The EPC-event is intended instead as "describing preconditions and postconditions of functions" [19], that is, in terms of state. This overloading of the same label for different semantics, as well as the lack of a clear relation between `event-EPC` and `precondition` reveals an imprecise and non-agreed understanding of these concepts and of their relations within the community. This criticality is further confirmed when looking at the relations between the two notions of event and activity. While the *causality* essence of the *initiated_by* relation between

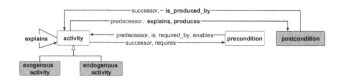

**Fig. 2.** Meta-model of events, activity, and pre-postcondition.

`activity` and `event-BPMN` reflects the *active* nature of the `event-BPMN`, the *predecessor* and *successor* relations between `activity` and `event-EPC` confirms their *temporal* characterisation, the `activates` relation between `activity` and `event-EPC` is tricky. A state, indeed, is a passive element, that cannot activate or cause anything by itself. The `activate` relation, however, refers to the complex notion of ARIS EPC event, which combines the two notions of `event-EPC` and `event-BPMN`.

Another issue emerging from the taxonomy extracted from the *LB meta-model* is related to the ORGANISATIONAL/DATA components. Indeed, the model reveals subsumption cycles between `actor`, `role` and `resource`, thus resulting in the equivalence of the three elements. These sumbsumption cycles and the consequent equivalence relation, due to the way in which elements and relations extracted from the literature have been composed in the *LB meta-model*, reveals that the community does not completely agree yet on the semantics of some ORGANISATIONAL/DATA elements and on the relations among them. This is especially true for the `resource` element that in the taxonomy of the *LB meta-model* shows a hybrid nature. Indeed, besides its ORGANISATIONAL (a `resource` *is_a* `role`) and DATA nature (`resource` *is_an* `artifact`), the `resource` element has also a BEHAVIOURAL nature (`resource` *is_a* `precondition`).

Finally, the *LB meta-model* captures mostly "standard" aspects of business processes and ignores elements related other dimensions of business processes such as, the decision rules and collaboration aspects underlying process models.

## 5    Towards an Ontologically Grounded Meta-model Refinement

In this section we address the critical aspects identified at the end of Sect. 4 trying to propose ontologically grounded solutions. In particular we focus here on the notions of state and event, and the notion of resource. For what concerns the scarce presence of important notions, in particular goal and value, we only note here that these absences should be filled, and that we plan to do it in the future starting from works such as [1, 28] and [23], respectively.

*Events, Activities, and States.* As already noted in Sect. 4, the different meta-models analysed associate, at type (i.e., conceptual) level, two different semantics to the term "event", which we resolved by explicitly renaming this element into event-BPMN and event-EPC. This overloading would become even more complex if we would take into account also the token (i.e., execution) level (mentioned for instance in [27]), where the term event is used to denote specific executions of activities and is close to the meaning of event as used in an "event log". This semantic overloading is somehow not a surprise for the BPM community, where the term "event" is used to denote elements that can pertain the type level, the token level, something that happens in time, a trigger that has causal power, and pre-postconditions.[5]

In this paper we concentrate our analysis mainly on the way "event" is used, in the different meta-models at type level. Nonetheless, it is easy to notice that, from an ontological point of view, events are often understood as elements happening at token level, that is, specific occurrences in time (see e.g., [8]). Then, what are event-BPMN and event-EPC? By looking at the language specification of BPMN, event-BPMN can be explained in terms of "a pattern of behaviour", that is, an activity type, which is an abstract entity [8].[6] Indeed event-BPMN, similarly to activities in that language, can be realised at token level by event occurrences (they happen in time), and can be repeated again and again in several process executions. What seems to differentiate the two notions in BPMN is more the fact that events "happen" in the world while activities denote pieces of works that a company (or a process owner more in general) should perform. Our proposal, therefore, is to borrow some concepts from the domain of statistics and conceive them as a sort of *exogenous* activity type, in contrast to the activities that happen within the process owner boundaries, that we rename *endogenous* activity type. This is a first analysis that may be further refined as these boundaries in BPMN are not always clear and events in BPMN are used to denote both elements with an "active" flavour (e.g., sending a message) as well as elements with a more "passive" flavour (e.g., exceptions or timers), whose differences should be accounted for. Nonetheless, we consider event-BPMN as an activity type as all these elements would be considered as "a pattern of behaviour" at type level according to [8] and not elements happening at token level.

If we move to ARIS EPCs, the analysis is slightly more complex. On the one hand, event-EPC is used as pre-postconditions which seem to be conceived as states. On the other hand, event-EPC is also described as an *activator* of activities. These two views are, from an ontological point of view, incompatible, as states cannot have causal power characteristics. Indeed, although states can be involved in causal relations, they cannot cause anything per-se [9]. Consider in a loan application process, "To have the credit history" is a state which acts as precondition for the "assess eligibility" activity, but that precondition alone cannot cause the assessment of eligibility. In this respect, the relation precondition

---

[5] See e.g., the definitions of event at https://www.businessprocessglossary.com/11516/event.

[6] The work of Galton [8] considers the differences between events and processes, the latter are the general counterpart of activities (see e.g., [20]).

*enables* activity found in the *LB meta-model*[7] appears to be more adequate than the one of event-EPC *activates* activity. Inspired by the analyses in [3] and [9], in this paper we propose to solve this inconsistency by viewing event-EPC as a specific pre-postcondition, and thus removing it, together with the *activates* relation from the diagram. Nonetheless, we strongly believe that this causal notion involving activities should be further investigated. Indeed, this double view of the notion of event-EPC, together with the higher presence of the notion of precondition w.r.t. the one of postcondition in the analysed meta-models, seem to suggest a need to incorporate some notion of "trigger" (distinct from a notion of state) that can explain (cause) the activation of activities within a business process. Instead, when discussing causal relations we can note that, although activities cannot cause directly anything (e.g., create) at type level, they have a sort of causal power, as they can *explain* why a certain activity type can cause something else, such as a state or other activities. Figure 2 summarises the refactoring of the two notions of event-BPMN and event-EPC explained above. Filled boxes represent newly added entities, and boldface has been used to denote newly added relations. Note, that we have included also postconditions to the diagram, and the relations that pertain this entity. Also, we have transferred the relations between event-EPC and activity to the appropriate relations between pre-postconditions and activity.

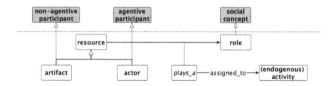

**Fig. 3.** Meta-model of resources.

*The Organisational/Data Component.* To start disambiguating the ORGANISA-TIONAL/DATA component, let us start by analysing the notion of resource. Similarly to what happened with the term event, also resources are defined, in the BPM community, in many different ways such as "[...] items necessary for a team to understand a problem and implement solutions [...]", "Agent used to perform activities [...]", "People, equipment, or materials required or used to accomplish an activity. [...]", and "Assets that is consumed in the operations [...]"[8]. All of these views upon resource are somehow included in Fig. 1, however in an overly rich and redundant manner that overlaps also with other elements such as artifact and actor.

---

[7] Although the label "enable" seems to be more suitable at token level, in this paper we retain it in the meta-model to represent the relation between precondition and activity.

[8] See e.g., the definitions of resource at: https://www.businessprocessglossary.com/8450/resources.

State-of-the-art ontological analysis in the context of Enterprise Modelling and manufacturing has classified resources in terms of *roles* that entities play within the context of an activity [5,7,24]. While an in-depth analysis of the notion of role is beyond the scope of this paper we can rely on the ones that have already been undertaken in literature, such as [17,18]). What we can retain here is the assumption that roles are dependent upon other entities for their existence and can be played, in context and time, by agentive (e.g., a person) and non-agentive (e.g., a data object) participants. Thus, roles can be conceived of variously including as *social concepts* that *describe* what that role is and in terms of *relations* [17,18].

In Fig. 3 a refactoring of the ORGANISATIONAL/DATA component based on the notion of "resource in terms of role it plays" is depicted. For the sake of clarity, the filled boxes denote reference concepts in the upper ontology DOLCE [16] in its extension for roles as social concepts [18] and in the analysis of business process participants [2]. In this diagram a business process resource *plays_a* role when it is *assigned_to* (endogenous) activities[9]. Note that we used association classes to reify the *plays_a* relation, to denote that the object denoting a resource playing a role is assigned to an activity. An actor is an agentive business process participant and an artifact is a non-agentive participant, and both can have *physical* and/or *non-physical* characteristics. Note that the association between the resource and the role occurs within the boundaries of activity, which somehow plays here the role of context in the definition of something as a resource [5,24].

A final comment is devoted to the resource *is-a* precondition relation found in the *LB meta-model*. While this relation must be deemed wrong, as a resource is not usually seen as a state, it is nonetheless true that the existence of resources with certain characteristics and capabilities can act as preconditions to the execution of certain activities. As such this relation should be further investigated.

# 6 Related Works

To the best of our knowledge, no work has been carried out so far specifically investigating and analysing the existing literature related to business process meta-models. However, a variety of sources exist that attempt to bring clarity to certain aspects of business process and modelling. Some of these papers are focused on the *creation of business process meta-models* and are indeed included in the list of the primary studies. For example, in both List et al. [14] and Söderström et al. [27] conceptual frameworks of business process are proposed in order to evaluate or compare and translate modelling notations. In the work of Heidari et al. [12], a general meta-model is developed starting from the elements of seven business process modelling languages. The language independent meta-model is finally compared and analysed with an ontology.

---

[9] Here we focus on resources that are assigned to activities within the process owner boundaries.

Several papers have been focusing on the *ontological analysis* of business process modelling and related fields. The works in [2,3,5,7,24] have been already discussed in reference to our work in Sect. 5 and are not described here for lack of space. In Sanfilippo et al. [25] an ontological analysis of event and activity constructs in BPMN is presented. In [26], Santos Jr. et al. presented an ontological analysis of ARIS EPCs using the UFO ontology [10] for the semantic interpretation of the elements. In particular, they focused on the analysis of function, event and rule. Focusing on works independent from specific modelling languages, in [11] Guizzardi et al. propose an ontological analysis of events. The analysis is performed considering the UFO ontology and, although the paper is not committed with the specific representation of events in business process modelling, the research analyses conceptual models, reference frameworks and domain ontologies also in the area of business process modelling. Other works (e.g., [22]) analise business process modelling using the Bunge Wand and Weber ontology [29] as reference framework. Concerning goals, the work in [1] provides a classification of business process goals from the point of view of participants, while the work in [28] analyses and integrates notion of goal and soft-goal in business process modelling. A careful evaluation of how to complement our work with the ones listed here is left for future works.

## 7    Conclusion

In this work a business process meta-model extracted from state-of-the-art proposals through a systematic literature review is presented, together with a preliminary ontological analysis of notions such as events, preconditions and resources. Although the single meta-models proposed in literature were individually consistent, combining them into a unique *LB meta-model*, allowed us to identify criticalities, to carry on a first analysis of these criticalities, and to propose possible solutions. This analysis gave us the opportunity to clarify, from an ontological perspective, well-known issues concerning the use of labels as *event* and *resource* and to investigate these interpretations within and outside the BPM community.

In the future we plan to further extend this work by addressing unsolved issues highlighted in Sect. 5. For instance, we would like to investigate the notion of "trigger" in relation to activities, as well as to analyse business process elements neglected in the individual meta-models, such as *goal* and *value*.

These investigations can provide a first step in the direction of a well-thought and agreed view on multi-perspective business process components at the conceptual level. This view would be beneficial not only for the development of new notations and systems, but also for improving the interoperability of existing notations and information systems.

# References

1. Adamo, G., Borgo, S., Di Francescomarino, C., Ghidini, C., Guarino, N.: On the notion of goal in business process models. In: Ghidini, C., Magnini, B., Passerini, A., Traverso, P. (eds.) AI*IA 2018. LNCS (LNAI), vol. 11298, pp. 139–151. Springer, Cham (2018). https://doi.org/10.1007/978-3-030-03840-3_11

2. Adamo, G., Borgo, S., Di Francescomarino, C., Ghidini, C., Guarino, N., Sanfilippo, E.M.: Business processes and their participants: an ontological perspective. In: Esposito, F., Basili, R., Ferilli, S., Lisi, F. (eds.) AI*IA 2017. LNCS, vol. 10640, pp. 215–228. Springer, Cham (2017). https://doi.org/10.1007/978-3-319-70169-1_16

3. Adamo, G., Borgo, S., Di Francescomarino, C., Ghidini, C., Guarino, N., Sanfilippo, E.M.: Business process activity relationships: is there anything beyond arrows? In: Weske, M., Montali, M., Weber, I., vom Brocke, J. (eds.) BPM 2018. LNBIP, vol. 329, pp. 53–70. Springer, Cham (2018). https://doi.org/10.1007/978-3-319-98651-7_4

4. Adamo, G., Ghidini, C., Di Francescomarino, C.: What's my process model composed of? A systematic literature review of meta-models in BPM. ArXiv abs/1910.05564 (2019, submitted for publication)

5. Azevedo, C.L.B., Iacob, M., Almeida, J.P.A., van Sinderen, M., Pires, L.F., Guizzardi, G.: Modeling resources and capabilities in enterprise architecture: a wellfounded ontology-based proposal for archimate. Inf. Syst. **54**, 235–262 (2015)

6. Brereton, P., Kitchenham, B.A., Budgen, D., Turner, M., Khalil, M.: Lessons from applying the systematic literature review process within the software engineering domain. J. Syst. Softw. **80**(4), 571–583 (2007)

7. Fadel, F.G., Fox, M.S., Gruninger, M.: A generic enterprise resource ontology. In: Proceedings of 3rd IEEE Workshop on Enabling Technologies: Infrastructure for Collaborative Enterprises, pp. 117–128, April 1994

8. Galton, A.: The ontology of states, processes, and events. In: Proceedings of the 5th Interdisciplinary Ontology Meeting, pp. 35–45. Keio University Open Research Centre for Logic and Formal Ontology (2012)

9. Galton, A.: States, processes and events, and the ontology of causal relations. In: Proceedings of the Seventh International Conference on Formal Ontology in Information Systems. FOIS 2012, Frontiers in Artificial Intelligence and Applications, vol. 239, pp. 279–292. IOS Press (2012)

10. Guizzardi, G., Wagner, G.: Using the unified foundational ontology (UFO) as a foundation for general conceptual modeling languages. In: Poli, R., Healy, M., Kameas, A. (eds.) Theory and Applications of Ontology: Computer Applications, pp. 175–196. Springer, Dordrecht (2010). https://doi.org/10.1007/978-90-481-8847-5_8

11. Guizzardi, G., Wagner, G., de Almeida Falbo, R., Guizzardi, R.S.S., Almeida, J.P.A.: Towards ontological foundations for the conceptual modeling of events. In: Ng, W., Storey, V.C., Trujillo, J.C. (eds.) ER 2013. LNCS, vol. 8217, pp. 327–341. Springer, Heidelberg (2013). https://doi.org/10.1007/978-3-642-41924-9_27

12. Heidari, F., Loucopoulos, P., Brazier, F.M.T., Barjis, J.: A meta-meta-model for seven business process modeling languages. In: IEEE 15th Conference on Business Informatics. CBI 2013, pp. 216–221. IEEE Computer Society (2013)

13. Kitchenham, B., Charters, S.: Guidelines for performing systematic literature reviews in software engineering. Technical report, EBSE 2007–001, Keele University and Durham University Joint Report (2007)

14. List, B., Korherr, B.: An evaluation of conceptual business process modelling languages. In: Proceedings of the 2006 ACM Symposium on Applied Computing (SAC), pp. 1532–1539. ACM (2006)
15. Mannhardt, F.: Multi-perspective process mining. In: Proceedings of the Dissertation Award, Demonstration, and Industrial Track Co-Located with 16th International Conference on Business Process Management (BPM 2018). CEUR Workshop Proceedings, vol. 2196, pp. 41–45 (2018). http://CEUR-WS.org
16. Masolo, C., Borgo, S., Gangemi, A., Guarino, N., Oltramari, A.: WonderWeb deliverable D18 ontology library (final). Technical report, IST Project 2001–33052 WonderWeb: Ontology Infrastructure for the Semantic Web (2003)
17. Masolo, C., Guizzardi, G., Vieu, L., Botazzi, E., Ferrario, R.: Relational roles and qua-individuals. In: Proceedings of the AAAI Symposium on Roles, an Interdisciplinary Perspective. AAAI Press (2005)
18. Masolo, C., et al.: Social roles and their descriptions. In: Proceedings of the 9th International Conference on Principles of Knowledge Representation and Reasoning (KR2004), pp. 267–277. AAAI Press (2004)
19. Mendling, J.: Event-driven Process Chains (EPC). Metrics for Process Models. LNBIP, vol. 6, pp. 17–57. Springer, Heidelberg (2008). https://doi.org/10.1007/978-3-540-89224-3_2
20. Mourelatos, A.P.D.: Events, processes, and states. Linguist. Philos. **2**(3), 415–434 (1978)
21. Object Management Group: Business Process Model and Notation (BPMN) version 2.0 (2011). https://www.omg.org/spec/BPMN/
22. Recker, J., Rosemann, M., Indulska, M., Green, P.F.: Business process modeling-a comparative analysis. J. AIS **10**(4), 1 (2009)
23. Sales, T.P., Guarino, N., Guizzardi, G., Mylopoulos, J.: An ontological analysis of value propositions. In: 21st IEEE International Enterprise Distributed Object Computing Conference, EDOC 2017, pp. 184–193. IEEE Computer Society (2017)
24. Sanfilippo, E.M., et al.: Modeling manufacturing resources: an ontological approach. In: Chiabert, P., Bouras, A., Noël, F., Ríos, J. (eds.) PLM 2018. IAICT, vol. 540, pp. 304–313. Springer, Cham (2018). https://doi.org/10.1007/978-3-030-01614-2_28
25. Sanfilippo, E.M., Borgo, S., Masolo, C.: Events and activities: is there an ontology behind BPMN? In: Proceedings of the 8th International Conference on Formal Ontology in Information Systems. FOIS 2014. Frontiers in Artificial Intelligence and Applications, vol. 267, pp. 147–156. IOS Press (2014)
26. Santos Jr., P.S., Almeida, J.P.A., Guizzardi, G.: An ontology-based semantic foundation for ARIS EPCs. In: Proceedings of the 2010 ACM Symposium on Applied Computing (SAC), pp. 124–130. ACM (2010)
27. Söderström, E., Andersson, B., Johannesson, P., Perjons, E., Wangler, B.: Towards a framework for comparing process modelling languages. In: Pidduck, A.B., Ozsu, M.T., Mylopoulos, J., Woo, C.C. (eds.) CAiSE 2002. LNCS, vol. 2348, pp. 600–611. Springer, Heidelberg (2002). https://doi.org/10.1007/3-540-47961-9_41
28. Soffer, P., Wand, Y.: On the notion of soft-goals in business process modeling. Bus. Process Manage. J. **11**(6), 663–679 (2005)
29. Wand, Y., Weber, R.: Toward a theory of the deep structure of information systems. In: ICIS, p. 3 (1990)
30. Weske, M.: Business Process Management. Concepts, Languages, Architectures. Springer, Cham (2012). https://doi.org/10.1007/978-3-642-28616-2

# Mining User Opinions to Support Requirement Engineering: An Empirical Study

Jacek Dąbrowski[1,2]([✉]) [iD], Emmanuel Letier[1] [iD], Anna Perini[2] [iD],
and Angelo Susi[2] [iD]

[1] University College London, London, UK
{j.dabrowski,e.letier}@cs.ucl.ac.uk
[2] Fondazione Bruno Kessler, Trento, Italy
{dabrowski,perini,susi}@fbk.eu

**Abstract.** App reviews provide a rich source of user opinions that can support requirement engineering activities. Analysing them manually to find these opinions, however, is challenging due to their large quantity and noisy nature. To overcome the problem, automated approaches have been proposed for so-called opinion mining. These approaches facilitate the analysis by extracting features discussed in app reviews and identifying their associated sentiments. The effectiveness of these approaches has been evaluated using different methods and datasets. Unfortunately, replicating these studies to confirm their results and to provide benchmarks of different approaches is a challenging problem. We address the problem by extending previous evaluations and performing a comparison of these approaches. In this paper, we present an empirical study in which, we evaluated feature extraction and sentiment analysis approaches on the same dataset. The results show these approaches achieve lower effectiveness than reported originally, and raise an important question about their practical use.

**Keywords:** Mining user reviews · Requirement engineering · Feature extraction · Sentiment analysis · Empirical study

## 1 Introduction

App reviews is a rich source of user opinions [1,2,14,17]. These opinions can help developers to understand how users perceive their app, what are users' requirements, or what are users' preferences [1,2,14]. Not surprisingly, knowing user opinions is an important information need developers seek to satisfy [2,4]. The information can affect different software engineering practices [1,14].

Analysing app reviews to find user opinions, however, is challenging [14,17]; Developers may receive thousands of reviews per day [1,14,17]. Moreover, these reviews contain mostly noise [17,19]. Consequently, the possibility of using these opinions to support engineering activities is obstructed [1,14].

© Springer Nature Switzerland AG 2020
S. Dustdar et al. (Eds.): CAiSE 2020, LNCS 12127, pp. 401–416, 2020.
https://doi.org/10.1007/978-3-030-49435-3_25

To address the problem, studies in requirement engineering proposed a few opinion mining approaches [10, 12, 13, 16]. These approaches facilitate mining user opinions by performing two tasks: extracting features discussed in reviews and identifying their associated users' sentiments [12, 16]. In particular, two approaches have become adopted in the community [17], GuMa [12][1] and SAFE [11].

Unfortunately, replicating the studies to confirm their results and to compare their approaches is a challenging problem. In fact, different methods and datasets have been used. The unavailability of their annotated datasets and evaluation procedures challenge their replicability even more [11–13, 21, 22].

The aim of the study is to address the problem by extending previous evaluations and performing comparison of these app review analysis approaches. We consider the following research questions to answer:

**RQ1:** What is the effectiveness of feature extraction approaches?
**RQ2:** What is the effectiveness of feature-specific sentiment analysis approaches?

To answer them, we conducted an empirical study in which we evaluated three approaches: GuMa [12], SAFE [11] and ReUS [10]. We evaluated them in performing feature extraction and sentiment analysis tasks using our annotated dataset.

The primary contributions of the study are: (i) an empirical evaluation expanding previous evaluations of the opinion mining approaches, (ii) a comparison of the approaches performing feature extraction and feature-specific sentiment analysis, and (iii) a new dataset of 1,000 reviews annotated with 1,521 opinions [7].

The remainder of the paper is structured as follows: In Sect. 2, we introduce terminology and the problem, then we give an overview of the opinion mining approaches we evaluate. In Sect. 3, we present scenarios motivating opinion mining. In Sect. 4, we present our study design. The results are detailed in Sect. 5, and the findings are discussed in Sect. 6. In Sect. 7, we provide threats to validity, then we discuss related works in Sect. 8. Conclusion is given in Sect. 9.

## 2    Background

This section introduces terminology and the formulation of opinion mining problem. It also provides an overview of approaches we evaluated.

### 2.1    Terminology and Problem Formulation

**Definition 1 (Feature and Feature Expression).** A feature is a user-visible functional attribute of an app that is intentionally provided. Attributes are typically functionalities (e.g., "send message"), modules providing functional capabilities (e.g., "user account") or design components (e.g., "UI") that can be utilized to perform tasks. A feature expression is a non-empty set of words $f = \{w_1, ..., w_m\}$ describing a feature in an app review. Further on in the text, we refer to a feature expression as a feature for the sake of simplicity.

---

[1] We refer to the approach using abbreviations derived from their authors' surnames.

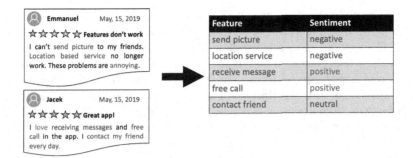

**Fig. 1.** Opinion mining

**Definition 2 (Sentiment).** A sentiment $s$ is a user attitude which can be either *positive, negative* or *neutral*.

**Definition 3 (Opinion).** An opinion is a tuple $o = (f, s)$, where $f$ is a feature in a review $r$, $s$ is a sentiment referencing to $f$ in $r$.

**Problem 1 (Opinion Mining).** Given a set of reviews $R = \{r\}$ on an app $a$, the opinion mining problem is to find a multi-set of all the opinions $O = \{o\}$ in a set of reviews $R$.

Figure 1 illustrates opinion mining problem. The problem can be decomposed into two sub-problems, feature extraction and feature-specific sentiment analysis:

**Problem 1.1 (Feature Extraction).** Let $R = \{r\}$ be a set of reviews on an app $a$. Find a multi-set of all the features $F = \{f\}$ in a set of reviews $R$.

**Problem 1.2 (Feature-specific Sentiment Analysis).** Consider a set of pairs $\{(f, r)\}$ where $f$ is a feature in a review $r$. Find a multi-set $S = \{s\}$ where $s$ is a sentiment referring to $f$ in $r$.

## 2.2   Approaches for Mining User Opinions

In our study, we selected three approaches: GuMa [12], SAFE [13] and ReUS [10]. We selected GuMa and SAFE as they are state-of-the-art approaches widely known in RE community [9,17,22]. We opted for ReUS [10] as the approach achieves a competitive performance in the context of opinion mining and sentiment analysis research [10,16]. We also have its original implementation.

**GuMa** performs feature extraction and feature-specific sentiment analysis. These tasks are performed independently of each other. To extract features, the approach relies on a collocation finding algorithm. For predicting sentiment, the approach uses the SentiStrength tool [23]. First, the approach predicts the sentiment of a sentence, then assigns sentiments to features in the sentence. Unfortunately, GuMa's source code and evaluation data set are not available. We have therefore re-implemented GuMa's approach using SentiStrength for sentiment analysis. We have tested that our implementation is consistent with GuMa's original implementation on examples in the original paper.

**SAFE** supports feature extraction, but not sentiment analysis. The approach extracts features based on linguistics patterns, including 18 part-of-speech patterns and 5 sentence patterns. These patterns have been identified through manual analysis of app descriptions. The approach conducts two main steps to extract features from a review: text preprocessing and the application of the patterns. Text preprocessing includes tokenizing a review into sentences, filtering-out noisy sentences, and removing unnecessary words. The final step concerns the application of linguistic patterns to each sentence to extract app features. We used the original implementation of the approach in our study.

**ReUS** exploits linguistics rules comprised of part-of-speech patterns and semantic dependency relations. These rules are used to parse a sentence and perform feature extraction and feature-specific sentiment analysis. Both tasks are performed at the same time. Given a sentence, the approach extracts a feature and an opinion word conveying a feature-specific sentiment. To determine the sentiment, the approach exploits lexical dictionaries. We used the original implementation of the approach, and set up it to identify one out of three sentiment polarities.

## 3   Motivating Scenarios

We describe three use cases in which the use of opinion mining can provide benefits. They are inspired by real-world scenarios, which were analysed in previous research [1, 2, 14].

**Use Case 1 (Validation by Users).** In any business endeavour, understanding customer opinions is an important aspect; app development is no exception [2, 14]. Knowing what features users love or dislike can give project managers an idea about user acceptance of these features [1, 2]. It can also help them draw a conclusion whether invested efforts were worth it [14]. As an example, imagine the development team changed core features in WhatsApp (e.g. video call). The team may want to know what users say about these features so that they can fix any glitches as soon as possible and refine these features. Mining user opinions could help them discover What are the most problematic features? or How many users do report negative opinions about a concrete feature (e.g. video call)?

**Use Case 2 (Supporting Requirements Elicitation).** Imagine now that WhatsApp receives negative comments about one of their features (e.g. group chat). It can be intimidating for developers to tackle a problem if they have to read through a thousand reviews. Using an opinion mining approach, developers could discover the issue within minutes. App mining tools could group reviews based on discussed features and their associated user's sentiment. Developers could then examine reviews that talk negatively about a specific feature (e.g. group chat). This could help developers understand user concerns about a problematic feature, and potentially help eliciting new requirements.

**Use Case 3 (Supporting Requirements Prioritization).** When added with statistics, user opinions can help developers prioritize their work [1,2,14]. Suppose the team is aware about problems with certain features which are commented negatively. Finding negative opinions mentioning these features could help them to compare how often these opinions appears, for how long these opinions have been made, and whether their frequency is increasing or decreasing. This information could provide an evidence of their relative importance from a users' perspective. Such information is not sufficient to prioritize issues, but it can provide useful evidence-based data to contribute to prioritization decisions.

For these scenarios having a tool that (i) mines user opinions and (ii) provides their summary with simple statistics could help the team to evolve their app.

## 4  Empirical Study Design

This section describes the empirical study design we used to evaluate the selected approaches. We provide the research questions we aimed to answer, the manually annotated dataset and evaluation metrics used to this end.

### 4.1  Research Questions

The objective of the study was to evaluate and compare approaches mining opinions from app reviews. To this end, we formulated two research questions:

**RQ1:** What is the effectiveness of feature extraction approaches?
**RQ2:** What is the effectiveness of feature-specific sentiment analysis approaches?

In RQ1, we evaluated the capability of the approaches in correctly extracting features from app reviews. In RQ2, we investigated the degree to which the approaches can correctly predict sentiments associated with specific features. A conclusive method of measuring the correctness of extracted features/predicted sentiments is by relying on human judgment. We used our dataset in which opinions (feature-sentiment pairs) have been annotated by human-coders (see Sect. 4.2). We compared extracted features/predicted sentiments to those annotated in ground truth using automatic matching methods (see Definition 4.3). In answering the questions, we report precision and recall.

### 4.2  Manually Annotated Dataset

This section describes the manually annotated dataset we created to answer RQ1 and RQ2 [7]. To create this datatset, we collected reviews from previously published datasets [18,24] and asked human-coders to annotate a selected samples of these reviews.

**Table 1.** The overview of the subject apps

| App name | Category | Platform | #Reviews |
|---|---|---|---|
| Evernote | Productivity | Amazon | 4,832 |
| Facebook | Social | Amazon | 8,293 |
| eBay | Shopping | Amazon | 1,962 |
| Netflix | Movies & TV | Amazon | 14,310 |
| Spotify Music | Audio & Music | Google Play | 14,487 |
| Photo editor pro | Photography | Google Play | 7,690 |
| Twitter | News & Magazines | Google Play | 63,628 |
| Whatsapp | Communication | Google Play | 248,641 |

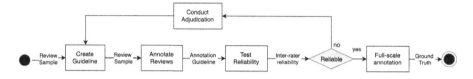

**Fig. 2.** The method for ground truth creation

## A) Data Collection

We have selected reviews from datasets used in previous review mining studies [18,24]. We selected these datasets because they include millions of English reviews from two popular app stores (i.e., Google Play and Amazon) for different apps, categories and period of times. We selected 8 apps from these datasets, 4 apps from Google Play and 4 from Amazon app stores. For each subject app, we also collected their description from the app store. Table 1 illustrates the summary of apps and their reviews we used in our study. We selected subject apps from different categories to make our results more generalizable. We believe that the selection of popular apps could help annotators to understand their features, and to reduce their effort during the annotation.

## B) Annotation Procedure

The objective of the procedure was to produce an annotated dataset that we use as ground truth to evaluate the quality of solutions produced by feature extraction and sentiment analysis approaches [20]. Figure 2 illustrates the overview of the procedure. Given a sample of reviews, the task of human-coders was to label each review with features and their associated sentiments.

We started by elaborating a guideline describing the annotation procedure, the definition of concepts and examples. We then asked two human-coders[2] to label a random sample of reviews using the guideline [7]. We evaluated the

---

[2] The first author and an external coder who has no relationship with this research. Both coders have an engineering background and programming experience.

**Table 2.** Statistics of the ground truth for 1,000 reviews for 8 subject apps.

| | App name | | | | | | | | Overall |
|---|---|---|---|---|---|---|---|---|---|
| | Evernote | Facebook | eBay | Netflix | Spotify | Photo editor | Twitter | WhatsApp | |
| *Reviews* | | | | | | | | | |
| No. reviews | 125 | 125 | 125 | 125 | 125 | 125 | 125 | 125 | 1,000 |
| Avg. review length | 48.30 | 37.90 | 32.54 | 43.46 | 23.62 | 12.38 | 15.79 | 14.47 | 28.59 |
| No. sentences | 367 | 327 | 294 | 341 | 227 | 154 | 183 | 169 | 2,062 |
| Avg. sentence length | 16.45 | 14.49 | 13.84 | 15.93 | 13.00 | 10.05 | 10.79 | 10.70 | 13.85 |
| Sentence per review | 2.94 | 2.62 | 2.35 | 2.73 | 1.82 | 1.23 | 1.46 | 1.35 | 2.06 |
| *Sentiment* | | | | | | | | | |
| No. sentiments | 295 | 242 | 206 | 262 | 180 | 96 | 122 | 118 | 1,521 |
| No. positive | 97 | 49 | 95 | 79 | 32 | 39 | 5 | 20 | 416 |
| No. neutral | 189 | 168 | 102 | 159 | 122 | 47 | 93 | 84 | 964 |
| No. negative | 9 | 25 | 9 | 24 | 26 | 10 | 24 | 14 | 141 |
| *Features* | | | | | | | | | |
| No. features | 295 | 242 | 206 | 262 | 180 | 96 | 122 | 118 | 1,521 |
| No. distinct features | 259 | 204 | 167 | 201 | 145 | 80 | 99 | 100 | 1,172 |
| No. single-word features | 82 | 80 | 78 | 94 | 69 | 39 | 39 | 49 | 530 |
| No. multi-word features | 213 | 162 | 128 | 168 | 111 | 57 | 83 | 69 | 991 |
| Feature per review | 2.36 | 1.94 | 1.65 | 2.10 | 1.44 | 0.77 | 0.98 | 0.94 | 1,52 |
| *Agrmt.* | | | | | | | | | |
| $F_1$ measure | 0.76 | 0.73 | 0.77 | 0.75 | 0.67 | 0.78 | 0.79 | 0.83 | 0.76 |
| Fleiss' Kappa | 0.64 | 0.77 | 0.77 | 0.55 | 0.75 | 0.86 | 0.69 | 0.80 | 0.73 |

reliability of their annotation using the inter-rater agreement metrics $F_1$ and Fleiss' Kappa [5,6]. $F_1$ is suitable for evaluating text spans' annotations such as feature expressions found in reviews; Fleiss' kappa is suitable to assess inter-rater reliability between two or more coders for categorical items' annotations such as users' sentiment (positive, negative, or neutral). We evaluated inter-rater agreement to ensure the annotation task was understandable, unambiguous, and could be replicated [20]. When disagreement was found, the annotators discussed to adjudicate their differences and refined the annotation guidelines. The process was performed iteratively, each time with a new sample of reviews until the quality of the annotation was at an acceptable level [6]. Once this was achieved, annotators conducted a full-scale annotation on a new sample of 1,000 reviews that resulted in our ground truth.

## C) Ground truth

Table 2 reports statistics of our ground truth. These statistics concern subject app reviews, annotated opinions (feature-sentiment pairs) and inter-rater reliability measures. The average length of reviews and sentences is measured in words. Statistics of opinions are reported separately for features and sentiments. The number of features has been given for all the annotated features, distinct ones, and with respect to their length (in words). The number of sentiments has been described including their number per polarity.

The ground truth consists of 1,000 reviews for 8 subject apps. In total, 1,521 opinions (i.e., feature-sentiment pairs) have been annotated. Their sentiment

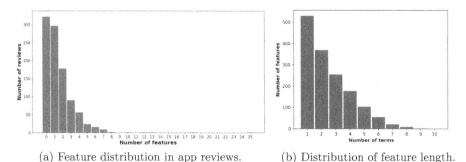

(a) Feature distribution in app reviews.  (b) Distribution of feature length.

**Fig. 3.** Feature distribution in app reviews, and feature length distribution.

distribution is unbalanced: most feature-sentiment pairs are neutral. Among 1,521 annotated features, 1,172 of them are distinct (i.e. mentioned only once).

The feature distribution in app reviews can be found in Fig. 3a. A large number of reviews do not refer to any specific feature. 75% of reviews refers to no feature or to only one or two features. Fig. 3b provides the feature length distribution. The median length for a feature is 2 words, 75% of features has between 1 and 3 words, and nearly 5% has more than 5 words.

### 4.3 Evaluation Metrics

We used precision and recall metrics [6] to answer RQ1 and RQ2. We used them because feature extraction is an instance of information extraction problem [6], whereas sentiment analysis can be seen as a classification problem [16].

*A) Evaluation Metrics for Feature Extraction*

In answering RQ1, precision indicates the percentage of extracted features that are true positives. Recall refers to the percentage of annotated features that were extracted. An extracted feature can be true or false positive. True positive features correspond to features that were both extracted and annotated; False positives are features that were extracted but not annotated; Annotated but not extracted features are called false negative. To determine whether an extracted feature is true or false positive, we compared them with annotated features in the ground truth. To this end, we used the following feature matching method:

**Definition 4 (Feature Matching).** Let $\Gamma$ be the set of words in a review sentence and $f_i \subseteq \Gamma$ be the set of words used to refer to feature $i$ in that sentence. Two features $f_1, f_2 \subseteq \Gamma$ match at level $n$ (with $n \in \mathbb{N}$) if and only if (i) one of the feature is equal to or is a subset of the other, i.e. $f_1 \subseteq f_2$ or $f_2 \subseteq f_1$, and (ii) the absolute length difference between the features is at most $n$, i.e. $||f_1| - |f_2|| \leq n$.

**Table 3.** RQ1. Results for feature extraction at varied levels of feature matching.

| App name | Exact Match (n = 0) | | | | | | Partial Match 1 (n = 1) | | | | | | Partial Match 2 (n = 2) | | | | | |
|---|---|---|---|---|---|---|---|---|---|---|---|---|---|---|---|---|---|---|
| | GuMa | | SAFE | | ReUS | | GuMa | | SAFE | | ReUS | | GuMa | | SAFE | | ReUS | |
| | P | R | P | R | P | R | P | R | P | R | P | R | P | R | P | R | P | R |
| Evernote | 0.06 | **0.13** | **0.07** | 0.08 | **0.07** | 0.08 | 0.15 | **0.35** | **0.22** | 0.24 | 0.19 | 0.20 | 0.17 | **0.39** | **0.32** | 0.35 | 0.27 | 0.29 |
| Facebook | 0.03 | 0.07 | 0.03 | 0.03 | **0.09** | **0.09** | 0.10 | **0.28** | **0.15** | 0.17 | **0.15** | 0.14 | 0.13 | **0.36** | **0.23** | 0.26 | 0.20 | 0.19 |
| eBay | 0.04 | **0.07** | 0.04 | 0.05 | **0.06** | 0.06 | 0.14 | **0.26** | **0.22** | **0.26** | 0.14 | 0.14 | 0.17 | 0.32 | **0.34** | **0.39** | 0.22 | 0.21 |
| Netflix | 0.03 | **0.13** | 0.03 | 0.03 | **0.06** | 0.07 | 0.11 | **0.45** | **0.19** | 0.21 | 0.18 | 0.21 | 0.13 | **0.55** | **0.27** | 0.29 | 0.25 | 0.29 |
| Spotify | 0.05 | 0.10 | 0.05 | 0.04 | **0.15** | **0.13** | 0.18 | **0.37** | **0.24** | 0.23 | 0.23 | 0.20 | 0.21 | **0.43** | **0.36** | 0.34 | 0.29 | 0.26 |
| Photo editor | 0.12 | 0.11 | 0.12 | 0.09 | **0.14** | **0.13** | 0.26 | 0.25 | **0.34** | **0.27** | 0.23 | 0.21 | 0.29 | 0.27 | **0.38** | **0.30** | 0.27 | 0.25 |
| Twitter | **0.06** | **0.19** | **0.06** | 0.07 | 0.02 | 0.02 | 0.16 | **0.49** | **0.23** | 0.24 | 0.11 | 0.11 | 0.18 | **0.58** | **0.35** | 0.36 | 0.27 | 0.26 |
| WhatsApp | 0.05 | **0.21** | **0.11** | 0.11 | 0.06 | 0.06 | 0.14 | **0.56** | **0.32** | 0.33 | 0.19 | 0.20 | 0.16 | **0.64** | **0.39** | 0.40 | 0.24 | 0.25 |
| Mean | 0.05 | **0.13** | 0.06 | 0.06 | **0.08** | 0.08 | 0.15 | **0.37** | **0.24** | 0.24 | 0.18 | 0.18 | 0.18 | **0.44** | **0.33** | 0.34 | 0.25 | 0.25 |

### B) Evaluation Metrics for Feature-Specific Sentiment Analysis

In answering RQ2, precision indicates the percentage of predicted sentiments that are correct. Recall refers to the percentage of annotated sentiments that are predicted correctly. To determine whether predicted sentiments are correct, we compared them with annotated ones in the ground truth.

We measured precision and recall for each polarity category (i.e. positive, neutral and negative). We also calculated the overall precision and recall of all three sentiment polarities. To this end, we used the weighted average of precision and recall of each polarity category. The weight of a given polarity category was determined by the number of annotated sentiments with the sentiment polarity.

## 5 Results

**RQ1: What is the effectiveness of feature extraction approaches?**
To answer RQ1, we compared extracted features to our ground truth using feature matching at levels 0, 1 and 2 (see Definition 4). We selected these levels as extracted and annotated features may differ by a few words but still indicating the same app feature. We then computed precision and recall at these levels. Table 3 reports precision and recall for each approach at different matching levels (best in bold). The results show the approaches achieved low precision, recall given Exact Match. For all three approaches, precision and recall increase when we loosen the matching criteria to partial matching with $n = 1$ or 2. The growth can be attributed to the changed numbers of true positives (TPs), false positives (FPs) and false negatives (FNs) when $n$ increases. Figures 4 shows their behavior as the matching level $n$ increases; $\Delta TPs = -\Delta FPs = -\Delta FNs$ when $n$ increases.

**RQ2: What is the effectiveness of feature-specific sentiment analysis approaches?**
In answering RQ2, we report the effectiveness of ReUS and GuMa in feature-specific sentiment (see Sect. 4.3). To this end, we compared predicted and annotated sentiments, and exploited a subset of the ground truth with opinions

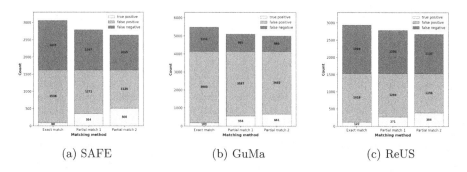

(a) SAFE     (b) GuMa     (c) ReUS

**Fig. 4.** RQ1. No. TPs, FPs and FNs as the level of features matching changes.

**Table 4.** RQ2. Dataset used for evaluating feature-specific sentiment analysis.

| Dataset | # opinions | # positive | # neutral | # negative |
|---|---|---|---|---|
| Exact Match | 122 | 56 | 52 | 14 |
| Partial Match 1 | 271 | 97 | 149 | 25 |
| Partial Match 2 | 384 | 120 | 226 | 38 |
| All Annotated | 1521 | 416 | 964 | 141 |

(feature-sentiment pairs) we used to answer RQ1. Indeed, since ReUS predicts sentiments only for extracted features, we considered only true positive features obtained in answering RQ1 and formed three datasets, each corresponding to true positive features (and their sentiment) from Exact Match, Partial Match$_1$ and Partial Match$_2$. Table 4 reports for each dataset the total number of opinions, and their breakdown to polarity categories. We also evaluated GuMa with these datasets and with all the annotated opinions in our ground truth.

The answer to RQ2 can be given at two levels of details, the overall effectiveness of predicting a sentiment, and the effectiveness of predicting a specific polarity (e.g., positive). We report our results at both levels of details.

*Overall Effectiveness.* Table 5 reports the number of correct predictions, and weighted precision/recall for inferring overall sentiment (best in bold). We can observe that ReUS achieves higher precision and recall than GuMa for Exact Match dataset, whereas both approaches have similar performances on the Partial Match$_1$ and Partial Match$_2$ datasets.

*Specific Effectiveness.* In Table 6, we report the metrics showing the effectiveness of the approaches in predicting specific polarities (best in bold). The results show that on positive opinions ReUS achieves higher precision while suffering from lower recall. Conversely, on neutral opinions GuMa provides better precision but lower recall than ReUS. When looking at the approaches, the analysis of the results revealed that none of the approaches was able to reliably assess the sentiment of negative options. Both approaches were good at discriminating between positive and negative opinions. Most incorrect predictions were caused by misclassifying positive/negative sentiment with neutral one and vice versa.

# 6 Discussion

The results indicate that the approaches have limited effectiveness in mining user opinions. Our findings bring into question their practical applications.

**Table 5.** RQ2. Results for feature-specific sentiment analysis (overall).

| Dataset | Approach | # correct prediction | Precision | Recall |
|---|---|---|---|---|
| Exact Match | ReUS | **85** | **0.74** | **0.70** |
| | GuMa | 77 | 0.65 | 0.63 |
| Partial Match 1 | ReUS | **184** | 0.69 | **0.68** |
| | GuMa | 176 | **0.72** | 0.65 |
| Partial Match 2 | ReUS | **265** | 0.69 | **0.69** |
| | GuMa | 252 | **0.73** | 0.66 |
| All Annotated | ReUS | – | – | – |
| | GuMa | **958** | **0.73** | **0.63** |

**Table 6.** RQ2. Results for feature-specific sentiment analysis (per each polarity).

| Dataset | Approach | Positive | | | Neutral | | | Negative | | |
|---|---|---|---|---|---|---|---|---|---|---|
| | | # correct prediction | Precision | Recall | # correct prediction | Precision | Recall | # correct prediction | Precision | Recall |
| Exact Match | ReUS | 35 | **0.90** | 0.62 | **45** | 0.60 | **0.87** | 5 | **0.62** | 0.36 |
| | GuMa | **47** | 0.68 | **0.84** | 21 | **0.68** | 0.40 | **9** | 0.41 | **0.64** |
| Partial Match 1 | ReUS | 47 | **0.80** | 0.48 | **131** | 0.66 | **0.88** | 6 | **0.43** | 0.24 |
| | GuMa | **86** | 0.61 | **0.89** | 73 | **0.85** | 0.49 | **17** | 0.40 | **0.68** |
| Partial Match 2 | ReUS | 53 | **0.80** | 0.44 | **205** | 0.68 | **0.91** | 7 | **0.41** | 0.18 |
| | GuMa | **107** | 0.59 | **0.89** | 122 | **0.86** | 0.54 | **23** | 0.38 | **0.61** |
| All Annotated | ReUS | – | – | – | – | – | – | – | – | – |
| | GuMa | **355** | 0.52 | **0.85** | **510** | **0.87** | 0.53 | **93** | 0.36 | **0.66** |

*A) Feature Extraction*

In our experiment, feature extraction methods have lower precision and recall than previously reported [10,12,13]. SAFE was reported with 0.71 recall [13]. Our results show the approach achieves 0.34 recall for the least rigorous evaluation strategy. The majority of features extracted by GuMa are incorrect. Although GuMa initially reported precision and recall of 0.58 and 0.52 [12], our experiment found lower figures of 0.18 precision and 0.44 recall.

Although the difference may be due to our re-implementation of the GuMa method, we have taken great care in implementing the method as described in the paper as rigorously as possible. Unfortunately, the original Guma implementation was not available for comparison. We believe ReUS suffered from low precision and recall because it was designed to extract features from product reviews in an online commerce website (Amazon) rather than from app reviews in app stores [16]. Our findings support a conjecture that the original evaluation procedures of SAFE and GuMa led to over-optimistic results. The limitations of these procedures have been questioned recently [21, 22]. These procedures did not define a feature matching strategy [21], relied on a subjective judgment [13, 22], and used a biased dataset [12, 21, 22]. We hope our new annotated dataset and description of our evaluation method will contribute to improving the quality of feature extraction techniques and their evaluations.

### B) Feature-Specific Sentiment Analysis

Our investigation of results (RQ2) concludes that the overall effectiveness of the approaches is promising (see Table 5). However, it reveals that their precision and recall differ considerably by sentiment class (positive, negative, or neutral). The approaches provide satisfactory performance for predicting positive and neutral sentiments. But they suffer from inaccurate predictions for negative sentiments. Overall, we are surprised by the comparable effectiveness of both approaches. We expected ReUS to outperform GuMa. ReUS exploits a sophisticated technique to detect an opinion word in a sentence that carries a feature-specific sentiment; GuMa makes predictions based on a simplified premise that a feature-specific sentiment corresponds to the overall sentiment of a sentence.

### C) Implication on Requirement Engineering Practices

Identifying what precision and recall app review mining techniques should have to be useful for requirements engineers in practice is an important open question [3]. In principle, a tool facilitating opinion mining should synthesize reviews so that the effort for their further manual analysis would be negligible or at least manageable. Clearly, this effort depends on a scenario the approach intends to support. Given a scenario of prioritizing problematic features, a developer may seek for information about the number of specific features that received negative comments, for example to understand their relevance. To this end, both information about extracted features and their predicted sentiments should be accurate and complete. Our results, however, show that feature extraction techniques generate many false positives. Given the large number of extracted features, filtering out false positives manually may not be cost-effective. We may imagine that the problem could be partially addressed using a searching tool [8]; Requirements engineers could use the tool to filter out uninteresting features (including false positives) and focus on those of their interest.

However, other issues remain unsolved. Feature extraction techniques fail to identify many references to features (they have low recall), and sentiment analysis techniques perform poorly for identifying feature-specific negative sentiments.

# 7    Threats to Validity

**Internal Validity.** The main threat is that the annotation of reviews was done manually with a certain level of subjectivity and reliability. To overcome the risk we followed a systematic procedure to create our ground truth. We prepared an annotation guideline with definitions and examples. We conducted several trial runs followed by resolutions of any conflicts. Finally, we evaluated the quality of the annotation using inter-rater agreement metrics.

**External Validity.** To mitigate the threat, we selected reviews for popular apps belonging to different categories and various app stores. These reviews are written using varied vocabulary. We, however, admit that the eight apps in our study represent a tiny proportion of all the apps in the app market. Although our dataset is comparable in size to datasets in previous studies [10,12,13], we are also exposed to sampling bias.

**Table 7.** The summarized differences between our study and related works.

| Criterion | | Our study | SAFE [13] | GuMa [12] | ReUS [10] |
|---|---|---|---|---|---|
| Evaluation | No. Approaches | **3** | 2 | 1 | 1 |
| | Feature extraction | **Yes** | **Yes** | No | **Yes** |
| | Sentiment analysis | **Yes** | – | **Yes** | **Yes** |
| | Method | **Automatic** | Manual | Manual | **Automatic** |
| Ground Truth | Released | **Yes** | No | No | No |
| | No. Apps | **8** | 5 | 7 | – |
| | No. Reviews | 1000 | 80 | **2800** | 1000 |
| | No. App Stores | **2** | 1 | **2** | - |
| | Dataset analysis | **Yes** | No | No | **Yes** |

**Construct Validity.** To mitigate the threat, we used precision and recall metrics that are extensively used for evaluating the effectiveness of information extraction and classification techniques.

# 8    Related Works

Previous work have proposed benchmarks for app review analytics (e.g. [15,21]) but with objective different than ours.

Table 7 shows the differences between our study and previous works, pointing out the different criteria that guided the evaluations, which are grouped into Evaluation and Ground Truth categories. The first includes criteria such as the number of evaluated approaches, evaluated tasks and a method type used for their evaluation. The latter includes characteristics of datasets.

In our study, we evaluated three approaches: SAFE, GuMa and ReUS. We assessed them in addressing problems of feature extraction and sentiment analysis. Johann et al. [13] also compared SAFE to GuMa [12]. Our study extends their evaluation by including ReUS [10]. Unlike the original study [12], we evaluated GuMa in performing a feature extraction rather than modeling feature topics. We also compared the approach to ReUS in inferring a feature-specific sentiment.

We used a different methodology for evaluating SAFE and GuMa [12,13]; The correctness of their solutions has been evaluated manually [12,13]. The judgement criteria, however, has not been defined. Such a procedure suffered from several threats to validity such as human error, authors' bias and the lack of repeatability [22]. To address the limitations, we adopted automatic matching methods and defined explicit matching criteria.

The ground truth in our study differs from that used in previous works. Unlike Dragoni et al. [10], we evaluated ReUS using app reviews. The authors used a dataset composed of comments for restaurant and laptops. As Johann [13] and Guzman [12], we created an annotated dataset for the evaluation. We, however, used a systematic procedure and assessed the quality of ground truth using acknowledged measures [16,20]. Previous studies did not report a systematic annotation procedure [13] nor measured the quality of their annotation [12]. Their datasets were not analyzed nor made public [12,13].

## 9    Conclusion

Mining user opinions from app reviews can be useful to guide requirement engineering activities such as user validation [1,2,19], requirements elicitation [1,2], or requirement prioritization [1]. However, the performance of app review mining techniques and their ability to support these tasks in practice are still unknown.

We have presented an empirical study aimed at evaluating existing opinion mining techniques for app reviews. We have evaluated three approaches: SAFE [13] relying on part-of-speech parsing, GuMa [12] adopting a collocation-based algorithm, and ReUS [10] exploiting a syntactic dependency-based parser. We have created a new dataset of 1,000 reviews from which 1,521 opinions are specific features were manually annotated. We then used this dataset to evaluate the feature identification capabilities of all three approaches and the sentiment analysis capabilities of GuMa and ReUS.

Our study indicates that feature extraction techniques are not yet effective enough to be used in practice [9,21] and that have lower precision and recall than reported in their initial studies. Our study also indicates that feature-specific sentiment analysis techniques have limited precision and recall, particularly for negative sentiments. We hope our novel annotated dataset [7] and evaluation method will contribute to improving the quality of app review mining techniques.

## References

1. AlSubaihin, A., Sarro, F., Black, S., Capra, L., Harman, M.: App store effects on software engineering practices. IEEE Trans. Softw. Eng. 1 (2019)

2. Begel, A., Zimmermann, T.: Analyze this! 145 questions for data scientists in software engineering. In: 36th International Conference on Software Engineering, pp. 12–13 (2014)

3. Berry, D.M., Cleland-Huang, J., Ferrari, A., Maalej, W., Mylopoulos, J., Zowghi, D.: Panel: context-dependent evaluation of tools for NL RE tasks: recall vs. precision, and beyond. In: 2017 IEEE 25th International Requirements Engineering Conference (RE), pp. 570–573, September 2017

4. Buse, R.P.L., Zimmermann, T.: Information needs for software development analytics. In 34th International Conference on Software Engineering, pp. 987–996 (2012)

5. Croft, B., Metzler, D., Strohman, T.: Search Engines: Information Retrieval in Practice, 1st edn. Addison-Wesley Publishing Company, Boston (2009)

6. Cunningham, H., Maynard, D., Tablan, V., Ursu, C., Bontcheva, K.: Developing language processing components with GATE version 8. University of Sheffield Department of Computer Science, November 2014

7. Dabrowski, J.: Manually annotated dataset and an annotation guideline for CAiSE 2020 paper, November 2019. https://github.com/jsdabrowski/CAiSE-20/

8. Dąbrowski, J., Letier, E., Perini, A., Susi, A.: Finding and analyzing app reviews related to specific features: a research preview. In: Knauss, E., Goedicke, M. (eds.) REFSQ 2019. LNCS, vol. 11412, pp. 183–189. Springer, Cham (2019). https://doi.org/10.1007/978-3-030-15538-4_14

9. Dalpiaz, F., Parente, M.: RE-SWOT: from user feedback to requirements via competitor analysis. In: Knauss, E., Goedicke, M. (eds.) REFSQ 2019. LNCS, vol. 11412, pp. 55–70. Springer, Cham (2019). https://doi.org/10.1007/978-3-030-15538-4_4

10. Dragoni, M., Federici, M., Rexha, A.: An unsupervised aspect extraction strategy for monitoring real-time reviews stream. Inf. Process. Manage. **56**(3), 1103–1118 (2019)

11. Gu, X., Kim, S.: "What parts of your apps are loved by users?" (T). In: 30th International Conference on Automated Software Engineering, pp. 760–770 (2015)

12. Guzman, E., Maalej, W.: How do users like this feature? a fine grained sentiment analysis of app reviews. In: Gorschek, T., Lutz, R.R., (eds.) RE, pp. 153–162. IEEE Computer Society (2014)

13. Johann, T., Stanik, C., Maalej, W.: Safe: a simple approach for feature extraction from app descriptions and app reviews. In: 2017 IEEE 25th International Requirements Engineering Conference, pp. 21–30 (2017)

14. Johanssen, J.O., Kleebaum, A., Bruegge, B., Paech, B.: How do practitioners capture and utilize user feedback during continuous software engineering? In: 2019 IEEE 27th International Requirements Engineering Conference (2019)

15. Lin, B., Zampetti, F., Bavota, G., Di Penta, M., Lanza, M., Oliveto, R.: Sentiment analysis for software engineering: how far can we go? In: 40th International Conference on Software Engineering, pp. 94–104 (2018)

16. Liu, B.: Sentiment Analysis and Opinion Mining. Synthesis Lectures on Human Language Technologies. Morgan & Claypool Publishers, San Rafael (2012)

17. Martin, W., Sarro, F., Jia, Y., Zhang, Y., Harman, M.: A survey of app store analysis for software engineering. IEEE Trans. Software Eng. **43**(9), 817–847 (2017)

18. McAuley, J., Targett, C., Shi, Q., van den Hengel, A.: Image-based recommendations on styles and substitutes. In: 38th International Conference on Research and Development in Information Retrieval, pp. 43–52. ACM (2015)

19. Pagano, D., Maalej, W.: User feedback in the appstore: an empirical study. In: RE, pp. 125–134. IEEE Computer Society (2013)

20. Pustejovsky, J., Stubbs, A.: Natural Language Annotation for Machine Learning - A Guide to Corpus-Building for Applications. O'Reilly, Sebastopol (2012)
21. Shah, F.A., Sirts, K., Pfahl, D.: Is the SAFE approach too simple for app feature extraction? a replication study. In: Knauss, E., Goedicke, M. (eds.) REFSQ 2019. LNCS, vol. 11412, pp. 21–36. Springer, Cham (2019). https://doi.org/10.1007/978-3-030-15538-4_2
22. Shah, F.A., Sirts, K., Pfahl, D.: Simulating the impact of annotation guidelines and annotated data on extracting app features from app reviews. In: International Conference on Software Technologies, ICSOFT (2019)
23. Thelwall, M., Buckley, K., Paltoglou, G., Cai, D., Kappas, A.: Sentiment strength detection in short informal text. J. Am. Soc. Inform. Sci. Technol. **61**(12), 2544–2558 (2010)
24. Vu, P.M., Nguyen, T.T., Pham, H.V., Nguyen, T.T.: Mining user opinions in mobile app reviews: a keyword-based approach (T). In: Proceedings of the 2015 30th IEEE/ACM International Conference on Automated Software Engineering (ASE) ASE 2015, pp. 749–759 (2015)

# Patterns for Certification Standards

Kevin Delmas⑩, Claire Pagetti⁽✉⁾⑩, and Thomas Polacsek

ONERA, Palaiseau, France
`claire.pagetti@onera.fr`

**Abstract.** One of the absolute preconditions for a safety-critical system to enter the market is to be issued a *certificate* by the regulating authorities. To this end, the "applicant" must demonstrate the compliance of its product with the domain's standards. The high complexity of this process has led applicants to rely on *assurance cases* made for certification in the medical, nuclear, or aeronautic domains. In this paper, we propose a generic method that guides the applicant through the specification of assurance cases for a complex standard. Unlike existing works focused on a single context, our objective is to provide an approach that is both generic and domain-agnostic. In order to illustrate this new approach, we present the results of its application on a real-world case study, which pointed out new issues and led to improvements.

## 1  Introduction

**Context.** Safety-critical systems, i.e. systems with the potential to endanger a person's life, are often subject to a *certification process*. In practice, any *applicant* requesting the certification of a system is in charge of convincing a *certification authority* that their product is compliant with the regulatory requirements. When the authorities are positively convinced, they deliver a certificate that authorizes its operation. Examples of such authorities include: the European Medicines Agency (EMA) and the Food and Drug Administration (FDA), for drug evaluation; or the European Aviation Safety Agency (EASA) and the Federal Aviation Administration (FAA), for civil aviation safety.

To support applicants in this task, expert committees, composed of companies, certification authorities and academics, have defined standards, guidelines or recommendations (that will be simply referred as standards in the sequel)[1]. These standards are complex documents, which provide high-level certification objectives to be fulfilled and often require experts to understand precisely what is expected by the certification. Moreover, there are two main types of standards: those which only define objectives without imposing any method in order to give some leeway to applicants in their development and validation; and conversely those which impose some high-level process not easy to implement.

**Assurance Cases for Certification.** Practically, an applicant must provide all the elements concerning the design of the system and the Verification and

---

[1] Examples of standards are DO178, ARP4754 for aeronautics, ISO 26262 for automotive and EC 62366, EC 62304 for medical devices.

© Springer Nature Switzerland AG 2020
S. Dustdar et al. (Eds.): CAiSE 2020, LNCS 12127, pp. 417–432, 2020.
https://doi.org/10.1007/978-3-030-49435-3_26

Validation (V&V) operations that have been carried out. In addition, they must also *argue* why these are sufficient to address all of the certification authority's concerns. In this context, for applicants (and system designers), the problem is to argue well and, for the certification authority, the problem is to evaluate an argument. As [4] points out for reliable systems, the system must provide a service that can legitimately be trusted, with trust being established through plausible links between the evidence provided and the fact that the system provides the expected service.

In order to cope with the complex activities associated with certification, industries are increasingly relying on *assurance cases*. An assurance case can be defined as *"an organized argument that a system is acceptable for its intended use with respect to specified concerns"* [33]. In practice, to build an assurance case, the applicant is free to organize their argumentation and to use any kind of format. However, especially in the safety world, practitioners rely on dedicated formalisms such as the *Goal Structuring Notation* (GSN) [18,26]. In addition, several works [7,27,39] suggest a pattern approach to design assurance case. In engineering, the design pattern approach is a way of describing a recurring problem and its associated solution based on best practices [2,10]. In a certification context, these assurance case patterns consist of a generic assurance case that lists, for a given claim, the associated evidences and the justification of why the claim could be concluded. Those patterns are then instantiated for a particular product and usage domain.

**Towards a Generic Method to Build Assurance Cases.** Even though the literature provides assurance case notations and consensus on the necessity of patterns approach, there is almost no work, apart from [13,42], on how to make a pattern. In fact, designing assurance case patterns and instances is really challenging and requires numerous skills. So the aim of this paper is to propose a method for designing certification assurance case patterns.

Through various projects, we have already had the opportunity to design patterns in the medical field, embedded aeronautical systems and assembly line [5,7,32]. In all these projects, the design process was not clearly defined so the construction of the patterns was quite tedious and time-consuming. This is the reason why we tried to define a method that is as generic as possible. This method was designed using a trial and error approach. Of course, we did not design our process from scratch, but we gradually enriched the process and defined the practices (roles and wording) step by step.

After presenting the general context and notations in Sect. 2, we define, in Sect. 3, a method to design patterns for certification standards. In Sect. 4, we detail the lessons learned when applying the method on a specific standard. Section 5 is dedicated to related work and we conclude in Sect. 6.

## 2  Background and Motivation

### 2.1  Certification

An applicant must provide a *compliance demonstration* that its product is compliant with the standards where a compliance demonstration is a set of assurance cases, each applying to a high-level objective. High-level objectives are usually defined as a sort of a reachable goal (sometimes process-oriented activities) and there is no indication on how to achieve the goal. Since nothing is imposed on the manner to develop or validate a product, applicants can rely on numerous solutions to fulfill an objective. For example, for the certification of a kettle, an objective may indicate that it is necessary to identify all scenarios where a user may be injured and show how those situations are mitigated. The ways to proceed (both for hazard identification and mitigation means validation) are not fixed by the standard. For instance, if, to reduce the risk of burns, the designer has put on a handle that remains always cold, it is up to them to demonstrate that this indeed mitigates the risk.

Any standard comes with an intrinsic complexity: high-level objectives are not always easy to understand and are very generic, rationales are not always provided, etc. Moreover, a compliance demonstration encompasses all the concerns of the certification authority, such as safety, security [3] or dependability [41]. This means that certification activities involve several people that need to have transverse and large spectrum knowledge of the product, the process and/or the V&V activities. Such a complexity can be a real obstacle, especially for small companies, to enter in safety critical markets. Thus, offering more tractable approaches is mandatory and our work is a way.

## 2.2  Assurance Cases

In order to help applicant organize their documentation, several works propose to structure argumentation demonstration with assurance cases and some adequate notations. We can cite for instance, on the academic side, GSN [18,26], *Claim-Argument-Evidence* [8], *Justification Diagram* [32] and, on the standardization organism side, *Structured Assurance Case Meta-model* [30].

All of these notations organize in diagrammatic form the various elements, formal and informal, that contribute to the justification of a result. These frameworks are all based on the model of the British philosopher Stephen Toulmin [36]. His purpose was to define a structure to help assess the validity of a judgement issued on the basis of justifications. In Toulmin's model, any argumentation is composed of a conclusion, namely the *claim*, and facts on which the claim is based. Basically, Toulmin has a legalistic view: to argue well amounts to stating a claim based on facts. In addition to these facts, Toulmin adds information about the reasoning process. This information clarifies why the inference is acceptable, why a set of justifications lead to a conclusion. Typically, in the legal field, this information corresponds to a reference to an article of law. Toulmin writes that this distinction "*is similar to the distinction drawn in the law courts between questions of fact and questions of law*". Toulmin called this additional information a *warrant*. Warrants are therefore what allow the passage from facts to claim, they justify the inference. Distinguishing between facts and warrants is not always easy. Warrants relate to the strength of the argumentation, they are general, whereas reasons depend more on data related to the context. To these three concepts, Toulmin adds other notions for the qualification of the conclusion and the backing of the warrants.

All assurance case notations focus on the three concepts: claim, warrant and fact, although terminology is sometimes changed, for example *strategy* is used in place of warrant in GSN [18]. We have chosen an agnostic notation approach based on a textual syntax (kind of abstract syntax) compliant with all existing notations (kind of concrete syntax). We rename fact as *evidence* because our argumentation does not really refer to established facts but to documents, for instance calculation results, test reports or expert judgements. The notation is hierarchical since an evidence of one pattern may also be the claim of another one. A final evidence refers to a terminal element that does not become a claim for another pattern. Such a final evidence could be a document or an analysis.

```
Claim: All hazards identified
Warrant: Analysis acceptable by the
authority
Evidence:
  (E1) Means for correctness
  (E2) Means for completeness
```

**Fig. 1.** Pattern example for the kettle

```
Claim: All hazards identified
Warrant: Functional Hazard Analysis
Evidence:
  (E1) Correctness: external safety
experts reviews
  (E2) Completeness: former accidents
database
```

**Fig. 2.** Instance example for the kettle

Figure 2 is a possible assurance case, for the kettle example, that answers part of the objective on identifying the hazards. To establish the claim, the justification relies on a Functional Hazard Analysis, a classical safety technique to extract hazards. Such an analysis, to be trustworthy, requires reaching a certain correctness level, based here on a double review by a second experts' team (E1), and also on a certain level of completeness, based here on checking the list with known accidents (E2).

For Toulmin, the notion of warrant is the cornerstone of reasoning. Indeed, it gives the rational and explains why a conclusion can be assessed. Even if some practitioners tend not to use the notion of warrant, it is difficult to evaluate an argument where the warrant is not explicit, in particular for an auditor. For us, even a simple aggregation with an "*and*", like a decomposition strategy for warrant, needs to be explicit. Indeed, a simple conjunction, such as "*and*" between evidence, can hide more complex mechanisms (e.g. check that the evidences are not contradictory or check whether they are sufficient).

### 2.3   Patterns Notation

[21] promoted the use of a collection of assurance case patterns, with the aim of rationalizing and reusing elements from previous assurance cases. The authors of [19] provide a format, including meta-data, that allows to capture and reuse patterns. In the case of medical devices, the authors [40] explain all the advantages

of using patterns in standards; and their arguments are valid in any application domain.

Figure 1 shows an assurance case pattern (also referred as justification pattern) for the identification of all kettle hazards. A possible instantiation of the pattern is given Fig. 2. The pattern is generic and could be reused for other products that need a risk analysis.

## 2.4   Justification Pattern Elicitation Problems

Building an assurance case, pattern or instance, is not an easy task. Each pattern can be seen as a guide that lists the necessary elements to meet an objective. The design of a pattern must involve experts who will define the patterns according to their technical domain knowledge and of the established good practices, standards, quality requirements, etc. The main pitfall is the introduction of mistakes during the design of the patterns, which are meant to guarantee the validity of the reasoning.

The problem when it comes to making justification patterns is to think in terms of inference, that is, determine whether or not it is acceptable to pass from a set of justifications to a given claim and to elicitate why this inference is correct. Experts tend to cling to their technical knowledge and how different activities are organized; whereas claims often target quality and safety reached levels. *Critical Thinking* [16] and the usage of *guide words* (as done in some methodologies like HAZOP[2] [20]) may support the experts in their task.

There are many cognitive biases that influence human reasoning. Among them, there is a tendency to consider one's own subjective interpretation as the truth about reality. Research in psychology has shown that one of the implications of this cognitive bias is our inability to judge our understanding and ignorance of what we know. In other words, we think we understand and have valid explanations for phenomena that we do not really understand. On sensitive subjects, the situation is such that we can greatly overestimate the quality of our justifications and reasoning [9]. However, it is possible to compensate for this bias through dialogue. As many studies have confirmed, group reasoning in a collaborative way is more effective than individual reasoning, especially for reasoning and logic problems[3] [23,37].

Regarding legitimacy, the experts must be considered as experts in their field by the people who will use the patterns. This legitimacy can only be acquired through credentials and recognition of competence by peers. In practice, the legitimacy comes from expert's resume, from the projects he has already collaborated on. Thus, an expert is most often someone who has already participated in system certification and/or made recognized contributions (usually in industrial

---

[2] HAZOP for *HAZard and OPerability analysis* is an industrial risk analysis method.
[3] Moshman and Geil showed on a reasoning problem, with a cohort of 20 groups and 32 individuals, that 75% of the groups found the right answer for only 9.4% of individuals [29]. It should also be noted that groups build more sophisticated, qualitatively, arguments than an individual.

conferences). The question of legitimacy arises with regard to the certification authority. It is the authority who will ultimately decide whether a person is an expert or not.

Finally, from our experience, patterns are very well received and accepted in a group (e.g. company) if they were collaboratively designed by experts working on the side of the applicant and experts belonging to the certification authority.

## 3   A Method to Design Certification Pattern

Our objective is to define a method to help applicant build a repository of justification patterns dedicated to their specific standard(s). To each objective is associated a pattern. Since correctness and completeness of a pattern can be altered by process flaws and psychological biases, the method concentrates on detecting and correcting these flaws as much as possible.

### 3.1   Process

Our method is based on a long process to construct justification patterns via several expert meetings. The process, given in Fig. 3, is composed of four iterative steps described below. Note that for a given claim, several patterns may exist since a same claim may be justified in several ways.

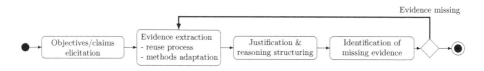

**Fig. 3.** A first pattern design process

**Objectives/Claim Elicitation.** Identify the certification objectives the product or process must comply to. Each objective is considered to be a top-level claim. As the process is iterative, some justifications (evidences) defined during an iteration may become a claim.

**Evidence Extraction.** There are mainly two cases for eliciting evidence: either the applicant has some experience on the claim and can rely on existing practices that have already been applied and convinced the authority. In which case, they can transform the process as a pattern and this corresponds typically to the classic design pattern approach where the pattern captures good practices and well-known solutions. Or the standard applies to a new technology or a new method, in which case experts have to find a fully new solution which can rely on methods coming from any other relevant domain. The result of this activity is an unorganized set of evidences (new claims or final evidences).

**Justification and Reasoning Structuring.** The activity consists in taking all identified evidences and articulating the inference, or different inferences, that lead(s) to the claim. This step defines the structure of the pattern and the associated warrants.

**Identification of Lack of Evidence or End of the Process.** When structuring the pattern, the experts may observe that some elements are missing in their reasoning, meaning that evidences are missing. The most common problem is to *forget some final evidences or intermediate claims* to sustain the objective. Thus, between two meetings, the experts must individually think on the patterns they have designed together, looking for mistakes, problems and missing elements possibly introduced during justification structuring. Alternating group and individual works is very important[4]. Indeed, collaborative reasoning facilitates individual cognitive progress, but it is also important for experts to take stock: team influences more individuals than individual influences team [22]. Any doubt should be discussed and traced at the next meeting, not to ask the same question several times. A lack of evidence can be a clue of some missing process, method or practices that, at first glance, seems not to sustain the objective but after deeper inspection provides some lack of evidences.

## 3.2   Organization

Designing patterns is both an individual and a collective task. To this end, meetings are organized. The purpose of these meetings is to engage in the construction of a common reference framework and to compare points of view. From there, a *justification pattern design team* (denoted *design team* in the remainder of the paper) will be able to collectively elicit justification patterns. The team should be small, three to five persons. Small teams encourage *dialogical* interaction (conversation between two people). To tackle the problem of deducting reasoning, psychological studies have shown that dialogical and small groups are very effective [22,23,37]. During the constitution of the design team, one must take into account the psychological biases of system experts. Especially for experts involved in the design of a system whose compliance to the certification objectives depends on the designed patterns. These experts are susceptible to confirmation bias (as identified in [24]) and thus may try to build assurance cases enforcing the compliance of their own system (a typical case of such a bias is illustrated in the accident report [12]).

During meetings, the experts must have all the necessary information: the standard, all the technical documentation, the past experiences. To create the patterns, the team must be able to share a common medium and *"draw"* patterns together (e.g. white board with markers). In order for the experts to work

---

[4] In a sense, we are quite close to the Delphi method [28] here since, between two meetings, the experts think alone, in isolation, about what has been collectively produced, the synthesis, and give their feedback at the next meeting. However, unlike the Delphi method, in our method much of the work is done during group meetings.

individually between meetings, it is also important to have minutes of meeting that include the patterns and detailed explanations of the elements of the patterns.

We recommend to have a design team composed of one *facilitator* managing the meetings and recording the patterns and *experts* designing the pattern.

**Facilitator Role.** The facilitator should help determine whether or not it is acceptable to pass from a set of justifications to a given claim. The study of such reasoning has expanded in North America since the 1970s, particularly since the publication of *Logical Self-defense* [16]. In this book, the authors attempt to define a systematic approach to studying informal argumentation. Thus, in recent years, all research that relates to non-formal reasoning has been called *Informal Logic, Critical Thinking* and *Argumentation.* To support the experts in their task of eliciting and explaining the inference, the facilitator must be very familiar with Critical Thinking. There is no need for the facilitator to be an expert in the areas covered by the standard, but they will still need to know the vocabulary and the context in order to communicate easily with the experts. Indeed, a minimum of technical knowledge is required for the experts to express their ideas without always having to explain technical issues. The facilitator is thus paramount in identifying a misuse of the pattern formalism that can lead to the following threats to pattern validity: introduction of *unnecessary evidence*, the *lack of evidence* and *fallacious inference*. If several members of the team are familiar with the Critical Thinking, we recommend alternating the role between meetings.

**Expert Role.** An expert must be a specialist in the field covered by the standard and, more precisely, a specialist in the V&V methods used to define the pattern. Indeed, the justifications and warrant of a pattern are generally related to V&V operations and results. To ensure the acceptance of the patterns, the expert must have credentials recognized by their peers and by the certification authority. Involving recognized experts prevents the design of incorrect patterns due to a *poor knowledge* of the application domain in which the pattern is intended to be used. An expert could be a well-known practitioner, a researcher or a member of the certification authority. Note that, it is better to have both practitioners and members of the authority in the team. Indeed the heterogeneity of the experts can address two threats by helping to identify *missing patterns* and avoiding a *non-holistic view*. A non-holistic view is when the pattern does not treat the whole problem but only adopts the point of view of the applicant or of the certification authority.

### 3.3   Wording

The way the design team brainstorms has a major impact on the avoidance of common mistakes. Hence, we define *guide words* and *avoid words* to promote an argumentation thinking mindset rather than a temporal thinking one and to ensure that warrants are not forgotten.

**Temporal Thinking.** One of the major difficulties when developing a pattern is to elicit an inference and not a process. Again, experts know how the system has been designed and they are tempted to graft the development process to the justification pattern. Writing a sequence of actions can lead to simply paraphrasing a process and thus concealing the underlying rationale justifying the claim. The claim is no longer the result of an argument, but of a series of activities and this does not sustain the claim. This threat of *temporal thinking* can be mitigated if the meeting participants avoid using all vocabulary relating to time. In other words, experts should try not to use the words: follow, after, before, then, etc. Instead, the facilitator should question the experts and direct them towards reformulation using the wording: *"the conclusion of"*, *"needs"*, *"is based on"*, etc.

**Warrantless Approach.** Experts may be familiar with formal logic and tend to build a proof tree instead of a pattern representing informal argumentation. This formal thinking usually leads to *logical* warrants, a symptomatic case is logical decomposition (the claim is the conjunction of the evidence). Of course, if one is able to express the argumentation in a formal way then this formal proof should be a final evidence and does not need to be represented as an argumentation pattern. Nevertheless, the facilitator must seek carefully this kind of warrants since it may conceal the actual warrant that allows the passage from evidence to claim. In the context of argumentation, the experts should avoid warrants containing only logical connectors: *"and"*, *"or"*, *"entails"*, etc.

## 4  Case Study

We have applied our method on the CAST-32A [6], that serves as a guideline to certify multi-core processor-based systems in avionics. All embedded platforms until now relied on mono-processor hardware or very specific dual-core. In the coming years, only multi-core processor hardware will be available on the market and the airframers will have no choice but to embed these new architectures. Since the CAST-32A is a new guideline, there is currently no process to refer to and applicants must create their argumentation from scratch. This is a perfect opportunity to apply our method.

### 4.1  Application of the Method

The *Design team* was composed of: 1. a senior expert on multi-core processor architectures, predictable programming and the mainstream aeronautics validation and verification process; 2. a junior safety expert of the safety assessment of technical systems; 3. a facilitator with a solid experience in justification pattern design and familiar with the overall V&V process used in aeronautics.

During the project, the justification pattern design team had a meeting once every two weeks, and each member individually took some time to ponder on the work that was done.

By the end, the design team defined 15 patterns[5] that address 5 high-level objectives of the guideline (some objectives, such as those that are purely organizational, have not been addressed in the context of this project).

## 4.2   Justification Pattern for RU3

Let us describe one of the objectives, namely RU3 (for *resource usage 3*) and part of the associated patterns. This objective concerns interference situations, which are feared situations where software can encounter strong slowdowns.

**Objective RU3.** *The applicant has identified the interference channels that could permit interference to affect the software applications hosted on the multicore processor cores, and has verified the applicant's chosen means of mitigation of the interference.*

Claim: RU3
Warrant: (W1) Check completeness of interference and mitigation
Evidence:
  (E1) Identification and classification of interferences
  (E2) Verified mitigation means

**Fig. 4.** Pattern for RU3

Claim: E1
Warrant: (W2) Platform stressing strategy
Backing: Architecture mastering
Evidence:
  (E3) Interference identification
  (E4) Effect classification
Given: Configuration, temporal constraints

**Fig. 5.** Pattern for E1

Fig. 4 shows its transcription as a pattern. Evidence (E1) states that the existing interferences have been identified and classified. Focusing on (E1), Fig. 5, it has been achieved because there was a stressing benchmark analysis that has collected the effects of each interference (strategy (W2)). Those effects can be expressed in different units (e.g. delay, bandwidth). Evidence (E3) points to a report that summarizes which interferences have been identified, how they have been identified, and why the identification is sound and complete. Evidence (E4) points to a safety report that details the acceptable effects on the hosted applications. From this information, the applicant has defined adequate means of mitigation to prevent, for instance, unacceptable effects. Evidence (E2) collects all those means of mitigation, how they mitigate each unacceptable interference and how they were verified. The applicant can argue the compliance with RU3 because an expert, who masters the architecture, has reviewed and double-checked that each interference has been correctly mitigated (W1).

---

[5] Available at https://w3.onera.fr/phylog/patterns.

## 4.3   Lessons Learned

**The Facilitator Supports the Elicitation of Patterns.** Both experts clearly reported that the facilitator helped them understand the argumentation approach. When designing the first patterns, experts tended to not know how to express the warrant, to skip it, and to describe a process rather than an argument. Interestingly, the further the project progressed, the more the experts understood how to operate. However, although the experts became familiar with the approach, a facilitator was always needed. By being outside of the context, facilitators rephrase the discussions and question the foundations of what may seem obvious to experts (by using, for example, the Douglas Walton's critical questions [11]). In the future, it would be preferable to define more precisely the skills of the facilitator as well as the way in which meetings should be conducted. To do this, we can take inspiration from, for example, [28].

**Wording Importance.** The wording was really necessary to prevent the experts falling in false reasoning. It helped counter the tendency to express what needs to be done rather than what leads to a justification.

**Process/Patterns Evaluation.** To evaluate the process, we must turn to an evaluation of the produced patterns. At the end, the design team presented the justification patterns in a workshop, the participants of which were: two contributors to the CAST-32A, five well-known experts from the aeronautics industry and three certification authority members.

The overall feedback was very positive. For industrial experts, the patterns are very useful and help clarify some implicit / ambiguous textual rationales. Moreover, because they give concrete evidence, they simplify discussion between stakeholders. Industrial experts also gave some suggestions to prepare certification audits with the patterns. For CAST-32A contributors, the patterns were compliant with the writers' perspective. They confirmed that patterns highlight some elements that were only in the writers' minds. In fact, the design team has extracted the implicit structure of the sentences, the main elements expected to be supplied and made explicit the reasoning of the writers. For certification authority members, patterns provide a framework for legible and clear presentation of justifications and their rationale.

Of course, the patterns were not free of defects (some evidences were missing and some warrants were not explicit enough). In addition, it appeared that an additional pattern would be useful for easing the discussion and moving around the other patterns. The conclusion we can draw from this evaluation is that there is one step missing from our process. We could add an expert committee assessment to our process. In this new process, the assessment committee would become the validation team. At the end, this team would be involved in a validation activity and would address the following challenges:

– *fallacious reasoning:* find conditions where the warrants do not sustain the claim. Those conditions can either be considered as rebuttal and must be integrated into the patterns, or disclose a flaw to be corrected;

- *lack of evidence:* find conditions where the evidences are not sufficient to sustain the claim. In that situation, the design team should identify them out of the processes, methods and practices;
- *missing patterns:* find another way to establish the claim. This may look challenging since this requires designing a new pattern but it can be addressed by trying some slight modifications of the existing patterns and assessing the validity of this new version.

## 5   Related Work

If there are many notations to structure an assurance case, there are fewer works addressing the justification patterns elicitation. In [42], the authors focus on security requirements and propose a tool to manage these requirements. In addition, they are interested in capturing the rationality of these requirements by using Toulmin's scheme. While they give some key elements to produce such models, they do not go into the details (role, wording, etc.) of the elicitation method. In another field, [13] are interested in safety arguments and provide a guide on how to build a GSN diagram properly, but no elicitation method is proposed. In the avionic context, the authors of [43,44] propose a UML profile, namely SafeUML, dedicated to safety requirements for an aeronautics guideline. This profile defines a set of stereotypes to model specific concepts associated to safety. The purpose of their approach is to facilitate communication between safety experts, software developers and certification authorities. Regarding the links with our approach, the different certification objectives are seen as requirements in SafeUML. Tractability between requirements and design choices is achieved by a stereotype *"rationale"* which has a text field to give an explanation. So, the use of our patterns could easily be added to SafeUML. Indeed, their application, linked to the rationale, would model more precisely this explanation of why a design meets a certification objective.

This idea of having a modeling framework to organize the certification elements is not new. It was particularly highlighted by [1,25]. Among the works on compliance to a regulation, we can mention, for example, the SafetyMet metamodel safety oriented [38] or the UML stereotype developed by [31]. In the second case, with the UML stereotype-based approach, the authors give a generic approach to model a safety certification standard and make the link between the concepts of the system designer and those of the standard. Their method consists in supporting modeling a safety standard in their UML profile, then to make the link, according to precise rules materialized by OCL constraints, between the domain model and the certification model. This work, as identified by [1], models the *structure* of the standard to provide an organization of the elements provided by the applicant to satisfy the standard. However this work does not clarify the *intent* of the objectives of standard, this task being assigned here to the experts who will model the safety standard.

Still in the field of modeling, [14] propose to add an argumentative dimension to a combine model of i* and Nomòs [35] with the *Acceptability Evaluation* *framework* [17]. The purpose here is to capture expert discussions to determine whether the requirements in systems are compliant with a standard or whether there are irregularities. Unlike us, the authors focus here on an argumentation with contradictory points of view and the certification of a specific system, not to eliciting requirements from the standard.

Seeking to capture variability in regulatory texts, [34] propose a formalism to model conditions and exceptions in a regulation. In addition, their framework also allows them to express alternatives that are compliant with the standard. We could imagine a link between their approach and ours. Indeed, sometimes, for one certification objective, several justification patterns could be applicable. Depending on the chosen pattern, it is necessary to guarantee new sub-objectives which are the evidences of the pattern. Representing these alternatives and all the possible solutions could be a significant help for system designers.

Finally, close to our work, [15] use a Goal-Oriented approach to refine guideline objectives. This method allows clarify law and certification terms, that are subject to interpretation. However, unlike us, they do not attempt to highlight the rationality that allows us to conclude from sub-objectives to the main claim. Clearly explaining this, in particular by means of a warrant, is crucial for the certification authority side that is rarely taken into account as identified by [1].

## 6  Conclusion

This paper introduced a method to guide the design justification patterns by experts. The method has been applied to a new position paper written for multicore processor and allowed design several patterns accepted by end users.

Repeatability and reproducibility are the main limitations of our approach. For the moment, even if the method results from a long standing experience, we have only used it on the CAST-32A. In the future, to consolidate the method, we will ask a new team to define patterns for the same standard and compare the results. As there are many ways to develop an argument, we will have to define the notion of equivalence between two patterns. A second axis of consolidation is to define patterns for another standard with the same team.

Future work will also need to address more deeper the problems of biases (anchoring, availability, bandwagon effect, halo effect, overconfidence, etc.) that may arise and their mitigation. To do this, we will have to rely on methods and works on expert knowledge elicitation.

Eventually, the current method does not characterize the assurance level provided by a given pattern nor an assessment of its cost. Our future works need to provide guidelines to document such impact to support the trade-off analysis of the applicant when several patterns are applicable. The question of how to instantiate a pattern is also an important issue and we will provide guidelines to help applicants on this matter as well as a method to conduct efficient certification audits with justification patterns and instances.

# References

1. Akhigbe, O., Amyot, D., Richards, G.: A systematic literature mapping of goal and non-goal modelling methods for legal and regulatory compliance. Requirements Eng. **24**(4), 459–481 (2018). https://doi.org/10.1007/s00766-018-0294-1
2. Alexander, C., Ishikawa, S., Silverstein, M.: A Pattern Language: Towns, Buildings Construction. Oxford University Press, Oxford (1977)
3. Alexander, R., Hawkins, R., Kelly, T.: Security assurance cases: motivation and the state of the art (2011)
4. Avizienis, A., Laprie, J., Randell, B., Landwehr, C.E.: Basic concepts and taxonomy of dependable and secure computing. IEEE Trans. Dependable Sec. Comput. **1**(1), 11–33 (2004)
5. Bieber, P., et al.: MIMOSA: towards a model driven certification process. In: Proceedings of European Congress Embedded Real Time Software And Systems (2016)
6. Certification Authorities Software Team: Multi-core Processors - Position Paper. Technical report CAST 32-A, Federal Aviation Administration (2016)
7. Duffau, C., Polacsek, T., Blay-Fornarino, M.: Support of justification elicitation: two industrial reports. In: Krogstie, J., Reijers, H.A. (eds.) CAiSE 2018. LNCS, vol. 10816, pp. 71–86. Springer, Cham (2018). https://doi.org/10.1007/978-3-319-91563-0_5
8. Emmet, L., Cleland, G.: Graphical notations, narratives and persuasion: a pliant systems approach to hypertext tool design. In: Proceedings of Hypertext and Hypermedia, HYPERTEXT 2002 (2002)
9. Fisher, M., Keil, F.C.: The illusion of argument justification. J. Exumlperimental Psychol. Gen. **143**(1), 425 (2014)
10. Gamma, E., Helm, R., Johnson, R., Vlissides, J.: Design Patterns: Elements of Reusable Object-oriented Software. Addison-Wesley Longman Publishing, Boston (1995)
11. Godden, D.M., Walton, D.: Argument from expert opinion as legal evidence: critical questions and admissibility criteria of expert testimony in the American legal system. Ratio Juris **19**(3), 261–286 (2006)
12. Haddon-Cave, C.: The Nimrod Review: an independent review into the broader issues surrounding the loss of the RAF Nimrod MR2 aircraft XV230 in Afghanistan in 2006, report, vol. 1025. Derecho International (2009)
13. Hawkins, R., Kelly, T., Knight, J., Graydon, P.: A new approach to creating clear safety arguments. In: Dale, C., Anderson, T. (eds.) Advances in Systems Safety. Springer, London (2011). https://doi.org/10.1007/978-0-85729-133-2_1
14. Ingolfo, S., Siena, A., Mylopoulos, J., Susi, A., Perini, A.: Arguing regulatory compliance of software requirements. Data Knowl. Eng. **87**, 279–296 (2013)
15. Ishikawa, F., Inoue, R., Honiden, S.: Modeling, analyzing and weaving legal interpretations in goal-oriented requirements engineering. In: Proceedings of International Workshop on Requirements Engineering and Law (2009)
16. Johnson, R.H., Blair, J.A.: Logical Self-Defense (Key Titles in Rhetoric, Argumentation, and Debate Series), 1st edn. International Debate Education Association, Brussels (2006)
17. Jureta, I., Mylopoulos, J., Faulkner, S.: Analysis of multi-party agreement in requirements validation. In: Proceedings of International Requirements Engineering Conference - RE 2009 (2009)
18. Kelly, T., Weaver, R.: The goal structuring notation - a safety argument notation. In: DNS 2004 Workshop on Assurance Cases (2004)

19. Kelly, T.P., McDermid, J.A.: Safety case construction and reuse using patterns. In: Daniel, P. (ed.) Safe Comp 97. Springer, London (1997). https://doi.org/10.1007/978-1-4471-0997-6_5

20. Kletz, T.: Hazop & Hazan - Identifying and Assessing Process Industry Hazards. Institution of Chemical Engineers, New York (1999)

21. Knight, J.: Advances in software technology since 1992. In: National Software and Airborne Electronic Hardware Conference, ser. FAA (2008)

22. Laughlin, P.R.: Collective induction: twelve postulates. Organ. Behav. Hum. Decis. Process. **80**(1), 50–69 (1999)

23. Laughlin, P.R., Hatch, E.C., Silver, J.S., Boh, L.: Groups perform better than the best individuals on letters-to-numbers problems: effects of group size. J. Pers. Soc. Psychol. **90**(4), 644 (2006)

24. Leveson, N.G.: The use of safety cases in certification and regulation (2011)

25. Lewis, R.: Safety case development as an information modelling problem. In: Dale, C., Anderson, T. (eds.) Safety-Critical Systems: Problems Process and Practice. Springer, London (2009). https://doi.org/10.1007/978-1-84882-349-5_12

26. McDermid, J.A.: Support for safety cases and safety arguments using SAM. Reliab. Eng. Syst Saf. **43**(2), 111–127 (1994)

27. Méry, D., Schätz, B., Wassyng, A.: The pacemaker challenge: developing certifiable medical devices (dagstuhl seminar 14062). In: Dagstuhl Reports. vol. 4, no. 2 (2014)

28. Meyer, M.A., Booker, J.M.: Eliciting and Analyzing Expert Judgment: A Practical Guide. SIAM, Philadelphia (2001)

29. Moshman, D., Geil, M.: Collaborative reasoning: evidence for collective rationality. Think. Reason. **4**(3), 231–248 (1998)

30. OMG: Structured assurance case meta-model (SACM). Technical report Object Management Group (2013)

31. Panesar-Walawege, R.K., Sabetzadeh, M., Briand, L.: A model-driven engineering approach to support the verification of compliance to safety standards. In: Proceedings of International Symposium on Software Reliability Engineering (2011)

32. Polacsek, T.: Validation, accreditation or certification: a new kind of diagram to provide confidence. In: Proceedings of International Conference on Research Challenges in Information Science, RCIS (2016)

33. Rinehart, D.J., Knight, J.C., Rowanhill, J.: Current practices in constructing and evaluating assurance cases with applications to aviation. Technical report NASA (2015)

34. Siena, A., Jureta, I., Ingolfo, S., Susi, A., Perini, A., Mylopoulos, J.: Capturing variability of law with *Nómos* 2. In: Atzeni, P., Cheung, D., Ram, S. (eds.) ER 2012. LNCS, vol. 7532, pp. 383–396. Springer, Heidelberg (2012). https://doi.org/10.1007/978-3-642-34002-4_30

35. Siena, A., Mylopoulos, J., Perini, A., Susi, A.: Designing law-compliant software requirements. In: Laender, A.H.F., Castano, S., Dayal, U., Casati, F., de Oliveira, J.P.M. (eds.) ER 2009. LNCS, vol. 5829, pp. 472–486. Springer, Heidelberg (2009). https://doi.org/10.1007/978-3-642-04840-1_35

36. Toulmin, S.E.: The Uses of Argument, 1st edn. Cambridge University Press, Cambridge (1958). Updated Edition (2003)

37. Trognon, A., Batt, M., Laux, J.: Why is dialogical solving of a logical problem more effective than individual solving?: a formal and experimental study of an abstract version of Wason's task. Lang. Dialogue **1**(1), 44–78 (2011)

38. de la Vara, J.L., Panesar-Walawege, R.K.: SafetyMet: a metamodel for safety standards. In: Moreira, A., Schätz, B., Gray, J., Vallecillo, A., Clarke, P. (eds.) MODELS 2013. LNCS, vol. 8107, pp. 69–86. Springer, Heidelberg (2013). https://doi.org/10.1007/978-3-642-41533-3_5

39. Wassyng, A., Joannou, P., Lawford, M., Thomas, M., Singh, N.K.: New standards for trustworthy cyber-physical systems. In: Omanovsky, A., Ishikawa, F. (eds.) Trustworthy Cyber-Physical Systems Engineering, pp. 337–368. Addison-Wesley Longman Publishing, New York (2016). Chap 13

40. Wassyng, A., et al.: Can product-specific assurance case templates be used as medical device standards? IEEE Des. Test **32**(5), 45–55 (2015)

41. Weinstock, C.B., Goodenough, J.B., Hudak, J.J.: Dependability cases. Carnegie-Mellon Univ Pittsburgh Pa Software Engineering Inst, Technical report (2004)

42. Yu, Y., Franqueira, V.N., Tun, T.T., Wieringa, R.J., Nuseibeh, B.: Automated analysis of security requirements through risk-based argumentation. J. Syst. Softw. **106**, 102–116 (2015)

43. Zoughbi, G., Briand, L., Labiche, Y.: A UML profile for developing airworthiness-compliant (RTCA DO-178B), safety-critical software. In: Engels, G., Opdyke, B., Schmidt, D.C., Weil, F. (eds.) MODELS 2007. LNCS, vol. 4735, pp. 574–588. Springer, Heidelberg (2007). https://doi.org/10.1007/978-3-540-75209-7_39

44. Zoughbi, G., Briand, L., Labiche, Y.: Modeling safety and airworthiness (RTCA DO-178B) information: conceptual model and UML profile. Softw. Syst. Model. **10**(3), 337–367 (2011). https://doi.org/10.1007/s10270-010-0164-x

# Information Extraction and Graph Representation for the Design of Formulated Products

Sagar Sunkle[1]([✉]), Krati Saxena[1], Ashwini Patil[1], Vinay Kulkarni[1],
Deepak Jain[2], Rinu Chacko[2], and Beena Rai[2]

[1] Software, Systems, and Services Group, TCS Research, Pune, India
{sagar.sunkle,krati.saxena,ab.patil2,vinay.vkulkarni}@tcs.com
[2] Physical Sciences Group, TCS Research, Pune, India
{deepak.jain3,rinu.chacko,beena.rai}@tcs.com

**Abstract.** Formulated products like cosmetics, personal and household care, and pharmaceutical products are ubiquitous in everyday life. The multi-billion-dollar formulated products industry depends primarily on experiential knowledge for the design of new products. Vast knowledge of formulation ingredients and recipes exists in offline and online resources. Experts often use rudimentary searches over this data to find ingredients and construct recipes. This state of the art leads to considerable time to market and cost. We present an approach for formulated product design that enables extraction, storage, and non-trivial search of details required for product variant generation. Our contributions are threefold. First, we show how various information extraction techniques can be used to extract ingredients and recipe actions from textual sources. Second, we describe how to store this highly connected information as a graph database with an extensible domain model. And third, we demonstrate an aid to experts in putting together a new product based on non-trivial search. In an ongoing proof of concept, we use 410 formulations of various cosmetic creams to demonstrate these capabilities with promising results.

**Keywords:** Formulated products · Design · Ingredients · Recipe · Information extraction · Conceptual model · Graph database · Neighbourhood · Creams · Cosmetics

## 1 Introduction

The formulated products industry is an emerging global market of around 1400bn Euro focusing on an array of ubiquitous products used in daily life world over. Despite this scale, the advent of information systems in this sector is still nascent. State of the art in the design of formulated products relies heavily on experiential knowledge of the experts who consult various sources of information perfunctorily [8]. Formulations of organic formulated products contain ingredients that undergo a step-by-step procedure with actions such as heating, cooling, stirring,

© Springer Nature Switzerland AG 2020
S. Dustdar et al. (Eds.): CAiSE 2020, LNCS 12127, pp. 433–448, 2020.
https://doi.org/10.1007/978-3-030-49435-3_27

mixing, and so on to obtain specific target properties, both physical and chemical [5,19]. Suppose a cosmetic company decides to introduce a new face cream. A team of experts on payroll has a general idea that a face cream requires an emulsifier and an emollient. An emulsifier is an ingredient that promotes dispersion of immiscible liquids while forming the cream, and an emollient imparts skin-soothing effect in the end product. The team would proceed by finding similar formulations for a face cream, choose ingredients that are representative of the said functionalities, and put together a recipe using appropriate actions.

This seemingly straightforward process takes months because the information sources are often not well organized and scattered over offline and online media such as handbooks, articles, journals, and websites, respectively. A vast number of ingredients exists representing multiple functionalities, possessing different names depending on different nomenclatures. Similar formulations show the composition of these ingredients, as well as numerous actions performed on them. Still, the synonyms/other names of the ingredients or their functionalities, reside in different sources and must be consulted separately.

There are necessarily two requirements for solving this problem one, the gathering of information from multiple sources, and two, enabling non-trivial searches and analyses of such information for the product design activity. This problem has been recognized in recent years by the EU Formulation Network[1] and the American Chemical Society[2], both of which have come up with roadmaps and offerings featuring more organized information sources.

We propose to cater to the above-stated requirements using specialized information extraction techniques and graph representation, respectively. The research in formulated products, as well as information systems in the chemical sector, often assumes a database of all/majority of the constituents of formulations under consideration as we will discuss in the next section. In comparison, our approach provides the method and tools to create such a database to aid the expert in designing new products.

We demonstrate our approach using 410 cream formulations obtained from the Volumes 1 to 8 of the book cosmetic and toiletry formulations by Flick [6]. The formulated product design activity requires informed access to ingredients and their other names, their weight ranges, their functionalities, knowledge of how to combine them and actions performed on them with specific conditions. Considering this, our specific contributions are as follows:

1. **Extraction.** In Sect. 3, we propose to use state of the art open information extraction (Open IE) as well as dependency parsing techniques augmented with dictionaries and stacking to obtain what we refer to as action-mixture/ingredient-condition (A-M-C) structures from the recipe texts of formulations. We extract product name, ingredients, and their weights using regular expressions. For information such as other names for given ingredients and their functionalities, we extract the information from relevant websites as shown in Fig. 1.

---

[1] EU Formulation Network https://formulation-network.eu/.
[2] Formulus by American Chemical Society https://www.cas.org/products/formulus.

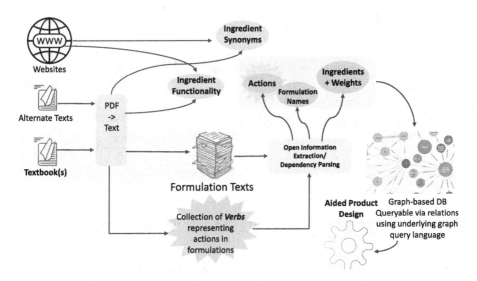

**Fig. 1.** Extraction, storage, and retrieval of formulations

2. **Storage.** We present a conceptual model for storing the details of each cream as a node in a graph database in Sect. 4. The extensibility offered by graph database means that not only creams as a kind of cosmetic product, but details of other formulated products can also be easily accommodated in this database. As illustrated in Fig. 1, our tool takes the formulation text as input and generates insertion queries on top of the base graph. We store ingredient synonyms and ingredient functionalities separately as simple lists.

3. **Retrieval and Design Aid.** SQL-like queries over the graph database and the A-M-C structures, along with queries on synonym and functionality lists, enable finding relatedness of ingredients, functionalities, and products, resulting in what we refer to as neighbourhoods. In Sect. 5, we show how we use these neighbourhoods step by step to aid the expert in composing variants of the intended products.

We begin by presenting the background on formulated products industry and the use of information systems therein in the next section.

## 2    Background and Related Work

**Formulated Products Industry.** We come across many formulated products in our daily lives in the form of cosmetics, personal care, detergents and other household and professional care products, foods, adhesives, fuels and fuel additives, lubricants, paints, inks, dyes, coatings, pesticides, construction materials, and medicines and pharmaceutical products. Individual ingredients used within a formulation may be incorporated to provide active functionality and enhanced

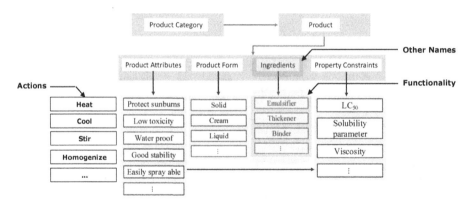

**Fig. 2.** Information and knowledge required for Formulation Design, adapted from [19]

delivery or as a protective or stabilizing agent. The idea of active or primary ingredients and other or secondary ingredients leads to the notions of mandatory and optional functionality in the design of formulated products as we will discuss in Sect. 5.

**Design of Formulated Products.** In the search for a new formulation, an expert must refer to the already existing recipes to make rational judgments when choosing the ingredients, their respective quantities and the procedure to follow to get a stable formulation that has the desired chemical functions. Several approaches have been proposed toward optimal design of formulated products [3–5,7,8,13,18,19]. These approaches suggest using knowledge from experience, models or databases to choose a product form such as cream; then select functionality of ingredients such as a solvent; generate candidates for each chosen ingredient functionality and finally combine the ingredients [19]. In most of these approaches, the assumption is that either a relevant database/ knowledge-base is available or created manually. State of the art, therefore, relies mainly on experts finding similar formulations using standard file search and compilation. Without any knowledge support tools, formulated product development becomes iterative and time-consuming without a list of acceptable ingredients and actions to be applied to them [13].

**Requisite Information and Sources.** Zhang et al. describe the kinds of knowledge and information that is required in formulated product design [19]. As illustrated in Fig. 2, in addition to product attributes, product form, ingredients, and property constraints; functionality of ingredients, actions associated with ingredients and their other names are also required. The product form and the product attributes describing functional requirements, indicate the main reason why a consumer may want to buy a product, e.g., a sunscreen lotion must protect skin from sunburns and skin ageing. On the other hand, the functionality of an ingredient, i.e., whether it is an emulsifier or a thickener, is the crucial factor when designing the product since other ingredients are chosen based on it. An important consideration when synthesizing ingredient-functionality list is

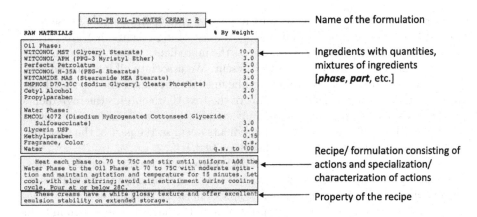

**Fig. 3.** Structure of a formulation from a textual source [6]

that several different names refer to a single ingredient. In such cases, an ingredients dictionary, such as [14] can be used as one source of collating different names of the same ingredient. Once experts finalize a set of ingredients, then it is possible to use techniques like mixed-integer programming to incorporate heuristics and compute possible variants [2,17].

**Extraction of Requisite Details.** Previous attempts at extracting formulation constituents have focused on inorganic materials [10,11,15], which are distinct from organic materials in formulated products like creams, meaning that recipe actions are not reactions between chemicals. To the best of our knowledge, ours is the first attempt at applying information extraction techniques to organic formulated products. In the next section, we elaborate our approach in extracting formulation constituents.

## 3   Extraction of Formulation Constituents

An organic chemical formulation text usually contains the name of the formulation, ingredients, mixtures (if any), weights or proportions of ingredients, and actions to be performed on the ingredients and mixtures, with conditions such as specific temperatures or states as shown in Fig. 3. We refer to these details as constituents of a formulation. We first cover the extraction of ingredient details followed by the processing of recipe text.

### 3.1   Extraction of Ingredients, Mixtures, and Ingredient Weights

To extract ingredients and ingredient weights, it helps to preserve the layout while transforming the PDF files to text format, which we achieve using the Apache PDFBox API. With a preserved layout, the ingredient and its weight occur in a single line of text. Additionally, the formulation may use the ingredients as a part of a mixture. To recognize the mixture indicators separately, we prepare a small list of mixture phrases. The list we use contains indicator phrases like phase a, phase b, phase c, oil phase, water phase, part a, part b, part c, and part d. These indicator phrases appear in a line followed by the list of ingredients that are part of that mixture, as shown in Fig. 3. To process the ingredients as part of the mixture, we first identify if a mixture phrase is present. We associate all ingredients with the current mixture obtained from that line until we encounter the next mixture. To ensure that we only consider the part of the text that contains the ingredients for the processing of ingredients, we apply simple sentence (boundary) detection (SBD)[3]. As illustrated in Fig. 3, the ingredients occur in the part of the text that is NOT a set of sentences (whereas the recipe text is).

To recognize the weight fractions of each ingredient, we use a regular expression. The regular expression is `\d+\s*\.\s*\d+|q.s.|as\s*desired` in Python. The `\s*` flag takes care of multiple white spaces between the integer and the fraction part of an ingredient's weight represented by the flag `\d`. The + sign in front of the flag indicates more than one digits in the integer part of the weight. Words such as q.s. (indicating the amount which is needed) can be added as more of such phrases are encountered.

### 3.2    Extraction of Actions from Recipe Texts

The recipe text describes actions performed a) on the ingredients individually or b) ingredients as a part of a mixture, and c) on the mixtures if the mixtures are present, as shown in Fig. 3.

The critical problems faced in extracting A-M-C structures are that a) the recipes contain instructions which are imperative sentences, and b) objects may be alluded to but could be missing from the sentences [9,15]. Since the sentences are instructions, they begin with an instructional verb and therefore often lack a subject (from the typical subject-verb-object structure of a sentence). Additionally, with the flow of instructions, the previous object acted upon is often implicitly considered without explicitly mentioning it in the next instruction.

Given that we need to associate actions with ingredients, we choose techniques that return set of subject-verb-object* (SVO*) triples from a given sentence. While other similar attempts in inorganic materials synthesis procedure extraction have used dependency parsing, we also use open information extraction or open IE[4]. An open IE implementation returns a triple of subject-verb-object*. Specific implementations may return individual triples, replicating the subject and verb for each object if there are many objects. Open IE models are often trained by bootstrapping on other open IE models which could have been trained on manually extracted triples from sentences.

Our observation is that open IE, as well as dependency parsing[5], fail for imperative or instructional sentences returning an incorrect SVO triple. We solve this problem by prepending "You should" to each instructional sentence. So that

---

[3] Spacy Sentence Boundary Detection https://spacy.io/usage/spacy-101.

[4] AllenNLP Open IE https://demo.allennlp.org/open-information-extraction.

[5] Spacy Dependency Parser https://spacy.io/usage/linguistic-features/#dependency-parse.

sentence like "Heat each phase to 70 to 75C and stir until uniform." from Fig. 3 reads as "You should heat each phase to 70 to 75C and stir until uniform". To solve the second problem, that of missing objects, we introduce a novel mechanism of using a stack as explained later in this section.

Additionally, we make use of a dictionary of verbs that are representative of actions performed on ingredients and/or mixtures. We compile the list using the 410 files and applying SBD and open IE to identify the verbs. Some of the example verbs are maintain, heat, add, stir, moisturize, cool, extract, demineralize, mix, disperse, blend, emulsify, select, distil, chelate, and so on. We use a total of 129 lemmatized verbs. As we will demonstrate in Sect. 6, we found that using a verb list is critical for accurate mapping of actions to ingredients/mixtures.

Figure 4 shows control flows for both open IE and dependency parsing for the extraction of what we refer to as Action Mixture/Ingredient Condition (henceforth A-M-C) structures.

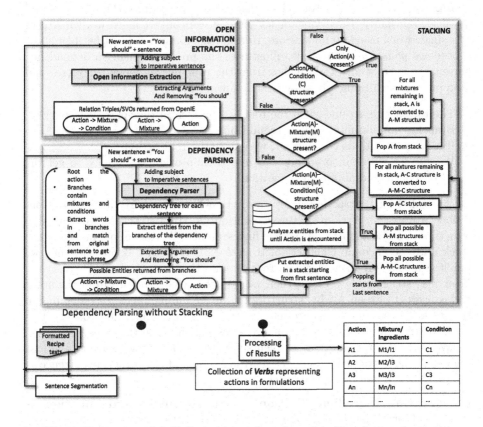

**Fig. 4.** Extraction of A-M-C structures from formulated product recipe text

**Using Open IE with Stacking.** Open IE model returns multiple (and possibly overlapping) triples of up to 4 values each; first value is the subject of the sentence, the second value is the verb of the sentence, the third value is the first object of the sentence, and the fourth value is the second object of the sentence. We illustrate the complete process of applying open IE to extract A-M-C structure in Fig. 4. We process each triple to separate actions and ingredients.

Depending on the SVO triple returned, if action and two arguments are present, then we find all mixtures (from the mixtures dictionary) and ingredients (from earlier processing). If a mixture or an ingredient exists, we push it to a stack, and the action and the two arguments represent the current A-M-C structure. If a mixture or an ingredient does not exist, then the two arguments (values apart from the action verb) contain conditions. In this case, we use all mixtures from the stack and process output as action, mixture or ingredient, and the two arguments as a single entry, which now represents an A-M-C. If a triple only contains one argument, then we use all mixtures from the stack and process output as action, mixture or ingredient, and single argument to represent the A-M-C.

**Using Dependency Parser with Stacking.** To recognize the mixtures and conditions properly using dependency parsing, we convert multi-word mixtures to a single word using an underscore. In this case, a mixture identifier like *phase a* becomes *phase_a*. Figure 4 also illustrates the process of using a dependency parser. We extract all the branches from the root in the dependency tree and then process each branch based on the following rules:

- The root is the action (when the root is a verb from the verbs dictionary).
- Branches contain mixtures and conditions.
- If a branch contains two actions, we ignore the root action.
- We extract words in branches and match from original sentence to get the correct phrase to obtain the condition.

The rule-based extraction returns an Action-Mixture (A-M), an Action-Condition (A-C) or an Action-Mixture-Condition (A-M-C) structure. We push the structure to a stack starting from the first sentence. Words are popped from the stack until we encounter an action. If an A-M-C structure is present, then we pop it as a result. If an A-M structure is present, then we pop the A-M structure. If an A-C structure is present, then we pop the A-C structure from the stack and convert it into an A-M-C structure for all the unique mixtures remaining in the stack. Otherwise, if we encounter only A, then we pop A and convert it to an A-M structure for all the unique mixtures remaining in the stack.

We carry out the above steps recursively from the last sentence to the first sentence. The extracted results get rearranged according to their occurrence in the text, thus maintaining the order of actions.

**Constructing Ingredient Dictionary for Synonyms and Functionalities.** We observe that there are scarce offline resources to collect synonyms or other names of an ingredient as well as their functionalities but several online resources including ingredient entries at Wikipedia and specialized databases like the EU Cosmetic Ingredient Database[6]. We apply web scraping to several online resources to construct ingredient-synonyms and ingredient-functionality dictionaries.

---

[6] EU CosIng https://ec.europa.eu/growth/sectors/cosmetics/cosing_en.

A total of 2633 ingredients exist in 410 formulations, out of which 1086 are unique, and 333 ingredients repeat more than once. Chemical names are more prominently available in public datasets as opposed to an ingredient name occurring in a formulation. We were able to find chemical names for 447 ingredients. We search for sources such as Wikipedia[7], PubChem[8] [12], Chebi[9], and ChemSpider[10] to gather the desired information. The extracted data contains:

- IUPAC (International Union of Pure and Applied Chemistry) name, Synonyms, Chemical formula, Smiles (a representation of the chemical), PubChem CID, and *uses* or *application* section or functionalities from Wikipedia.
- Chemical Formula and PubChem CID from PubChem.
- Link to Chebi and ChemSpider from Wikipedia.

In the following sections, we present the storage and retrieval of the formulation constituents that we have extracted.

## 4   Storing Formulations as Graphs

Figure 5 shows the graph conceptual/domain model for cosmetic and toiletry formulations. In Fig. 5, the node FormulationType indicates the high-level formulation category. Since all our formulations are of creams which are of the type cosmetic and toiletry, for all 410 formulations under consideration, we set the label name of the FormulationType to *cosmetic and toiletry*.

| | |
|---|---|
| Type of formulation | `FormulationType name: 'Cosmetic and Toiletry'` |
| Category within a type formulation | `FormulationCategory name: 'Creams'` |
| Name of the formulation | `Formulation name: 'acid ph. oil-in-water cream - b'` |
| Ingredients with quantities, mixtures of ingredients [*phase*, *part*, etc.] | `Ingredient name: 'witconol mst (glyceryl stearate)',` `quantity:'10.0'` `(:Mixture (name : 'oil phase'))` |
| Recipe/ formulation consisting of actions and specialization/ characterization of actions | `RecipeText RecipeActionGraph` `RecipeActionGraphStringRepr` `Action name : 'heat', node_id:'1')-[:Uses]->` `(:Constituent name : 'each phase')-[:UnderCondition]->` `(:Condition name : 'to 70 to 75c'),` |

| Get the formulations containing 'Cetyl Alcohol' as one of the ingredients | Get quantity of all ingredients of the name 'Cetyl Alcohol' | Get action graph of all "all purpose" creams |
|---|---|---|
| `MATCH (f:Formulation)-` `[:HasIngredient]->(ingd:Ingredient)` `WHERE ingd.name CONTAINS 'Cetyl Alcohol'` `RETURN COUNT(f.name) as nnumFormulations, collect(f.name) as Formulations` | `MATCH (f:Formulation)-` `[:HasIngredient]->(ingd:Ingredient)` `WHERE ingd.name CONTAINS 'Cetyl Alcohol'` `RETURN f.name as Formulation,` `ingd.name as IngredientName,` `ingd.quantity as WeightQT` | `MATCH (f:Formulation)-` `[:HasRecipeStringRepr]-` `>(r:RecipeActionGraphStringRepr)` `WHERE f.name CONTAINS "all purpose"` `RETURN f.name, r.repr` |

**Fig. 5.** Graph domain model (with formulation details from Fig. 3) and queries

---

[7] E.g., cetyl alcohol entry at Wikipedia https://en.wikipedia.org/wiki/Cetyl_alcohol.
[8] at PubChem https://pubchem.ncbi.nlm.nih.gov/compound/1-Hexadecanol.
[9] at Chebi https://www.ebi.ac.uk/chebi/searchId.do?chebiId=16125.
[10] at ChemSpider http://www.chemspider.com/Chemical-Structure.2581.html.

There are two reasons to choose a graph database. First, in contrast to relational databases, where join-intensive query performance deteriorates as the size of dataset increases, while a graph database performance tends to remain relatively constant, even as the dataset grows [1,16].

Second, graphs are also naturally additive, implying that we can add new nodes to represent hierarchies or taxonomies, new kinds of relationships between nodes, new nodes, and new subgraphs to an existing structure without disturbing current queries and application functionality [16].

```
MATCH (a:FormulationCategory) where a.name='Creams'
CREATE (a)-[:HasFormulation]->(f:Formulation {name:'acid-ph oil-in-water cream - b'}),
(f)-[:Source]->(:Source {name:'Vol1-1081.txt'}),
(f)-[:HasIngredient]->(:Ingredient {name:'witconol mst (glyceryl stearate)', quantity:'10.0'})-[:PartOf]->(:Mixture {name:'oil phase'}),
(f)-[:HasIngredient]->(:Ingredient {name:'witconol apm (ppg-3 myristyl ether)', quantity:'3.0'})-[:PartOf]->(:Mixture {name:'oil phase'}),
(f)-[:HasIngredient]->(:Ingredient {name:'perfecta petrolatum', quantity:'5.0'})-[:PartOf]->(:Mixture {name:'oil phase'}),
(f)-[:HasIngredient]->(:Ingredient {name:'witconol h-35a (peg-8 stearate)', quantity:'5.0'})-[:PartOf]->(:Mixture {name:'oil phase'}),
(f)-[:HasIngredient]->(:Ingredient {name:'witcamide m a a (stearamide mea stearate)', quantity:'3.0'})-[:PartOf]->(:Mixture {name:'oil phase'}),
(f)-[:HasIngredient]->(:Ingredient {name:'emphos d70-30c (sodium glyceryl oleate phosphate)', quantity:'0.5'})-[:PartOf]->(:Mixture {name:'oil phase'}),
(f)-[:HasIngredient]->(:Ingredient {name:'cetyl alcohol', quantity:'2.0'})-[:PartOf]->(:Mixture {name:'oil phase'}),
(f)-[:HasIngredient]->(:Ingredient {name:'propylparaben', quantity:'0.1'})-[:PartOf]->(:Mixture {name:'oil phase'}),
(f)-[:HasIngredient]->(:Ingredient {name:'emcol 4072 (disodium hydrogenated cottonseed glyceride sulfosuccinate) glycerin usp', quantity:'3.0'})
-[:PartOf]->(:Mixture {name:'water phase'}),
(f)-[:HasIngredient]->(:Ingredient {name:'methylparaben', quantity:'0.15'})-[:PartOf]->(:Mixture {name:'water phase'}),
(f)-[:HasIngredient]->(:Ingredient {name:'fragrance, color', quantity:'q.s.'})-[:PartOf]->(:Mixture {name:'water phase'}),
(f)-[:HasIngredient]->(:Ingredient {name:'water', quantity:'q.s.'})-[:PartOf]->(:Mixture {name:'water phase'}),
(f)-[:HasRecipe]->(g:RecipeActionGraph)],
(g)-[:Contains]->(a1:Action {name:'heat', node_id:'1'})-[:Uses]->(:Constituent {name:'phase'})-[:UnderCondition]->(:Condition {name:'each to 70 to 75c'}),
(g)-[:HasStartNode]->(a1),
(g)-[:Contains]->(a2:Action {name:'stir', node_id:'2'})-[:Uses]->(:Constituent {name:'phase'})->(:Condition {name:'until uniform'}),
(g)-[:Contains]->(a3:Action {name:'add', node_id:'3'})-[:Uses]->(:Constituent {name:'water phase+oil phase'})
-[:UnderCondition]->(:Condition {name:'to the oil phase at 70 75c with moderate agitation'}),
(g)-[:Contains]->(a4:Action {name:'maintain', node_id:'4'})-[:Uses]->(:Constituent {name:'phase+water phase+oil phase'})
-[:UnderCondition]->(:Condition {name:'agitation temperature for 15 minutes'}),
(g)-[:Contains]->(a5:Action {name:'let', node_id:'5'})-[:Uses]->(:Constituent {name:'phase+water phase+oil phase'})
-[:UnderCondition]->(:Condition {name:'with slow stirring'}),
(g)-[:Contains]->(a6:Action {name:'avoid', node_id:'6'})-[:Uses]->(:Constituent {name:'phase+water phase+oil phase'})
-[:UnderCondition]->(:Condition {name:'air entrainment during cooling cycle'}),
(g)-[:Contains]->(a8:Action {name:'pour', node_id:'8'})-[:Uses]->(:Constituent {name:'phase+water phase+oil phase'})
-[:UnderCondition]->(:Condition {name:'at or below 28c'}),
RETURN f.name
```

**Fig. 6.** Generated query for formulation in Fig. 3

In case we were storing the details of a non-cosmetic and toiletry formulation, we would begin by adding a node of type FormulationType and setting the name property appropriately. Next, the node FormulationCategory captures the specific type of cosmetic and toiletry formulation, in our case, creams (or cream). Typically, for other cosmetic and toiletry formulations like antiperspirants and deodorants, we would set the name accordingly.

We generate and execute the combined MATCH and CREATE query[11] parts as shown in Fig. 6 for each formulation, such that we process a formulation text, generate a query and execute it to add a specific formulation to the graph.

This graph structure lends itself to intuitive queries. We show some example queries at the bottom of Fig. 5. Note the queries to find all the formulations containing the ingredient Cetyl Alcohol, and the weights of Cetyl Alcohol in those formulations. Another query shown in Fig. 5 retrieves ingredients of all creams of the specific kind such as *all purpose* or *skin whitening*.

In theory, having built a database of formulations of a specific type (with FormulationType nodes and the specific instances thereof), it is possible to query the details of similar FormulationCategory nodes and their constituents. This kind of query ability paves the way to the first step of intelligent design of formulated products as we show next.

---

[11] Cypher Query Language for Neo4j Graph Database https://neo4j.com/developer/cypher-query-language/.

# 5    Aiding Experts in Design of Formulated Products

Now that we have a database (and in effect a method to create such a database), it is possible to start planning the creation of a design variant as follows:

1. Given a specific kind of FormulationCategory, query the functionalities it usually contains.
2. For each functionality, query all the Ingredient instances associated with it.
3. Query the weight ranges of the ingredients via the quantity attribute.
4. Finalize the set of ingredients and/or mixtures.
5. Query the actions generally performed on each ingredient as a standalone or as a part of a mixture from the A-M-C structures stored as RecipeAction-Graph instances.
6. Order the actions suitably to arrive at a complete formulation variant.

We prepare the following set of *neighbourhoods* as an aid to the expert:

– ingredients that never occur together, as well as those that occur together
– bidirectional neighbourhoods for functionality-ingredient and ingredient-actions, enabling to query functionality and actions of an ingredient and vice versa

It is possible to further cluster or rank the neighbourhoods of ingredients in terms of their functionalities, ingredients in terms of actions performed on them, and actions in terms of ingredients to which they apply.

# 6    Validation and Discussion

We describe validation of extraction, storage, and aided product design below.

**Validating the Extraction of A-M-C Structures.** To validate the extraction of A-M-C structures from the formulation recipes, we manually label recipes from 175 out of 410 formulation texts in terms of A-M-C structures. Figure 7 shows the F1 scores and score bins for both open IE and dependency parsing with and without a verb list and the stacking mechanism. The techniques, when combined, produce the best scores, as seen in Fig. 7.

For string similarity computation, we use an implementation of Levenshtein distance in Python[12].

We compute a similarity score and consider the prediction correct when the score is above a threshold of 75%. This threshold enables accommodating any small differences in the prediction and truth strings. If the predicted result contains more actions than truth, then we count them as false positives. If an action is missing from the predicted result, we count it as a false negative.

If we do not use the verb list, both open IE and dependency parser tag all possible verbs as actions. If we do not use the stacking mechanism, then the specific implementation misses out on mixtures or ingredients in most recipes,

---

[12] Fuzzywuzzy String Matching https://github.com/seatgeek/fuzzywuzzy.

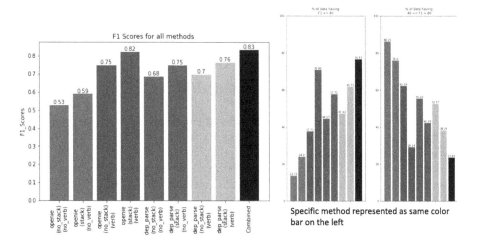

**Fig. 7.** F1 scores and score bins of extraction methods

where they are not explicitly mentioned. Consequently, when we use both the verb list and the stacking mechanism on top of open IE and dependency parser, we get better F1 scores.

In the combined approach, we use both open IE and dependency parsing with the verb list and the stacking mechanism. Based on observations, we use two rules: a) choose actions from the method that gives more number of actions, and b) for each action, we choose the more descriptive mixture and condition, so that we don't miss out any information that may have been lost when using the specific extraction technique.

The score bins show that the combined method achieves more than 80% F1 score for three fourth of the set of 175 formulations.

**Validating Neighbourhood Computation.** The top of Fig. 8 shows the ingredients that never occur together, as well as those that occur together, esp. in the same phase or mixture. Such neighbourhoods or clusters of ingredients are useful because using the membership within a specific ingredient-ingredient neighbourhood, the choice of other ingredients can be informed.

At the bottom of Fig. 8, the results already explicate useful insights that tend to be implicit knowledge even if well understood. Functionalities such as emollients and viscosity controlling dominate due to formulations being creams of various kinds. Water, Propylene Glycol, Fragrance, Triethanolamine, and Cetyl Alcohol are the most common ingredients and Heat, Add, and Cool are some of the most frequently occurring actions.

On top of such neighbourhoods, we can also relate functionalities of ingredients to specific kinds of formulations and thereby to formulation categories. For instance, massage cream instances tend to contain ingredients with anti-static, binding, buffering, and denaturant functionalities, among others. Similarly,

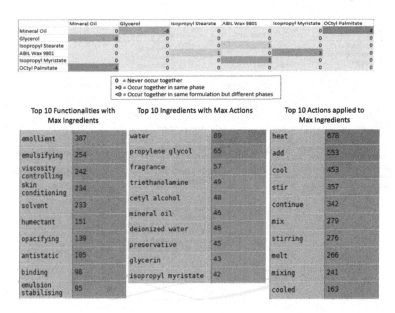

**Fig. 8.** (Top) Ingredient-ingredient neighbourhood (Bottom) Statistics from functionality-ingredient, ingredient-actions and actions-ingredients neighbourhoods

chamomile cream instances tend to contain functionalities such as bulking, humectant, and plasticizer among others.

**Validating Product Variant Generation Aid.** We show an example of an aided variant generation process in Fig. 9 using a tool based on our approach. Our tool aids the formulator (expert) in making rational decisions regarding ingredient choices and helps him/her arrive at a possible recipe to be followed using the actions generally associated with the chosen ingredient.

For example, if a user wanted to design a variant of a face cream then the tool takes face cream as input product type and returns the count of face cream recipes in the database (11, in this case) along with the various ingredient functionalities associated with the face cream recipes. The user then has the option to specify the functionality to be explored, say emollient. Based on the functionality chosen, the tool returns 33 possible ingredient choices for this functionality from 11 face cream formulations. Given the possible emollient choices, the user then selects one or more ingredients based on experience such as Isopropyl Myristate based on the knowledge that it is a liquid of low viscosity, absorbs quickly and also acts as a permeation enhancer. After selection of the emollient Isopropyl Myristate, the tool outputs 10 ingredients which occurred together with this ingredient and their respective functionalities. The user can opt to choose optional functionality like anti-ageing similarly. We check the novelty of the combination by ensuring that this combination does not occur in any of the 410 cream recipes.

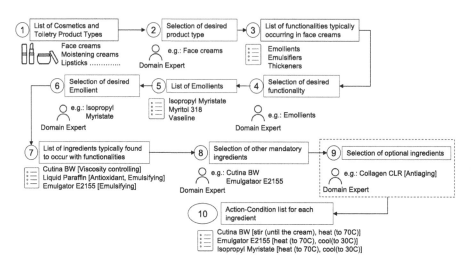

**Fig. 9.** Product design variant generation example

Once the formulator chooses all required ingredients, the tool outputs a list of A-M-C structures associated with each ingredient. The common A-M-C structures across all the chosen ingredients direct the formulator to the overall recipe steps. A possible recipe obtained as illustrated in Fig. 9 is as below:

```
Phase A: Isopropyl Myristate 10-35%, Cutina BW 0.1-2%,
Emulgator E2155 2-6%
Phase B: Water 55-75%, Collagen CLR 1-10%
Procedure: Heat Phase A and Phase B to about 70c.
Add Phase A to Phase B.
Continue stirring until the cream is emulsified.
Cool down to approximately 30c.
```

In the following, we briefly touch upon the limitations of our approach.

**Extraction Limitations.** Both open IE and dependency parsing incorrectly process a) gerund verb forms such as *mixing* in "disperse ... using high-speed mixing", and b) passive sentences, resulting in inaccurate triples and therefore, incorrect results. Similarly, if a sentence contains multiple actions as in "melt A and bring to about 70C", the processing fails to separate melting and bringing about as two different actions. We are currently extending annotated data by first creating A-M-C structures with our techniques and then manually correcting them. We plan to use machine learning techniques to overcome these limitations to some extent.

**Data Availability Limitations.** In spite of these aids, it is not possible to predict the final properties of the designed variant as in how adding or removing an ingredient affects the properties of the formulated product. Additionally, the sequence of recipe steps to be followed cannot be ascertained independently with just the A-M-C structures for the ingredients. We are currently compiling a set of heuristics to tackle these limitations.

# 7 Conclusion

Formulated products industry presents considerable opportunities for information systems such as one that we have detailed and demonstrated. Although it is tough to obtain and store details of every ingredient, its functionality, and kinds of products where it is useful, our approach provides a step in that direction, mainly if the user focuses on a specific product type like a cream or a coating.

# References

1. Angles, R., Gutierrez, C.: Survey of graph database models. ACM Comput. Surv. (CSUR) **40**(1), 1 (2008)
2. Arrieta-Escobar, J.A., Bernardo, F.P., Orjuela, A., Camargo, M., Morel, L.: Incorporation of heuristic knowledge in the optimal design of formulated products: application to a cosmetic emulsion. Comput. Chem. Eng. **122**, 265–274 (2019)
3. Bernardo, F.P., Saraiva, P.M.: A conceptual model for chemical product design. AIChE J. **61**(3), 802–815 (2015)
4. Conte, E., Gani, R., Ng, K.M.: Design of formulated products: a systematic methodology. AIChE J. **57**(9), 2431–2449 (2011)
5. Dionisio, K.L., et al.: The chemical and products database, a resource for exposure-relevant data on chemicals in consumer products. Sci. Data **5**, 180125 (2018)
6. Flick, E.W.: Cosmetic and Toiletry Formulations, vol. 1–8. Elsevier (1989–2014)
7. Gani, R., Ng, K.M.: Product design-molecules, devices, functional products, and formulated products. Comput. Chem. Eng. **81**, 70–79 (2015)
8. Hill, M.: Chemical product engineering–the third paradigm. Comput. Chem. Eng. **33**(5), 947–953 (2009)
9. Kiddon, C., Ponnuraj, G.T., Zettlemoyer, L., Choi, Y.: Mise en place: unsupervised interpretation of instructional recipes. In: Proceedings of the 2015 Conference on Empirical Methods in Natural Language Processing, pp. 982–992 (2015)
10. Kim, E., Huang, K., Jegelka, S., Olivetti, E.: Virtual screening of inorganic materials synthesis parameters with deep learning. NPJ Comput. Mater. **3**(1), 1–9 (2017)
11. Kim, E., Huang, K., Saunders, A., McCallum, A., Ceder, G., Olivetti, E.: Materials synthesis insights from scientific literature via text extraction and machine learning. Chem. Mater. **29**(21), 9436–9444 (2017)
12. Kim, S., et al.: Pubchem substance and compound databases. Nucleic Acids Res. **44**(D1), D1202–D1213 (2016)
13. Lee, C., Choy, K.L., Chan, Y.: A knowledge-based ingredient formulation system for chemical product development in the personal care industry. Comput. Chem. Eng. **65**, 40–53 (2014)
14. Michalun, M.V., DiNardo, J.C.: Skin Care and Cosmetic Ingredients Dictionary. Cengage Learning, Boston (2014)

15. Mysore, S., et al.: Automatically extracting action graphs from materials science synthesis procedures. arXiv preprint arXiv:1711.06872 (2017)
16. Robinson, I., Webber, J., Eifrem, E.: Graph Databases. O'Reilly Media, Inc., Newton (2013)
17. Wibowo, C., Ng, K.M.: Product-centered processing: manufacture of chemical-based consumer products. AIChE J. **48**(6), 1212–1230 (2002)
18. Zhang, L., Fung, K.Y., Wibowo, C., Gani, R.: Advances in chemical product design. Rev. Chem. Eng. **34**(3), 319–340 (2018)
19. Zhang, L., Fung, K.Y., Zhang, X., Fung, H.K., Ng, K.M.: An integrated framework for designing formulated products. Comput. Chem. Eng. **107**, 61–76 (2017)

# Information Systems Engineering

# Resource-Based Adaptive Robotic Process Automation

## Formal/Technical Paper

Renuka Sindhgatta[1]([✉]), Arthur H. M. ter Hofstede[1], and Aditya Ghose[2]

[1] Queensland University of Technology, Brisbane, Australia
{renuka.sr,a.terhofstede}@qut.edu.au
[2] University of Wollongong, Wollongong, Australia
aditya.ghose@uow.edu.au

**Abstract.** Robotic process automation is evolving from robots mimicking human workers in automating information acquisition tasks, to robots performing human decision tasks using machine learning algorithms. In either of these situations, robots or automation agents can have distinct characteristics in their performance, much like human agents. Hence, the execution of an automated task may require adaptations with human participants executing the task when robots fail, to taking a supervisory role or having no involvement. In this paper, we consider different levels of automation, and the corresponding coordination required by resources that include human participants and robots. We capture resource characteristics and define business process constraints that support process adaptations with human-automation coordination. We then use a real-world business process and incorporate automation agents, compute resource characteristics, and use resource-aware constraints to illustrate resource-based process adaptations for its automation.

**Keywords:** Robotic process automation · Declarative constraints · Resource characteristics

## 1 Introduction

Business process automation (BPA) provides the ability to coordinate tasks and distribute them to resources (humans or software systems) according to certain logical or temporal dependencies [1]. Tasks in a business process are often either *manual* and performed by human participants, or *system-supported* and executed by software systems. Robotic process automation (RPA) strives to automate frequent and repetitive manual tasks performed by human participants using *robots* by mimicking their interactions with IS systems [2,3].

Until recently, one of the criteria for the selection of tasks for automation has been a high level of repetition requiring limited human judgment. However, advances in artificial intelligence and learning algorithms have extended the ambit of automation capabilities [3]. The type of automation can vary

S. Dustdar et al. (Eds.): CAiSE 2020, LNCS 12127, pp. 451–466, 2020.
https://doi.org/10.1007/978-3-030-49435-3_28

in complexity with an automation agent or robot simply mimicking a human information acquisition activity (such as logging into a website and retrieving information for a warehouse management system), to providing decision support to human participants (e.g. a learning algorithm predicting inventory in a warehouse), to carrying out the necessary action (e.g. ordering and updating inventory). RPA technology focuses on the development of robots or 'software programs' having limited support for the design and characterisation of robots performing a task. As an example, in a real world process, a robot (or bot) extracting educational qualifications from a tax exemption request document may have lower accuracy when dealing with acronyms entered by claimants resulting in erroneous output. In such situations, the case execution needs to adapt suitably by having a human participant supervise the task performed by the robot.

There are several reasons why it is important to characterize robots in addition to human participants. First, the characteristics of robots and human participants influencing the execution of a process can be distinct and it is necessary to acquire an understanding during the design phase. For example, considering and characterizing the resource based on the ability to manage workload is critical for human participants but is of little significance for the design of robots (given their capacity is much larger than humans). Second, in line with human-automation studies that detail human interactions with automation agents [4,5], business process execution requires adaptation based on the resources and their characteristics to support different levels of automation: 1) with a robot not capable for performing a task, or 2) capable of performing a task with human assistance or 3) act autonomously and perform a task independently. Process tasks, process participants (humans and robots), and the coordination between process participants needs to be modelled as part of the design phase of the RPA development life-cycle [6]. Third, by taking resource characteristics and process adaptation into account during process design one is able to systematically determine the degree to which automation of the process is feasible. The paper makes the following contributions:

– It outlines a design approach that considers distinct resources (humans and robots) and their characteristics to support different levels of automation, and
– It describes a real-world business process based on a process event log and realizes it using different robots.

The paper is organised as follows. A brief overview of previous studies on resource characteristics and their extension in the context of RPA (Sect. 2) is followed by the introduction of distinct levels of automation and resource-based constraints required to support such levels of automation (Sect. 3). Different levels and types of automation are presented using a real world process and its event log (Sect. 4). Related work (Sect. 5) is followed by a brief conclusion and avenues for future work.

## 2    Resource Types and Characteristics

The organizational perspective of a business process tends to focus on the human participants and the constraints that need to be met at both design time (assignment) and run time (allocation) for tasks to be performed by certain human resources [7]. Our work broadens the typical focus of the organizational perspective by considering various other types of resources and how they can be involved in the execution of tasks.

**Resource Types.** We consider three types of resources participating in a business process:

- *Human Agent (HA)*: A human resource is capable of executing all types of (manual) tasks of the process.
- *Robotic Agents (RA)*: Robotic agents are robots, i.e. specialised software programs, that automate *information acquisition* tasks or information gathering tasks. In many scenarios, the RA mimics human interactions on user interfaces by reading the output of interface screens and entering values into such screens [3]. The RA functions like any software system and does not change (or learn) unless the software program is re-written. As observed by Scheepers, Lacity, and Willcocks [3], RAs often automate a subset of tasks and hence are used in conjunction with other resources.
- *Intelligent Agents (IA)*: The notion of an intelligent agent has been envisioned for over three decades. Intelligent agents automate *information analysis* and decision-making tasks. IAs improve their performance through learning [8]. In the scope of this paper, we refer to intelligent agents as agents that use statistical machine learning techniques and learn from observed data [9]. However, the approach scales to agents using other approaches to learning and decision making.

There can be other types of resources needed for executing a business process such as data resources, hardware resources, and other information systems. The focus of this work is limited to the resources automating tasks performed by human participants.

**Resource Characteristics.** Previous studies have presented various characteristics of human resources for allocation of tasks (referred to as criteria, ability, or profiles in existing literature). Table 1 summarizes different characteristics of a resource based on a prior systematic literature review [14]. Pika, Leyer, Wynn, *et al.* [10] present a detailed and fine-grained definition of various resource characteristics or behaviour, but for our study, we refer to those presented in the aforementioned literature review.

The significance of each of the resource characteristics for different types of resources is presented in Table 1. By significance, we mean the importance of the various characteristics when allocating a task to a resource. *Preference* and *Collaboration* are not primary characteristics for an IA or an RA as automation

**Table 1.** Literature-based resource characteristics for assigning or allocating tasks

| Resource characteristics | Significance | | | Description |
|---|---|---|---|---|
| | HA | IA | RA | |
| Expertise, skills | ✓ | ✓ | ✓ | The demonstrated capability of a resource to perform a task [10] |
| Preference | ✓ | ✗ | ✗ | The tendency for choosing particular types of work or for involving particular resources [11] |
| Collaboration | ✓ | ✗ | ✗ | The degree to which resources work well together [12] |
| Workload | ✓ | ✗ | ✗ | The average number of activities started by a given resource but not completed at a moment in time [10] |
| Availability | ✓ | ✗ | ✗ | The resource is available to perform an activity within a specific time frame [12] |
| Suitability | ✓ | ✓ | ✓ | The inherent qualification of the resource to perform a task [13] |
| Authorization | ✓ | ✓ | ✓ | Constraints on, or privilege of, a specific person or role to execute a task or case [14] |
| Experience | ✓ | ✓ | ✓ | Experience is collected by performing the task [15] |
| Performance (quality) | ✓ | ✓ | ✓ | Number of activities/cases completed with a given outcome by the resource [10] |
| Duration (time) | ✓ | ✗ | ✗ | The average duration of activities or cases completed by a resource [10] |

resources do not have a personal preference or choice (unless programmed as a part of the software code). *Duration* and *Workload* are constant and known at design time for an IA and RA, as compared to human participants with varying completion times [16]. Furthermore, unlike human participants with work schedules, an IA or an RA is always available. Resource characteristics such as expertise, preference, workload, or suitability may influence other resource characteristics such as experience, performance (quality) and duration (time).

In the context of automation, we present a subset of important resource characteristics relevant for the three types of resources to enable human-automation interactions. These measures can be determined using distinct data sources: process event logs, IA test results, or RA software specifications. Given a set of tasks $A$, a set of resources $R$ executing the tasks, and a set of process attributes $\mathcal{D} = \{d_1, \ldots, d_{|\mathcal{D}|}\}$, a subset of resource characteristics are presented:

**Suitability** is the inherent quality of a resource $r \in R$, to perform a task $a \in A$. The suitability of a resource [13] can be determined for a process attribute value $d_i \in \mathcal{D}$, with a value $D_{val}(d_i) = v_i$.

$suitability(r, a, d_i, v_i) \rightarrow [0, 1]$, is the suitability of resource $r$ for task $a$, for an attribute $d_i$ with its value $v_i$

For example, in an IT support process, a resource of type RA may not be suitable to perform the task 'apply patch' for a specific operating system. 'Operating system' is the process attribute which could take its value from the set

$\{ubuntu, redhat, \ldots, windows10\}$. Similarly, in a loan application process, a loan approval task for a higher amount may mandate an HA due to a business requirement. Suitability can be determined based on agent specification and implementation, or can be determined based on the organization model attributes such as role, department, or cost of the resource.

**Experience:** Performing a task activates the experience of a resource [15]. "Experience can be possessed and increased by a [resource] through performing that task" [15]. Event logs can be used to compute the experience of a resource. Consider an event log $\mathcal{L}$ consisting of a set of events occurring during window length $\kappa$. Each event $e \in \mathcal{L}$, is associated with a resource $res(e) = r$, task $task(e) = a$ and process attribute values $attr\_val(e, d_i) = v_i$. The number of task completions $a$ by resource $r$, having a process attribute $d_i$ with value $v_i$ indicates the experience of the resource.
$experience(r, a, d_i, v_i) = |\{e | res(e) = r \wedge task(e) = a \wedge attr\_val(e, d_i) = v_i\}|$

**Performance:** Automation agents are more susceptible to resource specific errors i.e. errors made by resources when performing a task [17]. Performance measure of an IA can be computed based on the algorithms implemented such as F1-score, root mean square error, precision, or precision@k [18]. These measures can be computed during the training and testing of the algorithms. The performance of agent $r$, on task $a$, with a process attribute $d_i$ having value $v_i$ can be computed using the measure specific to the implemented algorithms. $performance(a, r, d_i, v_i) \rightarrow [0, 1]$.

We illustrate the computation of the performance measure for an IA that uses a supervised classification algorithm [9]. A common metric for evaluating the performance of a classifier is the F1-score which considers precision and recall measures. These measures are computed on a test data set where the predictions of the classifier are compared to the true values to arrive at the confusion matrix. Table 2 shows the confusion matrix of the classifier, where each row represents the actual true value, and each column contains the predicted value. Hence, the values of the diagonal elements represent the degree of correctly predicted classes. The confusion is expressed by the false predicted off-diagonal elements, as they are confused for another class or value. Based on the confusion matrix, it is evident that the classifier performance is poor when identifying the label or class 'B'. In scenarios where the IA predicts class 'B', it would be necessary for an HA to intervene and verify the task completion. Hence, this section highlights

**Table 2.** Illustrative confusion matrix of a classifier

|  |  | Predicted class | | | |
|---|---|---|---|---|---|
|  |  | A | B | C | F1-score |
|  | A | 25 | 2 | 3 | 0.69 |
| Actual class | B | 10 | 10 | 10 | 0.47 |
|  | C | 7 | 0 | 23 | 0.69 |

the need for capturing fine grained resource characteristics for specific **domain attributes and their values** ($d_i$ and $v_i$), as the automation support could vary with these characteristics.

# 3   Process Adaptations for Levels of Automation

The notion of human participants and robots working together and requiring suitable interventions has been presented in human-automation studies acknowledging that "... automation is not all or none but can vary across a continuum of levels, from the lowest level of fully manual performance to the highest level of full automation" [4]. Taxonomies proposing the categorization of automation on different point scales, referred to as Levels of automation (LOA), have lower levels representing manual or no automation and higher levels representing increased automation [5]. While these scales vary from 3 LOA to 11 LOA, they can generally be broken down into three broad categories: (i) levels where the task is primarily performed by a human, (ii) levels where the human-agent interaction is high during task execution and (iii) levels with low human involvement. Table 3 summarizes the broad categories of automation levels.

**Table 3.** Levels of automation

| Scale | Description |
|---|---|
| Full automation | The automation agent carries out the action |
| Supervisory control | The automation agent carries out the action, the human may intervene if required |
| Decision support | The automation agent cannot perform the action but can provide support to the human |
| Manual | The automation agent offers no assistance |

In the context of RPA, at lower levels of automation (decision support), an HA would often be required to execute the task again after its completion by an IA or RA. At higher levels of automation, HAs exercise a supervisory role intervening only if necessary (failures, errors, or poor execution quality). Progress through different levels of automation is dependent on certain characteristics or attributes of the robots such as their performance and experience. Human verification tasks may be added dynamically during process execution based on resource characteristics of the IAs or RAs. Consequently, one or more resource characteristics can be used to design conditions for an HA to intervene.

## 3.1   Declarative Constraints for Process Adaptation

We use Declare, a declarative business process specification language to illustrate the process adaptations to support different levels of automation and interactions between the different types of resources [19]. Our approach can be supported

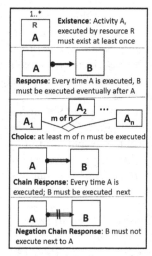 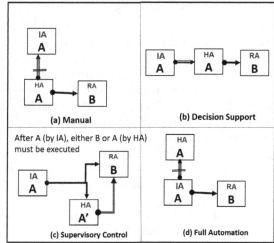

**Fig. 1.** Some Declare constraints and constraints supporting different LOA.

using any declarative specification that orchestrates control-flow through a definition of constraints and is not limited by the specification language. Declare constraints are grouped into four categories, as shown in Fig. 1: (i) Existence constraints, (ii) Choice constraints, (iii) Relation constraints, and (iv) Negation constraints. The different levels of automation for activity $A$ is shown in Fig. 1:

- *Manual:* An HA executes activity $A$, which is followed by activity $B$ eventually. Activity $A$ must not be immediately executed by an $IA$ after it was just executed by an HA. Activity $B$ can be performed by any resource type. An RA is chosen in the example to illustrate the interplay between different resource types.
- *Decision Support:* An IA executes activity $A$, which is immediately followed by an HA executing $A$, and is eventually followed by the execution of activity $B$. Thus, the execution by an IA is overridden by an HA (as the IA may not have much experience with, or a poor track record, performing $A$).
- *Supervisory Control:* An IA executes activity $A$ which can be followed by either activity $B$, or an activity strongly related to $A$ ($A'$ in the figure), e.g. a redo or a quality check, this time performed by an HA. Activity $A'$ is performed by an HA, and this has to be followed by activity $B$.
- *Full Automation:* An IA executes activity $A$, which is followed by activity $B$ eventually. Activity $A$ must not be immediately executed by an HA after it was just executed by an IA.

### 3.2 Syntax for Resource-Aware Declarative Constraints

To support automation based on types of resources and resource characteristics, we extend Declare with fine-grained resource-aware constraints. Existing work extends Declare with multiple perspectives beyond the control-flow perspective and includes data, resource roles, and time [20,21]. We need additional constraints to support human and automation agent interactions as well as process adaptations based on resource types and their characteristics. Hence, we extend Declare and define the syntax of resource-aware declarative specification through key extensions to Declare using abstract syntax notation [22].

A process model consists of an *ActivitySet*, and a *ConstraintSet* applied to the activities. An *ActivitySet* has one or more *Activity*. Each *Activity* has a label, a set of one or more *Resource* permitted to perform the activity, input and output *Data*. We use $\mathbb{N}$ and $\mathbb{S}$ to represent Integer and String types respectively.

Each *Resource* has a *Role* corresponding to role, a *ResourceType*, and a set of resource characteristics, *ResourceChar*.

$$Resource \triangleq ro : Role, rt : ResourceType; \quad ResourceCharSet \triangleq ResourceChar^*$$
$$rcs : ResourceCharSet$$
$$Role \triangleq \mathbb{S} \qquad\qquad\qquad ResourceType \triangleq HA \mid RA \mid IA$$

A resource characteristic *ResourceChar* is an attribute name and a value pair as discussed in Sect. 2.

$$ResourceChar \triangleq ra : ResourceAttribute \quad ResourceAttribute; \triangleq identifier$$
$$rv : Value \qquad\qquad\qquad Value \triangleq [0...1]$$

The *ConstraintSet* is a set of Declare *Constraint*. A constraint can be a unary or a binary constraint. Constraints operate on a set of *ActivityContext*.

$$Constraint \triangleq UnaryConstraint \mid BinaryConstraint$$

A *UnaryConstraint* refers to the (i) existence, and (ii) choice constraints. *Degree*, states the number of times, an *ActivityContext* must be executed for *existence* or *absence* constraint. For *choice* and *exclusive_choice*, it is the number of activities to be executed from *ActivityContextSet*.

$$UnaryConstraint \triangleq uc : UConstraint; \qquad UConstraint \triangleq Exist \mid Absence$$
$$acset : ActivityContextSet; \qquad\qquad \mid Exactly \mid Choice$$
$$n : Degree; \qquad\qquad\qquad \mid Exclusive\_Choice$$
$$ActivityContextSet \triangleq ActivityContext^* \qquad Degree \triangleq \mathbb{N}$$

*BinaryConstraint* represents the Declare binary constraint and comprises of a *BConstraint*, a source *ActivityContext* and a set of target *ActivityContext*.

$$BinaryConstraint \triangleq bc : BConstraint; \qquad BConstraint \triangleq Response \mid Neg\_Response$$
$$ac : ActivityContext; \qquad\qquad \mid Chain\_Response$$
$$acset : ActivityContextSet \qquad\qquad \mid Neg\_Chain\_Response$$

The *ActivityContext* is composed of an *Activity*, an *ExpressionSet*. Each *Expression* describes conditional expressions on the *ResourceAttribute* of the

*ResourceChar*. The Expression can be a Constant or another *Binary* expression. A *Binary* expression contains two expressions and an Operation.

$$ActivityContext \triangleq a:\ Activity,\ exps:\ ExpressionSet$$
$$ExpressionSet \triangleq Expression^*$$
$$Expression \triangleq \text{Constant} \mid Binary \mid ResourceAttribute$$
$$Binary \triangleq exp\_1, exp\_2:\ Expression;\ \text{op: Operation}$$

# 4  Evaluation and Results

The objective of this section is to illustrate our approach using two scenarios. In both scenarios, an IA is simulated, and the resource characteristics of the IA are computed using historical data. The levels of automation are configured by defining constraints on resource characteristics. The achievable levels of automation are illustrated based on the resource constraints. For the first scenario, we choose a business process event log and identify a task that can be automated by an IA. We measure two resource characteristics: performance and experience and illustrate the four levels of automation. The second scenario depicts a service-oriented chatbot (or IA) deployment considering bot-human partnerships. Here, we measure the performance of the chatbot and define two levels of automation. Lack of temporal information in the data limits our ability to measure other resource characteristics such as experience. In this experiment, we illustrate the flexibility of defining levels of automation and identifying achievable levels of automation with the chatbot.

**1. Business Process Intelligence Challenge 2014 (BPIC 2014):** The BPIC 2014 event log[1] comprises of events capturing the interaction management and incident management of a large bank. The interaction management process is triggered when a customer has an IT issue and calls a service desk agent (SDA). The SDA identifies the relevant IT element having the issue (known as configuration item or CI), the urgency and priority of the issue. If the SDA is unable to resolve the issue, an incident is created, thus initiating the incident management process. The incident is assigned to a team suitable for resolving the incident. Given the data available in the event log, we choose the automation of the activity 'Assign the team' of an incident which in the current process is manually done by an SDA. Identification of the activities for automation is carried out during the design phase of an automation life-cycle [6] and is out of the scope of this work. We choose this task for the purpose of illustration.

**Resource Characteristics:** In this study, the performance and experience (both resource characteristics) of the IA executing the task 'Assign Team' are presented. We use the BPIC 2014 interaction log and incident activity log for this purpose. Each event in the interaction log represents an interaction and

---

[1] https://www.win.tue.nl/bpi/doku.php?id=2014:challenge.

contains information entered by a SDA: the type and sub-type of CI, the component, the urgency and priority of the interaction. An incident is created using details of the corresponding interaction. Assignment of an incident to a team is captured in the incident activity log. The incident activity log may contain multiple teams corresponding to a single incident. Such a scenario occurs if there are multiple assignments, caused by an error made by an SDA, or an incident requires several teams to resolve. For this study, we consider incidents involving a single team. The event log contains 46086 incidents resolved over a period of 6 months, of which 13257 are handled by a single team and used to build the IA. To simulate a real-life situation where an IA is trained using historical data and applied to executing process instances, we split the data temporally, with the first 10,000 incidents ( 80%) used for building the IA. The remaining 20% of the data (2651 incidents) is considered to be unseen data replicating the scenario of an IA when deployed. The IA is a Random Forest classifier, trained using a training, cross-validation and test data. The overall accuracy of the classifier is 72.6%. Any suitable machine learning classifier can be used, as depicting the best performing classifier is not the goal of our experiment. The input features of the classifier based on the information available in the event log, are the CI name, CI type, and component of the incident. The team of the incident is the class or output feature. The F1-score representing the performance of the IA is computed. Figure 2 shows the normalized confusion matrix for a subset of the teams (due to space constraints) on the test data as detailed in Sect. 2. The *performance* of the classifier is high when predicting certain teams (e.g. TEAM0003, TEAM0015) vis-a-vis others (notably TEAM0031, TEAM0044).

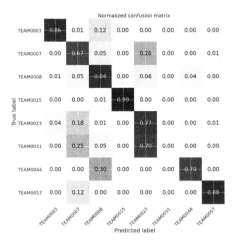

**Fig. 2.** Confusion matrix of the random forest classifier predicting teams

The experience of the IA is computed as the number of incidents handled by the IA, having a specific type, sub-type of the CI and the component (indicating a specific task). The IA would start with zero experience and accumulate experience as time progresses. We use min-max normalisation to limit experience values to a $[0, 1]$ range. The pre-processed logs, the training data and the source code for replicating the results are available at https://git.io/JePaI.

**Resource-aware Constraints:** To illustrate different levels of automation and a progression from a low level to a higher level of automation, we present resource-aware constraints for 'Assign Team' task.

When the IA is deployed, if the performance of IA is low on a task (or incident), an HA will execute the task again with no assistance from IA (Manual). In Fig. 3(a), this is captured as a *chain_response* between two 'Assign Team' tasks, first task performed by an IA, followed by another task performed by an HA. When an IA is deployed anew, experience is low and hence, the trust in automation is low. In such a scenario, if the performance is high, the IA may provide recommendations to an HA, but the task will be executed by an HA (Fig. 3(b)). An increase in the experience of IA will result in an increase in level of automation (Fig. 3(c)). Here, an HA performs a supervisory role and executes

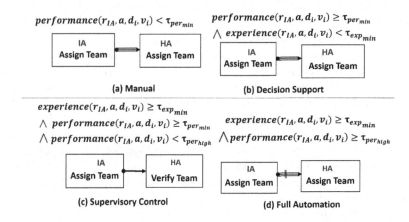

**Fig. 3.** Configuring resource-aware constraints enables achieving different LOA

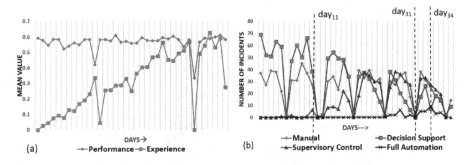

**Fig. 4.** (a) The mean values of resource characteristics for all incidents. (b) Levels of automation configured using resource characteristics.

a verification task 'Verify Team'. When the performance and experience of the IA are higher than a threshold, the highest level of automation is possible (Fig. 3(d)). Thus, the proposed approach suggests the possibility of having different levels of automation for different case attributes and their values. The thresholds for the resource characteristics are domain dependent and their choice results in a trade-off between the performance of the overall process and the levels of automation that can be achieved. In this experiment, we used threshold values to illustrate the ability to configure levels of automation. Generally speaking, such values are domain-dependent, but here they were heuristically determined. A methodological guideline to identify thresholds, which is yet to be developed, would take into account trade-offs between different resource characteristics and identify the implications on process performance and automation levels.

**Levels of Automation:** We simulate the scenario of deploying the IA. For every event in the new or unseen data, the performance of the IA is computed by considering the predicted team and the f1-score (or performance) for the predicted team. The normalized experience of the IA is computed considering the domain attributes (type, sub-type of CI, and component). The experience of the IA is updated daily for each incident, and the average experience is presented in Fig. 4(a). We observe a drop in the experience on $day_{31}$, when new tasks with different values of domain attributes are created by the SDA. This arrival of new tasks causes a decrease in the experience of the IA for those tasks, thus illustrating the need for measuring resource characteristics for specific tasks. Using the resource-aware constraints, levels of automation for the IA can be assessed for each incident (Fig. 4(b)). The distribution of levels of automation changes as time progresses. As shown by two markers, on $day_{11}$, the experience of the IA is be low for most domain attributes and values, and hence the automation of the task is distributed as 38% at Manual, 53% at Decision Support, 9% at Supervisory Control, and 0% at Full Automation. However, on $day_{34}$, the distribution changes with 37% of tasks executed manually, 10% at Decision Support, 40% at Supervisory Control and 13% at Full automation. The thresholds used for the purpose of illustration are: $\tau_{exp_{min}} = 0.4, \tau_{per_{min}} = 0.5, \tau_{per_{high}} = 0.8$. This example does not provide a benchmark on levels of automation that can be achieved but illustrates the need for configuring such automation levels.

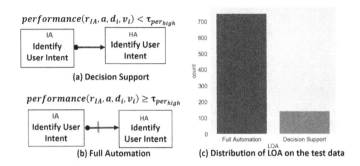

**Fig. 5.** (a), (b) resource constraints for LOA. (c) Distribution of LOA.

**2. Chatbot Intent Classification:** In this scenario, we illustrate use of resource constraints on an IA to customise LOA. Consider the scenario of a chatbot service answering the queries of customers. A chatbot would need to identify the goal or intent of the customer based on the customer query or utterance, a problem commonly referred to as 'intent classification'. If the performance of the chatbot in classifying the intent is high, the chatbot responds to the user query. If the performance is lower than the threshold, the customer query is handed over to a human participant. Hence, in this scenario there are two levels of automation - `Decision Support` or `Full automation` (Fig. 5). It would be useful to identify achievable levels of automation based on the frequency of distribution of user intents from past conversations and the performance achieved by the IA in relation to these user intents. To simulate this scenario, we consider the widely used public dataset ATIS (Airline Travel Information System) [23]. An IA is trained to classify intents and its performance is computed for each intent using the confusion matrix. The test data of ATIS is used, the user intents are predicted and the performance of IA is determined for each intent. Based on the performance of the IA on the predicted user intents, and a set performance threshold ($\tau_{per_{high}} \geq 0.95$), the achievable distribution of LOA is determined (Fig. 5(c)). The dataset, the training, and the testing of the classifier as well as the source code with further explanations are available at https://git.io/JeXmt.

## 5  Related Work

Recent studies on RPA have focused on the design phase presenting techniques to identify candidate tasks for automation [6]. This work similarly focuses on the design phase of the RPA development life-cycle and proposes to consider and broaden the organizational perspective of process automation design. Use of Artificial Intelligence (AI) and Machine learning to enable robots to do complex tasks has been discussed in previous work [3,24]. In this work, we distinguish types of resources and their characteristics in terms of suitability for execution of different types of tasks.

The need for robots and human participants to collaboratively work as part of BPA has been discussed [24] but has not gained sufficient attention. In this work, we present a domain-independent approach towards human-automation interactions, as such interaction requirements may vary across different domains [4,5] and thus need tailoring. The human-automation levels of interactions are supported using declarative process specification constraints.

Declarative specification supports ad-hoc compositions based on control-flow constraints of a business process [19,25]. Declare, a declarative language for process specification, has been further enhanced to support various perspectives by considering constraints on data [26], organizational roles [27], time [21], and all perspectives together [20]. Our work extends a declarative specification with additional resource-aware constraints that are important to support different automation levels and types of resources.

There have been extensive studies focusing on resources and their characteristics [10–12,14,15]. Resource characteristics are used for the allocation of tasks to resources [13, 28, 29]. The focus of these studies has been human participants. Furthermore, the primary objective of task allocation is to improve efficiency. In this work, we consider distinct types of resources and their characteristics from the perspective of supporting automation.

# 6    Conclusion and Future Work

The recent body of work on RPA has acknowledged the need to identify tasks that can be automated by robots and the need to consider the interplay between robots and human participants. In this paper, we introduce different types of resources and resource characteristics. We present declarative process constraints that enable interplay between resources taking their types and characteristics into account, thus supporting different levels of automation. This work provides a starting point for supporting more advanced forms of automation in business processes and for exploring more sophisticated ways of engaging resources in business processes.

**Limitations and Future Directions:** Choices made as part of run-time adaptation involving different resource types and different resource characteristics represents a complex *trade-off space*. While the current paper does not address this question, developing the machinery to support the identification of this space and reasoning over this space remains an interesting direction for future work. The monitoring machinery that flags the need for resource adaptation could, in principle, be quite sophisticated, involving the tracking of (potentially incremental) progress towards the achievement of functional goals and non-functional objectives (key performance indicators or KPIs). This too is something that our current proposal does not fully address and remains an avenue for future work.

# References

1. Dumas, M., Rosa, M.L., Mendling, J., Reijers, H.A.: Fundamentals of Business Process Management. Springer, Heidelberg (2013). https://doi.org/10.1007/978-3-642-33143-5. ISBN 978-3-642-33142-8
2. Lacity, M., Willcocks, L.P.: Robotic process automation at telefónica O2. MIS Q. Execut. **15**(1) (2016)
3. Scheepers, R., Lacity, M.C., Willcocks, L.P.: Cognitive automation as part of Deakin University's digital strategy. MIS Q. Execut. **17**(2) (2018)
4. Parasuraman, R., Sheridan, T.B., Wickens, C.D.: A model for types and levels of human interaction with automation. IEEE Trans. Syst. Man Cybern. Part A **30**(3), 286–297 (2000)
5. Vagia, M., Transeth, A.A., Fjerdingen, S.A.: A literature review on the levels of automation during the years. What are the different taxonomies that have been proposed? Appl. Ergon. **53**, 190–202 (2016)
6. Jimenez-Ramirez, A., Reijers, H.A., Barba, I., Del Valle, C.: A method to improve the early stages of the robotic process automation lifecycle. In: Giorgini, P., Weber, B. (eds.) CAiSE 2019. LNCS, vol. 11483, pp. 446–461. Springer, Cham (2019). https://doi.org/10.1007/978-3-030-21290-2_28

7. Cabanillas, C., Resinas, M., del-Río-Ortega, A., Cortés, A.R.: Specification and automated design-time analysis of the business process human resource perspective. Inf. Syst. **52**, 55–82 (2015)
8. Russell, S.J., Norvig, P.: Artificial Intelligence - A Modern Approach, 3rd edn. Pearson Education, London (2010)
9. Mohri, M., Rostamizadeh, A., Talwalkar, A.: Foundations of Machine Learning. MIT Press, Cambridge (2012). ISBN 978-0-262-01825-8
10. Pika, A., Leyer, M., Wynn, M.T., Fidge, C.J., ter Hofstede, A.H.M., van der Aalst, W.M.P.: Mining resource profiles from event logs. ACM Trans. Manage. Inf. Syst. **8**(1), 1:1–1:30 (2017)
11. Bidar, R., ter Hofstede, A., Sindhgatta, R., Ouyang, C.: Preference-based resource and task allocation in business process automation. In: Panetto, H., Debruyne, C., Hepp, M., Lewis, D., Ardagna, C.A., Meersman, R. (eds.) OTM 2019. LNCS, vol. 11877, pp. 404–421. Springer, Cham (2019). https://doi.org/10.1007/978-3-030-33246-4_26
12. Huang, Z., Lu, X., Duan, H.: Resource behavior measure and application in business process management. Expert Syst. Appl. **39**(7), 6458–6468 (2012)
13. Kumar, A., et al.: Dynamic work distribution in workflow management systems: how to balance quality and performance. J. Manage. Inf. Syst. **18**(3), 157–194 (2002)
14. Arias, M., Munoz-Gama, J., Sepúlveda, M.: Towards a taxonomy of human resource allocation criteria. In: Teniente, E., Weidlich, M. (eds.) BPM 2017. LNBIP, vol. 308, pp. 475–483. Springer, Cham (2018). https://doi.org/10.1007/978-3-319-74030-0_37
15. Kabicher-Fuchs, S., Mangler, J., Rinderle-Ma, S.: Experience breeding in process-aware information systems. In: Salinesi, C., Norrie, M.C., Pastor, Ó. (eds.) CAiSE 2013. LNCS, vol. 7908, pp. 594–609. Springer, Heidelberg (2013). https://doi.org/10.1007/978-3-642-38709-8_38
16. Nakatumba, J., van der Aalst, W.M.P.: Analyzing resource behavior using process mining. In: Rinderle-Ma, S., Sadiq, S., Leymann, F. (eds.) BPM 2009. LNBIP, vol. 43, pp. 69–80. Springer, Heidelberg (2010). https://doi.org/10.1007/978-3-642-12186-9_8
17. Reichert, M., Weber, B.: Enabling Flexibility in Process-Aware Information Systems - Challenges, Methods. Technologies. Springer, Heidelberg (2012). https://doi.org/10.1007/978-3-642-30409-5
18. Sokolova, M., Japkowicz, N., Szpakowicz, S.: Beyond accuracy, F-score and ROC: a family of discriminant measures for performance evaluation. In: Sattar, A., Kang, B. (eds.) AI 2006. LNCS (LNAI), vol. 4304, pp. 1015–1021. Springer, Heidelberg (2006). https://doi.org/10.1007/11941439_114
19. Pesic, M., Schonenberg, H., van der Aalst, W.M.P.: DECLARE: full support for loosely-structured processes. In: 11th IEEE Conference on EDOC, pp. 287–300 (2007)
20. Burattin, A., et al.: Conformance checking based on multi-perspective declarative process models. Expert Syst. Appl. **65**, 194–211 (2016)
21. Ramirez, A.J., Barba, I., Fernández-Olivares, J., Valle, C.D., Weber, B.: Time prediction on multi-perspective declarative business processes. Knowl. Inf. Syst. **57**(3), 655–684 (2018)
22. Meyer, B.: Introduction to the Theory of Programming Languages. Prentice- Hall, London (1990). ISBN 0-13-498510-9
23. Tür, G., Hakkani-Tür, D., Heck, L.P.: What is left to be understood in ATIS? In: 2010 IEEE Spoken Language Technology Workshop, pp. 19–24 (2010)

24. van der Aalst, W.M.P., Bichler, M., Heinzl, A.: Robotic process automation. BISE **60**, 269–272 (2018). https://doi.org/10.1007/s12599-018-0542-4. ISSN 1867–0202

25. Schönig, S., Cabanillas, C., Jablonski, S., Mendling, J.: A framework for efficiently mining the organisational perspective of business processes. Decis. Support Syst. **89**(C), 87–97 (2016). ISSN 0167–9236

26. Montali, M., Chesani, F., Mello, P., Maggi, F.M.: Towards data-aware constraints in declare. In: 28th ACM SAC 2013, pp. 1391–1396 (2013)

27. Jiménez-Ramírez, A., Barba, I., del Valle, C., Weber, B.: Generating multi-objective optimized business process enactment plans. In: Salinesi, C., Norrie, M.C., Pastor, Ó. (eds.) CAiSE 2013. LNCS, vol. 7908, pp. 99–115. Springer, Heidelberg (2013). https://doi.org/10.1007/978-3-642-38709-8_7

28. Kumar, A., Dijkman, R., Song, M.: Optimal resource assignment in workflows for maximizing cooperation. In: Daniel, F., Wang, J., Weber, B. (eds.) BPM 2013. LNCS, vol. 8094, pp. 235–250. Springer, Heidelberg (2013). https://doi.org/10.1007/978-3-642-40176-3_20

29. Havur, G., Cabanillas, C., Mendling, J., Polleres, A.: Resource allocation with dependencies in business process management systems. In: La Rosa, M., Loos, P., Pastor, O. (eds.) BPM 2016. LNBIP, vol. 260, pp. 3–19. Springer, Cham (2016). https://doi.org/10.1007/978-3-319-45468-9_1

# A Variability-Driven Analysis Method
# for Automatic Extraction of Domain Behaviors

Iris Reinhartz-Berger[✉] and Sameh Abbas

Information Systems Department, University of Haifa, Haifa, Israel
iris@is.haifa.ac.il, samih1079@gmail.com

**Abstract.** Domain engineering focuses on modeling knowledge in an application domain for supporting systematic reuse in the context of complex and constantly evolving systems. Automatically supporting this task is challenging; most existing methods assume high similarity of variants which limits reuse of the generated domain artifacts, or provide very low-level features rather than actual domain features. As a result, these methods are limited in handling common scenarios such as similarly behaving systems developed by different teams, or merging existing products. To address this gap, we propose a method for extracting domain knowledge in the form of *domain behaviors,* building on a previously developed framework for behavior-based variability analysis among class operations. Machine learning techniques are applied for identifying clusters of operations that can potentially form domain behaviors. The approach is evaluated on a set of open-source video games, named apo-games.

**Keywords:** Domain engineering · Systematic reuse · Variability analysis

## 1 Introduction

As systems grow and evolve over time and system development become challenging, it may help learn from existing relevant systems in the domain and create flexible, adaptable, and reusable artifacts. This can be done by performing domain engineering, which focuses on modeling common (and variable) knowledge in an application domain[1] for the purpose of understanding phenomena in the domain and supporting systematic reuse [9]. As this is a tedious and error-prone task, different methods have been proposed to automate it, e.g., by detecting or extracting features – prominent or distinctive user-visible aspects, qualities or characteristics of a system or systems [2].

Most automatic feature extraction methods assume similar system variants that were typically created following cloning scenarios, e.g., clone-and-own in which variants are formed by copying existing artifacts and adapting them to the requirements at hand. This assumption may narrow the uses to various software evolution scenarios, neglecting common scenarios, such as systems developed by different teams yet sharing similar

---

[1] The term domain has many interpretations: business domain, environment, application domain and more. Hereafter, we refer to domain as application domain.

© Springer Nature Switzerland AG 2020
S. Dustdar et al. (Eds.): CAiSE 2020, LNCS 12127, pp. 467–481, 2020.
https://doi.org/10.1007/978-3-030-49435-3_29

behaviors or attempts to integrate and merge existing products. Moreover, most of the existing methods provide low-level features rather than actual domain features [6] and hence their ability to help develop and maintain systems, as well as to promote reuse, is limited.

Of the different kinds of features, domain behaviors may help extract reusable services and interfaces. We define *domain behavior* as a transformation of state variables (attributes) of interest in the domain of discourse. Consider as an example the domain of applications for renting physical spaces, such as offices and houses. *Renting* can be considered a domain behavior, which transforms a state variable named *space_status* from *available* to *occupied*. This observation calls for supporting corresponding renting services as the variety of physical spaces and renting policies may be large.

In this paper, we aim to identify domain behaviors for the purpose of increasing reuse across similarly behaving systems, which do not necessarily share similar implementations. To this end, we build on a previously developed framework for *behavior-based variability analysis*, which identifies three mechanisms among behaviorally similar operations: parametric, subtyping, and overloading. Using this framework, we apply machine learning techniques for identifying clusters of operations that form domain behaviors. Particularly, our method gets object-oriented code of different systems and returns a list of domain behaviors that need to be maintained for the management of the input systems and the development of additional systems in the domain. The approach is evaluated using a set of apo-games, which are open-source video games developed in JAVA [14].

The rest of the paper is structured as follows. Section 2 presents the existing behavior-based variability analysis framework, while Sect. 3 introduces the suggested approach for extracting domain behaviors. Section 4 presents preliminary results and Sect. 5 reviews and discusses the related work with respect to the current research. Finally, Sect. 6 summarizes and highlights some future research directions.

## 2 Behavior-Based Variability Analysis

Features in general and domain behaviors in particular can be extracted from different system artifacts, such as domain information, requirements, design models, and source code [2]. The most available and reliable artifacts are source code, as they can be found in open source or proprietary repositories and represent faithfully the actual system intensions and functionality. Many of the source code artifacts are written in an object-oriented language, whose main elements are classes that exhibit operations.

In a previous work, we have suggested a tool-supported framework for analyzing variability of behaviors in object-oriented code [22]. The tool, named VarMeR – Variability Mechanisms Recommender [21], follows a three-step process: behavior extraction, behavior comparison, and variability analysis. These steps are briefly overviewed and exemplified next.

## 2.1 Behavior Extraction

Taking an external point of view, a (system) *behavior* is a transformation of state variables (attributes) from an initial state to a final state as a result of an external event[2]. A behavior is represented via two descriptors, shallow and deep, as defined below.

**Definition 1.** A *shallow descriptor* depicts the interface of the behavior. Formally expressed, a shallow descriptor is a pair (inOut, params), where *inOut* is a pair (bn, rt) – *bn* is the behavior name and *rt* is its returned type, and *params* is a set of pairs (pn, pt) – *pn* is the name of a parameter passed to the behavior and *pt* is its type.

**Definition 2.** A *deep descriptor* represents the transformation done to the state variables as a result of the behavior. Formally expressed, a deep descriptor is a pair (attUse, attMod), where *attUse*/*attMod* are sets of pairs (an, at) – *an* is the name of an attribute (state variable) used (read)/modified (written) by the behavior and *at* is its type, respectively.

As an example, assume two behaviors: office renting and house renting[3]. *Office renting* gets the client who rents the office and updates accordingly the clients list and the office availability status. Availability is checked based on the range of possible number of employees and the office status. *House renting* also gets the customer details, but updates only the customers list. Availability is checked based on the number of available beds. Both behaviors return whether they succeed or fail. Table 1 presents the shallow and deep behaviors of these operations.

**Table 1.** Examples of behavior representation

| Descriptor | Component | Office renting | House renting |
|---|---|---|---|
| Shallow | InOut | (rent, Boolean) | (rent, Boolean) |
|  | Params | (c, Client) | (c, Customer) |
| Deep | AttUse | (clients, ArrayList) (minEmployees, int) (maxEmployees, int) (status, OfficeStatus) | (customers, ArrayList) (beds, int) |
|  | AttMod | (clients, ArrayList) (status, OfficeStatus) | (customers, ArrayList) |

The behavior extraction is done through common static program analysis techniques. Particularly, we use Program Dependence Graph representation [12] to extract the deep descriptors from class operations in object-oriented code.

---

[2] The terms states and external events are defined in Bunge-Wand-Weber ontology as follows [28]: a *state* is a vector of values of state variables of a thing at a particular point in time; and *external event* is a change in the state of a thing as a result of an action of another thing.

[3] Due to space limitations, code examples from our running example are not included in the paper and can be found at https://sites.google.com/is.haifa.ac.il/varmer/ (additionals).

## 2.2 Behavior Comparison

In this step, the extracted behaviors are compared using similarity measures. The comparison of the low-level components, namely, inOut, params, attUse, and attMod, may be based on semantic nets or statistical techniques [17], whereas behavior comparison is done component-pairwise, namely, behaviors which have similar shallow and deep descriptors are the most similar. We categorize similarity mappings as follows.

**Definition 3.** Let B1, B2 be the components of the shallow/deep descriptors of behaviors b1, b2, respectively. Given a similarity mapping m:B1 × B2 → {0,1}, the corresponding behavior descriptors are claimed to follow[4]:

1. *USE* (abbreviation for use-as-is) – for each $c1 \in$ B1 there is exactly one $c2 \in$ B2 such that $m(c1, c2) = 1$ and for each $c2 \in$ B2 there is exactly one $c1 \in$ B1 such that $m(c1, c2) = 1$.
2. *REF* (abbreviation for refinement) – there is at least one $c1 \in$ B1 such that there are $c2, c2' \in$ B2 satisfying $m(c1, c2) = m(c1, c2') = 1$.
3. *EXT* (abbreviation for extension) – there is at least one $c2 \in$ B2 such that there is no $c1 \in$ B1 satisfying $m(c1, c2) = 1$.

The above mappings allow for a variety of relations between behaviors. Of those, behaviors whose shallow descriptors are related via USE are of special interest, since they intuitively correspond to the case when the behavior intensions as manifested by their interfaces are similar, but not necessarily identical. We thus distinguish between three types of potential mechanisms. These mechanisms, which are inspired by the notion of polymorphism in object-oriented programming, are defined below.

**Definition 4.** Let b1, b2 be two behaviors and m – a similarity mapping on their components. If the behavior shallow descriptors follow USE, then the behaviors are claimed to follow:

1. *Parametric* – if the behaviors' deep descriptors also follow USE.
2. *Subtyping* – if the behaviors' deep descriptors follow REF and/or EXT.
3. *Overloading* – if the behaviors' deep descriptors follow neither of USE, REF, or EXT.

Returning to our example, consider the office and house renting behaviors. They can be considered subtyping, as their shallow descriptors are related via USE, while their deep descriptors via EXT (office status has no counterpart) and REF (beds can be mapped to both min and max employees, as all are meant to estimate space capacity).

## 2.3 Variability Analysis

In the last step, the comparison results are percolated from the behavior level to the entities which exhibit them. In object-oriented terms, classes with similarly behaving

---

[4] In practice similarity have values in the range [0, 1]. Thus, we define all similarity values exceeding a pre-defined threshold as mapped to 1 ("similar") and all others – to 0 ("different").

operations are similar, and systems with similarly behaving classes are similar. The similarity relations are visualized as graphs whose nodes are entities (systems, classes, or even sub-systems or packages) and the edges represent the potential appropriateness of applying the different polymorphism-inspired mechanisms: parametric, subtyping, and overloading.

**Definition 5.** A *similarity graph* is a graph G = (V, E; w), where:

- V is a set of nodes of the same type (e.g., systems, classes, or operations). Each node holds its origin (e.g., system.class.operation).
- $E \subseteq V \times V$ is a set of edges.
- w: $E \rightarrow [0,1]^3$ is a weighting function that maps each edge to a triplet representing the parametric, subtyping, and overloading similarities of the connected vertices, respectively.

The weighting function on the level of behaviors (operations) always returns 1 (if the edge exists). On higher levels of abstractions, e.g., classes or systems, the weighting function reflects the fractions of operations which have counterparts. For example, let $C_1$ and $C_2$ be two classes exhibiting operations $\{o_{1i}\}_{i=1..n}$, $\{o_{2j}\}_{j=1..m}$, respectively. Then:

$$w(C_1, C_2) = \frac{\left|\{o_{1i} \in C_1 : \exists o_{2j} \in C_2 s.t. w(o_{1i}, o_{2j}) = 1\}\right| + \left|\{o_{2j} \in C_2 : \exists o \in C_1 s.t. w(o_{1i}, o_{2j}) = 1\}\right|}{m+n}.$$

An example of VarMeR outcome at the class level is shown in Fig. 1. Each system is visualized in a unique color. All classes depicted in yellow (House, Amenity, and Customer), for example, belong to RentCom. The classes House and Room of Find-Roommate, Office of WeWork, and House of RentCom similarly behave, as they all exhibit renting and availability checking operations. The two classes named Amenity (one of WeWork and the other of RentCom) and the class Facility of FindRoommate also share similar behaviors for managing amenities/facilities.

The class Roommate on the other hand is not similar (enough) to the classes Client and Customer, due to behaviors related to gender preferences exhibited only by the former class. This VarMeR outcome implies which types of assets need to be developed and reused in the systems: physical spaces (houses, rooms, and offices), amenities/facilities, and two types of stakeholders (clients/customers and roommates). Note that the slide bars at the top of the screen enables separately controlling similarity thresholds for each one of the mechanisms, directly affecting VarMeR recommendations. The sign "-" denotes a value lower than the corresponding specified threshold. Zooming into the classes, VarMeR can show the corresponding similar behaviors (not shown here, due to space limitation).

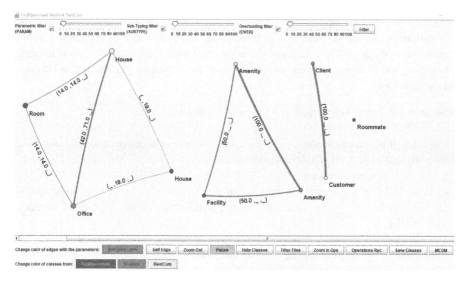

**Fig. 1.** A snapshot of VarMeR

# 3   The Suggested Approach for Extracting Domain Behaviors

VarMeR results in many recommendations. In order to extract (system) behaviors "of interest" in the domain of discourse rather than just similarly behaving operations, we apply machine learning. An overview of the suggested approach is depicted in Fig. 2. It is composed of three steps: (i) pre-processing – where behavior is extracted after the code is cleaned, e.g., by removing redundant code which may result from applying a cloning scenario; (ii) clustering similar behaviors, where sets of similar operations are suggested as potential domain behaviors; and (iii) domain behavior mining, where meaningful domain behaviors are extracted using machine learning techniques based on metrics of operations' characteristics.

The first pre-processing step was elaborated above. It further uses static analysis techniques to remove trivial operations, such as getters and setters, and redundant operations which may result from cloning. The rest of the section is devoted to the two other steps – clustering similar behaviors and mining domain behaviors, which together provide the core contributions of the suggested approach.

## 3.1   Clustering Similar Behaviors

In [23] we introduced an extension of the hierarchical agglomerative clustering algorithm for grouping similar behaviors. As behaviors may be related via different similarity types, namely, parametric, subtyping, and overloading, and hence have different similarity values, we suggested incorporating multi criteria decision making (MCDM) methods [27] into a clustering algorithm in order to group similar behaviors. A typical input of MCDM is a decision matrix, whose rows are the alternatives to be considered and its columns are the criteria. The cell [i,j] holds the evaluation given to alternative i with

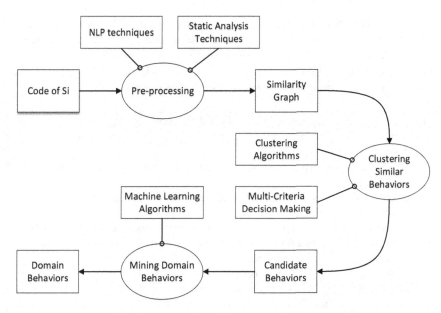

**Fig. 2.** An overview of the suggested approach

respect to criterion j. SAW – Simple Adaptive Weighting, for example, is an intuitive decision-making technique in which calculation is established based on a simple addition of scores that represent the goal achievement under each criterion, multiplied by some predefined weights [19]. In our context, we can weight parametric higher than subtyping and subtyping higher than overloading, in order to align preferences with the less effort required for adaptation. Table 2 exemplifies *part* of a decision matrix for selecting edges from the graph depicted in Fig. 1.

**Table 2.** *Part* of a decision matrix for selecting edges from the graph in Fig. 1

| Alternative | p | s | o | SAW score |
|---|---|---|---|---|
| (RentCom.Customer, WeWork.Client) | 1 | 0 | 0 | 3.00 |
| (RentCom.Amenity, WeWork.Amenity) | 1 | 0 | 0 | 3.00 |
| (RentCom.Facility, WeWork.Amenity) | 0.5 | 0 | 0 | 1.50 |
| (RentCom.House, FindRoommate.Room) | 0.14 | 0.14 | 0 | 1.03 |
| (FindRoommate.Room, WeWork.Office) | 0.14 | 0.14 | 0 | 1.03 |
| (WeWork.Office, FindRoommate.House) | 0 | 0.18 | 0 | 0.78 |

As similarity between operations may be accidental, namely, operations that happen to have similar interfaces and handle (use and modify) a similar set of state variables, we suggest here analyzing behavior similarity in the context of classes which own the operations. Listing 1 presents the pseudo code of the suggested clustering method for identifying similarly behaving classes. This method incorporates MCDM considerations, namely, it continues merging clusters which are suggested by a MCDM technique as best alternatives till a predefined threshold is reached.

Given a cluster of similarly behaving classes, we identify its potential domain behaviors as the maximal induced connected subgraphs of operations.

**Inputs:** G – a similarity graph at the class level, th – a similarity threshold, lnk – a linkage criterion (e.g., min, max, or avg for single, complete, or average linkage, respectively)

**Used structure:**

C is a set of clusters, where each cluster is a set of classes (namely, C is a set of sets).

D is a decision matrix

S is a triplet (C1, C2, score), where C1, C2 are clusters and score is a number.

**Used functions:**

C.initialize (G) – creates a set of |V| clusters, in each cluster a single node from the graph G.

D.create (C, G, lnk) – creates a decision matrix based on the given set of clusters, the similarity graph G, and the linkage metric lnk.

MCDM (D) – operates the MCDM methods on the decision matrix D and returns the alternative with the highest score including its score.

C.merge (C1, C2) – returns the set of clusters C, where C1 and C2 are merged and all other clusters are the same.

```
C.initialize (G)
Repeat
    D.create (C, G, lnk)
    S = MCDM (D)
    If (S.score > th)
        C.merge (S.C1, S.C2)
Until (S.score ≤ th)
return C
```

**Listing 1.** Pseudo code of clustering and identifying similarly behaving classes

**Definition 6.** Given a similarity graph $G = (V, E; w)$ and a cluster of similarly behaving classes $C \subseteq V$. A *candidate domain behavior* for cluster C is a maximal connected subgraph of $G|_C$ (i.e., the reduction of the similarity graph G to vertices in C).

Figure 3 exemplifies candidate domain behaviors for space rental applications.

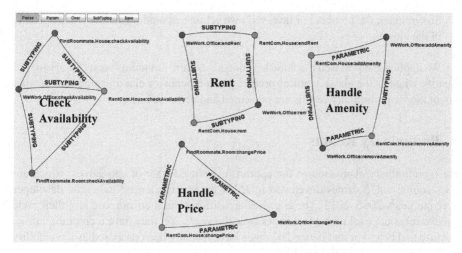

**Fig. 3.** Examples of candidate domain behaviors

### 3.2 Mining Domain Behaviors

The next stage is classifying whether the identified clusters, namely, the candidate domain behaviors, are indeed domain behaviors. The classification is commonly done by a human domain expert, but we explore in this study whether characteristics related to similarity, flow, and size of behaviors may provide good prediction. Thus, we identify three possibilities in which clusters may be mapped to domain behavior(s): specific, general, or irrelevant, as formalized below. For a cluster C and a domain behavior d, we denote C → d if C corresponds to d (namely, if a candidate domain behavior is indeed a domain behavior).

**Definition 7.** Let C be a cluster of similar behaviors (which may be obtained as a result of the previous step).

- C is *specific* if C → d for some (single) domain behavior d.
- C is *general* if there are different domain behaviors $d_1,\ldots,d_k$ such that $C = C_1 \cup \ldots \cup C_k$ and $C_i \to d_i$ for i = 1 to k.
- C is *irrelevant* if C is not specific neither general, i.e., there is no domain behavior d such that C → d or $C_i \to d_i$ where $C_i \subseteq C$.

As the set of domain behaviors is not known while conducting domain engineering, we now aim to build an automated classifier based on the above definition. The features which we hypothesize to be relevant for the classification belong to three categories:

1. Similarity-related: the normalized numbers of parametric, subtyping, and overloading relations *within* the cluster.
2. Flow-related: the minimal, maximal, and average numbers of operations invoking and being invoked by operations *within* the cluster.

3. Size-related: the numbers of involved instructions, operations, classes, and systems in the cluster.

We applied a supervised machine learning algorithm – random forest [5], in order to identify whether the above features predict domain behavior classification and to what extent. Some preliminary results are presented and discussed next.

## 4 Preliminary Results

For a preliminary evaluation of the approach, we used a set of apo-games, which are open-source video games developed in JAVA by an experienced industrial developer over the years 2006–2012. These games are different in their purpose and their code underwent some evolutionary changes over the years. Yet they have a common infrastructure and behavior and hence 20 games have recently been proposed as a variability reverse engineering challenge [14].

We selected two categories of the apo-games: 5 navigation games and 8 puzzle games. The characteristics of these games are summarized in Table 3. For each category, we extracted and created a similarity graph, using the semantic similarly metric proposed in [17]. We further clustered similar behaviors as described in Sect. 3.1, and collected and recorded the values of the features discussed in Sect. 3.2. 60 clusters were generated for the puzzle games and 62 – for the navigation games. Two human experts independently classified the 122 clusters into specific, general, and irrelevant domain behaviors, and discussed their classification till full agreement was reached. See Table 4 for characteristics of the resultant classification.

Overall, the initial candidate domain behaviors generated by our approach seem to be relevant (specific or general). Only few clusters (11.6% of puzzle and 4.8% of navigation) were found irrelevant. These were clusters containing low-level operations which seem unsuitable for being considered as domain behaviors. Several clusters (15% for puzzle and 16% for navigation) were found general, i.e., including operations which span across multiple domain behaviors.

While it may be possible to reduce the numbers of irrelevant and general clusters, we claim that complete avoidance is impossible, as operations and domain behaviors are assumed to be at different levels of abstraction. Thus, for automatization of domain behavior classification, we ran random forest in the WEKA framework [11] with the commonly used 5-fold cross-validation. The results are depicted in Table 5.

High F-measure values were obtained for specific clusters in both domains (0.891 and 0.911 for puzzle and navigation, respectively), demonstrating the potential for correctly extracting domain behaviors automatically. Irrelevant clusters were precisely classified, but had lower recall in both domains (0.286 and 0.667 for puzzle and navigation, respectively). Both precision and recall for the general category in both domains were relatively low. These results may be attributed to the low numbers of examples of these categories in the sample.

**Table 3.** Characteristics of the apo-games selected for evaluation (The values at the SLOC column are presented after cleaning redundant code, which is not used in given games and resulted from cloning the code of similar games.)

|  | Name | SLOC | Goal |
|---|---|---|---|
| Puzzle | ApoBot | 5,029 | To program a bot to turn the blue fields into red |
|  | ApoNotSoSimple | 5,770 | A clever but tricky puzzler with a possibility to build levels and publish them |
|  | ApoRelax | 4, 934 | To rearrange parts so that they give a picture |
|  | ApoSimple | 17,865 | To eliminate colored circles |
|  | ApoSlitherLink | 4,986 | To draw a closed path without intersections and ramifications of edges between the points of a grid |
|  | ApoSnake | 3,765 | A snake game with more than 30 levels and a possibility to upload more |
|  | ApoStarz | 5,039 | To return stars to their proper places |
|  | ApoSudoku | 4,119 | A Sudoku game |
| Navigation | ApoCommando | 8,053 | To make the player reach a goal by entering commands (such as "jump") in a command line |
|  | ApoIcarus | 4,466 | To reach the sun with Icarus by jumping from cloud to cloud without falling down or getting caught by an opponent |
|  | ApoIcejumpReloaded | 6,624 | Not to fall into the water as long as possible |
|  | ApoImp | 3,804 | To reach a Christmas tree, move gifts, beam around and climb |
|  | ApoMario | 15,801 | To navigate to the end of the level |

**Table 4.** Numbers of the candidate domain behaviors

|  | Puzzle games | Navigation games |
|---|---|---|
| Specific | 44 | 49 |
| General | 9 | 10 |
| Irrelevant | 7 | 3 |
| Total | 60 | 62 |

The most meaningful features for classification are mainly size-related (particularly the number of involved classes within the clusters) and flow-related (particularly the number of operations invoking operations within the clusters). These features look into the impact of the clustered operations across systems (apo-games) and thus are good predictors for domain behaviors. However, it should be noted that both of our considered

**Table 5.** Classification results

| | Class (Category) | Precision | Recall | F-Measure | ROC area | Strongest features |
|---|---|---|---|---|---|---|
| Puzzle | Specific | 0.854 | 0.932 | 0.891 | 0.807 | • size-related (# of classes, systems) <br> • similarity-related (overloading) <br> • flow-related (invoked by) |
| | General | 0.600 | 0.667 | 0.632 | 0.855 | |
| | Irrelevant | 1 | 0.286 | 0.444 | 0.642 | |
| | Weighted avg. | 0.833 | 0.817 | 0.800 | 0.795 | |
| Navigation | Specific | 0.885 | 0.939 | 0.911 | 0.841 | • size-related (# of classes) <br> • flow-related (invoked by, invokes) |
| | General | 0.625 | 0.500 | 0.556 | 0.862 | |
| | Irrelevant | 1 | 0.667 | 0.800 | 0.989 | |
| | Weighted avg. | 0.848 | 0.855 | 0.848 | 0.852 | |

domains are in the context of games. Indeed, we found behaviors common to the two categories of games, including behaviors dealing with buttons, images, mouse, audio/sound and more. Puzzle game behaviors further include level management and string manipulations, whereas navigation game behaviors also address entities, such as obstacles and enemies, locations and motions. Further investigation of generalizability of our method to other domains is needed. Particularly, running experiments in additional domains will help better isolate the important features that are not domain-specific.

## 5   Related Work

### 5.1   Variability Analysis

An important context in which domain engineering is commonly conducted is that of software product lines, which are families of systems that share common assets allowing systematic reuse [4, 18]. Apel et al. [1] provide a comprehensive overview of technical terms and techniques in the software product line engineering field from a feature-oriented perspective. Commonly, feature is a basic unit for commonality and variability analysis. In a recent literature review [2], feature detection is identified as the first phase of product line reengineering (followed by variability analysis and artifact transformation). In [13], three related tasks are mentioned: (1) feature identification – for determining the features that exist in a system based on a set of artifacts, revealing their dependencies and documenting the result (e.g., [15]); (2) feature location – for finding the artifacts (commonly source code) that implement a feature [8, 25]; and (3) feature mapping – for documenting the connection between a feature and its implementation (or realization). Of those, our suggested approach is mostly similar to feature identification. However, differently from existing methods, such as But4Reuse [15], which suggests features that are blocks of source code and thus actually low-level features, our approach provides more high-level domain features in the form of domain behaviors that may better support the development of reusable assets across systems.

Another context for application of variability analysis techniques is clone detection. Clones are segments of code that are similar according to some definition of similarity. Bellon et al. [3] identify three types of clones: Type 1 – exact copy without modifications (except for white space and comments); Type 2 – syntactically identical copy (only variable, type, or function identifiers were changed); and Type 3 – copy with further modifications (statements were changed, added, or removed). Other types of clones, such as semantic clones, structural clones, function clones, and model-based clones, are also mentioned in the literature [20, 24]. The main drawback of such approaches in our context is that they do the comparison (i.e., the similarity analysis) on the low level of implementations. Our approach, which takes a behavioral view, can better deal with analysis of artifacts which similarly behave but are differently designed (e.g., offices and houses).

### 5.2 Machine Learning in the Context of Systematic Reuse

While an increasing number of works apply machine learning techniques in software engineering [16, 29], works in the context of software reuse are scarcer. In the context of variability analysis, Ghofrani et al. [10] present a conceptual framework for clone detection using convolutional neural networks. In the context of software product lines, Safdar et al. [26] present an approach for mining rules for automatic configuration which combines multi-objective search with machine learning. Stefano and Menzies [7] performed a case study on a reuse data set using three different styles of learners: association rule, decision tree induction, and treatment and found some procedures which should significantly improve the odds of a reuse program succeeding. To the best of our knowledge, our approach is the first to apply machine learning techniques in the context of automatic support of domain engineering.

## 6   Summary and Future Research

Automatically supporting domain engineering is a challenging problem due to the required expert knowledge which heavily varies from one domain to another. So far most existing methods either assume high similarity of variants, or provide very low-level features which can mainly be used in cloning scenarios. This paper takes a new angle into the problem, proposing a method for extracting domain knowledge in the form of domain behaviors. The method builds on a previously developed framework for behavior-based variability analysis, applying on top of it clustering and machine learning techniques for domain behavior mining. The approach is evaluated on a subset of apo-games, open-source video games recently proposed as a variability reverse engineering challenge. Overall the results are promising in the sense of obtaining automatic classifiers for meaningful domain behaviors. Yet the obtained results are highly dependent on the availability of datasets annotated by human experts and the correctness of their annotations. One immediate direction for future research is considering unsupervised learning approaches and convolutional neural networks to reduce this dependency.

Another immediate direction for future research relates to improvement of the method design and its evaluation, including: (1) exploring additional clustering, MCDM, and machine learning techniques; (2) performing evaluation in additional domains, e.g., in the automotive or manufacturing sector; (3) conducting more large scale empirical studies for evaluating the suggested approach in different settings; and (4) comparing the approach to the state-of-the-art feature extraction methods.

Finally, we intend to further extend the approach to support systematic reuse, e.g., by guiding the creation of reusable artifacts or services, using the identified domain behaviors. We envision this to be done using code manipulation techniques such as refactoring. Extension of the behavior-based framework is also considered, in order to support further mechanisms whose shallow descriptors are not related via USE.

**Acknowledgement.** The authors would like to thank Anna Zamansky for her advice to the formal parts and her help in the evaluation of the approach.

# References

1. Apel, S., Batory, D., Kästner, C., Saake, G.: Feature-Oriented Software Product Lines. Springer, Heidelberg (2016). https://doi.org/10.1007/978-3-642-37521-7
2. Assunção, W.K.G., Lopez-Herrejon, R.E., Linsbauer, L., Vergilio, S.R., Egyed, A.: Reengineering legacy applications into software product lines: a systematic mapping. Empir. Softw. Eng. **22**(6), 2972–3016 (2017). https://doi.org/10.1007/s10664-017-9499-z
3. Bellon, S., Koschke, R., Antoniol, G., Krinke, J., Merlo, E.: Comparison and evaluation of clone detection tools. IEEE Trans. Softw. Eng. **33**(9), 577–591 (2007)
4. Clements, P., Northrop, L.: Software Product Lines. Addison-Wesley, Boston (2002)
5. Cutler, A., Cutler, D.R., Stevens, J.R.: Random forests. In: Zhang, C., Ma, Y. (eds.) Ensemble Machine Learning, pp. 157–175. Springer, Boston (2012). https://doi.org/10.1007/978-1-4419-9326-7_5
6. Debbiche, J., Lignell, O., Krüger, J., Berger, T.: Migrating the Java-based apo-games into a composition-based software product line. In: 23rd International Systems and Software Product Line Conference (SPLC), Challenge Track (2019)
7. Di Stefano, J.S., Menzies, T.: Machine learning for software engineering: case studies in software reuse. In: 14th IEEE International Conference on Tools with Artificial Intelligence, ICTAI 2002, Proceedings, pp. 246–251. IEEE, November 2002
8. Dit, B., Revelle, M., Gethers, M., Poshyvanyk, D.: Feature location in source code: a taxonomy and survey. J. Softw. Evol. Process **25**(1), 53–95 (2013)
9. Falbo, R.D.A., Guizzardi, G., Duarte, K.C.: An ontological approach to domain engineering. In: Proceedings of the 14th International Conference on Software Engineering and Knowledge Engineering, pp. 351–358. ACM, July 2002
10. Ghofrani, J., Mohseni, M., Bozorgmehr, A.: A conceptual framework for clone detection using machine learning. In: IEEE 4th International Conference on Knowledge-Based Engineering and Innovation (KBEI), pp. 0810–0817. IEEE, December 2017
11. Holmes, G., Donkin, A., Witten, I.H.: Weka: a machine learning workbench (1994)
12. Krinke, J.: Identifying similar code with program dependence graphs. In: Proceedings Eighth Working Conference on Reverse Engineering, pp. 301–309. IEEE, October 2001
13. Krüger, J., Berger, T., Leich, T.: Features and how to find them: a survey of manual feature location. In: Mistrik, I., Galster, M., Maxim, B. (eds.) Software Engineering for Variability Intensive Systems: Foundations and Applications. Taylor & Francis Group, LLC/CRC Press (2018)

14. Krüger, J., Fenske, W., Thüm, T., Aporius, D., Saake, G., Leich, T.: Apo-games: a case study for reverse engineering variability from cloned Java variants. In: Proceedings of the 22nd International Conference on Systems and Software Product Line-Volume 1, pp. 251–256. ACM, September 2018

15. Martinez, J., Ziadi, T., Bissyandé, T.F., Klein, J., Traon, Y.L.: Bottom-up technologies for reuse: automated extractive adoption of software product lines. In: Proceedings of the 39th International Conference on Software Engineering Companion, pp. 67–70. IEEE Press, May 2017

16. Menzies, T.: Practical machine learning for software engineering and knowledge engineering. In: Handbook of Software Engineering and Knowledge Engineering: Volume I: Fundamentals, pp. 837–862 (2001)

17. Mihalcea, R., Corley, C., Strapparava, C.: Corpus-based and knowledge-based measures of text semantic similarity. American Association for Artificial Intelligence, AAAI 2006, pp. 775–780 (2006)

18. Pohl, K., Böckle, G., van Der Linden, F.J.: Software Product Line Engineering: Foundations, Principles and Techniques. Springer, Heidelberg (2005). https://doi.org/10.1007/3-540-289 01-1

19. Qin, X., Huang, G., Chakma, A., Nie, X., Lin, Q.: A MCDM-based expert system for climate-change impact assessment and adaptation planning – a case study for the Georgia Basin. Can. Expert Syst. Appl. **34**(3), 2164–2179 (2008)

20. Rattan, D., Bhatia, R., Singh, M.: Software clone detection: a systematic review. Inf. Softw. Technol. **55**(7), 1165–1199 (2013)

21. Reinhartz-Berger, I., Zamansky, A.: VarMeR – a variability mechanisms recommender for software artifacts. In: CAiSE-Forum-DC, pp. 57–64 (2017)

22. Reinhartz-Berger, I., Zamansky, A.: A behavior-based framework for assessing product line-ability. In: Krogstie, J., Reijers, Hajo A. (eds.) CAiSE 2018. LNCS, vol. 10816, pp. 571–586. Springer, Cham (2018). https://doi.org/10.1007/978-3-319-91563-0_35

23. Reinhartz-Berger, I., Abbas, S., Zamansky, A.: Towards polymorphism-inspired recommendation on software product line artifacts. In: Proceedings of Models and Evolution Workshops, MODELS 2019 (2019)

24. Roy, C.K., Cordy, J.R., Koschke, R.: Comparison and evaluation of code clone detection techniques and tools: a qualitative approach. Sci. Comput. Program. **74**(7), 470–495 (2009)

25. Rubin, J., Chechik, M.: A survey of feature location techniques. In: Reinhartz-Berger, I., Sturm, A., Clark, T., Cohen, S., Bettin, J. (eds.) Domain Engineering, pp. 29–58. Springer, Heidelberg (2013). https://doi.org/10.1007/978-3-642-36654-3_2

26. Safdar, S.A., Lu, H., Yue, T., Ali, S.: Mining cross product line rules with multi-objective search and machine learning. In: Proceedings of the Genetic and Evolutionary Computation Conference, pp. 1319–1326. ACM, July 2017

27. Velasquez, M., Hester, P.T.: An analysis of multi-criteria decision making methods. Int. J. Oper. Res. **10**(2), 56–66 (2013)

28. Wand, Y., Weber, R.: On the deep structure of information systems. Inf. Syst. J. **5**(3), 203–223 (1995)

29. Zhang, D., Tsai, J.J. (eds.): Machine Learning Applications in Software Engineering, vol. 16. World Scientific Inc. Publishers, USA (2005)

# Mutation Operators for Large Scale Data Processing Programs in Spark

João Batista de Souza Neto[1]([🖂]) [iD], Anamaria Martins Moreira[2] [iD],
Genoveva Vargas-Solar[3] [iD], and Martin Alejandro Musicante[1] [iD]

[1] Department of Informatics and Applied Mathematics (DIMAp),
Federal University of Rio Grande do Norte, Natal, Brazil
jbsneto@ppgsc.ufrn.br, mam@dimap.ufrn.br
[2] Computer Science Department (DCC), Federal University of Rio de Janeiro,
Rio de Janeiro, Brazil
anamaria@dcc.ufrj.br
[3] University Grenoble Alpes, CNRS, Grenoble INP, LIG-LAFMIA, Grenoble, France
genoveva.vargas@imag.fr

**Abstract.** This paper proposes a mutation testing approach for big data processing programs that follow a data flow model, such as those implemented on top of Apache Spark. Mutation testing is a fault-based technique that relies on fault simulation by modifying programs, to create faulty versions called *mutants*. Mutant creation is carried on by operators able to simulate specific and well identified faults. A testing process must be able to signal faults within mutants and thereby avoid having ill behaviours within a program. We propose a set of mutation operators designed for Spark programs characterized by a data flow and data processing operations. These operators model changes in the data flow and operations, to simulate faults that take into account Spark program characteristics. We performed manual experiments to evaluate the proposed mutation operators in terms of cost and effectiveness. Thereby, we show that mutation operators can contribute to the testing process, in the construction of reliable Spark programs.

**Keywords:** Big data · Spark programs · Mutation testing · Mutation operators

## 1 Introduction

The intrinsic characteristics of data and associated processing environments introduce challenges to the development of *big data* processing programs. These programs need to deal with data *Volume*; *Velocity* in which data is produced;

This study was financed in part by the Coordenação de Aperfeiçoamento de Pessoal de Nível Superior - Brasil (CAPES) - Finance Code 001.

S. Dustdar et al. (Eds.): CAiSE 2020, LNCS 12127, pp. 482–497, 2020.
https://doi.org/10.1007/978-3-030-49435-3_30

*Variety* of representation and *Veracity* level of the data. These technical characteristics, allied to the *Value* of the knowledge obtained by processing big data (the *five V's* [18]), have contributed to the development of systems and frameworks adapted to big data processing.

Existing frameworks adopt either control flow [4,6] or data flow approaches [3, 26,28]. In both cases, frameworks provide a complete and general execution environment that automates lower level tasks (processing and data distribution and fault tolerance), allowing developers to (mostly) concentrate on the algorithmic aspects of big data programs.

Reliability of big data processing programs becomes important, due to the fine-grain tuning required, regarding both the programming logic and particularly, their extensive use of computational resources [12]. This introduces the need to verify and validate programs before running them in production in a costly distributed environment. In this context, software testing techniques emerge as important and key tools. Testing big data processing programs is an open issue that is receiving increasing attention [5,20]. There exist only few works on functional testing of big data programs, most of them address testing of programs built using control flow based programming models like MapReduce [20].

This paper addresses big data programming testing by exploring the application of Mutation Testing on Apache Spark programs. Mutation testing is a fault-based technique that explores the creation of erroneous versions of a program, called *mutants*, to generate and evaluate tests. Mutants are created by applying modification rules, called mutation operators, that define how to create faulty versions from a program. In this paper, we present a set of mutation operators based on the data flow model of Apache Spark programs. We manually applied our mutation operators in an experiment to show the feasibility of mutation testing in Spark programs and to make a preliminary assessment of application costs and effectiveness of the proposed mutation operators. The results of these experiments agree with the preliminary results obtained using a prototype, currently under development[1].

This paper is organized as follows: Sect. 2 describes works that have addressed some aspects of big data program testing. Section 3 introduces the main concepts of mutation testing adopted in our work. Section 4 introduces Apache Spark and presents the set of mutation operators that we designed for Spark programs. Section 5 describes our experimental setting and discusses results. Section 6 concludes the paper and discusses future work.

---

[1] The description of the prototype is out of the scope of this paper. The interested reader can refer to https://github.com/jbsneto-ppgsc-ufrn/transmut-spark for technical details of the tool.

## 2    Related Work

The emerging need of processing big data together with the democratization of access to computing power has led to the proposal of environments providing solutions that ease the development of big data processing programs at scale. Even if these environments prevent programmers from dealing with the burden of low level control issues (e.g. fault tolerance, data and process distribution), programming must still consider several details regarding data flow (e.g., explicit data caching, exchange, sharing requests). Thus, testing methodologies must be proposed considering the particular characteristics of big data.

The testing of big data processing programs has gained interest as pointed out in [5] and [20]. Most work has focused on performance testing since performance is a major concern in a big data environment given the computational resources required [20]. Regarding functional testing, few works have been done, most of them being concentrated on MapReduce [20], leaving an open research area for testing big data programs on other models and technologies.

The work in [8] applies symbolic execution to search for test cases and data. It proposes to encode MapReduce correctness conditions into symbolic program constraints which are then used to derive the test cases and test data. The proposal in [16] applies a similar technique to test *Pig Latin* [22] programs. The MRFlow technique in [19] builds a data flow graph to define the paths to test and uses *graph-based testing* [1] to search for test cases in MapReduce.

Concerning data flow systems, most of the them support unit test execution for their programs. The work in [14] provides a framework that supports execution of unit testing and property checking of Spark programs. The tool does not provide support for the design of test cases, which is a critical part of the testing process. The area is still lacking techniques and tools that exploit the characteristics of big data processing programs, showing that more research needs to be done. Mutation testing provides criteria for the systematic design of test cases. In this context, our work explores both the design and application of mutation testing in Spark.

## 3    Mutation Testing

Mutation testing is a fault-based technique based on creating variants of a program, called *mutants*, simulating common faults inserted through simple modifications to the original program [1]. Mutants can be used to design test cases that identify the simulated faults or to assess the quality of an already implemented test set by looking if it can identify erroneous behaviors generated by the mutants. Different studies [11,21,25] have shown the effectiveness of mutation testing by comparing it with other testing criteria and techniques.

A general mutation testing process is shown in Fig. 1. Given a source program assumed to be nearly correct (developed by a competent programmer), Mutation Generation consists in creating variations of the program ( *Mutants*), by introducing changes or *mutations* to the source code. Examples of classic mutations include the replacement of literals in the program (*value mutations*); substitution of operators in expressions or conditions (*decision mutations*) and the deletion or duplication of statements (*statement mutations*) [1]. This phase of the testing process is strongly dependent on the model or language of the program being tested and on a number of *mutation operators*, rules which define how to derive mutants from the original program. The task of generating mutants of a given program can be automated using parsing and source-to-source code generation techniques.

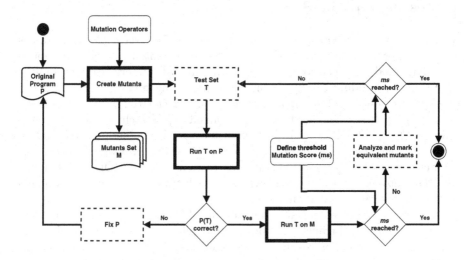

**Fig. 1.** Mutation testing process (Adapted from [1]).

The production of test cases is the next stage of the process. In this step input data, corresponding to each test case, is defined for the program and its mutants. The results of executing the test cases with each mutant are compared with the results obtained by the original program. A mutant is said to be *killed* if its results differ from those of the original program for some test case. The goal of a test set is then to kill as many mutants as possible. This indicates that the test set was able to detect the potential inserted code defects. Mutants that produce the same results as the original program, no matter which input data is provided, cannot be killed and are said to be *equivalent* to the original program.

Given a program $P$ and a set of test cases $T$, a *mutation score* is given by:

$$ms(P,T) = \frac{DM(P,T)}{M(P) - EM(P)}$$

where $DM(P,T)$ is the number of killed mutants; $M(P)$ is the number of mutants and $EM(P)$ is the number of mutants that are *equivalent* to $P$. The mutation score measures the quality of the test set. This score is used to decide whether to produce more test cases, to improve the test set or to stop the testing process.

Mutation testing is strongly influenced by the programming model, language and framework of the target program. Thus, mutation operators and tools have been developed to support mutation testing for different contexts as shown in [13]. Such contexts include mutation operators and tools for programs in specific languages like C [23] and Java [17], aspect-oriented programs [10] and web services [15]. To the best of our knowledge, there is no previous work addressing mutation testing for data flow programs in the context of big data processing.

# 4    Testing Apache Spark Programs

Apache Spark is a general-purpose analytics engine for large-scale data processing on cluster systems [28]. It adopts a data flow-oriented programming model with data models, execution plans and programming interfaces with built in operations as building blocks for big data processing programs. Spark is centered on the concept of *Resilient Distributed Dataset* (RDD) [27], a read-only, fault-tolerant data collection that is partitioned across a cluster. RDDs can be processed by two kinds of operations: transformations and actions. Transformations are operations that result in a new RDD from processing another one. Actions are operations that generate values that are not RDDs or that save the RDD into an external storage system. Spark transformations are evaluated under a lazy strategy when an action is called.

A Spark program is defined as a set of initial RDDs loaded from an external storage, a sequence of transformations to be applied on these RDDs and actions that trigger the program execution. The sequence of operations implementing a Spark program is represented by a *Directed Acyclic Graph* (DAG) which acts as execution plan defining dependencies between transformations and representing the program data flow. These aspects are key elements for developing specific testing methodologies.

Spark provides a set of transformations for a wide variety of data processing operations. These transformations are described by a high-level interface with input parameters, which are functions that are applied to process elements on the RDD, and outputs. We classify transformations into families, according to the type of processing operation: *Mapping*, apply functions to map one element of the RDD to another (*e.g.*, map and flatMap); *Filtering*, filter elements based on predicate functions that determine whether an element should remain in the RDD (*e.g.*, filter); *Aggregation*, aggregate elements applying a binary function on the RDD elements (*e.g.*, reduceByKey and aggregateByKey); *Set*, operate like mathematical set operations on two RDDs (*e.g.*, union and intersection); *Join*, make a relational-like join between two RDDs (*e.g.*, (inner) join and leftOuterJoin); and *Ordering*, for operations that sort the elements on the RDD (*e.g.*, sortBy and sortByKey). We call unary transformations those that operate on a single RDD and binary transformations those that operate on two RDDs.

In order to propose a fault based approach for testing Apache Spark programs, we first studied representative example programs and the framework documentation to identify common faults or mistakes. Within Spark's programming approach, a program is defined by a *(i)* data flow that defines data transmission, sharing, caching and persistence strategies to be adopted by processes running on cluster components; and *(ii)* data processing operations. Considering this characteristic of Spark programs we have classified faults that can emerge within these complementary aspects and proposed a fault taxonomy. This taxonomy was then used as reference to the definition of the mutation operators that are a key element of our mutation testing based approach[2]. The mutation operators we propose have been designed considering the Spark data flow model and its operations (transformations). These components are independent of the programming language chosen to develop Spark programs (which can be done in Scala, Java or Python). Thus, our mutation operators are agnostic to the programming language and can be applied to any program that follows the data flow model of Spark. The next sections introduce these operators and their experimental validation.

## 4.1   Mutation Operators for Apache Spark Programs

Mutation operators are rules that define changes on a program to add simulated faults. These operators are designed to mimic common faults, such as a missing iteration of a loop or a mistake in an arithmetical or logical expression, or to prompt testers to follow common test heuristics, such as requiring a test where a specific action is executed [1].

Common faults and mistakes in Spark programs are generally related to the incorrect definition of the data flow of a program, such as calling transformations in a wrong order, and mistakes in specific transformations, such as calling the wrong transformation or passing the wrong parameter.

In this paper, we propose two groups of mutation operators: *data flow* and *transformations*. Data flow operators define modifications in the sequence of transformations of a program (*i.e.*, altering the flow of data between transformations). Transformation operators define modifications in specific groups of transformations, like replacing a transformation by another or changing a parameter. This section introduces these operators intuitively see their formal definition in [9].

**Mutation Operators for the Data Flow:** Operators in this class change the sequence of operations that defines the data flow of a Spark program.

*Unary Transformations Replacement (UTR)* - Replace one unary transformation for another with the same input and output signature (RDD types).

*Unary Transformation Swap (UTS)* - Swap the calls of two transformations of the program, provided that they have the same input and output signature.

---

[2] The fault taxonomy of Spark programs and the mutation operators formalization are out of the scope of this paper, but are described in [9].

*Unary Transformation Deletion (UTD)* - Bypass a transformation that has the same RDD type as input and output.

We also define operators similar to UTS and UTR, adapted to binary transformations: *Binary Transformation Swap* (BTS) and *Binary Transformations Replacement* (BTR).

To illustrate the mutation operators for data flow, let us consider the excerpt from a Spark program presented in Fig. 2. In this program we manipulate an integer RDD (input: RDD[Int]). Line 1 filters the even numbers of the dataset. Then, each number is mapped to its square (line 2). Finally, the RDD is sorted (line 3). All the mutants generated for this program by our data flow mutation operators are presented in Table 1. In that table, only the lines affected by the mutation are included. For instance, applying the UTS operator to the transformations in lines 1 and 2, results in the mutant 7 of Table 1. In this mutant, the filter transformation that was called on line 1 is swapped with the map transformation that was called on line 2 in the original program.

```
1    val even = input.filter(x => x % 2 == 0)
2    val square = even.map(x => x * x)
3    val sorted = square.sortBy(x => x)
```

**Fig. 2.** Example of part of a Spark program.

**Table 1.** Mutants generated with the data flow mutation operators.

| Id | Operator | Lines | Mutation |
|----|----------|-------|----------|
| 1 | UTR | 1 | val even =input.map( x =>x * x ) |
| 2 | UTR | 1 | val even =input.sortBy( x =>x ) |
| 3 | UTR | 2 | val square =even.filter( x =>x % 2 ==0 ) |
| 4 | UTR | 2 | val square =even.sortBy( x =>x ) |
| 5 | UTR | 3 | val sorted =square.filter( x =>x % 2 ==0 ) |
| 6 | UTR | 3 | val sorted =square.map( x =>x * x ) |
| 7 | UTS | 1,2 | val even = input.map(x => x * x)<br>val square = even.filter(x => x % 2 == 0) |
| 8 | UTS | 1,3 | val even = input.sortBy(x => x)<br>val sorted = square.filter(x => x % 2 == 0) |
| 9 | UTS | 2,3 | val square = even.sortBy(x => x)%<br>val sorted = square.map(x => x * x) |
| 10 | UTD | 1 | val even =input |
| 11 | UTD | 2 | val square =even |
| 12 | UTD | 3 | val sorted =square |

**Mutation Operators for Transformations:** In this class of operators, changes are made in specific transformations in a Spark program. Table 2 provides examples of mutants that are generated with the operators presented below.

**Table 2.** Mutants generated with the transformation mutation operators.

| Id | Operator | Line | Mutation |
|----|----------|------|----------|
| 1 | MTR | 2 | val square =even.map(x =>0) |
| 2 | MTR | 2 | val square =even.map(x =>1) |
| 3 | MTR | 2 | val square =even.map(x =>Int.MaxValue) |
| 4 | MTR | 2 | val square =even.map(x =>Int.MinValue) |
| 5 | MTR | 2 | val square =even.map(x =>−(x * x)) |
| 6 | FTD | 1 | val even =input |
| 7 | NFTP | 1 | val even =input.filter(x =>!(x % 2 ==0)) |
| 8 | STR | – | val rdd3 =rdd1.intersection(rdd2) |
| 9 | STR | – | val rdd3 =rdd1.subtract(rdd2) |
| 10 | STR | – | val rdd3 =rdd1 |
| 11 | STR | – | val rdd3 =rdd2 |
| 12 | STR | – | val rdd3 =rdd2.union(rdd1) |
| 13 | DTD | – | val rdd4 =rdd3 |
| 14 | DTI | 1 | val even =input.filter(x =>x % 2 ==0).distinct() |
| 15 | DTI | 2 | val square =even.map(x =>x * x).distinct() |
| 16 | DTI | 3 | val sorted =square.sortBy(x =>x).distinct() |
| 17 | ATR | – | val rdd4 =rdd3.reduceByKey((x, y)=>x) |
| 18 | ATR | – | val rdd4 =rdd3.reduceByKey((x, y)=>y) |
| 19 | ATR | – | val rdd4 =rdd3.reduceByKey((x, y)=>x + x) |
| 20 | ATR | – | val rdd4 =rdd3.reduceByKey((x, y)=>y + y) |
| 21 | ATR | – | val rdd4 =rdd3.reduceByKey((x, y)=>y + x) |
| 22 | JTR | – | val rdd4 = rdd3.leftOuterJoin(rdd2)<br>.map(x => (x._1,<br>(x._2._1, x._2._2.getOrElse("")))) |
| 23 | JTR | – | val rdd4 = rdd3.rightOuterJoin(rdd2)<br>.map(x => (x._1,<br>(x._2._1.getOrElse(0), x._2._2))) |
| 24 | JTR | – | val rdd4 = rdd3.fullOuterJoin(rdd2)<br>.map(x => (x._1,<br>(x._2._1.getOrElse(0), x._2._2.getOrElse("")))) |
| 25 | OTD | 3 | val sorted =square |
| 26 | OTI | 3 | val sorted =square.sortBy(x =>x, ascending =false) |

*Mapping Transformation Replacement (MTR)* - for each mapping transformation (map, flatMap) in the program, replace the mapping function passed as a parameter to that transformation by a different mapping function. We propose a mapping function that returns a constant value of the same type as the original, or makes some modification to the value returned by the original function. For example, for a mapping function that operates on integers, we can replace this function by one that returns zero or another that reverses the sign of the value returned by the original. In Table 3 we present mapping values of basic types and collections that can be returned by the mutant mapping function. To illustrate the MTR operator, consider the mapping transformation applied in line 2 of Fig. 2. The operator generates mutants 1–5 in Table 2.

**Table 3.** Mapping values for basic and collections types.

| Type | Mapping value |
|---|---|
| Numeric | $0, 1, MAX, MIN, -x$ |
| Boolean | $true, false, \neg x$ |
| String | " " |
| List | $List(x.head), x.tail, x.reverse, Nil$ |
| Tuple | $(k_m, v), (k, v_m)$ |
| General | $null$ |

Description: $x$ represents the value generated by the original mapping function; $k$ and $v$ represents the key and value generated by the original mapping function in case of Key-Value tuples; $k_m$ and $v_m$ represents modified values for the key and value, which is the application of other mapping values respecting the type.

*Filter Transformation Deletion (FTD)* - for each filter transformation in the program, create a mutant where the call to that transformation is deleted from the program. For example, considering the filter transformation in line 1 of Fig. 2, applying the FTD operator generates the mutation of line 6 in Table 2.

*Negation of Filter Transformation Predicate (NFTP)* - for each filter transformation in the program, replace the predicate function passed as a parameter to that transformation by a predicate function that negates the result of the original function. For the filter transformation in line 1 of Fig. 2, the NFTP operator generates the mutation 7 in Table 2.

*Set Transformation Replacement (STR)* - for each occurrence of a set transformation (union, intersection and subtract) in a program, create five mutants: (1–2) replacing the transformation by each of the other remaining set transformations, (3) keeping just the first RDD, (4) keeping just the second RDD, and (5) changing the order of the RDDs in the transformation call. For example, given the following excerpt of code with a union between two RDDs:

```
val rdd3 = rdd1.union(rdd2)
```

The application of the STR operator to this transformation creates the five mutants, described by lines 8–12 in Table 2.

*Distinct Transformation Deletion (DTD)* - for each call of a distinct transformation in the program, create a mutant by deleting it. As the distinct transformation removes duplicated data from the RDD, this mutation keeps the duplicates. For example, the application of DTD in the following excerpt of code generates the mutant 13 of Table 2:

```
val rdd4 = rdd3.distinct()
```

*Distinct Transformation Insertion (DTI)* - for each transformation in the program, create a mutant inserting a distinct transformation call after that transformation. Applying DTI to the transformations presented in Fig. 2 generates the mutants 14–16 of Table 2.

*Aggregation Transformation Replacement (ATR)* - for each aggregation transformation in the program, replace the aggregation function passed as a parameter by a different aggregation function. We propose five replacement functions. For an original function $f(x, y)$, the replacement functions $f_m(x, y)$ are defined as: (1) a function that returns the first parameter ($f_m(x, y) = x$); (2) a function that returns the second parameter ($f_m(x, y) = y$); (3) a function that ignores the second parameter and calls the original function with a duplicated first parameter ($f_m(x, y) = f(x, x)$); (4) a function that ignores the first parameter and calls the original function with a duplicated second parameter ($f_m(x, y) = f(y, y)$); and (5) a function that swaps the order of the parameters ($f_m(x, y) = f(y, x)$), which generates a different value for non-commutative functions. For example, considering the following excerpt of code with an aggregation transformation (reduceByKey) and an aggregation function that adds two values, the application of ATR generates the mutants 17–21 of Table 2.

```
val rdd4 = rdd3.reduceByKey((x, y) => x + y)
```

*Join Transformation Replacement (JTR)* - for each occurrence of a join transformation ((inner) join, leftOuterJoin, rightOuterJoin and fullOuterJoin) in the program, replace that transformation by the remaining three join transformations. Additionally, a map transformation is inserted after the join to adjust the typing of the new join with the old one. This is necessary because depending on the join type, the left side, right side, or both can be optional, which makes the resulting RDD of the new join slightly different from the previous one. So we adjust the type of the resulting RDD to be of the same type as the original join. For example, replacing the join transformation by leftOuterJoin makes right-side values optional. To keep type consistency with the original transformation, we map empty right-side values to default values, in case of basic types, or null, otherwise.

To illustrate the JTR operator, let us consider the following code snippet where two RDDs are joined. Assume that rdd3 is of type RDD[(Int, Int)] and that rdd2 is of type RDD[(Int, String)]. The resulting RDD of this join (rdd4) is of type RDD[(Int, (Int, String))]. Applying JTR to this transformation generates the mutants 22–24 of Table 1. Taking mutant 22 as an example, replacing join with leftOuterJoin, the resulting RDD is of type RDD[(Int, (Int, Option[String]))]. Thus, the map following the leftOuterJoin serves to set the value of type Option[String] to String. When this value is empty (None), we assign the empty string (""").

val rdd4 = rdd3.join(rdd2)

*Order Transformation Deletion (OTD)* - for each order transformation (sortBy and sortByKey) in the program, create a mutant where the call to that transformation is deleted from the program. For example, considering the order transformation called in line 3 of Fig. 2, the application of OTD generates the mutant 25 of Table 2.

*Order Transformation Inversion (OTI)* - for each order transformation in the program, create a mutant where the ordering of that transformations is replaced by the inverse ordering (ascending or descending). Applying OTI to the same order transformation of Fig. 2 generates the mutant 26 of Table 2, where the ascending ordering that is true by default was changed for false.

## 5   Experiments

We conducted experiments to evaluate the cost and effectiveness of the proposed mutation operators. We selected a set of eight representative Spark programs[3] to apply the mutation testing process described in Fig. 1. These programs perform common data analysis such as text and log analysis, queries on tabular datasets inspired by the benchmark presented in [2], and data exploration and recommendation based on the collaborative filtering algorithm [24]. These programs were selected to explore the features necessary to apply the operators, such as having data flow and transformations commonly used in Spark programs and that could be modified in the testing process.

The experiments presented in this section show a first assessment of the mutation operators. The process described in Fig. 1 was strictly followed, by manually executing each step. For each code to be tested, and each applicable mutation operator, the source was edited to simulate the application of the operator, generating a mutant. A script was then executed to run each mutant. Test cases were developed incrementally to kill the mutants. Comparison of the results with the original program and metrics calculation were also executed manually. Once we implemented a prototype mutation testing tool, the results of these experiments evaluated and results were corroborated.

Finally, we performed a cost analysis based on the number of mutants generated and tests needed to kill all mutants ($ms = 100\%$). We also analyzed the effectiveness of the mutation operators by identifying the operators that generated mutants that were killed by most of the tests and operators that generated mutants that were harder to kill. Table 4 summarizes the results for each

---

[3] The programs used in the experiments of this work are publicly available at https://github.com/jbsneto-ppgsc-ufrn/spark-mutation-testing-experiments.

program, showing the number of transformations in each program, number of mutants, number of tests created, number of killed mutants, number of equivalent mutants, and mutation score ($ms$).

**Table 4.** Total of mutants and tests per program.

| Program | Transformations | Mutants | Tests | Killed | Equiv. | $ms$ (%) |
|---|---|---|---|---|---|---|
| NGramsCount | 5 | 27 | 5 | 20 | 5 | 100 |
| ScanQuery | 3 | 12 | 3 | 12 | 0 | 100 |
| AggregationQuery | 3 | 15 | 3 | 11 | 2 | 100 |
| DistinctUserVisitsPerPage | 4 | 16 | 2 | 10 | 6 | 100 |
| MoviesRatingsAverage | 5 | 25 | 4 | 22 | 3 | 100 |
| MoviesRecomendation | 12 | 37 | 5 | 33 | 4 | 100 |
| JoinQuery | 11 | 27 | 6 | 25 | 2 | 100 |
| NasaApacheWebLogsAnalysis | 7 | 55 | 4 | 49 | 6 | 100 |
| **Total** | **50** | **214** | **32** | **182** | **28** | – |

Table 5 summarizes the results aggregated for each mutation operator. It shows the total number of mutants generated by the operator, the number of equivalent mutants and the *killed ratio*[4]. The killed ratio shows how easy it was to kill the mutants generated with that mutation operator. Thus, operators with a low ratio generated mutants harder to kill (they required more specific tests). This measures the effectiveness of the mutation operator because mutants that are not killed trivially (get killed by any test) simulate faults that are not easily revealed.

**Table 5.** Total of mutants and killed ratio per mutation operator.

| Mut. Op. | # of Mutants | # of Equiv. | Killed Ratio (%) | Mut. Op. | # of Mutants | # of Equiv. | Killed Ratio (%) |
|---|---|---|---|---|---|---|---|
| UTS | 11 | 2 | 67,6 | STR | 10 | 2 | 34,4 |
| BTS | 1 | 0 | 75,0 | DTI | 31 | 10 | 27,7 |
| UTR | 22 | 2 | 39,0 | DTD | 1 | 0 | 25,0 |
| BTR | 2 | 0 | 37,5 | ATR | 20 | 4 | 46,4 |
| UTD | 6 | 0 | 32,0 | JTR | 6 | 3 | 22,2 |
| MTR | 82 | 5 | 76,1 | OTI | 4 | 0 | 30,0 |
| FTD | 7 | 0 | 34,4 | OTD | 4 | 0 | 20,0 |
| NFTP | 7 | 0 | 65,6 | | | | |

The mutation operators for data flow (UTS, BTS, UTR, BTR and UTD) were responsible for 19,6% of the generated mutants. The number of mutants

---

[4] The killed ratio is the ratio between the number of tests that killed the generated mutants and the total number of tests that were executed with those mutants.

generated by each of these operators depends on the number of transformations that have the same input dataset type and the same output dataset type. The number of mutants generated by UTS and BTS is equal to the number of two-by-two combinations between these transformations. In the case of the UTR and BTR, the number of mutants depends on the number of permutations of these transformations. The UTD generates a number of mutants equal to the number of transformations that have input and output datasets of the same type. From these operators, UTR, BTR and UTD generated the most relevant mutants since their mutants were killed by fewer tests.

The MTR operator generated the largest number of mutants (38,3% of total). Mapping operations are common in big data processing programs, which explains the number of mutants. The number of mutants depends on the type to which data is being mapped according to Table 3. For example, a mapping transformation that generates a numeric value will generate five mutants since we define five mapping values for numeric types. Analyzing the total, the mutants generated with the MTR were the easiest to kill, as we can see in Table 5. Individually, the mappings for 1, with numeric types, and $List(x.head)$ and $Nil$, in list type, obtained the best results with ratios below 70%.

The operators FTD and NFTP, related with filter transformations, and OTD and OTI, related with order transformations, generate a number of mutants equal to the number of transformations of the respective types. A subsumption relationship between FTD and NFTP, and between OTD and OTI was observed in the results. All tests that killed FTD mutants also killed NFTP mutants, just as all tests that killed OTD mutants also killed OTI mutants, but the opposite in both cases was not observed. This indicates that the FTD and OTD operators are stronger than the NFTP and OTI operators, which in turn indicates that when FTD and OTD are applied, the NFTP and OTI operators are not required.

The operator DTI generated 14.5% of all mutants, being the second operator that generated the most mutants. DTI is the most applicable operator because it can be applied after any transformation considering the resulting dataset is always the same type as the original. This operator also generated the largest number of equivalent mutants. This occurs because in some cases the operator is applied after aggregation transformations, so the repeated data had already been aggregated and the dataset no longer had duplicate data. In general, the DTI operator generated relevant mutants considering they were killed by less than 30% of the tests. The number of mutants generated with DTD is equal to the number of distinct transformations called in the program. In our experiment, only one program used distinct, which explains the existence of only one mutant.

ATR generated 11,2% of the mutants in the experiment. The number of mutants it generates is proportional to the number of aggregation transformations in the program, with five mutants for each transformation. The ATR operator has helped to improve the test set because it requires testing with diverse data to aggregate in order to kill the mutants. All equivalent mutants generated by ATR in our experiments were generated by the commutative replacement $(f_m(x,y) = f(y,x))$ because all aggregation functions applied in the programs were commutative. Even so, the commutative replacement mutation is useful because aggregation operations in distributed environments must be commutative to be deterministic [7]. Thus, this mutation can ensure that the commutative property is being taken into account in the testing process.

The mutation operators for binary transformations STR, for set-like transformations, and JTR, for join transformations, generate mutants proportional to the number of these types of transformations. A set transformation generate five mutants, whereas a join transformation generates three mutants. Both operators force the creation of test cases that include two input datasets with diversified data, containing data common to both as well as data not shared between them. In this manner, STR and JTR contribute to the improvement of the test set as they require nontrivial test data. This can be seen in Table 5 which shows that the killed ratio was 34,4% for STR and 22,2% for JTR, which we consider relevant results.

In general, the results showed a reasonable cost estimation for the mutation operators proposed in this work and the viability of their application in the mutation testing process. The number of mutants generated depends on the amount of transformations in the program and their types. The analysis of these aspects, as well as an analysis of the results shown in Table 5, such as the killed ratio, can be used as a reference to the selection of the operators to apply to the mutation testing of big data processing programs.

## 6   Conclusions and Future Work

The development of big data processing programs has gained interest in recent years. The distributed environment and computational resources required to run such programs make their costs high, which makes it necessary to validate and verify them before production. This paper addressed this issue by proposing the application of mutation testing to big data programs based on data flow systems.

We proposed a set of 15 mutation operators that take into account characteristics and operations of data flow systems to model changes in Spark programs and simulate faults. We applied these operators in an experiment to show their feasibility and make a first assessment of costs and effectiveness. The results showed the feasibility to apply mutation testing and design test cases for big data programs, at a reasonable cost. The experiment also hinted at the quality of mutation operators by showing which operators generated mutants, and hence faults, which were more difficult to identify, thus leading to more interesting test cases. This was revealed by the *killed ratio* for each operator in Table 5.

Our approach is complementary to traditional mutation testing criteria developed for Scala, Java and Python. The mutation analysis at the workflow level has several advantages. First, it reflects the two-level organization of Apache Spark programs, where the programmer defines the basic processing blocks (transformation) and the composition of these blocks (data flow). We designed our testing criteria to deal with this composition. Second, it can be used in addition to traditional mutation testing at the programming language level. Finally, it can be generalised to other data flow big data processing frameworks which have similarities in program definition and operations. Thus, we plan to do experiments to apply the proposed mutation operators for testing programs in other data flow frameworks such as Apache Flink [6], DryadLINQ [26] and Apache Beam [3].

Our work has shown that mutation testing can be successfully applied to big data processing programs by designing mutation operators specific to this class of programs. However, due to the effort required for generation, execution and analysis of the mutants, mutation testing is dependent on automation so that it can be viable. Thus, we are consolidating our prototype to automate the process of generation and execution of mutants, to assist the mutation testing of big data programs. Moreover, we plan to evaluate the effectiveness of our mutation operators by comparing the test sets created in the process with other test coverage criteria (e.g., input space partitioning and logic coverage [1]).

# References

1. Ammann, P., Offutt, J.: Introduction to Software Testing, 2nd edn. Cambridge University Press, New York (2017)
2. AMPLab: Big Data Benchmark (2019). https://amplab.cs.berkeley.edu/benchmark/
3. Apache Foundation: Apache Beam: An advanced unified programming model (2016). https://beam.apache.org/
4. Apache Foundation: Apache Hadoop Documentation (2019). https://hadoop.apache.org/docs/r2.7.3/
5. Camargo, L.C., Vergilio, S.R.: MapReduce program testing: a systematic mapping study. In: Chilean Computer Science Society (SCCC), 32nd International Conference of the Computation (2013)
6. Carbone, P., Ewen, S., Haridi, S., Katsifodimos, A., Markl, V., Tzoumas, K.: Apache Flink: stream and batch processing in a single engine. IEEE Data Eng. Bull. **38**(4), 28–38 (2015)
7. Chen, Y.-F., Hong, C.-D., Lengál, O., Mu, S.-C., Sinha, N., Wang, B.-Y.: An executable sequential specification for spark aggregation. In: El Abbadi, A., Garbinato, B. (eds.) NETYS 2017. LNCS, vol. 10299, pp. 421–438. Springer, Cham (2017). https://doi.org/10.1007/978-3-319-59647-1_31
8. Csallner, C., Fegaras, L., Li, C.: New ideas track: testing mapreduce-style programs. In: Proceedings of the 19th ACM SIGSOFT Symposium and the 13th European Conference on Foundations of Software Engineering, pp. 504–507. ACM (2011)
9. De Souza Neto, J.B.: An approach to mutation testing of big data processing programs. Thesis Proposal, Federal University of Rio Grande do Norte (2019). (in Portuguese). https://archive.org/details/prop-doc-joao-ufrn
10. Ferrari, F.C., Maldonado, J.C., Rashid, A.: Mutation testing for aspect-oriented programs. In: 2008 1st International Conference on Software Testing, Verification, and Validation, pp. 52–61, April 2008
11. Frankl, P.G., Weiss, S.N., Hu, C.: All-uses vs mutation testing: an experimental comparison of effectiveness. J. Syst. Softw. **38**(3), 235–253 (1997)
12. Garg, N., Singla, S., Jangra, S.: Challenges and techniques for testing of big data. Procedia Comput. Sci. **85**, 940–948 (2016). International Conference on Computational Modelling and Security (CMS 2016)

13. Jia, Y., Harman, M.: An analysis and survey of the development of mutation testing. IEEE Trans. Softw. Eng. **37**(5), 649–678 (2011)
14. Karau, H.: Spark testing base (2019). https://github.com/holdenk/spark-testing-base
15. Lee, S.C., Offutt, J.: Generating test cases for XML-based Web component interactions using mutation analysis. In: Proceedings 12th International Symposium on Software Reliability Engineering, pp. 200–209, November 2001
16. Li, K., Reichenbach, C., Smaragdakis, Y., Diao, Y., Csallner, C.: SEDGE: symbolic example data generation for dataflow programs. In: 2013 28th IEEE/ACM International Conference on Automated Software Engineering, pp. 235–245 (2013)
17. Ma, Y.S., Offutt, J., Kwon, Y.R.: MuJava: an automated class mutation system. Softw. Test. Verif. Reliab. **15**(2), 97–133 (2005)
18. Marr, B.: Big Data: Using SMART Big Data, Analytics and Metrics to Make Better Decisions and Improve Performance. Wiley, Hoboken (2015)
19. Morán, J., de la Riva, C., Tuya, J.: Testing data transformations in MapReduce programs. In: Proceedings of the 6th International Workshop on Automating Test Case Design, Selection and Evaluation, pp. 20–25. ACM (2015)
20. Morán, J., de la Riva, C., Tuya, J.: Testing MapReduce programs: a systematic mapping study. J. Softw. Evol. Process **31**(3), e2120 (2019)
21. Offutt, A.J., Pan, J., Tewary, K., Zhang, T.: An experimental evaluation of data flow and mutation testing. Softw. Pract. Exper. **26**(2), 165–176 (1996)
22. Olston, C., Reed, B., Srivastava, U., Kumar, R., Tomkins, A.: Pig Latin: a not-so-foreign language for data processing. In: Proceedings of the 2008 ACM SIGMOD International Conference on Management of Data, pp. 1099–1110. ACM (2008)
23. Richard, H.A., et al.: Design of mutant operators for the C programming language. Technical report (1989)
24. Sarwar, B., Karypis, G., Konstan, J., Riedl, J.: Item-based collaborative filtering recommendation algorithms. In: Proceedings of the 10th International Conference on World Wide Web, pp. 285–295. ACM, New York (2001)
25. Walsh, P.J.: A measure of test case completeness (software, engineering). Ph.D. thesis, State University of New York at Binghamton, Binghamton, NY, USA (1985)
26. Yu, Y., et al.: DryadLINQ: a system for general-purpose distributed data-parallel computing using a high-level language. In: Proceedings of the 8th USENIX Conference on Operating Systems Design and Implementation, pp. 1–14. USENIX Association (2008)
27. Zaharia, M., et al.: Resilient distributed datasets: a fault-tolerant abstraction for in-memory cluster computing. In: Proceedings of the 9th USENIX Conference on Networked Systems Design and Implementation, p. 2. USENIX Association (2012)
28. Zaharia, M., Chowdhury, M., Franklin, M.J., Shenker, S., Stoica, I.: Spark: cluster computing with working sets. In: Proceedings of the 2nd USENIX Conference on Hot Topics in Cloud Computing, HotCloud 2010, p. 10. USENIX Association (2010)

# Recommendations for Evolving Relational Databases

Julien Delplanque[1,2(✉)], Anne Etien[1,2], Nicolas Anquetil[1,2],
and Stéphane Ducasse[1,2]

[1] Univ. Lille, CNRS, Centrale Lille, Inria UMR 9189 - CRIStAL, Lille, France
{julien.delplanque,anne.etien,nicolas.anquetil}@inria.fr
[2] INRIA Lille Nord Europe, Villeneuve d'Ascq, France
stephane.ducasse@inria.fr

**Abstract.** Relational databases play a central role in many information systems. Their schemas contain structural and behavioral entity descriptions. Databases must continuously be adapted to new requirements of a world in constant change while: (1) relational database management systems (RDBMS) do not allow inconsistencies in the schema; (2) stored procedure bodies are not meta-described in RDBMS such as PostgreSQL that consider their bodies as plain text. As a consequence, evaluating the impact of an evolution of the database schema is cumbersome, being essentially manual. We present a semi-automatic approach based on recommendations that can be compiled into a SQL patch fulfilling RDBMS constraints. To support recommendations, we designed a meta-model for relational databases easing computation of change impact. We performed an experiment to validate the approach by reproducing a real evolution on a database. The results of our experiment show that our approach can set the database in the same state as the one produced by the manual evolution in 75% less time.

**Keywords:** Relational database · Meta-model · Semi-automatic evolution · Impact analysis

## 1 Introduction

Relational Database (DB) schemas contain structural entity descriptions (*e.g.,* tables and columns), but also sometimes descriptions of behavioral entities such as views (*i.e.,* named **SELECT** queries), stored procedures (*i.e.,* functions written in a programming language), triggers (*i.e.,* entity listening to events happening on a table and reacting to them), etc. Structural and behavioral entities are referencing each others through foreign keys, function calls, or table/column references in queries.

Continuous evolution happens on databases [21] to adapt to new requirements of a world in constant change. When databases evolve, problems are twofold:

© Springer Nature Switzerland AG 2020
S. Dustdar et al. (Eds.): CAiSE 2020, LNCS 12127, pp. 498–514, 2020.
https://doi.org/10.1007/978-3-030-49435-3_31

*Issue 1: Relational database management systems (RDBMS) do not allow schema inconsistencies.* The consistency of databases is ensured by the RDBMS *at any moment.* This feature makes the evolution of the database complicated because the database runs during the evolution and continues to ensure its consistency. For other kinds of software, the program is stopped during source code edition. Thus, the program can be temporarily in an inconsistent state.

*Issue 2: Stored procedure bodies are not meta-described* in RDBMS such as PostgreSQL. Unlike references between tables, columns, constraints or views that are kept and managed through metadata, stored procedures bodies are considered only as text and existing references they make are not known. This second problem slightly alters the first one as inconsistencies can be introduced but only in stored procedures (dangling references).

For example, to remove a column from a table, different cases occur:

(i) If the column is not referenced, the change can be performed.
(ii) If the column is a primary key and is referenced by a foreign key in another table, the removal is not allowed.
(iii) If the column is referenced in a view, either the change is refused or the view must be dropped. In the latter case, views referencing the one to drop must also be transitively dropped.
(iv) If the column is referenced in a function, change can be performed but an error might arise at execution.

Cases (ii) and (iii) result from the first issue whereas the second issue leads to case (iv). This shows that the consequences of even a small change can be complex to handle, particularly cases (iii) and (iv). Such changes need to be anticipated to comply with the constraints imposed by the RDBMS. Meurice *et al.* studied the history of three applications using databases [14]. They conclude that the impact of renaming or removing a table or a column on programs using the database is not trivial. To ease the evolutions of the database and the management of their impacts on related programs, the authors provide a tool to detect and prevent program inconsistencies under database schema evolution. Their approach has two major drawbacks: First, only a small number of evolutions of the database are taken into account (removing and renaming table or column); second, internal programs stored in behavioral entities such as views or stored procedures are not studied.

In this paper, we propose a tool automating most modifications required after applying a change on a database, similar to a refactoring browser [18,19]. We do not consider only refactorings [5], which are by definition behavior preserving, but also deal with other evolutions as illustrated by the above example. Thus, we use the term *change* rather than *refactoring.*

We propose an approach based on a meta-model to provide recommendations to database architects. The architects initiate a change and, based on impact analysis, our tool proposes recommendations to the architect. Those recommendations allow the model to reach a consistent state after the change – new changes are induced and new recommendations provided until a stable state is reached. Finally, when the architect accepts the various changes, an analysis is done to generate a patch containing all the SQL queries to perform these changes.

This article is organized as follows. Section 2 sets the context and defines the vocabulary. Section 3 introduces the behavior-aware meta-model used to represent relational databases. Section 4 describes our approach based on impact computation and recommendations to generate SQL evolution patch. It also shows an example of how our approach manages such evolutions illustrated with one evolution operator. Section 5 validates our approach by using our implementation to reproduce an evolution that was performed by an architect on a real database. Section 6 discusses related work. Finally, Sect. 7 concludes this article by summarizing our results and proposing future work.

## 2   Setting the Context

Before getting into the meta-model and approach explanations, let us set the context in which the approach is designed.

*Database Schema:* The concept of database schema commonly refers to the way data are organized in a database (through tables and referential integrity constraints for relational databases). However, RDBMSs also allows one to define behavior inside the database (*e.g.,* stored procedure), and this behavior might be used to constrain data (*e.g.,* triggers or CHECK constraints). Thus, since there is a fine line between the schema as described before and the behavior, in this article when the terms *database schema* or *schema* are used, they refer to both structural and behavioral entities.

*Impact of a Change:* Changing a database will probably affect its structure and behavior. The *impact* of such a change is defined as the set of database entities that potentially need to be adapted for the change to be applied. For example, RemoveColumn's impact set includes constraints applied to the column.

*Recommendation:* Once the *impact of a change* has been computed, decisions might need to be taken to handle impacted entities, for example dropping views in cascade in the scenario proposed in the introduction. In the context of this paper, we call each of these potential decisions a *recommendation*. For example, if one wants to remove a column, we recommend to remove the NOT NULL constraint concerning this column.

Note that Bohnert and Arnold definition of *impact* [1] mixes the set of impacted entities and the actions to be done to fix such entities (in the context of this paper, we call these actions "recommendations"): "Identifying the potential consequences of a change, or estimating what needs to be modified to accomplish a change". To avoid confusion, we decided to use a specific word for each part of the definition.

We identified two kinds of constraints involved in a relational database: (1) data constraints are responsible for data consistency. 5 types of such constraints are available: "primary key", "foreign key", "unique", "not-null" and "check". (2) schema constraints are responsible for schema consistency and 3 types of such constraints are available: "a table can have a single primary key", "a column can not have the same constraints applied twice on it" and "foreign key can not reference a column that has no primary key or unique constraint".

*Database Schema Consistency:* The RDBMS ensures the consistency of the database schema. This notion of consistency is characterized by the fact that schema constraints are respected and no dangling reference is allowed (except in stored procedure).

Our approach works on a model of the database schema. Using a model allows one to temporarily relax schema constraints and dangling references constraint for the sake of evolution. It allows the developer to focus on changes to be made and not on how to fulfill schema consistency constraints and avoid dangling references at any time.

*Operator:* An operator represents a change to the database schema. It may impact several entities and require further changes to restore the schema in a consistent state after its application. RemoveColumn is an example of operator.

*Entity-Oriented Operator:* An entity-oriented operator applies on an element of the model that does not represent a reference. This kind of operator has the particularity to be translatable directly as one or many SQL queries that implement it. An example of such operator is RemoveColumn.

*Reference-Oriented Operator:* A reference-oriented operator applies on an element of the model representing a reference. RDBMSs do not reify references. Thus, such concepts are implicit and only exist in the source code of DB entities. Because of that, they can not be directly translated as SQL queries. Instead, they need to be converted to entity-oriented operator by interpreting them and generating updated versions of the source code of concerned entities. An example of such operator is ChangeReference Target.

## 3    A Behavior-Aware Meta-Model for Relational Databases

This section presents our meta-model for relational databases. It takes into account both structural and behavioral entities of the database as well as their relationships.

### 3.1   Meta-model Objectives

As discussed in the introduction, modifying the structure of a database implies adapting the behavior (*i.e.* program) depending on it. Thus, the development of the meta-model is driven by two objectives:

1. Model the structure and behavior of the database.
2. Ease the computation of entities impacted by a change.

Objective 1 is fulfilled by modeling tables, columns and constraints. We also model behavioral entities such as CRUD[1] queries, views (*i.e.,* named SELECT query stored in the database), stored procedures, and triggers. Objective 2 is fulfilled by *reifying references* between structural and behavioral entities. The details of these modeling choices are given in Sect. 3.4.

The implementation of the meta-model is available on github[2]. The meta-model is instantiated by analysing meta-data provided by the RDBMS and parsing the source code of entities that are not meta-described. The source code of the meta-data reader[3] and the parser[4] available on github as well.

### 3.2   Structural Entities

Figure 1 shows the structural part of the meta-model. To ease reading, for this UML diagram and the following, inheritance links have straight corners while other links are rounded; classes modeling structural entities are red (such as Table); classes modeling behavioral entities are orange (such as StoredProcedure); and classes modeling references are white.

A StructuralEntity defines the structure of data held by the database or defining constraints applied on these data (*e.g.,* Table, Column, Referential integrity constraint, etc.). The containment relation between Table and Column is modeled through ColumnsContainer which is an abstract entity. This entity also has subclasses in the behavioral part of the meta-model (see Sect. 3.3). A Column has a type. This relation is modeled through a TypeReference. A Column can also be subject to Constraints. Depending on whether a Constraint concerns a single or multiple columns, it inherits from, respectively, ColumnConstraint or TableConstraint. Six concrete constraints inherit from Constraint: PrimaryKey, ForeignKey, Unique, Check (a developer-defined constraint, described by a boolean expression), NotNull, and Default (a default value assigned when no value is explicitly provided, it can be a literal value or an expression to compute). Note that Check and Default constraints also inherit from BehavioralEntity because they contain source code.

---

[1] Create Read Update Delete query in SQL: INSERT, SELECT, UPDATE, DELETE.

[2] https://github.com/juliendelplanque/FAMIXNGSQL.

[3] https://github.com/olivierauverlot/PgMetadata.

[4] https://github.com/juliendelplanque/PostgreSQLParser.

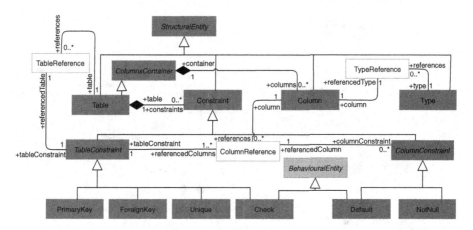

**Fig. 1.** Structural entities of the meta-model.

## 3.3  Behavioral Entities

A behavioral entity is an entity holding behavior that may interact with StructuralEntities. Figure 2 shows the behavioral part of the meta-model. The main entities are as follows.

View is a named entity holding a SELECT query. StoredProcedure is an entity holding developer-defined behavior which includes queries and calls to other StoredProcedure. A StoredProcedure contains Parameter(s) and LocalVariable(s). These entities can be referenced in clauses of queries that are contained in StoredProcedures or Views. Trigger represents actions happening in response to event on a table (*e.g.,* row inserted, updated or deleted). CRUDQuery(ies) contain multiple clauses depending on the query. For the sake of readability, we did not include the clause classes in the diagram. In a nutshell, the containment relation between CRUD queries and clauses are: SelectQuery contains With, Select, From, Where, Join, Union, Intersect, Except, GroupBy, OrderBy, Having, Limit, Offset, Fetch clauses. InsertQuery contains With, Into, Returning clauses. UpdateQuery contains With, Update, Set, From, Where, Returning clauses. DeleteQuery contains With, Delete, From, Where, Returning clauses. Each clause holds some References to structural or behavioral entities. The references made to structural or behavioral entities from clauses are detailed in Sect. 3.4. DerivedTable is an anonymous query usually used in another query but can also appear in the body of a StoredProcedure.

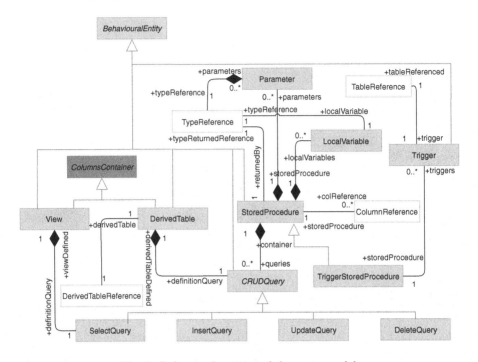

**Fig. 2.** Behavioral entities of the meta-model.

### 3.4   References

The third and last part of the meta-model represents links between entities. It allows one to track relations between behavioral and structural entities. To simplify the approach, all references have been reified. For example, a column is thus referenced through a ColumnReference, a local variable through a LocalVariableReference and a stored procedure through a StoredProcedureCall.

## 4   Description of the Approach

To evolve a database, the database architect formulates changes on some of its entities. These changes impact other entities that, in turn, need to evolve to maintain the database in a consistent state. To handle evolutions induced by the initial changes, we developed a 3-step approach. The implementation of this approach is available on github[5].

A. *Impact computation*: The set of *impacted* entities is computed from the change. The next step treats impacted entities one by one.

---

[5] https://github.com/juliendelplanque/DBEvolution.

B. *Recommendations selection*: Second, depending on the change, and the *impacted* entity, our approach computes a set of *recommendations*. These *recommendations* are presented to the database architect that chooses one when several are proposed. This introduces new changes that will have new impacts. Steps A. and B. are recursively applied until all the *impacts* have been managed.

C. *Compiling operators as a valid SQL patch*: Finally, all operators (the recommendations chosen by the architect) are converted as a set of SQL queries that can be run by the RDBMS. The set of SQL queries is used to migrate the database to a state in which the initial architect's change has been applied.

### 4.1   Impact Computation

To compute the entities potentially affected by a change, one needs to collect all the entities referencing this changed entity. For example, if a Column is subject to a modification, our approach identifies the *impacted* entities by gathering all the ColumnReferences concerning this column. The *impact* of the change corresponds to the sources of all ColumnReferences since they can potentially be affected by the modification.

### 4.2   Recommendations Selection

For each operator, the set of impacted entities is split into disjoint sub-sets called *categories*. For each of these *categories*, one or several *recommendations* are available. We determinated those recommendations by analysing how to handle them according to database schema constraints.

The output of step 4.1 combined with this step (4.2) is a tree of operators where the root is the change initiated by the architect and, each other node corresponds to an operator chosen among *recommendations*.

### 4.3   Compiling Operators as a Valid SQL Patch

Once all the *impact sets* have been considered and *recommendations* chosen, our approach generates a SQL patch. This patch includes queries belonging to the SQL data definition language (DDL). These queries enable migrating the database from its original state to a state where the initial operator and all induced operators have been applied.

We stress that, during the execution of any operator of the patch, the RDBMS cannot be in inconsistent state. This constraint is fundamentally different from source code refactoring where the state of the program can be temporarily inconsistent. Therefore, each operator must lead the database to a state complying with schema consistency constraints. Else the RDBMS will forbid the execution of the SQL patch. For this purpose, the tree of operators resulting from the previous step has to be transformed into a sequence of SQL queries.

The tree resulting from the step described in Sect. 4.2 is composed of operators on references. However, DDL queries only deal with entities. Thus, reference-oriented operators are transformed into entity-oriented operators. As the RDBMS does not allow inconsistencies, operators concerning a given behavioral entity of the database are aggregated into a single operator per view and per stored procedure. This aggregation is performed in two steps: 1. all reference-oriented operators are grouped according to the entity to which belongs to the source code in which the reference appears, and 2. for each group of reference-oriented operators, we create the new version of the source code for this entity. To do so, we iterate the list of reference-oriented operators and update the part of the source code corresponding to the reference to make it reflect the change implemented by the operator. Once the iteration is complete, a new version of the source code has been built with no more dangling reference.

Those entity-oriented operators are ordered to comply with RDBMS constraints of consistency and serialized as SQL queries. Technical details related to this serialization are not provided in this paper because of space limitation.

### 4.4   Example

To explain the proposed process, let us take a small example. Consider the simple database shown in Fig. 3. In this database, there are two tables, t1 with two columns t1.b, t1.c and t2 with column t2.e. Additionally, one stored procedure s() and three views v1, v2 and v3 are present. On this figure, dependencies between entities are modeled with arrows. These dependencies arrows are a generalization over the various kinds of reference entities of the meta-model. For example, the arrow between s() and t1 is an instance of TableReference and the arrow between s() and b is an instance of ColumnReference. Views and functions have source code displayed inside their box. In this source code, a reference to another entity of the database is underlined.

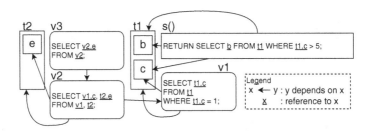

**Fig. 3.** Example database.

The architect wants to rename the column c of table t1 as d.

*Impact Computation.* First, we compute the impact of this change. Column c of table t1 is referenced three times: *(i)* in the WHERE clause of the SELECT query of the stored procedure s(); *(ii)* in the WHERE clause of the query defining view v1; and *(iii)* in the SELECT clause of the query defining view v1. Each of these clauses is added in the *impact* of renaming t1.c as t1.d.

*Recommendations Selection.* For each of the three *impacted entities, recommendations* are produced. For the WHERE clause of the stored procedure s(), the recommendation is to replace the reference to column t1.c with a new one corresponding to t1.d. The result of replacing this reference will be the following source code: RETURN SELECT b FROM t1 WHERE t1.d > 5;. From this operator, the impact is computed but is empty which stops the recursive process.

The recommendation concerning the WHERE clause of v1 is the same: replacing the reference to t1.c by a reference to t1.d. Again, there is no further impact for this operator.

For the reference to t1.c in the SELECT clause of view v1, two recommendations are proposed to the architect: either aliasing the column and replacing the reference (*i.e.,* replacing SELECT t1.c by SELECT t1.d AS c) or replacing the reference (*i.e.,* replacing SELECT t1.c by SELECT t1.d). In the latter case, the column c in view v1 becomes d; it is no longer possible to refer to v1.c. Consequently, the second recommendation leads to rename column v1.c. If the architect choose to replace the reference without aliasing, the recursive process continues: new impacts need to be computed and new changes to be performed. The SELECT clause of view v2 is impacted. Two recommendations are again provided: either aliasing the column and replacing the reference or just replacing the reference. In this case, the architect chooses to alias the column and replace the reference. Thus, the rest of the database can continue to refer to column c of view v2. Figure 4 illustrates this step.

*Compiling Operators as a Valid SQL Patch.* Figure 5 illustrates the patch generation step. References-oriented operators resulting from the recommendations are transformed into entity-oriented operators. For this purpose, operators concerning the same sourced entity are aggregated. Operators (3) and (4) concern the same sourced entity, v1. They are thus aggregated into ModifyViewQuery(v1). At the end, there is a single operator per entity to be modified.

The resulting list of operators is ordered and converted to a SQL patch.

## 5  Experiment

Our university department uses an information system to manage its members, teams, thematic groups, etc. with 95 tables, 63 views, 109 stored procedures and 20 triggers. This information system is developed by a database architect.

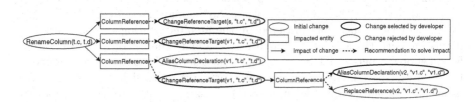

**Fig. 4.** Recommendations selection.

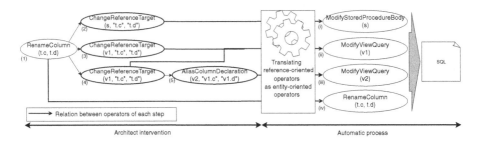

**Fig. 5.** Compiling operators as a valid SQL patch.

Before each migration, he prepares a road map containing, in natural language, the list of operators initially planned for the migration. We observed that these road maps are not complete or accurate [4]. Following a long manual process, the architect writes a SQL patch (*i.e.*, a text file containing queries) to migrate from one version of the database to the next one.

The architect gave us access to these patches to do a post-mortem analysis of the DB evolutions. One of the patches implements the renaming of a column belonging to a table that is central to the DB. This is interesting because it is a non-trivial evolution.

We had the opportunity to record the architect's screen during this migration [4]. We observed that the architect used a trial-and-error process to find dependencies between entities of the database. He implements part of the patch and runs it in a transaction that is always rolled back. When the patch fails in between, the architect uses the gained knowledge to correct the SQL patch. Using this methodology, the architect built incrementally the SQL patch implementing the patch during approximately 1 h. The patch is ∼200 LOC and is composed of 19 SQL statements. To validate our approach, we regenerate this SQL patch with our tool but without the architect's expertise. Then, we compare our resulting database with the one obtained by the architect.

## 5.1 Experimental Protocol

The goals of the experiment are multiple: (*i*) to illustrate on a concrete case the generation of a SQL patch; (*ii*) to compare the database resulting from our approach with the one originally written by the architect; and (*iii*) to estimate the time required to generate a SQL patch as compared to the manual generation.

Based on the road map written by the architect and the comments in the patch we extracted the operators initiated by the architect during this migration. A discussion with the architect allowed us to validate the list of initial operators: RenameColumn(person.uid, login), RemoveFunction(key_for_uid(varchar)), Remove-Function(is_responsible_of(int4)), RemoveFunction(is_responsible_of(int4,int4)), Re-nameFunction(uid(integer), login(integer)), RenameLocalVariable(login.uidperson, login.loginperson), RemoveView(test_member_view). Details on these operators can be found at: https://hal.inria.fr/hal-02504949v1.

The experiment consists in choosing these operators in our tool and following the *recommendations* it proposes. Potentially several *recommendations* might be proposed, particularly as whether to create aliases in some referencing queries or to rename various columns in cascade (see example in Sect. 4.4). The architect told us that, as a rule, he preferred to avoid using aliases and renamed the columns. These were the only decision we had to do during the experiment.

We finished the experiment by executing the SQL patch generated by our tool on an empty (no data) copy of the database. Note that having no data in the database to test the patch might be a problem for operators modifying data (*e.g.*, changing the type of a column implies converting data to the new type). However, in the case of our experiment no operator modifies data stored in the database. First, we checked whether the generated patch ran without errors. Second, we compared the state of the database after the architect's migration and ours. For this, we generated a dump of the SQL schema of both databases and compared these two dumps using a textual diff tool. Third, we also considered the time we spent on our migration and the one used by the architect when he did his.

## 5.2    Results

We entered the seven operators listed previously in our tool and let it guide us through the decision process to generate the SQL migration patch.

Fifteen decisions were taken to choose among the proposed recommendations. They all concerned the renaming or aliasing of column references. From this process, the tool generated a SQL patch of $\sim$270 LOC and 27 SQL statements.

To answer the goals of the experiment listed previously: *(i)* The generated SQL patch was successfully applied on the database. *(ii)* The diff of the two databases (one being the result of the hand-written patch and the other being the result of the generated patch) showed a single difference: a comment in one function is modified in the hand-written version. Such changes are not taken into account by our approach. *(iii)* Encoding the list of changes and taking decisions took approximately 15 min. This corresponds to about 25% of the time necessary to the architect who has a very good knowledge of his database to obtain the same result.

## 5.3    Discussion

Validating tools predicting the impact of a software change is not easy. Evidence of that claim can be found in Lehnert's meta-review [10]. On the 18 approaches reviewed by Lehnert using either call graphs or program dependency graph techniques, only six have experimental results about the size of the system, time, precision and recall. And only one of these has results on all the metrics together.

Accessing industrial databases with their evolutions is more difficult than accessing source code. Since databases are usually at the core of company business, companies are reluctant to provide their schema. The database schema evolutions are not systematically recorded in tools such as version control systems (VCS) probably because the integration between relational database and VCS is poor. Finding database administrators willing to devote some time to our experiment can also be challenging.

It is also possible to analyze the co-evolution between the source code of a database and the source code of its clients. Analyzing only the behavior inside the database has the advantage that the precision is better as queries are usually not built dynamically. When queries are built dynamically via string concatenation, it is hard to determinate what query is executed in the end. However, it is possible to build query dynamically from inside the database (via `PERFORM` query). We do not handle these kinds of query at the moment but it would be possible to use an approach similar to Meurice et al. approach [14].

Note that our approach has been applied on AppSI database but is does not rely on AppSI specificities. DBEvolution relies on the meta-model and operators definitions to provide recommendations for a given change. We can import other databases as model in our tool. For example, we were able to load Liquidfeedback database schema[6] in our tool and we can use DBEvolution on it to get recommendations.

# 6    Related Work

Our work needs to be compared to *impact analysis* and *database schema evolution* research fields.

*Impact Analysis.* Since the first paper introducing Impact Analysis by Bohnert and Arnold [1], the research field has been widely investigated by the scientific community. Meta-analyses on this topic exist, *e.g.,* Lehnert did a review of software change impact analysis in 2011 [10]. We focus on work adapting impact analysis techniques to relational databases as discussed below.

Karahasanovic and Sjøberg proposed a tool, called SEMT, to find impacts of object-database schema changes on applications [9]. Their tool allows one to identify and visualize the impact. It uses an improved version of the transitive closure algorithm. It also provides a language to graphically walk the impact graph.

Gardikiotis and Malevris [6] proposes an approach to estimate the impact of a database schema change on the operability of a web application. To achieve that, they proposed a tool named DaSIAn (Database Schema Impact Analyzer) based on their approach. This tool finds CRUD queries and stored procedures affected by a change on the database schema. The authors also presented an approach assessing impact on client applications from schema changes [7]. They used this approach to assess both affected source code statements and affected test suites in the application using the database after a change in the database.

---

[6] https://liquidfeedback.org.

Maul *et al.* [13] created a static analysis technique to assess the impact of changing a relational database on its object-oriented software clients. They implemented Schema Update Impact Tool Environment (SUITE) which takes the source code of the application using the database and a model of the database schema as input. Then, they queried this model to find out the part of the source code application impacted when modifying an entity of the database.

Nagy *et al.* [15] compared two methods for computing dependencies between stored procedures and tables in a database: One using Static Execute After/Before relations [8] and the other analysing CRUD queries and schema to find database access and propagate this dependency at the stored procedure level. The authors concluded that the two approaches provide different results and should thus be used together to assess dependencies safely.

Liu *et al.* [11,12], proposed a graph called attribute dependency graph to identify dependencies between columns in a database and parts of client software source code using it. They evaluated their approach on 3 databases and their clients written in PHP. Their tool presents to the architect an overview of a change impact as a graph.

Similarly to approaches covered by Lehnert meta-analysis, the validations for impact analysis on databases are usually quite weak because it is a difficult task. To position our approach, it uses static analysis to determine the impact of a change on an entity. This information is directly available in our model because we reify the references between entities. As explained previously, our approach considers that if you change an entity, all entities referencing it are potentially impacted. That set of impacted entities is decomposed into categories and a recommendation is provided for each of them.

*Recommendations for Relational Database Schema Evolution.* Sjøberg's work [20] quantifies schema evolution. They studied the evolution of a relational database and its application forming a health management system during 18 months. To do so they used "the Thesaurus" tool which analyses how many screens, actions and queries may be affected by a potential schema change. This tool does not propose recommendations to users but rather shows code locations to be manually modified. Their results suggest that change management tools are needed to handle this evolution.

Curino *et al.* [2,3] proposed PRISM, a tool suite allowing one to predict and evaluate schema modification. PRISM also propose database migration feature through rewriting queries and application to take into account the modification. To do so, they provide a language to express schema modification operators, automatic data migration support and documentation of changes applied on the database. They evaluated their approach and tool on Wikimedia showing it is efficient. In PRISM approach, the operators are limited to modification on structural entities of the database, whereas our approach also deals with change on behavioral entities.

Papastefanatos *et al.* [16,17] developed Hecataeus, a tool representing the database structural entities, the queries and the views, as a uniform directed graph. Hecataeus allows user to create an arbitrary change and to simulate it to predict its impact. From this perspective, it is close to the aim of our tool. The main difference is that our approach ensures no inconsistency is created at some point during database evolution. It is not clear how Hecataeus addresses this problem in these papers.

Meurice *et al.* [14] presented a tool-supported approach that can analyze how the client source code and database schema co-evolved in the past and to simulate a database change to determine client source code locations that would be affected by the change. Additionally, the authors provide strategies (recommendations and warnings) for facing database schema change. Their recommendations describe how to modify client program source code depending on the change performed on the database. The approach presented has been evaluated by comparing historical evolution of a database and its client application with recommendations provided by their approach. From the historical analysis the authors observed that the task of manually propagating database schema change to client software is not trivial. Some schema changes required multiple versions of the software application to be fully propagated. Others were never fully propagated. We argue that, according to what we observed in previous research [4] and the research made in this article, propagating structural change to behavior entities of the database is a hard task as well.

Compared to previous approaches, DBEvolution brings as a novelty that any entity can be subject to an evolution operator. In particular, stored procedures can be modified and DBEvolution will provide recommandations for the modification. The other way around, modifying a structural entity will provide recommandations to accomodate stored procedures with the change. Such capability is absent from above approaches.

## 7   Conclusion

We have developed an approach to manage relational database evolution. This approach addresses the two main constraints that a RDBMS sets: 1. *no schema inconsistency is allowed during the evolution* and 2. *stored procedures bodies are not described by meta-data.* Addressing these problems allowed us to provide three main contributions: i. a meta-model for relational databases easing the computation of the impact of a change, ii. a semi-automatic approach to evolve a database while managing the impact, and iii. an experiment to assess that our approach can reproduce a change that happened on a database used by a real project with a gain of 75% of the time. These results show that this approach is promising to build the future of relational databases integrated development environments.

Our future works are threefold. First, we would like to extend the set of operators supported by our implementation. More specifically, we want higher-level operators such as: *historize column* which will modify the database schema to keep track of the history of the values of a column through the database life.

Second, the evolution has been reproduced by us which might bias our results in terms of time to implement a change. Indeed, as we have little knowledge on the DB, it is possible that an expert using our tool would be faster than us. Thus, we would like to do another experiment where we compare the performances of an architect using our tool with the performances of an architect using typical tools to implement an evolution.

Finally, some operators will require to transform or move data stored in the database (for example moving a column from a table to another). We plan to support such operators in our methodology by generating CRUD queries in addition to the DDL queries already generated by the operators.

# References

1. Arnold, R.S., Bohnert, S.: Software Change Impact Analysis. IEEE Computer Society Press, Los Alamitos (1996)
2. Curino, C., Moon, H.J., Zaniolo, C.: Automating database schema evolution in information system upgrades. In: Proceedings of the 2nd International Workshop on Hot Topics in Software Upgrades, p. 5. ACM (2009)
3. Curino, C.A., Moon, H.J., Zaniolo, C.: Graceful database schema evolution: the prism workbench. Proc. VLDB Endow. **1**(1), 761–772 (2008)
4. Delplanque, J., Etien, A., Anquetil, N., Auverlot, O.: Relational database schema evolution: an industrial case study. In: 2018 IEEE International Conference on Software Maintenance and Evolution (ICSME) (2018). https://doi.org/10.1109/ICSME.2018.00073. http://rmod.inria.fr/archives/papers/Delp18c-ICSME-DatabaseSchemaEvolution.pdf
5. Fowler, M., Beck, K., Brant, J., Opdyke, W., Roberts, D.: Refactoring: Improving the Design of Existing Code. Addison Wesley, Boston (1999)
6. Gardikiotis, S.K., Malevris, N.: DaSIAn: a tool for estimating the impact of database schema modifications on web applications. In: 2006 IEEE International Conference on Computer Systems and Applications, pp. 188–195. IEEE (2006)
7. Gardikiotis, S.K., Malevris, N.: A two-folded impact analysis of schema changes on database applications. Int. J. Autom. Comput. **6**(2), 109–123 (2009)
8. Jász, J., Beszédes, Á., Gyimóthy, T., Rajlich, V.: Static execute after/before as a replacement of traditional software dependencies. In: 2008 IEEE International Conference on Software Maintenance, pp. 137–146. IEEE (2008)
9. Karahasanovic, A., Sjoberg, D.I.: Visualizing impacts of database schema changes-a controlled experiment. In: 2001 Proceedings IEEE Symposia on Human-Centric Computing Languages and Environments, pp. 358–365. IEEE (2001)
10. Lehnert, S.: A review of software change impact analysis, p. 39. Ilmenau University of Technology (2011)
11. Liu, K., Tan, H.B.K., Chen, X.: Extraction of attribute dependency graph from database applications. In: 2011 18th Asia Pacific Software Engineering Conference (APSEC), pp. 138–145. IEEE (2011)
12. Liu, K., Tan, H.B.K., Chen, X.: Aiding maintenance of database applications through extracting attribute dependency graph. J. Database Manage. **24**(1), 20–35 (2013)
13. Maule, A., Emmerich, W., Rosenblum, D.: Impact analysis of database schema changes. In: 2008 ACM/IEEE 30th International Conference on Software Engineering, ICSE 2008, pp. 451–460. IEEE (2008)

14. Meurice, L., Nagy, C., Cleve, A.: Detecting and preventing program inconsistencies under database schema evolution. In: 2016 IEEE International Conference on Software Quality, Reliability and Security (QRS), pp. 262–273. IEEE (2016)

15. Nagy, C., Pantos, J., Gergely, T., Besz'edes, A.: Towards a safe method for computing dependencies in database-intensive systems. In: 2010 14th European Conference on Software Maintenance and Reengineering (CSMR), pp. 166–175. IEEE (2010)

16. Papastefanatos, G., Anagnostou, F., Vassiliou, Y., Vassiliadis, P.: Hecataeus: A what-if analysis tool for database schema evolution. In: 2008 12th European Conference on Software Maintenance and Reengineering, CSMR 2008, pp. 326–328. IEEE (2008)

17. Papastefanatos, G., Vassiliadis, P., Simitsis, A., Vassiliou, Y.: HECATAEUS: regulating schema evolution. In: 2010 IEEE 26th International Conference on Data Engineering (ICDE), pp. 1181–1184. IEEE (2010)

18. Roberts, D., Brant, J., Johnson, R.E., Opdyke, B.: An automated refactoring tool. In: Proceedings of ICAST 1996, Chicago, IL, April 1996

19. Roberts, D.B.: Practical Analysis for Refactoring. Ph.D. thesis, University of Illinois (1999). http://historical.ncstrl.org/tr/pdf/uiuc_cs/UIUCDCS-R-99-2092.pdf

20. Sjøberg, D.: Quantifying schema evolution. Inf. Softw. Technol. **35**(1), 35–44 (1993)

21. Skoulis, I., Vassiliadis, P., Zarras, A.: Open-source databases: within, outside, or beyond Lehman's laws of software evolution? In: Jarke, M., et al. (eds.) CAiSE 2014. LNCS, vol. 8484, pp. 379–393. Springer, Cham (2014). https://doi.org/10.1007/978-3-319-07881-6_26

# A Combined Method for Usage of NLP Libraries Towards Analyzing Software Documents

Xinyun Cheng, Xianglong Kong$^{(\boxtimes)}$, Li Liao, and Bixin Li

School of Computer Science and Engineering, Southeast University, Nanjing, China
{yukicheng,xlkong,lliao,bx.li}@seu.edu.cn

**Abstract.** Natural Language Processing (NLP) library is widely used while analyzing software documents. The numerous toolkits result in a problem on NLP library selection. The selection of NLP library in current work commonly misses some objective reasons, which may pose threats to validity. And it is also not clear that whether the existing guideline on selection still works for the latest versions. In this work, we propose a solution for NLP library selection when the effectiveness is unknown. We use the NLP libraries together in a combined method. Our combined method can utilize the strengths of different NLP libraries to obtain accurate results. The combination is conducted through two steps, i.e., document-level selection of NLP library and sentence-level overwriting. In document-level selection of primary library, the results are obtained from the library that has the highest overall accuracy. Through sentence-level overwriting, the possible fine-gained improvements from other libraries are extracted to overwrite the outputs of primary library. We evaluate the combined method with 4 widely used NLP libraries and 200 documents from 3 different sources. The results show that the combined method can generally outperform all the studied NLP libraries in terms of accuracy. The finding means that our combined method can be used instead of individual NLP library for more effective results.

**Keywords:** Natural Language Processing · NLP library selection · Software document

## 1 Introduction

Software documents are important sources of knowledge in an information system. The documents (e.g., requirement documents, design documents or logs) are commonly written in natural language by some developers or automatically created by generators for different purposes. To obtain the information contained in software documents, many researchers directly use state-of-the-art Natural Language Processing (NLP) libraries to carry out the tasks [11,21,26]. There are

---

Technical paper.

S. Dustdar et al. (Eds.): CAiSE 2020, LNCS 12127, pp. 515–529, 2020.
https://doi.org/10.1007/978-3-030-49435-3_32

several high-quality NLP libraries which are widely used in both industry and academia, such as NLTK[1], spaCy[2], Stanford CoreNLP[3], Google's SyntaxNet[4], OpenNLP[5] and so on. ALL the NLP libraries can provide API supports for the common NLP tasks (e.g., tokenization and part-of-speech tagging). The rich sources of candidates result in a new problem on the selection of suitable NLP library while analyzing documents. In most cases, the selection of NLP library is subjective [22,28,29,32]. And the results from different NLP libraries may also be different, the subjective selection may pose threats to validity [17].

To solve the problem, Omran and Treude propose an empirical study to give a guideline for choosing appropriate NLP libraries [17]. The guideline is expressed as the best choice of NLP libraries for a specific type of software documents. The effectiveness of NLP libraries is influenced by the NLP task and the source. For example, spaCy performs best on Stack Overflow text with nearly 90% of tokens tagged correctly in the experiments, while it is significantly outperformed by Google's SyntaxNet when parsing GitHub ReadMe text. However, the guideline cannot always help researchers to choose the best NLP library for a specific task. There are three reasons for the possible inaccuracy. First, there exist a great variety of software documents in real world [4,13,20], and it is too tedious to produce an universal guideline for all the types of software documents. Second, the NLP libraries are optimized continuously, the existing guideline may be inaccurate in some upcoming scenarios. Third, different types of software documents may be analyzed together in some cases [6,31], the individual selection of different NLP libraries on different documents and NLP tasks may weaken the automation.

Since it is impractical to summarize an universal and continuously updated guideline of NLP library selection, we turn to investigate a method to use them together. In this paper, we propose a combined method which can utilize the strengths of different NLP libraries to achieve more effective results. The combined method is expected to generate more accurate results than single NLP library. To obtain the combined results, we firstly choose the whole results from the NLP library which has the highest overlapping degree. The overlapping degree of a NLP library defined in our work is the average proportion of identical outputs (e.g., tokens or part-of-speech tags) among the results achieved by it and any other NLP library individually. The overlapped results have high possibility to be correct due to the high quality of the studied NLP libraries. When the primary NLP library is selected in the first step, we identify the result of each sentence. The results of low-overlap sentences within a document are overwritten with the fine-gained improvements from other NLP libraries.

Our study has two main novel aspects. First, we conduct an empirical study to check whether the existing guideline fits to different versions of NLP libraries

---

[1] http://www.nltk.org/.

[2] https://spacy.io/.

[3] https://nlp.stanford.edu/nlp/.

[4] https://opensource.google.com/projects/syntaxnet.

[5] http://opennlp.apache.org/.

and different documents. The subjects include 4 publicly available NLP libraries and 200 documents from 3 different sources. The results confirm that the existing guideline should be updated with the evolution of NLP libraries and the change of given documents. Furthermore, each NLP library can generate its own exclusive correctness. This finding inspires us to extract correct results from different libraries to achieve a better effectiveness. The combined method for usage of NLP libraries brings the second novelty of our work. It contains two steps, i.e., document-level selection of NLP library and sentence-level overwriting. We evaluate the combined method according to a handmade benchmark in our study. The results show that our method can outperform any individual library in terms of accuracy on tokenization and part-of-speech tagging. The numeric promotion is around 2%. Due to the high quality of the studied NLP libraries, the improvements are meaningful in practice. And the majority of correct NLP results come from the outputs of primary NLP library. These findings mean that our combined method can be used instead of individual NLP library for more effective results in the analysis of software documents.

To sum up, this paper makes the following contributions.

- We conduct an empirical study to investigate the effectiveness of NLP libraries, and prove that the existing guideline should be updated with the evolution of libraries and each library has its own exclusive results.
- We propose a method to combine the strengths of different NLP libraries, and the combined method can outperform any individual NLP library in the experiments.

## 2   Background

In the section, we discuss some background knowledge of our method, i.e., NLP Library, NLP task and software document.

### 2.1   NLP Libraries and Tasks

There are a lot of NLP libraries in both academia and industry, and the publicly available libraries are very popular in the analysis of software documents. Among them, we introduce several widely used NLP libraries in this section. NLTK is a platform for building Python programs to work with human language data. It provides a suite of text processing libraries. SpaCy is another free open-source library for NLP which is called "Industrial-Strength Natural Language Processing in Python". Stanford CoreNLP is a set of open-source Java NLP tools developed by Stanford University. Google's SyntaxNet is a new open-source natural language parsing model which is developed by Google. Apache OpenNLP is a toolkit based on machine-learning for processing natural language text.

NLP tasks denote the various purposes of analyzing documents. We list 3 frequently used NLP tasks as follow. Tokenization is the process of dividing a string into several parts [30]. The resulting tokens will be used in other tasks. When processing texts in English, tokenization of strings is impacted by the rules on processing punctuations. Stop words removal is designed to save storage space and improve search efficiency, some words or phrases will be filtered while processing natural language texts. These stop words or phrases are commonly insignificant. Part-of-speech is a basic grammatical property of a vocabulary. Part-of-speech tagging is the process of determining the grammatical category of each word in a given sentence and tagging it [5,18], the tags are usually used in syntactic analysis and information retrieval.

## 2.2 Software Documents

Documents in software life-cycle may contain both oral words and formal statements. The formal documents are usually generated by some approaches, and the human-written documents may have a low degree of formalization. According to the different degree of formalization, we introduce three types of software documents as below.

Feature requests are requirements of new features which are received by developers in order to modify the code and documents [26]. The documents of feature requests can be extracted from JIRA[6] (an issue and project tracking system). There is not a standard of the formalization of the language in the documents of feature requests. ReadMe Files are written by the developers to help other people understand the projects. Developers can author the files in different languages. ReadMe files are more formal than descriptions of feature requests. Java API documentation is quite different from the documents mentioned above. Java API documentation has their own structures and not as casual as the descriptions of feature requests. Moreover, Java API documentation contains many code elements which may obey the rules of grammar in daily expression. It is the official text provided by the community[7]. Therefore, it can be treated as formal software documents. In this work, we apply the four NLP libraries on three types of software documents to conduct tokenization and part-of-speech tagging.

## 3  Approach

It is hard to predict the accuracy of NLP libraries while analyzing software documents, especially for the people which are not professional at NLP. Since the subjective selection of NLP libraries may result in threats to the validity, and random selection may obtain unexpected NLP results, we want to propose a combined method to utilize the strengths of different NLP libraries. The overall framework of our combined method is illustrated in Fig. 1. The combined method mainly consists of two stages: document-level selection of NLP library and sentence-level overwriting. In this section, we present the details of our approach in sequence.

---

[6] https://www.atlassian.com/software/jira.
[7] https://docs.oracle.com/javase/7/docs/api.

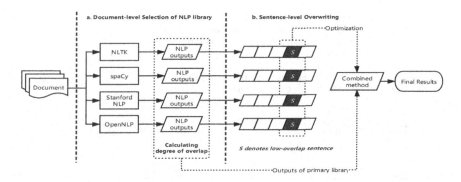

**Fig. 1.** Overall framework of the combined method

## 3.1   Document-Level Selection of NLP Library

For the given documents, we firstly apply NLTK, spaCy, Stanford CoreNLP and OpenNLP to produce four sets of results independently. Then we calculate the degree of overlap for each studied NLP library. The NLP library with highest degree of overlap is selected as primary library, its outputs are transfered to the next step as primary outputs. Document-level overlapping degree of a NLP library defined in our experiment is the average proportion of identical outputs (e.g., tokens or part-of-speech tags) among the results achieved by it and any other NLP library individually. The degree of overlap between NLP library $i$ and $j$ is calculated as

$$o_{i,j} = \frac{|\{Outputs_i\} \bigcap \{Outputs_j\}|}{|\{Outputs_i\}| + |\{Outputs_j\}|} \cdot 2 \tag{1}$$

where $o_{i,j}$ denotes the degree of overlap between NLP library $i$ and $j$, $\{Outputs_i\}$ and $\{Outputs_j\}$ are the sets of all the annotations generated by NLP library $i$ and $j$, respectively.

The document-level overlapping degree of library $i$ is calculated as

$$O_i = \frac{\sum_{j=1}^{k-1} o_{i,j}}{k-1} \tag{2}$$

where $O_i$ denotes the document-level overlapping degree of library $i$, and $k$ is the total number of studied NLP libraries.

We show the process of calculating document-level overlapping degree through a case. Figure 2 shows an example of document from Java API Documentation. The document contains 14 sentences, and we list the 2 selected sentences in the figure. For the whole document, NLTK, spaCy, Stanford CoreNLP and OpenNLP identify 244, 246, 242 and 246 tokens, respectively. Table 1 presents the results of document-level overlapping degrees on part-of-speech tagging. In the table, the first column presents the studied NLP libraries, and overlapping degrees of the paired NLP libraries are shown in column 2 to 5. The last column

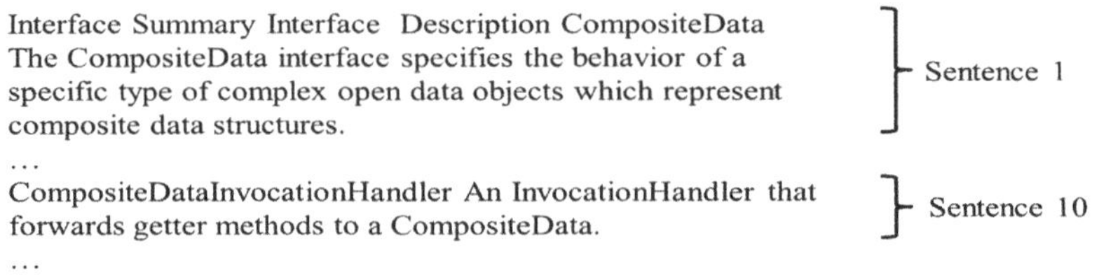

Interface Summary Interface  Description CompositeData
The CompositeData interface specifies the behavior of a
specific type of complex open data objects which represent
composite data structures.
...
CompositeDataInvocationHandler An InvocationHandler that
forwards getter methods to a CompositeData.
...

}— Sentence 1

}— Sentence 10

**Fig. 2.** Document from JavaDoc of javax.management.openmbean

presents the document-level overlapping degree. The data within parentheses in
row 2 to 5 denotes the number of identical tags for each pair of NLP libraries.
In this case, NLTK gets the highest document-level overlapping degree, so we
select NLTK as primary library.

**Table 1.** Document-level overlapping degree of NLP libraries on POS tagging

| Document | NLTK (244) | spaCy (246) | CoreNLP (242) | OpenNLP (246) | Overlapping degree |
|----------|-----------|-------------|---------------|---------------|--------------------|
| NLTK | – | 0.89 (218) | 0.84 (203) | 0.87 (213) | **0.87** |
| spaCy | 0.89 (218) | – | 0.82 (199) | 0.87 (214) | 0.86 |
| CoreNLP | 0.84 (203) | 0.82 (199) | – | 0.81 (197) | 0.82 |
| OpenNLP | 0.87 (213) | 0.87 (214) | 0.81 (197) | – | 0.85 |

The reason for choosing a primary library is shown as follows. The studied
NLP libraries are all widely used and well maintained by professional teams.
So the expected effectiveness of these NLP libraries is high enough to ensure
that the identical overlapping results in their outputs are highly possible to be
correct. The selected NLP library in this step is supposed to have the best overall
effectiveness. We also record the results of each sentence separately, which will
be analyzed in the next step.

## 3.2   Sentence-Level Overwriting

After document-level selection, we obtain a primary NLP library which has the
best overall performance. Then we try to investigate the fine-gained improvements on sentences. Due to the complex features of software documents, the
primary NLP library may not perform better than other NLP libraries on every
sentence within the document.

To locate the potential sentences, we calculate the overlapping degree of the
primary NLP library for each sentence by treating it as an individual document. We apply the same formula as the previous step on each sentence. Once
the sentence-level overlapping degree of a particular sentence is less than the
document-level overlapping degree of the document it belongs to, we mark it
as low-overlap sentence. The outputs of primary NLP library on low-overlap

**Table 2.** Sentence-level overlapping degree of NLP libraries on POS tagging

| Sentence 10 | NLTK (11) | spaCy (11) | CoreNLP (11) | OpenNLP (11) | Overlapping degree |
|---|---|---|---|---|---|
| NLTK | – | 0.64 (7) | 0.73 (8) | 0.64 (7) | 0.67 |
| spaCy | 0.64 (7) | – | 0.82 (9) | 0.64 (7) | 0.70 |
| CoreNLP | 0.73 (8) | 0.82 (9) | – | 0.73 (8) | 0.76 |
| OpenNLP | 0.64 (7) | 0.64 (7) | 0.73 (8) | – | 0.67 |

sentences are highly possible to have great space for improvements. For the low-overlap sentence, we overwrite its primary outputs with another set of results from the library which has highest overlapping degree on it.

Table 2 presents the overlapping degree of sentence 10 in this above case. We can find that the primary library NLTK obtains 0.67°, which is smaller than the document-level degree (i.e., 0.87). And Stanford CoreNLP gets the highest overlapping degree on it, so we overwrite the primary outputs on sentence 10 with the annotations generated by Stanford CoreNLP. In this case, the tag of token *getter* changes from adjective to noun.

---

**Algorithm 1:** Combined usage of NLP libraries

**Input** : Given Document $D$, candidate NLP libraries $\{NLP\}$
**Output:** Combined NLP results

1  $InitialResultsSet\{InitialR\} \leftarrow$ Analyze($NLP$, $D$);
2  **for** *each* $NLP_i \in \{NLP\}$ **do**
3      **for** *each* $(R_i, R_j) \in InitialR$ **do**
4        | Document-level overlapping degree $O(d_{ij}) \leftarrow$ Compare($(R_i, R_j)$) ;
5      **end**
6      $O(d_i) \leftarrow \sum_{j=1}^{|\{NLP\}|-1} O(d_{ij})$ / $(|\{NLP\}| - 1)$ ;
7  **end**
8  $NLP_{primary} \leftarrow \{NLP_i, \max(O(d_i))\}$ ;
9  **for** *each* $d \in \{D\}$ **do**
10     **for** *each* $s \in \{d\}$ **do**
11       **for** *each* $NLP_k \in \{\{NLP\}\text{-}NLP_{primary}\}$ **do**
12         | $O(s_{primary,k}) \leftarrow$ Compare($(R_{primary}, R_k)$) ;
13       **end**
14       $O(s_{primary}) \leftarrow \sum_{k=1}^{|\{NLP\}|-1} O(s_{primary,k})$ / $(|\{NLP\}| - 1)$ ;
15       **if** $O(s_{primary}) < O(d)$ **then**
16         | $\{S_{improve}\} \leftarrow (s, R_s)$;
17       **end**
18     **end**
19 **end**
20 $FinalResults \leftarrow$ Combine($R_{primary}$, $\{S_{improve}\}$);
21 **return** $FinalResults$

---

The NLP library may have some exclusive correctness, which usually occur on some controversial spots. If we directly use sentence-level overlapping degree to combine the results, the exclusive results will be totally overwritten. In our method, we can keep parts of the exclusive correctness, which are extracted when other NLP libraries cannot generate the same wrong results. Algorithm 1 shows the details of our combined method. $O$ () represents the calculation of overlapping degree, and $R()$ denotes the related results of the subject. The document-level selection of NLP library is implemented in line 2 to line 8, $NLP_{primary}$ denotes the primary NLP library. The sentence-level overwriting is implemented in line 9 to line 19.

## 4   Experiment

We propose a combined method for usage of NLP libraries to obtain more accurate NLP results than individual NLP library. The outputs generated by our method may include NLP annotations from several different NLP libraries. We discuss the effectiveness of our method in this section.

### 4.1   Research Questions

Our experiments investigate the following research questions.

– **RQ1:** Does the existing guideline for NLP library selection still work for the latest version of NLP libraries?
– **RQ2:** How effective is the combined method compared with individual NLP library?

To answer RQ1, we evaluate the guideline according to the comparison of NLP libraries on different documents in our study. RQ2 evaluates the effectiveness of our method compared with individual NLP library on tokenization and part-of-speech tagging. We also want to discuss the contributions of the two sources of information in our final results.

### 4.2   Subjects

To answer the above two research questions, we conduct experiments with four state-of-the-art NLP libraries and several documents from three different sources.

**Selection of NLP Libraries.** In the literature, there are a wide variety of NLP libraries used in different studies. Since our method focuses on analysis of software documents, we select several publicly available NLP libraries according to empirical results in existing work [17]. In their work, NLTK achieves the best overall results on tokenization, and spaCy performs better than other NLP libraries on part-of-speech tagging. They also make a systematic literature review of 1,350 conference papers in the area of software engineering [17]. Their results show that Stanford CoreNLP is the most frequently used NLP library. Furthermore, we add a new NLP library in our experiments, i.e., Apache OpenNLP. Apache OpenNLP is another widely used NLP library and it is proved to have a good performance on text chunking and other NLP tasks [2]. Finally, we select NLTK (version 3.4), spaCy (version 2.0.18), Stanford CoreNLP (version 3.9.2) and OpenNLP (version 1.9.1) as NLP libraries in our experiments. These NLP libraries are used as either individual NLP library or a source of outputs in the combined method. The releasing time between our studied NLP libraries and the existing work [17] is more than 2 years, which may result in different performance.

**Selection of Software Documents.** We select several software documents from feature requests in Jira, ReadMe files on GitHub and Java API documentation randomly to evaluate the effectiveness of our method. For feature requests, we select 160 descriptions from 8 Apache projects[8], i.e., AXIF2, CXF, Hadoop HDFS, Hadoop Common, Hadoop MapReduce, Hbase, Maven and Struts2. These projects are widely used in research of software engineering [26,32], and we select 20 feature requests from each project. For ReadMe files, we randomly select 20 projects on Github[9] and remove Github markdown and code snippets in the selected documents. For Java API documentations, 20 APIs of Java7 are randomly selected. The total number of tokens from the selected software documents is around 40,000.

**Selection of NLP Tasks.** We select two NLP tasks in our experiments, i.e., tokenization and part-of-speech tagging. There are two reasons for this selection. One reason is that these NLP tasks are widely used in the literatures [3,9,11, 14,23,25]. Once researchers want to analyze software documents, tokenization and part-of-speech tagging are highly possible to be applied. The other reason is that both the two tasks can produce individual outputs, which can help us to conduct a quantitative assessment easily.

### 4.3   Experimental Steps

For each NLP task, we perform the following steps:

- To control the size of inputs from different sources, the selected 200 documents (i.e., 160 descriptions of feature requests, 20 ReadMe files and 20 API documents) are repartitioned into 100 new documents. There are about 400 tokens in each document. All the documents are used to analyze the overlapping degree of the studied techniques, and help to evaluate the existing guideline on NLP library selection.
- The four NLP libraries are applied to analyze the preprocessed documents for tokenization and part-of-speech tagging, respectively.
- To obtain the benchmark of correct NLP results, 20 students in our group conduct manual tokenization and part-of-speech tagging. Due to the limitation of human labor, we only collect 50 documents (i.e., about 10,000 tokens in total) to build the benchmark. We also perform a cross-validation to identify the controversial spots. The threshold value of controversy is set as 0.5 overlapping degree, i.e., more than 10 students generate different annotations on it. We obtain 82 controversial results in total, and the final results

---

[8] https://projects.apache.org/.
[9] https://github.com/.

are determined through our discussion. For the other parts of studied documents, the handmade benchmarks are generated by results with the highest degree of overlap.
- We apply the two-steps method on the collected 50 documents, and discuss the effectiveness of our combined method and the four NLP libraries based on the handmade benchmark generated in the above step.

### 4.4   Experimental Results

### RQ1 Evaluation of the Existing Guideline
To evaluate the accuracy of tokenization and part-of-speech tagging for the studied NLP libraries, we compare the generated results with manual annotations. Table 3 and Table 4 show the results of comparison on tokenization and part-of-speech tagging, respectively. In the tables, column 1 lists all the studied libraries, column 2 presents the number of identical results from the outputs of NLP libraries and manual benchmark, column 3 presents the total number of results generated by NLP libraries. Column 4 presents the accuracy of each studied technique, i.e., the ratio of identical results to all the results. Columns 2 to 4 present the results on feature request, columns 5 to 7 present the results on ReadMe file, and columns 8 to 10 present the results on JavaDoc. We list the results of four individual NLP libraries at rows 3 to 6. And the last two rows in the tables present the results of our combined method which will be discussed in RQ2. From the data in Table 3 and Table 4, we have the following observations.

**Table 3.** Comparison on tokens (NLP libraries vs. Manual benchmark)

|  | Feature request | | | ReadMe file | | | JavaDoc | | |
|---|---|---|---|---|---|---|---|---|---|
|  | Identical | All | ACC | Identical | All | ACC | Identical | All | ACC |
| NLTK | 2484 | 2545 | **98%** | 3154 | 3238 | **98%** | 4209 | 4256 | **99%** |
| spaCy | 2453 | 2580 | 96% | 3113 | 3335 | 95% | 4188 | 4348 | 97% |
| Stanford CoreNLP | 2478 | 2529 | **98%** | 3170 | 3243 | **98%** | 4222 | 4245 | **99%** |
| OpenNLP | 2382 | 2535 | 94% | 3080 | 3218 | 96% | 4105 | 4221 | 97% |
| Combined method | 2496 | 2543 | 99% | 3171 | 3215 | 99% | 4219 | 4243 | 99% |
| Overall improvement | | | **1%** | | | **1%** | | | **0%** |

First, Stanford CoreNLP and NLTK perform best in terms of accuracy of tokenization on software documents. This finding is different with the existing guideline [17]. In that work, NLTK performs best on all kinds of software documents. Stanford CoreNLP performs worse than NLTK. Second, OpenNLP is the most effective NLP library on part-of-speech tagging in our experiments. While in the existing work [17], spaCy outperforms other NLP libraries on part-of-speech tagging except on Readme files. Based on the findings, we can infer that the guideline of NLP library selection should be updated with the change of releasing version and given documents.

**Table 4.** Comparison on POS tags (NLP libraries vs. Manual benchmark)

| | Feature request | | | ReadMe file | | | JavaDoc | | |
|---|---|---|---|---|---|---|---|---|---|
| | Identical | All | ACC | Identical | All | ACC | Identical | All | ACC |
| NLTK | 2165 | 2545 | 85% | 2807 | 3238 | 87% | 3701 | 4256 | **87%** |
| spaCy | 2241 | 2580 | **88%** | 2851 | 3335 | 87% | 3732 | 4348 | **87%** |
| Stanford CoreNLP | 2123 | 2529 | 84% | 2717 | 3243 | 84% | 3549 | 4245 | 84% |
| OpenNLP | 2197 | 2535 | 87% | 2842 | 3218 | **89%** | 3665 | 4221 | 87% |
| Combined method | 2308 | 2528 | 91% | 2931 | 3227 | 91% | 3824 | 4252 | 90% |
| Overall Improvement | | **3%** | | | **2%** | | | **3%** | |

---

**Finding 1** *The guideline of NLP library selection should be updated with the change of releases and given documents.*

---

## RQ2 Effectiveness of the Combined Method

Table 5 presents the data of overlapping degree. In the tables, column 1 lists all the six pairs of NLP libraries, while columns 2 to 4 and columns 6 to 8 present the percentages of identical tokens/tags to the average number of tokens/tags generated by the two NLP libraries. Column 5 and column 9 present the average percentages of identical tokens/tags for each pair of NLP libraries. The performance of studied NLP libraries is close to each other on both tokenization and part-of-speech tagging.

Comparing the results in Table 4 and Table 5, we find that the accuracy of part-of-speech tagging is higher than the overlapping degree of the paired NLP libraries in most cases. The promotion on accuracy of all the four NLP libraries indicates that every library has its own exclusive correctness on part-of-speech tagging. This finding inspires us to combine the exclusive correctness of each NLP library to achieve an improved effectiveness. The only one exception occurs on the overlapping degree of NLTK and OpenNLP on part-of-speech tags. They obtain 88% overlapped results, that is higher than the accuracy (i.e., 87%) in Table 4. We check the exception manually, and find that it is caused by the identical wrong results generated by the two libraries.

**Table 5.** Degree of overlap on tokens and part-of-speech tags

| | Tokens | | | | Part-of-speech tags | | | |
|---|---|---|---|---|---|---|---|---|
| | Feature request | ReadMe | JavaDoc | **Avg** | Feature Request | ReadMe | JavaDoc | **Avg** |
| NLTK vs. spaCy | 92% | 95% | 97% | 95% | 79% | 84% | 85% | 83% |
| NLTK vs. CoreNLP | 95% | 88% | 99% | 94% | 75% | 71% | 82% | 76% |
| NLTK vs. OpenNLP | 93% | 94% | 98% | 95% | 82% | 84% | 88% | 85% |
| spaCy vs. CoreNLP | 89% | 94% | 97% | 94% | 74% | 79% | 83% | 79% |
| spaCy vs. OpenNLP | 89% | 94% | 96% | 93% | 80% | 85% | 86% | 84% |
| CoreN vs. OpenNLP | 90% | 87% | 98% | 92% | 77% | 75% | 84% | 79% |

Based on the degree of overlap in Table 5, we apply the combined method to generate results through document-level selection and sentence-level overwriting. The final results on tokenization and part-of-speech tagging are showed in last two rows in Table 3 and Table 4. According to the comparison of results, the combined method outperforms the studied libraries in most cases of tokenization and part-of-speech tagging. The exceptions occur in tokenization of Java API documentations by NLTK and Stanford CoreNLP. They already obtains a really high accuracy of tokenization, so the improvements from other NLP libraries cannot help too much in this case. Our combined method can achieve slight improvements on tokenization and part-of-speech tagging on the basis of state-of-the-art NLP libraries. Since the initial results of the NLP libraries already have high quality, the 2% promotion is small but meaningful. The promotion means that our combined method is better than the best selection of independent NLP library. We can use the combined method instead of any individual NLP library in the analysis of software documents.

---

**Finding 2** *The combined method can generally outperform the individual NLP libraries in terms of effectiveness. The promotion on accuracy is around 2%.*

---

To evaluate the contribution of two steps in our combined method, i.e., document-level selection of NLP library and sentence-level overwriting, we analyze the proportion of each source in the final correct results. In our experiments, 1% of correct tokens and 4% of correct part-of-speech tags come from the improvements in sentence-level overwriting, and the other correct results are generated by the primary NLP library in document-level selection. Document-level selection plays a more important role than sentence-level overwriting in terms of contribution to correct results. However, the improvements of our combined method on individual NLP library mainly come from the sentence-level overwriting. The studied NLP libraries are all high-qualified toolkits with their own exclusive correctness. This is the main reason that we do not simply treat each sentence as an individual document and combined the results with highest sentence-level overlapping degree into the results of a document. The final outputs should mainly inherit the results of a primary NLP library. In this way, we can keep some exclusive correctness in the final results.

---

**Finding 3** *The majority of correct NLP results come from the outputs of primary NLP library. The meaningful improvements of our combined method on individual NLP library come from sentence-level overwriting.*

---

# 5   Related Work

## 5.1   Analyzing Software Artifacts with NLP Libraries

The NLP-related researchers have proposed many meaningful works for the analysis of documents [7,10,12,15,24]. These jobs are mostly designed to obtain accurate results of tokenization and part-of-speech tagging. Some works are already considered in the widely used NLP libraries [1,8]. However, for the researchers who are not professional at NLP, the common solution for NLP tasks is using state-of-the-art NLP libraries. To solve the problem on selection of NLP libraries, we propose a combined method to utilize the strengths of different NLP libraries.

## 5.2   Empirical Study on NLP Libraries

There are also several works which focus on the empirical comparison of current NLP libraries. Tian and Lo [27] conduct a comparison of the effectiveness of part-of-speech tagging on bug reports. In their work, Stanford CoreNLP performs better than other toolkits. To investigate the impacts of NLP toolkits on analyzing different texts, Pinto et al. [19] compared the results of tokenization and another three NLP tasks achieved by four NLP libraries. Olney et al. [16] investigated the accuracy of 9 part-of-speech taggers on more than 200 source code identifiers Omran et al. [17] compared the results of tokenization and part-of-speech tags achieved by four NLP libraries. Compared to their work, we select three types of software documents, along with four publicly available NLP libraries in this paper. We aim to check the effectiveness of the existing guideline, rather than the comparison of current NLP libraries. According to our results, each NLP library has its own exclusive results. This finding inspires us to investigate a combined method.

# 6   Conclusion

This paper evaluates the existing guideline on NLP library selection with 4 publicly available NLP libraries and 200 documents. The results report that the guideline should be updated continuously and each library has its own exclusive results. Based on these findings, we turn to investigate a combined method to utilize the strengths of different libraries. The evaluation confirms that our combined method can outperform any individual NLP library in the experiments. In future, we will conduct the study on more NLP tasks with additional NLP libraries and different software documents to improve the combined method.

**Acknowledgments.** This work is supported in part by the National Key R&D Program of China under Grant 2018YFB1003900, in part by National Natural Science Foundation of China under Grant 61402103, Grant 61572126 and Grant 61872078, and in part by Open Research Fund of Key Laboratory of Safety-Critical Software Fund (Nanjing University of Aeronautics and Astronautics), under Grant NJ2019006.

# References

1. Abebe, S.L., Tonella, P.: Natural language parsing of program element names for concept extraction. In: Proceedings of the 18th IEEE International Conference on Program Comprehension, pp. 156–159 (2010)
2. Arora, C., Sabetzadeh, M., Goknil, A., Briand, L C., Zimmer, F.: Change impact analysis for natural language requirements: an NLP approach. In: Proceedings of the 23rd IEEE International Requirements Engineering Conference, pp. 6–15 (2015)
3. Asaduzzaman, M., Roy, C.K., Monir, S., Schneider, K.A.: Exploring API method parameter recommendations. In: Proceedings of IEEE International Conference on Software Maintenance and Evolution, pp. 271–280 (2015)
4. Swathi, B.P., Anju, R.: Reformulation of natural language queries on source code base using NLP techniques. Int. J. Adv. Comput. Technol. **8**(2), 3047–3052 (2019)
5. Brill, E.: A simple rule-based part of speech tagger. In: Proceedings of the 3rd Applied Natural Language Processing Conference, pp. 152–155 (1992)
6. Cao, Y., Zou, Y., Luo, Y., Xie, B., Zhao, J.: Toward accurate link between code and software documentation. Sci. China Inf. Sci. **61**(5), 1–15 (2018). https://doi.org/10.1007/s11432-017-9402-3
7. Capobianco, G., Lucia, A.D., Oliveto, R., Panichella, A., Panichella, S.: Improving IR-based traceability recovery via noun-based indexing of software artifacts. J. Softw.: Evol. Process **25**(7), 743–762 (2013)
8. Gimpel, K., et al.: Part-of-speech tagging for Twitter: annotation, features, and experiments. In: Proceedings of the 49th Annual Meeting of the Association for Computational Linguistics: Human Language Technologies, pp. 42–47 (2011)
9. Gupta, R., Pal, S., Kanade, A., Shevade, S.K.: DeepFix: fixing common C language errors by deep learning. In: Proceedings of the 31st AAAI Conference on Artificial Intelligence, pp. 1345–1351 (2017)
10. Gupta, S., Malik, S., Pollock, L.L., Vijay-Shanker, K.: Part-of-speech tagging of program identifiers for improved text-based software engineering tools. In: Proceedings of the 21st IEEE International Conference on Program Comprehension, pp. 3–12 (2013)
11. Hu, X., Li, G., Xia, X., Lo, D., Jin, Z.: Deep code comment generation. In: Proceedings of the 26th Conference on Program Comprehension, pp. 200–210 (2018)
12. Jiang, W., Huang, L., Liu, Q., Lü, Y.: A cascaded linear model for joint Chinese word segmentation and part-of-speech tagging. In: Proceedings of the 46th Annual Meeting of the Association for Computational Linguistics, pp. 897–904 (2008)
13. Khamis, N., Witte, R., Rilling, J.: Automatic quality assessment of source code comments: the JavadocMiner. In: Hopfe, C.J., Rezgui, Y., Métais, E., Preece, A., Li, H. (eds.) NLDB 2010. LNCS, vol. 6177, pp. 68–79. Springer, Heidelberg (2010). https://doi.org/10.1007/978-3-642-13881-2_7
14. Kim, K., et al.: FaCoY: a code-to-code search engine. In: Proceedings of the 40th International Conference on Software Engineering, pp. 946–957 (2018)
15. Lynn, T., Scannell, K.P., Maguire, E.: Minority language Twitter: part-of-speech tagging and analysis of Irish tweets. In: Proceedings of the Workshop on Noisy User-generated Text, pp. 1–8 (2015)
16. Olney, W., Hill, E., Thurber, C., Lemma, B.: Part of speech tagging java method names. In: Proceedings of IEEE International Conference on Software Maintenance and Evolution, pp. 483–487 (2016)

17. Al Omran, F.N.A., Treude, C.: Choosing an NLP library for analyzing software documentation: a systematic literature review and a series of experiments. In: Proceedings of the 14th International Conference on Mining Software Repositories, pp. 187–197 (2017)

18. Petrov, S., Das, D., Mcdonald, R.: A universal part-of-speech tagset. Comput. Sci. **1**(3), 2089–2096 (2011)

19. Pinto, A.M., Oliveira, H.G., Alves, A.O.: Comparing the performance of different NLP toolkits in formal and social media text. In: Proceedings of the 5th Symposium on Languages, Applications and Technologies, pp. 3:1–3:16 (2016)

20. Reinhartz-Berger, I., Kemelman, M.: Extracting core requirements for software product lines. Require. Eng. **25**(1), 47–65 (2019). https://doi.org/10.1007/s00766-018-0307-0

21. Reiss, S.P.: Semantics-based code search. In: Proceedings of the 31st International Conference on Software Engineering, pp. 243–253 (2009)

22. Rodriguez, C., Zamanirad, S., Nouri, R., Darabal, K., Benatallah, B., Al-Banna, M.: Security vulnerability information service with natural language query support. In: Advanced Information Systems Engineering, pp. 497–512 (2019)

23. Santos, A.L., Prendi, G., Sousa, H., Ribeiro, R.: Stepwise API usage assistance using n-gram language models. J. Syst. Softw. **131**, 461–474 (2017)

24. Shokripour, R., Anvik, J., Kasirun, Z.M., Zamani, S.: Why so complicated? Simple term filtering and weighting for location-based bug report assignment recommendation. In: Proceedings of the 10th Working Conference on Mining Software Repositories, pp. 2–11 (2013)

25. Thung, F., Oentaryo, R.J., Lo, D., Tian, Y.: WebAPIRec: recommending web apis to software projects via personalized ranking. IEEE Trans. Emerg. Top. Comput. Intell. **1**(3), 145–156 (2017)

26. Thung, F., Wang, S., Lo, D., Lawall, J.L.: Automatic recommendation of API methods from feature requests. In: Proceedings of the 28th IEEE/ACM International Conference on Automated Software Engineering, pp. 290–300 (2013)

27. Tian, Y., Lo, D.: A comparative study on the effectiveness of part-of-speech tagging techniques on bug reports. In: Proceedings of the 22nd IEEE International Conference on Software Analysis, Evolution, and Reengineering, pp. 570–574 (2015)

28. Tripathy, A., Rath, S.K.: Application of natural language processing in object oriented software development. In: Proceedings of International Conference on Recent Trends in Information Technology (2014)

29. van der Aa, H., Di Ciccio, C., Leopold, H., Reijers, H.A.: Extracting declarative process models from natural language. In: Giorgini, P., Weber, B. (eds.) CAiSE 2019. LNCS, vol. 11483, pp. 365–382. Springer, Cham (2019). https://doi.org/10.1007/978-3-030-21290-2_23

30. Webster, J.J., Kit, C.: Tokenization as the initial phase in NLP. In: Proceedings of the 14th International Conference on Computational Linguistics, pp. 1106–1110 (1992)

31. Witte, R., Sateli, B., Khamis, N., Rilling, J.: Intelligent software development environments: integrating natural language processing with the eclipse platform. In: Butz, C., Lingras, P. (eds.) AI 2011. LNCS (LNAI), vol. 6657, pp. 408–419. Springer, Heidelberg (2011). https://doi.org/10.1007/978-3-642-21043-3_49

32. Xu, C., Sun, X., Li, B., Lu, X., Guo, H.: MULAPI: improving API method recommendation with API usage location. J. Syst. Softw. **142**, 195–205 (2018)

# Query-Based Metrics for Evaluating and Comparing Document Schemas

Evandro Miguel Kuszera[1,2(✉)], Letícia M. Peres[2(✉)],
and Marcos Didonet Del Fabro[2(✉)]

[1] Federal University of Technology - Paraná, Dois Vizinhos, PR, Brazil
`evandrokuszera@utfpr.edu.br`
[2] Federal University of Paraná, Curitiba, PR, Brazil
`{lmperes,marcos.ddf}@inf.ufpr.br`

**Abstract.** Document stores are frequently used as representation format in many applications. It is often necessary to transform a set of data stored in a relational database (RDB) into a document store. There are several approaches that execute such translation. However, it is difficult to evaluate which target document structure is the most appropriate. In this article, we present a set of query-based metrics for evaluating and comparing documents schemas against a set of existing queries, that represent the application access pattern. We represent the target document schema and the queries as DAGs (Directed Acyclic Graphs), which are used to calculate the metrics. The metrics allow to evaluate if a given target document schema is adequate to answer the queries. We performed a set of experiments to calculate the metrics over a set of documents produced by existing transformation solutions. The metric results are related with smaller coding effort, showing that the metrics are effective to guide the choice of a target NoSQL document structure.

**Keywords:** RDBs · Document stores · Metrics · Evaluation

## 1 Introduction

Relational databases (RDB) are widely used to store data of several types of applications. However, they do not meet all requirements imposed by modern applications [18]. These applications handle structured, semi-structured and unstructured data, and RDBs are not flexible enough, since they have a predefined schema. In these scenarios, NoSQL databases [16] emerged as an option. They differ from RDB in terms of architecture, data model and query language [16]. They are generally classified according to the data model used: document, column family, key-value or graph-based. These databases are called schema-free, since there is no need to define a schema before storing data. This flexibility facilitates rapid application development and makes it possible to structure the data in different ways. One of the most used NoSQL format are document stores.

RDB and document stores will be used together for a long period of time, being necessary to investigate strategies to convert and migrate schema and

© Springer Nature Switzerland AG 2020
S. Dustdar et al. (Eds.): CAiSE 2020, LNCS 12127, pp. 530–545, 2020.
https://doi.org/10.1007/978-3-030-49435-3_33

data between them. Different approaches have been presented to convert RDB to NoSQL document stores [4, 8, 9, 17, 20]. Some of them consider just the structure of the RDB in the conversion process [17, 20]. While others also consider the access pattern of the application [4, 8, 9]. However, none of the approaches is concerned with the evaluation and the comparison of the output document structure against the existing queries that need to be adapted and then executed. Often, expert user knowledge is the only guarantee that the produced document is appropriate.

The work from [5] presents eleven metrics to evaluate the structure of document oriented databases. These metrics were based on those proposed in [14] and [10] to evaluate XML schemas. Such evaluation is important to guide the choice of an adequate document structure. However, the approach has no specific metrics for assessing the queries access pattern against document structure. Despite not having a formal schema, a document has a structure used by the queries to retrieve data. We consider that the document structure can be used as an abstraction to represent a schema.

In this paper, we present a set of query-based metrics to evaluate a NoSQL document schema in relation to a set of queries that represent the application access patterns. We use DAGs (Directed Acyclic Graphs) to represent the queries and the document schemas. DAGs as schema have already been used in a previous approach to converting RDB to NoSQL nested models [11]. Since it is possible to produce different data schemas in an RDB to NoSQL conversion scenario, it is important to have a procedure to choose the most appropriate one. To help with this, we show how to use the query-based metrics alone or in combination to evaluate and compare candidate NoSQL schemas.

We performed a set of experiments to validate the metrics, using as input a set of NoSQL schemas generated from an existing RDB, and a set of queries previously defined on the same RDB. All NoSQL schemas were generated using RDB to NoSQL conversion rules already proposed in the literature. After computing the metrics, we migrate the RDB data to a MongoDB instance, according to the schemas previously generated. Then, we measure the necessary query coding effort/maintenance. The conversion showed that the metrics are effective to guide on the choice of an appropriate document structure.

The contributions of this paper are summarized as follows:

- A set of metrics to evaluate and compare document schema against a set of queries that represent the application access patterns, **prior to the execution** of an RDB to document transformation.
- A query score *QScore* and a schema score *SScore*, enabling to combine related metrics.
- A comparison of 4 different RDB to NoSQL document conversion approaches from the literature, through the query-based metrics and a set of previously defined queries.

The remainder of this paper is organized as follows: Sect. 2 presents background about RDB to NoSQL conversion approaches and how we represent

NoSQL document schemas as DAGs. In Sect. 3 we present our query-based metrics. Section 4 shows how to combine the query-based metrics to evaluate and compare NoSQL document schemas. Section 5 deals with experiments and results. Related work is given in Sect. 6. Finally, conclusions and future work are provided in Sect. 7.

## 2    Background

Different works present approaches for converting RDB to NoSQL document [4,8,9,17,20]. The works [17,20] are automatic solutions that receive as input the RDB metadata and E-R diagrams, respectively. [17] presents an algorithm that considers the dependencies between tables and the number of PKs and FKs during the conversion process. [20] presents an algorithm that uses the dependencies between tables, however, the data nesting is performed only in the FK to PK direction.

The approaches [4,8,9] are semi-automatic. The user needs to provide additional information about the RDB to guide the translation. In these approaches, in addition to the E-R diagram, the user provides a kind of table classification. This table classification is used to decide which tables should be embedded together. The work from [4] develops an algorithm and four kinds of tables: *main*, *subclass*, *relationship* and *common*. The conversion algorithm uses this classification to nest the subclass and common tables in the main table. Relationship tables are converted using references. The approach from [9] has a different classification composed of four classes: *codifier*, *simple entity*, *complex entity* and *N:N-link*. Besides the classification, the user must provide the "table in focus", that represents the target NoSQL entity. The algorithm builds a tree with the related tables. Finally, in [8], they are based on the creation of tags to guide the process. The user annotates the E-R diagram with tags (*frequent join*, *modify*, *insert* and *big size*) that represent the data and query characteristics. From these tags the algorithm decides to use embedded documents or references in the conversion.

In a previous work, we created an approach to convert RDB to NoSQL nested models [11]. We use a set of DAGs (Directed Acyclic Graphs) to capture the source RDB and the target NoSQL document structure, which is an abstraction used to represent a NoSQL schema. Each DAG lists a set of RDB tables which are transformed into one NoSQL entity (document structure). Through our approach we use the DAGs to represent the process of converting RDB to NoSQL document from the works cited at the beginning of this section.

A DAG is defined as $G = (V, E)$, where the set of vertices $V$ is related with the tables of the RDB and the set of edges $E$ with the relationships between tables. The direction of the edges defines the transformation flow. Each DAG may be seen as a tree, where the root vertex is the target entity. The path from one leaf vertex to the root vertex defines one transformation flow. Each vertex contains the metadata of its respective RDB table, including the table name, fields and primary key. The edge between two vertices encapsulates relationship data between two tables, including primary and foreign keys and which entity is on the *one* or *many* side of the relationship. Through the DAG, we specify the de-normalization process from a set of related tables to produce a NoSQL entity. There are works with similar idea, but with different strategies [8,20].

Similarly, a NoSQL entity (document structure) is also represented by a DAG. The root vertex is the first level of the collection and the remaining vertices are the nested entities. The direction of the edges defines the direction of nesting between entities. Besides that, the edge encapsulates nesting type information, including embedded objects or array of embedded objects types. Through a set of DAGs it is possible to represent a NoSQL schema, where each DAG represents the structure of a collection. We define a NoSQL schema as $S = \{DAG_1, ..., DAG_n | DAG_i \in C\}$, where $C$ is the set of collections of $S$.

## 3   Query-Based Metrics

This section presents our query-based metrics. We define six metrics to measure the coverage that a particular NoSQL document schema has in relation to a set of queries representing the application access pattern. The metrics are used to identify which schema has the appropriate access pattern required by the application. First, we present the key definitions and terminologies required to introduce the query-based metrics. Then, we present the set of metrics.

### 3.1   Queries and Paths

The following are the key definitions and terminologies used in this paper.

**Query as DAG.** A query is defined as $q = (V_q, E_q)$, where $V_q$ is a set of vertices, representing the query tables, and $E_q$ is a set of edges, representing the join conditions between query tables. The query $q \in Q$, where $Q$ is the set of queries.

We define two rules to convert an SQL *SELECT* statement into a DAG. SQL statements including sub-queries and *full outer join* clauses are not supported.

– **Rule 1:** if the statement has only one table, then a DAG with one vertex representing the table is created.
– **Rule 2:** if the statement has two or more tables, then it is necessary to define which table is the root vertex of the DAG. After that, the other tables are added to the DAG according to the join conditions of the statement.

To identify the join condition in Rule 2, we parse the SQL statement. Then, we apply one of the following subrules to determine which table is the root vertex:

– **Rule 2.1:** if it is a left join, returns the leftmost table in the FROM clause.
– **Rule 2.2:** if it is a right join, returns the rightmost table in FROM clause.
– **Rule 2.3:** if it is an inner join, returns the first table in the FROM clause.

**Path, Sub Path and Indirect Path.** We define the types of paths considered in the metrics to evaluate the schemas and queries DAGs:

- **Path:** a path $p$ is a sequence of vertices $v_1, v_2, ..., v_j$, such that $(v_i, v_{i+1}) \in V_q$, $1 \le i \le j-1$, $v_1$ is the root vertex and $v_j$ is the leaf vertex of the $DAG$. This sequence of vertices may be called the path from the root vertex to the leaf vertex.
- **Sub Path:** considering a path $p = (v_1, v_2, ..., v_k)$ and, for any $i$ and $j$, such that $1 \le i \le j \le k$, a subpath of $p$ is defined as $p_{ij} = (v_i, v_{i+1}, ..., v_j)$, from vertex $i$ to vertex $j$.
- **Indirect Path:** Considering a path $p = (v_1, v_2, ..., v_k)$ and, for any $i$, $y$ and $j$, such that $1 \le i \le y \le j \le k$, an indirect path relative to $p$ is defined as $p_{ind} = (v_i, v_{i+1}, ..., v_j)$, where $\exists v_y \in p : v_y \notin p_{ind}$. That is, an indirect path $p_{ind}$ is the one where all its vertices and edges are contained in path $p$, but there are additional intermediate vertices in $p$ that separate one or more vertices of $p_{ind}$.

In addition, to make the query-based metric definitions more clear, we use the following terms: $V_q$, $V_s$ and $V_c$ are the vertex set of a given query, schema and collection (or DAG), respectively. $P_q$, $P_s$ and $P_c$ are the path set (all paths from root to leaves) of a given query, schema and collection, respectively.

## 3.2 Direct Edge Coverage

*Direct Edge* (1) measures query edge coverage against the edges of a given schema collection, considering the direction of edges (e.g. $a \to b$). $E_{dq}$ and $E_{dc}$ denote the set of query and collection edges considering the direction of the edges. Schema coverage (2) is the maximum value found when applying *DirectEdge* metric for each schema collection $c \in C$.

$$DirectEdge(c, q) = |(E_{dq} \cap E_{dc})|/|E_{dq}| \qquad (1)$$

$$DirectEdge(q) = Max(C, q, DirectEdge) \qquad (2)$$

The function *Max* is a higher-order function that receives a set of elements (e.g., collection set $C$), the query $q$ and the metric function (e.g., *DirectEdge*). It applies the metric for all elements of the collection and the query $q$ and it returns the higher value. It is used in other metrics in the remaining of the paper.

## 3.3 All Edge Coverage

*All Edge* (3) measures edge coverage between the query and schema collection, regardless of edge direction (e.g. $a \to b$ or $a \leftarrow b$). $E_q$ and $E_c$ denote the query and collection edges, respectively. Schema coverage (4) is the maximum value found when applying *AllEdge* metric for each schema collection ($c_i$).

$$AllEdge(c, q) = |(E_q \cap E_c)|/|E_q| \qquad (3)$$

$$AllEdge(q) = Max(C, q, AllEdge) \qquad (4)$$

## 3.4    Path Coverage

The *Path Coverage* metric measures the coverage of query paths in relation to the collection paths. A query may have one or more paths (e.g. $q_6$ in the Fig. 3 has two paths). Through the *Path Coverage* it is possible to measure the coverage of the query paths relative to the collection paths (5). The Path Coverage for all the schema (6) is the maximum value found when applying the metric for each collection.

$$Path(c, q) = |(P_q \cap P_c)|/|P_q| \tag{5}$$

$$Path(q) = Max(C, q, Path) \tag{6}$$

## 3.5    Sub Path Coverage

Through the *Sub Path Coverage* metric, it is checked if the query paths are present in the collection as subpaths (7). We define the *existSubPath* function that receives as parameters a query path ($qp \in P_q$) and a set of paths, where the set of paths is the paths of a given collection ($P_c$). The function returns 1 if the query path was found or 0 if it was not found as a subpath. It is possible to measure the sub path coverage of all the schema by applying the metric for each collection (8). The result is the higher value returned.

$$existSubPath(qp, P_c) = \begin{cases} 1 & found\ qp\ as\ subpath\ in\ P_c \\ 0 & not\ found\ qp\ as\ subpath\ in\ P_c \end{cases}$$

$$SubPath(c, q) = \frac{\sum_{i=1}^{|P_q|} existSubPath(qp_i, P_c)}{|P_q|} \tag{7}$$

$$SubPath(q) = Max(C, q, SubPath) \tag{8}$$

## 3.6    Indirect Path Coverage

Through the *Indirect Path* metric, it is checked if the query paths are present in the schema as indirect paths (as defined in Sect. 3.1). To find indirect paths in the schema we define the function *existIndPath*, that receives as parameters the query path ($qp$) and a set of collections' paths ($P_c$). If there is an indirect path in the collection that matches the query path, the function returns 1, otherwise it returns 0. In (9) we measure the indirect path coverage relative to the collection level, and in (10) relative to the schema, by applying the metric for each collection, where the largest value returned represents the schema coverage.

$$existIndPath(qp, P_c) = \begin{cases} 1 & found\ qp\ as\ an\ indirect\ path\ in\ P_c \\ 0 & not\ found\ qp\ as\ an\ indirect\ path\ in\ P_c \end{cases}$$

$$IndPath(c, q) = \frac{\sum_{i=1}^{|P_q|} existIndPath(qp_i, P_c)}{|P_q|} \qquad (9)$$

$$IndPath(q) = Max(C, q, IndPath) \qquad (10)$$

### 3.7   Required Collections Coverage

The *Required Collections* (11) metric returns the smallest number of collections required to answer a given query. The function $createCollectionPaths(q)$ returns a set of paths that consists of collections that have the entities required to answer the query.

$$ReqColls(q) = min(createCollectionPaths(q)) \qquad (11)$$

The metrics presented above enable to independently evaluate the queries. In the next section we describe how to combined them to provide a broader evaluation.

## 4   Combining the Metrics

In this section we present how to combine the metrics for measuring the overall coverage of a schema with respect to a set of input queries. First, it is necessary to calculate a *QScore*, which denotes a score per metric, or per combination of related metrics, per query. This score enables to set up weights to prioritize the importance of specific metrics. Second, we calculate a *SScore*, which is a score for a set of queries over a given schema. The results are used to rank the input schema. These scores are explained in the following sections.

### 4.1   Query Score (QScore)

The *QScore* yields a single value per metric, or a value that combines related metrics. The score is calculated for a given metric and a given query $q_i$. The *QScore* for metrics *DirEdge*, *AllEdge* and *ReqColls* is the same value returned by the metric:

$$QScore(DirEdge, q) = DirEdge(q) \qquad (12)$$

$$QScore(AllEdge, q) = AllEdge(q) \qquad (13)$$

$$QScore(ReqColls, q) = ReqColls(q) \qquad (14)$$

However, the *QScore* for metrics *Path*, *Sub Path* and *Indirect Path* is a unique value and is namely as *Paths*. It returns the highest value among the three metrics, taking into account the depth of each path and an additional weight, as defined below:

$$path_v = Path(q_i) * w_p \qquad (15)$$

$$subpath_v = (SubPath(q_i) * w_{sp})/depthSP(q_i) \qquad (16)$$

$$indpath_v = (IndPath(q_i) * w_{ip})/depthIP(q_i) \qquad (17)$$

$$QScore(Paths, q_i) = max(path_v, subpath_v, indpath_v) \qquad (18)$$

First, the metric value is weighted according to its path type, divided by the smallest depth in which the root vertex of path is located in the schema. The depth is obtained by a specific function for each metric. The weights $w_p$, $w_{sp}$ and $w_{ip}$ are used to set up a priority between *Path*, *Sub Path* and *Indirect Path* metrics. The method for calculating *QScore* is inspired by the results of [6], where the authors state that the depth of the required data in the collection and the need to access data stored at different levels of the collection produce negative impact. As the *Path* metric denotes the exact match between query path and collection path (with $depth = 1$), one possibility is to set the $w_p$ with the highest value, followed by smaller values for $w_{sp}$ and $w_{ip}$. In this way, schemas with exact match are prioritized. Another aspect is related to data redundancy that NoSQL schemas may present: a query path can be found as a *Path*, *Sub Path*, and *Indirect Path* in the schema. Then, by defining distinct weights and using path depth, we can prioritize a particular type of path coverage. For better readability, we assign each calculation to a specific variable (15–17), which is then used to calculate the *QScore* (18).

## 4.2   Schema Score (SScore)

*SScore* denotes the schema score for a given metric (except *ReqColls*) as the sum of the *QScore* values for all the queries, where each query $q_i$ has a specific weight $w_i$, and the sum of all $w_i$ is equal to 1. Following the same idea of the *QScore*, it has a single value for *Path*, *SubPath*, and *IndPath*, which is the sum of its corresponding *QScore*. It is defined below:

$$SScore(metric, Q) = \sum_{i=1}^{|Q|} QScore(metric, q_i) * w_i \qquad (19)$$

The *SScore* for *ReqColls* metric is a ratio between the number of queries and the number of collections required to answer them. A schema that answers each input query through only one collection has *SScore* equal to 1. It decreases when the number of collections increases. It is defined as follows:

$$NC = \sum_{i=1}^{|Q|} QScore(ReqColls, q_i)$$

$$SScore(ReqColls, Q) = \frac{|Q|}{NC} \qquad (20)$$

$NC$ is the number of collections required to answer all input queries, which is the sum of all $QScore$. The expression for calculating $SScore$ above is based on the schema minimality metric presented in [3].

These scores show the coverage provided by the schema for each query, where we can identify which queries require the most attention or are not covered by the schema. The $SScore$ field provides an overview of how well the schema fits the query set. Since the metrics are not independent, we do not define a single expression to calculate the overall score of the schema. The goal here is to provide the user with a methodology for evaluating NoSQL schema using the proposed metrics. Still, the user can use the metrics independently, according to their needs and application requirements.

## 5    Experimental Evaluation

In this section we present the experiments to evaluate our query-based metrics in an RDB to NoSQL documents conversion scenario, where different NoSQL schemas are generated from the input RDB. In order to generate the candidate NoSQL schemas we select four RDB to NoSQL conversion approaches from the literature. The input queries represent the application's access pattern over the RDB, and are then known a priori. The goal is to show how to use the query-based metrics to assist the user in the process of evaluation, comparison and selection of the appropriate NoSQL schema before executing the data migration. In the following sections we detail the execution of each of these steps.

### 5.1    Creating NoSQL Schemas from Conversion Approaches

We select four RDB to NoSQL document approaches from the literature, that define different ways to convert relational data to nested data [8,9,17,20]. These approaches were chosen because they contain the most diverse set of translation rules. We apply the translation rules on the RDB of Fig. 1 to generate a set of NoSQL schemas using our DAG approach to represent them. So, we create one schema for each approach and set a label from A to D to identify them.

Figure 2 shows the graphical representation of the generated NoSQL schemas. The vertices with gray background color represent the collections of the schemas (root vertex). We can see that schemas differ in number of collections and arrangement of entities. As a result, we have all approaches represented by the same format, which allows us to evaluate and compare them objectively.

### 5.2    Defining the Evaluation Scenario

The schemas are evaluated considering the best matching between the queries access patterns and the schema structure. We use *Path, SubPath, IndPath,*

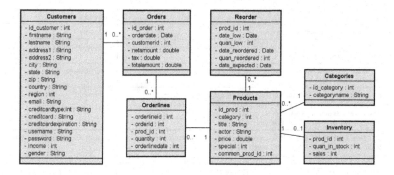

**Fig. 1.** Input RDB

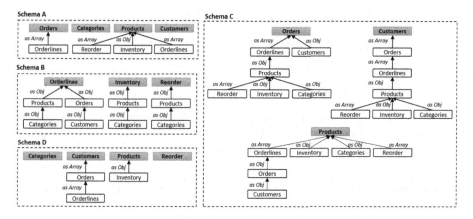

**Fig. 2.** Generated NoSQL schemas by approach

*DirEdge*, *AllEdge* and *ReqColls* metrics to check if the entities are (or not) nested according to the access pattern. To calculate *SScore* and *QScore*, we assigned the same weight for all queries and for all *paths* metrics ($w_p = 1; w_{sp} = 1; w_{ip} = 1$). This means that all queries and types of path coverage have the same priority. The depth where query path starts is also considered in the calculation, prioritizing schemas where the entities are closest to the root of the DAG. However, the user can define different weights and turn off the depth of path, according to their needs.

The seven queries used to evaluate the schemas are presented in Fig. 3. These queries have been chosen because they contain different access patterns. We show the queries in SQL and also as DAG paths, which are produced according to the translation rules from Sect. 3.1. Each query DAG contains the data path of each SQL statement, but alternative DAGs could be built to represent different access patterns.

| ID | SQL | DAG Paths |
|----|-----|-----------|
| q1 | **select \* from** customers **where** id_customer = 1; | Customers |
| q2 | **select \* from** products **inner join** inventory **on** products.id_prod = inventory.prod_id **where** id_prod = 1; | Products\Inventory |
| q3 | **select \* from** orders **left join** orderlines **on** orderlines.orderid = orders.id_order **where** id_order = 1; | Orders\Orderlines |
| q4 | **select \* from** customers    **left join** orders **on** customers.id_customer = orders.customerid    **left join** orderlines **on** orders.id_order = orderlines.orderid **left join** products **on** orderlines.prod_id = products.id_prod **where** orderdate between '2009-01-01' and '2009-01-02'; | Customers\Orders\Orderlines\Products |
| q5 | **select \* from** products **left join** orderlines **on** products.id_prod = orderlines.prod_id **left join** orders **on** orderlines.orderid = orders.id_order **left join** customers **on** orders.customerid = customers.id_customer **where** products.price **between** 29 **and** 30; | Products\Orderlines\Orders\Customers |
| q6 | **select \* from** orders o **left join** customers c **on** o.customerid = c.id_customer **left join** orderlines ol **on** ol.orderid = o.id_order **where** orderdate between '2009-01-01' and '2009-01-02'; | Orders\Customers Orders\Orderlines |
| q7 | **select \* from** inventory **right join** orderlines **on** inventory.prod_id = orderlines.prod_id **where** orderid = 1; | Orderlines\Inventory |

**Fig. 3.** Input queries used to evaluate the NoSQL schemas

### 5.3   Experimental Results

In this section we present the metrics result and the impact on query coding effort for each schema[1]. Finally, preliminary results on query execution time are presented. Table 1 summarizes all results and is used by the sections below.

**Metrics Result.** Table 1 shows the $QScore$ for the $Paths$, $DirEdge$, $AllEdge$ and $ReqColls$ metrics, by query. $Paths$ is calculating taking into account the $Path$, $SubPath$, and $IndPath$ metrics (see Sect. 4.1). The $SScore$ is also shown. Considering the paths coverage, schema $C$ has the highest score 0.93. This means $C$ best matches the access pattern of the query set. Following are the schemas $A$, $D$ and $B$, with schema $B$ having the worst $SScore = 0.08$.

We use path metrics to identify which schema best covers the queries. For instance, in schema $C$, the queries $q_1 - q_6$ are 100% covered by the schema through the $Path$, $SubPath$ or $IndPath$ metrics. Only $q_7$ is penalized for starting at level 2 of the $Orders$ collection, resulting in lower $QScore$ (0.5). In contrast, in the schema $B$ we identify only the queries $q_1$ and $q_6$ that match paths metrics, but both queries are penalized by the level where they are located in the schema. For example, to answer $q_1$ is necessary traverse the $Orderlines$ collection to find $Customers$ entity, at level 3. If we look at schema $B$, we notice that the $Orderlines$, $Inventory$, and $Reorder$ collections are inverted in relation to the query access pattern. As a result, there is no coverage for the path metrics for queries $q_2 - q_5$ and $q_7$.

Using the metrics $DirEdge$ and $AllEdge$, we verify the degree to which the entities in the schema are related to each other, as required by the access pattern of the queries. For example, schema $C$ has the highest $DirEdge$ score

---

[1] The tool implemented and all the results are available for download at: https://github.com/evandrokuszera/nosql-query-based-metrics.

**Table 1.** Query-based metrics result, by schema

Schema A

| Query | Paths | DirEdge | AllEdge | ReqColls | LoC | Stages | Time |
|---|---|---|---|---|---|---|---|
| q1 | 1.0 | 0.0 | 0.0 | 1 | 5 | 1 | 0.0 |
| q2 | 1.0 | 1.0 | 1.0 | 1 | 11 | 2 | 0.0 |
| q3 | 1.0 | 1.0 | 1.0 | 1 | 5 | 1 | 0.0 |
| q4 | 0.0 | 0.3 | 0.3 | 3 | 92 | 11 | 0.06 |
| q5 | 0.0 | 0.3 | 0.3 | 3 | 73 | 11 | 0.89 |
| q6 | 0.5 | 0.5 | 0.5 | 2 | 19 | 6 | 0.02 |
| q7 | 0.0 | 0.0 | 0.0 | 1 | 27 | 5 | 0.06 |
| SScore | 0.50 | 0.45 | 0.45 | 0.58 | 232 | 37 | 1.03 |

Schema B

| Query | Paths | DirEdge | AllEdge | ReqColls | LoC | Stages | Time |
|---|---|---|---|---|---|---|---|
| q1 | 0.3 | 0.0 | 0.0 | 1 | 16 | 3 | 0.06 |
| q2 | 0.0 | 0.0 | 1.0 | 1 | 21 | 2 | 0.02 |
| q3 | 0.0 | 0.0 | 1.0 | 1 | 48 | 2 | 0.05 |
| q4 | 0.0 | 0.3 | 1.0 | 1 | 66 | 7 | 0.07 |
| q5 | 0.0 | 0.66 | 1.0 | 1 | 50 | 5 | 0.19 |
| q6 | 0.25 | 0.5 | 1.0 | 1 | 41 | 6 | 0.11 |
| q7 | 0.0 | 0.0 | 0.0 | 2 | 23 | 4 | 0.06 |
| SScore | 0.08 | 0.21 | 0.71 | 0.88 | 265 | 29 | 0.55 |

Schema C

| Query | Paths | DirEdge | AllEdge | ReqColls | LoC | Stages | Time |
|---|---|---|---|---|---|---|---|
| q1 | 1.0 | 0.0 | 0.0 | 1 | 10 | 2 | 0.0 |
| q2 | 1.0 | 1.0 | 1.0 | 1 | 12 | 2 | 0.0 |
| q3 | 1.0 | 1.0 | 1.0 | 1 | 11 | 2 | 0.0 |
| q4 | 1.0 | 1.0 | 1.0 | 1 | 15 | 2 | 0.03 |
| q5 | 1.0 | 1.0 | 1.0 | 1 | 15 | 2 | 0.06 |
| q6 | 1.0 | 1.0 | 1.0 | 1 | 13 | 2 | 0.01 |
| q7 | 0.5 | 0.0 | 0.0 | 1 | 27 | 5 | 0.06 |
| SScore | 0.93 | 0.71 | 0.71 | 1.0 | 103 | 17 | 0.16 |

Schema D

| Query | Paths | DirEdge | AllEdge | ReqColls | LoC | Stages | Time |
|---|---|---|---|---|---|---|---|
| q1 | 1.0 | 0.0 | 0.0 | 1 | 10 | 2 | 0.0 |
| q2 | 1.0 | 1.0 | 1.0 | 1 | 12 | 2 | 0.0 |
| q3 | 0.5 | 1.0 | 1.0 | 1 | 13 | 3 | 0.02 |
| q4 | 0.0 | 0.67 | 0.66 | 2 | 55 | 9 | 0.08 |
| q5 | 0.0 | 0.0 | 0.66 | 2 | 89 | 12 | 35.91 |
| q6 | 0.25 | 0.5 | 1.0 | 1 | 25 | 5 | 0.03 |
| q7 | 0.0 | 0.0 | 0.0 | 2 | 37 | 8 | 0.09 |
| SScore | 0.39 | 0.45 | 0.62 | 0.70 | 241 | 41 | 36.12 |

and *AllEdge* score, which means that it has the closest access pattern to the query set. In contrast, schema $B$ has the highest *AllEdge* score (same value as schema $C$) and the smallest *DirEdge* score, which means that entities are related to each other in the schema $B$ according to the query structure, but the relationship direction is inverted, so it does not correspond properly to the access pattern of queries. For example, the collection *Orderlines* has part of the relationships between entities corresponding to the $q_4 - q_6$ query structure ($DirEdge > 0$), but for the remaining queries, schema $B$ is inverted.

For *ReqColls* metric, the schema $C$ has the best result, with $SScore = 1.0$. This means that all queries are answered accessing a single collection. Then, the schemas are ranked as: $C$, $B$, $D$ and $A$. This result is due to schema $C$ being the most redundant schema, in which the three collections encapsulate all RDB entities, but using a different nesting order.

**Query Coding Effort.** We measured the impact on query coding effort for each schema, to asses if it is related with metrics results. To measure the coding effort, we use the number of lines of code (LoC) required to manually implement the query. While they could be automatically generated, they would need to be maintained during the application life cycle. The goal here is to check whether high *SScore* schemas have less query implementation complexity.

We created four target database instances in MongoDB[2] according to schemas $A$, $B$, $C$ and $D$. MongoDB was selected because it is a widely used document store. We use our Metamorfose framework to migrate data from RDB to MongoDB. After that, we implement all queries of Fig. 3 using the MongoDB *aggregation pipeline* framework, that uses the concept of data processing pipelines. Each pipeline consists of stages, where each stage transforms the documents what goes through it.

The LoC for each query was obtained by the MongoDB *explain* command, with a standardized query format, facilitating line count. In addition to LoC, we counted the number of stages used in the pipeline to fetch and project documents according to the query DAG structure. Table 1 shows the LoC of each query by schema. Considering the total LoC per schema, schema $C$ has the smallest value (103), followed by schemas $A$, $D$, and $B$. When considering the number of query pipelines, schema $C$ has the lowest value, followed by schemas $B$, $A$, and $D$. In this case, $B$ takes second place because its structure has no nested arrays, so no extra stages are required to unwind arrays of documents.

Analyzing *SScore* results for *Paths*, *DirEdge*, and *AllEdge* metrics together with the aggregate LoC and *Stages*, we can verify that schemas with higher *Paths* and *DirEdge* scores require less lines of code when implementing queries. For metric *AllEdge* this is not always true. This metric shows whether the entities in the schema are related as the query access pattern. However, the relationship may exist, but the direction may not match the pattern specified in the query (case of schema $B$). In this case, more effort is required to project the data according to the query pattern.

---

[2] https://www.mongodb.com.

To summarize, the expert user can evaluate and compare schema options before executing the translation from an RDB to a NoSQL document stores, by applying the set of defined metrics and scores. Through these metrics we check if the entities are (or not) nested according to the query access pattern. We also check which queries need to fetch data from different collections, so the user can decide which schemas to prioritize. We generated a set of queries and the LoC metrics reflect the results of our metrics.

**Query Execution Time.** We measured query execution time to verify if it is related with the metrics results. The last column of Table 1 shows the average execution time in seconds (each query was executed 30x). It is worth noting that query time for $q_1 - q_3$ returned zero for some schemas because the search field is the index of collection. The results show that schema $C$ is the most adapted, followed by schemas $B$, $A$, and $D$. Schema B is the second one, even though it did not match the queries access pattern. The reason is due to the execution time of $q_5$ for schemas $A$ and $D$. For both schemas, it is necessary to perform the MongoDB *lookup* operation (similar to SQL left join). In $A$, there is a *lookup* operation between *Orders*, *Products* and *Customers*, and in $D$ between *Products* and *Customers*. In both cases, the fields used in the *lookup* are located in nested arrays, which has significant impact, especially for schema $D$, where the *lookup* field is located inside two nested object arrays. However, these results are preliminary and need further investigation, where we plan to extend our metrics set to consider the impact on data nesting, document size, collection size, and the use of indexes have on query performance.

## 6   Related Work

Different works present formal definitions for NoSQL document data models [1,2,19]. In [2], they present NoAM, the NoSQL Abstract Model that use as the main modelling unit the concept of aggregates (set of entities) and is driven by application use cases (functional requirements). [1] and [19] present approaches that transform a conceptual model (UML) into NoSQL physical model. These approaches consist in methodologies for defining NoSQL schemas according to user-supplied parameters. However, they do not provide means to evaluate the schema produced. Our approach aims to evaluate the NoSQL schema in relation to a set of queries that represent the access pattern of the application.

There are works defining optimized schemas for column-family [7,13] and document [8,12,15] oriented NoSQL databases. In [7] they present Graph based Partition Algorithm (GPA) approach, that groups high affinity schema attributes in the same column family to avoid loading unnecessary data to answer queries. In a similar way, [13] describes a cost-based approach to schema design that recommends a column-family NoSQL schema suitable for the application queries. The authors of [12] and [8] present a conversion approach for generating NoSQL document logical schema considering a previously provided conceptual model and the expected workload of the application. Our query-based metrics approach can be used to evaluate and compare the output schemas of these works.

Considering the utilization of metrics, the work from [5] presents a metric set to evaluate schemas of NoSQL document databases. It was based on the works [14] and [10], that present structural metrics to evaluate XML documents. Eleven structural metrics are defined to evaluate NoSQL Document schemas and to assist the user in the process of selecting the most appropriate schema. Our work is partially inspired by [5]. The way the authors represent the NoSQL schema is similar to our approach based on DAGs. However, our approach has a different purpose, which is to evaluate and compare NoSQL schemas based on queries that represent the application access pattern instead of evaluating only the schema structure. To the best of our knowledge, our work is the first that presents a set of query-base metrics used to evaluate and compare NoSQL document schemas using a set of queries.

## 7    Conclusions

We presented a solution to evaluate how adequate a NoSQL document schema is with respect to a set of queries representing the application access patterns. Our approach is used as a guide on the choice of the most adequate target document schema in a scenario of RDB to NoSQL document transformation. The queries and the set of target schemas are represented as DAGs.

We define a set of query-based metrics, which are calculated based on the input DAGs (queries and schemas). The metrics enable to identify how the target document schema covers the input original queries. The metrics can be analyzed individually, or collectively, using a score per metric (*QScore*), or a score per schema (*SScore*), enabling specialized analysis.

We applied the metrics on a set of schemas produced by existing RDB to NoSQL transformations solutions. The evaluation of these different transformation approaches was only possible because we adopted the DAGs as a common unified format. This also means that the approach is technology independent. We executed all transformation scenarios, to confirm that the metrics can be related to the coding effort of the queries, with respect to the LoC measure. In addition, if the choice of a given output schema is not possible, the metrics may guide the re-factoring of the existing queries. As future work, we aim to extend the evaluation to integrate with cost-based approaches.

## References

1. Abdelhedi, F., Ait Brahim, A., Atigui, F., Zurfluh, G.: MDA-based approach for NoSQL databases modelling. In: Bellatreche, L., Chakravarthy, S. (eds.) DaWaK 2017. LNCS, vol. 10440, pp. 88–102. Springer, Cham (2017). https://doi.org/10.1007/978-3-319-64283-3_7
2. Bugiotti, F., Cabibbo, L., Atzeni, P., Torlone, R.: Database design for NoSQL systems. In: Yu, E., Dobbie, G., Jarke, M., Purao, S. (eds.) ER 2014. LNCS, vol. 8824, pp. 223–231. Springer, Cham (2014). https://doi.org/10.1007/978-3-319-12206-9_18

3. Cherfi, S.S.-S., Akoka, J., Comyn-Wattiau, I.: Conceptual modeling quality - from EER to UML schemas evaluation. In: Spaccapietra, S., March, S.T., Kambayashi, Y. (eds.) ER 2002. LNCS, vol. 2503, pp. 414–428. Springer, Heidelberg (2002). https://doi.org/10.1007/3-540-45816-6_38
4. Freitas, M.C.d., Souza, D.Y., Salgado, A.C.: Conceptual mappings to convert relational into NoSQL databases. In: Proceedings of the 18th ICEIS (2016)
5. Gómez, P., Roncancio, C., Casallas, R.: Towards quality analysis for document oriented bases. In: Trujillo, J.C., et al. (eds.) ER 2018. LNCS, vol. 11157, pp. 200–216. Springer, Cham (2018). https://doi.org/10.1007/978-3-030-00847-5_16
6. Gómez, P., Casallas, R., Roncancio, C.: Data schema does matter, even in NoSQL systems! In: 2016 IEEE Tenth RCIS, pp. 1–6, June 2016
7. Ho, L., Hsieh, M., Wu, J., Liu, P.: Data partition optimization for column-family NoSQL databases. In: 2015 IEEE International Conferene on SmartCity, pp. 668–675 (2015)
8. Jia, T., Zhao, X., Wang, Z., Gong, D., Ding, G.: Model transformation and data migration from relational database to MongoDB. In: IEEE BigData, pp. 60–67 (2016)
9. Karnitis, G., Arnicans, G.: Migration of relational database to document-oriented database: structure denormalization and data transformation. In: 2015 7th ICCI-CSN, pp. 113–118 (2015)
10. Klettke, M., Schneider, L., Heuer, A.: Metrics for XML document collections. In: Chaudhri, A.B., Unland, R., Djeraba, C., Lindner, W. (eds.) EDBT 2002. LNCS, vol. 2490, pp. 15–28. Springer, Heidelberg (2002). https://doi.org/10.1007/3-540-36128-6_2
11. Kuszera, E.M., Peres, L.M., Fabro, M.D.D.: Toward RDB to NoSQL: transforming data with metamorfose framework. In: Proceedings of the 34th ACM/SIGAPP Symposium on Applied Computing, SAC 2019, pp. 456–463 (2019)
12. de Lima, C., dos Santos Mello, R.: A workload-driven logical design approach for NoSQL document databases. In: Proceedings of the 17th iiWAS (2015)
13. Mior, M.J., Salem, K., Aboulnaga, A., Liu, R.: NoSE: schema design for NoSQL applications. In: 2016 IEEE 32nd ICDE, pp. 181–192 (2016)
14. Pusnik, M., Hericko, M., Budimac, Z., Sumak, B.: Xml schema metrics for quality evaluation. Comput. Sci. Inf. Syst. **11**, 1271–1289 (2014)
15. Reniers, V., Van Landuyt, D., Rafique, A., Joosen, W.: Schema design support for semi-structured data: finding the sweet spot between NF and De-NF. In: 2017 IEEE International Conference on Big Data (Big Data), pp. 2921–2930 (2017)
16. Sadalage, P.J., Fowler, M.: NoSQL Distilled: A Brief Guide to the Emerging World of Polyglot Persistence, 1st edn. Addison-Wesley Professional, Boston (2012)
17. Stanescu, L., Brezovan, M., Burdescu, D.D.: Automatic mapping of MySQL databases to NoSQL MongoDB. In: 2016 FedCSIS, pp. 837–840, September 2016
18. Stonebraker, M., Madden, S., Abadi, D.J., Harizopoulos, S., Hachem, N., Helland, P.: The end of an architectural era (it's time for a complete rewrite). In: Proceedings of 33rd VLDB, University of Vienna, Austria, 23–27 September 2007, pp. 1150–1160 (2007)
19. Li, X., Ma, Z., Chen, H.: QODM: a query-oriented data modeling approach for nosql databases. In: 2014 IEEE WARTIA, pp. 338–345 (2014)
20. Zhao, G., Lin, Q., Li, L., Li, Z.: Schema conversion model of SQL database to NoSQL. In: 2014 Ninth 3PGCIC, pp. 355–362 (2014)

# Invited Keynote Talk

# Data Sovereignty and the Internet of Production

Matthias Jarke[(✉)]

Informatik 5, RWTH Aachen and Fraunhofer FIT,
Ahornstr. 55, 52074 Aachen, Germany
jarke@dbis.rwth-aachen.de

**Abstract.** While the privacy of personal data has captured great attention in the public debate, resulting, e.g., in the European GDPR guideline, the sovereignty of knowledge-intensive small and medium enterprises concerning the usage of their own data in the presence of dominant data-hungry players in the Internet needs more investigation. In Europe, even the legal concept of data ownership is unclear. We reflect on requirements analyses, reference architectures and solution concepts pursued by the International Data Spaces Initiative to address these issues. The second part will more deeply explore our current interdisciplinary research in a visionary "Internet of Production" with 27 research groups from production and materials engineering, computer science, business and social sciences. In this setting, massive amounts of heterogeneous data must be exchanged and analyzed across organizational and disciplinary boundaries, throughout the lifecycle from (re-)engineering, to production, usage and recycling, under hard resource and time constraints. A shared metaphor, borrowed from Plato's famous Cave Allegory, serves as the core modeling and data management approach from conceptual, logical, physical, and business perspectives.

**Keywords:** Data sovereignty · Data spaces · Digital shadows · Internet of Production

## 1 Introduction

The term "data sovereignty" is hotly debated in political, industrial, and privacy communities. Politicians understand sovereignty as national sovereignty over data in their territory, when it comes to the jurisdiction over the use of big data by the big international players.

One might think that data industries dislike the idea because – in whatever definition – it limits their opportunities to exploit "data as the new oil". However, some of them employ the vision of data sovereignty of citizens as a weapon to abolish mandatory data privacy rules as limiting customer sovereignty by viewing them as people in need of protection in an uneven struggle for data ownership. For exactly this reason, privacy proponents criticize data sovereignty as a tricky buzzword by the data industry, aiming to undermine the principles of real self-determination and data thriftiness (capturing only the minimal data necessary for a specified need) found in

© Springer Nature Switzerland AG 2020
S. Dustdar et al. (Eds.): CAiSE 2020, LNCS 12127, pp. 549–558, 2020.
https://doi.org/10.1007/978-3-030-49435-3_34

many privacy laws. The European GDPR regulation follows this argumentation to some degree by clearly specifying that you are the owner of all personal data about yourself.

Surprising to most participants, the well-known Göttingen-based law professor Gerald Spindler, one of the GDPR authors, pointed out at a recent Dagstuhl Seminar on Data Sovereignty (Cappiello et al. 2019) that this personal data ownership is the *only* formal concept of data ownership that legally exists in Europe. In particular, the huge group of knowledge-intensive small and medium enterprises (SMEs) or even larger user industries in Europe are lacking coherent legal, technical, and organizational concepts how to protect their data- and model-based knowledge in the globalized industrial ecosystems.

In late 2014, we introduced the idea to extend the concept of personal data spaces (Halevy et al. 2006) to the inter-organizational setting by introducing the idea of *Industrial Data Spaces* as the kernel of platforms in which specific industrial ecosystems could organize their cooperation in a data-sovereign manner (Jarke 2017; Jarke and Quix 2017). The idea was quickly taken up by European industry and political leaders. Since 2015, a number of large-scale German and EU projects have defined requirements (Otto and Jarke 2019). Via numerous use case experiments, the International Data Space (IDS) Association with currently roughly 100 corporate members worldwide has evolved, and agreed on a reference architecture now already in version 3 (Otto et al. 2019). Section 2 gives a brief overview of this reference architecture, its philosophy of "alliance-driven data ecosystems", and a few of the technical contributions required to make it operational.

As recently pointed out by Loucopoulos et al. (2019), the production sector offers particularly complex challenges to such a setting due to the heterogeneity of its data and mathematical models, the structural and material complexity of many products, the globalized supply chains, and the international competition. Funded by the German "Excellence Competition 2019", an interdisciplinary group of researchers at RWTH Aachen University therefore started a 7-year Excellence Cluster "Internet of Production" aiming to address these challenges in a coherent manner. Section 3 presents an overview of key concepts and points to ongoing work on specific research challenges.

## 2    Alliance-Driven Ecosystems and the International Data Space

### 2.1    Keystone-Driven vs. Alliance-Driven Data Ecosystems

Several of the most valuable firms worldwide create value no longer by producing their own output but by orchestrating the output of others. Following modern versions of early medieval port cities and more recently phone companies, they do this by creating network effects by creating platforms which serve as two-sided or multi-sided markets (Gawer 2014).

In the best-known cases within the software industries, such as Apple, Amazon, or Facebook, but also domain-specific ones like Uber or Flixbus, there is a keystone player defining and running the platform. The typical strategy here is a very high early marketing investment to gain as many early adopters as possible, thus achieving quickly a dominant market position and being able to exploit extremely rich data sets as a basis for analytics, advertising, or economies of logistics. Design requirements engineering for this kind of platforms was already discussed in (Jarke et al. 2011).

More recently, however, driven by the goals of exploiting the opportunities of platforms but also preserving organizational data sovereignty, we are seeing the appearance of platform-based ecosystems organized and governed by alliances of cooperating players. Examples in Europe include a smart farming data ecosystem initiated by the German-based farm equipment producer Claas together with farming and seed-producing partners, which was recently joined by Claas' fiercest competitor John Deere.

Another example is an ongoing effort by VDV, the German organization of regional public transport organization, to set up an alliance-driven data ecosystem for intermodal traffic advice, ticketing, and exception handling in competition to efforts by big keystone players such as Flixbus, Deutsche Bahn, or even Google Maps based on Aachen's Mobility Broker metadata harmonization approach (Beutel et al. 2014).

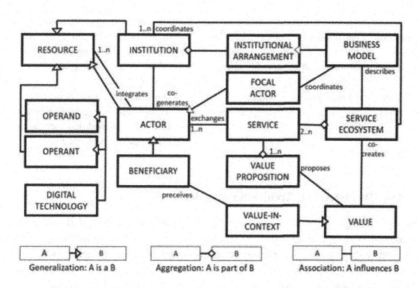

**Fig. 1.** Business model analytics based on service-dominant logic

Beyond the core importance of such a domain-specific meta model, the creation of platform business models is a key success factor. Yoo et al. (2010) already pointed out that, in contrast to traditional business model approaches, the "currency" of multi-sided markets can be an exchange of services rather than a purely financial one. In Pfeiffer et al. (2017), we therefore developed a business model development approach based on their service-dominant business logic and validated it in this intermodal travel ecosystem (cf. Fig. 1). In Otto and Jarke (2019), we employed a literature analysis and elaborate focus groups with industrial partners from the IDS Association in order to identify the main commonalities and differences (Table 1), extending an earlier discussion of platform evolution by Tiwana et al. (2010).

**Table 1.** Alliance and keystone-driven ecosystem design (Otto and Jarke 2019)

| Theoretical concept | Keystone-driven | Alliance-driven |
|---|---|---|
| Platform architecture | Architecture determined by goals of keystone firm | Architecture determined by shared interest of multiple owners (leading to decentral data storage, for example) |
| Platform boundary resource | Mainly technical boundary resources (APIs, SDKs etc.), supported by "social" boundary resources (e.g. training for developers) | Data as a boundary resource of "dual" nature, i.e. requiring both technical processing and functional use; many social boundary resources, such as working groups, task forces |
| Platform design | Core developed by platform owner, then extended by complementors | Consensus oriented design process with focus on "common denominator" |
| Platform ecosystem stages | 1) Innovation, 2) Adoption, 3) Scaling | 1) Adoption, 2) Innovation, 3) Scaling |
| Ecosystem governance | Start with limited number of sides and limited options for interaction between them, then increase number of sides and options for interaction | Start with complex ecosystem (i.e. multi-stakeholder setting), then reduce to core ecosystem and extend it later on depending on roll-out requirements |
| Regulatory instruments | Mainly pricing instruments, accompanied by non-pricing instruments | Dominated by non-pricing instruments; integration of pricing instruments scheduled for scaling phase; data governance |

## 2.2   The IDS Reference Architecture Model

In this subsection, we summarize some of the fundamental design decisions of the International Data Space approach to alliance-driven data ecosystems design. The full description with, e.g., a complete information model of the approach can be found in (Otto et al. 2019) from which the figures in this section have been excerpted.

With its focus on sovereign and secure data exchange, the IDS Architecture takes up aspects of several other well-known architectural patterns for data exchange, as shown in Fig. 2. It is different from the data lake architectures employed by most keystone-driven data platforms which emphasize rapid loading and pay-as-you-go data integration and knowledge extractions, but does embed such functionalities as service offerings whose usage, however, can be limited with enforced and monitored usage policies. On the other side, blockchains can be considered one extreme of such enforcements in a decentralized setting aiming at full transparency and provenance tracking, whereas the IDS architecture emphasizes the sovereign definition of usage policies by the individual players, plus agreed policies for a Data Space.

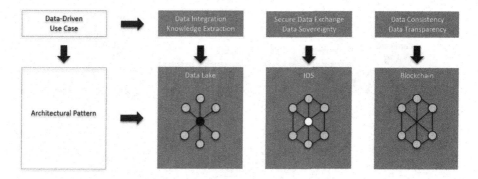

**Fig. 2.** Comparison of IDS architectural goals with other data-driven architectures

Membership of an actor (organizational data management entity, cloud, or service provider) is established by two core technical elements, as illustrated in Fig. 3: firstly, the data exchange (only) under agreed Usage Policies (shown as print-like IDS boxes on the links in the figure), and secondly by more or less "trusted" IDS Connectors. These combine aspects of traditional wrapper-mediators for data integration with trust guarantees provided by a hierarchy of simple to very elaborate security mechanisms.

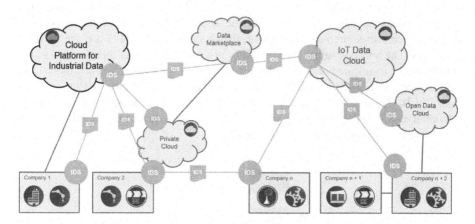

**Fig. 3.** IDS connectors and usage policy links form the technical core of IDS

Within the IDS projects, at least four different usage policy enforcement strategies have been developed (Eitel et al. 2017), all accessible via the conceptual model of the ODRL (Open Digital Rights Language) accepted by W3C in 2015. The usage control specifications support model-based code generation and execution based on earlier work by Pretschner et al. (2005). Figure 4 shows how security elements for policy definition (PDP) and policy management (PMP) in the linkage between connectors interact with policy execution points (PEP) in the IDS Connectors from which they can be propagated even to certain specific data items within the protected internal sphere of a company.

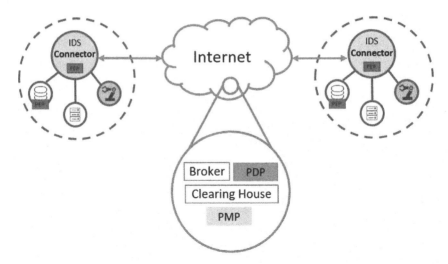

**Fig. 4.** Usage policy definition, management and execution in the link between IDS subsystems

In Fig. 1, we referred to the service-dominant business logic underlying most alliance-driven data ecosystems including the IDS. Obviously, as in other trust-intensive inter-organizational settings (Gans et al. 2003), the individual actors and linkages should be carefully defined at the strategic level, for which conceptual modeling techniques such as i* strategic dependencies (Yu 2011) are the obvious candidates. The analysis summarized in (Otto and Jarke 2019) has therefore led to the inclusion of an i*-inspired actor dependency network of important roles and their (task) dependencies (Fig. 5). In the Reference Architecture Model version 3.0 report (Otto et al. 2019), this is further elaborated with business process model patterns for the individual tasks, and governance mechanisms for the organizational infrastructure underlying data ecosystem set-up and operation.

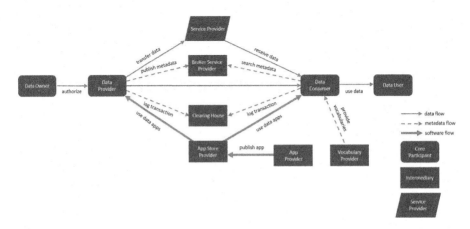

**Fig. 5.** Actor-dependency network in the IDS Reference Architecture

## 3  Towards an "Internet of Production"

Typical IDS use cases so far have been relatively limited in their organizational and technical complexity. A number of more ambitious and socially complex variants, such as Medical Data Spaces for cross-clinic medical and biomedical research have started and are accelerated by the demand caused by the CoVid-19 crisis.

However, probably the most complex application domain tackled so far is production engineering, the subject of our DFG-funded Excellence Cluster "Internet of Production". In this 7-year effort, 27 research groups from production and materials engineering, computer science, business and social sciences cooperate to study not just the sovereign data exchange addressed by the IDS Architecture in a fully globalized setting, but also the question of how to communicate between model- and data-driven approaches of vastly different disciplines and scales. In this setting, massive amounts of heterogeneous data must be exchanged and analyzed across organizational and disciplinary boundaries, throughout the lifecycle from (re-)engineering, to production, usage and recycling, under hard resource and time constraints.

Figure 6 illustrates this complexity with a few of the different kinds of data, but most importantly with three different lifecycles that have traditionally hardly communicated in the nowadays necessary speed of feedback cycles among them.

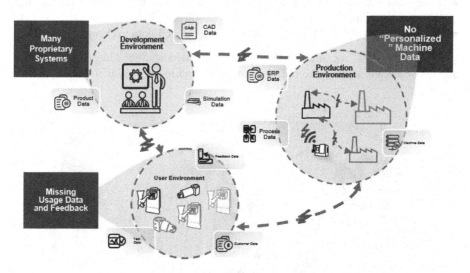

**Fig. 6.** Interacting cycles of data exchange in the Internet of Production

As one use case, we are considering the introduction of low-cost electric vehicles to the market. The engineering of such completely new cars requires numerous different specialties and supplier companies to collaborate and exchange data worldwide. To be financially viable, their production will take place in many small factories which can already be profitable with, say, 2.000 cars a year, rather than the traditional 200.000.

But this raises the question how the many small factories all over the world can exchange best practices, and provide feedback to the development engineers for perhaps culture-specific design improvements. Last not least, only the usage experience with buying and operating the novel vehicles will really show what works, what is attractive for customers, what are their ideas for improving the design but perhaps also the production process of the cars. And all of this must happen in an iterative improvement cycle which runs at least 5–10 times the speed of traditional automotive innovation, in order to have a successful vehicle before the venture capital runs out.

In addition to the challenges mentioned in Sect. 2, the computer science perspective on Fig. 6 yields extreme syntactic and semantic heterogeneity combined with very high data volume, but often also highly challenging real-time velocity requirements, and a wide variety of model-driven and data-driven approaches. Thus, all the V's of Big Data are present in this setting in addition to sovereign data exchange.

Building a complete Digital Twin for such a setting appears hopeless. We need a new kind of data abstraction with the following properties:

- Support for model-driven as well as data-driven approaches, and combinations thereof, across a wide range of different scientific disciplines.
- Relatively small size, in order to be easily movable anyplace between cloud and edge computing.
- Executable according to almost any real-time demand, with reasonable results on at least the most important perspective to the problem at hand.
- Suitable as valorized objects in an IDS-like controlled data exchange ecosystem.

In other words, we must find a common understanding addressing the open question what are actually the objects moving around in an Industrial Data Space.

**Fig. 7.** Plato's Cave Allegory

The intuition for our solution to this question came from an unexpected corner, Greek philosophy. In its famous Allegory of the Cave illustrated in Fig. 7, Plato (ca. 400 B.C.) showed the limits of human knowledge by sketching a scenery in which humans are fixed in a cave such that they can only see the shadows of things happening in the outside world cast by natural light or by fires lit behind the phenomena (it is funny to note that he even invented the concept of Fake News using human-made artefacts instead of real-world objects between the fire and the shadow).

Anyway, the shadows are obviously highly simplified data-driven real-time enabled abstractions which are, however, created under specific illuminations (=models) such as sunlight or fire. We therefore named our core abstraction *Digital Shadows*, a suitably compact result of combining context-specific simplified models and data analytics. Formally, Digital Shadows can be seen as a generalization of the view concept in databases where the base data as well as the (partially materialized) views are highly dynamic and complex objects.

Once we had invented this abstraction, we found that there already exist quite a number of useful Digital Shadow examples, among them quite well-known ones like the combinations of shortest path algorithms and real-time phone location data shown in navigation systems like TomTom, the flexible combination of Petri net process modeling with event mining algorithms in process mining (Van der Aalst 2011), or abstractions used in real-time vision systems for autonomous driving or sports training.

Within the Excellence Cluster "Internet of Things", we have been demonstrating the usefulness on complex examples from machine tooling control with extreme real-time constraints, optimizing the energy-intensive step of hot rolling ubiquitous in steel-based production chains, plastics engineering, and laser-based additive manufacturing.

Rather than going into details here, we point to some companion papers elaborating specific issues including the Digital Shadow concept itself and some early validation experiments (Liebenberg and Jarke 2020), the design of an initial physical infrastructure emphasizing the dynamic positioning and secure movement of Digital Shadows as well as base data within a novel infrastructure concept (Pennekamp et al. 2019), logical foundations of correct and rapid data integration in connectors or data lakes (Hai et al. 2019), model-driven development (Dalibor et al. 2020) and the creation of a RDF-based metadata infrastructure called FactDag (Gleim et al. 2020) aimed at interlinking the multiple Digital Shadows in a holistic knowledge structure.

**Acknowledgments.** This work was supported in part by the Fraunhofer CCIT Research Cluster, and in part by Deutsche Forschungsgemeinschaft (DFG, German Research Foundation) under Germany's Excellence Strategy – EXC-2023 Internet of Production – 390621612. I would like to thank numerous collaborators in these projects, especially Christoph Quix and Istvàn Koren (deputy area coordinators for the IoP infrastructure), the overall IDS project manager Boris Otto, and my IoP co-speakers Christian Brecher, Günter Schuh as well as IoP manager Matthias Brockmann.

# References

Beutel, M.C., Gökay, S., Kluth, W., Krempels, K.-H., Samsel, C., Terwelp, C.: Product oriented integration of heterogeneous mobility services. In: IEEE 17th International Conference Intelligent Transportation Systems (ITSC), Qingdao, China (2014)

Cappiello, C., Gal, A., Jarke, M., Rehof, J.: Data ecosystems–sovereign data exchange among organizations. Dagstuhl Rep. **9**(9), 66–134 (2019)

Dalibor, M., et al.: Model-driven development of a digital twin for injection molding. In: Proceedings CAiSE 2020, Grenoble, France (2020, to appear)

Eitel, A., et al.: Usage control in the industrial data space. Fraunhofer IESE Report 056.17/E (2017)

Gans, G., Jarke, M., Kethers, S., Lakemeyer, G.: Continuous requirements management for organization networks – a (dis-)trustful approach. Requirements Eng. **8**(1), 4–22 (2003)

Gawer, A.: Bridging different perspectives on technological platforms—towards and integrative framework. Res. Policy **43**(7), 1239–1249 (2014)

Gleim, L., Pennekamp, J., Liebenberg, M., et al.: FactDAG – formalizing data interoperability in an internet of production. IEEE Internet Things J. **4**(7), 3243–3253 (2020)

Hai, R., Quix, C., Wang, D.: Relaxed functional dependency discovery in heterogeneous data lakes. In: Laender, A.H.F., Pernici, B., Lim, E.-P., de Oliveira, J.P.M. (eds.) ER 2019. LNCS, vol. 11788, pp. 225–239. Springer, Cham (2019). https://doi.org/10.1007/978-3-030-33223-5_19

Halevy, A., Franklin, M., Maier, D.: Principles of data space systems. In: Proceedings 25th ACM SIGMOD-PODS, pp. 1–9 (2006)

Jarke, M.: Data spaces: combining goal-driven and data-driven approaches in community decision and negotiation support. In: Schoop, M., Kilgour, D.M. (eds.) GDN 2017. LNBIP, vol. 293, pp. 3–14. Springer, Cham (2017). https://doi.org/10.1007/978-3-319-63546-0_1

Jarke, M., Loucopoulos, P., Lyytinen, K., Mylopoulos, J., Robinson, W.: The brave new world of design requirements. Inf. Syst. **36**(7), 992–1008 (2011)

Jarke, M., Quix, C.: On warehouses, lakes, and spaces – the changing role of conceptual modeling for data integration. In: Cabot, J., Gómez, C., Pastor, O., Sancho, M.-R., Teniente, E. (eds.) Conceptual Modeling Perspectives, 231-245. Springer, Heidelberg (2017). https://doi.org/10.1007/978-3-319-67271-7_16

Liebenberg, M., Jarke, M.: Information systems engineering with digital shadows – concept and case studies. In: Proceedings CAiSE 2020, Grenoble, France (2020, to appear)

Loucopoulos, P., Kavakli, E., Chechina, N.: Requirements engineering for cyber physical production systems. In: Giorgini, P., Weber, B. (eds.) CAiSE 2019. LNCS, vol. 11483, pp. 276–291. Springer, Cham (2019). https://doi.org/10.1007/978-3-030-21290-2_18

Otto, B., Jarke, M.: Designing a multi-sided data platform: findings from the international data spaces case. Electron. Markets **29**(4), 561–580 (2019)

Otto, B., Steinbuß, S., Teuscher, A., Lohmann, S., et al.: Reference Architecture Model Version 3.0. International Data Spaces Association, Dortmund (2019)

Pfeiffer, A., Krempels, K.-H., Jarke, M.: Service-oriented business model framework – a service-dominant logic based approach for business modeling in the digital era. In: Proceedings 19th ICEIS Conference (Porto 2017), vol. 3, pp. 361–372 (2017)

Pennekamp, J., Glebke, R., Meisen, T., Quix, C., et al.: Towards an infrastructure enabling the internet of production. In: IEEE International Conference Industrial Cyber-Physical Systems (ICPS 2019), Taipei, TW, pp. 31–37 (2019)

Plato: Allegory of the Cave. The Republic VII (ca. 400 B.C.)

Pretschner, A., Hilty, M., Basin, D.: Distributed usage control. Commun. ACM **49**(9), 39–44 (2005)

Tiwana, A., Konsynski, B.R., Bush, A.: Platform evolution – co-evolution of platform architecture, governance, and environmental dynamics. Inf. Syst. Res. **21**(4), 675–687 (2010)

Van der Aalst, W.: Process Mining – Discovery, Conformance, and Enhancement of Business Processes. Springer, Heidelberg (2011). https://doi.org/10.1007/978-3-642-19345-3

Yoo, Y., Henfridsson, O., Lyytinen, K.: The new organizing logic of digital innovation – an agenda for information systems research. Inf. Syst. Res. **21**(4), 724–735 (2010)

Yu, E.: Modeling strategic relationships for process reengineering. In: Yu, E., et al. (eds.) Social Modeling for Requirements Engineering. Springer, Heidelberg (2011)

# Tutorials

# Volunteer Design of Data Warehouse

Sandro Bimonte[(✉)]

INRAE, TSCF Clermont Ferrand, 9 Avenue Blaise Pascal, 63178 Aubiere,
France
sandro.bimonte@inrae.fr

**Abstract.** Data Warehouse (DW) design methodologies have been widely
investigated in literature. Nowadays, with the advent of crowdsourcing systems,
more and more volunteers collect data for scientific purposes (i.e. citizen science). Involving volunteers in the DW design process raises several research
issues that are discussed in this tutorial. In particular, we detail our volunteer
DW design methodology based on ad-hoc elicitation methods, rapid prototyping, and collaborative design.

**Keywords:** Citizen science · Data warehouse · OLAP

## 1 Topic and Novelty

Data Warehouse (DW) design methodologies have been widely investigated in literature [5]. Nowadays, with the advent of crowdsourcing systems, more and more volunteers (amateurs and/or professionals) collect data for scientific purposes (i.e. citizen
science) [4]. The key to success in citizen science is fully involving volunteers in the
scientific project. Therefore, it is important to provide volunteers with results about
their collected data, which are really understandable and fitting with their wishes. Thus,
there is a need to change the classical "top-down" approach of citizen science, which
defines volunteers as active data producers and passive analysis consumers, to a
"bottom-up" approach where volunteers also play an active role in the definition of
what and how to analyze the collected data. Some studies investigate warehousing and
OLAPing crowdsourcing data, but to the best of our knowledge only some recent
works [3, 6] focus on effectively putting volunteers in the DW design process (i.e.
volunteer design of DW), which raises some new methodological and technological
issues.

## 2 Goal and Objectives

Volunteers, contrary to common usual DW decision-makers [2], have very low
knowledge of DW fundamentals, they are partially involved in the DW project, they
have a medium understanding of the project goals, they have difficulties to reach a
unified vision of the analysis goals, the have a low proficiency in the subject matter,
they are quite available to the elicitation session, and they are numerous and geo-
graphically distributed. Therefore, main principles for DW design must be revisited in

© Springer Nature Switzerland AG 2020
S. Dustdar et al. (Eds.): CAiSE 2020, LNCS 12127, pp. 561–562, 2020.
https://doi.org/10.1007/978-3-030-49435-3

such new context ("*How handle the requirement elicitation step with these particular decision-makers?*", "*How grant the respect of timeline of the DW project?*", etc.).

The main goal of this tutorial is to provide a set of methodological and technical answers to the above described questions concerning the volunteer design of DW. By means of a real case study concerning the biodiversity in agriculture, issued from the French ANR project VGI4bio [3], this tutorial:

- describes the benefits of the volunteer design of DW compared to classical DW approaches from decision-makers point of view,
- details the methodological issues of the volunteer design of DW from requirement elicitation to implementation providing some theoretical solutions [2],
- presents the set of tools we have developed from 2013 to implement our methodology (the UML profile ICSOLAP[1] [1]; the rapid DW prototyping tool[2] [1]; the integration of wiki and OLAP tool [3]; and finally the collaborative DW design tool[3] [6])
- details the results of some experiments we have conducted to validate our theoretical and implementation proposals [3].

**Acknowledgement.** This work is supported by the French ANR project VGI4bio ANR-17-CE04-0012. The author would like to thank different all people that participate to this work.

# References

1. Bimonte, S., Edoh-Alove, E., Nazih, H., Kang, M., Rizzi, S.: ProtOLAP: rapid OLAP prototyping with on-demand data supply. In: DOLAP 2013, pp. 61–66 (2013)
2. Bimonte, S., Antonelli, L., Rizzi, S.: Requirement-driven data warehouse design based on enhanced pivot tables. Requirements Eng. (to appear)
3. Bimonte, S., Rizzi, S., Sautot, L., Fontaine, B.: Volunteered multidimensional design to the test: the farmland biodiversity VGI4Bio project's experiment. In: DOLAP 2019 (2019)
4. Newman G., Wiggins A., Crall A.: Citizen science futures: emerging technologies and shifting paradigms. Front. Ecol. Environ. **10**, 298–304
5. Romero, O., Abelló, A.: A survey of multidimensional modeling methodologies. IJDWM **5**(2), 1–23 (2009)
6. Sakka, A., Bimonte, S., Sautot, L., Camilleri, G., Zaraté, P., Besnard, A.: A volunteer design methodology of data warehouses. In: ER 2018, pp. 286–300 (2018)

---

[1] https://www.youtube.com/watch?v=2VQUrmU1yYk.

[2] https://www.youtube.com/watch?v=WNHEwi4e3bg.

[3] https://www.youtube.com/watch?v=GTzHVLyaI_Q&feature=emb_title.

# Design of Service-Dominant Business Models for a Digital World

Paul Grefen[✉] and Oktay Turetken

Eindhoven University of Technology, Eindhoven, The Netherlands
{p.w.p.j.grefen, o.turetken}@tue.nl

**Keywords:** Service-dominant business · Business model design ·
Digital world

## 1 Introduction

Service-dominant business (SDB) thinking is a relatively new approach for business engineering. It emphasizes the added value created in integrated solution delivery to customers by the use of assets and individual services, instead of putting the emphasis on the assets or individual services themselves. Service-dominant thinking (or value-based business thinking) receives extensive attention in the current digital age, in which asset-based thinking is moved to the background (for example by asset virtualization). Examples can easily be found in many domains, such as the mobility domain (like car sharing models), the entertainment domain (like streaming music and movie delivery models), the document management domain (like virtualized printing solutions), etcetera.

The BASE/X methodology places the SDB paradigm explicitly in the context of agile business collaborations that are required for solution delivery in complex, dynamic markets (Grefen and Türetken 2018). BASE/X links business model design explicitly to business strategy design, business process design and business service design, as well as to the design of distributed information systems supporting the execution of business processes and business services (Grefen 2015). This holistic approach provides a bridge in the field of service-dominant business engineering between topics that have been rather disparate so far. Example business domains in which BASE/X has been broadly applied are urban mobility, advanced transport and logistics, and smart manufacturing (Industry 4.0).

## 2 Service-Dominant Business Model Concept

Even though there has been ample attention for business model design in general (for example in the context of the well-known Business Model Canvas technique), there is far less work on the design of service-dominant business models. The specific characteristics of SDB make traditional business modeling techniques less usable.

S. Dustdar et al. (Eds.): CAiSE 2020, LNCS 12127, pp. 563–565, 2020.
https://doi.org/10.1007/978-3-030-49435-3

One of the techniques in the BASE/X methodology is the Service-Dominant Business Model Radar (SDBM/R). The SDBM/R technique has been explicitly designed for the specification of service dominant business models in a collaborative setting of business networks (Türetken and Grefen 2017, Türetken et al. 2019). More specifically: it is centered on a value-in-use that is co-produced by a business network for a customer segment; it takes a network-centric perspective for business collaboration; it assumes a dynamic market by default and hence is positioned in the BASE/X framework as an enabler of business agility.

## 3   Service Dominant Business Model Design

Service-dominant business model design in the BASE/X approach takes a highly network-centric perspective in modeling collaboration, favoring an outside-in view over an inside-out view for collaboration between business entities (including the customer). For this reason, the SDBM/R technique uses a circular business model representation (that was the reason for the label 'radar') that organizes all participating business actors in a peer-to-peer fashion.

The actors are drawn in the form of pie slices around the central value-in-use that is co-produced for the customer actor. Around this central value-in-use, the representation uses three concentric circular lanes that intersect with all actors. The inner lane represents the value contributions of each actor to the central value-in-use, the middle lane represents the co-production activities that each actor performs to generate its value contribution, and the outer lane represents the costs and benefits involved with these activities (addressing both financial and non-financial costs and benefits).

Designing service dominant business models in the SDBM/R technique is an interactive, iterative process with the active participation of at least the main stakeholders in the business model. The design process with its simple, low-tech tooling supports quick prototyping and evolution of business model designs in hands-on workshop settings. Experience shows that the technique is easily picked up by relative novices in business model design. Despite their 'approachable character', SDBM/R models are a solid basis for operationalization of business models into conceptual business process models representing the practical business operations in collaborative networks required to actually implement the intended business (Suratno et al. 2018).

## References

1. Grefen, P.: Service-Dominant Business Engineering with BASE/X: Business Modeling Handbook. CreateSpace Independent Publishing Platform, USA (2015)
2. Grefen, P., Türetken, O.: Achieving Business Process Agility through Service Engineering in Extended Business Networks. BPTrends (2018)
3. Türetken, O., Grefen, P.: Designing service-dominant business models. In: Proceedings of the 25th European Conference on Information Systems, pp. 2218–2233. AIS (2017)

4. Türetken, O., Grefen, P., Gilsing, R., Adali, O.: Service-dominant business model design for digital innovation in smart mobility. Bus. Inf. Syst. Eng. **61**(1), 9–29 (2019). https://doi.org/10.1007/s12599-018-0565-x

5. Suratno, B., Ozkan, B., Turetken, O., Grefen, P.: A method for operationalizing service-dominant business models into conceptual process models. In: Shishkov, B. (ed.) BMSD 2018. LNBIP, vol. 319, pp. 133–148. Springer, Cham (2018). https://doi.org/10.1007/978-3-319-94214-8_9

# Using the Four-Component Instructional Design Model (4C/ID) for Teaching Complex Learning Subjects in IS

Monique Snoeck[(✉)] [iD] and Daria Bogdanova [iD]

Research Center on Information Systems Engineering, KU Leuven,
Naamestraat 69, 3000 Leuven, Belgium
{monique.snoeck, daria.bogdanova}@kuleuven.be

**Abstract.** The 4C/ID is an instructional design model for complex learning. Despite the 4C/ID model being particularly relevant for information systems teaching, we believe the model is not really known in this community. In this tutorial we review 4C/ID's main building blocks and illustrate their application for requirements engineering and conceptual modelling. Using a rich method such as 4C/ID could be overwhelming as the conscious use of instructional design methods forces one to more carefully reflect on learning goals and students' mental processes. However, in return the increased understanding of students' cognitive processes allows reaping the benefit of instructional design methods. The goal of the tutorial is to offer guidance in where to start, and how to gradually expand the application of this interesting model to one's teaching.

**Keywords:** 4C/ID · Instructional design · Requirements engineering · Conceptual modelling

Many topics in IS teaching are truly complex: students need to be able to handle complex multi-faceted problems that may have multiple solutions. Especially in the presence of larger groups of students, this poses challenges to teachers, as in such kind of courses student have a high demand for personal feedback. A good instructional design may satisfy to a certain extent students' need for personal feedback, by ensuring that series of task are well-scaffolded, and students have the needed supportive and just-in-time information.

The goal of the tutorial is to provide an overview of the 4C/ID model, and to exemplify how it can be applied to teach requirements engineering and conceptual modelling. 4C/ID[1] is an instructional design model for complex learning, which was developed by Jeroen van Merriënboer [1]. Complex learning subjects are characterized by the fact that many solutions exist for a single problem, and that different paths can be followed to achieve the solution. While the model was initially developed in the context of medical education, the model has been widely applied in various educational contexts. Despite 4C/ID being particularly relevant for IS teaching, we believe the model is not really known in this community. Using a rich method such as 4C/ID could

---

[1] https://www.4cid.org/about-4cid.

© Springer Nature Switzerland AG 2020
S. Dustdar et al. (Eds.): CAiSE 2020, LNCS 12127, pp. 566–568, 2020.
https://doi.org/10.1007/978-3-030-49435-3

be overwhelming. The goal of the tutorial is therefore to offer guidance in where to start, and how to gradually expand the application of this interesting model to one's teaching.

One of the four main building blocks of 4C/ID are authentic tasks, meaning that each task should have the characteristics of a real-life task. This is likely the easiest starting point for applying 4C/ID. As performing real-life tasks right away is too difficult for students, some phasing and support is required. A typical phasing would be to offer a worked example first, and then let students gradually take on more and more parts of the solution process. The exact phasing needs to be built on a set of clear learning goals. A well-developed learning goals framework for conceptual modelling based on Bloom's taxonomy as guidance can be found in [2, 3].

The three remaining building blocks of 4C/ID are: supportive information, which is the information that is always available to learners; part-task practice, which is aimed at training "mechanical skills" such as the use of tools; and Just-in-time information, which is the information that is presented when needed. For each of these blocks, we review how they can be implemented in practice, in particular by making use of automation. Part-task practice can e.g. be implemented by means of small exercises targeting "frequently occurring errors" [3, 4]. Just-in-time information can e.g. be automated feedback as described in [5, 6].

Richer instructional design theories such as 4C/ID which specifically targets complex learning are inspirational to perform more fundamental changes in how one teaches a course. The conscious use of instructional design methods forces one to more carefully reflect on learning goals and students' mental schemas. In return the increased understanding of students' cognitive processes allows reaping the benefit of instructional design methods. Our research has demonstrated that applying the different concepts of 4C/ID results in better learning and better teaching [4, 6–8].

# References

1. Van Merriënboer, J.J.G., Kirschner, P.A.: Ten Steps to Complex Learning: A Systematic Approach to Four-Component Instructional Design. Routledge
2. Bogdanova, D., Snoeck, M.: Domain modelling in bloom: deciphering how we teach it. In: Poels, G., Gailly, F., Serral Asensio, E., Snoeck, M. (eds.) PoEM 2017. LNBIP, vol. 305, pp. 3–17. Springer, Cham (2017). https://doi.org/10.1007/978-3-319-70241-4_1
3. Bogdanova, D, Snoeck, M.: CaMeLOT: an educational framework for conceptual data modelling. Int. J. Appl. Earth Obs. Geoinf. (2019)
4. Bogdanova, D., Snoeck, M.: learning from errors: error-based exercises in domain modelling pedagogy. In: Buchmann, R.A., Karagiannis, D., Kirikova, M. (eds.) PoEM 2018. LNBIP, vol. 335, pp. 321–334. Springer, Cham (2018). https://doi.org/10.1007/978-3-030-02302-7_20
5. Sedrakyan, G., De Weerdt, J., Snoeck, M.: Process-mining enabled feedback: 'tell me what I did wrong' vs. 'tell me how to do it right'. Comput. Hum. Behav. **57**, 352–376 (2016)
6. Sedrakyan, G., Snoeck, M., Poelmans, S.: Assessing the effectiveness of feedback enabled simulation in teaching conceptual modeling. Comput. Educ. **78**, 367–382 (2014)

7. Deeva, G., Snoeck, M., De Weerdt, J.: Discovering the impact of students' modeling behavior on their final performance. In: Buchmann, R.A., Karagiannis, D., Kirikova, M. (eds.) PoEM 2018. LNBIP, vol. 335, pp. 335–350. Springer, Cham (2018). https://doi.org/10.1007/978-3-030-02302-7_21

8. Strecker, S., Baumöl, U., Karagiannis, D., Koschmider, A., Snoeck, M., Zarnekow, R.: Five inspiring course (re-)designs: examples of innovations in teaching and learning bise. Bus. Inf. Syst. Eng. **61**(2), 241–252 (2019)

# Open Source Software and Modern Information Systems: A Tutorial

Anthony I. Wasserman$^{(\boxtimes)}$ (iD)

Carnegie Mellon University – Silicon Valley, Moffett Field,
CA 94035, USA
tonyw@acm.org

**Keywords:** FOSS · Open source · OSPO · OSI · Information systems

## Extended Abstract

The adoption and use of free and open source software (FOSS) has grown remarkably over the past 22 years since the term "open source" was coined and the Open Source Initiative (OSI) was formed. The OSI wrote the Open Source Definition and now serves as the steward for that definition and the software licenses that comply with that definition. The OSI, along with the Free Software Foundation (FSF), are the leading proponents for the central freedoms of FOSS, giving its users the right to read, copy, change, and distribute the software. These freedoms are essential to enabling community development of open source software.

The FSF has described the free software movement as a successful social movement that has arisen from computing culture, driven by a worldwide community of ethical programmers dedicated to the cause of freedom and sharing. Until the last decade, FOSS was largely the province of technologists and developers, with very little adoption by governments, industry, and other organizations.

Today, though, the picture is very different. There are millions of high-quality community-based and foundation-supported projects that are freely available for adoption and use under OSI licenses. These projects include some of the world's most popular software systems, including the Firefox browser, the LibreOffice suite, WordPress, and the Apache HTTP server. In addition, there are hundreds of successful commercial open source companies (see the COSSCI list at https://oss.capital) that provide commercial support for FOSS projects, with RedHat (now part of IBM) as the largest of these. There's ample evidence, and general agreement, that the best FOSS code is equal in quality, if not better than, closed proprietary code.

As a result, governments, organizations, and companies have widely adopted FOSS software. More than 90% of companies use open source, both for internal use and in the products and services that they provide to their customers. Most software startups avoid using proprietary software, and build their products on a foundation of FOSS software. Companies also see FOSS as a way to attract developers, and to demonstrate their support for FOSS. Similarly, FOSS is widely used in academia and the broader research community, with academic projects often released as FOSS.

© Springer Nature Switzerland AG 2020
S. Dustdar et al. (Eds.): CAiSE 2020, LNCS 12127, pp. 569–570, 2020.
https://doi.org/10.1007/978-3-030-49435-3

Many companies have now moved up the FOSS adoption curve, going from initial experimentation through using FOSS in its products and then contributing FOSS code to various projects and releasing their own FOSS projects, such as Cassandra and Tensor Flow. As this use has grown, companies have learned to manage their use of FOSS, often creating an Open Source Project Office (OSPO). One significant outcome of this shift is that FOSS has long moved from being a "copycat" of proprietary software to being the basis for innovative advances; much of the leading software in areas such as management of large data sets, microservices, and Internet of Things (IoT) are open source. More than a third of all servers worldwide, and all supercomputers, run Linux. On the consumer side, more than 80% of all smartphones run the Linux-based Android system, with many vendors adding their own enhancements to the foundation code.

The latter part of this tutorial addresses the transformation of modern information systems development. Not long ago, information systems were built with proprietary software and deployed to run in a server environment. Now, however, more and more in-house systems and commercial products and services are designed to run in the cloud, with the code running on one or more virtual machines running on one or more "real" processors and storage mechanisms owned and managed by a cloud services provider. The operating system and data management tools are typically FOSS components, with an organization putting its effort into its unique features, rather than the commodity features. Organizations must adapt new development practices to work in this new environment.

The tutorial continues with a review of some areas and specific FOSS tools and components that modern information system developers are using to design, develop, and deploy their systems in this environment. Topics covered include development methods and tools, architectures for the cloud, data management platforms, analytics and machine learning systems.

The tutorial concludes with a discussion of some of the challenges in adopting and using FOSS technology, and some forecasts for future FOSS adoption and use, leaving sufficient time for attendee questions and discussion.

# Tutorial on Process Performance Management

Adela del-Río-Ortega$^{(\boxtimes)}$ and Manuel Resinas

Universidad de Sevilla, Sevilla, Spain
{adeladelrio,resinas}@us.es

**Abstract.** Business process performance management (PPM), aims at assessing the achievement of strategic and operational goals and supporting decision-making for the continuous optimisation of business processes. To carry out this evaluation, information systems must provide mechanisms to support the modelling, gathering, visualisation and analysis of a set of indicators that evaluate performance-relevant data of one or several business processes. Unfortunately, up to date, there is not a well-established holistic standard or a set of good practices that guide these tasks. Instead, this is usually done based on the experience and intuition of the process owners, CIOs, CEOs and domain experts, often applying ad-hoc techniques and tools. This tutorial will offer participants the opportunity to get to know and use in a practical setting a set of guidelines and techniques, based on existing well-grounded literature from both academic and industrial researchers, that address the modelling, evaluation analysis and visualisation of performance indicators.

**Keywords:** Process performance indicators · Visualization · KPIs

## 1 Overview

The evaluation of process performance plays a key role in obtaining information on the achievement of their strategic and operational goals and forms the basis for consistent and continuous process optimisation. To carry it out, a performance measurement strategy must be implemented so that business processes (BPs) can be continuously improved. Its implementation in an organisation is closely related to its information systems since they should provide mechanisms to support the modelling, gathering, visualisation and analysis of a set of process performance indicators (PPIs). PPIs are quantifiable metrics that allow an evaluation of the efficiency and effectiveness of business processes and can be measured directly by data generated within the process flow. For instance, one could have a PPI for an order to cash process that specifies that its resolution time should be less than 20 working days in order to keep customer satisfaction.

This work has received funding from the European Commission (FEDER) and the Spanish and Andalusian R&D&I programmes (PAIDI 2020, RTI2018-101204-B-C22 (OPHELIA), P18-FR-2895 (EKIPMENT-PLUS)).

S. Dustdar et al. (Eds.): CAiSE 2020, LNCS 12127, pp. 571–572, 2020.
https://doi.org/10.1007/978-3-030-49435-3

Concerning the modelling of PPIs, there is sometimes the misconception that a closed set of indicators such as cycle time, waiting time or process cost are the only indicators that are relevant for all kinds of processes. However, the modelling of PPIs can be much more complex. First, it involves not only defining the metric that is going to be used, but also other attributes such as the target value of the PPI, its scope, or the business goals to which it is related [3]. These task is supported by several guidelines. (1) A PPI must satisfy the SMART criteria, which stands for: Specific, Measurable, Achievable, Relevant, and Time-bounded. (2) PPIs themselves must be efficient, i.e., it must be worth the measuring effort from a cost/benefit viewpoint. The amount of PPIs must also be efficient, where a balance between information need and information overload has to be met. (3) PPIs must be defined according to the vocabulary used in the specific domain and in a language comprehensible by the different stakeholders. (4) They must keep traceability to the business process they are defined for. (5) They must be amenable to automation. (6) The set of PPIs should include two types of indicators [1], namely *lag* indicators, which establishes a goal that the organisation is trying to achieve, and *lead* indicators, which operationalise lag indicators by measuring actions that performers can do to achieve the lag indicator.

Once a system of PPIs has been defined, data sources, methods and instruments need to be established in order to gather the required data to calculate their values. Gathering methods can be classified into evidence-based methods, commonly using the data recorded by existing information systems, and subjective methods like interviews or questionnaires, among others.

The last part of PPM is the visualisation and analysis of performance data for two purposes. First, monitoring it to be able to quickly learn whether the performance is moving to the right direction so that appropriate actions are taken. Second, diagnosing it in order to be able to spot points of potential improvement, where visual interfaces designed for data exploration and analysis are used. Regardless of the purpose, well-known knowledge on visual perception should be exploited to create effective visualisations that serve these purposes [2].

The main goal of this tutorial is to give a theoretical and practical perspective on how to properly model process performance measures aligned with the business strategy, how to gather information related to PPIs and compute them based on it, and how to address the business performance analysis and visualisation, including dashboards.

# References

1. Estrada-Torres, B., et al.: Measuring performance in knowledge- intensive processes. ACM Trans. Internet Technol. **19**(1), 1–26 (2019). Article 15
2. Few, S.: Information Dashboard Design: The Effective Visual Communication of Data. O'Reilly Media Inc., Sebastopol (2006)
3. del-Río-Ortega, A., Resinas, M., Durán, A., Bernárdez, B., Ruiz-Cortés, A., Toro, M.: Visual ppinot: a graphical notation for process performance indicators. Bus. Inf. Syst. Eng. **61**(2), 137–161 (2017). https://doi.org/10.1007/s12599-017-0483-3

# Author Index

Abbas, Sameh  467
Adamo, Greta  384
Alhazmi, Ahoud  101
Aljubairy, Abdulwahab  101
Amaral de Sousa, Victor  117
Anquetil, Nicolas  498

Barros, Alistair  3
Benatallah, Boualem  199
Bibow, Pascal  85
Bidar, Reihaneh  54
Bimonte, Sandro  561
Bogdanova, Daria  566
Böhmer, Kristof  283
Bouguelia, Sara  199
Brabra, Hayet  199
Breitenbücher, Uwe  20, 134
Burnay, Corentin  117

Carmona, Josep  299
Cetina, Carlos  353
Chacko, Rinu  433
Cheng, Xinyun  515

Dąbrowski, Jacek  401
Dalibor, Manuela  85
Daniel, Florian  134
De Alwis, Adambarage Anuruddha
    Chathuranga  3
de Souza Neto, João Batista  482
del-Río-Ortega, Adela  571
Delmas, Kevin  417
Delplanque, Julien  498
Di Francescomarino, Chiara  384
Didonet Del Fabro, Marcos  530
Domingo, África  353
Ducasse, Stéphane  498

Echeverría, Jorge  353
Engels, Gregor  36
Etien, Anne  498

Fahrenkrog-Petersen, Stephan A.  252
Falazi, Ghareeb  134

Fani Sani, Mohammadreza  234
Fernandes de Macêdo, José Antônio  185
Fidge, Colin  3

Ghidini, Chiara  384
Ghose, Aditya  451
Grefen, Paul  563

Hadar, Irit  368
Herschel, Melanie  153
Hopmann, Christian  85

Jain, Deepak  433
Janssen, Dominik  252
Jarke, Matthias  70, 549
Jazayeri, Bahar  36

Képes, Kálmán  20
Kong, Xianglong  515
Koschmider, Agnes  252
Kulkarni, Vinay  433
Kumar, Akhil  268
Küster, Jochen  36
Kuszera, Evandro Miguel  530

La Rosa, Marcello  299
Lamparelli, Andrea  134
Landsiedel, Olaf  252
Leemans, Sander J. J.  217
Letier, Emmanuel  401
Leymann, Frank  20, 134
Li, Bixin  515
Li, Shu'ang  268
Liao, Li  515
Liebenberg, Martin  70
Lin, Leilei  268
Lin, Li  268
Linhares Coelho da Silva, Ticiana  185

Mainz, Ben  85
Mannhardt, Felix  252
Martins Moreira, Anamaria  482

Metzger, Andreas   169
Mühlhäuser, Max   319
Musicante, Martin Alejandro   482

Nolle, Timo   319
Nuñez von Voigt, Saskia   252

Oppold, Sarah   153
Outmazgin, Nesi   368

Pagetti, Claire   417
Palm, Alexander   169
Pastor, Óscar   353
Patil, Ashwini   433
Peres, Letícia M.   530
Perini, Anna   401
Pika, Anastasiia   334
Pohl, Klaus   169
Polacsek, Thomas   417
Polyvyanyy, Artem   3, 217

Qian, Chen   268

Rai, Beena   433
Reinhartz-Berger, Iris   467
Resinas, Manuel   571
Rinderle-Ma, Stefanie   283
Rodriguez, Carlos   199
Rumpe, Bernhard   85

Saxena, Krati   433
Schmalzing, David   85
Schmitz, Mauritius   85
Schwichtenberg, Simon   36
Seeliger, Alexander   319

Sheng, Quan Z.   101
Sindhgatta, Renuka   54, 451
Snoeck, Monique   117, 566
Soffer, Pnina   368
Sunkle, Sagar   433
Susi, Angelo   401

Taymouri, Farbod   299
ter Hofstede, Arthur H. M.   54, 451
Thoma, Nils   319
Tschorsch, Florian   252
Turetken, Oktay   563

van Zelst, Sebastiaan J.   234
van der Aalst, Wil M. P.   234
Vargas-Solar, Genoveva   482

Wang, Jianmin   268
Wasserman, Anthony I.   569
Weder, Benjamin   20
Weidlich, Matthias   252
Wen, Lijie   268
Wild, Karoline   20
Wortmann, Andreas   85
Wynn, Moe T.   334

Yaghoubzadehfard, Mohammadali   199
Yussupov, Vladimir   134

Zamanirad, Shayan   199
Zhang, Wei Emma   101
Zimmermann, Olaf   36
Zong, Zan   268
Zschornack Rodrigues Saraiva, Felipe   185

Printed in the United States
By Bookmasters